Marketing
Investment
Real Estate

Marketing
Investment
Real Estate

Finance
Taxation
Techniques
Third Edition

Stephen D. Messner
Irving Schreiber
Victor L. Lyon
Robert L. Ward

PRENTICE
HALL CCIM

PRENTICE-HALL, INC., Englewood Cliffs, New Jersey 07632

COMMERCIAL-INVESTMENT REAL ESTATE COUNCIL™
of the REALTORS NATIONAL MARKETING INSTITUTE®
of the NATIONAL ASSOCIATION OF REALTORS®
Chicago, Illinois

Printed in the United States of America

10 9 8 7 6 5 4 3 2

ISBN 0-13-557893-0 01

PRENTICE-HALL INTERNATIONAL (UK) LIMITED, *London*
PRENTICE-HALL OF AUSTRALIA PTY. LIMITED, *Sydney*
PRENTICE-HALL CANADA INC., *Toronto*
PRENTICE-HALL HISPANOAMERICANA, S.A., *Mexico*
PRENTICE-HALL OF INDIA PRIVATE LIMITED, *New Delhi*
PRENTICE-HALL OF JAPAN, INC., *Tokyo*
PRENTICE-HALL OF SOUTHEAST ASIA PTE. LTD., *Singapore*
EDITORA PRENTICE-HALL DO BRASIL, LTDA., *Rio de Janeiro*

Preface

This book concerns itself with the process of including real estate in a total investment program in order to achieve an investor's goals. As we move midway into the decade of the 1980s, this task is becoming increasingly important and relevant. Income-producing and/or speculative real estate have long been recognized as having a useful investment potential for a broad range of investors with different needs and investment objectives. Now, even greater numbers of investors and institutions are turning to real estate over other forms of direct and indirect investment media because of the flexibility and return potential that it offers when transactions are properly structured.

The national economy has experienced record levels of inflation during the past several years and many forms of real estate investments represent an ideal hedge against the shrinking purchasing power of the dollar. In addition, real estate is often purchased because of the tax advantages it holds for certain categories of investors. Also, real estate has long been linked with the advantages associated with leveraged financing; even during periods of tight money it is possible to finance real estate purchases through lender participation.

All of these developments create new opportunities for well-qualified investment real estate brokers to provide counsel to a growing number of clients. To meet the investment objectives of their clients, brokers must be aware of market developments and be equipped with the specialized tools of analysis necessary to cope with ever-changing market conditions. It is to this end that this book was written.

Understanding and knowledge of the new techniques and tools presented here will assure the broker a viable role in the client team—attorney, accountant and REALTOR® (as depicted in the cover logo). The broker's role is multifaceted; it can be the traditional one of the seller's agent or one of providing counseling services for which a fee rather than a commission is paid. Whatever the case, it is clear that the role of the commercial-investment real estate broker is expanding in both breadth and complexity.

Thorough mastery of investment principles and techniques and their applications can best be achieved through the educational courses which lead to the professional designation CCIM (Certified Commercial-Investment Member) of the REALTORS NATIONAL MARKETING INSTITUTE®. These courses constitute the best in professional education and training and produce some of the most competent real estate investment brokers in the country. *Marketing Investment Real Estate* is the primary textbook for these courses.

However, *Marketing Investment Real Estate* is also intended to be an independent entity. It can be used before, during and after the courses or can stand on its own. While primarily addressed to the commercial-investment real estate broker for use in marketing real estate to clients, it will also be of value to the investor and his direct advisors. Accountants and attorneys will find this book a reference of great value in their work for real estate investment clients. In any case, it is intended to be read from cover to cover so that the comprehensiveness of a thorough, uniform analytical approach is understood. Only then should it be used as a reference in checking a particular tax treatment or financing technique to be applied to a specific property.

By using the methods described in this book, knowledgeable brokers will be able to extend their skills to serve many more clients than in the past and serve all their clients in a more professional manner than has ever before been possible.

Acknowledgments

The preparation of the third edition of *Marketing Investment Real Estate* involved the efforts of several individuals who provided suggestions, reviewed draft materials, typed a succession of drafts, did editorial work and performed other important tasks. Rather than list the many, many people who were involved in various degrees with the production of this book, the authors would like to single out two individuals who deserve special thanks and recognition.

Helene Berlin of the REALTORS NATIONAL MARKETING INSTI-TUTE® editorial staff should be acknowledged for the highly professional manner in which she edited and coordinated the manuscript through to final bound books. This revision effort was complicated by the enactment of major tax legislation at a time when the final draft was ready for printing. The efficient and timely manner in which these problems were solved are due in large part to Helene. She possesses a unique combination of patience, perseverance and diplomacy which is an inspiration to those of us who work with her.

Greg Pinto, a University Scholar at the University of Connecticut, assisted in making the changes necessary to update illustrations and numerical examples so that they reflect the most recent tax treatment.

Many thanks to these individuals and to the many other people who were instrumental in the production of the revised text.

Storrs, CT
1985

About the Authors

REALTOR Stephen D. Messner, D.B.A., is Associate Dean and Professor of Finance and Real Estate in the School of Business Administration at the University of Connecticut. He also served as Head, Finance Department from 1972 through 1985, and Director of the Center for Real Estate and Urban Economic Studies from 1969 through 1977. Dr. Messner co-authored the first and second editions of *Marketing Investment Real Estate* and *Analyzing Real Estate Opportunities* both published by the COMMERCIAL-INVESTMENT REAL ESTATE COUNCIL of the REALTORS NATIONAL MARKETING INSTITUTE and *Industrial Real Estate* published by the Society of Industrial REALTORS and has contributed articles to *real estate today* and the *Commercial Investment Real Estate Journal.* In addition, he is the author of more than 50 other books, articles and monographs and has served as the Marketing Institute's educational consultant on Commercial-Investment courses since 1972. Dr. Messner holds the CCIM and SRPH designations.

   Irving Schreiber, B.B.A. and J.D., is a certified public accountant and a member of the New York State bar. He is a former Professor of Taxation and Director of the Tax Institute, School of Professional Accountancy, C. W. Post Center of Long Island University, New York. In addition, he is the author and/or editor of more than 30 books and looseleaf services in tax and related fields. Mr. Schreiber, a co-author of the first and second editions of *Marketing Investment Real Estate,* is a frequent lecturer and moderator of professional taxation seminars.

   REALTOR Victor L. Lyon, CCIM, is Chairman of the Board of Victor L. Lyon, Inc., REALTORS of Tacoma, Washington, and is a past president of REALTORS NATIONAL MARKETING INSTITUTE. A co-author of the previous editions of *Marketing Investment Real Estate,* REALTOR Lyon, a CCIM and a Certified Real Estate Brokerage Manager (CRB), is a senior instructor for the Commercial-Investment courses of the Marketing Institute and has served as the chairman of the Commercial-Investment Division. In addition, he holds the MAI, CRE, and SRS designations. Mr. Lyon is a recipient of the Distinguished Service Award from the NATIONAL ASSOCIATION OF REALTORS.

   REALTOR Robert L. Ward, CCIM, is a partner in Community Shopping Centers, one of the largest developers of strip shopping centers in Florida. He is a past chairman of the Commercial-Investment Council of REALTORS NATIONAL MARKETING INSTITUTE and a senior instructor of the Marketing Institute's Commercial-Investment courses, also serving on instructor development and faculty committees. REALTOR Ward is a co-author of *Analyzing Real Estate Opportunities,* published by the Marketing Institute.

Contents

Contents

Contents

Chapter 11   Exchanges   **286**

Contents

Contents

Marketing
Investment
Real Estate

Section I

Real Estate Investment and Finance

Chapter 1

Nature and Scope
of Investments

Introduction

This is a text about real estate investments, the impact of the federal income tax on such investments and a rational approach to analyzing and comparing the relative benefits of real estate investment opportunities. In a broader sense, it is a book on real estate investment decision-making, since the goal of the analysis generally is to help an investor make a choice from alternative investments. It is appropriate at the outset, however, to consider the larger scope of investment, including how and why investing is undertaken, the problems of investment risks, basic investment characteristics or attributes and investment alternatives. Such analysis will enable the real estate broker or investor to compare different types of available investments and the expected results of each. The real estate broker must be familiar with the entire spectrum of investments to make a meaningful analysis of the present or potential position of a client or prospect.

Investing in the 1980s

At no time over the past 50 years has it been more important to understand the principles of real estate investment analysis and decision-making. As we entered the 1980s, investors faced unparalleled problems. The United States economy was in the early stages of what appeared to be a major recession, inflation was rampant, and public efforts to fight both economic foes caused major upheavals in the money and capital markets.

Most small investors were in a quandary, having to choose from an ever-growing array of investment alternatives—precious metals and gems, art, railroad cars, oil drilling interests plus a variety of new securities and funds (trusts) entering the investment arena. In addition, the general trend of reducing special tax benefits or shelters and plugging tax loopholes for investors, which was prevalent in the 1970s, continued to influence the relative desirability of certain investments. Real estate retained many of the tax advantages lost by other forms of investments. The Economic Recovery Tax Act of 1981 added even further advantages to real estate as an investment. The Deficit Reduction Act of 1984 produced minor reductions in these advantages, but real estate investments retained the major tax advantages gained in earlier years.

The extremely volatile and uncertain market conditions, coupled with a significant increase in the nature and choice of investment vehicles, create an intensely competitive environment for the real estate broker. The broker must be able to understand the investment implications of a variety of investments if he is to best serve the investor.

Nature of investing

What is an investment?

The answer to this question is understood by most people probably in only a general way. One dictionary, for example, defines an investment as an "expenditure of money for income or profit; capital outlay." Most people understand that investment involves the commitment of money or other property (the capital outlay) in the hope of earning future income or profit on that outlay. However, specific investments and the elements affecting them raise more complex questions for which answers may not be as readily available.

The range of possible investments is, of course, quite broad. Placing money into a savings account is an investment, as is the purchase of corporate or government bonds. The purchase of some types of life insurance is considered an investment insofar as there is a buildup in cash surrender value. Similarly, the purchase of an annuity is a form of investment. The purchase of stock in a corporation or a mutual fund is an investment, as is the contribution of capital to a proprietorship or partnership business. Last, but not least, of course, real estate, in its many forms, is an investment.

When an individual commits funds for a property with the combined expectation of direct benefit from use plus future investment return, the classification of the activity is somewhat less well defined than the examples above. This phenomenon is common with commercial-investment property (vacation rental property, an owner-occupied duplex, owner-occupied retail buildings, etc.) and can also be found with certain other tangible property (paintings, jewelry, antiques and other collector items). The problem here is much more than simply one of definition; it centers on the decision-making criteria used in acquiring or disposing of the property, which may be confounded by the multiple objectives of use and investing.

The *primary* purpose of a pure investment is future income or profit. The profit or income an investor expects from an investment can take two basic forms: (1) income earned in the form of interest, dividends or rents; (2) profit realized from appreciation in value (when the investment property is sold for more than it cost).

Who invests?

One quite remarkable feature of the economic system of the United States, with its ability to produce an enormous and varied quantity of goods and services, is that a major portion of this capacity is made possible by private investments. In a private enterprise economy such as ours, the buildings and machines necessary for production can be purchased only through sacrifices in present consumption and through the desire and ability of some to save and to invest their savings for the future.

The overwhelming majority of the population is engaged in some form of investing. As disposable personal income in the United States has risen, so have the number and proportion of people who have funds in excess of their current consumption requirements. Indeed, for the past several decades the number of savers and investors has grown at a rate much higher than the population itself. Today in our economy, savings and investment capital emanate not from a select few but from the large and growing number of middle-income individuals and families.

Accompanying this growth in the number of investors has been the growth in the country's financial intermediaries: banks, life insurance companies, savings and loan associations, pension funds, etc. This growth has been in the size and, consequently, the importance of such institutions and in the variety of investment vehicles they offer. Recent changes have occurred whereby increasing numbers of investors are channeling their funds *directly* into investments such as real estate, tangible personal property and open-market securities (U. S. Treasury Bills) without using financial intermediaries.

The forecast for the future seems clear enough. There will be even greater numbers of investors. Investors will be more sophisticated and will have increasing amounts of information and media to aid them in their investment pursuits. Finally, there will be an ever-increasing number of investors seeking to invest their funds directly rather than utilizing financial intermediaries, and they will face an ever-expanding selection of investment alternatives.

Why do people invest?

While the answer to this question seems all too obvious, the point should be emphasized that ''making a profit'' is neither a definitive enough nor comprehensive enough goal to be helpful in assessing the rationale for investing. In our free enterprise economy, individuals interact with business firms by supplying both labor and capital in exchange for wages, salaries, interest and dividends. The cash receipts from business are then used by individuals to meet and satisfy basic consumption needs and desires. Consumption, however, has a variety of monetary costs. While food and clothing typically can be purchased with current earnings, other items such as housing, automobiles, education, etc., can be purchased only through borrowing or savings, or both. Most individuals save a portion of current income so that they might provide for future consumption; as a result these people face investment decisions regularly. Thus, it is to make possible future consumption that people save and invest in the present.

People purchase commercial-investment real estate for a variety of reasons. Obviously, some people buy property because they intend to use it themselves. But even those who purchase income-producing property to rent to others may have reasons other than dollar return when they make the acquisition. Pride of ownership—the romance of brick and mortar—can be an important factor in purchasing commercial property. An investor may take great pride in the purchase of a locally prominent office building that he can show friends.

Other investors look to commercial property to provide gainful employment through management, construction, repair, etc. Monetary return may be of secondary importance to this group of buyers. Still other buyers may have a combination of goals in mind when selecting commercial real estate including portfolio diversification, control of a highly leveraged property and tax shelter.

Investment alternatives

A large number of investment alternatives are available to the typical investor; these alternatives can be categorized in several ways. Here is one way to categorize investment alternatives:[1]

    Direct Investment Alternatives
        Fixed-principal investments
            Cash
            Savings accounts
            Marketable savings certificates
            Corporate bonds
            Government bonds
        Variable-principal securities
            Preferred stocks
            Common stocks
            Convertible securities
            Warrants
            Options
        Nonsecurity investments
            Real estate
            Mortgages
            Commodities
            Business ventures
            Art, antiques and other valuables
    Indirect Investment Alternatives
        Pension funds
        Insurance company portfolios
        Investment companies
        Trust funds

The primary division between types of investments—direct and indirect —differentiates between those investment alternatives in which the individual makes the actual investment decisions for himself and those in which he does not. Indirect investments are those in which the individual has little or no say.

Of the direct investments, the fixed-principal investments are those in which the principal amount or terminal value is known (fixed) with complete certainty. Perhaps the best example of this class is the bond that has a set value at maturity.

Variable-principal securities have no fixed or certain terminal value, and the laws of supply and demand produce periodic changes in principal value (price). Common stock, for example, has neither a fixed income nor a fixed market price.

Nonsecurity investments include a broad range of vehicles, but their common characteristic is that while they are direct investments under the definition used above, they are not classified as securities. One might argue that the mortgage instrument is a near-security in that it is traded in secondary markets, but there are many types of mortgage loans and many different ways to invest directly in mortgages. The other nonsecurities are more clearly of the tax-sheltered variety in which certain of the income tax provisions can offer significant tax advantages to classes of investors.

With indirect investment alternatives individuals have virtually no, or at most very little, influence or control over the actual selection of investments. Some have called this the "money management industry," which is growing rapidly in our economy.[2]

Investment attributes

Although it is generally true that the primary reason individuals and institutions invest is to create future wealth and thus provide for future consumption, there are a variety of other reasons. Because particular investors have different needs and desires that must be satisfied by the investments they undertake, it follows that there are basic factors or attributes of each investment that somehow relate to its ability to meet a particular investor's objectives. As a practical matter, many institutional investors are restricted to some extent in the types of investments they make. In some cases they are legally restricted, but equally important to individuals as well as institutional investors are such factors as habits, historical precedent, tradition and, simply, sound judgment; those factors prompt investors to limit their selection to certain investments.

Investment attributes are directly related to investment objectives. Rational financial planning requires that each investor carefully consider and specifically identify his investment objectives within the context of his personal needs along with any legal restrictions he might face when he invests for others. Thus, we might think of attributes in terms of the ability of an investment to provide investment benefits.

For the typical investor the five most important investment attributes are the following:

Risk
Liquidity
Return
Manageability
Taxability

Risk

In terms of relative importance, risk may be the most important attribute of an investment for most investors. Risk is generally defined in terms of the degree of certainty with which return from the investment is expected. An extreme example would be cash which remains uninvested. The return is absolutely certain to be zero; there is complete safety and thus no risk. Most investors think of certainty of receiving principal invested back as their highest priority and are concerned only secondarily with receipt of income.

Risk may be further defined according to type. There are four distinct categories:

Purchasing power risk relates to the extent to which an investment is subject to losses (or gains) in the purchasing power of dollar amounts received as income or as return of principal. With price levels moving steadily upward, most investors have come to think of this form of risk as almost sure uncertainty as to *loss* of purchasing power, referring to this as "inflation risk." This attitude has been substantially reinforced by the double-digit inflation of the late 1970s and early 1980s. It should be remembered, however, that there have been periods of downward price movement (during the Depression of the 1930s and in some isolated instances in the mid-1970s), and during these periods purchasing power actually increased.

Most commonly, high purchasing power risk is associated with those investments offering a fixed income, even though this risk affects income and principal in the same way. Investments with a high degree of purchasing power risk are bonds, mortgages, savings accounts and other fixed (or limited) income investments. Investing in common stock and real estate is generally considered the most practical and effective protection against this form of risk.

Fixed income investments are not protected against inflation or loss of purchasing power. Once an annuity with a fixed dollar amount is purchased, that is the dollar amount which will be received regardless of future changes in the purchasing power of the dollars received. This also holds true for the interest rate called for in bonds; only the *amount* specified by the bond will be paid at each interest period (the interest rate will not go up). Furthermore, the amount received at maturity will be the amount paid for the bond except when purchased at a discount. Preferred stock falls into the same category as bonds since the dividends called for are generally fixed as a percentage of the par value of the stock.

Common stock, on the other hand, is deemed to be a hedge against inflation on the theory that the market value of the stock will reflect any inflationary factors in the economy. This may hold true for the entire spectrum of common stocks but may not apply to any one particular stock. Furthermore, when interest rates increase in an inflationary period, common stock prices may decline as was dramatically demonstrated in 1974.

Various business investments may reflect the pressures of inflation since the price at which the products or services are sold by the business will be subject to the same inflationary pressures.

Real estate prices generally have reflected the inflationary spiral in recent years. It also has become quite common for real estate leases to include escalation clauses calling for increased rents to offset increases in the cost of living.

Financial risk   This form of risk is measured in terms of the uncertainty concerning the financial ability of the investment to return principal and income in the future. The popular rating systems, such as Moody's and Standard and Poor's, base their grading systems of securities on the relationship between the amount of funds an issuer has to satisfy security holders and the amount of funds required to meet those demands.

Business risk   This form of risk is often confused with "financial risk" because the two are so closely interrelated. Business risk, however, refers to the uncertainty associated with the profit potential of the property or business, while financial risk relates to the capital structure that is used to finance the assets of the firm. For example, the business risk associated with drilling for oil is separate from the manner by which the venture is financed.

Interest rate (money rate) risk   This form of risk relates to the impact of changes in future interest rates on investment value. When interest rates fall, the market price of existing mortgages increases; conversely, when interest rates rise, the value of existing mortgages falls. Even the most secure investments from the standpoint of financial risk—U.S. Government Bonds—are highly subject to changes in interest rates, as evidenced by the significant drop in long-term government bond prices during the first half of 1980 when interest rates hit new highs. In general, the greater the financial safety of the investment, the greater the investment rate risk. For example, high grade bonds suffer most from changes in interest rates.

Risk and return by type of investment

It is generally accepted that risk and return on the investment have a direct relationship to each other. That is, the higher the expected return, the greater the risk. In contrast, risk is low when guaranteed (or practically guaranteed) returns are involved.[3] Thus, the risk factor is low for savings accounts, life insurance and annuities and relatively low for corporate and municipal bonds. The effective interest rate (not necessarily the rate called for by the bond but the effective rate determined by the combination of the interest rate called for by the bond, the price at which the bond is selling and the time left to maturity of the bond) will reflect the relative risk attributed to the bond.

Corporate stock is more difficult to classify with respect to risk since it may have widely varying degrees of risk. Stock of a regulated public utility is generally considered less risky than the stock of a new, unproven company just entering the field. The latter may have more "action" among stockholders looking for dramatic increases, but the risk is more substantial.

Partnerships, syndicates and other forms of ownership in business ventures also have varying degrees of risk. Again, the risk and rate of return are directly related. Investments in speculative oil drilling, for example, may be very risky (in terms of the percentage of wells that do strike oil) but the return may be substantial. The cost of an investment in a proven well will be much higher than in a wildcat venture because the risk is much less.

Real estate investments also run the gamut of degrees of risk. A property with a long-term lease from a national tenant is considered far less risky than one with a lease with only three years remaining. Some other factors that affect the degree of risk in a real estate investment may be unknown at the time the investment is undertaken. Changes in the economic viability of the neighborhood, changes in zoning, increases in real estate taxes, possible condemnation of the property and increases in interest rates all are examples of factors that affect risk.

Liquidity

Another factor important to many investors is the ability to convert an investment into cash or its equivalent rapidly and with little, if any, loss of principal. This attribute is called "liquidity." An example of a highly liquid investment would be a savings account that has no penalty for withdrawal before a specified date. Thus, not only can conversion take place quickly and easily, but also there is no loss whatsoever in the amount of principal invested at the time the investment is terminated.

Liquidity is important to both individual and institutional investors since liquid assets may be needed to meet unexpected expenses or in order to take advantage of unforeseen opportunities that are particularly favorable. A closely related attribute that may meet these requirements is "marketability," or the capability of the investment to find a ready market where the asset may be sold even at a possible loss of principal. Under this definition an asset that is liquid must also be marketable, but assets that are marketable are not necessarily liquid.

Money in a savings bank, investment bonds, life insurance and annuities all are considered to be relatively liquid. They are already in the form of cash or may be converted into cash very quickly and generally with little or no loss of principal. This is in contrast to the characteristic of "marketability" where there is a ready and active market for the quick sale of the investment, although the sale price may be well below the original amount invested. Investments in common stocks listed on the New York Stock Exchange may be highly marketable but the price at which they are traded may fluctuate widely from week to week. Such securities would therefore be considered marketable but not liquid.

Investments in oil, cattle and other business ventures may be neither liquid nor marketable. An interest (especially a minority interest) in a closely held business (one held by only a few owners) may be difficult to sell at any price.

Real estate is generally not considered to be liquid and is often not marketable compared with other investment alternatives. Certainly it is not as readily salable as is stock trading on the New York Stock Exchange. However, cash is often available from a real estate investment without the necessity of a sale. Real estate, traditionally, is among the best types of security for a loan; mortgages on real estate are generally readily available. If property has increased in value, the immediate availability of this increase to the owner may be realized without his actually selling the property; he can usually borrow against it by refinancing the property.

Return: dollar and rate

Not surprisingly, the *periodic income* from and the *appreciation* of the investment are two of its most important attributes. Generally, income and appreciation are combined into a measure of return that can be expressed as a periodic dollar amount or as a periodic rate measured as a percentage of amount invested. Investors are pressured to seek the highest return on their investment possible, commensurate with the risk they are willing to assume and other important attributes they desire.

Fixed income investments, while relatively free of risk, generally have no appreciation factor. The return on the investment is there (in the form of interest or dividends), but the dollar value of the capital investment remains unchanged. If a person deposits $10,000 in a savings bank and receives 5 percent interest per year, the original $10,000 investment grows only by the amount of the interest earned. If a person buys an annuity that pays $100 a month for the rest of his life, that is exactly what he will receive (except in the case of variable annuities whose periodic payouts are geared to the value of the equity securities in which the annuity company invests). The amount payable at the maturity of a bond is generally its face amount. So unless the bonds are purchased at a discount there is no capital appreciation. Interest is paid during the life of the bond, but when it matures the investor receives only the amount originally paid.

Stocks may have a substantial appreciation factor. This will vary according to the nature of the stock, the industry involved, the expectations of investors for that particular industry, the position of the company in that industry, the inflation factor in the economy and many other intangibles that continue to baffle students of the stock market. Many stocks have been known to double, triple and quadruple in value in comparatively short periods of time; others have nose-dived in similarly short periods.

Investments in oil, gas, cattle, etc. may have some appreciation, especially if the price of the end products is influenced by inflation and other market conditions. Each of these specialized forms of investment has its own combination of periodic income and appreciation potential, and generalizations here would be hazardous.

Real estate, especially during the past 25 years, has shown remarkable increases in value because of a variety of factors such as increasing population and wealth, limitations on the quantity of land available, availability of mortgage money, inflation, and the special tax advantages available to real estate investors. As with other forms of investments, there is no point in generalizing, but the basic economic characteristics of real estate provide persuasive rationale for an expectation of long-term appreciation.

Manageability

The manageability of an investment is the extent to which it requires monitoring and periodic change. As a rule, real estate investments require much more management than, for example, a savings account or even common stocks. It is possible, however, to acquire the services of professional management and thereby reduce the burdens and risk of management.

In the context of this discussion "management" refers to the management of the investment as a segment of an investment portfolio, and not management of the operation of the business entity or property that may represent the investment. Probably every investment has a charge for management built into it when it does not require direct management by the investor. An investment in a savings bank does not seem to require management by the investor at all. However, the bank has to select the properties on which it will grant mortgage loans and determine what other investments and loans it may make. The cost of this management reduces the net return to the bank and, therefore, to the investor. Admittedly, this management cost is almost negligible as far as each individual depositor in the bank is concerned.

Stocks and bonds require careful and constant management regarding both the selection of individual stocks or securities and the timing of purchase and sale. The management may be supplied by the investor himself, by professional management available from brokers or by professional managers hired for a fee. An investor may try to avoid the management problem and, in effect, hire professional management by investing in mutual funds. But here, too, professional management must be paid since each mutual fund has a professional management advisor who is paid a fee from the assets of the fund based upon the size of the fund's portfolio.

Other types of investments, such as those in oil, gas and cattle, require management, and the investor often is not experienced in this role. Hence, included in the fee he pays for his investment is a charge for management.

For small properties, the investor may be his own manager. For large properties, he will generally need professional management help and should take this fact into consideration when analyzing the return he can expect from his investment.

Taxability

The effect of income tax is well known, for it is only the after-tax dollar that is spendable by the investor. The federal government (and many states) takes its share of income via income tax, and the investor gets what remains. Not all sources of income are taxed alike. The tax on some types of profit may even be deferred, as in the case of exchanges. Some investments have certain built-in tax advantages (such as accelerated cost recovery) which reduce the tax impact on the income produced. Finally, certain investments deemed desirable from a public policy standpoint are encouraged through tax credits.

In general, dividends, rents and interest are taxable as ordinary income, with the exception of the interest on municipal bonds. However, the accounting measure of taxable rental income is reduced by depreciation deductions (requiring no cash outlay) which, in turn, can boost after-tax cash flows to the investor.

Annuity income is partially taxed since part of the annuity is merely a return of the capital investment. However, the taxable portion is taxed as ordinary income.

Income from the participation in a business venture as a sole proprietor or partner is taxable as ordinary income. Income from the sale of oil, gas or other minerals is subject to ordinary income tax, but a depletion allowance reduces the income subject to tax.

Gain from the sale (or exchange when applicable) of investment property is generally taxable as a capital gain. That means that these gains are taxable at 40 percent of the rate that applies to ordinary income and at no time at a total rate exceeding 20 percent (40 percent of net capital gains times the 50-percent maximum tax rate).

In addition to the special tax advantages enjoyed by real estate through the use of accelerated methods of cost recovery and the availability of capital gains treatment on the sale or exchange of real estate at a profit, another tax advantage lies in the tax-deferred exchange. Real estate that has appreciated in value may be exchanged for other real estate with the tax on the appreciation deferred to a later time. Income tax on the appreciation may be avoided altogether if the property acquired in the exchange, or some other property acquired in still another exchange for this acquired property, is held until death.

Notes

1. Keith V. Smith and David K. Eiteman, *Essentials of Investing* (Homewood, IL: Richard D. Irwin, Inc., 1974), pp. 4-7.

2. Smith and Eiteman, p. 7.

3. Nearly the entire issue of *The Real Estate Appraiser and Analyst,* vol. 44, no. 6, November-December, 1978, is devoted to the issue of the relationship of real estate investment yields to other alternative investments in the money and capital markets.

Chapter 2

Real Estate Investments

Introduction to commercial-investment brokerage

The previous chapter dealt with the characteristics found in all forms of investments. This chapter will focus specifically on the nature and scope of real estate investments. The real estate broker must deal with and therefore be aware of a number of investor and user needs and desires. These needs and desires may be satisfied by acquiring interests in a wide variety of investment properties, ranging from raw land to small duplex multifamily units to massive shopping center developments. The interests that may be acquired in this large array of alternative properties also may take many forms such as lessee, sublessor, equity owner, mortgagee, etc. The overwhelmingly large number of combinations open to the broker in meeting the objectives of his client makes his task both complex and challenging.

Spectrum of income-producing property

The spectrum of real estate investments is quite broad, ranging from residential income properties to commercial and industrial properties and to farms and land. The following list is illustrative of the real estate investment spectrum. Any of these properties could be owned by users or held by investors for rental income.

> Residential income
>> Apartment houses
>>> Garden
>>> High-rise
>> Hotels
>> Motels
>> Rest homes
> Commercial
>> Professional buildings (doctors, lawyers and other professionals)
>> Office buildings
>> Shopping centers
>>> Regional

Community
Local
Single purpose buildings
Theatres
Bowling alleys
Free-standing retail stores
Service stations
Industrial
Warehouses
Industrial parks
Manufacturing facilities
Utility company buildings—power plants, steam generation plants
Farms and land
Recreation land—lots for single-family residences
Subdivision land
Residential lots zoned for multiple dwellings
Commercially zoned land
Industrially zoned land
Raw acreage
Farms
Ranches

Clients

Being knowledgeable about the types of properties in the market is only part of the real estate investment broker's responsibility. He also must be aware of the people in the market who might utilize the services of a broker and what motivates them to invest in real estate.

On one side of the market are the sellers, or disposers, of property. These people provide the basic inventory for the broker. In many cases, the disposition of the property is by sale or exchange, and usually the principal motivation is that the property no longer meets the investment goals of the owner.

In other cases, the owner of the property has a problem that can be solved by refinancing the property, by improving the management of the property or by taking some other action that improves property performance in terms of his objectives.

On the other side of the real estate market equation are those persons or institutions who wish to acquire real estate. The motivations for acquisition generally focus on financial gain, but may also include a variety of other personal reasons such as the desire to be directly involved in the creation and management of a business enterprise, pride of ownership, etc. The range of skills is represented by first-time, totally inexperienced buyers to highly sophisticated, well trained representatives of major corporations.

Thus, the professional commercial-investment broker must understand the needs, motivations and objectives of a wide variety of sellers and buyers of investment property. He must be able to assist his clients, whether buyers or sellers, in selecting that strategy which has the highest probability of achieving the individual client's objectives.

Types of interest in real estate

Real estate interests can be divided in a number of ways. One form is a fee ownership interest which is the outright ownership of the property (subject, in many instances, to encumbrances such as loans for which the property is security).

Parts or all of the fee, however, may be leased to lessees who, in turn, may sublease part or all of their leasehold interests. A lessee also may construct improvements on the leased property (for which he may be entitled to deduct depreciation or amortization expenses). However, at the termination of the lease, the improvement reverts to the lessor unless otherwise provided for in the lease contract.

There is also the interest of the lender—the mortgagee. He may be entitled to foreclose on the mortgage loan, acquire the property and then sell it should there be a default on the loans on that property. In the case of mortgagees, there may be several mortgagee positions, each with a different interest. The first loan on the property has the first lien. If a second lender has made a loan, he stands in line behind the first mortgagee and has no claim against the property until the first mortgagee's loans have been satisfied.

In addition, there may be other liens against a property. For example, if the owner has a judgment against him, the judgment holder may have a lien against the property, which means he has a claim against the proceeds of sale for the amount of his lien. There also may be a mechanic's lien against the property for unpaid amounts to those who have made repairs or have done other work on the property.

Finally, the property may be subject to easements—the rights of others to make certain use of the property. An example would be the right of a telephone company to string telephone lines across part of the land.

Forms of ownership

The ownership of a fee or other interests may be by an individual or by several persons in the form of joint ownership, a partnership, a trust or a corporation. The manner in which real estate, or an interest in real estate, is owned often has great tax significance, as illustrated in Chapter 8.

An individual investor generally seeks to have tax losses generated by the real estate investment available to offset his other taxable income. An individual or partnership form of ownership accomplishes this purpose best.

On the other hand, if real estate is producing ordinary income and the investor already has considerable taxable income, it may be preferable to have the income taxable to a corporation.

Corporate ownership presents other problems. The corporation is a separate entity and pays its own tax on any income it earns. However, the income remaining after tax, if paid to the stockholders by way of dividends, is taxable to the stockholders; as a result, income may be taxed twice.

Accumulating after-tax income in the corporation is not necessarily a long-term solution. The corporation may become subject to a penalty tax for unreasonably accumulating earnings and profits. There also are problems of disposing of corporate-owned property or getting that property back into the hands of the stockholders. Many of these problems can be solved, but astute planning prior to acquisition is preferable.

Both the tax problems and tax-saving opportunities that evolve from the proper form of ownership are mentioned here to alert the reader to the importance of the ownership form. Too often not enough attention is paid to this aspect of real estate investment; too often an investor acts without regard to all of the consequences, only to discover at some later date that he is faced with possible tax liabilities that otherwise could have been avoided.

Factors affecting real estate investments

The investment factors of risk, appreciation, marketability, liquidity and management were discussed in Chapter 1. They are discussed in more detail here with respect to how they affect real estate investments.

Risk

Risk is one of the most vital factors to consider in any investment. As previously indicated, in virtually all cases the greater the risk element the greater the expected return must be in order to attract investors. This element of risk is itself composed of component parts—namely the quantity, the quality and the durability of the future income stream produced by the property.

Quantity If all other factors are equal, a property that is estimated to produce $6,000 of income will be less valuable than a similar property estimated to produce $10,000 of income over the same period of time, assuming equal probability of attainment.

Quality A rooming house for transients and a small industrial warehouse, both producing the same amount of net income, are not necessarily worth the same amount. The warehouse normally will be deemed more valuable because the quality of its income stream is more reliable than that of the rooming house.

17

Durability A parcel of property having two years remaining on its lease may not be as valuable as one with 15 years still to run on its lease. The concept of durability also may be related to the economic life of the property.

In essence, then, risk is the chance an investor takes that he will not earn as much as he anticipates. His return from his investment will vary directly with the degree of risk. High risk tends to yield high income and low risk tends to produce low income.

Appreciation

Another characteristic inherent in real estate investments is that of increment or appreciation. Part of the reason for the importance of appreciation is inflation, the decrease in the value of money. In the case of land, however, much of this appreciation is caused by the law of supply and demand. Except for certain limited instances where man has been able to reclaim land from the sea and lakes, there is only a certain amount of land on earth; this cannot be increased. At the same time, the population of the earth is increasing steadily. There is, therefore, an increased need or demand for whatever land is available. As the ratio of supply and demand changes, so does the value of the commodity—in this case land. Because of these factors, it often is true that the value of land and buildings can increase—appreciate— even though there is physical deterioration to the improvement occurring at the same time.

Liquidity and marketability

Liquidity is another basic characteristic of real estate investment property. This characteristic includes two elements: the loan potential and the sale potential. Real estate is particularly well suited to financing. The property is virtually immovable in the case of buildings and virtually indestructible in the case of land. Traditionally, lending sources have been willing to make loans secured by real estate. After the income from a parcel has enabled its owner to pay off his mortgage loans, it is possible for him to place a new mortgage on the property. Proceeds of this new loan will be tax-free to him at that time.

Often, with real estate, there is no instant market. An owner desiring to sell his real estate often must wait a considerable period of time before he gets his desired price. This differs markedly from the case of an owner of a stock who can merely telephone his broker and have the sale of his stock completed within minutes of his instructions to sell. But, perhaps because of the slowness of the real estate market, real estate usually is not subject to short cycles of upward and downward trends in prices, as is the securities market.

Sources of financing are as varied as man's imagination. Conventional sources are the commercial banks, savings and loan associations and insurance companies. In addition, there are union welfare funds, pension programs, profit-sharing and other kinds of employee-benefit and retirement funds (both public and private) and some charitable and educational institutions that may be interested in placing such loans for their investment portfolios. Not to be overlooked is the seller of the property. He may be willing to take a purchase-money mortgage that will provide sufficient financing to complete a transaction. In some cases, the necessary financing can come from the brokers handling the transaction.

Property management

A sometimes neglected characteristic of a real estate investment is the requirement of property management, which may be necessary in varying degrees, from the mere receipting of one check a month to the full-time responsibility for a large building. In some cases, the investor may be buying a full-time job if suitable local property management is not available.

In computing return on investment, the investor should remember to charge a cost for management (even if he does it himself and has no cash outlay) in order to determine true return on the capital invested. Often professional management is worth the out-of-pocket cash outlay. Professional management usually knows when to increase or decrease rents and provides protection, such as tax escalator and cost-of-living index clauses, that the lessor might not ordinarily think of. Professionals have the ability to guide and counsel the investor on proper timing for selling or exchanging. On the other hand, sometimes the personal attention of an owner-manager can counteract the forces of a depressed market. This largely depends on the management skills of the professional or the owner.

Special factors affecting real estate

Three special factors particularly applicable to real estate investments should be noted. They are tax shelter through cost recovery, leverage and exchange or installment sale potential.

Cost recovery

Under the provisions of the 1984 Deficit Reduction Act, capital costs for property held for trade or business may be deducted as expenses over an 18-year period. This deduction is based on the entire adjusted basis of an improvement on the property, which includes the amount of any loans on the property (see Chapter 8 for an explanation of basis). Thus, if a property improvement (assume the land is leased) were purchased and the improvement was worth $100,000—$10,000 cash and $90,000 mortgage—the deduction often may be computed by the accelerated method which permits the recovery of basis for tax purposes in a relatively short time. This is because deductions in the early years are large and diminish over time.

The importance of the cost recovery deduction is that it requires no cash outlay, yet it reduces the income from the property that is subject to tax. Further, such deductions taken can exceed real depreciation in the property, thereby creating tax-free dollars because of income tax savings. (If the deduction exceeds the income from the property, the excess deduction may be applied to reduce other taxable income the property owner may have.) Since a dollar of tax that does not have to be paid is, in essence, a form of income, the deduction helps to produce more after-tax dollars from a real estate investment than would be available were the same amount of income earned from another form of investment which does not allow for such deductions.

The relationship between the tax accounting concept of *income* and the investment concept of *cash flows* is shown in Figure 1 for a single year. Assume that the property improvement cited above produced a net operating income (NOI) of $10,000.

As shown in Figure 1, the shelter of "income" from the real estate that otherwise would be taxed immediately may be seen as a three-step process, depending upon how large the cost recovery deduction is:

1. Cost recovery shelters, first of all, the principal portion of the Annual Debt Service (ADS) since this is a cash outflow that is not deductible as an expense.

2. If the amount of cost recovery exceeds principal reduction (as in the example above), the next portion of "income" that is sheltered is the Cash Flow Before Tax (CFBT).

3. To the extent that total cost recovery exceeds the sum of principal reduction and CFBT, other income unrelated to the property is sheltered.

Leverage

As was previously mentioned, real estate is well suited to financing; traditionally it has been very good security for loans. As such, real estate can be acquired or carried with a smaller percentage of cash outlay by the owner than most other investments.

The ability to finance the purchase or carrying of real estate gives rise to leverage. Leverage arises because all appreciation of the property belongs to the property holder even though there may be substantial loans against the property. Similarly, all of the income belongs to him—regardless of the amounts of the loan.

Figure 1 Income and Cash Flows

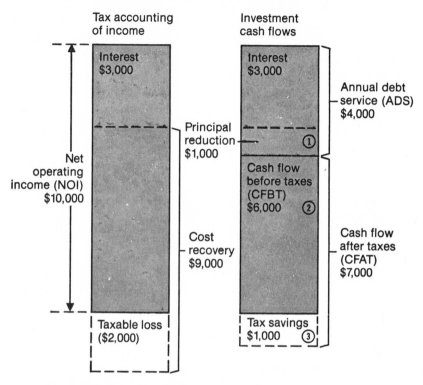

Tax accounting of income

Investment cash flows

Interest $3,000

Interest $3,000

Annual debt service (ADS) $4,000

Principal reduction $1,000 ①

Net operating income (NOI) $10,000

Cash flow before taxes (CFBT) $6,000 ②

Cost recovery $9,000

Cash flow after taxes (CFAT) $7,000

Taxable loss ($2,000)

Tax savings $1,000 ③

Note: ①, ②, ③ see text, page 20

Examples

1. Assume a property available today for $100,000 will sell for $150,000 five years from now. If the property is bought for $100,000 cash, the buyer will subsequently realize a $50,000 profit or a 50-percent increase of his investment. Suppose, however, the buyer is able to obtain a $90,000 mortgage, committing only $10,000 of his own money. When he sells the property for $150,000 and pays off the $90,000 mortgage, he will be left with $60,000, or a 500-percent increase of his investment. (The cost of the transaction and the loan for the five-year period have been ignored here for the purpose of keeping the example simple.)

2. Leverage has its negative side, too. If the investor puts up $10,000 of his own money and borrows $90,000 and if the value of the property then falls to $90,000, his entire $10,000 investment will be wiped out.

3. Leverage is also present in terms of the current income from the property. Suppose the net operating income from the property in the previous example amounts to $5,000. If the investor puts up $100,000 in cash, he will see a 5-percent return on his investment. If he puts up only $10,000 in cash, he will see a 50-percent return on his investment. (Again, we are ignoring the cost of the loan and the effect of income taxes so as not to complicate this illustration.)

Exchange or installment sale of property

Investment real estate can be exchanged[1] on a tax-deferred basis, a possibility not available with many other popular investment alternatives (see Chapter 11). Even if the property is sold, the gain on sale may be prorated over several tax periods through the vehicle of the installment sale (see Chapter 10). In either case, these options provide owners additional factors to consider before they dispose of property.

Notes

1. For a complete volume on exchanges, including tax implications, see Mark Lee Levine, *Real Estate Exchanges* (Chicago: REALTORS NATIONAL MARKETING INSTITUTE®, 1981).

Chapter 3

Fundamentals of Discounted Cash Flow Analysis

Valuation of income-producing properties

Meaning of value

Of central importance in the analysis of any investment is the determination of "value." Real estate brokers, appraisers, investors and users are concerned with estimates of value for existing or proposed property developments. Those desiring an estimate of value have a variety of purposes; thus there is also a variety of definitions for value. In essence, the definition of value is a function of the purpose for which an estimate of value is sought.

For example, the well-known real estate appraiser, Alfred Ring, lists the following as representing only *a few* of the many types of "value" in common use today.[1]

Economic value	Sale value
Stable value	Salvage value
Appraised value	Intrinsic value
Potential value	Extrinsic value
Book value	Tax value
Sound value	Use value
Fair value	Rental value
Real value	Speculative value
True value	Reproduction value
Depreciated value	Nuisance value
Warranted value	Liquidation value
Face value	Mortgage value
Cash value	Improved value
Capital value	Insurance value
Exchange value	Leasehold value

The economist typically views "value" as the point of intersection on a supply and demand curve. The residential broker may consider the value of a property he represents as being the price the property will bring from an informed buyer after the property has had reasonable exposure in an active

23

and competitive market. The appraiser may view the value of a property in a variety of ways: (1) as having the same value as a comparable property already in existence and sold in the marketplace; (2) as having a value equal to the cost of reproducing a given property with equivalent utility; and (3) as having the same value as an investment with a similar income stream. These all are related concepts of *market value*. To the user of the property, "value" is related to the specific purpose for which a property is utilized and the productivity achieved in this use. To the typical investor, however, "value" is the present worth of the anticipated future income stream or cash benefits that would accrue from the investment. The primary focus of this book is *investment value*. To the extent that a buyer is typical of investors in the market who are most likely to purchase an income-producing property, investment value may equal market value.

Amenity properties versus income-producing properties

For amenity properties, such as owner-occupied homes, the value of the property most often derives from the right to use the realty. Payment for the property typically comes from income and/or wealth totally unrelated to the property itself. The approval of a mortgage loan on such a property is generally based on the owner's ability to meet mortgage payments, not on the property's ability to generate income.

In contrast, income-producing properties provide a stream of payments from the rental of the property that may be used as the basis of its purchase price and as the security for mortgage financing. Typically, the investor collects rents and pays the necessary expenses of operation, such as property taxes and maintenance. What remains is available to pay financing charges. The balance provides a return to the investor for assuming the risk of ownership. In the case of real estate investments, like all other forms of investments, the investor is concerned with *cash* received in the future in return for cash or its equivalent invested in the present. Tax benefits from the ownership of real estate, the impact of financing and financial leverage, depreciation, etc., all are factors that influence the after-tax cash flows accruing from a property. Once the after-tax cash flows are determined or estimated, it is still necessary to decide which alternative stream of future income is most valuable to a specific investor.

Even if the investor chooses to use the property rather than rent it, the rental payments that would have been paid to obtain a comparable property represent a savings to the investor/user/owner. The savings, in turn, may be used to support the purchase and financing of the property. In either case, whether the investor rents the income property to another or uses the property himself, the value of the property may be derived as the present worth of the estimated income from rents to be received by the investor (actual or imputed rent) plus the present worth of the estimated proceeds from selling the property.

Capitalization of income

The basis used to estimate the value of income-producing real estate is the potential income it can produce in the future. The process of converting future income into a single present value is called capitalization. Value is a direct function of income. Therefore, any change in anticipated future income affects the capitalized value (present value) of the income.

Future income streams are capitalized into single values so that investors may have a consistent basis to compare investment alternatives. The primary selection criterion of the investor should be based upon some measure of the stream of income from rental payments plus proceeds from the eventual sale of the property compared with the initial cash (down payment) invested to receive this future income. Reduced to its simplest terms, the cash that a buyer is willing to invest for an income-producing property is directly related to the income that is estimated to be received and the rate of return that is desired.

Example

If $100,000 were invested today at an annual interest rate of 10 percent, the investment would accrue to a value of $110,000 by the end of the first year. If this total amount is considered to represent both return *of* the original investment ($100,000) and return *on* the investment ($10,000), the "return on" portion is indeed 10 percent and the earnings may be withdrawn and enjoyed with no effect on the original investment. This process of earning and withdrawal can take place endlessly as long as (1) only the "return on" portion is withdrawn and (2) the original investment amount ($100,000) can be reinvested each and every year at 10 percent. Stated another way, an income of $10,000 per year capitalized at 10 percent suggests that the investment value is $100,000.

This example represents the most simplistic form of income capitalization, perpetuity capitalization. The stream of equal payments are received at the end of each period (usually one year) for infinity. The capitalization rate must be consistent with the periods. In the example, the cash flows of $10,000 were received at the end of each year. The capitalization rate was 10 percent per year. Symbolically this may be stated as:

$$V = \frac{I}{R}$$

V = value or present worth of the future rights to periodic income
I = periodic net income
R = rate of capitalization

This formula represents the most basic building block to an understanding of the investment process. However, the preceding illustration deals with the very simple case of capitalization in perpetuity where the principal is assumed to remain unchanged over an indefinite period. Although raw land may provide an excellent example of realty that could produce such a regular income stream, the more common investment situation involves capitalization of uneven cash flows over a term. To better understand the process whereby income received for a finite term is capitalized into a single present value, it is necessary to introduce the concept and technique of compound interest and discounting.

Compound interest and discounting

Every financial investment produces a stream of cash flows, or spendable dollars. The cash flows created by alternative investments are rarely equal in size or duration. Compound interest and discounting techniques are used to adjust cash flows for comparison on a par basis. These techniques are widely used in many financial fields, including investment real estate, mortgage lending, banking, corporate finance and securities investment. Compound interest and discounting methods are used to: (1) compare investment alternatives, (2) compare anticipated investment performance to the investor's financial objectives and (3) compare investment performance under alternative assumptions that affect the cash flows.

Investor motivation

When comparing investment alternatives with comparable risks associated with the return *on* and return *of* capital, the rational investor is motivated by two basic preferences. They are simply summarized as:

more is better than less

and

sooner is better than later.

More is better than less

This investor preference has two basic aspects. First, when given alternative investment opportunities of comparable risk that require an equal capital investment and have the same timing of cash flows, the investor will prefer the investment that produces the most cash. Consider the two
comparisons of four investments below.

Example

The initial investment in each case is $1,000. The parentheses indicate that the cash flow is paid by the investor, or that it is a negative cash flow. Time Period 0 is the time the initial investment is made. Other cash flows are assumed to be received at the end of period (EOP) unless otherwise indicated.

Time Period (EOP)	Investment A	Investment B
0	($1,000)	($1,000)
1	–0–	–0–
2	–0–	–0–
3	$1,800	$1,500

Investment A is superior because the same investment of $1,000 will produce more return of funds at the end of the investment holding period.

Time Period (EOP)	Investment C	Investment D
0	($1,000)	($1,000)
1	600	500
2	600	500
3	600	500

Investment C is superior because each cash flow is more than those of Investment D.

The second aspect of the assumption that more is better than less is that an investor will prefer to invest less to acquire the same cash benefits. In the preceding example, Investment A was better than Investment B. Investment A would be even more desirable if it were acquired for $800 instead of $1,000. The same reasoning is applicable to Investment C compared with Investment D. Compound interest and discounting techniques could be used to determine how much less would have to be paid for Investment B or D, respectively, to produce the better return to the investor.

Sooner is better than later

Among investment alternatives with comparable risk and which produce equal cash flows the investor will prefer the alternative that produces cash flows sooner.

27

Example

Investment A is more desirable than Investment E below since the cash flow is received one period sooner. There is no compensation for waiting the additional period; therefore, receiving the cash flow sooner is better.

Time Period (EOP)	Investment A	Investment E
0	($1,000)	($1,000)
1	–0–	–0–
2	–0–	–0–
3	$1,800	–0–
4	–0–	$1,800

Investment E would be more appealing if it cost less at Time Period 0 and/or produced more income at end of period (EOP) 4.

Compare Investment A with Investment C to determine which is preferable. The cost of each alternative is $1,000. The holding period is the same for each alternative. The total cash flows are $1,800 for both investments.

Time Period (EOP)	Investment A	Investment C
0	($1,000)	($1,000)
1	–0–	600
2	–0–	600
3	$1,800	600
Total Positive Cash Flows	$1,800	$1,800

The rational investor would prefer Investment C because a portion of the total cash flows are received sooner. There is no compensation from Investment A for forgoing the earlier payments available from Investment C. Investment A might be better if it cost less or produced a larger cash flow at EOP 3.

Time value (or cost) of money

The time value of money is the preference to have money now rather than receive the same amount in the future. It is exemplified by the interest charged on borrowed funds. A lender makes a loan as an investment. In return for extending funds to a borrower, the lender will receive the original funds loaned (return *of* capital) plus interest (return *on* capital). The interest rate represents the time value of money to the lender. The lender can invest the funds with any credit-worthy borrower at the going interest rate. The interest rate, in this case, would be the lender's *opportunity cost* of capital. That is, the lender would forgo the interest charge by not seizing a suitable investment opportunity (i.e., a loan to a credit-worthy borrower).

Cash flows can be converted to a present value—capitalized—with a specified interest rate as shown in the example below.

Example

A lender will loan $1,000 for one year at 12 percent interest. The loan plus interest will be paid in full at the end of the year (EOY) 1. The lender therefore will receive $1,000 plus $120 (12 percent of $1,000) or $1,120 at EOY 1. The ratio of the amount invested now ($1,000) to the lump sum amount to be received at EOY 1 ($1,120) is:

$$\frac{\$1,000}{\$1,120} = 0.892857 \text{ or } 89.29\%$$

Given this ratio, a lender or other investor who requires a 12-percent return on money could compute the present value of a lump sum of money to be received at the end of one year. The process of computing the present value of cash flows is called discounting. For example, the present value of $10,000 to be received at the end of one year to an investor requiring a 12-percent return on capital is:

$$
\begin{array}{r}
\$10,000.00 \\
\times\ 0.892857 \\
\hline
\$8,928.57
\end{array}
$$

An investor requiring a 12-percent return on capital would be indifferent to receiving $8,928.57 now or receiving $10,000 one year from now.

In summary, there are two basic aspects to time value of money calculations. First, cash flows can be *compounded* to determine an amount to be received in the future, or a future value $\boxed{\text{FV}}$.[2] Second, anticipated cash flows to be received in the future can be *discounted* to determine the present value $\boxed{\text{PV}}$ at the beginning of the first relevant time period. A specific interest rate $\boxed{\text{i}}$ is required for both compound interest and discount calculations as well as the number of compounding periods $\boxed{\text{n}}$.

Concept of compound interest

In the preceding example, the time period used to illustrate the time value of money was one year, with interest paid only once during the one-year period. This is generally referred to as simple interest since interest was earned only on the original investment. However, investment opportunities with compound interest are generally available. Compounding occurs when periodic earnings are reinvested each period along with the original investment. It is difficult to compare alternative investments with different investment compounding periods.

Example

Suppose that two investment alternatives were presented as follows: (1) an investment of $100 that returns $160 at the end of five years; (2) an investment of $100 that returns $112 at the end of one year. One simple means of comparing these two investment alternatives is to convert the five-year investment to an annual simple rate. Since the investment returns 60 percent per five-year period, the average annual rate is 60 percent divided by five—12 percent per annum. Since the one-year investment likewise returns 12 percent per annum, it would appear that the two investments produce the same return.

This comparison precludes the possibility of reinvesting both principal and interest at the end of each year for five years when selecting the one-year investment. This is exactly the same investment amount and duration as the five-year investment since annual interest earned is not withdrawn but reinvested. Both investments would then involve the commitment of $100 for a duration of five years with no cash returns to the investor until the end of the fifth year. In the case of reinvestment each year, the following would occur.

Year	Investment Beginning of Year (BOY)	Interest Rate	Interest Earned During Year	Investment Amount Plus Interest Earned EOY
1	$100.00	.12	$12.00	$112.00
2	112.00	.12	13.44	125.44
3	124.44	.12	15.05	140.49
4	140.49	.12	16.86	157.35
5	157.35	.12	18.88	176.23

Thus, if the one-year investment is selected *and* the investor is able to reinvest the annual proceeds at the 12-percent rate over the five-year term, the $100 investment would grow to an amount of $176.23, or $16.23 more than the simple five-year investment that returns only $160.

Comparing alternative investments

The rate of return for nearly all investments may be measured in terms of *annual return* on invested capital, with compounding assumed when the capital invested is not returned within one year. Thus, the concept of compound interest and discounting is fundamental to evaluating investments in general, and real estate investments specifically. Compound discounting not only reflects the investor's preference for returns sooner rather than later but also includes in the cost of waiting the assumption that the investor has the opportunity to reinvest both principal and earnings each period.

If the investment choice is simple, such as the choice of investing $1,000 today and receiving either $1,100 one year from today or $1,100 two years from today, no measurement is actually needed. However, investment alternatives are seldom that simple. For example, consider the problem of measuring the annual rate of return for the following investment alternatives, each of which costs $10,000.

Cash Receipts from Alternative Investments

End of Year	Discounted Mortgage	Five-Year Note	Stock	Insurance Annuity	Land
1	$ 1,627.45	–0–	$ 1,000	$1,000	–0–
2	1,627.45	–0–	1,000	each	–0–
3	1,627.45	–0–	1,000	year	–0–
4	1,627.45	–0–	1,000	to	–0–
5	1,627.45	$16,105.10	1,000	perpetuity	–0–
6	1,627.45	–0–	1,000		–0–
7	1,627.45	–0–	1,000		–0–
8	1,627.45	–0–	1,000		–0–
9	1,627.45	–0–	1,000		–0–
10	1,627.45	–0–	11,000		$25,937.42
Total Receipts	$16,274.50	$16,105.10	$20,000	∞	$25,937.42

The problem here is to convert each of these cash flows to a common base so that they may be compared. In order to deal with this type of measurement problem, compound interest and discount techniques must be used. The calculation required may be performed with a wide variety of preprogrammed, hand-held, financial calculators. However, the following explanations use compound interest and discount tables to illustrate the concepts associated with the calculations.

Compound interest and discount calculations

Proper use and understanding of compound interest and discount tables is a prerequisite to grasping the measurement of investment rates of return, present value and a number of other calculations commonly used in real estate investment analysis. Today, most calculations are made using an electronic financial calculator. However, the compound interest and discount tables present a complex "picture" that is not possible with the typical single line display of a hand-held calculator. For this reason a rather detailed presentation will be made of such tables, their construction and their real estate applications.

Appendix A of this book contains selected compound interest tables from Part II of the fourth edition of Ellwood's *Tables for Real Estate Appraising and Financing*.[3] The sample tables shown are 5 percent and 10 percent (monthly, quarterly, semiannual and annual factors) and are used for purposes of illustration. You also may use them to follow the examples in this chapter. The full set of tables contained in Ellwood has monthly, quarterly, semiannual and annual factors for rates of interest in .25-percent increments from 3 percent to 12 percent. In addition, factor tables in 1-percent increments are available from 13 percent through 30 percent. Each table contains six columns as follows:

Column	Function of the Dollar (Factor)
1	Amount of 1 at compound interest
2	Accumulation of 1 per period
3	Sinking fund factor
4	Present value, reversion of 1
5	Present value, ordinary annuity of 1 per period
6	Installment to amortize 1

1. Amount of 1 at compound interest (column 1)   The fundamental building block of all compounding and discounting calculations is the future value of a sum compounded at a specific interest rate per period. A time deposit or savings account is a common example. Consider a savings account deposit of $10,000 at 10-percent interest per annum, compounded annually, which is left on deposit for two years. Since the interest is compounded annually, the interest earned EOY 1 will also earn interest during Year 2.

The balance EOY 1 will be:

$$\$10,000 + (\$10,000 \times .10) = \$10,000 + \$1,000 = \$11,000$$

This equation may be restated as:

$$\$10,000 \ (1 + .10) = \$11,000$$

Interest will be earned on the total balance of $11,000 during Year 2. The balance EOY 2 will be:

$$\$11,000 \ (1 + .10) = \$12,100$$

This equation may be restated as:

$$\underbrace{\$10,000 \ (1 + .10)} \times (1 + .10) = \$12,100$$

Calculation of balance
EOY 1 from above

This is equal to:

$$\$10,000 \ (1 + .10)^2 = \$12,100$$

The general formula for this calculation is:

$$\boxed{FV} = \boxed{PV} (1 + i)^n$$

where:

$\boxed{PV}$ = amount invested at the present

$\boxed{i}$ = interest rate per period (effective rate)

$\boxed{n}$ = number of compounding periods

$\boxed{FV}$ = future value at the end of n compounding periods.

The expression $(1 + i)$ is called the base. The base with the exponent n is part of all six functions of the dollar (listed on page 32). The base is the mathematical translation that expresses the *return of* capital (1) and the *return on* capital (i). Note that if the interest rate is 0, the base would equal 1, just the return of capital.

$$\boxed{FV} = \boxed{PV} \quad (1 \quad + \quad i)^n$$
$$\uparrow \qquad\qquad \uparrow$$
$$\text{return } of \ \boxed{PV} \quad \text{return } on \ \boxed{PV}$$

Rates of return (e.g., interest rates, bond yields) usually are stated as annual rates. However, the compounding periods frequently are less than one year. For example, savings accounts may be compounded quarterly, monthly or daily. The *effective rate* (i) or interest rate per period must be consistent with the length of the compounding period. Therefore, the annual interest rate is divided by the number of compounding periods per year. The effective rate is the rate actually applied to the investment balance *each* period. In the case of the investment in the preceding example, here are the effective rates for some alternative compounding periods:

Compounding Period	Annual Rate		Per Year		Effective Rate (*i*)
Annual	10%	÷	1	=	10%
Semiannual	10%	÷	2	=	5%
Quarterly	10%	÷	4	=	2.5%
Monthly	10%	÷	12	=	0.8333%

The number of compounding periods (*n*) during the investment horizon (holding period) must be consistent with the effective rate (*i*). Therefore, the total number of compounding periods is equal to the number of compounding periods per year multiplied by the number of years (*N*) during the investment horizon. Continuing with the same example, the number of compounding periods in the two-year investment horizon are summarized below.

Compounding Period	Investment Horizon (Years)		Compounding Periods Per Year		Total Compounding Periods (*n*)
Annual	2	×	1	=	2
Semiannual	2	×	2	=	4
Quarterly	2	×	4	=	8
Monthly	2	×	12	=	24

The effect of different compounding periods is illustrated in the following table. It is a summary of the future value ($\boxed{\text{FV}}$) of the $10,000 invested for two years at 10-percent interest per year with different compounding periods. The effective rates and total compounding periods were calculated in the preceding tables.

Compounding Periods (EOP)	Amount of 1 at Compound Interest		Period in Time	
	Calculation	Factor	$\boxed{\text{PV}}$	$\boxed{\text{FV}}$
Annual	$(1 + .10)^2$	1.210000	× $10,000	= $12,100.00
Semiannual	$(1 + .05)^4$	1.215506	× $10,000	= $12,155.06
Quarterly	$(1 + .025)^8$	1.218403	× $10,000	= $12,184.03
Monthly	$(1 + .00833)^{24}$	1.220390	× $10,000	= $12,203.90

Note that the future value increases as the number of compounding periods per year increases. This could be expected because the return *on* investment is added to the balance sooner and therefore earns interest for a longer time.

The compound interest formula for compounding periods may be generalized as:

$$\boxed{FV} = \boxed{PV}\,(1 + I/p)^{N \times p}$$

where:

I = annual interest rate
N = number of years
p = number of compounding periods per year

therefore,

$$\frac{I}{p} = i = \text{effective rate of interest earned per period}$$

$$N \times p = n = \text{total number of compounding periods}$$

From the example, the $10,000 invested at 10-percent interest per year, compounded monthly, is:

$$\$10,000 \times \left(1 + \frac{.10}{12}\right)^{2 \times 12} = \$10,000 \times (1 + .008333)^{24} = \$12,203.90$$

This is a restatement of the results from the table above.

The factors in the summary above can be found in Column 1 of the tables in Appendix A of this book. Refer to the pages showing 10 percent for this example. Then turn to the 10-percent table with the appropriate compounding periods per year (e.g., monthly). The factors are listed for each period during the first year, then each year for at least 25 years, depending on the interest rate. The number of years is found in the left-hand column. The total number of compounding periods (n) for each year is found in the right-hand column. The amount of 1 at compound interest for two years at 10-percent interest per year, compounded monthly, will be found on the 10-percent monthly compound interest table, in Column 1, next to Year 2. There you will find the calculated factor of 1.220390.

The factors are computed for $1.00. Simply multiply by the number of dollars of the investment to determine the appropriate quantity. Our example, thus far, has used an investment of $10,000. Using the appropriate table, the future value $\boxed{FV}$ of $10,000 invested at 10 percent, compounded monthly for seven years, would be:

$$\$10,000 \times 2.007920 = \$20,079.20$$

└─factor from Column 1 of 10 percent monthly table

Indeed, the calculated value is:

$$\$10,000 \times \left(1 + \frac{.10}{12}\right)^{7 \times 12} = \$20,079.20$$

The $\boxed{\text{FV}}$ for seven years, \$20,079.20, is greater than the $\boxed{\text{FV}}$ for two years, \$12,203.90. This would be expected since the investor waited longer to receive the money. One interpretation of the foregoing is that an investor with an opportunity cost of capital of 10 percent that could be compounded monthly would be indifferent to having \$10,000 today, \$12,203.90 at the end of two years or \$20,079.20 at the end of seven years.

The amount required by an investor in the future will increase as the interest rate (or opportunity cost of capital) increases. If an investor could earn 12 percent compounded monthly on the \$10,000, instead of 10 percent, the \$12,203.90 would not be sufficient compensation EOY 2. The investor would require the $\boxed{\text{FV}}$ of \$10,000 compounded monthly at 12 percent for two years. That amount is:

$$\$10,000 \times \left(1 + \frac{.12}{12}\right)^{2 \times 12} = \$12,697.35$$

$\boxed{\text{FV}}$ of \$10,000 @ 10%, compounded monthly = $\underline{\$12,203.90}$

Difference = \$493.45

The investor would acquire an additional \$493.45 EOY 2 if the required interest rate were 12 percent instead of 10 percent.

The characteristics of any amount at compound interest are the same. Many investments produce cash flows with more than one amount to be received in the future. If the income stream has equal payments received at the end of equal time periods it is easy to calculate the future value based on the mathematics of the amount of 1 at compound interest.

2. Accumulation of 1 per period (column 2) is used to calculate the future value of *equal* payments invested at the *end* of each period for a total of *n* compounding periods at *i* interest rate per period. To illustrate, the $\boxed{\text{FV}}$ of five equal payments of \$1,200 invested at the end of each year for five years, compounded annually at 10 percent, could be calculated as five separate investments, as follows:

Year	Time Invested (years)	Column 1 factor	Amount Invested	$\boxed{\text{FV}}$
1	4	1.464100	× \$1,200.00 =	\$1,756.92
2	3	1.331000	× \$1,200.00 =	\$1,597.20
3	2	1.210000	× \$1,200.00 =	\$1,452.00
4	1	1.100000	× \$1,200.00 =	\$1,320.00
5	0	1.000000	× \$1,200.00 =	\$1,200.00
Totals		6.105100		\$7,326.12

Payments are made at the end of each period. Therefore, no interest is earned during the first period. It is as if the first payment were made at the beginning of year (BOY) 2. The last payment is made at the end of the investment term; accordingly, no interest is earned on the last payment. The total balance EOY 5 will be $7,326.12 which is equal to the sum of the Column 1 factors multiplied by the amount of the payment:

$$\$1,200 \times 6.105100 = \$7,326.12$$

The sum of amount of 1 at compound interest (Column 1 factor) for each period at a specific interest rate is equal to the accumulation of 1 per period in Column 2. Compare the factors above with those found in the 10-percent annual compound interest table. This is most apparent on the annual tables. The Column 1 factors for each compounding period less than one year are listed for the first year only (i.e., the column factor for an amount invested at compound interest for 13 months is not listed).

The formula to calculate the factor for the accumulation of one per period is:

$$\boxed{FV} = \left[\frac{(1 + i)^n - 1}{i} \right]$$

The effective rate (i) must be consistent with the total number of compounding periods (n). The factor for the preceding example is:

$$\left[\frac{(1 + .10)^5 - 1}{.10} \right] = 6.105100$$

The future value of n equal payments made at the end of each period, compounded at i interest rate, is:

$$\boxed{FV} = \boxed{PMT} \left[\frac{(1 + i)^n - 1}{i} \right]$$

Compare $1,200 invested at the end of each year for five years compounded annually at 10 percent with monthly investments of $100 compounded monthly at 10 percent per year for five years. The $\boxed{FV}$ of the latter is:

$$\$100 \left[\frac{(1 + .10/12)^{5 \times 12} - 1}{.10/12} \right] = \$7,743.71$$

As we saw above, the $\boxed{FV}$ of the annual compounding is $7,326.12.

The same total funds are invested each year (100×12 months = $1,200); however, the investor begins to earn interest at the end of the first month and the interest is compounded more frequently. Therefore, shorter compounding periods with comparable payments will produce a greater future value.

Two generalizations are consistent with the characteristics of an amount invested at compound interest. First, an increase in the number of compounding periods and, consequently, the number of periodic payments will increase the future value. This is because more payments will earn more interest for more compounding periods. Second, as the periodic effective rate increases, the future value of the accumulated equal investments per period also increases. Each payment will then earn more interest.

3. Sinking fund factor (column 3) is used to calculate the equal payments required to be invested at i interest rate per period at the end of each period for n periods that will grow to a specified future value. This is similar to the accumulation of 1 per period, except that the future value is known and the payment is unknown. Thus the accumulation of 1 per period (Column 2) and the sinking fund factor (Column 3) are reciprocals.

Suppose that an investor required $7,743.71 at the end of five years. In order to achieve this financial goal, equal payments will be invested monthly at 10 percent per year compounded monthly. It has been determined that $100 invested each month at 10 percent per year, compounded monthly, will grow to $7,743.71. Recall that the formula for the accumulation of 1 per period is:

$$\boxed{FV} = \boxed{PMT}\left[\frac{(1+i)^n - 1}{i}\right]$$

The reciprocal formula to calculate the sinking fund factor is:

$$\boxed{PMT} = \frac{\boxed{FV}}{\left[\dfrac{(1+i)^n - 1}{i}\right]} = \boxed{FV}\left[\frac{i}{(1+i)^n - 1}\right]$$

The computation to determine the equal monthly payment that will grow to $7,743.71 in five years, compounded at 10 percent per month, is:

$$\$7,743.71\left[\frac{.10/12}{(1+.10/12)^{5 \times 12} - 1}\right] = \$7,743.71 \times 0.012913 = \$100$$

Note that i is the effective rate per month, which is 10 percent divided by 12 months per year. There are five years multiplied by 12 months per year, or 60 monthly investments. That is, n equals 60. The factor (0.012913) for $1 may be found under Column 3 in the 10-percent monthly table.

The periodic payment will decrease if periodic investment earns more interest during the investment horizon. Compare the $100 per month in the example to the monthly payment required to grow to the same future value of $7,743.71 at 12 percent per year.

$$\$7,743.71\left[\frac{.12/12}{(1+.12/12)^{5 \times 12} - 1}\right] = \$94.82$$

The periodic payment declines as the number of payment periods (n) increases. For example, compare the annual payment, compounded at 10 percent, required to grow to $10,000 in five years and ten years.

For five years:

$$\$10{,}000 \left[\frac{.10}{(1 + .10)^5 - 1} \right] = \$1{,}637.97$$

For ten years:

$$\$10{,}000 \left[\frac{.10}{(1 + .10)^{10} - 1} \right] = \$627.45$$

This relationship is apparent from the factors listed in the tables. For any effective rate, the sinking fund factor is 1.000000 for the first period since one payment made at the end of one period does not earn any interest. The factors decline as the number of periods increase.

4. Present value reversion of 1 (column 4)   shows the amounts that must be invested at present to grow to a specific value at the end of n periods at i effective rate. This is the reciprocal of the amount of 1 at compound interest (Column 1). For example, an investor wishes to know how much should be invested now, at 10-percent interest compounded annually, to have $10,000 EOY 2. The formula for the present value reversion of 1 is:

$$\boxed{\text{PV}} = \boxed{\text{FV}} \left[\frac{1}{(1 + i)^n} \right]$$

The solution to the problem is then:

$$10{,}000 \left[\frac{1}{(1 + .10)^2} \right] = 10{,}000 \times 0.826446 = \$8{,}264.46$$

The investor would have to invest $8,264.46 at 10 percent compounded annually to grow to $10,000 EOY 2. Stated another way, an investor with an opportunity to invest money at 10 percent compounded annually would be indifferent to having $8,264.46 today or receiving $10,000 EOY 2. The factor of 0.826446 will be found in Column 4 of the 10-percent annual table.

Determining the present value of money to be received in the future is called discounting. The opportunity cost of capital, 10 percent in the example above, is the discount rate. As demonstrated in Chapter 4, the present value of cash flows is a valuable measure to determine the relative benefits of investment alternatives.

The impact of effective rates and investment duration on the present value reversion of 1 is inversely related to the amount of 1 at compound interest. The present value of a sum to be received in the future is less if the investor must wait longer to receive the money. That is, the present value of $10,000 to be received EOY 10 is less than if it were to be received EOY 2. Remember that "sooner is better than later."

The present value of a future lump sum of money is less if the number of compounding periods per year is greater. Compare $8,264.46, the present value of $10,000 to be received EOY 2, *discounted* at 10 percent and compounded annually, to the same terms except for monthly compounding:

$$\$10,000 \left[\frac{1}{(1 + .10/12)^{2 \times 12}} \right] = \$8,194.10$$

The present value is less for the monthly compounding.

The present value of a future cash flow decreases as the discount rate increases. Compare $8,264.46 from above with the present value of $10,000, discounted at 12 percent with annual compounding for two years:

$$\$10,000 \left[\frac{1}{(1 + .12)^2} \right] = \$7,971.94$$

5. Present value of an ordinary annuity (column 5)   shows the present value of an ordinary annuity—a stream of equal payments made at the end of equal time periods—as the sum of the present value of each individual payment (Column 4). For example, the present value of $1,000 to be received at the end of each year for five years and discounted at 10 percent annually is:

Year	PMT	PV of 1 Factor	PV
1	$1,000.00 ×	0.909091	= $ 909.09
2	$1,000.00 ×	0.826446	= 826.45
3	$1,000.00 ×	0.751315	= 751.31
4	$1,000.00 ×	0.683013	= 683.01
5	$1,000.00 ×	0.620921	= 620.92
Total		3.790786	$3,790.79*

*Rounding error results from alternative methods of computation.

An investor with a 10-percent cost of capital would be indifferent to receiving an ordinary annuity of $1,000 at the end of each year for five years or the lump sum of $3,790.79 today.

The formula to calculate the present value of an ordinary annuity is:

$$\boxed{PV} = \boxed{PMT} \left[\frac{1 - \dfrac{1}{(1 + i)^n}}{i} \right]$$

Using the same example, the present value would be calculated as:

$$\$1,000 \left[\frac{1 - \frac{1}{(1 + .10)^5}}{.10} \right] = \$1,000 \times 3.790787 = \$3,790.79$$

The factor 3.790787 will be found in Column 5 of the 10 percent annual table.

As with all compound interest and discount problems, the number of periods, n, and the effective periodic rate, i, must be consistent. For example, the present value of $250 received at the end of each calendar quarter and discounted at 10 percent per year for five years is:

$$\$250 \left[\frac{1 - \frac{1}{(1 + .10/4)^{4 \times 5}}}{.10/4} \right] = 250 \times 15.589162 = \$3,897.29$$

Notice that the present value of the four quarterly payments per year for five years of $250 discounted at 10 percent quarterly is greater than the $\boxed{PV}$ of five annual installments of $1,000 discounted at the same rate. That is because the cash flow starts at the end of one calendar quarter compared to one calendar year.

The $\boxed{PV}$ of an ordinary annuity decreases as the discount rate increases. Compare $3,897.29, the $\boxed{PV}$ of $250 received at the end of each calendar quarter for five years and discounted at 10 percent per year, to the same cash flow discounted at 12 percent:

$$\$250 \left[\frac{1 - \frac{1}{(1 + .12/4)^{4 \times 5}}}{.12/4} \right] = \$250 \times 14.877475 = \$3,719.37$$

The $\boxed{PV}$ of an ordinary annuity increases as the number of payments increases. However, since the payments to be received in the distant future have a smaller $\boxed{PV}$ than do earlier payments, the $\boxed{PV}$ increases by smaller and smaller increments as the term increases.

Ordinary annuity payments are assumed to be received at the end of each period. The $\boxed{PV}$ of an *annuity due,* an equal stream of periodic payments received at the beginning of each period, is the $\boxed{PV}$ of an ordinary annuity times the base $(1 + i)$. Using the previous example, the present value of $250 received at the beginning of each calendar quarter discounted at 12 percent is:

$$\$250 \left[\frac{1 - \frac{1}{(1 + .12/4)^{4 \times 5}}}{.12/4} \right] (1 + .12/4) = \$3,830.95$$

6. Installment to amortize 1 (column 6) shows the equal periodic payment required to provide the return of and return on capital invested at present for a specified number of periods, n, at the effective rate, i. This is the reciprocal of the present value of an annuity. Recall from the first example in the preceding section that the present value of $1,000 received at the end of each year for five years, discounted at 10 percent, is:

$$\$1,000 \times 3.790786 = \$3,790.79$$

The installment to amortize $3,790.79 with five equal installments including interest of 10 percent per year could be calculated from the above as:

$$\$3,790.79 \left[\frac{1}{3.790786} \right] = \$1,000$$

The general formula for the installment to amortize is:

$$\boxed{\text{PMT}} = \boxed{\text{PV}} \left[\frac{i}{1 - \dfrac{1}{(1 + i)^n}} \right]$$

Using this formula for the example above, the installment to amortize is:

$$\$3,790.79 \left[\frac{.10}{1 - \dfrac{1}{(1 + .10)^5}} \right] = \$3,790.79 \times .263797 = \$1,000$$

The payment will decrease as the number of payments per year increases. Compare $1,000, the annual installment to amortize $3,790.79 at 10 percent in five years, to the monthly installment required for the same investment:

$$\$3,790.79 \left[\frac{.10/12}{1 - \dfrac{1}{(1 + .10/12)^{5 \times 12}}} \right] = \$3,790.79 \times 0.021247 = \$80.54$$

The payment also will decrease if the number of years to amortize is increased. Compare the monthly payment above to a monthly payment for the same investment to be amortized in ten years:

$$\$3,790.79 \left[\frac{.10/12}{1 - \dfrac{1}{(1 + .10/12)^{10 \times 12}}} \right] = \$3,790.79 \times 0.013215 = \$50.10$$

The payment increases as the effective rate increases. Using the example above, the monthly payment to amortize $3,790.79 in ten years at 12 percent per year is:

$$\$3{,}790.79 \left[\cfrac{.12/12}{1 - \cfrac{1}{(1 + .12/12)^{10 \times 12}}} \right] = \$3{,}790.79 \times .014347 = \$54.39$$

The installment to amortize presumes payments are made at the end of each period. The same investment would be amortized with a smaller payment if each installment were received at the beginning of the period. The payment made at the beginning of the period is equal to the payment made at the end of the period divided by the base. Using the first example, the installment at the beginning of each year (including the first year) required to amortize $3,790.79 in five years at 10-percent interest per year is:

$$\frac{\$1{,}000}{(1 + .10)} = \$909.09$$

Financial calculators and computers

The preceding discussion on compound interest and discounting problems is intended to present the conceptual framework for all quantitative financial analysis. The formulas are presented to enable the reader to become familiar with the impact of rate and term on unknown values. The time value of money calculations can be performed on a wide variety of financial calculators and computers. Modern technology has produced inexpensive, preprogrammed calculators with a wide range of financial functions. Even the most simple can perform the calculations we have explored in this chapter. More sophisticated equipment combines the same basic calculations to save steps for the user.

It is important to understand the conceptual framework of time-value of money calculations in order to use financial calculators effectively. Skill with compound interest and discounting concepts will enable the analyst to comprehend the nature of any cash flow problem and, therefore, establish a valid approach to the solution. The results of *appropriate* calculations will be reasonable to the analyst. In contrast, the potential applications of these tools will be substantially limited for those who attempt to solve compound interest and discounting problems mechanically, with a few keystroke sequences on their particular calculators.

In general, financial calculators have five financial keys identified by the same symbols used in the preceding section ($\boxed{\text{n}}$, $\boxed{\text{i}}$, $\boxed{\text{PV}}$, $\boxed{\text{PMT}}$, $\boxed{\text{FV}}$). Most financial calculators will solve for any one unknown value when given three specified values. The number of periods, $\boxed{\text{n}}$, and the effective rate, $\boxed{\text{i}}$, always must be consistent with regard to compounding periods. The present value of a sum, $\boxed{\text{PV}}$, is always assumed to be invested or available at the immediate beginning of the time horizon of the cash flows (i.e., now); henceforth in this book, $\boxed{\text{PV}}$ will be paid or re-

Figure 2   Summary of Compound Interest and Discount Factors

Function of the Dollar (Factor)	Column	Known Values	Unknown Value	Result of Increasing	
				n	i
Amount of 1 at compound interest	1	$\boxed{PV}$, i, n	$\boxed{FV}$	↑	↑
Accumulation of 1 per period	2	$\boxed{PMT}$, i, n	$\boxed{FV}$	↑	↑
Sinking fund factor	3	$\boxed{FV}$, i, n	$\boxed{PMT}$	↓	↓
Present value reversion of 1	4	$\boxed{FV}$, i, n	$\boxed{PV}$	↓	↓
Present value of an ordinary annuity	5	$\boxed{PMT}$, i, n	$\boxed{PV}$	↑	↓
Installment to amortize 1	6	$\boxed{PV}$, i, n	$\boxed{PMT}$	↓	↑

where:

$\boxed{PV}$ = Present value of a single sum available immediately

$\boxed{FV}$ = Future value of a single sum to be received in the future

$\boxed{PMT}$ = Payment to be received at the end of each period

i = effective periodic interest rate

n = number of periods

↑ = increase

↓ = decrease

---

ceived at time period zero. Payments, $\boxed{PMT}$, are always assumed to be equal and occur at the end of each equal compounding period *including* the last period. Many financial calculators have some simple adjustment or procedure to convert computations for payments made at the beginning of each period, as with an annuity due. In this book, the reader will always be informed when payments are received at the beginning of each period. Otherwise it can be assumed that payments are made at end of the period. The future value, $\boxed{FV}$, of a sum will be received at the end of the period.

When cash flows include an ordinary annuity and a future value, FV and PMT are *not* added together.

As we have seen, the compound interest tables list factors for any combination of compounding periods, effective rates and number of years. Financial calculators can compute factors and subsequent values for terms and effective rates that are not included in the tables. To calculate any of the six factors, refer to the summary table on page 44. Use the value of $1 in place of the known dollar amount (PV, PMT or FV) and solve for the unknown value.

Example

To calculate the Column 6 factor, the installment to amortize 1, for a loan at 12-percent interest per year with payments every five months for ten years, input $1 for PV and solve for PMT. The known values for this problem are:

$$PV = \$1$$
$$n = 10 \text{ years} \times (12 \div 5) = 24 \text{ periods}$$
$$i = 12\% \div (12 \div 5) = 5\% \text{ per period}$$

The calculated factor for the installment to amortize 1 is:

$$PMT = 0.072471$$

The quantity $(12 \div 5)$ is the number of five-month periods per year. Notice that this need not be an integer value. There are indeed 24 five-month periods in ten years: $(24 \times 5 = 120$ months; 120 months $\div$ 12 months per year $= 10$ years).

Many financial calculators compute values to several decimal places. Some calculators round results if the next significant digit is greater than or equal to five; some do not. The use of rounded or unrounded intermediate values can easily cause a slight rounding error in the final result. The reader is urged not to become distressed by minor discrepancies between values caused by rounding.

Examples (compounding)

1. **Future value at compound interest** A survey of land sales over the past 15 years indicates that comparable land to the subject site has

increased in value at a rate of 5 percent per year. If this trend continues, what would the estimated sales price be in five years for a property worth $15,000 today?

The known values are:

$$\boxed{PV} = \$15,000$$
$$\boxed{n} = 5 \text{ periods}$$
$$\boxed{i} = 5\% \text{ per period}$$

$\boxed{FV}$ is unknown. It is computed to be:

$\boxed{FV}$ of $15,000, five years at 5% per year = $19,144.22

2. Future value at compound interest   An investor pays $100,000 for a vacant site in January, 1971. In January, 1981, the site is sold for $250,000. At what annual compound rate of interest did the value of the land increase?

The known values are:

$$\boxed{PV} = \$100,000$$
$$\boxed{FV} = \$250,000$$
$$\boxed{n} = 10 \text{ years}$$

The effective rate is unknown. It is computed to be:

$$\boxed{i} = 9.60\%$$

Determine the annual interest rate for the problem above if semiannual compounding were assumed. Now the number of periods is:

$$\boxed{n} = 10 \times 2 = 20 \text{ periods}$$

Recall that *i* is the effective rate *per period*. The periodic effective rate is calculated to be:

$$\boxed{i} = 4.69\%$$

The annualized rate is two times the semiannual effective rate since there are two compounding periods per year.

$$2 \times 4.69\% = 9.38\%$$

Notice that this rate is less than the rate with annual compounding of 9.60 percent. This could be expected since there are more compounding periods for the semiannual rate.

3. Accumulation of 1 per period   An investor has leased a site for use as a parking lot. The lessee agreed to pay all expenses, including property tax, in the net lease contract. The lessor is to receive a ground rent of $250 per month for nine years with the first payment to begin one month after signing the lease. If the lessor were to invest the monthly rental proceeds at an annual rate of 12 percent compounded monthly, how much would be in the investment account at the end of the lease?

The known values are:

$$\boxed{\text{PMT}} = \$250 \text{ per month}$$
$$\boxed{\text{n}} = 9 \text{ years} \times 12 = 108 \text{ periods}$$
$$\boxed{\text{i}} = 12\% \div 12 = 1\% \text{ per period}$$

The $\boxed{\text{FV}}$ is unknown. It is calculated to be:

$$\boxed{\text{FV}} = \$48,223.14$$

4. Sinking fund factor   An investor purchases an apartment building that is projected to need a new roof which will cost $15,000 in five years. How much must be invested at the end of each calendar quarter, at 10-percent interest per year, so that the necessary capital for the roof will be accumulated?

The known values are:

$$\boxed{\text{FV}} = \$15,000$$
$$\boxed{\text{n}} = 5 \text{ years} \times 4 = 20 \text{ periods}$$
$$\boxed{\text{i}} = 10\% \div 4 = 2.5\% \text{ per period}$$

The $\boxed{\text{PMT}}$ is the unknown value. It is calculated to be:

$$\boxed{\text{PMT}} = \$587.21$$

Note that 20 investments multiplied by $587.21 is $11,744.20; thus $15,000 less $11,744.20, or $3,255.80, is the amount of interest earned over the five-year period.

Examples (discounting)

1. Present value at compound interest   An investor is considering the purchase of a "remainder" (the interest in a property which matures at the end of another estate). The property is under lease for the next seven years. The investor estimates that the value of the fee interest at the end of the lease will be $50,000. What should the investor be willing to pay for the remainder interest today if the required rate of return on invested capital is 15 percent?

The known values are:

$$\boxed{\text{FV}} = \$50,000$$
$$\boxed{\text{n}} = 7 \text{ periods}$$
$$\boxed{\text{i}} = 15\% \text{ per period}$$

The $\boxed{\text{PV}}$ is unknown. It is calculated to be:

$$\boxed{\text{PV}} = \$18,796.85$$

If an investor were to invest \$18,796.85 today at 15 percent com-pounded annually, the investment would grow to the amount of \$50,000 by the end of seven years.

It is often helpful to identify each known factor (e.g., $\boxed{\text{PV}}$ or $\boxed{\text{i}}$) and determine which value is unknown when solving compound interest or discounting problems. When using the compound interest tables or a finan-cial calculator, it may be useful to refer to Figure 2 which summarizes the compound interest and discount factors in the preceding section.

All discounted cash flow analyses can be reduced to four simple questions:

1. How much money does the investment cost?
2. When is each payment made?
3. How much money does the investment produce?
4. When does the investor receive each cash flow?

The numerical answers to these questions may be summarized on a "t-chart" as follows:

EOY	\$
0	$\boxed{\text{PV}}$
1	$\boxed{\text{PMT}}$
2	$\boxed{\text{PMT}}$
3	$\boxed{\text{PMT}}$
↓	↓
n	$\boxed{\text{PMT}} + \boxed{\text{FV}}$

The left-hand column indicates the time period each payment is made or cash flow received. The end of time period 0 is, by definition, the present or the time at which the investment term begins. The periods, n, are consistent with the cash flows (i.e., monthly or annual). The heading in the example above indicates annual periods; EOY is End of Year. Cash flows are listed in the right-hand column. In this case, each periodic pay-ment is equal—an ordinary annuity. Thus $\boxed{\text{PMT}}$ is used. Unequal cash flows may replace the equal cash flows. An algebraic sign convention is used to distinguish cash payments from cash receipts. Payments are negative, indicated by the negative sign or parentheses. Cash receipts are positive. To illustrate, the t-chart for an investment that costs $10,000 and produces $1,000 at the end of each quarter (EOQ) for eight quarters plus a reversion of $12,000 at the end of the last period would be as follows:

EOQ	$
0	($10,000) amount *paid* for the investment
1	$1,000
2	$1,000
3	$1,000
↓	↓
(2 years × 4 quarters per year) 8	$1,000 + $12,000

2. Present value of an ordinary annuity   What is the present value of a leasehold interest of $2,650 per year for four years when discounted at 10 percent per year?

The known values are:

$$\boxed{\text{PMT}} = \$2,650$$
$$\boxed{n} = 4 \text{ periods}$$
$$\boxed{i} = 10\% \text{ per period}$$

The $\boxed{\text{PV}}$ is unknown. It is calculated to be:

$$\boxed{\text{PV}} = \$8,400.14$$

Now, suppose that the same stream of income were available in an investment ($2,650 per year for four years) but that the first payment would begin three years from today rather than one year from today. This is sometimes called a deferred annuity. In essence, this problem could be solved in three different ways, as follows:

	Method 1 Addition of Reversion Factors		
EOY	Column Factor (10%)	Cash Flows	Present Value
2	—	0	0
3	.751315	$2,650	$1,990.98
4	.683013	2,650	1,809.98
5	.620921	2,650	1,645.44
6	.564474	2,650	1,495.86
Total	2.619723	—	$6,942.26

2.619723 × $2,650 = $6,942.27

49

The known values are:

$$\boxed{FV} = \$2,650 \text{ received four times}$$
$$\boxed{n} = 3, 4, 5 \text{ and } 6$$
$$\boxed{i} = 10\%$$

The sum of the four $\boxed{PV}$s is unknown. It is calculated to be:

$$\boxed{PV}_{n=3} = \$1,990.98$$
$$\boxed{PV}_{n=4} = 1,809.99*$$
$$\boxed{PV}_{n=5} = 1,645.44$$
$$\boxed{PV}_{n=6} = \underline{1,495.86}$$
$$\text{Total} = \$6,942.27$$

*Differs from above due to rounding.

Method 2
Subtraction of Annuity Factors

This approach may be viewed as removing or subtracting out those periods for which no cash flows are received.

Column 5 Factor	4.355261
10%, $n = 6$	
Column 5 Factor	− 1.735537
10%, $n = 2$	
	2.619724
	× $2,650
	$6,942.27

Note that the factor calculated by subtracting annuity factors is the same as that arrived at in Method 1 by adding reversion factors.

For a financial calculator, this method is a three-step process: (1) calculate the present value of a six-year annuity; (2) calculate the present value of a two-year annuity; (3) subtract the $\boxed{PV}$ of the six-year annuity from the $\boxed{PV}$ of the two-year annuity.

For Steps 1 and 2 the known values are:

$$\boxed{PMT} = \$2,650$$
$$\boxed{n} = 6 \text{ (for step 1) and 2 (for step 2)}$$
$$\boxed{i} = 10\%$$

The solution is:

Step 1	$\boxed{PV}$ of 6-year annuity	$11,541.44
Step 2	$\boxed{PV}$ of 2-year annuity	− 4,599.17
Step 3	$\boxed{PV}$ of deferred annuity	$6,942.27

```
                              Method 3
                       Calculating Deferred Annuity
─────────────────────────────────────────────────────────────
 The logic employed in this method is that at a 10% discount rate:

   EOY │   $   ⎫                        EOY │    $
   ────┼───────                         ────┼─────────
    1  │   0   ⎪                          1 │    0
    2  │   0   ⎪                          2 │ $8,400.14
    3  │ 2,650 ⎬    equals
    4  │ 2,650 ⎪
    5  │ 2,650 ⎪
    6  │ 2,650 ⎭

            Column 5 Factor            3.169865
            10%, n = 4

            Column 4 Factor          ×  .826446
            10%, n = 2
                                     ───────────
                                       2.619722
                                     ×  $2,650
                                     ───────────
                                      $6,942.26
```

Method 3 may be accomplished with two steps on a calculator. First, calculate the $\boxed{\text{PV}}$ of the four-year annuity as though it were not deferred. In essence, this $\boxed{\text{PV}}$ occurs *one year prior* to the first future payment $\boxed{\text{PMT}}$ to be received; in this example, the time period of the $\boxed{\text{PV}}$ would be EOY 2 as seen above.

The known values for Step 1 are:

$$\boxed{\text{PMT}} = \$2,650$$
$$\boxed{n} = 4 \text{ periods}$$
$$\boxed{i} = 10\%$$

The $\boxed{\text{PV}}$ of the regular annuity is calculated to be:

$$\boxed{\text{PV}} = \$8,400.14$$

Since the above $\boxed{\text{PV}}$ is equivalent to the annuity to be received EOY 2, the $8,400.14 becomes the $\boxed{\text{FV}}$ for Step 2. Thus, the known values for Step 2 are:

$$\boxed{\text{FV}} = \$8,400.14$$
$$\boxed{n} = 2 \text{ periods}$$
$$\boxed{i} = 10\% \text{ per period}$$

The $\boxed{\text{PV}}$ of the deferred annuity is calculated to be:

$$\boxed{\text{PV}} = \$6,942.26$$

51

3. Installment to amortize   What is the monthly payment for a $100,000 mortgage loan at 12 percent for a term of 30 years?

The known values are:

$$\boxed{PV} = \$100,000$$
$$\boxed{n} = 30 \times 12 = 360 \text{ periods}$$
$$\boxed{i} = 12\% \div 12 = 1\% \text{ per period}$$

The $\boxed{PMT}$ is unknown. It is calculated to be:

$$\boxed{PMT} = \$1,028.61$$

Another example of the use of the installment to amortize would be a situation where a portion of a real estate investment must be recovered over a finite time period. Assume a situation where an investor pays $10,000 for a site and builds a $90,000 warehouse on it. Assume that the land value remains stable to perpetuity and that the warehouse has an economic life of 25 years. What would be the proper *annual net rental* on a 25-year contract if the investor requires a 10-percent return before taxes?

This may *seem* much more complex than the previous problem but it is not. The $90,000 structure in this problem is treated as though it were a loan to be repaid with interest over its economic life. Thus, the annual rent must include the following:

Rental of land	
(10% of $10,000)	$ 1,000.00
Rental of structure	

The known values are:

$$\boxed{PV} = \$90,000$$
$$\boxed{n} = 25 \text{ periods}$$
$$\boxed{i} = 10\% \text{ per period}$$

The $\boxed{PMT}$ is calculated to be:

$\boxed{PMT} = \$9,915.13$	+ 9,915.13
Required annual net rental	$10,915.13

4. Perpetuity   In the previous problem it was presumed that the site would produce $1,000 net rental each year to perpetuity. Thus, at a 10-percent discount rate, the present value of the site is $10,000 ($1,000 ÷ .10). But what if the stream of income to perpetuity is deferred? For example, what is the present value of a perpetual income stream of $1,000 which begins at EOY 5 instead of EOY 1 when discounted at 10 percent?

Method 1					
	Subtraction of an Annuity				
EOY	$			EOY	$
1	1,000 received *each year* to perpetuity	minus		1 2 3 4	1,000 1,000 1,000 1,000

This is the same three-step process used in the preceding deferred annuity example. First, calculate the $\boxed{PV}$ of the perpetuity. Second, calculate the $\boxed{PV}$ of a four-year annuity. Third, the $\boxed{PV}$ of the deferred perpetuity is the $\boxed{PV}$ of the perpetuity less the $\boxed{PV}$ of the four-year annuity.

Step 1: The $\boxed{PV}$ of the perpetuity is:

$$\boxed{PV} = \frac{\boxed{PMT}}{\boxed{i}} = \frac{\$1,000}{.10} = \$10,000$$

Step 2: The known values for the annuity are:

$$\boxed{PMT} = \$1,000$$
$$\boxed{n} = 4$$
$$\boxed{i} = 10\%$$

The $\boxed{PV}$ of the annuity is:

$$\boxed{PV} = \$3,169.87$$

Step 3: The $\boxed{PV}$ of the deferred annuity is:

$\boxed{PV}$ of perpetuity (from Step 1)	$10,000.00
$\boxed{PV}$ of annuity (from Step 2)	− 3,169.87
$\boxed{PV}$ of deferred perpetuity	$ 6,830.13

The logic employed is that the present value of an ordinary perpetuity assumes that the income stream begins at EOY 1. If it begins at a later time, the present value of the amounts not received must be subtracted from the present value of an ordinary perpetuity.

Method 2					
	Calculating Deferred Perpetuity				
EOY	$			EOY	$
1	0			1	0
2	0			2	0
3	0	equals		3	0
4	0			4	10,000
5	1,000—received *each year* to perpetuity				

Thus, the calculation becomes that of a simple single sum reversion of $10,000 to be received at EOY 4.

The known values are:

$$\boxed{FV} = \$10,000$$
$$\boxed{n} = 4$$
$$\boxed{i} = 10\%$$

The $\boxed{PV}$ of the deferred perpetuity is:

$$\boxed{PV} = \$6,830.13$$

5. Combinations of cash flows   Calculate the present value of the following annual cash flows for an investor with an opportunity cost of capital of 15 percent.

EOY	$
0	0
1	$10,000
2	10,000
3	10,000
4	10,000
5	10,000 + 150,000

The unknown value is $\boxed{PV}$. This problem may be solved by adding the present value of two cash flows, the five-year annuity and the future sum received EOY 5:

EOY	$		EOY	$		EOY	$
0	0		0	0		0	0
1	$10,000		1	$10,000		1	0
2	10,000		2	10,000		2	0
3	10,000	equals	3	10,000	plus	3	0
4	10,000		4	10,000		4	0
5	10,000 + 150,000		5	10,000		5	$150,000

The known values for the annuity are:

$$\boxed{PMT} = \$10,000$$
$$\boxed{n} = 5 \text{ periods}$$
$$\boxed{i} = 15\% \text{ per period}$$

The $\boxed{PV}$ is calculated to be:

$$\boxed{PV} \text{ annuity} = \$33,521.55$$

The known values for the reversion are:

$$\boxed{FV} = \$150,000$$
$$\boxed{n} = 5 \text{ periods}$$
$$\boxed{i} = 15\% \text{ per period}$$

The $\boxed{PV}$ is calculated to be:

$$\boxed{PV} \text{ reversion} = \$74,576.51$$

The $\boxed{PV}$ of all the cash flows is the sum of the calculated present values of each component of the cash flows. The $\boxed{PV}$ is then:

$\boxed{PV}$ annuity	$ 33,521.55
$\boxed{PV}$ reversion	+ 74,576.51
$\boxed{PV}$ of all cash flows	$108,098.06

An investor who requires a 15-percent return on invested capital would pay $108,098.06 for an investment that would produce these cash flows.

Mortgage calculations

Calculation of the *size* of periodic (generally monthly) payments, over a given term, necessary to amortize fully a mortgage loan has already been illustrated. Another very useful application of the compound interest tables is the calculation of mortgage *balances* over the term of the loan.

The typical mortgage loan contract can be considered from the standpoint of both the lender and the borrower. To the borrower, the mortgage loan represents a loan amount received in the present in return for level payments in the future over a specified term. In contrast, the lender views the loan as an investment outlay in the present in return for a series of equal cash flows over a specific term in the future.

Example

In the previous section, we worked with an example of a mortgage loan of $100,000 at 12 percent with monthly payments for a term of 30 years. The monthly payment necessary to amortize this loan was found to be $1,028.61. From the standpoint of the investor (lender) in this example, the initial mortgage loan amount represents the *present value* of the 30-year stream of monthly payments of $1,028.61, discounted at their opportunity cost of capital, 12 percent. Therefore, the known values are:

55

$$\boxed{\text{PMT}} = \$1,028.61$$
$$\boxed{\text{n}} = 30 \times 12 = 360 \text{ periods}$$
$$\boxed{\text{i}} = 12\% \div 12 = 1\% \text{ per period}$$

The $\boxed{\text{PV}}$ is calculated to be:

$$\boxed{\text{PV}} = \$100,000$$

(Actual calculation is $99,999.75 because of rounding cents in the payment).

Since the periodic payments on a mortgage loan can be viewed as an ordinary annuity, it is very simple to calculate the balance of the mortgage loan to any point in time over the life of the mortgage. This is the present value of the remaining stream of payments when discounted at the mortgage lending rate. For example, after ten years of payments (120 payments of $1,028.61) have been made, 20 years (240 payments) remain. Therefore, the known values for calculating the balance of the mortgage loan at EOY 10 are:

$$\boxed{\text{PMT}} = \$1,028.61$$
$$\boxed{\text{n}} = 240 \text{ periods (the remaining payments)}$$
$$\boxed{\text{i}} = 1\% \text{ per period}$$

The loan balance EOY 10 is calculated to be:

$$\boxed{\text{PV}} = \$93,417.76$$

The lender would be indifferent to receiving either the remaining loan payments or the present value of those payments discounted at the mortgage lending rate. The foregoing presumes there are no prepayment penalties or "lock-in" clauses.

In the analysis of real estate investments, it is often necessary to calculate both future mortgage balances and annual accumulated interest. This may be done for the same loan as shown in the table on page 57.

The procedure used to construct the preceding table was (1) calculate the mortgage balances for each of the ten subsequent periods using the remaining terms of 29 years through 20 years respectively; (2) subtract from each year the balance from the previous year-end balance to obtain the second column, "Principal Reduction"; (3) calculate amount of annual payment by multiplying 12 times the monthly payment; and (4) find "Interest Expense" by subtracting the principal reduction from the "Annual Payment."

Year	EOY Mortgage Balance	Principal Reduction	Annual Payments	Interest Expense
0	$100,000.00	0	0	0
1	99,636.87	$ 363.13	$12,343.32	$11,980.19
2	99,227.97	408.90	12,343.32	11,934.42
3	98,767.21	460.76	12,343.32	11,882.56
4	98,248.01	519.20	12,343.32	11,824.12
5	97,662.97	585.04	12,343.32	11,758.28
6	97,003.73	659.24	12,343.32	11,684.08
7	96,260.88	742.85	12,343.32	11,600.47
8	95,423.82	837.06	12,343.32	11,506.26
9	94,480.60	943.22	12,343.32	11,400.10
10	93,417.76	1,062.84	12,343.32	11,280.48

Summary

This chapter has been devoted to a systematic presentation of the concepts and techniques of compound interest and discounting. The tools and applications presented here can serve as a useful reference and guide to the real estate investment broker.

It simply is not possible to understand the ever-changing world of real estate finance and investment without a thorough working knowledge of the compound interest and discount tables and their many applications. There is no doubt that the investment problems and instruments of tomorrow will be different from those of today; however, the tools discussed in this chapter will be used to create the many innovations of the future. The time spent now in mastering these tools should be considered a sound *investment* which will pay great dividends in the future.

Notes

1. Alfred A. Ring, *The Valuation of Real Estate* (Englewood Cliffs, NJ: Prentice-Hall, Inc., 1970), p. 6.

2. All abbreviations in boxes, such as $\boxed{FV}$ and $\boxed{PV}$, relate both to the compounding and discounting variables and to the financial keys on the typical financial calculator. This is done in an attempt to link together the concepts and the mechanical calculations.

3. L. W. Ellwood, *Ellwood Tables for Real Estate Appraising and Financing*, 4th ed. (Chicago: American Institute of Real Estate Appraisers, 1977).

Chapter 4

Measuring Investment Returns

One of the most critical considerations in the analysis of real estate investments is the measure of investment desirability. Over the years, many measures have been used to indicate the relative profitability of alternative real estate investments. The interesting dilemma is that different approaches or methods of measuring relative investment desirability produced both different relative rankings and different indicators of investment returns. It is not the purpose of this chapter to critique all past practices and techniques of analysis since this topic has already been discussed in various publications.[1] It is worthwhile noting, however, some of the principal weaknesses of traditional techniques.[2]

Investment in real estate involves making choices among many other investment alternatives. These choices must be made within the context of investment objectives. Real estate investors, like all investors, are concerned with providing for future consumption for themselves and/or others by limiting present consumption. Their selection of a particular investment to meet this end takes into account several investment characteristics such as risk, return on investment, timing and duration of cash flows. Most traditional measures of return are ill-equipped to provide a clear and unequivocal indication of investment desirability in view of the variety of investment characteristics that may be important to a single investor.

A general shortcoming of traditional methods of measuring investment returns from real estate is the failure to account for the realities of the marketplace. There are several instances of this weakness. For example, it is common to measure the return on a real estate investment on a before-tax basis. This may be extremely misleading since each real estate transaction offers unique income tax effects. Although most investors are aware that the federal income tax is a significant expense item of most investments, it is often ignored in selecting an investment. This may be because small, middle-income investors assume that they are not really tax sensitive or believe that all investments are affected proportionally by the income tax. Also, the returns of the most common investment alternatives to real estate are stated in before-tax terms. Many investors considering savings accounts or certificates of deposit as investment alternatives tend to forget that the annual interest on those investments will be treated as ordinary income for tax purposes. Even common stocks and corporate bonds are evaluated by many investors on the basis of before-tax yields.

In addition, some techniques ignore the timing of cash flows from the investment while others "stabilize" a single-year income and thus distort the importance of timing. Still other techniques utilize nonmarket rates as "opportunity costs" in a practical world where markets exist. Finally, other approaches omit consideration of the impact of financing when measuring returns to the equity investor.

Present value and internal rate of return

Because of the many shortcomings related to those techniques which distort or disregard the timing of cash flows, there has been a significant move toward the use of the Internal Rate of Return (IRR) as the standard measure of return on equity investments in real estate. This widespread acceptance can be explained by the advantages offered by this measure of return:

1. It is simple to understand and compute.

2. It is the "standard" among most financial institutions and has been widely used for mortgage loan rates, bond rates, etc.

3. It is provided in a convenient form—a rate—which can readily be used as the criterion of comparison for alternative investments.

In Chapter 3, several investment alternatives were presented:

Cash Receipts from Alternative Investments

End of Year	Discounted Mortgage	Five-Year Note	Stock	Insurance Annuity	Land
1	$1,627.45	-0-	$ 1.000	$1,000	-0-
2	1,627.45	-0-	1,000	each	-0-
3	1,627.45	-0-	1,000	year	-0-
4	1,627.45	-0-	1,000	to	-0-
5	1,627.45	$16,105.10	1,000	perpetuity	-0-
6	1,627.45	-0-	1,000	↓	-0-
7	1,627.45	-0-	1,000		-0-
8	1,627.45	-0-	1,000		-0-
9	1,627.45	-0-	1,000		-0-
10	1,627.45	-0-	11,000	↓	$25,937.42
Total Receipts	$16,274.50	$16,105.10	$20,000	∞	$25,937.42

By now, with the use of the compound interest and discount tables, it should be clear that each of the alternative investments above has a **59** present value of $10,000 when discounted at an annual rate of 10 percent. Since the cost of purchasing each alternative is exactly $10,000, the rate of return to the investor is 10 percent—that discount rate which reduces the sum of all future amounts to be received to exactly the amount of the initial investment.

Cash flow as the focus of analysis

All real estate investments may be viewed as cash flows. Subsequent chapters of this text are devoted to methods of determining or estimating the cash flows from real properties with particular emphasis on the effect of depreciation method, form of ownership, age and type of property and various other factors that influence the after-tax cash flows. It is the function of the compound interest and discount factors to determine both investment value and/or rate of return on the various investment alternatives available to the investor.

Within the context of the present value tables, estimated cash flows from real estate investments are treated as though they are *sums certain to be received.* That is, when future cash flows are discounted to the present, the discounting process makes no specific allowance for risk. Even the use of relatively higher discount rates, while having the effect of producing relatively lower present values, does not actually take into account the element of risk associated with the specific property. When comparisons are made among the present values and/or rates of return among investment alternatives, the alternatives should represent cash flows of similar risk and duration.

Future cash flows are also treated as though they represent dollars with the same purchasing power as those of the present. Since future cash flows are discounted to the present and compared with present dollar outlays, such comparisons are valid only when constant dollars are assumed.

Present value

The present value or present worth of an interest in a real property investment may be defined as the sum of all future benefits accruing to the owner of the interest when such benefits are discounted to the present by an appropriate discount rate. In the case of investment real estate, "future benefits" are expressed as *cash flows* which may be both receipts and outlays. As a general proposition, the present value of any interest in real estate may be estimated if the *amount* and *timing* of cash flows and the appropriate *discount rate* are known.

Any form of cash flow, whether level, increasing or variable, may be converted to a simple present value figure. Negative cash flows are discounted in the same manner as positive cash flows, with the sum of such flows subtracted from the sum of positive flows.

Example

Compare the following present value calculations of different cash flows discounted at 15 percent, all of which total $100,000, to be computed over a six-year period.

Present Value of Cash Flows

	Investment A		Investment B		Investment C	
EOY	CF	PV	CF	PV	CF	PV
1	$ 85,000	$73,913	$ 1,000	$ 870	$ 25,000	$21,739
2	5,000	3,781	2,000	1,512	25,000	18,904
3	4,000	2,630	3,000	1,973	25,000	16,438
4	3,000	1,715	4,000	2,287	(25,000)	(14,294)
5	2,000	994	5,000	2,486	25,000	12,429
6	1,000	432	85,000	36,748	25,000	10,808
	$100,000	$83,465	$100,000	$45,876	$100,000	$66,024

One interpretation of the foregoing is that an investor who requires a 15-percent return on investment would pay $83,465 for Investment A, $45,876 for Investment B and $66,024 for Investment C. The *investment value* of each group of cash flows depends upon the discount rate and is the worth of a forecast stream of cash flows to a specific investor. Recall from Chapter 3 that the present value of cash flows to be received in the future decreases as the discount rate increases. Thus, investors who have different yield requirements will employ different discount rates in estimating the investment value of a property.

Net present value

The net present value (NPV) of an investment is the sum of the present value of all future cash flows less the initial investment. The cash flows are discounted at the investor's *opportunity cost of capital*—that rate of discount that represents the yield the investor could obtain from the next best alternative investment of similar size, duration and risk.

Example

Suppose that each of the investments above are available at a cost of $50,000. The NPV of each of the three alternatives to an investor who has $50,000 to invest and requires a 15-percent return on investment are shown in the following table.

Investment	PV of Cash Flows @ 15% (from above)	minus	Initial Investment	equals	NPV
A	$83,465	–	$50,000	=	$33,465
B	45,876	–	50,000	=	(4,124)
C	66,024	–	50,000	=	16,024

Assuming that the risk associated with each alternative investment is comparable, Investment A is the best financial choice because it has the greatest NPV. We said above that an investor who required a 15-percent return on investment could pay $83,465 for Investment A. In that case, it would certainly be a higher yielding investment at a price of $50,000. Investment B, however, is unsuitable because the NPV is less than zero; therefore, the investor would not achieve the required rate of return of 15 percent on invested capital. Recall that it was only worth $45,876 to the investor; at that price it would yield exactly 15 percent.

The NPV of cash flows is affected by the discount rate because the present value of cash flows depends on the discount rate. The NPV increases as the discount rate decreases. For example, the NPV of the same three investment alternatives with a 12-percent opportunity cost of capital is summarized below.

Investment	PV of Cash Flows @ 12%	minus	Initial Investment	equals	NPV
A	$86,274	–	$50,000	=	$36,274
B	53,065	–	50,000	=	3,065
C	71,009	–	50,000	=	21,009

The ordinal ranking of the investment alternatives is the same as before. However, at the lower required return on investment of 12 percent, Investment B becomes acceptable.

Internal rate of return

The typical investor is concerned with the complete return *of* invested capital and an adequate return *on* investment. In general, this return on invested capital is expressed as an annual rate. The calculation of "rate of return" or "yield" of a real estate investment is an important measure of investment worth because it provides one basis for selecting among alternative investments. Since it is calculated from cash flows internal to a specific investment (the initial investment outlay and the future cash flows), it is frequently called the Internal Rate of Return (IRR).

The IRR of an investment may be defined as *that rate of discount at which the present value of all future cash flows is exactly equal to the initial capital investment.* Also, the IRR is the discount rate at which the NPV equals zero.

Three forms of IRR calculations are common in the analysis of real estate investments. The first represents the most simple form of investment return: a single sum returned for an initial investment. The second is a level annuity and the third is a stream of variable cash flows.

Examples

1. Single sum received   Find the IRR of an investment of $15,000 that returns $39,900 in seven years. This may be done with a financial calculator by solving for the unknown value of $\boxed{\text{i}}$ with the known values of:

$$\boxed{\text{PV}} = \$15,000$$
$$\boxed{\text{FV}} = \$39,900$$
$$\boxed{\text{n}} = 7 \text{ periods}$$

The IRR is calculated to be 15 percent.

The same result could be derived by using the compound interest tables (see Appendix A). Recall that the amount of 1 at compound interest, Column 1 factor (F_1), times the $\boxed{\text{PV}}$ equals the $\boxed{\text{FV}}$. In this case,

$$\boxed{\text{PV}} \times F_1 = \boxed{\text{FV}}$$
$$\$15,000 \times F_1 = \$39,900$$

Solving for the Column 1 factor:

$$F_1 = \frac{\$39,900}{\$15,000} = 2.66000$$

Thus, the solution will be found by looking for a Column 1 factor for seven years with annual compounding which equals 2.66000. This is found at an annual rate of approximately 15 percent. Thus, the IRR of this investment is 15 percent because at this discount rate the present worth of the

63

future amount to be received is equal to the initial investment. The present value reversion of 1, Column 4 factor (F_4), could have been used in a similar fashion to solve for IRR since it is the reciprocal of Column 1.

2. Level annuity received   Another common form of investment return is a level stream of income (ordinary annuity) in return for an initial investment. For example, find the IRR of an investment of $15,000 that returns $3,600 each year for seven years.

This may be done with a financial calculator by solving for the unknown value of $\boxed{i}$ with the known values of:

$$\boxed{PV} = \$15,000$$
$$\boxed{PMT} = \$3,600$$
$$\boxed{n} = 7 \text{ periods}$$

The IRR is calculated to be 14.95 percent.

Use of the tables would indicate the same approximate yield. Since both $\boxed{PV}$ and $\boxed{PMT}$ are known, the factor for either the present value of an ordinary annuity of 1 per period, Column 5 (F_5), or the installment to amortize 1, Column 6 (F_6), could be used. Solving for the Column 6 factor:

$$\boxed{PV} \times F_6 = \boxed{PMT}$$
$$\$15,000 \times F_6 = \$3,600$$
$$\frac{\$3,600}{\$15,000} = 0.24000$$

This is very close to the Column 6 factor for seven years of 0.240360 found in the 15-percent annual table. The actual IRR is slightly less than 15 percent because the installment to amortize 1 decreases as the interest rate decreases.

3. Variable cash flows   Calculation of the IRR of the investment forms illustrated above may be accomplished directly because the basic solution equation involves only one unknown. Variable cash flows, however, cannot be solved quite as readily from the tables; a "trial-and-error" process must be used to find that rate which discounts the future cash flows such that their sum equals the initial investment. Of course, IRR calculations with financial calculators can be greatly simplified.

Consider the investments discussed starting on page 61. They were ranked for an investor who has a required yield of 15 percent. Since the NPV is 0 for an investment discounted at the IRR, the IRR on an investment with a positive NPV is always greater than the discount rate used to calculate the present value of the cash flows. This is because NPV declines as the discount rate increases.

For example, look at Investment B:

Investment B

EOY	$		
0	($50,000)		
1	1,000	NPV @ 12% =	$3,065
2	2,000	NPV @ 15% =	($4,124)
3	3,000		
4	4,000		
5	5,000		
6	85,000		

Therefore, the yield to the investor who pays $50,000 for Investment B is less than 15 percent and greater than 12 percent. One way to estimate the IRR within a narrower range is to interpolate between the two rates.[3]

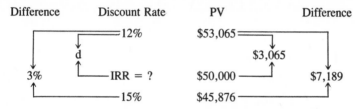

Difference	Discount Rate	PV	Difference
	12%	$53,065	
d			$3,065
3%	IRR = ?	$50,000	$7,189
	15%	$45,876	

Interpolation

Percentage Rate		Present Value Amount		
Smaller	.12	$53,065 ⟶		$53,065
Larger	.15	$45,876	Initial Investment	$50,000
Absolute Difference	[.03 ÷ 7,189]	×	3,065 =	.01279

Smaller Rate .12 + Interpolation Amount 0.1279 = .13279

The IRR to an investor will increase if the initial investment is decreased. At a cost of $50,000, the IRR of Investment B is 13.28 percent. The investor's IRR would be 15 percent if it were acquired for $45,876. This is consistent with the time value of money concepts. The present value of cash flows decreases as the discount rate increases. Recall that the IRR is the discount rate at which the present value of cash flows is equal to the initial investment. Therefore, in order for the present value of cash flows to equal a lower initial investment, the discount rate must be increased.

Periodic and annualized IRRs   The rate of return on an investment is usually stated as an annualized rate. The annualized IRR is merely the effective periodic IRR multiplied by the number of periods per year. This is the reverse process used to compute the effective periodic rate from an annual rate for compound interest and discounting problems.

Example

To compute the annualized IRR to a lender for a $100,000 loan with monthly payments of $1,028.61 to be received for the next 30 years, we must first find the monthly effective rate. The known values are:

$$\boxed{PV} = \$100,000$$
$$\boxed{PMT} = \$1,028.61$$
$$\boxed{n} = 30 \times 12 = 360 \text{ periods}$$

The monthly rate is computed to be 1 percent. The annualized rate is, thus:

$$12 \times 1\% = 12\%$$

Proof of IRR   The IRR is the return *on* each dollar each year that the dollar remains invested. It is *not* the rate earned by the total initial investment throughout the entire term of the investment.

Example

Consider a borrower with a bank line of credit. The IRR to the lender, or the cost of borrowing, is the interest rate on the *outstanding annual balance*. The annual cash flows are listed below. Negative cash flows are loan proceeds paid to the borrower. Positive cash flows represent payments of interest and principal reduction by the borrower.

EOY	$
0	($10,000)
1	2,000
2	(5,000)
3	–0–
4	18,029

The IRR is calculated to be 10 percent. The loan schedule is summarized below.

Year	Investment Balance BOY	10% Interest Due EOY	Principal Plus Interest	Cash Flows of Lender	Balance EOY
1	($10,000)	$1,000	$11,000	$2,000	$ 9,000
2	(9,000)	900	9,900	(5,000)	14,900
3	(14,900)	1,490	16,390	–0–	16,390
4	(16,390)	1,639	18,029	18,029	–0–

The original loan balance of $10,000 earns $1,000 interest EOY 1. The borrower's $2,000 payment is allocated to $1,000 interest and $1,000 principal reduction. The new balance EOY 1 of $9,000 earns $900 interest and the lender advances an additional $5,000 to the borrower EOY 2, so the new balance is $14,900 ($9,000 + $900 + $5,000). Interest of $1,490 is added to the new balance of $14,900 EOY 3. The borrower does not make a payment at EOY 3. The interest earned during Year 4 on the new balance of $16,390 is $1,639. The total loan balance, including interest, is $18,029 ($16,390 + $1,639), which is paid in full EOY 4. The investor (lender) earned 10 percent on each dollar that was invested each year.

This example is intended to demonstrate that the IRR is calculated like—and is directly comparable to—the typical loan in which interest charges are based upon the outstanding balance each payment period. Thus, the IRR is directly comparable to all compound interest (yield) measures.

Applications of IRR   The IRR is useful to measure the yield on capital remaining at risk in an investment. The impact on yield of alternative investment assumptions with respect to financing or taxation can be measured with IRR. The effective cost of borrowing—the lender's yield—for creative financing can also be measured with IRR to compare alternative financing. In general, the IRR is useful for measuring the *internal* performance of a particular investment.

Investment base

The discussion thus far has centered on the term "initial investment" as the cash outflow at risk at the initial period. In the definition of IRR, it is necessary to specify an initial amount of cash advanced. As we have said, the IRR is defined as that rate of discount which, applied to all future cash flows, produces present values whose sum is exactly equal to the initial investment.

In the case of a conventional new investment with the familiar form,

EOP	Cash Flows (CF)
0	(Initial Investment)
1	CF
↓	↓
n	CF + Sales Proceeds

the initial investment is relatively simple to measure—it is the cash outlay made to "purchase" the future cash flow stream. Sometimes, however, the initial investment is more difficult to identify and/or measure.

For example, would it be accurate to conclude that you had nothing invested in a building lot that you acquired in a trade of an item (such as an automobile) that was received as a gift? What if, instead, the automobile were purchased at considerably less than its fair market value?

In both of these situations, the basic issue is not what *cash* was actually advanced to acquire the building lot but rather what *cash value* was sacrificed to acquire the lot. In the instance above of a gift traded for a building lot, the amount in cash that could be obtained (on the average) for the car in the open competitive market (*after* any taxes due are paid) would be the proper measure of the initial investment. Since "initial investment" is generally used to refer to a cash flow, we will use the term *investment base* to refer to the after-tax cash value of a good or service used to acquire an investment.

This procedure is simply an example of the concept of "opportunity cost" whereby the "cost" of employing a good or service in one use is measured by the amount of cash that could have been received had it been employed in the next best alternative use. In the first instance above, the "cost" of trading the car for the land was the amount in cash that would have been obtained in a normal outright sale plus the amount of taxes due, if any.

In the second instance of a car purchased at less than its cash value (for whatever reason), the "investment base" of the land would be the cash value of the car at the time of the trade regardless how much cash was actually paid to obtain the car. The use of an improper measure of investment base to evaluate potential alternatives is a common error in investment decision-making.

Example

Consider the situation whereby a stock is purchased for $100 per share and has earnings of $15 per year for several years. There is a tendency to measure the "yield" as 15 percent ($15 ÷ $100) in spite of market changes in the value of the stock over the holding period. For example, after three years of ownership, the investor may view the stock as earning a highly competitive yield of 15 percent because he is still using the historic purchase price or book value as the measure of "investment base." However, if the stock were currently selling for $160 in the marketplace and the investor could obtain $145 per share after paying capital gains tax and brokerage fees, the true current yield for investment comparison purposes would be approximately 10 percent. If the investor could obtain a stock with similar risk characteristics and growth potential yielding 12 percent after broker's commissions, he would improve the investment yield by doing so:

$$\begin{array}{r} \$145 \\ \times\ .12 \\ \hline \$17.40 \end{array}$$ Net cash received from sale

Per share is more than $15 per share

In general, the *investment base* of Property A already owned and being used to acquire Property B (as in an exchange) is:

1. Cash value of Property A if it were sold outright

2. Less taxes and commissions that would be due from the sale and mortgage debt outstanding at time of the sale.

If additional cash were paid to supplement the value of Property A in acquiring Property B, this would increase the investment base measured above by the amount of the cash. If cash were received at the time of the trade, either through refinancing or to balance the trade, it would reduce the investment base accordingly.

Selecting among alternative investments

Problems with the use of IRR

Although IRR is widely used as a measure of investment return, there are a variety of problems connected with relying on IRR as the exclusive criterion of investment desirability. Before critiquing some of the procedural problems inherent in quantifying the relative yield advantage of one real estate investment alternative over another, let us weigh again at least two other considerations that should be taken into account when selecting (or guiding the selection of) investments: risk and nonfinancial elements. The following discussion is based upon the assumption that investments being compared are of *similar risk* so that an explicit measure of risk is not necessary. As indicated earlier in this text, present value discount factors are not an acceptable means of adjusting for the risk inherent in an investment.

Turning to the particular weaknesses of the IRR as a measure of investment desirability, five problems are apparent.

69

1. **Lack of unique yield** Conventional investments involve an initial outlay of capital with future receipts. For such investments, there can be one and only one IRR. For nonconventional investments, where the future net cash flow stream contains both receipts and outlays, the calculation may become more complex. Under certain circumstances, a given investment may have multiple IRRs or no IRR within the realm of real numbers.[4] Whenever this occurs, it is clear that the use of the IRR as the criterion of investment selection can be misleading.

Example

The IRR of the following cash flows is either 0 percent, 100 percent or 200 percent.

EOY	$
0	(25,000)
1	150,000
2	(275,000)
3	150,000

2. **Discounting negative cash flows** In the standard approach to the calculation of IRR, negative cash flows are discounted at the same internal rate as are positive cash flows. However sound this approach may be from a mathematical standpoint, it generally makes little financial sense. The discount rate for negative cash flows should be that rate at which funds could be invested in the present so as to be available to meet future outlay requirements. It seems most reasonable to discount future negative cash flows by that rate which represents the best estimate of the investor's after-tax yield on relatively safe investments so that the amount set aside in the present would have a reasonable guarantee of increasing in value to the amount needed as an outlay in the future.[5]

3. **Initial investment** Directly related to the procedure of discounting future outlays is the problem of improperly identifying the true initial investment. In the typical IRR approach, the outlay in the present is the measure of the initial investment. However, this does not take into account outlays (investments) in the future that may be necessary to continue the investment. The typical real estate investor is concerned not only with the initial capital investment needed to acquire an interest in the real estate, but he is also interested in capital requirements occurring prior to the future obligations that may not be met either by borrowing and/or by positive cash flows.

Example

Suppose that a developer is considering a project that offers the following cash flows after taxes and after borrowing:[6]

EOY	$	
0	($230,000)	Initial investment
1	($500,000)	Future outlays
2	($500,000)	
3	$2,000,000	Future receipt

The IRR on this investment is approximately 30 percent. However, note that the investor is, in effect, discounting $1 million of future outlays at 30 percent so that it represents a present "cost" of only $680,000. The key question here is: Could the developer reasonably expect to invest $680,000 in the present in order to meet solid obligations of $500,000 in one year and $500,000 at the end of the second year? The answer is yes only if he could invest the $680,000 in some form of investment that is relatively liquid and has an after-tax yield of 30 percent. Without belaboring the argument, it would seem clear that an *after-tax* rate of between 5 and 7 percent would be more realistic. If 5 percent were used, the "adjusted" rate could be calculated as follows.

EOY	$
0	($230,000) + ($929,705) = ($1,159,705) Adjusted initial investment
1	–0–
2	–0–
3	$2,000,000

Adjusted IRR = 20%

The substantial drop in IRR took place because of the different manner in which negative cash flows in the future were discounted. In addition, the initial investment is increased by $929,705. It is the contention here that these adjustments represent a significant improvement over the simple IRR procedure.

4. **Reinvestment of cash proceeds** When the IRR is used to choose between mutually exclusive investment alternatives, the implicit assumption is that the cash proceeds from the investments can be reinvested at the calculated IRR. If the timing of the cash flows differs among the investments being compared, the IRR may provide an invalid indicator of investment desirability.

Example

Consider the following choice between two investments.

EOY	Investments	
	A	B
0	($10,000)	($10,000)
1	–0–	$11,000
2	–0–	–0–
3	–0–	–0–
4	–0–	–0–
5	$20,114	$ 2,074

If the IRR is calculated for each of the above investments, the yield of Investment A is 15 percent, while the yield of Investment B is 20 percent. The investments look quite similar; they both require the same initial investment and they are both for a duration of five years. Using IRR as the basis for investment selection, B is preferable to A. However, this presumes that the investor's goal is to maximize rate of return or at least choose that investment alternative among several which has the highest IRR. What this approach does not consider are the *reinvestment* opportunities that should be taken into account in most investment decisions. Investment A involves only one cash flow received in the future while Investment B involves two. The question that should be asked when making investment comparisons of this type is: At what rate can the investor invest his intermediate cash flows? Suppose that the investor could hope to achieve a yield of only 10 percent on the EOY 1 cash flow from Investment B. A direct comparison of the result would be as follows:

EOY	Investments	
	A	B
0	($10,000)	($10,000)
1	–0–	$11,000 ─┐
2	–0–	–0– │ Reinvested
3	–0–	–0– │ at 10%
4	–0–	–0– ↓
5	$20,114	$ 2,074 + $16,105 = $18,179

Clearly, the investor would have increased his future wealth position by a substantially greater amount by selecting Investment A rather than Investment B *if* he could reinvest his intermediate cash flows at a rate of only 10 percent. So, to make investment choices that reflect true market conditions, the reinvestment rate should be explicitly considered in the analysis of alternatives, and it should not be assumed that the rate to be earned on reinvested funds is exactly equal to the IRR.

5. Size differences in investments   The size of an investment can influence the return in a number of ways. Implicit in the use of IRR is that investments being compared are both *divisible* and *replicable*. That is, the use of IRR carries with it the assumption that any size cash flow can be reinvested at the constant IRR and that a given investment may be undertaken or replicated at any time and on any size scale. Obviously, this is seldom possible in the real world.

Example

Assume the following mutually exclusive investment alternatives.

EOY	Investments	
	A	B
0	($10,000)	($15,000)
1	–0–	–0–
2	–0–	–0–
3	–0–	–0–
4	–0–	–0–
5	$30,518	$40,541

If the IRR is calculated for each of the alternative investments, the yield of Investment A is 25 percent and the yield of B is 22 percent. If we rely exclusively upon IRR in the selection of one of these investments, A would be selected because it has the higher IRR. However, the real issue here is what the investor would do with the incremental investment (the $5,000 difference between the two initial investments) if he were to select Investment A. If we assume that the investor could select either A or B, we must likewise assume that he has the larger of the two investment amounts available to invest. Under these circumstances, it is critical to the investment decision to make an explicit estimate of the rate of return that the differential investment might earn, and then incorporate that rate in the decision. For example, if the investor could earn only 10 percent on the differential $5,000 initial investment, the following case would result.

	Investments			
EOY	A			B
	Original (25%) + Differential (10%) = Total			
0	($10,000) +	($5,000) =	($15,000)	($15,000)
1	–0–	–0–	–0–	–0–
2	–0–	–0–	–0–	–0–
3	–0–	–0–	–0–	–0–
4	–0–	–0–	–0–	–0–
5	$30,518 +	$8,053 =	$38,571	$40,541

Thus, the investor would have been better off selecting Investment B with the lower IRR than selecting Investment A and investing the remaining $5,000 at 10 percent. The key question again is: What is the *actual* market rate that the investor can expect to invest his differential cash flows?

Another size-related issue is the implicit assumption made when using the IRR as an investment criterion for mutually exclusive investment alternatives that any future cash flow (negative or positive), *regardless of size*, can be reinvested at the IRR. Within the realm of real world investment opportunities it is clear that the dollar size (as well as the duration) of an investment is related to the yield. This market phenomenon is well known and widely observed, yet is ignored by the IRR measure.

Introduction to the financial management rate of return

In view of the shortcomings and deficiencies of the use of IRR in many investment decisions, an alternative model called the Financial Management Rate of Return (FMRR) was developed.[7] This model was specifically developed around the assumption that the primary goal of the investor is to maximize his long-run wealth position. Although this may not be his only goal, it is generally consistent with other goals he may have. This model is based upon the terminal value rate of return concept which has existed in economics and finance literature for some time.[8]

In particular, the FMRR is a specialized version of the geometric mean rate of return and is thus directly consistent with the goal of long-run wealth maximization.[9] It is described as "specialized" because the structure of the model has been modified to include as many of the unique characteristics of the real estate market as possible. FMRR makes the following assumptions:

1. *Only cash flows after financing and taxes from the property under evaluation are considered.* The fact is ignored that other sources of

74

cash (such as other properties owned by the investor) may be available in future years to meet cash outflow requirements on the given property, as is the possibility of the investor meeting such payments through the use of unsecured credit.

2. *Funds can be invested at any time in any amount at a safe after-tax rate* (i_L) *and withdrawn when needed.* This would represent highly liquid holdings at modest after-tax yields, comparable to a savings account. The key points here are safety to principal and stability of interest with the ability to make any size investment, however small.

3. *Funds can also be invested in "run of the mill" real estate projects of comparable risk at after-tax rates* (i_R) *above the safe rate.* The stipulation here is that such investments must be in minimum quantities of R dollars and such investments may not be liquidated to meet other cash requirements during the period under analysis.

These assumptions allow the model to recognize market realities and to simulate the actions of a rational financial manager. Real investments are *not* completely divisible; they require a certain minimum level of investment and typically cannot be liquidated without significant loss. At the same time, returns are higher than those of the safe rate. The variables are defined in terms of "run of the mill" projects so that i_R will represent the minimum acceptable return at the given level of risk for an investment of R. Defined in this manner, i_R also represents the minimum return which could be earned by reinvesting cash thrown off early in a project's life. Hence, the main test of the appropriateness of i_R used in a given application of the model is whether the analyst is confident that numerous investment projects would be available yielding at least that rate; if not, i_R should be lowered until such confidence is achieved.

Derivation of the basic FMRR model

The FMRR was designed to overcome the deficiencies of the IRR outlined previously. More specifically, it is designed to do the following:

1. Avoid the possibility of a nonunique or ambiguous solution by converting the cash flows into a conventional investment format.

2. Make explicit those assumptions implicit in the use of IRR regarding the discounting of outflows and the reinvestment of inflows. In essence, this eliminates the problems associated with cash flow reinvestment assumptions, variations of rate with size of investment and reinvestment and recognition of true initial investment.

Example

A simple example can be used to demonstrate the calculation and use of the FMRR model, using only after-financing and after-tax cash flows to show how they are treated within this model:

EOY	$	
0	($10,000)	
1	($50,000)	
2	($50,000)	
3	$30,000	IRR = 25.2%
4	($20,000)	
5	$30,000	
6	$250,000	

Step 1. Remove all future outflows by utilizing prior inflows where possible In this example, if $19,048 of the $30,000 received at EOY 3 were invested at a safe rate (i_L) of 5 percent, it would grow to $20,000 by EOY 4 and be available to meet the $20,000 outflow requirement at that point in time.

The cash flows, therefore, are changed as follows.

EOY	$	Modified Cash Flows
0	($10,000)	($10,000)
1	($50,000)	($50,000)
2	($50,000)	($50,000)
3	$30,000 + ($19,048)	$10,952
4	($20,000) ⟵ 5%	–0–
5	$30,000	$30,000
6	$250,000	$250,000

Step 2. Discount all remaining outflows to the present at the safe rate In this example, the $50,000 payments at EOYs 1 and 2 are discounted to the present at a rate of 5 percent. The cash flows are changed as follows.

EOY	$	Modified Cash Flows
0	($10,000) + ($47,619) + ($45,352)	($102,971)
1	($50,000) ⟵ 5%	–0–
2	($50,000) ⟵ 5%	–0–
3	$10,952	$10,952
4	–0–	–0–
5	$30,000	$30,000
6	$250,000	$250,000

Note that this reflects the fact that the actual investment amount to be made or assumed by the investor is $102,971, not $10,000.

Step 3. Compound forward those positive cash flows remaining at the appropriate rate   In this example, assume R is equal to $10,000 and i_R is 10 percent. Thus, cash flows received at EOYs 3 and 5 will be compounded forward at $i_R = 10$ percent. The cash flows are again changed as follows.

EOY	$	Modified Cash Flows
0	($102,971)	($102,971)
1	–0–	–0–
2	–0–	–0–
3	$10,952 ──── 10% ──┐	–0–
4	–0–	–0–
5	$30,000 ── 10% ─┐ ↓	–0–
6	$250,000 + $33,000 + $14,577	$297,577

Therefore:

FMRR = 19.4% (the rate at which $102,971 grows to $297,577 in six years)
IRR = 25.2%(the rate which discounts all future cash flows such that
the sum of the present values is equal to $10,000)

The difference between these two measures of yield is entirely explained by the explicit estimates made for the various rates utilized within the FMRR calculation as compared with the assumption of the IRR approach, in which all relevant rates (i.e., safe rates and reinvestment rates) are exactly equal to the calculated IRR. Alternately stated, FMRR is the forecast compound rate of growth of the investor's wealth, measured in dollars, with reinvestment assumptions consistent with the particular investor's financial management strategy, including consideration of cash flows external to the investment under consideration. In contrast, recall that IRR is the return on each dollar each year that the dollar remains at risk in an investment.

Use of FMRR to compare investment alternatives

Real estate investment alternatives often require different initial investments and have different anticipated holding periods. It is appropriate, therefore, to adjust cash flows for time and size disparities among investment alternatives under consideration for comparison on a par basis. As with all preceding examples, the investment alternatives below are assumed to have comparable risk and all cash flows shown are after-tax. Usually, investments will have intermediate periodic cash flows. They are adjusted   **77** independently, as demonstrated above. The adjusted cash flows are then compared.

Example

To illustrate the final adjustment process, compare the cash flows from the previous example (henceforth Investment A) to Investment B, an investment in raw land that costs $130,000. Assume that holding costs are $1,000 per year and that sale proceeds EOY 5 are projected at $331,000. The cash flows and adjusted cash flows for Investment B are shown below.

EOY	Investment B	
	$	Modified Cash Flows
0	($130,000) + ($3,546)*	($133,546)
1	($1,000)	–0–
2	($1,000)	–0–
3	($1,000)	–0–
4	($1,000) 5%	–0–
5	($1,000) + $331,000	$330,000

*PV of an ordinary annuity of $1,000 per year for four years discounted at 5 percent.

The IRR of Investment B is 20 percent compared to 25.2 percent for Investment A. Note that the initial investments are not equal for A and B, nor are the holding periods. If Investment B is indeed an alternative, the investor must have $133,546 to invest. If A were acquired, it is assumed that the balance of investment capital would be invested at 10 percent for the longest holding period, six years. The holding period of A is six years compared to five years for Investment B. The cash available at EOY 5 for Investment B will be reinvested at a forecast 10 percent. The adjustments to cash flows for comparison of the two investment alternatives are summarized in the following two tables:

EOY	Investment A	
	Modified CF	Adjusted for Comparison
0	($102,971) + ($30,575)	($133,546)
1	–0–	–0–
2	–0–	–0–
3	–0– 10%	–0–
4	–0–	–0–
5	–0–	–0–
6	$295,577 + $54,165	$351,742

EOY	Investment B	
	Modified CF	Adjusted for Comparison
0	($133,546)	($133,546)
1	–0–	–0–
2	–0–	–0–
3	–0–	–0–
4	–0–	–0–
5	$330,000 ── 10% ──┐	–0–
6	–0– $363,000 ↓	$363,000

The alternative investments can now be compared on a par basis. The table below summarizes the cash flows and investment measures. Note that the IRR alone would not have indicated the investment alternative which would produce the maximum amount of future wealth with the foregoing financial management assumptions.

EOY	Investment A		Investment B	
	$	Adjusted for Comparison	$	Adjusted for Comparison
0	($10,000)	($133,546)	($130,000)	($133,546)
1	($50,000)	–0–	($1,000)	–0–
2	($50,000)	–0–	($1,000)	–0–
3	$30,000	–0–	($1,000)	–0–
4	($20,000)	–0–	($1,000)	–0–
5	$30,000	–0–	($1,000) + $331,000	–0–
6	$250,000	$351,742	–0–	$363,000
IRR	25.2%		20.0%	
FMRR		17.5%		18.1%

Investment B will produce the greatest future wealth EOY 6. Calculation of the actual FMRR is not even required for this decision once the cash flows have been adjusted. The appropriate financial choice is simply that alternative which will provide the most dollars at the end of the investment time horizon.

It should be noted here that the 10-percent rate for reinvestment of the sale proceeds from Investment B may be understated. The $330,000 available EOY 5 may very well have been reinvested in another property that would produce a higher yield. This assumption could have been imputed into the analysis easily by compounding the future wealth EOY 5 from Investment B at a greater rate of perhaps 20 percent since this was the yield on the last investment. The safe rate(s) and reinvestment rate(s) must be consistent, after-tax rates. Do not use a *before*-tax bond yield for a safe rate with an analysis of cash flows *after* tax.

Other applications of the FMRR

One of the more interesting and useful applications of the FMRR is in determining the "optimal holding period" of an investment. The holding period of a real estate investment has traditionally been determined by the IRR, which is especially ill-suited to the task. In addition, the FMRR can be used in selecting among mutually exclusive alternative investments and in selecting from a mix of alternatives when investment funds are rationed.

There are several other applications of the FMRR that can be most helpful in real estate investment decision-making. It is not within the scope of this chapter to detail such applications, but the concerned reader is referred to the Messner-Findlay article for some extensions or modifications of the basic FMRR model.[10]

Notes

1. For an exposition of some of the traditional and conventional methods of measuring the return on real estate investments and their respective shortcomings, see James R. Cooper, *Real Estate Investment Analysis* (Lexington, MA: Lexington Books, 1974), Ch. 1; Stephen E. Roulac, "Truth in Real Estate Reporting," *Real Estate Review*, Spring, 1974, pp. 90-95; and Victor Lyon, "ABC's of Investment Analysis," *real estate today*, February, 1980, pp. 20-25.

2. Much of the following discussion is based on Stephen D. Messner and M. Chapman Findlay, "Real Estate Investment Analysis: IRR Versus FMRR," *The Real Estate Appraiser*, July-August, 1975, pp. 5-20.

3. See Appendix B for a further discussion of interpolation.

4. See Messner and Findlay, pp. 8-9 for numerical examples of nonconventional investments and the phenomenon of multiple yields. See also Donald J. Valachi, "More on the Arithmetic of Multiple and Imaginary Rates of Return," *The Real Estate Appraiser and Analyst*, Vol. 46, No. 5, September-October, 1980, pp. 19-22.

5. Messner and Findlay, pp. 9-11.

6. Messner and Findlay, pp. 10-11.

7. The FMRR was developed by M. Chapman Findlay and Stephen D. Messner of the School of Business Administration, the University of Connecticut, Storrs, Connecticut, in 1973. Jay W. Levine, working with Realtron Corporation, assisted the originators to relate and adapt their model to problems found in the real estate investment market. An explanation of this model was first published as *Determination and Usage of FM Rate of Return,* 1973, by Realtron Corporation, Detroit. An expanded version was presented by Findlay and Messner at the Eastern Finance Association meetings in April, 1975, at the University of South Carolina. Subsequently, the model has been refined and much discussed in real estate literature. For example, see Guilford C. Babcock, M. Chapman Findlay and Stephen D. Messner, "FMRR and Duration: Implications for Real Estate Investment Analysis," *AREUEA Journal,* Vol. 4, No. 3, Winter, 1976, pp. 49-67; M. Chapman Findlay, Stephen D. Messner and R. Tarantello, "Risk Analysis in Real Estate," *The Real Estate Appraiser and Analyst,* Vol. 45, No. 4, July-August, 1979, pp. 27-38; M. Chapman Findlay, Carl W. Hamilton, Stephen D. Messner and Jonathan S. Yormark, "Optimal Real Estate Portfolios," *AREUEA Journal,* Vol. 7, No. 3, Fall, 1979, pp. 298-317; and M. Chapman Findlay, Stephen D. Messner and R. Tarantello, *FMRR Simulation Model and User Manual* (Storrs, CT: Center for Real Estate and Urban Economic Studies, 1980).

8. Gene Dilmore, *The New Approach to Real Estate Appraising* (Englewood Cliffs, NJ: Prentice-Hall, Inc., 1971), pp. 122-23.

9. H. Latane, "Criteria for Choice Among Risky Ventures," *Journal of Political Economy,* April, 1959, pp. 144-55.

10. Messner and Findlay, pp. 18-20. See also Note 7 of this chapter.

Chapter 5

Estimation of Real Estate Cash Flows (Forecasting)

Introduction to forecasting

Thus far the major emphasis of this text has been on the process of converting forecast future cash flows (income receipts) into present value estimates by using the mathematical process of compound discounting. The mathematical logic employed in discounting future cash flows is fundamentally essential in analyzing real estate investments. Of equal importance, however, is the process by which the future cash flows of a specific property (or group of properties) are estimated. Generally, this process stands in marked contrast to the inexorable precision of the discounting process. Since estimates of cash flows generated by real estate necessarily involve estimates of the future, they are more often than not significantly less precise than the mathematical technique used to discount them to the present.

The estimation of future cash flows for income-producing real estate requires a variety of judgments and assumptions concerning the future. Among these are judgments concerning the property itself, the future of the neighborhood in which it is located, the general market conditions that will prevail in the future and their impact on the specific property, future developments in the federal income tax laws that may influence the after-tax cash flows of the property and myriad other factors which may affect the cash flows of the specific property over time. The point is that the task of income estimation typically requires both experience in and knowledge of the operation of the real estate market. It is not simply an extrapolation of the known market behavior of preceding years, nor can the estimation problem be refined completely to objective statistical probabilities. In its final form, the estimate of future benefits from an investment in real estate must relate to the *amount, timing, duration* (or term) and *stability* of after-tax cash flows to be received by the investor.

This process may be viewed as more an art than a science because of the variety of types of real estate income. The income from a long-term net lease is simplest to define because the lease itself usually states the rental stream. This estimation could become more complicated if a percentage rent is also required. At the other extreme, the income from a vacant portion of land, encumbered with debt, can account for a negative income stream created by real estate taxes and loan payments, until the land is sold.

Between these extremes is the apartment building, the store building or other improved real estate with short-term leases where the owner pays all or most of the expenses. Other examples include vacant buildings as well as properties to be developed where all income and expense items must be estimated and projected.

Income estimation as a brokerage tool

Distinctions between residential and investment property

At the outset, it is important to recognize the differences between marketing investment property and residential property. By understanding the differences, the broker presenting an investment property can readily see the most effective means of making such a presentation.

Residential properties that are owner-occupied are paid for from income unrelated to the property and are purchased to satisfy the functional and structural arrangement needed by the purchaser. These properties must have the floor plan and amenities that are of personal importance to the buyer. He is interested in the size of the home, the number of bedrooms and the room arrangement. Neighborhoods, the local school system, available transportation, churches, shopping, social and recreational facilities and, perhaps, the view from his living room window are important considerations. Real estate brokers stress these items in showing a home intended for owner occupancy.

In selling residential properties, a market data approach is typically used in determining market value and/or price. Market value is determined by the sale prices of similar properties. In some cases, replacement costs and the amount of actual depreciation that the property has already undergone might be considerations influencing residential property buyers.

When income-producing property is involved, the amenities, churches, neighborhood and view all are secondary considerations. Income-producing properties are purchased for their ability to produce an income stream, whether that income is operating income or potential capital gain on resale, or both, and are paid for with the income generated. The amenities and other factors that are so important with residential properties have importance for income-producing property only if they influence the stream of cash flows. Do they add to the quantity of that income; do they make the quality or the durability of that income any better?

Many brokers make the mistake of stressing only the physical characteristics of an investment property and/or its replacement cost when the purchaser is really interested in the future income benefits. The fact that the present owner has invested considerable sums in the property does not necessarily influence the potential buyer of investment property. If the income produced by the property will only justify a sale price of $175,000, the buyer does not care that the owner has actually invested $300,000 in the property and is "willing to let it go" for $250,000.

If, then, buyers purchase investment property for future income, it is absolutely imperative that the broker have all of the financial information about a property prior to marketing it. Just as a stock broker cannot market stock without a prospectus (operating history), a real estate broker cannot intelligently present a property if the owner will not produce an operating statement until a qualified buyer is found.

Appraiser versus investment broker

The task of the real estate appraiser is most often that of estimating the *market value* of a property; that is, the most probable selling price of the property under "normal" exposure to the market and under financing terms generally available for similar properties. Under the somewhat rigid definition utilized for market value, particularly in the legal context imposed by institutional mortgage lenders, property tax authorities and others, there is a single value at any point in time. Obviously, different opinions of market value among appraisers may prevail, but in concept there is only one correct market value for a given property at any one time.

In contrast, the investment broker is generally concerned with the value of a property to a specific potential investor or class of investors. Under these conditions, the analysis of value takes into account the estimated after-tax cash flows, the desired or required rate of return on the equity investment and the financing terms available on the property to the specific investor. This value estimate is *investment value;* it may be less than, equal to or greater than market value. For example, *if* the potential investor is also "typical" in terms of the group of investors most likely to purchase the property under the competitive market conditions required by the definition of market value, investment value will be exactly equal to market value.

Collection of property data

The first step in estimating the future cash flows that will be generated by a specific property is to collect the most recent operating data from the present owner. Obtaining financial information about previous years' operations, however, is not the broker's only responsibility. He must also be able to analyze and evaluate the information, process the data in an operating statement, convert the income stream to an estimate of value and, finally, interpret to the owner or client the consequences of owning the property under present and alternate financing arrangements.

Interview with owner

In his interview with the owner the broker must be adamant in his quest for information. Many owners only reluctantly divulge financial information about their property. Most agree to supply the information "when a qualified buyer is found."

It is only when the broker truly understands that buyers are buying the future income rather than the structure that he can insist on obtaining proper information from the owner *before* any potential purchaser is contracted. When owners understand what truly motivates a buyer, they will usually supply the necessary information. No one buys securities without a prospectus. In the same way, the public cannot be expected to purchase income property without a past history of its operations.

The broker cannot always depend on the owner's memory; he should insist on previous years' statements. The best information is usually obtained when the broker gets written authority from the owner's accountant for all the data needed. The owner's records will have validity but income tax statements will provide the best information. It is rare for income tax records to overstate income or understate expenses.

Property Inspection

Although the property will be sold mainly on the basis of the financial data, it is necessary that the broker also obtain physical data on the property. This will include type of construction, condition of the property, the size and area of the land and improvements. This information will be used as an aid in verifying incomes and expenses and for estimating value.

It is also important for the broker to inspect the neighborhood to observe if it is economically stable, dying or growing.

Depending on the type of property involved, the broker should also investigate all or some of the following facilities with respect to the property:

Public transportation
Highways and expressways
Interchanges
Power
Utilities
Railroad transportation
Schools
Taxation procedures

Revision of property data

The information the broker obtains from the owner may be 100 percent truthful and still not be valid. The owner, even if he is truthful, can only report what the property took in for the previous year or years and what expenses were incurred during the same years. He is not in a position to *evaluate* the data. This is the broker's task since he is interested in developing an operating statement that will closely reflect what the property might be expected to do under average management conditions during future years. Buyers, after all, are paying for future potential, not for past income.

It is possible that the indicated previous year's rents were unusually low or high. It is the broker's job to find out what rents *should be* for this type of property. It is also possible that last year's maintenance costs or taxes or any other particular expense might have been unusually high or low; the broker must then determine typical costs. Possibly, when all adjustments and revisions have been completed, not a single item of expense or income may be the same as indicated by the owner for previous years. However, such a revised operating statement supplied by the broker will more closely reflect what the property can be expected to do in the future, which is of utmost importance to any potential buyer.

The first step in revising property data is to analyze the information obtained from the owner and make certain obvious adjustments. For example, if the owner is occupying the building, it is necessary to determine what rent he would be paying if he were not the building's owner. If the broker is unable to evaluate what the rent should be, a notation should be made that the owner is not paying rent to occupy his space. The key point is that any items on the owner's income statement that fail to reflect the "market" should be modified.

The expenses should be evaluated to determine if they include any of the owner's personal expenses. It is possible that they could be legitimate tax deductions for the present owner yet not be true expenses involved in obtaining rent for the building.

Obtaining relevant market data

In order to make the necessary adjustments to the operating information supplied by the owner, the broker must investigate and/or be familiar with a variety of market data.

Rental information must be obtained. What do similar properties rent for per square unit per month or per year? Is a percentage rent applicable and, if so, how much? What are typical rent terms and provisions? How valid are the owner's stated rents as to quantity, quality and durability? What vacancy and credit loss factor should be applied? Are utilities included in the rent or are they paid for by the tenant? Do rent schedules of comparable buildings include comparable services or furnishings?

Expenses must be analyzed both individually and totally. Are the expenses indicated by the owner valid or should they be adjusted upward or downward? Are sufficient amounts allowed for taxes in districts that need new schools and other facilities? Are there proper amounts allowed as maintenance and repair expenses? Is the total expense-to-income ratio adequate?

The broker should also obtain from his own files or from contractors or other sources reconstruction costs for the type of building under study. He should also search the market for recent sales of similar properties and land. These figures will be needed for estimating market value.

Financial data provided by the owner must be verified as to accuracy and thoroughness. The broker should determine exact encumbrances, payments, interest rates and due dates. He should find out whether existing financial arrangements are by mortgage, trust deed or contract and determine the order of the liens. He must also determine if the existing loans may be assumed by a prospective purchaser and whether the seller will carry back any financing and on what terms.

Other important items of information the broker should include on the statement are assessed values of land, improvements and personal property, as well as the present owner's basis and depreciation schedule.

Organization of property data

For purposes of investment analysis, *cash flows* are used rather than accrual accounting concepts to measure benefits. Thus, non-cash flow "expenses" such as depreciation are *not* included in the measure of cash flows (although the impact of depreciation may be reflected through reduced tax outlays) while the cash outflow of debt repayment through mortgage amortization is not recorded as an accounting expense.

The typical cash flow statement for real estate is divided into the major categories of Gross Income (or Scheduled Rental Income), Gross Operating Income (Effective Rental Income), Operating Expenses, Net Operating Income, Cash Flow Before Tax and Cash Flow After Tax.

Gross income (scheduled rental income)

This is generally defined as the "rent roll" or annual market rental for the entire capacity of rentable space in the property. If the property is owner-occupied, a market rental would be imputed; if the property is under long-term lease, the contract rent would be the most appropriate measure of rent receipts. Present rents for the property may be higher, lower or approximately equal to market rents. It is important to determine (estimate) the *most probable* rent levels for the future; this is a critical first step in determining the future cash flows that the potential investor might expect to receive.

Effective rental income

As indicated, Gross Income is the annual amount that the property would produce *if* all rentable space were rented. In most cases, it is not reasonable to assume 100-percent occupancy of the property. In any case, the vacancy and credit losses of similar and competitive properties must be compared with those of the subject property so that reasonable expectations of the future rate can be made. In general, the rate is measured as the annual percentage of total rentable space that is vacant. This rate is then converted into an annual dollar amount and subtracted from Gross Income to obtain Effective Rental Income.

Gross operating income

To obtain the figure for Gross Operating Income, "other income" is added to the Effective Rental Income. Other income is income related to the property but not derived directly from the rental of building space. Examples would be income from the rent of parking space or income from concessions.

Operating expenses

Gross Operating Income, as defined, represents the total cash inflows to the property that are available to pay operating expenses (including income taxes), to cover annual debt service and to provide for a return on investment as well as a complete return *of* the investment over time. Operating expenses typically include the following.

Taxes   The major tax paid on real estate is property tax. This is a "fixed" expense in that it does not vary with occupancy but does (or can) change over time. Factors such as trends in the local or state property tax law and the frequency of reassessment can help in estimating likely future tax payments.

Insurance   Current quotations or estimates are needed on multiperil insurance for the property. The "prudent man" test should be applied in determining the extent of coverage.

Utilities   Today utility costs often increase at so rapid a pace that actual costs for the past year may significantly understate probable future costs. Utility companies may be able to provide some reliable estimates for the future based on past levels of consumption.

Licenses, permits and advertising A check should be made to determine what licenses and/or permits are needed, if any, to operate the property and their annual costs. Local property management companies and other owners can provide some comparable information on the annual cost of advertising utilizing signs, newspapers and other publications.

Management There are two kinds of property management: professional and resident. Professional management firms generally charge a percentage of Gross Operating Income. The use of a resident manager is required in many areas and is generally done in conjunction with a professional management firm when a large number of units is involved and/or when day-to-day requirements call for constant supervision. Market data are usually available on the cost of such management. The real problem is the tendency by an owner to omit consideration of this expense when he acts as manager and/or the prospective buyer is planning to do so.

Payroll and payroll taxes In addition to the payroll expense of regular employees used in operating the property, there is also the cost of payroll taxes, such as social security tax and workmen's compensation insurance.

Supplies This category of expense will vary significantly from one type of property to another, but similar properties should have similar relative supply expenses.

Services Special services required by the property such as rubbish collection and pool service must be included as operating expenses. Typically this category of expense is relatively small but, as in the case of "supplies," can vary greatly from one type of property to another.

Maintenance Actual maintenance and repair expenses for the subject property for the past few years can be used as a starting point for estimating future expenses. However, current trends in the market should be compared with recent costs. Market data can generally be obtained from local management firms; in addition, there are published data on several types of income-producing properties which provide average annual maintenance costs per unit of space.

Replacements Equipment and building parts with relatively short lives must be replaced periodically over the term of investment. Typical appraisal practice calls for prorating, or "stabilizing," such outlays on an annual basis. This is accomplished by dividing the replacement cost by the forecast economic life to obtain the annual amount needed to cover replacement. However, this appraisal treatment is technically incorrect for two reasons. From the standpoint of income tax calculations, the cost of replacements is a capital expenditure, *not* an expense, and must be depreciated over the economic life of the asset. Also, the practice of prorating the cash outlay over several annual periods distorts the actual cash flows used to measure investment value and return. Thus, the proper practice for investment analysis is to forecast *actual* cash flows for each year.

Net operating income

Net Operating Income is obtained by subtracting Operating Expenses from Gross Operating Income. This is *the* key measure of income used by appraisers and mortgage lenders when market value is sought because it is the measure of return *before* financing, taxes and capital recovery.

Cash flow before taxes (CFBT)

As indicated, Net Operating Income (NOI) represents an estimate of the typical year's income return to the *entire* property. When the property is financed with a mortgage loan, the NOI must provide for the Annual Debt Service associated with the loan. Thus, Cash Flow Before Taxes is obtained by subtracting the Annual Debt Service from the NOI.

Cash flow after taxes (CFAT)

This is the true "bottom line" of the annual return of the investment. Each year's income tax liability is subtracted from CFBT to obtain Cash Flow After Taxes. The calculation of income tax liability will be considered in subsequent chapters, but it is important to note that this may be (in fact, typically is) a negative figure. That is, accounting losses (because of the non-cash depreciation expense) may be used to reduce taxes that would be paid on other income.

Example

The following illustration is intended to show how data collected from both the present owner of an apartment property and from the marketplace may be used to develop cash flow estimates.

Owner's property data

The accounting records of a 28-unit apartment building for the past year showed the following:

Rental receipts		$51,000
Expenses		
Property taxes	$7,956	
Insurance	4,203	
Utilities	2,669	
Supplies	1,173	
Services	1,511	
Depreciation	5,000	
Interest	9,076	
		−31,588
Taxable income (accounting income)		$19,412

A physical inspection of the property indicated the following information:

The apartment building contained	26,500 sq. feet
garages	6,900 sq. feet
land (270 × 200)	54,000 sq. feet
apartment rooms	100

All this information was listed on an Annual Property Operating Data form showing the owner's statement, an example of which can be seen as Figure 19 in Chapter 12.

The owner's mortgage loan record indicates that the original mortgage loan of $200,000 is now eight years old. The interest rate of the loan is 6 percent, payable monthly, and the term of the loan is 20 years. Monthly payments on the loan are $1,432.80 and the present balance of the loan is $146,825.81.

Based upon this accounting record of the past year's income, NOI for the past year for the owner would be as follows:

Taxable income		$19,412
Plus:		
Depreciation	$5,000	
Interest	9,076	
		+14,076
Owner's Net Operating Income		$33,488

Broker's cash flow estimate (forecast of cash flows)

Up to this point the only thing that has been accomplished is the organization of the owner's accounting data relating to the building in a form that will allow comparison with market data. The next step is to compare the past year's performance with the performance of other similar apartment properties in the same market area.

The information submitted by the owner reflects the results of last year's operations. Last year's results may or may not be an indication of results in the future. Consequently an analysis must be made of what the *potential* income of the property is because the purchaser is really buying the future potential benefits of the property.

To test the validity of the income information submitted by the owner, the broker reconstructs a new operating statement based upon both the owner's statement and the market area. An example of a broker's forecast is shown on an Annual Property Operating Data form in Figure 21 in Chapter 12.

The first item needed is the Scheduled Rental Income. This is the income that the property would produce if rented at market or economic rents 100 percent of the time. To estimate Gross Scheduled Income, it is necessary to know what the typical rentals in the area are for this type of apartment. Studies may have to be made to determine unit rents on a square- or cubic-foot basis or per-room or per-apartment basis. In this case the broker's study indicates rents at $2.40 per square foot annually.

Thus, scheduled rental income would be $63,600 (26,500 square feet × $2.40).

The broker's studies also indicate that vacancies and credit losses are to be estimated at 6 percent or $3,816 ($3,800 rounded). This amount is subtracted from Scheduled Rental Income, resulting in Effective Rental Income of $59,800.

The broker finds that garage space rents at $96 per year and, because the property has only 14 garages, they have historically been fully rented in spite of changes in the building's occupancy rate. This source of "Other Income" is likely to provide $1,344 (14 garages × $96) per year. When this amount is added to Effective Rental Income, Gross Operating Income becomes $61,144.

Next, an analysis of expenses is in order. The taxes submitted on the Owner's Statement were $8,000. An analysis of the tax situation must be made to determine whether that figure will hold for the next few years. (For example, are the schools in the neighborhood adequate? Are there other improvements planned?) In this case, the broker estimates an annual tax cost of $8,400.

The broker asks his insurance agent to check the owner's reported premium of $4,200. It was determined that this amount was for a three-year policy, the average annual cost being $1,500.

A check with the utilities companies indicated an increase in utilities costs over those submitted by the owner. Therefore, the broker increases the utility cost figure to $2,700.

The broker determined that the present owner managed the property, collected the rents, did minor repairs and kept the lawn and garden. Investigation in the market area indicated that typical management costs were a 5-percent management fee plus an on-site manager rental allowance of $50 per month. Thus, total estimated management costs were approximately $3,700 per year.

Supplies were estimated at $120 per month, or $1,400 per year. Services were estimated to be $175 per month, or $2,100 per year. Maintenance costs were estimated at $140 per year per unit and miscellaneous costs at $50 per month.

It is now possible for the broker to calculate Net Operating Income for this property for a typical investor.

Scheduled rental income		$63,600
Less: Vacancy and credit losses		− 3,800
Effective rental income		$59,800
Plus: Other income		+ 1,344
Gross Operating Income		$61,144
Less: Operating expenses		
Taxes	$8,400	
Insurance	1,500	
Utilities	2,700	
Management	3,700	
Services	2,100	
Supplies	1,400	
Maintenance	3,920	
Other	600	−24,320
	$24,320	
Net Operating Income		$36,824

Obviously, the broker's cash flow estimate for the property is significantly different from the owner's accounting of the past year's income for the property. It must be noted that the broker's estimate is based primarily on current market conditions. Thus, the estimate of cash flow is essentially a "one-year" estimate for the property. Whether or not this may be safely extrapolated into the future beyond the first year depends on specific circumstances. In later chapters, we will examine further examples of the process whereby future income streams of properties can be estimated.

Chapter 6

Real Estate Financing

Introduction

Financing is often the most important element of a real estate transaction. Indeed, the finalization of many transactions can be contingent upon available financing. Even the market value of income-producing real estate is affected by current market financing availability and terms. Real estate purchase and sales agreements usually include at least one clause regarding the amount, term and rate of the financing to be acquired by the buyer. It is essential to understand the implications of the terms of financing in order to choose the most appropriate alternative for a specific borrower-investor.

Real estate, like most other forms of economic goods, may serve as collateral for loans. A key difference, however, is that real estate provides unique advantages to both lender and borrower which tend to make borrowing the rule of the real estate investment market rather than the exception. Of key importance to the lender is the fact that as security for a loan, most real estate has a long life (both physical and economic) and a fixed location.

The borrower may use debt financing for a variety of reasons. He may diversify risk by investing limited equity capital in several properties, in contrast to only one property. Equity funds may be retained for alternative uses that may provide a greater return or more financial security. Since debt financing is most often required to supplement the purchase price of the property, equity yield may be increased as a result of financial leverage—which is the primary topic of this chapter.

General financing characteristics

As one views the financing of real estate, certain outstanding characteristics that tend to set it apart from other types of financing become obvious. The relatively *long-term* nature of loans on real estate is unique. Of course, short-term construction loans are typical for development projects, but this is only a form of interim financing until the permanent loan is made. The durability of the property and its fixed location have made such long-term loans a standard of the industry. "Long terms" mean relatively small principal returned per annum and increased cash flows for the investor in real estate.

94

Related to the long-term nature of real estate loans are the special risks associated with such long-term commitments. A wide variety of factors in the neighborhood where the property is located, the urban area that provides the demand for the property's services and the national economy which is responsible for changes in purchasing power, federal government spending and monetary policy all affect the income-producing potential of a specific property. These must be taken into account by both the lender and the borrower-investor in making real estate finance decisions.

Also important to an understanding of real estate financing is the predominant instrument used in the market—the mortgage. The legal complexities surrounding the mortgage contract have tended to make real estate transactions relatively cumbersome and costly. In addition, mortgage terms, rates and conditions may vary significantly from location to location and time to time.

Real estate may be financed in a variety of ways other than simply through mortgage loans. Partnerships, syndicates and trusts may be created to accumulate the necessary equity funds. In addition, leasing is a popular alternative means of financing real estate.

Sources of real estate funds

The major sources of mortgage loans for real estate investments are life insurance companies, commercial banks, mutual savings banks and savings and loan associations. Other important financial operatives in the market are mortgage brokers and companies, real estate investment trusts and individual lenders.

Life insurance companies

Life insurance companies specialize in large long-term loans on major real estate development projects and represent the most important source of debt financing for major shopping center developments, office buildings and large multifamily projects. They have been the leaders in innovative financing techniques in this country and have, during the beginning of the 1980s, revived lender participation as a means of coping with double-digit inflation.

Commercial banks

Commercial banks also play a highly specialized role in real estate financing and have extended the scope of their activities in recent years. Although commercial banks do make mortgage loans, this has not been the area where they have had the greatest impact on the market. They are closely regulated with respect to their mortgage lending practices and by policy have not been as aggressive in mortgage lending as some other financial institutions even though their mortgage portfolios have increased in recent years. Their primary significance in the real estate market is in the area of short-term lending where they supply the vast majority of interim financing for real estate. They lend not only to developers during the construction phase of the project but also to other real estate lenders and investors such as mortgage brokers and companies.

Mutual savings banks

Most mutual savings banks are found on the east coast where they invest a major portion of their total portfolios in real estate. They are quite active in home mortgages and are also important local lenders for commercial and investment real estate. Like insurance companies, they have been somewhat innovative and creative in their lending procedures and are aided by being somewhat less regulated than are other mortgage lenders.

Savings and loan associations

Savings and loan associations are "home loan" specialists which originate most of their mortgage portfolios locally. They are by far the most important sources of single family mortgage loans in this country and have historically restricted the majority of their loan portfolios to this type of financing. In recent years, however, they have moved to diversify into other types of real estate investments including an emphasis on financing multi-family housing projects. By granting broader lending powers to savings and loans, the 1980 "deregulation act" passed by Congress added further stimulus to this move by savings and loans to finance investment properties.

Mortgage banking

The primary function of mortgage brokers and companies is to channel mortgage funds from large institutional investors to developers and other real estate owners and users. The "broker" serves as an intermediary between borrower and lender and receives a fee for these services. Mortgage bankers, on the other hand, use their own funds (or warehoused funds borrowed from commercial banks) to make mortgage loans.

Real estate investment trusts

REITs pool funds from investors to invest in real estate. Special conduit tax treatment allows earnings to "pass through" to shareholders without tax to the trust. Individual REIT investment portfolios may include one investment or any combination of the full spectrum of real estate investments, including long-term mortgages, short-term construction and development loans and equity investments in one or more types of real estate (shopping centers, apartment buildings, office buildings).[1]

Analyzing the impact of debt financing

The typical informed purchaser (user and/or investor) of income-producing property uses mortgage financing primarily so he can take advantage of leverage. In addition, the purchaser may also borrow to supplement equity capital to meet the relatively large initial investment amount usually required in the real estate market. The knowledgeable investor with the necessary funds to buy a real estate investment on a "free and clear" basis generally would *not* do so, even in the face of the apparently high interest rate charges of the 1980s.

Small investors, both individuals and syndicated groups formed to buy real estate investments, may require mortgage financing because they lack the necessary cash to buy on a completely equity basis. Businesses that acquire income properties for their own use frequently can pay for the properties from cash available within the firm. They usually elect not to do so, however, because of their need for working capital for the business and because they feel that their funds are more profitable when used in the business. Investors, whether users of the property or not, recognize that the *interest rates* on mortgages are usually lower than the overall rate of return (sometimes called the capitalization rate) on the property (the "cap" rate is the NOI divided by the selling price). Maximum borrowing can accomplish two objectives: (1) enhance equity yield (the annual rate of return on each dollar of equity funds invested) over what it would be without the use of borrowed funds and (2) extend available funds into other leveraged investments which can produce higher yields on those funds.

Nature of leverage

The term "leverage" refers to the use of borrowed funds which have a fixed cost to the borrower (or at least which have a portion of the borrowing cost fixed, as in equity participations) to complete the purchase of an investment property. Generally, the larger the percentage or ratio of borrowed funds to total value (or purchase price), the greater the amount of leverage.

Leverage may be represented visually by a diagram of a lever. The length of the lever is 100 percent of the cost of the investment. The portion financed with mortgage proceeds (m) plus the percentage equity investment (e) is equal to the total cost. To continue the analogy, the interest rate on borrowed funds (i) is the force applied to the end of the debt side of the lever and the yield to equity (y) is applied to the equity side. The force of the fulcrum is equal to the overall rate of return (R). The balanced lever would look like Figure 3.

Figure 3　Leverage

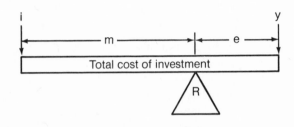

The following mathematical statement is true of the lever:

$$R = (m \times i) + (e \times y)$$

Example

To illustrate, a property that costs $100,000 with an NOI of $12,000 will be used throughout this chapter. Assume that the overall rate of return (R) is 12 percent ($12,000 ÷ $100,000). Assume that income and value will remain constant indefinitely. In this first instance, a buyer finances 75 percent of the purchase price with a 10-percent interest-only loan. Therefore, the equity investment is 25 percent of the price, or $25,000. Each year the equity investor will receive the NOI of $12,000 less the interest on the loan of $7,500 (10 percent of $75,000), or $4,500. The equity yield is:

$$\frac{\text{Cash flow to equity}}{\text{Equity investment}} \qquad \frac{\$4,500}{\$25,000} = 18\%$$

Notice that the equity yield exceeds the overall rate.
The leverage formula is valid:

$$12\% = (.75 \times 10\%) + (.25 \times 18\%)$$
$$12\% = 7.5\% + 4.5\%$$

This formula may be formatted as:

$$
\begin{array}{rl}
.75 \times 10\% = & 7.5\% \\
.25 \times 18\% = & \underline{4.5} \\
\overline{1.00} & 12.0\%
\end{array}
$$

This format, common in real estate, is called the *band of investment*. It is a useful guide to determining the impact of changes in the financing structure of an investment. Notice that all of the rates in the preceding example represent the return *on* capital since the property value is constant and the loan is not amortized. The return *of* all capital will occur upon disposition of the property. The equity yield will be affected by either a change in value or a change in NOI.

The leverage diagram and the band of investment formula identify several factors that affect the benefit of leverage. The overall rate is the maximum rate on debt financing available from property income. Net cash flow to the equity investor is a function of the interest rate on borrowed funds and the amount borrowed. The amount of equity funds required to buy a property decreases as the portion of borrowed funds increases. Band of investment analysis will indicate the impact on investment performance from a change in any of the previous factors.

Recall, from the lever analogy, that the force, or weight, on the ends of the lever are the rate on borrowed funds (i) and the equity yield (y), respectively. The diagrams in Figure 4 (p. 100) show a variety of combinations of loan amounts and resulting equity yields. The band of investment formuli are also shown. The interest rate is 10 percent in each case.

As with a real lever, the same force—interest rate—on one side of the fulcrum will be balanced with more force—equity yield—as leverage is increased. These numerical relationships are true only for this special case where income and value are assumed to remain constant.

Forms of leverage

Leverage may affect the equity yield in one of three ways. Financing may increase, decrease or have no effect on the investor's return. The equity yield was increased in each of the examples above. However, some interest rate and repayment terms may not benefit the investor financially.

Positive leverage is the term associated with financing that increases the equity yield. It will occur when the cost of debt financing—interest rate on borrowed funds—is *less* than the yield on the property without debt financing.

Example

In the example on page 98, the yield on the property without financing is 12 percent. The cash flow is like an interest-only loan where the investor pays $100,000 for the property to receive $12,000 at the end of each year

Figure 4 Loan Amounts and Equity Yields

Examples

1.

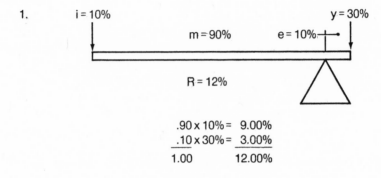

$$
\begin{array}{ll}
.90 \times 10\% = & 9.00\% \\
.10 \times 30\% = & 3.00\% \\
\hline
1.00 & 12.00\%
\end{array}
$$

2.

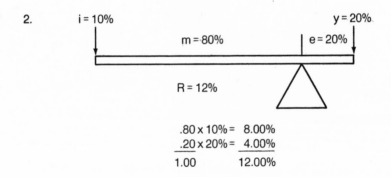

$$
\begin{array}{ll}
.80 \times 10\% = & 8.00\% \\
.20 \times 20\% = & 4.00\% \\
\hline
1.00 & 12.00\%
\end{array}
$$

3.

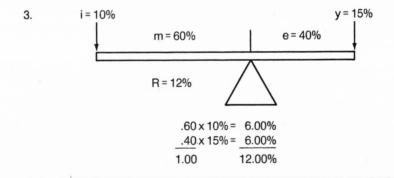

$$
\begin{array}{ll}
.60 \times 10\% = & 6.00\% \\
.40 \times 15\% = & 6.00\% \\
\hline
1.00 & 12.00\%
\end{array}
$$

until all capital is returned when the property is sold. The cash flow for a five-year holding period would be:

EOY	$
0	($100,000)
1	12,000
2	12,000
3	12,000
4	12,000
5	12,000 + $100,000

It was demonstrated on page 98 that the investor's yield was increased to 18 percent when a 75-percent interest-only loan at 10-percent interest was taken to purchase the investment. After financing, the equity investment to the investor is:

Total purchase price	$100,000
Less: loan proceeds	− 75,000
Equity investment	$25,000

Annual cash flows are:

NOI	$12,000	
Less: interest on loan*	7,500	(10% of $75,000)
Cash flows to equity	$4,500	

*Interest-only loan, no principal reduction

The investor's equity reversion is:

Sale price EOY 5	$100,000
Less: loan balance	− 75,000
Equity reversion	$25,000

Thus, the equity cash flows are:

EOY	$
0	($25,000)
1	4,500
2	4,500
3	4,500
4	4,500
5	4,500 + 25,000

The equity yield is 18 percent (IRR of the cash flows to equity) which is greater than the 12-percent return on the whole investment in the property. Therefore, this financing produces positive leverage.

Neutral leverage occurs when there is no change in equity yield as a result of using debt financing. It is the result of financing a property at the interest rate equal to the yield on the property had it not been financed.

Example

Using the same example as above, with an interest rate of 12 percent, the equity investment and reversion are the same, but the annual cash flows are:

NOI	$12,000	
Less: interest on loan	− 9,000	(12% of $75,000)
Cash flows to equity	$3,000	

The equity cash flows are:

EOY	$
0	($25,000)
1	3,000
2	3,000
3	3,000
4	3,000
5	3,000 + 25,000

The equity yield is 12 percent, equal to the return on the property without financing.

Negative leverage occurs when the equity yield is decreased as a result of debt financing at a cost *greater* than the yield to the property. When debt financing causes negative leverage, the equity yield will be maximized by minimizing the amount borrowed.

Example

Consider the same example with a loan at 14 percent. The annual equity cash flows are:

NOI	$12,000
Less: interest on loan	−10,500
Equity cash flows	$1,500

The equity cash flows are:

EOY	$
0	($25,000)
1	1,500
2	1,500
3	1,500
4	1,500
5	1,500 + 25,000

The equity yield is 6 percent which is less than the 12-percent yield on the property without financing.

Sources of financial benefit from leverage

Equity yield is influenced by either periodic cash flows or a lump sum received in the future, or a combination of both. The examples so far have illustrated the impact of periodic cash flows and financing on equity yield. The return *on* equity was produced solely by the annual cash flows to equity. All of the equity investment was returned upon disposition. But consider an investment that appreciates in value but has no periodic cash flows.

Example

A vacant site is acquired for $125,000. Two years later it is sold for $156,800. Assume all holding costs are equal to the rental income for a billboard on the property—therefore, NOI is 0. The overall rate of return is also 0. The net cash flows without financing are:

EOY	$
0	($125,000)
1	–0–
2	156,800

The yield (IRR) on this investment is 12 percent. Consider the same site financed with three alternative loans of $100,000. Interest is compounded annually and payable upon disposition for each loan. The interest rates are 10 percent for Loan A, 12 percent for Loan B and 14 percent for Loan C. The equity investment in each case is $25,000 ($125,000 less $100,000 loan). The equity reversions for each financing alternative are summarized below.

	Loan A	Loan B	Loan C
Interest Rate	10%	12%	14%
Sale Price of Land EOY 2	$156,800	$156,800	$156,800
Less: loan balance (principal + accrued interest)	121,000	125,440	129,960
Equity Reversion	$35,800	$31,360	$26,840

The cash flows to equity for each financing alternative are:

EOY	Loan A	Loan B	Loan C
0	($25,000)	($25,000)	($25,000)
1	–0–	–0–	–0–
2	35,800	31,360	26,840
IRR	19.7%	12.0%	3.6%
Leverage	Positive	Neutral	Negative

Loan A would produce the greatest return to equity. Note that band of investment analysis would not have been appropriate here since the overall rate is zero. The benefit of leverage is consistent with the comparisons of interest rates on the loans and the return from the property without financing, 12 percent. The interest rate below 12 percent produced positive leverage, the 12-percent loan produced neutral leverage and the 14-percent loan resulted in negative leverage.

Major financing variables

When borrowing is undertaken to finance the purchase of a real estate investment, several variable items are crucial:

1. Effective rate of interest on debt financing
2. Ratio of loan to value
3. Term of the loan (period over which the loan is made) and method of amortization
4. Ratio of annual debt service to net operating income (see section on Determination of Maximum Loan Amount, page 122)

Each of the variables listed above is included in every financing alternative for income-producing properties. In the following sections, we will isolate each to illustrate the impact on equity yield. In each example, property value and income are constant in order to isolate the impact of financing on equity yield.

Effective rate of interest

The interest rate paid for the use of money is one of the key variables in analyzing financing alternatives. The idea of increasing equity yield through borrowing is based upon the expectation that money can be borrowed at a rate of interest lower than the overall rate of return produced by the property. If this expectation is realized, that proportion of the total investment financed by the mortgage produces an additional amount that is available to the equity investor. This was demonstrated in the preceding discussion on positive, neutral and negative leverage.

Loan-to-value ratio (leverage factor)

The percentage that the loan represents of the property value or purchase price can also influence equity yield. The higher the proportion of total investment represented by borrowed funds, the *greater* the leverage. The leverage factor (L) is another means of expressing this and is simply the reciprocal of 1 minus the loan-to-value percentage.

Example

In the examples for positive, negative and neutral leverage, all loans were 75 percent of value; therefore, they each have the following leverage factor:

$$\frac{1}{1 - .75} = 4$$

In other words, the equity investment goes into the total investment four times. If an equity investor had $10,000 to invest and could borrow 75 percent of value, the leverage factor times equity available for investment determines the size of total investments:

$$4 \times \$10,000 = \$40,000$$

Viewed another way, if the investor can borrow 75 percent of the property value, the equity portion must be 25 percent (or, $1 - .75$). Thus, the leverage factor is simply the number of times the *equity* investment goes into the *total* investment.

The following table shows loan-to-value ratios and the corresponding leverage factors.

Loan-to-Value	Leverage Factor (L)
95%	20
90	10
85	6.7
80	5
75	4
70	3.3
65	2.9
60	2.5
55	2.2
50	2

Figure 5   Loan-to-Value Ratio and Leverage Factor

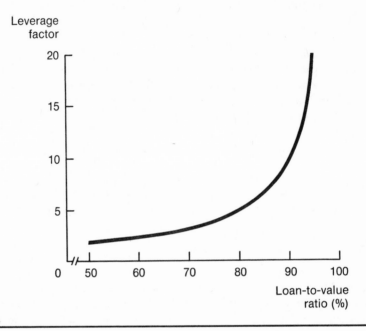

Note that the leverage factor changes in geometric terms as the loan-to-value changes by increments of five percentage points (see Figure 5). This demonstrates the power of leverage and also provides an alternative means of measuring the impact of leverage on equity yield.

Rather than the form:

$$R = (m \times i) + (e \times y)$$

we could define e as "$1 - m$" since $m + e = 1$. Alternatively:

$$R = (m \times i) + [(1 - m)y]$$

$$R - (m \times i) = (1 - m)\, y$$

$$y = \frac{R - (m \times i)}{1 - m}$$

Add and subtract i in the numerator:

$$y = \frac{R - (m \times i) + i - i}{1 - m} \text{ or } \frac{R - i + i - (m \times i)}{1 - m}$$

Factor the numerator:

$$y = \frac{(R - i) + i (1 - m)}{1 - m} = \left[\frac{R - i}{1 - m}\right] + i$$

Thus, an alternative means of solving for y is:

$$y = i + \left[\left(\frac{1}{1 - m}\right)\left(R - i\right)\right]$$

Note that:

$$\text{Leverage factor } (L) = \frac{1}{1 - m}$$

$$\text{Borrowing differential } (D) = R - i$$

Therefore:

$$y = i + (L \times D)$$

Thus, the equity impact of borrowing can be thought of as the product of two variables—the leverage factor (L) and the borrowing differential (D). Equity yield is determined by adding the cost of borrowing (i) to the equity impact.

Example

A property that sells for $80,000 has an NOI of $10,400, with a 90-percent loan at 11.5-percent interest. The impact of financing in this instance may be seen as:

$R = 13\%$ [$10,400 ÷ $80,000 = 13\%$]
$D = 1.5\%$ [$13\% - 11.5\% = 1.5\%$]
$L = 10$ [$1 ÷ (1 - .9) = 10$]

Where:

$$y = 11.5 + (10 \times 1.5) = 26.5\%$$

If the loan were only 80 percent, then:

$$y = 11.5 + (5 \times 1.5) = 19\%$$

The concepts of positive, neutral and negative leverage also may be demonstrated:

1. Positive leverage $i + (L \times D) = y$

     $.8 \times .11 = .088$
     $.2 \times .16$ $\underline{.032}$ or $11 + (5 \times 1) = 16\%$
                 $.120$

2. Neutral leverage

$$
\begin{array}{l}
.8 \times .12 = .096 \\
.2 \times .12 \quad \underline{.024} \\
 .120
\end{array}
\qquad \text{or} \quad 12 + (5 \times 0) = 12\%
$$

3. Negative leverage (positive return)

$$
\begin{array}{l}
.8 \times .13 = .104 \\
.2 \times .08 \quad \underline{.016} \\
 .120
\end{array}
\qquad \text{or} \quad 13 + [5(-1)] = 8\%
$$

4. Negative leverage (zero return)

$$
\begin{array}{l}
.8 \times .15 = .12 \\
.2 \times .0 \quad \underline{0} \\
 .12
\end{array}
\qquad \text{or} \quad 15 + [5(-3)] = 0
$$

5. Negative leverage (negative return)

$$
\begin{array}{l}
.8 \times .16 = .128 \\
.2 \times -.04 \quad \underline{-.008} \\
 .120
\end{array}
\qquad \text{or } 16 + [5(-4)] = -4
$$

Based upon the foregoing, certain generalizations can be made.

1. Under conditions of positive leverage ($D > 0$), the larger the leverage factor, the higher the equity yield.

2. Under conditions of neutral leverage ($D = 0$), the leverage factor has no impact on the equity yield, and the equity yield equals the overall rate ($y = R$).

3. Under conditions of negative leverage ($D < 0$), the larger the leverage factor, the lower the equity yield.

These equity yield generalizations are only valid with the assumptions that NOI and property value are constant and the loans are not amortized. However, this is an excellent preliminary step to a detailed analysis.

It should be obvious at this point that there is an infinite variety of interest rate/loan-to-value combinations that could be produced at any given equity yield.

Example

As in the case of an interest-only loan and a constant 20-percent equity yield, there are *many* other combinations that can produce the same equity yield.

$$90\% \times .1111 = 10.00\%$$
$$10\% \times .20 \quad = \quad \underline{2.00}$$
$$12.00\%$$

$$85\% \times .1059 = 9.00\%$$
$$15\% \times .20 \quad = \quad \underline{3.00}$$
$$12.00\%$$

$$80\% \times .1000 = 8.00\%$$
$$20\% \times .20 \quad = \quad \underline{4.00}$$
$$12.00\%$$

$$75\% \times .0933 = 7.00\%$$
$$25\% \times .20 \quad = \quad \underline{5.00}$$
$$12.00\%$$

$$70\% \times .0857 = 6.00\%$$
$$30\% \times .20 \quad = \quad \underline{6.00}$$
$$12.00\%$$

Property value and income are constant, as above, for these relationships. Notice that the interest rate declines as the loan-to-value ratio declines with the constant equity yield.

Amortization method and term

The "term" of the loan is the length of time over which there will remain some outstanding balance. The amortization of the loan is the periodic repayment of the principal plus interest. Three general types of amortization are common in the market.

1. *Straight mortgage loan* Only interest is paid during the term, and the entire amount of the original mortgage amount is paid at maturity.

2. *Fully amortized mortgage loan* This is the typical loan payment method whereby periodic (most often monthly) equal payments are made so that the loan is completely paid back at maturity.

3. *Partially amortized mortgage loan* The periodic payments of debt service are not sufficient to amortize the loan completely by its maturity; a lump sum payment, generally called a balloon payment, must be made to complete the return of all principal. This is often done by establishing the maturity of the loan for one period and setting the debt service payments for a longer period.

The impact of loan-to-value ratio and interest rate on equity yield have been demonstrated with interest-only loans. Amortization is the lender's return *of* capital. It can be imputed into the band of investment formula by replacing the interest rate (return *on* lender's capital) with the *loan constant* which is the return *of* plus the return *on* the lender's capital.

Calculation of the loan constant
The loan constant is defined as the ratio of annual debt service to loan proceeds.

109

Example

The loan constant for a $100,000 loan, at 10-percent interest with monthly payments of $877.57 for 30 years, is calculated as follows:

Annual debt service is:

Monthly payment	$877.57
Annual debt service	× 12
	$10,530.84

The loan constant is:

$$\frac{\text{Annual debt service}}{\text{Loan proceeds}} = \frac{\$10,530.84}{\$100,000.00} = .1053$$

Since the loan constant is a ratio, the Ellwood table Column 6 compound interest table factor (installment to amortize 1; see Appendix A) could be used. The factor for a 30-year loan at 10-percent interest with monthly payments is .008775. The loan constant would be:

Monthly payment for $1	.008775
	× 12
Annual loan constant	.1053

Given a loan constant and annual debt service, the loan proceeds can be calculated. Using the .1053 loan constant and annual debt service of $10,530.84, the loan proceeds are:

$$\frac{\$10,530.84}{.1053} = \$100,000 \text{ (rounded)}$$

Likewise, given the loan constant and loan proceeds, annual debt service may be calculated. The $100,000 loan with a loan constant of .1053 would have annual debt service of:

$$\$100,000 \times .1053 = \$10,530$$

The loan constant depends on both the term and interest rate of a loan. Thus, a particular constant has an infinite variety of interest rate-term combinations. The following table is a summary of such combinations for an $80,000 loan with annual payments of $8,800 and the balance EOY 10. The loan constant is .1100 ($8,800 ÷ $80,000) in each case.

Interest Rate	Term in Years*	Mortgage Balance EOY 10
5%	12.4	$19,626
6	13.5	27,277
7	14.9	35,787
8	16.9	45,232
9	19.8	55,691
10	25.2	67,250
11	∞	80,000

*The term (n) is calculated with the known values of interest rate (i), loan amount ($\boxed{PV}$ = 1) and the loan payment ($\boxed{PMT}$ = .1100).

The term increases as the interest rate increases because more of the **$8,800** payment is allocated to interest. At 11-percent interest, all of the **payment** is required for interest ($80,000 × 11% − $8,800). Thus, the constant for an interest-only loan is equal to the interest rate.

Loan constant and band of investment The loan constant is used in the band of investment formula in place of the interest rate for amortizing loans. Thus, the lender's return *of* capital is imputed into the formula. However, band of investment analysis will indicate the exact equity yield only in the special situation where income and property value are constant and the loan is payable interest-only.

Example

In the case of the $100,000 subject property with a constant NOI of $12,000, the indicated equity yield with the $80,000 loan and the .1100 loan constant is:

$$
\begin{array}{lr}
\text{Total investment} & 100\% \times .1200 = 12.00\% \\
\text{Mortgage interest \&} & \\
\quad \text{principal} & \underline{80\% \times .1100 = \ \ \underline{8.80}} \\
& 20\% \qquad\qquad 3.20\%
\end{array}
$$

$$
\text{Equity yield } \frac{3.20\%}{20\%} = 16.00\%
$$

The loan balance EOY 10 decreases as the interest rate decreases. Therefore, the equity reversion EOY 10 will increase as the interest rate decreases. The periodic cash flows will be the same since debt service is the same in each loan. The equity investment is $20,000 ($100,000 − $80,000) for the

111

Figure 6   Alternative Equity Yields with the Same Annual Debt Service and Loan Amount

Property value		Equity yields (IRR)	Loan interest rate	Mortgage balance
$20,000 Equity				
$80,000 Mortgage loan		16.0%	11%	$80,000
		18.6%	10%	$67,250
		20.6%	9%	$55,691
		22.1%	8%	$45,232
		23.3%	7%	$35,787
		24.2%	6%	$27,277
		25.1%	5%	$19,626

BOY 1   Time   EOY 10

subject property and annual cash flows to equity are $3,200. The following table summarizes the equity reversion EOY 10 for each loan shown in Figure 6. The IRR for equity yield is also calculated based on the $20,000 investment that produces $3,200 per year for ten years plus the reversion EOY 10.

Interest Rate	Sale Price EOY 10		Loan Balance EOY 10		Equity Reversion EOY 10	IRR
5%	$100,000	−	$19,626	=	$80,374	25.1%
6	100,000	−	27,277	=	72,723	24.2
7	100,000	−	35,787	=	64,213	23.3
8	100,000	−	45,232	=	54,768	22.1
9	100,000	−	55,691	=	44,309	20.6
10	100,000	−	67,250	=	32,750	18.6
11	100,000	−	80,000	=	20,000	16.0

Given equal loan constants and loan-to-value ratios, the yield to equity increases as the interest rate decreases as shown in Figure 6. The only difference in the cash flows for these financing alternatives is the equity reversion. As the loans are amortized, the equity in the property is increased. The loan balance is amortized faster with a lower interest rate. Therefore, both the equity reversion and equity yield increase as the interest decreases.

The loan constant, however, may not indicate which loan, among alternatives, will produce the greatest equity yield.

Example

For example, an investor may finance the subject property with one of the two alternatives below. Each requires annual payments.

	Loan Amount	Interest Rate	Term	Loan Constant
Loan A	$80,000	11%	17 yrs.	.1325
Loan B	$80,000	12%	35 yrs.	.1223

The equity investment is $20,000 with either loan. The equity cash flows and equity yields for both loans for a ten-year holding period are:

	Loan A	Loan B
Loan amount	$80,000	$80,000
Loan constant	× .1325	× .1223
Annual payment	$10,600	$9,784
NOI	$12,000	$12,000
Less: annual payment	10,600	9,784
Cash flows to equity each year	$1,400	$2,216
Sale price	$100,000	$100,000
Less: loan balance EOY 10	49,900	76,771
Equity reversion	$50,100	$23,229
Equity Yield (IRR) (rounded)	14.6%	12.0%

Loan A produced the higher yield, even though the loan constant was greater than the loan constant for Loan B. Notice the yield of 12 percent with Loan B, resulting from neutral leverage. Band of investment analysis would have indicated just the opposite result:

	Loan A	*Loan B*
Total investment	$100\% \times .12000 = 12.00\%$	$100\% \times .12000 = 12.00\%$
Mortgage interest and principal	$80\% \times .1325 = 10.60\%$	$80\% \times .1223 = 9.78\%$
Equity	20% 1.40%	20% 2.22%
Equity yield indicated by band of investment	$\dfrac{1.40\%}{20\%} = 7.00\%$	$\dfrac{2.22\%}{20\%} = 11.10\%$

The yield is understated because band of investment does not include provision for the increase in the equity resulting from loan amortization. Even though the constant (.1325) is greater than the overall rate (.1200) for Loan A, the equity yield is still greater. The investor benefits from positive leverage because the interest rate is less than the overall rate of the investment.

Holding Period   Two loans of $80,000 at 11-percent interest were used in the foregoing discussion. The 11-percent interest-only loan produced an equity yield of 16 percent in contrast to only 14.6 percent when the same 11-percent loan was amortized in 17 years over a 10-year holding period. The yield to equity is less with the amortizing loan because the equity investment is increased with each loan payment. Recall that IRR is the return on each dollar *invested*. Principal amortization is additional equity investment. Each dollar of principal amortization invested during the holding period is returned *without* any additional return when the property is sold. Therefore, the same cash flows produce a lower return on more dollars invested, compared to an interest-only loan. In short, the benefit of positive leverage (or cost of negative leverage) diminishes as leverage declines from loan amortization.

Since leverage changes with each loan payment of an amortizing loan, equity yield will be different for alternative holding periods. If the interest rate on borrowed funds is constant and financing produces positive leverage, the equity yield will decrease over time for an amortizing loan.

Example

The equity yields for several possible holding periods of the subject property financed with an $80,000 loan at 10-percent interest with annual payments of $9,397 for 20 years are summarized below. The equity investment is $20,000 and the annual cash flows are $2,603 ($12,000 − $9,397).

Holding Period	Sale Price	Loan Balance EOY		Equity Reversion	IRR
5 years	$100,000 −	$71,473	=	$ 28,527	18.9%
10 years	100,000 −	57,739	=	42,261	17.8
15 years	100,000 −	35,621	=	64,379	17.0
20 years	100,000 −	−0−	=	100,000	16.3

Notice that the equity reversion increases as the holding period increases. The equity yield decreases as the holding period increases because the benefit of positive leverage decreases as the loan is amortized. The equity yield is not affected by amortization for an interest-only loan. Since the outstanding loan balance for a loan at the same interest rate but longer amortization term will be greater with a shorter term, the equity yield for any holding period will be greater.

Below are five financing alternatives, each requiring annual payments, for our subject property:

Loan	Loan Amount	Rate	Term
A	$80,000	10%	Interest only
B	80,000	10%	30 Years
C	80,000	10%	20 Years
D	80,000	10.25%	30 Years
E	95,000	10%	20 Years

Recall that NOI and value are constant for the subject property. Therefore, the equity yield is not influenced by appreciation or increased income. Figure 7 (p. 116) plots the equity yields for Loans A, B and C.

Figure 8 (p. 117) shows Loan B compared to a new, higher-interest loan, Loan D, under the same assumptions. In this case, the loan-to-value ratio and amortization term are the same for either alternative. Only the interest rates are different—10 percent for Loan B; 10.25 percent for Loan D. As might be expected, the equity yield of Loan B, with the lower interest rate, is always greater, regardless of holding period.

Loan-to-value ratio will also influence the volitility of equity yield over time. With positive leverage, the equity yield will decline faster over time as the loan-to-value ratio is increased if all else is the same. The converse is true for negative leverage. Figure 9 (p. 119) compares Loan C ($80,000, 10 percent, 20 years) with yet another loan, Loan E, which represents a $95,000 loan at 10 percent fully amortized for 20 years.

Notice in Figure 7 that the equity yield is 20 percent for Loans A, B and C up to the first payment EOY 1. The loan balance and interest due are the same until that time. The yield for Loan A is constant at 20 percent because it is an interest-only loan. After the first year, the equity yield for any holding period will always be greater for the loan with the longer amortization term if all else is equal.

Figure 7   Equity Yield and Holding Period

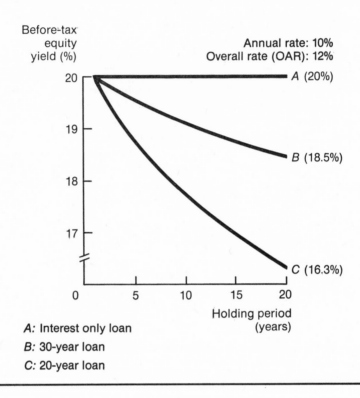

A: Interest only loan
B: 30-year loan
C: 20-year loan

The interest rate will have an effect on the equity as well as the amortization term. Figure 10 (p. 120) compares the equity yield from Loan C ($80,000, 10-percent interest, 20-year term) with that of Loan D, an $80,000 loan at 10.25-percent interest, 30-year term. The loan-to-value ratio is the same. However, Loan D's equity yield exceeds that of Loan C for any holding period over three years, even though the interest rate of Loan D is higher. The reason is apparent from Figure 10. The equity yield curve associated with Loan D does not decline as rapidly over time as it does with Loan C. Therefore, if the investor intends to hold the property more than three years without refinancing, Loan D would produce the higher yield.

Effective equity yield   Thus far in this chapter, the analyses of equity yield over time have assumed annual compounding periods. The equity yields (IRR) have been calculated from annual cash flows. The yield from annualized cash flows may be overstated, however, and may lead to the

Figure 8   Equity Yield and Holding Period

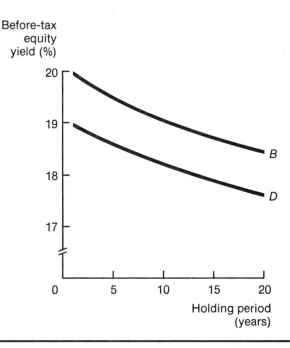

incorrect decision. This distortion is more apparent for short holding periods. The difference declines to a few basis points (a basis point is 1/100 of 1 percent, or 0.01 percent) for extended holding periods.

Example

Consider financing the subject property with either of the following loans. Assume equity investment of $20,000 and monthly NOI of $1,000 for the subject property.

Loan A $80,000 loan at 10-percent interest, with monthly payments of $1,057.21 for 10 years. Balance EOY 1 is $75,092.65.

Loan B $80,000 loan at 10-percent interest, with monthly payments of $702.06 for 30 years. Balance EOY 1 is $79,555.30.

The following table summarizes the *annualized* cash flows to the equity and the IRR for each loan assuming a sale price of $100,000 at EOY 1.

117

EOY	Loan A	Loan B
0 1	($20,000) (686.52) + 24,907.35	($20,000) 3,575.28 + 20,444.70
IRR	21.10%	20.10%

Loan A would seem the appropriate choice from the annualized analysis. The next table is a summary of the *monthly* cash flows and IRR for each loan.

EOM	Loan A		Loan B	
0 1 ↓ 12	($20,000) (57.21) ↓ (57.21) + 24,907.35		($20,000) 293.94 ↓ 293.94 + 20,444.70	
IRR (monthly) IRR (annualized)		1.59% × 12 19.08%		1.64% × 12 19.68%

It is apparent that Loan B would be the better choice, based on IRR. The IRR with Loan A was distorted by more than two percentage points for the one-year holding period. The difference between the equity yields for annualized cash flows and monthly cash flows EOY 30 for Loan B declines to 15 basis points (18.35 percent − 18.20 percent) from 42 basis points EOY 1 (20.10 percent − 19.68 percent). The analyst should be aware of this potential source of error. It should also be noted that the *range* of distortion declines as the term of the loan is extended.

Notice that Loan A produced positive leverage even though monthly cash flows are negative.

Conclusions

Certain observations and generalizations can be made from our analysis of debt financing:

1. "Simple" band-of-investment analysis is only valid for an interest-only loan with an interest rate *equal* to the annual mortgage constant.

2. The equity yield of the investment is greater than the overall rate of the investment if the interest rate on the loan is less than the overall rate.

118 3. As the interest rate on the loan goes down relative to the overall rate, the equity yield rises.

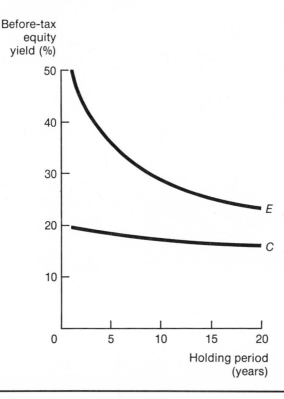

Figure 9   Equity Yield and Holding Period

4. Even though the mortgage constant is greater than the overall rate, there are still loan terms that can result in equity yields which exceed the overall rate of returns on the property.

5. Even lower debt service (mortgage constant) may not result in higher equity yields.

6. The equity yield declines over time for investments financed with loans that are amortized.

7. Loan constants are affected by both the interest rate and the amortization term. If the interest rate is constant, the loan constant decreases as the term increases. If the term is constant, the loan constant increases as the interest rate increases.

8. The benefit of positive leverage (or cost of negative leverage) increases as the loan-to-value ratio increases.

9. The benefit of positive leverage (or cost of negative leverage) increases as the loan term is increased.

119

Figure 10   Equity Yield and Holding Period

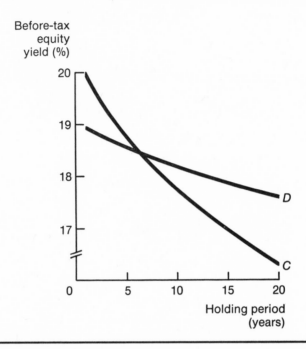

Although some generalization can be made, the specific alternative terms and conditions of the mortgage contract should be compared on the basis of cash flows in order to test for relative yield.

Mortgage underwriting

Fundamental to a discussion of the impact of debt financing on commercial/investment real estate is mortgage underwriting—the analysis and evaluation of a loan from the standpoint of the lender to determine the risk of making the loan using the real estate as collateral. Although this text will make no attempt at comprehensive coverage of this topic, certain key elements are critical to the broker/analyst who is involved in the process of acquiring funds to finance investment real estate.[2]

Risk aversion

Although the real estate serves as collateral for the mortgage loan, it is not the primary defense against loss to the lender. The typical lender does not want to obtain ownership of the property through foreclosure because of

default. This is really an extreme line of defense against loss of his investment position, one which can be very costly and time consuming and detrimental to good public relations. Basically, such lenders are not in the business of operating and/or selling commercial/investment real estate and usually like to avoid the necessity of doing so through the vehicle of foreclosure. This then points to the first line of defense—reducing the probability of default in payment of loan obligations in the first place.

The most direct means of ensuring prompt and continuous payment of a mortgage loan on an income-producing property is to forecast accurately the income flow from which the annual debt service will be paid. This is a principle applied widely in bond securities repayment as well as being a fundamental underwriting tenet.

Debt coverage ratio

Most lenders who finance investment real estate projects are concerned more with the relationship between Net Operating Income (NOI) and Annual Debt Service (ADS) than they are with the loan-to-value ratio. The reason for this is the general lack of agreement concerning the value of the property and/or the overall rate used to capitalize NOI.

The foundation of the market value or investment value of income-producing real estate is the future stream of income. The key to estimating the present value of this future income rests in estimates of the *size, timing, duration* and *stability* of future income flows. The process of converting these future income flows to a present value is a simple matter of capitalization at the appropriate rate. In the area of mortgage lending, the appropriate rate can sometimes present quite a problem, particularly when the overall rate on the property combines such factors as the tax situation of the typical investor, typical financing terms, appreciation and holding period. As indicated above, the lender is not interested in acquiring the property by default. That, in essence, is the *final* step in protecting loan capital. The first line of protection for the loan is the *income stream*, for it is from the income stream that the lender will be repaid. Loan payments include both interest on the loan and periodic principal payments. Thus, the lender is much more concerned with a careful examination and analysis of the validity of estimates of NOI than he is with estimates of the present market value of the property.

Lenders use a *debt coverage ratio* to compare ADS to NOI. The debt coverage ratio is the NOI divided by ADS:

$$\text{debt coverage ratio} = \frac{\text{NOI}}{\text{ADS}}$$

The lender's margin of safety—that debt payments can be met by property income—increases as the coverage ratio increases.

Example

A loan which requires ADS of $9,600, with an NOI of $12,000, would have a coverage ratio of:

$$\frac{\$12,000}{\$9,600} = 1.25$$

In this case NOI could decline 20 percent (from $12,000 to $9,600) before the lender would have to rely on the investor to contribute to debt service from other sources of funds.

Based upon experience, lenders may specify a maximum debt coverage ratio for particular types of property. In the case of an NOI that can be forecast with a high degree of accuracy with respect to size, timing and duration (such as a long-term completely net lease with a AAA tenant), the lender should require relatively less margin between NOI and ADS— a lower debt coverage ratio. Accordingly the debt coverage ratio should increase with the risk (uncertainty) associated with the NOI.

Determination of maximum loan amount

The analyst (lender, broker or investor) can determine the maximum loan available on an income property when the NOI, debt coverage ratio, loan term and interest rate are known. The loan amount will be the present value of the debt service discounted at the interest rate of the loan.

Example

A lender will make a 10-percent loan with monthly payments for 30 years. The required debt coverage ratio for the subject property by that lender is 1.25. NOI is $12,000. First determine the monthly payment:

$$\frac{NOI}{debt\ coverage\ ratio} = ADS$$

$$\frac{\$12,000}{1.25} = \$9,600$$

Monthly debt service (loan payments) are:

$$\frac{ADS}{12} = \frac{\$9,600}{12} = \$800\ per\ month$$

The maximum loan on the subject property is the present value of an annuity (the loan payments) at 10 percent per year with monthly compounding for 30 years. The known values are:

$$\boxed{\text{PMT}} = \$800 \text{ per period}$$
$$\boxed{\text{n}} = 30 \text{ years} \times 12 = 360 \text{ periods}$$
$$\boxed{\text{i}} = 10\% \div 12 = 0.83\% \text{ per period}$$
$$\boxed{\text{PV}} = ?$$

The maximum loan is calculated to be $91,160.66, rounded to $91,000.

Alternately, the loan amount could be calculated by dividing ADS by the loan constant. This procedure is demonstrated in the following section.

Additional underwriting considerations

In a broader context, the loan underwriting process includes (1) an estimate of the property value; (2) an evaluation of the risk associated with the income stream; (3) an assessment of the credit-worthiness of the borrower; (4) an appraisal of real estate and financial market conditions; and (5) determination of the interest rate, duration and size of the loan. The latter is the topic of this discussion.

A typical mortgage loan analysis might proceed in the following manner.

1. Analysis of NOI forecasts The lender examines the estimates of NOI in terms of size, timing, duration and stability. Based upon experience and knowledge of the market in which the property is (or is to be) located, forecasts of the future for the location and type of property and past experience in lending on this type of property in the same or similar locations, the lender will establish the required *safety margin* for the loan.

2. Determination of mortgage constant The previous analysis established the *duration* of the income stream of at least a range of years, perhaps between 30 and 35. The lender has also established, again within a range, the interest rate required on a current basis for long-term loans. Based upon this combination of term and interest rate an annual mortgage constant is estimated.

3. Mortgage loan amount The first approximation of the loan amount can be calculated by dividing the ADS by the mortgage constant.

Example

A numerical example of this process would be as follows:

$$\text{NOI} = \$12,000$$

Lender requires 20-percent margin (ADS must be at least 80 percent of NOI). Therefore the debt coverage ratio is 1.25 (1 ÷ .80)
Interest rate must be at least 10 percent
Term cannot exceed 25 to 30 years (monthly payments)
ADS = \$9,600 (80% × \$12,000)
Mortgage constant = .109044 to .105309

Loan amount: $\dfrac{\$9,600}{.109044} = \$88,038$ or \$88,000

to $\qquad \dfrac{\$9,600}{.105309} = \$91,160$ or \$91,000

Thus, the preliminary loan amount indicates an approximate range between \$88,000 and \$91,000. The most likely area of negotiation would be with the *term* of the loan.

4. Relationship between loan-to-value and ADS-to-NOI   It is immediately apparent that there is a direct relationship between the ratio of loan-to-value and the ratio of ADS to NOI. The direct link between these two is the overall rate of capitalization. When the mortgage constant and the overall rate are *equal,* the ratios of loan-to-value and ADS-to-NOI are exactly equal.

Example

$$\text{Loan} \qquad 80\% \times .12 = .096\%$$

$$\text{Equity} \quad 20\% \times .12 = \dfrac{.024}{.120\%}$$

$$\dfrac{\text{Loan}}{\text{Value}} = \dfrac{\$80,000}{\$100,000} = \dfrac{9,600}{12,000} = \dfrac{\text{ADS}}{\text{NOI}}$$

Other financing considerations

Balloon payment mortgages (partially amortized mortgages)

Generally speaking, mortgage payments include both interest and principal payments such that the original mortgage amount is completely repaid over the full term of the loan. Sometimes, however, the amortization schedule agreed upon by the borrower and lender provides for only partial reduction of the principal amount, with a "balloon" payment of the remaining principal at the end of the term.

124   Calculating periodic payment   A popular and easy way of calculating the periodic payment under such a mortgage contract is to agree upon a

rate and term but to calculate the mortgage payment based upon a somewhat longer term.

Example

Assume a 9-percent interest rate, a 15-year term, but monthly payments based on a 20-year amortization schedule. The annual mortgage
constant would be as follows.

The monthly constant for a 9-percent loan, for 20 years is .008997.

The annual constant is:

$$.008997 \times 12 = .107964$$

This is somewhat less than the constant of .121716 for the same loan
with a 15-year amortization schedule. The balloon payment due EOY 15
is equal to the present value $\boxed{PV}$ of payments for five years (20-year
amortization term less 15-year loan term) discounted at the interest rate
of 9 percent. For example, if $100,000 is loaned at the terms described
above, the payment is calculated from the following known values:

$$\boxed{PV} = \$100,000$$
$$\boxed{n} = 20 \times 12 = 240 \text{ periods (amortization term)}$$
$$\boxed{i} = 9\% \div 12 = 0.75\% \text{ per period}$$

The monthly payment is $899.73. The balloon payment due EOY 15
is the $\boxed{PV}$ calculated from the following known values:

$$\boxed{PMT} = \$899.73$$
$$\boxed{n} = 5 \times 12 = 60 \text{ periods (remaining amortization term)}$$
$$\boxed{i} = 9\% \div 12 = 0.75\% \text{ per period}$$

The balloon payment is $43,343.03.

Calculating the balloon payment Often during loan negotiations
for a balloon payment mortgage an amount that can be paid from NOI is
specified by the borrower rather than utilizing a specific amortization
schedule.

Example

Suppose that an $80,000 loan is desired by the mortgagor who in-
dicates that he can pay a maximum of $650 per month. The mortgagee is
willing to lend at 9 percent for 15 years with monthly payments. If the loan
were fully amortized over 15 years, the monthly payment would be $811.41.

Thus it will be necessary to create a balloon payment loan if the mortgage is to be made. The size of the balloon payment at the end of 15 years can be calculated from the following data:

$$\boxed{\text{PMT}} = \$650$$
$$\boxed{\text{n}} = 15 \times 12 = 180 \text{ periods (the term of the loan)}$$
$$\boxed{\text{i}} = 9\% \div 12 = 0.75\% \text{ per period}$$

The $\boxed{\text{PV}}$ is \$64,085.72, the amount amortized by the monthly payments over 15 years. The difference of \$15,914.28 (\$80,000.00 − \$64,085.72) will be compounded at the interest rate. The balloon payment is the future value $\boxed{\text{FV}}$ calculated from the following known values:

$$\boxed{\text{PV}} = \$15,914.28$$
$$\boxed{\text{n}} = 15 \times 12 = 180 \text{ periods}$$
$$\boxed{\text{i}} = 9\% \div 12 = 0.75\% \text{ per period}$$

The balloon payment is \$61,079.70.

Another way of viewing the process of partial amortization is to consider the total loan as two loans, an amortizing loan and an interest-only loan. In the case of the loan above, the payment would be calculated as follows:

Monthly payment to amortize \$40,000 at 9% in 15 years	\$405.71
Plus: Monthly interest only on remaining \$40,000 at 9%	+ 300.00
Total monthly payment	\$705.71

Mortgage participation financing

In 1967, and subsequently in 1980, a "lender's market" for mortgage funds was created by tight money market conditions which were part of a national effort to halt inflation.[3] Since lenders held the clear upper hand in their loan negotiations during these periods, they sought new ways to guard against inflation not only by increasing their yield through high fixed interest rates on the loans but also by participating in a part of the anticipated gain or profit which had heretofore been reserved for the equity investor. One of the more interesting aspects of this lending innovation was the uniqueness of each contract, with over 40 "standard" formulas in use by lending institutions.

Forms of lender participation Although there is a wide variety of contracts which provide the mortgage lender with some form or combination of forms of variable participation in the future benefits of the property, such interests can be classified in six basic forms, divided into two categories.

1. Income participations This type of participation grants the lender the right to share in some part of the cash flow to the property for a specified period of time, generally the term of the loan. It takes on three major forms:

- Percentage of gross rental income provides the lender with a fixed percentage for a specified period.

- Percentage of net income provides for a fixed percentage of the net income of the property.

- Percentage of cash flow provides for a share of either before- or after-tax cash flow (NOI less ADS).

2. Equity participation This type of participation grants rights to the lender that may endure beyond the term of the loan and may represent a true equity share of the property. The equity participation may or may not involve any direct investment by the lender beyond the amount of the loan.

- Percentage of equity reversion is the right to share in some future reversionary value such as that derived from refinancing or sale.

- Percentage of equity interest is a means by which the right to share in all of the equity benefits is transferred to the lender.

- Percentage of tax shelter is a means by which the lender acquires a right to use all or a part of the tax shelter associated with the mortgaged property.

Example

Assume a lending situation which involves a gross income participation where property has the following characteristics.[4]

Purchase price:	$1,100,000
Gross income:	$200,000
NOI:	$112,000
Mortgage loan:	Amount, $840,000
	Interest rate, 9%
	Term, 25 years with annual payments
	Annual debt service, $85,520
Forecast reversion:	EOY 10, $1,250,000
Lender participation:	4% of gross income for 25 years
	Desired return on participation income, 10%
Equity investor:	Desired yield, 12% to 15%
	Holding period of property, 10 years

In order to analyze the impact of the 4-percent gross income participation, find the respective yield for each of the interests in the property, in this case the mortgagee and the mortgagor.

Mortgagee's (Lender's) Interest

Initial mortgage loan (lender's investment)	$840,000
Lender's annual cash flows:	
Annual debt service	85,520
Participation income (4% × $200,000)	8,000
Total annual cash flows to lender	$93,520
Lender's reversion EOY 10	
Loan balance EOY 10	$689,350
PV of $8,000 per year participation for	
remaining 15 years (25-10) discounted	
at 10%	60,849
Total due lender EOY 10	$750,199

The lender's cash flows are summarized as:

EOY	$
0	($840,000)
1	93,520
2	93,520
3	93,520
4	93,520
5	93,520
6	93,520
7	93,520
8	93,520
9	93,520
10	93,520 + 750,199

The lender's yield, before tax, on these cash flows is 10.48 percent.

Mortgagor's (Equity) Interest

Equity investment	
Purchase price	$1,100,000
Less: mortgage proceeds	840,000
Equity investment	$260,000
Annual cash flows to equity	
NOI	$112,000
Less: total annual cash flows to lender	93,520
Annual cash flows to equity	$18,480
Equity reversion	
Sale price EOY 10	$1,250,000
Less: total due lender EOY 10	750,199
Equity reversion EOY 10	$499,801

The cash flows to equity are summarized as:

EOY	$
0	($260,000)
1	18,480
2	18,480
3	18,480
4	18,480
5	18,480
6	18,480
7	18,480
8	18,480
9	18,480
10	18,480 + 499,801

The yield to equity, before tax, is 12.29 percent, at a purchase price of $1,100,000.

The investment value of this property is equal to the sum of the present value $\boxed{PV}$ of cash flows to each interest discounted at the appropriate rate. In this case, the $\boxed{PV}$ of the lender's position is $840,000, the amount of the loan. If the equity investor requires a 15-percent before-tax yield, rather than 12 percent, the investment value of this property is:

$\boxed{PV}$ of lender's position	$840,000
$\boxed{PV}$ of equity cash flows discounted at 15%	216,290
Investment value of the property	$1,056,290

If this property were acquired for $1,056,290 under the assumptions listed above, the lender would earn 10.48 percent (IRR on lender's cash flows). The equity yield before tax would be 15 percent.

Wraparound mortgages

Calculation of yield   The wraparound mortgage is simply a refinancing device in which one lender uses the relatively low interest rate on an existing mortgage balance of another lender to advantage by creating a new mortgage instrument which incorporates the original loan. The wraparound lender advances the difference of the total wraparound loan less the balance on the existing loan. The borrower makes one payment on the total loan to the wraparound lender. The "wrap" lender assumes the existing, or underlying, loan and therefore makes the remaining payments. Often, the term of the wraparound loan will be less than or equal to the remaining term of the underlying loan. The "wrap" lender utilizes financial leverage to increase the yield over the nominal rate of the new loan.

This form of loan also can be seen in the situation of a land contract in which the owner/seller retains title until all (or a specified number) payments on the property have been made by the purchaser. In this situation, the seller may have or may acquire a mortgage loan on the property that is below the rate being paid by the purchaser.

Example

A lender is approached by a potential borrower who has a property with an existing mortgage loan. The original loan, now five years old, was for $150,000 with a 7.5-percent interest rate and monthly payments of $1,108.49 for 25 years. The borrower wishes to refinance; the new lender agrees to "wrap" the existing loan and advance a new wraparound loan for $160,000 at 8.5 percent with monthly payments of $1,288.36 for 25 years. What is the rate of return to the "wrap" lender if the loan is paid in full in ten years?

The first step is to identify the cash flows to the "wrap" lender.
The wraparound lender's investment is:

New loan amount	$160,000.00
Less: balance of underlying loan	
(after 5 years)	137,598.82
"Wrap" lender's investment	$ 22,401.18

The *monthly* cash flows to the "wrap" lender are:

Payment on $160,000, 25-year amortization at 8.5%	$1,288.36
Less: Payment on underlying loan	1,108.49
Net monthly cash flow to "wrap" lender	$179.87

The "wrap" lender's cash flow from the loan repayment is:

Balance of wraparound loan EOY 10	$130,832.90
Less: balance of underlying loan EOY 10	
(15 years after the loan was made)	93,384.18
Net balance due "wrap" lender	$ 37,448.72

The cash flows to each of the parties to this loan and the before-tax yields are summarized in the table on p. 131.

The cost of the loan to the borrower is 8.5 percent, the nominal rate of the loan. The underlying lender's yield is the nominal rate of 7.5 percent. Since the yield on the wraparound loan exceeds the interest rate on the underlying loan, the wraparound lender enjoys positive leverage. The wraparound lender's yield is 12.95 percent.

Notice that the cash flow to the underlying lender plus the cash flow to the wraparound lender is equal to the cash flow to the total wraparound loan for every period.

The wraparound lender's IRR is equal to the cost of borrowing the additional $22,401.18. It would be advantageous for the borrower to acquire the same $22,401.18 with another type of loan if the cost were less than 12.95 percent.

EOM	Total Wraparound Loan	Underlying Lender	Wraparound Lender
0	($160,000)	($137,598.82)	($22,401.18)
1	1,288.36	1,108.49	179.87
↓	↓	↓	↓
120	1,288.36 + 130,832.90	1,108.49 + 93,384.18	179.87 + 37,448.72
IRR (monthly)	0.708% × 12	0.625% × 12	1.08% × 12
IRR (annualized)	8.5%	7.5%	12.95%

Wraparound loan with specified yield to wraparound lender In some situations, the wraparound lender may make funds available at a specified before-tax yield. The borrower would need to know the effective interest rate on the total wraparound loan. This rate is calculated from the total cash flows to the borrower.

Example

Suppose the wraparound lender in the previous illustration required a 15-percent before-tax yield on the $22,401.18. The wraparound lender would require a monthly payment of $286.92 (amount to amortize $22,401.18 in 25 years at 15 percent). Treated as a separate loan, the wraparound lender's "balance" EOY 10 would be $20,500.42. Now the yield and cash flows are known for both lenders. The borrower's effective rate is calculated from the total of the cash flows (see table on p. 132).

The effective interest rate is 8.64 percent. The borrower would be better off only if a new first loan of $160,000 were available at less than 8.64 percent.

Mortgage discount points

It is common among mortgage lenders to require the payment of "discount points" on mortgage loans as a means of increasing yields. A discount point is, by definition, 1 percent of the face value of the mortgage at the time it is granted. Obviously, by requiring the payment of discount points at the time the loan is granted, the lender decreases the loan amount **131**

EOM	Underlying Lender	+	Wraparound Lender	=	Total Wraparound Loan
0	($137,598.82)	+	($22,401.18)	=	($160,000.00)
1	1,108.49	+	286.92	=	1,395.41
↓	↓		↓		↓
120	1,108.49 + 93,384.18	+	286.92 + 20,500.42	=	1,395.41 + 113,884.60
IRR (monthly)					0.720%
					× 12
IRR (annualized)	7%		15%		8.64%

without changing the flow of future debt service and, thus, increases the IRR on the loan.

Calculating yield In order to determine the effective interest rate (rate paid by the borrower if the borrower pays the points *or* the yield received by the lender) on a discounted mortgage, one has only to relate the actual amount loaned with the periodic mortgage payments and loan balance at the end of the loan duration. These are the lender's cash flows.

Example

A lender charges four points on the following loan:

Loan amount:	$125,000
Nominal interest rate:	10%
Amortization term:	25 years, monthly payments

The loan payment and balance at the end of the loan duration are based on the amount of the total loan, before discount points. The *nominal interest rate* (sometimes called coupon rate) is used to calculate the payment and balance. The *effective interest rate* is the actual cost of borrowing (nominal interest rate plus discount points).

The monthly payment, computed from the data above, is $1,135.88.

The lender's investment, net loan proceeds, is:

Face amount of loan	$125,000
Less: 4% discount	5,000
Net loan proceeds	$120,000

The effective interest rate of this loan, if it is paid in full EOY 25, is calculated on the following cash flows:

EOM	$	
0	($120,000)	Net loan proceeds
1	1,135.88	Monthly loan payment
↓	↓	
25 years × 12 = 300	$1,135.88	The balance is –0– EOY 25

The annualized effective interest rate is 10.53 percent. Note that this is the yield on the loan held to maturity. This calculation allocates the discount points over the total term of the loan. If the loan balance were paid before EOY 25, the effective interest rate would be greater since the same number of points would be "amortized" over a shorter term.

The effective yield on this loan, if it were paid in full after two years, would be computed from the debt service for 24 months and the loan balance EOY 2 of $122,508.89 (present value of $1,135.88 per month discounted at 10 percent for the remaining term of 23 years). The lender's cash flows are summarized as follows:

EOM	$
0	($120,000)
1	1,135.88
↓	↓
2 × 12 = 24	1,135.88 + 122,508.89

The annualized effective interest rate EOY 2 is 12.29 percent. As expected, it is greater than the nominal interest rate.

Figure 11 (p. 134) shows the effective interest rate for loan durations up to the full maturity of 25 years. The rate is very high for very short holding periods because the same number of discount points are paid for shorter periods as for long periods.

The effective interest rate is always greater than the nominal rate because of the discount points. Obviously, the effective interest rate is increased if the number of discount points is increased. Although caution should always be used with "rules of thumb" such as these, each point will increase the effective interest rate *about* ⅛ percent at maturity.

Calculating points to achieve a specified yield   The lender can calculate the discount for a loan, when the effective interest rate is specified, by subtracting the PV of cash flows to the lender discounted at the appropriate rate from the loan amount.

Example

Suppose the lender in the example above expected the loan to be paid in full EOY 10 and required an 11-percent yield.

Figure 11   Effective Interest Rate

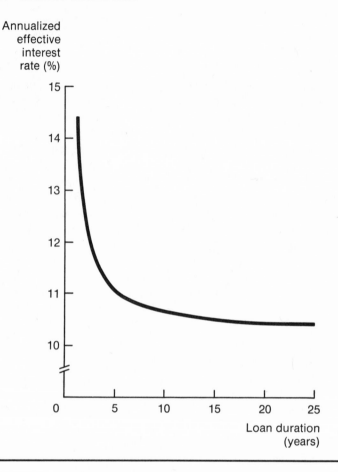

The loan balance EOY is \$105,702.08 (PV of \$1,135.88 per month discounted at 10 percent, the nominal rate, for the remaining term of 15 years).

The lender's cash flow is:

EOM	\$
0	PV = ?
1	\$1,135.88
↓	↓
10 × 12 = 120	1,135.88 + 105,702.08

The PV of these cash flows, discounted at 11 percent, the lender's re-
134   quired yield, is \$117,821.45. The discount is:

Loan amount	$125,000.00
Loan proceeds	− 117,821.45
Discount	$7,178.55

This translates to:

$$\frac{\$7,178.55}{\$125,000.00} = 5.74 \text{ points}$$

Thus, the effective interest rate is 11 percent for a $125,000 loan at a nominal interest rate of 10 percent, with monthly payments based on a 25-year amortization term *if* the loan is paid in full EOY 10.

Impact of holding period   When considering financing alternatives, it has been shown that the investor's anticipated holding period is an important variable. This is especially true with loans with discount points, since the effective interest rate changes over time. For a short holding period discounted loans may result in negative leverage on an investment. If the loan in the preceding example were used to finance a property which has a constant overall rate of return of 12 percent, for any holding period, the investor would have negative leverage for a short holding period (recall that the effective interest rate was 12.29 percent EOY 2). For longer holding periods, this loan may become the higher yielding alternative.

Example

Suppose an investor used the loan in the example above to finance a property that cost $165,000 with NOI of $19,800 (12 percent of $165,000). Value and NOI are assumed to be constant over time. The equity investment is:

Purchase price	$165,000
Less: loan proceeds (net of discount)	120,000
Equity investment	$45,000

Monthly cash flows to equity are:

NOI ($19,800 ÷ 12)	$1,650.00
Monthly loan payment	1,135.88
Monthly cash flows to equity	$514.12

The equity reversion EOY 2 is:

Sale price	$165,000.00
Loan balance EOY 2	122,508.89
Equity reversion EOY 2	$42,491.11

135

The cash flows to equity are summarized below.

EOM	$
0	($45,000)
1	514.12
↓	↓
2 × 12 = 24	514.12 + 42,491.11

The annualized before-tax equity yield is 11.21 percent. As expected, the investor had negative leverage for the two-year holding period. The before-tax equity yield EOY 25 is 14.74 percent.

Figure 12 (p. 138) shows the before-tax equity yield for holding periods up to 25 years, the term of the loan. Equity yields on this graph are calculated assuming that the property is sold at the end of the holding period. For example, if the property were sold EOY 2, the before-tax yield would be 11.21 percent (Point A).

Notice in Figure 12 that the equity yields for the shorter holding periods are very low, but increase rapidly year by year. This is the result of the very high effective interest rate on a loan with discount points for short holding periods.

The equity yield peaks during Year 11 (Point B). Two financing variables are affecting the yield. Leverage is declining over time which reduces the equity yield for longer holding periods, as discussed earlier in this chapter. The effective interest rate is also declining over time which in turn increases the equity yield. At holding period B, the impact of reduced leverage becomes greater than the impact of the decreased effective interest rates. Therefore, the equity yield will decline after 11 years. (Although the same principles apply to other similar financing situations, Figure 12 is unique to the assumptions described above.)

Prepayment penalties

A prepayment penalty is an additional charge by a lender due only if the loan is paid in full before the end of the minimum period. The extra charge will increase the lender's yield.

Example

Consider a $100,000 loan at 10-percent interest per year with monthly payments of $897.90. The lender requires a prepayment penalty of 2 percent of the outstanding balance if the loan is repaid before the end of ten years. The borrower plans to repay the loan balance of $95,000 EOY 5. The lender's cash flows are summarized below.

EOM	$
0	($100,000)
1	897.90
↓	↓
5 × 12 = 60	897.90 + 95,000 + 1,900

The prepayment penalty EOY 5 is $1,900 (2 percent × $95,000). The annualized effective interest rate is the IRR of these cash flows, 10.3 percent. The effective interest rate will decline to 10 percent when the prepayment penalty no longer applies as the loan balance (therefore, the penalty) declines over time.

Alternative mortgage instruments

High interest rates and shortages of available mortgage funds have inspired many innovative financing techniques and alternative mortgage instruments.[5] Some of these instruments require debt service that changes during the investment holding period. Fluctuations in mortgage interest rates (as with variable rate mortgages or renegotiable rate mortgages) may change the periodic payment or the loan balance at the end of the cash flow projection. These characteristics add risk (uncertainty) to the analysis. Unfortunately, specific changes in interest rates are impossible to forecast accurately. The analyst should be aware of the implications of financing variables on yield for alternative holding periods in order to estimate the impact of changes in financing terms in the future.

Summary

Debt financing of real estate investments is very common. The terms of mortgage loans have a great effect on the equity yield. The equity yield depends on the overall rate of return on the investment property and several financing variables including effective interest, loan-to-value ratio, terms of loan amortization and investment holding period.

The examples in this chapter have presumed constant property value and income to isolate the impact of debt financing to equity yield. In practice, income and property value are almost always expected to change in the future, and these changes can easily be imputed into the analysis. However, the ordinal ranking of alternative financing will be the same for any particular set of assumptions relevant to a specific property.

Equity yield, or lender's yield, is calculated from cash flows received. Typically, the process involves determining the initial investment, the periodic cash flows and the reversion at the end of the holding period. The yield is determined by calculating the IRR on the cash flows.

After-tax analysis of financing alternatives has been discussed briefly in this chapter. It is discussed in more detail in Section III of this book.

Figure 12   Equity Yields

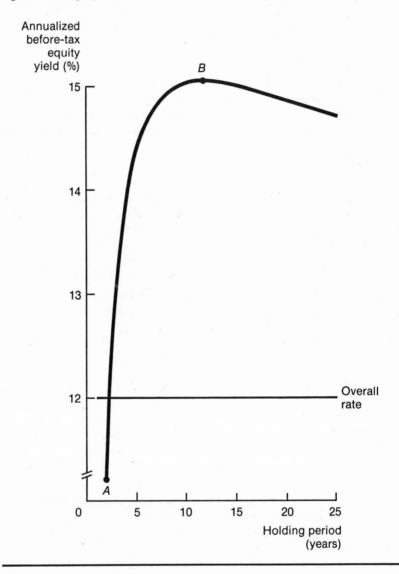

Notes

1. Gary Alan Brown, "Real Estate Investment Trusts," from *The Real Estate Handbook,* edited by Maury Seldin (Homewood, IL: Dow Jones-Irwin, 1980), pp. 686-87.

2. See Marshall Dennis, *Fundamentals of Mortgage Lending* (Reston, VA: Reston Publishing Co., 1978) for a much more complete discussion of this topic.

3. Much of the material and examples in this section are from Jerome J. Dasso, William N. Kinnard, Jr. and Stephen D. Messner, *Valuation and Analysis of Interests in Participation Financed Properties* (Chicago: Society of Real Estate Appraisers, 1972).

4. Dasso, Kinnard and Messner, pp. 21-22.

5. For more detailed discussion on this topic, see Arthur M. Weimer, Homer Hoyt and George F. Bloom, *Real Estate,* 7th ed. (New York: John Wiley & Sons, 1978), Ch. 15; and Donald R. Epley and James A. Miller, *Basic Real Estate Finance and Investments* (New York: John Wiley & Sons, 1980) Ch. 10-11.

Impact of Federal Income Tax on Real Estate Investment

Chapter 7

The Tax Process

While neither the investor nor the real estate broker is expected to be an income tax expert, familiarity with the general tax rules is essential for the purposes of determining motivation, comparison or consequences of an investment program. Such familiarity also should enable the broker or investor to read a tax report and understand its makeup and consequences.

Tax law background

Tax legislation is combined into a single immense section of the federal statutory law called the Internal Revenue Code. This Code is revised from time to time by Congress; some of these revisions are extensive. In recent years, our national legislators have been extremely active in revising the Code. Extensive changes in the tax law have been made by the Installment Sales Revision Act of 1980, the Economic Recovery Tax Act of 1981 (ERTA), the Tax Equity and Fiscal Responsibility Act of 1982 (TEFRA), the Subchapter S Revision Act of 1982, and the Tax Reform Act of 1984. It is estimated that the latest of these tax revisions made more than 1,200 changes in the tax law.

Congress also has created an administrative agency to collect the tax and interpret the tax law, the Internal Revenue Service (IRS). IRS has issued elaborate regulations and rulings interpreting the Internal Revenue Code. The federal courts also constantly review the Code, the regulations and the rulings as applied to complaining taxpayers in literally thousands of cases and have upheld, upset or altered those rules by court opinions and decisions.

As a result of an accumulation of legislation, administrative rulings and court opinions, a continuing and ever-changing mass of tax law has been developed. Although it takes full-time professional experts to research and interpret specific, complex situations, because the income tax is an escalating major cost of living item, the tax law should be understood by every income-earning individual. Everyone has the legal right to minimize his tax bill by prudent management of his affairs within the framework of the rules.

Nature of taxable income

The income tax is not imposed on *all* income; it is imposed only on *taxable income.* Taxable income is an amount arrived at by making adjustments to *gross income,* which the tax law defines as income from all sources.

For individuals, gross income is reduced by three categories of deductions: (1) business deductions, (2) personal deductions and (3) exemptions and dependency deductions. After reducing gross income by business deductions, the individual arrives at *adjusted gross income.* Adjusted gross income is then reduced by the amounts in Categories 2 and 3 above to arrive at taxable income. (For taxpayers other than individuals—corporations, for example—the intermediate adjusted gross income calculation does not occur.)

There are two reasons why the individual must first determine the amount of his adjusted gross income. The first deals with the personal deductions in Category 2. If these deductions add up to less than a flat amount allowed by the tax law, the taxpayer is entitled to deduct this flat amount (via a device called the *zero bracket amount*). If he uses the zero bracket amount, he determines his tax from IRS tables that relate to his adjusted gross income.

The second reason for determining adjusted gross income deals with limitations on medical expense, casualty loss, and charitable contribution deductions. The maximum amounts permitted to be deducted in these three categories are determined as percentages of adjusted gross income.

Adjusted gross income

Following is a list of the most typical sources of gross income for the individual and the deductions he may take in reducing this gross income to adjusted gross income:

Salary and wages   Among the deductions allowed are transportation and travel expenses, outside salesperson's expenses, moving expenses and contributions to IRAs.

Dividends   The law allows $100 of dividends ($200 on a joint return) to be excluded from gross income. Also, a taxpayer is permitted to receive $750 ($1,500 on a joint return) of nontaxable dividends from certain public utility companies if he takes the dividend in the form of stock and if he holds the dividend stock and the stock on which it was issued for one year. This rule terminates after 1985.

Interest   Excluded from gross income is interest on state and municipal bonds.

Pensions and annuities Formulas are provided for excluding from gross income portions of pensions and annuities that are considered a recovery of the taxpayer's costs of acquiring the pension or annuity.

Rents and royalties Depreciation and other expenses incurred in earning rents and royalties are deducted.

Sole proprietor's business income The cost of operation reduces the gross income.

Income from partnerships The partnership calculates its gross income, reduces it by the cost of operations and allocates the appropriate portion of the net amount to each partner.

Unincorporated farm The cost of operating reduces the gross income.

Sale and exchange of property Gain or loss is computed as the difference between the sale price and the adjusted basis of the property sold or exchanged. Only 40 percent of long-term gain is included in gross income. Some exchanges are tax free.

Alimony A taxpayer may deduct alimony paid from his gross income in arriving at adjusted gross income.

Itemized deductions

After arriving at adjusted gross income, the individual taxpayer may then take a series of itemized deductions from his adjusted gross income. These include certain medical expenses, charitable contributions, interest expenses, taxes paid and other costs. In lieu of taking these itemized deductions, the taxpayer can make use of the zero bracket amount. The zero bracket amount is explained later in this chapter.

Exemptions and dependency deductions

Finally, the individual taxpayer further reduces his income (to arrive at taxable income) by exemptions and dependency deductions. Each exemption and dependency deduction is $1,000, including one exemption for the taxpayer himself. An extra exemption is allowed for a taxpayer who is over 65, and another exemption is allowed for a taxpayer who is blind. On a joint return, each spouse is entitled to one exemption plus the exemption for being over 65 or blind.

Types of income

For federal income tax purposes, taxpayers may have two types of taxable income, ordinary income and capital gains. As will be demonstrated later in this chapter, certain capital gains are taxed at much lower effective rates than is ordinary income.

There is a third type of income a taxpayer may have: tax-exempt income. This income is usually in the form of interest on bonds or other obligations of states, cities and other subdivisions of a state (usually referred to as municipal bonds). It is also possible to have a gain or profit that is not recognized for tax purposes. While the gain is there, it is not taxable in the year in which it is realized. This often occurs when there is an exchange of like-kind property, usually real estate. (Exchanges are discussed in depth in Chapter 11.)

In the determination of whether certain gains from the disposition of real estate are to be treated as capital gains or ordinary income, the status of the taxpayer relative to the property is a vital factor. If he is deemed to be an *investor,* his gain will generally be a capital gain; however, if he is deemed to be a *dealer* in that property, his gain is ordinary income—income derived from the operation of his business.

Accounting methods

As we have seen, taxable income is determined by reducing gross income by allowable deductions and exemptions. However, there is a timing factor to be considered: *when* income or expense arises. The time when income is recognized or deductions are allowed depends on the accounting method used. There are two common, recognized methods of accounting, the accrual method and the cash method.

The accrual method

Considered the most accurate method, accrual accounting matches the income and expense attributable to a period of time, regardless of when the income is actually received or the expense paid. In other words, income is reported when everything that has to be done to entitle the recipient to the income has occurred. Similarly, an expense is deductible when everything has been done that requires the payment. The fact that the payment date is to occur prior to or after all the other events is disregarded.

Examples

1. Brown is a landlord and is entitled to receive $1,000 a month for the premises he rents to Green. Rent is payable on the first day of the month for that month. Green is delinquent in his rent payment and pays the De-

cember, 1984, rent in January, 1985. If Brown is on the accrual basis, he must report the December rent in 1984 even though he received payment in 1985. Even if (in the unusual event) the December rent were actually payable in 1985, Brown would still have to report the December rent as 1984 income.

2. Brown, the landlord in the previous example, has fuel oil delivered to him in 1984. He receives a bill for $950. Under the terms of his agreement with the vendor, payment is not due until 1985. Brown pays for the oil in 1985. On the accrual basis, Brown deducts the $950 in 1984.

The accrual method can be used by any taxpayer. It is, however, required if inventories are a substantial income-producing factor in a business.

For deductions claimed after July 18, 1984, a new concept—economic performance—has been added to the accrual method. Under this concept, an accrual basis taxpayer cannot accrue a deduction until economic performance has occurred. If, for example, the taxpayer's liability arises because the taxpayer is to receive property from another person, the economic performance occurs when the property is received. Thus, the new rule would not change the results in Example 2 above.

If the taxpayer's liability arises for services to be received from another person, economic performance occurs as the services are provided by the other person. Thus, if the services are provided over a period of more than one taxable year, the liability accruing in each year is limited to the amount of services received in that year. If the taxpayer's liability arises out of the use of property by the taxpayer (e.g., rent for the use of the premises), economic performance occurs as the taxpayer uses the property. Therefore, the rent is deductible in one taxable year only to the extent that it covers the use of the property during that year.

The cash method

Cash accounting is a much simpler method to use although it is not considered as scientifically accurate. It also permits greater flexibility in moving income and deductions from one year to another. Under this method, income is recognized and deductions are allowable when the actual payment takes place.

Examples

1. Going back to our first example above, since Brown did not receive the December, 1984 rent until 1985, as a cash-basis taxpayer he reports that rent as income in 1985, when he receives it.

2. In the second example, if Brown uses the cash method, he gets the deduction for the fuel payment in 1985, when he paid for it.

Section 467 rental agreements

Congress was disturbed by the fact that a cash-basis lessee included rent income only when payment was received and an accrual-basis lessee could deduct the rent on the basis of occupancy of the premises regardless of when payment was made. So, for rental agreements entered into after June 8, 1984, a new set of rules (applying to both lessor and lessee, regardless of their cash- or accrual-basis status) has been put into the law. This new set of rules applies if the rental agreement qualifies as a *Section 467 rental agreement.*

A rental agreement is a Section 467 rental agreement if *either* of the following two conditions exists:

1. Some amount of rent is payable in a future year for use of the property in a prior year. This rule applies if the future payment is made more than one year after the close of the taxable year in which the use of the property occurs.
2. The agreement calls for rent increases during the term of the lease.

Note, however, that if the total amount of the rents for the entire lease term is $250,000 or less, the agreement is *not* a Section 467 rental agreement.

If the rental agreement *is* a Section 467 rental agreement, the lessor and the lessee (regardless of the accounting method each uses) take into account each year the amount of rent allocable to that year by the rental agreement *plus* the present value of the rents to be paid in future years that are allocable to that year. IRS will issue regulations to explain how to compute the present value of the future rents.

In addition, interest is to be included for the amounts payable in future years that are allocable to the present year. In calculating the present value of future payments and of the interest, a rate equal to 110% of the applicable federal rate at the time the rental agreement was entered into (compounded semiannually) is used. The applicable federal rate, to be published by the IRS, is based on the rates paid on federal obligations.

Disqualified leaseback or long-term agreements

Special rules apply if a Section 467 rental agreement is a disqualified leaseback or long-term agreement—that is, if it has tax avoidance as a principal purpose and is either (1) part of a leaseback transaction, or (2) for a term that is greater than 75% of the statutory recovery period of the property. For real estate, the statutory recovery period is 18 years. A leaseback transaction involves a leaseback to any person (or relative of that person) who had an interest in the property at any time within two years before the leaseback.

If the disqualified leaseback or long-term agreement does not provide for rent allocations that meet the requirements for Section 467 rental agreements, the rent allocable to each year is the portion of the *constant rent amount* allocable to each year. The constant rent amount is the amount that, were it paid at the end of each lease period, would add up to a present value equal to the present value of all the rent payments called for in the agreement. (Present value is computed as set forth above for Section 467 rental agreements.)

The IRS is authorized to issue regulations spelling out circumstances in which the agreement will not be treated as a disqualified leaseback or long-term agreement. These circumstances include (1) rent amounts geared to price indices; (2) rents based on fixed percentages of the lessee's receipts; (3) reasonable rent holidays; and (4) changes in amounts paid by the lessor to third parties.

Recapture of prior understated income. If the transaction would have been a disqualified leaseback or long-term agreement but for the exceptions provided, the lessor may have ordinary income recapture on the disposition of the property. The recapture amount is calculated by first determining the amounts that would have been included as rent under the rules for Section 467 rental agreements. Subtracted from this amount is the actual amount of rents taken into account by the lessor during the period of the lease. The remaining amount is compared to the gain on the disposition. The lesser of these two amounts is the recapture amount.

Prepayments

The IRS has long taken a position (and it has been upheld by the courts) that prepayment of rent expense must be deducted over the period for which it was paid, *regardless of the accounting method used by the tenant*.

In addition, Congress has enacted legislation that now prevents a cash-basis taxpayer from deducting prepaid interest.

Constructive receipt

When the cash method is used, income may not be avoided merely by turning one's back to available income. Once payment is tendered or is available for the asking, the income is deemed to have been realized even though the actual payment has not been received. For example, when interest is credited to a savings bank account, it becomes income even though the amount is not withdrawn.

Once payment is tendered, it becomes income. Asking the payor to hold up on payment at that point is too late. However, it is permissible to arrange in advance when payment is to be due. For example, even though title will close in December, 1984, a real estate broker can arrange in advance for the seller to pay the broker's commission in 1985. If this arrangement is made as a condition for the broker's representation of the seller prior to the sale, the income will become 1985 income if the broker is a cash-basis taxpayer. On the other hand, if the commission was to be paid at the closing and at that time the broker says, "hold onto the money until next year and then pay me," he has constructive receipt in 1984.

Choosing and changing accounting methods

A taxpayer may choose the accounting method he desires (subject to the requirement that the accrual method be used when inventory is a substantial income-producing factor) on his first tax return for a business. Typically, individuals whose major (or sole) income is from wages and salaries use the cash method. Professionals (doctors, lawyers, accountants) and those in service businesses (real estate brokers, for example) use the cash method more often than not. Businesses that sell goods generally use the accrual method.

Once an accounting method has been chosen, the taxpayer must continue to use that method for that business unless he gets permission from the IRS to change. (When permission for change is granted, IRS generally requires certain adjustments and there may be additional tax to pay as a result. Often, this additional tax is permitted to be paid ratably over a number of years.)

Installment method

An exception to the cash and accrual method is the installment method. Under this method, gain on the sale of property is permitted to be reported ratably over the period of collection. This method applies when some portion (or all) of the sale price is to be paid in a year later than the year of sale. This is a very popular method for reporting gain on the sale of real estate. A complete discussion of the installment method is in Chapter 10.

Taxation of individuals' ordinary incomes

Typically, an individual's ordinary income will arise from salary or wages if he is an employee; this includes the executive or the stockholder who is employed by his own corporation. If he is self-employed or a partner in a partnership, his ordinary income will, in effect, be the net profits from the operation. Thus, we can say that the major source of an individual's ordinary income normally comes from his gainful occupation.

In addition, there are other types of ordinary income. Security income, dividends on stocks and interest on bonds or bank accounts are ordinary income. However, even a portion of security income may be tax exempt.

For individuals, $100 ($200 on a joint return) of dividends is not taxable. As previously mentioned, interest on municipal bonds is also not taxable.

Royalty payments are ordinary income, as are the taxable portions of annuity payments.

Real estate ownership can also create ordinary income. The ordinary income from real estate held for income-producing purposes is the real estate taxable income—gross income collected (rent) less depreciation, repairs and other expenses.

Because depreciation may exceed the total of the otherwise taxable income and the principal payments on the loan, it is possible to receive cash flow from the real estate and still have a net loss for tax purposes.

Examples

1.
Gross rents collected		$130,000
Less: Depreciation	$40,000	
Repairs and maintenance	15,000	
Other expenses—interest, real estate taxes, management	85,000	140,000
Net loss		($10,000)

Although there was a tax loss, the owner of the property could still end up with cash in hand if, for example, his cash outlay for principal payments (not deductible for tax purposes) was less than the deduction for depreciation (for which no cash outlay is required).

2. Assume in the preceding example that the owner paid $25,000 in mortgage principal payments during the year. His cash position would be as follows:

Gross rents collected		$130,000
Less cash outlays:		
Repairs and maintenance	$15,000	
Principal payment on mortgage	25,000	
Other expenses	85,000	125,000
Cash available to investor		$ 5,000

Thus, while he had a tax loss of $10,000, he also has cash in hand of $5,000.

The tax loss of $10,000 is fully deductible. That is, it reduces the other ordinary taxable income the property owner may have. Thus, if his ordinary income from gainful employment, dividends, interest, etc. totals $35,000 (after deductions and exemptions), his ordinary income will be reduced to $25,000 by applying the $10,000 taxable loss from the real estate investment.

Business income and farm income are reduced much the same way as income from rental property. All necessary reasonable costs are deducted from the gross amount to get the net amount added to ordinary income.

Deductions and exemptions

In computing the tax of an individual, we must first reduce his ordinary income by allowable deductions and exemptions. We have already seen that in determining a person's ordinary income (or loss) from rental real estate, we reduce his gross operating income from the property by his operating expenses, interest expense of loans on the property, and depreciation. But from the individual's total income (from gainful employment, securities and real estate, etc.) he may subtract personal deductions.

These personal deductions are made up of charitable contributions, medical expenses, interest (other than interest already deducted in arriving at real estate taxable income), taxes (other than federal income taxes and real estate taxes already deducted among the operating expenses of the real estate), casualty losses and other expenses related to investments or to the production of income. These are generally referred to as an individual's itemized deductions.

In lieu of itemized deductions, a taxpayer is permitted to deduct a minimum fixed amount. He will deduct this fixed amount if it is greater than the total of his itemized deductions. The device whereby he deducts the fixed amount is called the *zero bracket amount.*

The tax law subjects this fixed amount to a zero tax. If the taxpayer's adjusted gross income does not exceed $50,000, he can get the benefit of the zero bracket amount by using tax tables supplied by IRS. The tax indicated in these tables reflects the fact that the fixed amount was taxed at zero.

A taxpayer whose adjusted gross income exceeds $50,000 may still take advantage of the zero bracket amount if he does not itemize his deductions. He calculates his tax from the regular schedules, but those schedules are structured to impose a zero tax on the zero bracket amount. The zero bracket amounts are:

- $3,400 on a joint return ($1,700 for each spouse if a married couple files separate returns)
- $2,300 for single taxpayers and heads of households

In addition, the individual is entitled to a deduction for each exemption on his return. He gets one exemption for himself. If he files a joint return, he gets two, one for himself and one for his spouse. If either he or his spouse is blind, there is an extra exemption for each person who is blind. If either he or his spouse is over 65, there is an extra exemption for each spouse over 65. In addition, there is a deduction for each dependent the taxpayer has. A dependent is someone who is closely related to the taxpayer (son, daughter, father, mother and other enumerated relatives) who receives more than half of his support from the taxpayer and whose gross income is less than $1,000. (A son or daughter who is either under 19 or a full-time student is permitted to have any amount of gross income and still be a dependent as long as the parent furnished more than half of that child's support. In such a case, both parent and child may claim the exemption.) The amount of the deduction allowed for each exemption and each dependent is $1,000.

The tax rates applied to the amount on which the tax is computed (taxable income) depends on the taxpayer's marital status. The categories of taxpayers and the tax rate schedules they must use (see Figure 13) are as follows:

Unmarried taxpayers not qualifying as heads of households	Schedule I
Married taxpayers filing joint returns and certain widows and widowers with dependent children	Schedule II
Married persons filing separate returns	Schedule III
Taxpayers qualifying as heads of households	Schedule IV

The rates that apply to unmarried individuals who are not heads of households are about 20 percent greater than the rates applying to joint returns. The rates on heads of households are about halfway between the rates on unmarried individuals who are not heads of households and the rates imposed on joint returns.

Note that beginning in 1985, the tax rate tables will be adjusted each year to take inflation into account. Thus, the inclusive amounts of each tax bracket will be changed each year. The tables set forth in Figure 13 apply only to 1984.

Two-earner married couples

Because married couples must file either joint returns or separate returns calling for higher tax rates than the separate returns filed by unmarried persons, where each spouse earns approximately the same amount of income, their tax on a joint return may be greater than the total of the tax they would pay were each permitted to file a separate return using the tax rates that apply to single individuals. This phenomenon has been referred to as the "marriage penalty." Congress has taken steps to alleviate (but not eliminate) this so-called penalty.

A married couple filing a joint return is permitted to reduce its gross income, in arriving at adjusted gross income, by 10 percent of the earned income of the spouse with the lower earnings. However, the maximum deduction will be 10 percent of $30,000, or $3,000.

Computing the tax

As previously indicated, if the taxpayer is not claiming itemized deductions, and if his adjusted gross income does not exceed $50,000, he determines his tax from special tax tables provided by IRS. These tables take into account the taxpayer's filing status and the zero bracket amount applicable to him.

Those taxpayers who itemize their deductions and those who do not itemize but who have adjusted gross income in excess of $50,000 must compute their tax, using applicable tax rate schedules.

Those who itemize their deductions subtract from adjusted gross income the total amount of the itemized deductions. But before they deduct their itemized deductions from adjusted gross income, they must first reduce their total deductions by the zero bracket amount applicable to them. The reason for this is that the first bracket in the tax rate schedules is an amount equal to the zero bracket amount. That amount is taxable at zero percent. So, although the taxpayer reduces his itemized deductions by the zero bracket amount, an equivalent amount escapes tax in the computation. Therefore, he is not penalized.

After deducting itemized deductions from adjusted gross income, the result is further reduced by the amount claimed for exemptions and dependents, as already explained. The amount remaining after deductions for exemptions and dependents is the amount on which the taxpayer computes his tax, using the appropriate tax rate schedule.

Example

Assume that for 1984, Jones, an unmarried individual, has salary income of $25,000 and security income of $7,000. He has personal, itemized deductions of $4,000. To arrive at his taxable income, he first reduces his itemized deductions of $4,000 by the $2,300 zero bracket amount that applies to unmarried taxpayers filing separate returns. He reduces his $32,000 adjusted income (combined salary and security income) by the remaining $1,700 of itemized deductions, to $30,300. He further reduces this figure by his $1,000 exemption, to $29,300. Then, to find his tax, he goes to Schedule I of the tax rate schedule (see Figure 13).

In Schedule I, in the bracket "over $28,800 but not over $34,100," he will find the tax to be $5,705 plus 34 percent of the excess over $28,800. Since $29,300 exceeds $28,800 by $500, he will compute 34 percent of $500, or $170. Adding $170 to $5,705 yields $5,875. This is Jones' tax for 1984. (In Schedule I, the first $2,300 of Jones' income was subject to a zero tax, thus compensating him for reducing his itemized deductions by $2,300.)

Marginal and effective rates

In the example above, Jones paid a tax of $5,875. His total gross income (before deductions and exemptions) was $32,000. Jones' total tax was approximately 18 percent of his gross income. In effect, he kept 82 cents, after taxes, out of each dollar of gross income he acquired that year. Thus, it can be said that his overall tax rate was 18 percent.

On the other hand, because of the bracket system of imposing tax, the last $500 of Jones' income was subject to a tax of 34 percent. This is his *marginal* tax rate, the rate at which the next dollar of additional income would be taxed. Often, you hear the expression, "he's in the 34-percent bracket." That is an expression of the marginal rate.

How, then, should a broker or investor look at tax rates?

Given a specific set of current facts, anyone who knows the tax rates can determine the exact tax. However, in most situations, we are dealing with comparisons and forecasts on income-producing properties. We are determining the type and amount of income a property is expected to produce. Exact tax computations reflect specious accuracy because all of the other figures with which we are dealing are estimates. Thus, we can rely on marginal rates to a degree.

Keep in mind, however, that future rates are always subject to change. Beginning in 1985, the tax brackets in the rate tables will be adjusted for inflation—so-called indexing. (There have been attempts to do away with this indexing, but Congress resisted the repeal of indexing in the 1984 tax legislation. However, there may be future attempts to eliminate it.) This potential change in future tax rates must be taken into consideration in forecasting.

50 percent maximum marginal rate

The highest marginal rate applying to *any* taxable income is 50 percent. This maximum rate is an important consideration in planning for future years. Because only 40 percent of long-term capital gains are included in taxable income, the maximum marginal rate of 50 percent has the effect of imposing a maximum tax of only 20 percent on long-term capital gains (.40 x .50 = .20).

Taxation of individuals' capital gains

Capital gains receive special tax treatment. Capital gains result from the sale or exchange of capital assets or assets which, for tax purposes, are treated as capital assets. For the most part, property held for investment (by someone who is not a dealer in that type of property) is a capital asset. Stocks, bonds and vacant land may be capital assets. Similarly, other personal-use items not held for sale in business, such as a personal residence or personal car, are capital assets.

Figure 13 Tax Schedule*

Schedule I			
Single Taxpayers Not Qualifying as Heads of Households			
If the taxable income is:		The tax is:	
Over—	But not over—		of the amount over—
Not over $2,300		0	
$ 2,300	$ 3,400	11%	$ 2,300
$ 3,400	$ 4,400	$ 121 + 12%	$ 3,400
$ 4,400	$ 6,500	$ 241 + 14%	$ 4,400
$ 6,500	$ 8,500	$ 535 + 15%	$ 6,500
$ 8,500	$10,800	$ 835 + 16%	$ 8,500
$10,800	$12,900	$ 1,203 + 18%	$10,800
$12,900	$15,000	$ 1,581 + 20%	$12,900
$15,000	$18,200	$ 2,001 + 23%	$15,000
$18,200	$23,500	$ 2,737 + 26%	$18,200
$23,500	$28,800	$ 4,115 + 30%	$23,500
$28,800	$34,100	$ 5,705 + 34%	$28,800
$34,100	$41,500	$ 7,507 + 38%	$34,100
$41,500	$55,300	$10,319 + 42%	$41,500
$55,300	$81,800	$16,115 + 48%	$55,300
$81,800	—	$28,835 + 50%	$81,800

Schedule II			
Married Taxpayers Filing Joint Returns and Qualifying Widows and Widowers			
If the taxable income is:		The tax is:	
Over—	But not over—		of the amount over—
Not over $3,400		0	
$ 3,400	$ 5,500	11%	$ 3,400
$ 5,500	$ 7,600	$ 231 + 12%	$ 5,500
$ 7,600	$ 11,900	$ 483 + 14%	$ 7,600
$ 11,900	$ 16,000	$ 1,085 + 16%	$ 11,900
$ 16,000	$ 20,200	$ 1,741 + 18%	$ 16,000
$ 20,200	$ 24,600	$ 2,497 + 22%	$ 20,200
$ 24,600	$ 29,900	$ 3,465 + 25%	$ 24,600
$ 29,900	$ 35,200	$ 4,790 + 28%	$ 29,900
$ 35,200	$ 45,800	$ 6,274 + 33%	$ 35,200
$ 45,800	$ 60,000	$ 9,772 + 38%	$ 45,800
$ 60,000	$ 85,600	$15,168 + 42%	$ 60,000
$ 85,600	$109,400	$25,920 + 45%	$ 85,600
$109,400	$162,400	$36,630 + 49%	$109,400
$162,400	—	$62,600 + 50%	$162,400

*Beginning in 1985, the brackets will be adjusted each year to reflect inflation.

Figure 13 (continued)

Schedule III

Married Taxpayers Filing Separate Returns

If the taxable income is:		The tax is:	
Over—	But not over—		of the amount over—
Not over $1,700		0	
$ 1,700	$ 2,750	11%	$ 1,700
$ 2,750	$ 3,800	$ 115 + 12%	$ 2,750
$ 3,800	$ 5,950	$ 241 + 14%	$ 3,800
$ 5,950	$ 8,000	$ 542 + 16%	$ 5,950
$ 8,000	$10,100	$ 870 + 18%	$ 8,000
$10,100	$12,300	$ 1,248 + 22%	$10,100
$12,300	$14,950	$ 1,732 + 25%	$12,300
$14,950	$17,600	$ 2,395 + 28%	$14,950
$17,600	$22,900	$ 3,137 + 33%	$17,600
$22,900	$30,000	$ 4,886 + 38%	$22,900
$30,000	$42,800	$ 7,584 + 42%	$30,000
$42,800	$54,700	$12,960 + 45%	$42,800
$54,700	$81,200	$18,315 + 49%	$54,700
$81,200	—	$31,300 + 50%	$81,200

Schedule IV

Heads of Households

If the taxable income is:		The tax is:	
Over—	But not over—		of the amount over—
Not over $2,300		0	
$ 2,300	$ 4,400	11%	$ 2,300
$ 4,400	$ 6,500	$ 231 + 12%	$ 4,400
$ 6,500	$ 8,700	$ 483 + 14%	$ 6,500
$ 8,700	$ 11,800	$ 791 + 17%	$ 8,700
$ 11,800	$ 15,000	$ 1,318 + 18%	$ 11,800
$ 15,000	$ 18,200	$ 1,894 + 20%	$ 15,000
$ 18,200	$ 23,500	$ 2,534 + 24%	$ 18,200
$ 23,500	$ 28,800	$ 3,806 + 28%	$ 23,500
$ 28,800	$ 34,100	$ 5,290 + 32%	$ 28,800
$ 34,100	$ 44,700	$ 6,986 + 35%	$ 34,100
$ 44,700	$ 60,600	$10,696 + 42%	$ 44,700
$ 60,600	$ 81,800	$17,374 + 45%	$ 60,600
$ 81,800	$108,300	$26,914 + 48%	$ 81,800
$108,300	—	$39,634 + 50%	$108,300

There is a special rule for so-called Section 1231 assets which are non-inventory, depreciable assets and land used in a business. Property held for production of income, such as a rental apartment building, is a Section 1231 asset, as are factory buildings, warehouses, and machines used in business. If the asset was acquired after June 22, 1984, it has to have been held for more than six months prior to disposition to qualify as a Section 1231 asset. If it was acquired before June 23, 1984, it has to have been held more than one year to meet the Section 1231 definition. (The more-than-one-year holding period is scheduled to be reimposed for property acquired after 1987.) Net Section 1231 gains are treated as ordinary loss (subject to recapture). These rules are explained below.

Real estate held by dealers (i.e., held for sale to customers in the ordinary course of business) is neither a capital asset nor a Section 1231 asset. Gain or loss on a sale or exchange would result in ordinary income or loss (see Chapter 10).

Computing section 1231 gains and losses

We have said that Section 1231 gains receive capital gain treatment and Section 1231 losses are treated as ordinary losses. In a broad sense that is the tax rule. However, this explanation needs some modification. Actually, all the Section 1231 gains and losses that occur in one year are first aggregated to arrive at a *net* Section 1231 gain or loss. Then, if the net figure is a gain, it is treated as a capital gain; if the net result is a loss, it is treated as an ordinary loss. Thus, Section 1231 losses first offset Section 1231 gains before any net loss is applied against ordinary income.

The general rule that net Section 1231 gains are capital gains and net Section 1231 losses are ordinary losses has been modified by 1984 tax legislation. For taxable years beginning after 1983, a net Section 1231 gain will be treated as ordinary income to the extent of net Section 1231 losses that arose during the prior five years (but not before 1982). Thus, for example, if Jones had a $30,000 Section 1231 gain and a $10,000 Section 1231 loss in 1984, the $20,000 net gain would normally be treated as a capital gain. However, assume he had had a net Section 1231 loss of $5,000 in 1983 (which he used as an ordinary loss). In 1984, his $20,000 net Section 1231 gain is treated as consisting of $5,000 of ordinary income and $15,000 of capital gain.

Depreciation recapture and capital gains

When a Section 1231 asset is sold or exchanged, some "depreciation recapture" may result. It is only the gain remaining after deducting the depreciation recapture that is treated as a Section 1231 gain. The portion of the gain that is considered to be depreciation recapture is taxed as ordinary income. (When and how depreciation recapture arises and how to compute it is explained in Chapter 10.)

Calculating long- and short-term capital gains and losses

The favorable rates that apply to capital gains apply only to long-term capital gains. Long-term gains arise from the sale or exchange of property held for the required holding period. If the property being sold or exchanged was acquired prior to June 23, 1984, it must have been held for more than one year to qualify for long-term capital gain. If it was acquired after June 22, 1984, a holding period of more than six months will qualify for long-term treatment. (The holding period is scheduled to revert to "more than one year" for property acquired after 1987.)

All items that qualify for Section 1231 treatment automatically meet the long-term holding period requirement. Gains or losses from the sale or exchange of property held exactly one year or less (or exactly six months or less, in the case of acquisitions after June 22, 1984) are considered short-term gains or losses. Gains or losses from property that would qualify for Section 1231 status but for the fact that the holding period requirements have not been met are treated as ordinary income or losses.

Because of the new dual holding period requirements—depending on the date of acquisition—it behooves the taxpayer to analyze his transactions carefully. It is possible, for example, in 1984 to have a short-term transaction from the sale of a property held as long as exactly one year (acquired before June 23, 1984) and a long-term transaction from the sale of a property held for six months and one day (acquired after June 22, 1984).

In the following paragraphs we will look at how net long-term and short-term capital gains and losses are arrived at, by aggregating those gains and losses. However, keep in mind that the sale or exchange of property held for personal use—a personal residence, a car used for nonbusiness purposes, a ring, a boat, household furniture, etc.—gives rise to a long- or short-term capital gain when sold at a profit. But if such property is sold at a loss, the loss is *entirely nondeductible.* Such losses *do not* enter into the aggregating procedures described in the following paragraphs.

In determining the net long- and short-term gains or losses for the year, short-term capital gains are aggregated with short-term losses and long-term gains are aggregated with long-term losses.

If both categories end up with gains, the short-term gains are treated as ordinary income and the long-term gains get the special capital gains treatment. If both categories end up with losses, however, the rules for capital losses (different rules for corporations and individuals) apply. These rules are spelled out later in this chapter.

If one category ends up with a gain and the other with a loss, the gain and loss must be aggregated to arrive at a net long-term or short-term gain or loss. The net figure is then given the treatment described above for a net gain or loss of that nature. Of course, if all the transactions fall into only one category, the net gain or loss in that category gets the treatment previously described for that category.

Some examples are required to explain more fully the foregoing principles regarding the calculation of long- and short-term capital gains and losses.

Note In the following examples, items are classified as long-term or short-term based on holding periods that meet the requirements for each classification. Thus, it is possible that one item in the long-term category was held more than one year and another more than six months but not more than one year. Both could qualify as long-term transactions based on the date they were acquired. (See the discussion in the section above.)

Examples

1. Assume the following facts concerning four sales of capital assets by an investor:

Purchase Date	Sale Date	Cost or Basis	Sale Price	Long-Term Gain (Loss)	Short-Term Gain (Loss)
4/4/82	3/9/84	$10,000	$15,000	$5,000	
7/14/83	1/14/84	4,000	8,000		$4,000
2/14/84	6/8/84	5,000	4,000		(1,000)
6/25/84	12/28/84	20,000	17,000	(3,000)	
			Totals	$2,000	$3,000

Since both categories end up with gains, the $2,000 long-term capital gain gets the special capital gain treatment, while the $3,000 short-term gain is added to ordinary income as explained above.

2. Assume the following facts concerning four sales of capital assets:

Purchase Date	Sale Date	Cost or Basis	Sale Price	Long-Term Gain (Loss)	Short-Term Gain (Loss)
3/11/81	1/2/84	$10,000	$40,000	$30,000	
8/8/83	1/18/84	15,000	20,000		$5,000
2/4/83	9/19/84	20,000	16,000	(4,000)	
6/23/84	12/23/84	16,000	9,000		(7,000)
			Totals	$26,000	($2,000)
				(2,000)	
				$24,000	

In this case, one category (long-term) ends up with a gain, while the other (short-term) ends up with a loss. Therefore, the two results have to be aggregated, resulting in a long-term capital gain of $24,000. (This gain is eligible for the special long-term capital gain treatment.)

3. Assume the following facts:

Purchase Date	Sale Date	Cost or Basis	Sale Price	Long-Term Gain (Loss)	Short-Term Gain (Loss)
3/11/84	7/9/84	$10,000	$14,000		$4,000
8/31/83	9/1/84	40,000	45,000	$5,000	
5/6/84	10/10/84	10,000	2,000		(8,000)
10/8/83	11/4/84	16,000	10,000	(6,000)	
			Totals	($1,000)	($4,000)

Here, we have a loss in both categories. The capital loss treatment explained later in this chapter applies.

4. Assume the following facts:

Purchase Date	Sale Date	Cost or Basis	Sale Price	Long-Term Gain (Loss)	Short-Term Gain (Loss)
6/24/84	12/29/84	$ 4,000	$ 8,000	$4,000	
4/5/82	5/4/81	18,000	16,000	(2,000)	
3/12/84	1/14/84	3,000	6,000		$3,000
6/28/84	9/9/84	20,000	12,000		(8,000)
			Totals	$2,000	($5,000)
					2,000
					$(3,000)

As shown above, since we have a net gain in one category (long-term) and a net loss in the other (short-term), the two results must be aggregated, giving a net result of a net short-term loss of $3,000. The capital loss treatment explained later in this chapter applies.

5. At this point, let us consider the effect of Section 1231 transactions. Assume the following results from three Section 1231 transactions in 1984:

Transaction	Gain (Loss)
#1	$10,000
#2	(16,000)
#3	20,000
Net Result	$14,000

Since the result is a gain, the gain is treated as a long-term capital gain (assuming that there were no net Section 1231 losses in the prior years after

1982; see the explanation above, "Calculating Section 1231 Gains and Losses"). Therefore, we would include this gain as a long-term capital gain in making our calculations of net long- or short-term capital gains. In other words, this $14,000 gain would be listed as a long-term capital gain along with any other capital gains and losses we may have had for the year when we set up our calculation (in the same manner as in the prior examples). For instance, if in addition to the facts listed in Example 4, we also had the $14,000 Section 1231 gain computed in this example, we would get the following results:

Section 1231 Transaction	Gain (Loss)
#1	$ 10,000
#2	(16,000)
#3	20,000
Net Section 1231 gain	$ 14,000 ⟶

Capital Gains Transactions (from Example 4)

	Long-Term Gain (Loss)	Short-Term Gain (Loss)
	$ 4,000	
	(2,000)	
		$3,000
		(8,000)
	14,000 ←	
	$ 16,000	($5,000)
	(5,000) ←	
	$ 11,000	

If the aggregate of the Section 1231 transaction had been a loss, the loss would be a direct deduction against ordinary income and would have no effect on any of the other capital gain or capital loss transactions for the year.

Taxation of short-term capital gains

If, as a result of the calculations, the individual taxpayer ends up with a short-term capital gain, that gain is added to ordinary income. Short-term gains are not added to ordinary income until *after* all of the aggregation of capital gains and losses are first made (as in Examples 1–4 above). These short-term gains must first be offset against short-term, and possibly long-term, losses before being added to ordinary income.

Long-term capital gain treatment for individuals

Net long-term capital gains receive very favorable tax treatment. Simply put, only 40 percent of the net long-term capital gain is included in ordinary income. Technically, the taxpayer takes a deduction, against his long-term capital gain, of 60 percent of the gain and then includes the balance of the gain in his ordinary income.

Since the highest tax bracket in which any individual taxpayer's income can fall is 50 percent, by including only 40 percent of the net long-term capital gain in his income, the highest *effective* rate to which the entire net long-term capital gain can be subject is 20 percent (.40 of .50 = .20). In lesser brackets, of course, the net effective tax rate on net long-term capital gains is less than 20 percent. In the 45 percent tax bracket, for example, the effective rate on long-term capital gains is 18 percent.

Example

Smith has $48,000 of salary income and $5,400 of deductions. He and his wife file a joint return. They have no dependents.

In 1984, Smith sold investment real estate for $90,000 for which he had a basis of $60,000. He had held the property for more than one year, giving him a $30,000 long-term capital gain. He had no other capital gain or loss transactions (or Section 1231 transactions) in 1984.

Here is how Smith calculates his tax for 1984:

Salary income		$48,000
40% of $30,000 long-term capital gain		12,000
Total income		$60,000
Itemized deductions	$5,400	
Less: zero bracket amount	3,400	2,000
Subtotal		$58,000
Less: exemptions		2,000
Taxable income		$56,000

Tax computation (using Schedule II):

Taxable income	$56,000		
Tax on	45,800	is	$9,772
Tax on (38%) on excess over $45,800 or	10,200	is	3,876
Total tax			$13,648

If the full capital gain had been included in Smith's income, his total taxable income would have been $74,000. The tax would have been $21,048. If Smith had no capital gain at all, his taxable income would have been $44,000, and the tax would have been $9,178. If $9,178 is subtracted from $21,048, the result is $11,870, which would have been the tax on the $30,000 gain if the special long-term capital gain tax rules were not in effect. If we subtract $9,178 from the $13,648 tax that applies when only 40 percent of the long-term capital gain is included in taxable income, we get $4,470. That is the tax imposed on the long-term capital gain. Comparing that with the $11,870 that would have been the tax on the $30,000 gain if there were no special tax rule for long-term capital gains, it is quite obvious that there is a tax saving of $7,400.

Looked at another way, the effective tax rate applied to the $30,000 capital gain was 14.9 percent ($4,470 tax divided by the $30,000 gain). From the calculation above, we see that Smith's marginal tax bracket was 38 percent. Forty percent of the 44 percent marginal rate is 15.2 percent. (The differential between the 14.9 percent effective rate on the capital gain and the 15.2 percent rate based on a marginal rate of 38 percent is due to the fact that a portion of the capital gain actually fell into the next lower bracket of 33 percent.)

Any way you look at it, it is apparent that long-term capital gains get very favorable income tax treatment.

Treatment of capital losses for individuals

Net capital losses (both short- and long-term) may be used to offset ordinary income of up to $3,000. The losses remaining are then carried over to the following year and used as long- or short-term losses in that year. There is no limit on the number of years an individual may carry over a loss. But there is a difference between how a long-term loss and a short-term loss is used to offset the $3,000 of ordinary income. (Of course, if ordinary income is less than $3,000, the maximum amount that a capital loss may offset is the amount of the ordinary income.)

In applying capital losses as offsets against ordinary income, two dollars of long-term loss must be used to offset one dollar of ordinary income. Short-term losses offset ordinary income on a dollar-for-dollar basis. If a taxpayer has both short- and long-term losses, short-term losses are applied first in offsetting ordinary income. If the short-term losses are insufficient to offset $3,000 of ordinary income (or the total of ordinary income if that total does not exceed $3,000), then long-term losses (on a two-for-one basis) are applied.

The following examples illustrate these rules.

Examples

1. In 1984, Green has a long-term capital gain of $1,000 and a short-term capital loss of $6,000. After netting the two, he has a short-term loss of $5,000. His ordinary income is $12,000. He applies $3,000 of his short-term loss to reduce ordinary income to $9,000 and carries over $2,000 as a short-term capital loss to 1985.

2. In 1984, Black has $12,000 ordinary income but has a short-term gain of $1,000 and a long-term loss of $8,000. Now he has a net long-term loss of $7,000. In this case he has to use $6,000 of the $7,000 net long-term loss to offset $3,000 of ordinary income, reducing ordinary income to $9,000. He has $1,000 of long-term capital loss left which is carried over to 1985 as a long-term capital loss.

3. In 1984, Grey has ordinary income of $12,000, a short-term loss of $3,200 and a long-term loss of $400. She applies $3,000 of the short-term loss to reduce ordinary income to $9,000. And, she carries over to 1985 a short-term loss of $200 and a long-term loss of $400.

4. In 1984, Brown has ordinary income of $12,000, a short-term loss of $800 and a long-term loss of $4,800. He applies the $800 short-term loss to offset $800 of ordinary income. He has to use $4,400 of his long-term loss to offset $2,200 of ordinary income, thus offsetting a total of $3,000 of ordinary income. He has $400 of long-term capital loss to carry over to the next year.

Arithmetic of capital gains and losses

Because of the special rates that apply to net long-term gains and the limitations on applying net capital losses to offset ordinary income, good planning (when possible) is called for to keep taxes on these transactions to allowable minimums.

If a taxpayer has a single short-term loss and a single long-term gain in the same year, the short-term loss will offset the long-term gain dollar for dollar (in the aggregating process described earlier in this chapter). However, if the loss and the gain were realized in separate years, the short-term loss would offset ordinary income dollar for dollar (up to a maximum of $3,000 in one year), and, under the rules for taxing long-term gains, only 40 percent of that gain would be included in ordinary income.

If the nature of the gain and the loss were reversed (i.e., a short-term gain and a long-term loss), having them both in the same year could be an advantage. The long-term loss would offset the short-term gain, dollar for dollar. However, if the gain and loss occurred in separate years, the short-term gain would be taxed as ordinary income and it would take two dollars of long-term loss to offset one dollar of ordinary income (up to a maximum of $3,000 in one year).

There are other aspects of this "arithmetic":

Example

Assume a taxpayer has a $2,000 long-term capital loss already realized in 1984. He is in a position to acquire a $2,000 long-term gain before the end of the year or postpone it to 1985. If he takes the gain in 1984, it will be offset by the $2,000 loss he has already realized in 1984. However, if he postpones the gain, the $2,000 loss of 1984 will offset $1,000 of 1984 ordinary income (on a two-for-one basis). In 1985, the $2,000 gain will only create $800 of ordinary income (40 percent of the $2,000 long-term gain). Thus, if he takes both gain and loss in the same year, the $2,000 loss will, in effect, be offsetting $800 of ordinary income. But if he postpones the gain, the $2,000 loss will offset $1,000 of ordinary income. This result arises because only 40 percent of long-term gains are included in ordinary income, but net long-term capital losses offset ordinary income equal to 50 percent of the loss (up to a maximum of $3,000 per year).

When year's end approaches, therefore, it is a good idea to take an inventory of capital gains and losses already realized that year and to survey the potential gains and losses that can still be realized in that year or postponed to the following year. The arithmetic described above should then be applied to determine the desirability of realizing further capital gains and/or losses in the current year.

Of course, tax planning cannot be the only criterion for investment decisions. The reality of being able to postpone to next year a currently available gain or loss must be assessed. The market conditions may change, or a ready buyer may not be available later.

Sometimes postponement can be accomplished by entering into an installment sale. While the sale is made in the current year, the lion's share of the proceeds can be collected in the following year. The gain attributable to the proceeds collected in the following year would be taxable in that following year. Keep in mind, however, that installment sales can be used only to postpone gains, not losses. (The techniques and requirements for installment sale reporting are described in Chapter 10.)

Sales of personal residences

A personal residence is a capital asset. Sale at a gain results in a taxable capital gain. If the sale results in a net loss, the loss is not deductible at all (it does not even offset other capital gains) because losses on disposition of personal items are not deductible.

Although a gain on the sale of a personal residence is a taxable capital gain, there are two exceptions to this rule:

1. Gain is deferred when the proceeds of the sale are reinvested in another personal residence within a prescribed time.

2. Once in a lifetime, $125,000 of gain on the sale of a personal residence is completely tax free if certain conditions are met.

Deferral of the gain   Under this provision of the tax law, on the sale of a principal residence, the taxpayer calculates the gain in the usual way (the excess of the net sale price—sale price minus cost of sale—over the basis). Then, if he buys or builds another principal residence within a prescribed time, he compares the cost of the new residence with the *adjusted sale price* of the old residence. If the cost of the new residence is at least equal to the adjusted sale price of the old one, no part of the gain on the sale is taxable. If the cost of the new residence is less than the adjusted sale price of the old, that part of the gain on the sale which is equal to the *excess* of the adjusted sale price over the cost of the new residence is taxed.

The adjusted sale price of the old residence is the amount realized on its sale (sale price minus cost of sale) reduced by "fix-up" costs (costs incurred in repairing or improving the residence to assist in its sale). These "fix-up" costs must be for work done within 90 days before the taxpayer enters into a contract of sale for the old residence. And these costs must be paid no later than 30 days after title to the old residence is passed.

Example

Here are some facts about such a transaction:

Sale price of old residence	$100,000
Sale commissions	−6,000
Amount realized	94,000
Basis of old residence	−60,000
Gain on sale of old residence	$ 34,000
Amount realized on sale of old residence	$ 94,000
Fix-up costs	−8,000
Adjusted sale price of old residence	$ 86,000
Cost of new residence	−81,000
Excess of adjusted sale price of old residence over cost of new residence	$ 5,000

Thus, of the $34,000 gain realized on the sale of the old residence, $5,000 is treated as a capital gain subject to tax. The balance of the gain is not taxed. Although $29,000 of the gain is not taxed, we referred to the gain as being deferred. The reason is that the basis of the new residence is the cost of the new residence *minus* the gain that was not recognized on the sale of the old residence. Thus, while the new residence cost $81,000, its basis is only $52,000 ($81,000 minus the nontaxed $29,000 gain on the sale of the old residence.) That $29,000 may be taxable in the future when the second residence is sold (unless the subsequent sale is also tax free because of another reinvestment in a residence or the once-in-a-lifetime exemption, discussed below).

There are a number of technical requirements that must be met in order to avoid gain under the rules just described:

1. The old residence and then the new residence must be the taxpayer's *principal* residence. Thus, a summer home, used occasionally, will not qualify.
2. The purchase of the new residence must occur within a period that starts two years before the sale of the old residence and ends two years after that sale.

The purchase and sale of a cooperative or condominium apartment are treated the same as purchase and sale of a house under these rules.

Exclusion of gain once in a lifetime   If a personal residence is sold at a gain, the taxpayer can elect to have that gain considered completely tax free. The maximum amount of gain that can escape tax is $125,000. *The election to avoid the tax on the gain can be made only once in a taxpayer's lifetime.* At the time the election is made, the taxpayer or his spouse (if the property is held jointly and a joint return is filed) must be at least 55 years old and must have owned and used the property as a principal residence for a total of three years during the five-year period preceding the sale.

If a taxpayer sold a principal residence prior to July 26, 1978, and elected not to have part of the gain taxed (because he qualified for exclusion available under the law prior to that date), he is allowed to elect the up-to-$125,000 exclusion on a subsequent sale if he meets the tests of this new rule. However, once he elects this up-to-$125,000 exclusion, he cannot elect it again.

The taxpayer does not get this tax-free gain unless he *elects* to take it. If he intends to reinvest in another personal residence, he may prefer to defer the gain under the rule discussed previously. If the amount reinvested in the new residence (within two years) is sufficient to wipe out the entire gain on the sale of the old residence, there is no point in electing the once-in-a-lifetime tax-free treatment, and thereby lose the opportunity of using the election in the future.

Special tax computations for individuals

There are additional aspects to the computation of the income tax for individuals—a tax relief provision and another possible tax.

The relief provision involves income averaging. The other tax—the alternative minimum tax—may apply in certain cases.

Income averaging

The tax law recognizes that some taxpayers may have unusually high incomes in some years and that this can be inequitable since income tax is computed on an annual basis. To provide for tax relief in such situations, the concept of income averaging was introduced into the tax law. The intent of income averaging is to have the effect of averaging the current year's income with the income of the prior three years and to arrive at a tax that approaches the tax that would have applied had the income been earned ratably over the four years instead of being bunched into one year.

For many years, income averaging applied if the current year's income exceeded the prior four years' average income by more than 120 percent (and if the excess over 120 percent was greater than $3,000). For taxable years beginning after 1983, the rule has been changed. Income averaging applies if the current year's income exceeds the prior three years' average income by more than 140 percent (and if the excess over 140 percent is greater than $3,000).

In essence, under income averaging, if the current year's taxable income exceeds the prior three years' average taxable income by more than 140 percent, that excess over the 140 percent (if it is more than $3,000) is taxed at an overall rate that would apply to one-fourth of the excess. *Current* year's taxes are computed under income averaging. Prior years' taxes are not recalculated.

The income averaging procedure is as follows:

1. Determine the tax on that portion of the current year's taxable income that is equal to 140 percent of the prior three years' average taxable income (base income).

2. Determine the portion of the current year's taxable income that exceeds 140 percent of the prior three years' average taxable income. This is referred to as averageable income. Divide this amount by four.

3. Determine what the tax on this one-fourth of the averageable income would be if the one-fourth were added to the portion of the average year's income equal to 140 percent of the prior years' average taxable income.

4. Multiply by four the tax computed in Step 3.

5. Add the tax determined in Step 1 to the tax determined in Step 4. **169**
   That figure is the total tax due for the current year.

Example

Assume Gray has had a taxable income of $10,000 per year during the prior three years. In 1984, his taxable income is $85,000. Without income averaging, his tax in 1984 on $85,000 of taxable income (on a joint return) is $25,668. Applying the five-step income averaging procedure, his tax amounts to $16,969, a saving of $8,699, determined as follows:

1. Gray's average taxable income for the prior three years was $10,000; 140 percent of that is $14,000. The 1984 tax on $14,000 is $1,421.

2. $14,000 (140 percent of the prior three years' average taxable income) is subtracted from the $85,000 total taxable income of 1984. The remaining $71,000 (the averageable income) is divided by four, giving a figure of $17,750.

3. The $17,750 is added to the $14,000, giving a combined amount of $31,750. The 1984 tax computed on this amount is $5,308. This is the tax that results when one-fourth of the averageable income is added to 140 percent of the prior three years' average income. The tax of $1,421 (computed in Step 1) is subtracted from the $5,308 in order to determine what portion of this amount is attributable to the addition of one-fourth of the averageable income to the 140 percent of the prior three-year average taxable income. Thus, $3,887 is attributable to one-fourth of the averageable income.

4. Since the entire averageable income is to be taxed at the rate that applies to one-fourth of that averageable income when added to 140 percent of the prior three-year average income, the $3,887 determined in Step 3 is multiplied by four, resulting in a tax of $15,548.

5. In Step 1, the tax on $14,000 base income (or 140 percent of the prior three-year average taxable income) was determined. In Step 4, the tax on the excess $71,000 was determined. Hence, the total tax for 1984 is determined as follows:

Tax from Step 1	$ 1,421
plus	
Tax from Step 4	15,548
Total tax	$16,969

Alternative minimum tax

The alternative minimum tax is imposed in cases where a taxpayer has very large capital gains and/or very high deductions (usually associated with tax shelters). When these items are so substantial as to reduce a very large gross income to a very small taxable income, the alternative minimum tax is imposed.

As the word "alternative" implies, this tax is imposed *instead of* the regular tax. Therefore, the alternative minimum tax is imposed only if it is greater than the regular tax.

The alternative minimum tax is imposed on alternative minimum taxable income (AMTI). AMTI is calculated as follows:

The starting point is adjusted gross income. If there was a net operating loss deduction involved in arriving at the adjusted gross income, that loss is eliminated. From this adjusted gross income is subtracted:

1. Alternative net operating loss deduction. This is calculated by taking into account the alternative minimum taxable income (instead of regular taxable income) in intervening years when a loss from a prior year is being carried over.

2. Distributions from trusts deemed distributed in prior years under the so-called throwback rule.

3. Alternative minimum tax itemized deductions. These are the itemized deductions claimed for the regular tax with a number of modifications (details below).

After the subtractions from adjusted gross income are made, the balance remaining is added to the total of the taxpayer's tax preference items (these are explained below). The resulting total is then reduced by an exemption amount. The exemption amount is $40,000 on a joint return; $30,000 on a separate return of an unmarried individual; and $20,000 on a separate return of a married individual or on the return of a trust or estate.

The amount remaining after the exemption is subtracted is the AMTI which is subject to a flat tax of 20 percent. This is the alternative minimum tax which is then compared to the regular tax. The taxpayer must pay the larger of the two taxes.

Itemized deductions As indicated above, certain deductions can be itemized to arrive at AMTI. These are:

1. Medical expenses in excess of 10 percent of adjusted gross income.

2. Casualty losses in excess of 10 percent of adjusted gross income.

171

3. Charitable contributions.

4. Gambling losses.

5. Qualified interest paid. This includes interest paid on a principal residence and on a residence used by the taxpayer, his or her spouse, brother, sister, ancestor, or lineal descendant. Interest up to the amount of net income from investments is also deductible.

6. Estate tax applicable to income in respect of a decedent included in the tax return.

7. Trust and estate deductions for charitable set-asides.

Items of tax preference The total of the items of tax preference is included in calculating AMTI. This is the major area of vulnerability to the alternative minimum tax.

Probably the most important item of tax preference is the 60% portion of long-term capital gains that is omitted from taxable income in calculating the regular tax. The other tax preference items are:

1. Depreciation (or accelerated cost recovery) deducted on real property that exceeds the amount deductible under the straight line method.

2. Depreciation (or accelerated cost recovery) deducted on personal property subject to a lease, to the extent it exceeds the deduction allowed under the straight line method.

3. The $100 or $200 of dividends that can be excluded by an individual.

4. Excess of fair market value of stock acquired under an incentive stock option over the exercise price of the option.

5. Circulation expenses of publications deducted to the extent they exceed the amount that would be deductible if they were amortized over three years.

6. Mining exploration and development costs to the extent the deduction exceeds the amount that would be allowed if they were amortized over ten years.

7. Deduction for a certified pollution facility under 60-month amortization to the extent it exceeds the amount that would be deductible if the 60-month amortization were not chosen.

8. Excess of intangible drilling costs over net income from oil and gas properties.

172 9. Depletion in excess of basis of property at end of year.

10. Reserves for bad debts of financial institutions.

Example

To illustrate how the alternative minimum tax works, assume the following financial data for 1984 for William Harrison, an unmarried individual:

Salary	$ 70,000
Net long-term capital gain	350,000
Dividends received	25,100
Interest received	35,000
Investment in real estate partnership	(70,000)
Medical expenses	24,800
Interest paid	40,000
Contributions made	55,000
Casualty loss	40,100
Other business-related expenses	30,000

During the year, Harrison exercised an incentive stock option. The fair market value of the stock exceeded the exercise price by $20,000. Also, included in the $70,000 loss in the real estate partnership was $25,000 of depreciation in excess of the amount allowable under straight line.

Harrison calculates his regular tax as follows:

Salary		$ 70,000
40% of long-term capital gain		140,000
Dividends received (minus $100 exclusion)		25,000
Interest received		35,000
Investment in real estate partnership		(70,000)
Adjusted gross income		$200,000
Itemized deductions		
Medical expenses ($24,800 minus 5% of $200,000, or $10,000)	$ 14,800	
Interest paid	40,000	
Contributions	55,000	
Casualty loss ($40,100 minus $100 deductible and minus 10% of $200,000)	20,000	
Other business related deductions	30,000	
Total itemized deductions	159,800	
Less: zero bracket amount	2,300	
Net itemized deductions		157,500
Adjusted gross income minus net itemized deductions		42,500
Exemption		1,000
Taxable income		$ 41,500
Regular tax on $41,500		$ 12,068

He calculates the alternative minimum tax as follows:

Adjusted gross income		$200,000
Itemized deductions:		
Medical expenses ($24,800 minus 10% of		
adjusted gross income of $200,000)	$ 4,800	
Interest paid	40,000	
Contributions	55,000	
Casualty loss	20,000	
Total itemized deductions		119,800
Adjusted gross income minus itemized		
deductions		80,200
Tax preferences:		
Dividend exclusions		100
60% of long-term capital gain		210,000
Excess depreciation		25,000
Fair market value of stock option in excess of		
exercise price		20,000
Total		335,300
Minus exemption		30,000
Alternative minimum taxable income (AMTI)		$305,300
Alternative minimum tax (20% of AMTI)		$ 61,060

Since Harrison's alternative minimum tax of $61,060 is greater than his regular tax of $12,068, he has to pay the alternative minimum tax instead of the regular tax.

Taxation of partnerships

Partnerships and other joint, unincorporated ownership forms (which, for tax purposes, are treated as partnerships) are not separate taxable entities. The partners, be they individuals, corporations or other entities, report their shares of the partnership's ordinary income or loss and capital gains and losses on their own tax returns.

Partnership income or loss passes directly to the partners. While most tax elections (e.g. installment sale treatment) must be made by the partnership rather than by its partners, the partnership is not a tax-paying entity. Types of income and deductions which have a special tax significance retain their special characteristics as they pass through the partnership conduit. Consider the following illustration.

Example

David, Melissa, Michael and Jeffery form a real estate partnership. At the end of 1984, their partnership records disclose the following items of income and expenses.

Rental income		$25,000
Tax exempt interest income from municipal bonds		10,000
Operating expenses (before depreciation)		17,000
Depreciation (ACRS recovery)		5,000
Complete write-off for personal property		2,000
Charitable contributions		1,000

On their personal income tax returns, each of the partners will report his share of the income and special items of the partnership. Actual distribution of funds is not required from the partnership to the partners; each partner is taxed on his *distributive* share of the profits or losses and special items for the partnership taxable year that ends within his taxable year. The partnership will file an income tax return (actually, an information return) and will pay no tax. The tax returns of the four individual partners will reflect the following items of taxable income and deduction:

			Partnership	Each 25% Partner
Tax exempt income			$10,000	$2,500
Rent income		$25,000		
Operating expense	$17,000			
ACRS recovery	5,000			
		$22,000		
Net rent income			3,000	$750 income
Complete write-off for personal property			2,000	$500 deduction
Contributions			1,000	$250 deduction

Each partner shares in the profits and losses of the partnership as well as in certain special items. Thus, tax-free income passes through to each partner as tax-free income. Each partner must report his own share of the partnership's charitable contributions.

Since each partner picks up his share of the partnership's income or loss, the effect that the ACRS deduction has on the profit picture is reflected on each partner's own tax return. If, for example, the partnership had ACRS deductions of $10,000, it would have had a net loss from real estate operations of $2,000 and each partner would have reported a $500 loss on his own tax return. Any cash flow that the partnership earned could be distributed to the partners without causing any additional tax to them.

A taxpayer may completely write off the cost of personal property up to $5,000. This amount is stepped up to $7,500 for the years 1988 and 1989, and to $10,000 in 1990 and thereafter (see Chapter 9). A partnership may write off the cost of personal property up to the limit allowed for that year. Each partner has allocated to him his proportionate share of that write-off. He adds the amount allocated to him to any other complete write-offs he has taken for that year on property he acquired, or to any other allocations he received from other partnerships. The total amount he can deduct on his tax return may not exceed the limit applicable to that year.

Limited partnerships

The discussion thus far has dealt with general partnerships. Tax rules for limited partnerships are similar to general partnership tax rules.

While a partner in a limited partnership is taxed on his portion of the gain from the partnership, the amount of loss which he is permitted to deduct is limited to his basis for his partnership interest (this is usually the total amount he has placed at risk of the business plus his share of partnership earnings and minus partnership losses allocable to him and earnings which he withdrew from the partnership).

In addition, each partner usually may add to his basis his share of the partnership liabilities. This, of course, increases the basis against which he may deduct losses.

For a general partner this rule presents no problem. Since he has unlimited liability, his share of all partnership liabilities increases his basis. The limited partner, however, does not have unlimited liability; his liability is limited to his investment. Thus, conceptually, he has no share in the partnership's liabilities.

There is, however, a special rule dealing with nonrecourse liabilities (those liabilities on which the borrower is not personally liable; the creditor can only take the property mortgaged or other property which otherwise secures the loan if the loan is not repaid). These liabilities, to which the investor is not "at risk" (i.e., has no personal liability), cannot be added to an investor's basis for the purpose of determining deductible loss. This "at risk" rule applies to all investors, whether or not they are involved in a partnership.

The "at risk" rule does not apply to real estate investments, however. Thus, the mortgage is added to basis even though there is no personal liability (the mortgagee can look only to the property itself in the case of default).

The real estate exception to the "at risk" rule is of special significance to real estate limited partnerships. IRS has agreed that when a partnership has a nonrecourse loan outstanding, it is not a partnership liability but rather a liability of all the partners, including the limited partners. Hence, in a limited real estate partnership, the nonrecourse mortgage is allocated to both the general and the limited partners, thus increasing each limited partner's basis for his partnership interest. Losses generated by a real estate partnership can be allocated to the limited partnership investors. In determining how much of the allocated loss is deductible by him, a limited partner includes in his basis his share of the partnership's nonrecourse mortgage.

A fuller explanation of the application of the nonrecourse loan to the limited partner's basis is in Appendix C.

Partnership tax returns

Although partnerships do not pay income taxes, they are required to file information returns. A penalty is imposed for failure to file a timely partnership return (unless reasonable cause for such failure is shown). The penalty is $50 per month or fraction thereof (not to exceed five months' penalty) that the return is late. The penalty is then multiplied by the number of partners involved during the partnership's taxable year for which the return was due.

The statute of limitations for assessing tax deficiencies on partners and for claiming tax refunds by partners is lengthened beyond the regular limitation in some cases. This extension of the statute of limitations applies only to "federally registered partnerships"—those partnerships in which interests were offered for sale in an offering requiring Securities and Exchange Commission (SEC) registration or which are or have been subject to annual reporting requirements of the SEC.

Under the regular statute of limitations, assessment and refund time limitations are generally three years from the time a partner's tax return was due. The due date of the partnership information return is irrelevant for this purpose. For federally registered partnerships, the statute of limitations applied to each partner is four years after the *partnership return* is filed. This longer statute of limitations applies only to partnership items on each partner's personal tax return that arose in taxable years of the partnership beginning after 1978. To repeat—this new statute of limitations rule applies only in the case of federally registered partnerships.

After 1984, if a partner exchanges all or part of his partnership interest and receives amounts attributable to the partnership's unrealized receivables or appreciated inventory, the partnership must file an information return with IRS before January 31 of the year following the transaction. There is a $50 penalty for failure to file each information return. The reason for the information return is to make sure that the partner picks up the amounts allocable to the unrealized receivables or appreciated inventory as ordinary income (other gains on disposition of a partnership interest are treated as capital gains).

Income tax aspects of corporate ownership

The corporation is a separate *legal* and *taxpaying* entity. It has its own tax rate structure applying to ordinary income as follows:

Taxable Income	Tax Rates
$0 to $25,000	15%
Over $25,000 to $50,000	18%
Over $50,000 to $75,000	30%
Over $75,000 to $100,000	40%
Over $100,000	46%

After 1983, if a corporation has taxable income in one year of more than $1,000,000, it is subject to an additional tax. This additional tax is 5 percent of the taxable income over $1,000,000, to a maximum tax of $20,250. The $20,250 represents the maximum tax savings available in the first four corporate tax brackets (when the rates in those brackets are compared to the 46 percent rate applicable to income in excess of $100,000). In Congress's view, the tax savings in the first four brackets should apply only to small businesses. So, if a corporation has income in excess of $1,000,000, Congress wants to deprive it of the tax-rate advantages of the first four brackets.

If a real estate corporation has losses, created very often by virtue of large deductions for depreciation, these tax losses may not be utilized by the individual owners of the corporation on their own income tax returns. If such property was owned directly by the individuals, however, they would be entitled to use the excess real estate deductions to reduce their taxable income from other sources.

Although the corporation's losses are not available to its stockholders, a corporation having an accumulated deficit and current income tax losses, but also having an available cash flow might be able to make cash distributions to its shareholders that would not be taxable to them. These distributions would not be taxable at all to the extent that they did not exceed the shareholders' bases for their corporate stock. The rule is that a corporation which has *neither* current nor accumulated earnings and profits (a tax concept related to but not exactly the same as taxable income) may make distributions to its shareholders which will not be taxed as dividends. Such distributions are treated as a return of capital and, therefore, are not taxable at all to the extent that they reimburse the corporate shareholder for his investment in the stock of the corporation. Distributions received which exceed the tax basis for the stock are taxable, but as capital gains.

In determining a corporation's earnings and profits, for corporations' taxable years beginning after June 30, 1972, only straight line depreciation will be allowed. This does not mean that accelerated depreciation will not be allowed to be used to determine the taxable income of the corporation; it will be allowed to be used if the corporation is eligible to use it. But straight line will have to be used to find out how much earnings and profits the corporation has in order to determine how distributions to the stockholders are to be taxed. This means that while a corporation may have a loss due to accelerated depreciation, it may still have earnings and profits for determining whether a distribution to its stockholders is to be taxed as a dividend rather than a return of capital investment (or capital gain where the basis for the stockholder's stock has already been recovered via prior distributions).

For property acquired in 1981 or thereafter, the only way a taxpayer can have accelerated depreciation deductions is by using the ACRS recovery system (see Chapter 9). Because the concept of useful life is not used in ACRS (the deductions are calculated from government tables based on the classification of the property), the law provides specific useful lives on which the straight line depreciation is to be calculated. The straight line calculation for each year is the amount by which the earnings and profits are to be reduced that year, even though the larger ACRS deduction is the one that is used to calculate the taxable income for that year. The straight line lives that must be used to determine the amount which reduces earnings and profits are as follows:

3-year property	5 years
5-year property	12 years
10-year property	25 years
15-year property (public utility and real estate)	35 years
18-year real property	40 years*

*For taxable years beginning after September 30, 1984.

Should the real estate corporation realize taxable profits, however, any distribution of such after-tax profits to the shareholders as dividends will be taxed again. These earnings would be taxed first to the corporation and then again to the individuals.

Examples

1. In 1984, X Corporation has taxable income of $10,000. Its tax on that amount is $1,500. It distributes the remaining $7,500 to Mr. A, its sole shareholder, as a dividend. Mr. A must include the $7,500 in his own taxable income and pay a second tax.

To some extent this second tax can be avoided by the payment of salaries to the corporation's owners, provided such owners actually perform services and their compensation is reasonable. This payment reduces the income upon which the corporation pays taxes, thus removing these salaries from one layer of taxation and, to that extent, results in a single tax on that salary income.

2. In the preceding example, in which X Corporation had taxable income of $10,000, if Mr. A had performed services for the corporation and received a salary of $10,000 (or if his salary were increased by $10,000), the corporation would have no taxable income since it would get a $10,000 deduction for salaries paid. It would pay no tax but would distribute the entire $10,000 to Mr. A as salary. He would include the $10,000 in his own taxable income.

In this connection, it is important to recognize that if Mr. A's salary had been increased to a point at which it is deemed to be unreasonably high, the unreasonable portion would not be deductible. Hence, the unreasonable portion would be treated as if it were a dividend payment to Mr. A. Even if the salary is not unreasonably high, it may not be desirable for Mr. A to be taxed on an additional $10,000 if he is already in a high personal income tax bracket. It may be more desirable to have the corporation pay the tax and make no distribution of dividends to its shareholders. This raises a different tax problem.

If, even after the deduction of reasonable salaries to the shareholder-employees, the corporation still has taxable profits which it desires to shelter from double taxation by refusing to pay dividends, it may face another corporate tax. Such excess accumulation of earnings, beyond the reasonable needs of the business and in excess of $250,000, which are accumulated to avoid the tax on the shareholders, is subject to an additional tax. This is an annual tax at the rate of 27½ percent of the first $100,000 and 38½ percent of any excess of earnings beyond $100,000 unreasonably accumulated during the year. It is called an accumulated earnings tax.

Example

X Corporation has accumulated earnings of $250,000 on January 1, 1984. During 1984 it earns $50,000 *after all taxes* including federal income taxes.

Unless it can show a reasonable business need for the $300,000 accumulation of earnings or the lack of a purpose to avoid income tax to shareholders, the corporation will be subject to an additional tax of $13,750, 27½ percent of $50,000. If X Corporation pays a dividend of $50,000 to its shareholders, this tax will not be imposed. (This is a simplified version of a very complicated subject. For purposes of illustration certain technical adjustments have been omitted.)

Corporate tax on tax preferences

In addition to its regular tax, a corporation pays a tax of 15 percent on its tax preferences to the extent that they exceed the greater of (1) $10,000, or (2) the regular corporate income tax. Tax preferences are discussed in connection with the calculation of the alternative minimum tax for individuals in an earlier portion of this chapter.

Multiple corporations

As indicated above, there are four $25,000 tax brackets for a corporation (with tax rates ranging from 15 to 40 percent). Beyond $100,000 of income, all income is taxable at 46 percent. (If taxable income exceeds $1,000,000 an additional tax—up to $20,250—is also payable.) In addition, each corporation may accumulate up to $250,000 in earnings and profits without fear of being subject to the 27½-percent and 38½-percent penalty taxes explained above.

Consequently, if a corporate business can be divided into several corporations, each would have its own four brackets and each would have its own $250,000 "safe" earnings and profits accumulation. For example, if one corporation had $200,000 in taxable income, the second $100,000 would be subject to a 46-percent tax. If the same business were divided into four corporations, each would have only $50,000 of taxable income. Each would pay 15 percent tax on its first $25,000 of income, and 18 percent on its second $25,000. Obviously, the total tax paid by the four corporations would be considerably less than the tax on $200,000 earned by one corporation.

To prevent this practice, Congress treats certain groups of corporations (controlled by the same five or fewer persons) as if they were one corporation. Their incomes are combined and they calculate the tax as if the entire income were earned by one corporation. Similarly, this group of corporations as a whole is entitled to a total of $250,000 of "safe" accumulations of earnings and profits.

The S corporation

It was pointed out above that a corporation is a separate entity for tax purposes and its profits and losses do not pass through to its shareholders (except by way of dividends, which are first taxed on the corporate level). There is one form of corporation, however, that is treated much like a partnership. Its profits and losses *do* pass through to the shareholders without first being subject to a tax on the corporate level. This corporation is the S corporation.

Although the S corporation has been in the tax law since 1958, until 1982 it was not very useful for real estate operations. The reason? It could not have more than 20 percent of its gross receipts in the form of passive income. Passive income included rents (as well as dividends, interest, royalties, and capital gains), so that ruled out most real estate businesses.

Under a revision to the S corporation rules enacted in 1982, the passive income restriction no longer applies to taxable years beginning after 1982—unless the corporation had accumulated earnings from years prior to 1983. Thus, new corporations (which automatically have no prior earnings and profits) can elect S corporation treatment and not worry about passive income. (Corporations with pre-1983 accumulated earnings may not have passive income in excess of 25 percent of gross receipts in more than three consecutive years. If they do, they lose their S corporation status. And in the years they do have excess passive income, the corporation itself is subject to a tax. But these corporations can distribute their accumulated earnings and avoid the passive income restriction in the future.)

The income and losses of an S corporation pass through to the stockholders in proportion to their holdings (calculated on a daily basis during the year); the corporation itself pays no tax. The losses that pass through to each shareholder are deductible by him only to the extent of the basis of his stock in the corporation and the basis of any debt owed to him by the corporation. If the loss allocated to a shareholder exceeds his basis, the excess is deferred. It is deductible by him in a future year in which he acquires sufficient basis to cover the loss (as he would should he get an allocation of profits in a future year).

Corporate capital gains and losses also pass through to the shareholders as capital gains or losses. Specific items that affect a shareholder's tax return—e.g., charitable contributions, tax-exempt interest—pass through to the shareholder in that form.

An S corporation is a regular corporation (for state corporate law purposes) organized in the United States. To become an S corporation for tax purposes, the corporation must elect that status by filing a form with IRS. All the shareholders must consent to this election. An S corporation may not have more than 35 shareholders, none of whom may be a nonresident alien. It may have only one class of stock (but that class of stock may be divided into voting and nonvoting stock). All the shareholders must be individuals, estates, or certain classes of trusts. Furthermore, the corporation may not be part of an affiliated group eligible to file consolidated returns.

Taxation of corporate capital gains

Short-term, long-term and Section 1231 gains and loses for corporations are determined in the same manner as for individuals (see section on individual capital gains earlier in this chapter).

Net Section 1231 gains are included in long-term capital gains and *net* Section 1231 losses are deducted from ordinary income. Long-term gains and losses are aggregated separately, short-term gains and losses are aggregated separately and the results in the two categories are aggregated if one is a gain and the other is a loss. The final results are net short-term and/or long-term gains and losses.

Corporate net short-term capital gains These are added to ordinary income in the same manner as for individuals.

Corporate net long-term capital gains These are treated in one of two ways (the corporation chooses the method that results in the lower tax).

1. The full amount of the net long-term capital gains is added to ordinary income and taxed at ordinary income rates.

2. The corporate alternative tax is used. A flat 28-percent rate is applied to the net long-term capital gains. This tax is then added to the corporate tax computed on the ordinary income alone.

To understand the significance of the two methods, it must be remembered that the first $25,000 of corporate ordinary income is subject to a 15-percent tax and the next $25,000 to an 18-percent tax. Thus, the first $50,000 of corporate ordinary income is subject to lower tax rates than the 28-percent flat rate of the alternative tax for corporate capital gains. The alternative tax would not be used if the total corporate income did not exceed $50,000 *after* the capital gains were added.

If, by adding the capital gains to the ordinary income, the total exceeds $50,000, the excess would be taxable at 30 percent, which is greater than the alternative tax on capital gains. At that point, it is necessary to determine whether it is cheaper to use the alternative tax. When ordinary income is very small and the capital gain is relatively large, even though the total exceeds $50,000, it may still be cheaper to avoid the alternative tax because a great part of the capital gain would be subject to ordinary income rates of less than 28 percent.

It is not permissible to add part of the long-term capital gain to the corporation's ordinary income and apply the alternative tax to the other part. The *entire* long-term capital gain must either be added to ordinary income or be subjected to the alternative tax.

Examples

1. In 1984, White Corporation has $10,000 of ordinary income and a long-term capital gain of $5,000. Obviously, it will add the $5,000 to its ordinary income because that $5,000 will be subject to a tax of ònly 15 percent.

2. In 1984, Black Corporation has ordinary income of $80,000 and a long-term capital gain of $25,000. Again the choice is obvious. It will use the alternative tax of 28 percent for its $25,000 capital gain. Otherwise, $20,000

of the capital gain would be subject to a 40-percent tax and $5,000 to a 46-percent tax.

3. In 1984, Gray Corporation has ordinary income of $15,000 and a long-term capital gain of $40,000. Although, by adding the capital gain to ordinary income, $5,000 of the $55,000 total is subject to a 30-percent tax (which is greater than the alternative tax rate of 28 percent), it is still cheaper to add the capital gain to the ordinary income.

If the ordinary income approach is used, there is a total income of $55,000, taxable as follows:

$25,000 at 15%	$3,750
25,000 at 18%	4,500
5,000 at 30%	1,500
Total tax	$9,750

If the alternative tax is used, the tax would be computed as follows:

$15,000 of ordinary income at 15%	$ 2,250
40,000 capital gain at 28%	$11,200
Total tax	$13,450

Corporate net capital losses   Whether the corporation ends up with a net long-term loss, a net short-term loss or both, it cannot deduct any part of that loss against ordinary income of any year.

Net capital losses become carrybacks and carryovers in the form of *short-term* capital losses (regardless of whether they arose as long- or short-term). The loss may be carried back three years and forward five in the following manner.

If the loss arose in 1984, it would first be carried back to 1981. It is then determined whether, if that loss arose as a short-term capital loss in 1981, the corporation's taxable income would have been different. (If the corporation had net capital gains, long- or short-term in 1981, the short-term loss carried back to that year would affect that year's taxable income since part or all of those gains would be offset by the loss. If it had no net long- or short-term capital gains in 1981, the short-term capital loss carried back to 1981 would have no effect on 1981 taxable income.) If the loss carried back to 1981 *does* reduce the 1981 tax, the taxpayer corporation is entitled to a refund.

If the corporation is unable to use all of the carryback loss in 1981, the portion not used is then carried to 1982 and the procedure used for 1981 is repeated.

To the extent the loss is not used in 1982, it is carried to 1983 and again the procedure is repeated.

If there is still an unused capital loss carryback after applying it to the prior three years, it becomes a carryforward to the succeeding five years.

Thus, continuing our example, the unused loss would be available as a short-term capital loss in 1985. If there were not enough capital gains in 1985 to absorb the entire carryforward loss, the balance would be carried to 1986 as a short-term capital loss and then to 1987, 1988, and 1989 if necessary. After 1989, if the loss had not been absorbed by offsetting capital gains, it would no longer be available to the corporation for any purpose.

Corporate dispositions

Once the corporate form has been chosen as the form of ownership, not only are there tax problems during ownership (e.g. nonavailability of corporate losses to offset individual income) but additional tax problems also arise at the time it is decided to dispose of the property.

If the corporation sells the property, the gain or loss will be taxed to it, the corporate entity. What happens to the after-tax profits on the sale that remain in the corporation? They could be subject to a second tax if distributed to the shareholders. However, some tax relief provisions are available to those who have taken the proper steps to qualify for special corporate liquidations. In other cases, by way of corporate reorganization, tax may be deferred (as is the case of an exchange of like-kind properties) and a shareholder's investment diversified. Again, it is necessary to know the rules and make preparations to qualify. The rules and strategies involved in using corporate liquidations and reorganizations are set forth in Appendix E.

Chapter 8

Acquisitions

8

When an investment in real estate is made, a major decision involves the form of ownership.

If the property is being acquired by a single investor, he may take the property in his own name as sole owner or jointly with his spouse. Or, he may decide it would be better to have the property owned by a corporation even though he owns all the corporate stock. Where more than one person will own the property, it may be held in partnership, joint tenancy, tenancy in common or in a corporation. It is also possible to hold property in a trust.

When more than one form of ownership is available, which one should an investor choose? The answer is not simple. It depends on the investor's immediate and long-term goals, his current personal tax position and his expected tax position in the future (plus good guesses about the state of the tax law and the economy in the future). No intelligent decision can be made, however, without an understanding of the various forms of ownership and the tax consequences of each.

Another important factor in the acquisition of property is the establishment of *basis*. This is the starting point for the calculation of the important cost recovery (depreciation) deductions and the determination of gain or loss on ultimate disposition of property. Establishing basis depends on the application of the appropriate rule (drawn from a complex network of rules concerning different forms of acquisition). The second part of this chapter is an explanation of the rules of basis and their ramifications.

Forms and nature of ownership

The basic forms of ownership were discussed in Chapter 2. Following is a summary of the rights inherent in the various forms of ownership:

Form of Ownership	Rights Owner Has	Duration
Fee Simple	All	Infinite
Lease	Defined in terms of agreement	Usually terms of years
Easement	Specified by agreement, usage or state law	Infinite or specified
Life estate	Defined by agreement	Specified life

At this point, the nature of the *owner,* rather than the nature of his ownership *interest,* will be considered.

Individual ownership

Individual ownership refers to a person owning property in his or her own name. The danger of unlimited liability is often a deterrent to the use of this form of ownership. Where feasible, insurance may reduce or eliminate this risk. The factors which often tip the scales in favor of individual ownership are the income tax rules and the freedom of action it allows in making decisions regarding acquisition, management and disposition of the investment. However, an individual may have only a limited amount of capital at his disposal for use in any particular venture. For this reason, one of the other forms of ownership, which makes greater sums of capital available, is often preferred.

From a tax viewpoint, an advantage of individual ownership of investment or income-producing real property is the availability of substantial depreciation deductions which can be used to offset the owner's taxable income from other sources.

Example

Ms. A is unmarried and has net taxable income after deductions and exemptions of $55,300 in 1984. Her income tax bill on this amount is $16,115. If she were to invest in a propety which showed a tax loss of $30,000 due to large depreciation deductions, her taxable income would be reduced to $25,300 and her tax would be only $4,655—a savings (and thus an increase in available cash flow) of $11,460.

It would not be necessary for Ms. A to invest $30,000 in cash to produce a tax loss of that amount. Basis for real estate usually includes any mortgages on the property. So, if an investor could buy a building for $20,000 cash and $80,000 debt, the basis for depreciation of the building would still be $100,000.

Of course, if Ms. A had created a corporation and the corporation had purchased the property, the tax loss would not be available for use on her personal return even if she were the sole owner of the corporation. She would not have saved any personal income tax for that year. However, she might be able to use an S corporation and pass the loss through to herself. (The requirements for qualifying as an S corporation are discussed in Chapter 7.)

Joint ownership

Joint ownership is a type of concurrent ownership of property by several persons in which each joint owner possesses an undivided interest in the whole property. The joint ownership may be set up with or without a right of survivorship.

There are several types of joint ownership. A tenancy in common is one which does not involve any rights of survivorship. Upon the death of one of the co-owners, his heirs or his estate becomes the owner of his share.

In a joint tenancy there *is* the right of survivorship. Upon the death of one of the co-owners, his share passes to the other co-owner or owners. Sometimes this is referred to as a "joint tenancy with right of survivorship." Generally, no probate proceedings are required to effect the transfer to the surviving joint owners. Where a joint tenancy exists between spouses, it is often called a "tenancy by the entirety."

Who is entitled to the income from property held in joint ownership depends upon the provisions of law in the state where the property is located.

As in the case of individual ownership, the profits or losses of the jointly-owned property pass directly to the owners according to the state laws for picking up income or losses.

Tenancy in common is often preferable to a formal partnership because each owner picks up his income or loss directly, without regard to his co-owners. Each owner can make his own tax elections (e.g. accounting method, reinvestment of funds received as condemnation awards, fire insurance and other involuntary conversion proceeds). In a partnership, the partnership files an information return in which each partner's share of income and losses is revealed. Tax elections are made by the partnership and are binding on all partners. If one partner's tax return is examined (perhaps because of nonpartnership items on his individual return), the other partners may find that their returns will be examined too. With tenants in common, this result is less likely.

A problem arises, however, when the jointly-owned property is, in effect, a business (such as an active ownership of rental property where the co-owners also manage the property). In that case, although the legal form of ownership is a tenancy in common or a joint tenancy, for tax purposes the owners will be treated as partners and a partnership tax return will be required.

Since joint ownership is so similar to ownership by a partnership, many of the advantages and disadvantages are identical. However, those forms of joint ownership with rights of survivorship offer the additional advantage of avoiding probate on the death of one of the co-owners. At death, the decedent's interest passes automatically with no need for court proceedings.

If a joint tenancy is not between spouses, for estate tax purposes, the entire value of the joint property could be included in the gross estate of the first joint tenant to die. However, this amount is reduced by the percentage of consideration that was *not* supplied by the deceased joint tenant in acquiring the property.

However, for property acquired by husband and wife as joint tenants, only half the value of the joint property is included in the deceased spouse's estate regardless which spouse paid for the property. No formal gift had to have been made.

Community property

Under the laws of some states, property owned by married individuals is deemed to be property of both of them. Generally, property owned by them prior to their marriage is separate property and property acquired after the marriage is community property. Laws of states applying this type of ownership will vary and therefore will not be discussed in detail here. It is important, however, for the real estate broker to know and be able to explain to clients the effect of community property laws if they are applied in his state.

Federal income taxation of property held in this form of ownership, as in the case of other types of joint ownership, depends on state rules as to who is entitled to the income and who is liable for the expenses.

Partnerships

Partnerships have become a very important form of real estate ownership with the increasing popularity of syndications and "tax shelters." The partnership form of ownership permits the passing through of losses and income directly to the partners. Furthermore, the use of a limited partnership limits the investors' liabilities much in the same manner as the liabilties of corporate shareholders are limited. In real estate limited partnerships nonrecourse loans to the partnership can increase the limited partners' bases for their investments far beyond the amounts of their actual cash investments. (This is not true for other than real estate limited partnerships insofar as nonrecourse loans are concerned.)

The rules pertaining to limited partnerships are very complex, especially in view of recent IRS actions taken to curb what the government sees as abuses in this area. A comprehensive analysis of limited partnerships will be found in Appendix C.

Partnerships include all sorts of *unincorporated* businesses owned by more than one individual or entity. (In most states, corporations and other partnerships may also be partners in a partnership.)

Among the reasons for using a partnership to own investments is the increased availability of capital and skills arising from an association of more than one individual. A group of investors may be able to purchase a larger piece of property than can a single investor and have available a wider range of business skills, including managerial and financial talent.

On the other hand, it may be difficult to arrive at a consensus in making decisions for the group investment. Unless one member is given authority to act, the group may be hamstrung in efforts to act quickly to take advantage of rapidly changing business or market conditions.

Partnerships terminate at the death of a partner in absence of special arrangements to the contrary. Heirs and successors are usually entitled to an accounting for profits, but have no claim on specific partnership assets.

Partner's capital contributions   As a general rule, no gain or loss is recognized by either the partner or the partnership on contributions of either cash or property. The basis of the partner's interest in the partnership is the amount of money contributed plus that partner's adjusted basis in the property transferred. The partnership assumes the partner's basis in the property transferred.

If property is contributed to a partnership by a partner and no gain or loss is recognized and if the property is transferred to the partnership after March 31, 1984, special rules apply when the partnership disposes of that property:

1. If the partner contributed unrealized receivables, the partnership will realize ordinary income or loss on the disposition of these.

2. If the property was an inventory item in the hands of a partner (i.e., property held for sale in the ordinary course of business), the partnership will realize ordinary income or loss if it disposes of the property during the five-year period beginning on the date the property was contributed to the partnership. (This assumes, of course, that in the hands of the partnership the property is not an inventory item. This could occur when a partner who is a developer transfers buildings to the partnership which the partnership holds for rental income purposes. If the partnership held the property as inventory, it would realize ordinary income in any event even without the new provisions of the law.

191

3. If the contributed property had a built-in capital loss at the time of contribution (i.e., its fair market value was lower than the contributing partner's basis for that property), if the partnership realizes a loss on the disposition of the property, the loss will be a capital loss to the extent of the capital loss built into the contribution by the partner. This rule applies to losses occurring during the five-year period beginning on the date of the contribution of the property to the partnership.

In order to prevent inequities from arising between partners when appreciated property with a low tax basis is contributed to the partnership, the law permits the partnership agreement to provide for special allocations among the partners of depreciation, depletion or gain or loss with respect to the property.

However, if the partnership agreement did not make the special allocations, the contributed property was treated as having been purchased from the contributing partner. This meant that depreciation, depletion, gain, or loss arising from the contributed property was allocated among the partners in their general profit and loss-sharing ratios. Congress felt that there was room for abuse when the partnership agreement did not make the special allocations—gain might be allocated to a low-bracket partner, loss to a high-bracket partner. So, for the property transferred to a partnership after March 21, 1984, the special allocations that previously were "permitted" are now mandatory. IRS is to issue regulations explaining how the allocations are to be made.

In the formation of a real estate partnership a problem frequently arises when a promoter/developer receives a partnership capital interest in exchange for services. The IRS regulations take the position that the promoter/developer has received ordinary income to the extent of the fair market value of his services. This result might be avoided if the promoter/developer receives a partnership profits interest (the right to share in future partnership income) rather than a capital interest. In this manner, the tax would be postponed until he actually shares in the partnership income. However, the Tax Court and the Seventh Circuit Court have held that the promoter/developer will be taxed on the value of the income interest *upon receipt* if the profit interest has an ascertainable market value. (In the particular case the courts were considering, the promoter sold his interest three weeks after he got it, so the value was easily established.)

To the extent that an acquired interest in partnership capital results in taxable income, that partner's basis is increased by the amount of such income.

Partnership Limitation of liability and income tax consequences are determined by the nature of the partnership. A general partnership is one in which all partners share in profits or losses. There is no limitation of liability; partnership liabilities, to the extent they cannot be satisfied out of partnership assets, become claims against the individual partners. The partnership files an income tax return which is merely an information return. It pays no federal income tax. All of the income and deductions of a partnership flow through to the income tax returns of its partners.

A disadvantage of both the individual and general partnership form of ownership is the lack of limited liability. Each of the general partners places not only his partnership investment, but also all his other business investments and his personal assets as well, at the risk of the partnership venture. Each partner may be legally responsible for the business actions of *all* of the other partners in their conduct of the partnership business.

Another form of partnership is the limited partnership which is composed of both limited and general partners. The limited partnership must have at least one general partner. It is the general partner or partners who usually conduct the business of the limited partnership. (A limited partner may not participate in active management without risking his status in the limited partner classification and may then incur liabilities as a general partner. (Each limited partner's liability is restricted to the amount he has invested or is required to invest. Claims against the partnership which exceed partnership assets may be collected only from the general partners.

Possibly the greatest advantage of the limited partnership is that it enables larger amounts of capital to be invested than a single investor could raise on his own, while providing limited liability for the bulk of its investors without the formalities and often onerous tax burdens of the corproate form. Disadvantages of both the general and limited partnership may arise when their size becomes too great for efficient operation. Further, some complications may occur with respect to the transferability of the interests of retiring and deceased partners.

Syndicates

A syndicate is a combination of investors. It may be set up in the form of a corporation, a general partnership or a limited partnership.

Trusts

A trust is a legal arrangement sometimes used as a vehicle to hold property. It is not itself a legal entity; the trust *itself* does not own property. Rather, the trustee, sometimes called the fiduciary, is the legal owner of all trust property. He holds it for the benefit of someone else, the beneficiary. The person who sets up the trust arrangement by giving the property to the trustee to hold in trust is the grantor, settlor or creator.

Every trust must have one or more beneficiaries. They may get income from the trust and sometimes deductions. A beneficiary can have an income interest or a remainder interest in the trust property. If he has an income interest, he has a right to some or all of the trust's income as it is earned. If he has a remainder interest, he has a right to receive trust property at the termination of the trust.

Trusts are often used to separate the burdens of management from the benefits of ownership. For example, if a person wants to make a gift of income-producing real estate to someone who would not be capable or qualified to manage it (or to hire competent management) and to decide if and when the property should be sold or exchanged, the gift might be made to someone whose business acumen is respected by the donor, *in trust,* for the benefit of the intended beneficiary. The trustee will manage, or hire someone to manage, the property and make decisions about changing investments, while the beneficiary will receive the net income after expenses.

Some trusts are created by will; others are created by written instruments or deeds during the lifetime of the grantor, as *intervivos* (or lifetime) gifts. An advantage of the trust as a gift vehicle is that it can be used as an arrangement for testamentary disposition of assets yet to be set into operation during the life of the grantor. Thus, he can view, during his lifetime, the operation of his testamentary plan. If he has retained the right to revoke or to change the trust, he may alter his testamentary plan if it does not work as he had anticipated.

Since the powers of the trustee are set forth in the trust instrument and in the law of a particular state, the trust form is sometimes a little cumbersome in its operation. As with a corporation which may act only via its authorized officers, persons dealing with a trust should always be sure that the trustee is authorized to perform whatever acts he claims are within the scope of his authority. Consequently, copies of the trust instrument may often be required.

Federal income taxation of trusts is a rather complex topic. The income of a trust is sometimes taxed to the trustee; he pays the tax from the funds he holds in trust and not from his own personal funds. Sometimes it is taxed to the beneficiary and sometimes part of the trust income is taxed to the beneficiary and part to the trustee. In other instances trust income may even be taxed to the grantor. The determining factors are the terms of the trust instrument and sometimes local law. If the grantor gives property to a trustee but retains too much control over the property, then trust income will be taxed to him as though he still owned the property.

When the trust instrument requires all the income to be distributed to the beneficiary, that beneficiary will usually be taxed on all the trust's income, even if he has not actually received it. If, however, the trustee has discretion to distribute income to the beneficiary or hold it in the trust, the beneficiary is taxed only on the amount he actually receives and the trustee pays the tax on the income that is retained. A subsequent distribution of the income on which the trust was taxed may require an additional tax to be paid by the beneficiary. This is called the throw-back rule. Under this rule, if the trust paid less tax on the income it retained than the beneficiary would have paid had the income been distributed instead of retained, the difference in tax is paid upon ultimate distribution of the retained income.

Depreciation on property held by a trustee is generally allocated among the beneficiaries and the trustee in the same proportion in which the income is allocated. If local law or the trust instrument provides that the trustee must set aside a reserve for depreciation, the depreciation deduction is allocated to the trustee to the extent of trust income he retains. These principles are illustrated as follows.

Examples

1. A sets up a trust with T as the trustee and B as the beneficiary. According to the trust instrument, all the trust income is required to be distributed to B each year. In 1984, trust income consists of rent income of $7,000. Deductible expenses before depreciation amount to $4,000 and depreciation amounts to $1,000.

Here, the net income before depreciation is $3,000—$7,000 income minus $4,000 expenses. B is entitled to receive this $3,000. Were it not for the special rule allocating the depreciation deduction to the person getting the income, B would have to pay tax on $3,000 and the deduction for depreciation would go to the trustee since he is the legal owner of the property. Since the trustee has no income, the deduction would be wasted. Applying the special rule requires the allocation of all the depreciation deduction to the person getting the income. Therefore, B is required to pay tax on only $2,000—$3,000 net income less $1,000 depreciation deduction. T, as trustee, has zero taxable income and pays no tax.

2. If, using the facts above, T had been required by the trust instrument or by local law to set aside $1,000 as a reserve for depreciation, then B would only be entitled to receive $2,000—$3,000 income less $1,000 set aside for depreciation. B would pay tax on that $2,000. T, as trustee, would have $1,000 of income allocated to him and also $1,000 of depreciation expense, for a net result of zero taxable income and no tax due.

3. If the tax instrument had given T the right to withhold or distribute income to B at his own discretion and local law imposed no requirement as to a reserve for depreciation, the result for tax purposes would depend on how much, if any, of the trust income was actually distributed to B. If T distributed half of the net income to B, then B would be entitled to half the depreciation deduction. The final result, using the same facts, would be that the $2,000 would be taxable: half ($1,000) to B and the other half ($1,000) to T.

Corporate ownership

A corporation is a legal entity chartered by a state. (Each state has its own procedural rules that must be followed to create a corporation.) The corporation is a fictional person with certain unusual attributes such as unlimited life. It is a form of ownership particularly suited for use when large amounts of capital are required or desirable. A corporation enables centralized management to direct the investments of numerous owners called shareholders. The owners elect a board of directors which is responsible for the overall policy decisions of the corporation. It, in turn, appoints officers who are in charge of the corporation's everyday activities.

The corporate form is also available for small groups of owners—even one owner. Because it is a legal person, the corporation is often used to shield its owners from the dangers of business liabilities or reversals.

Example

X Corporation is owned solely by Mr. A. Mr. A buys an old house at 2 Main Street in his own name. X Corporation buys the house next door at 4 Main Street. Some children injure themselves on the broken steps leading up to each house.

The children who were injured on the steps leading to 2 Main, owned by Mr. A, can sue him for all he's worth. This includes assets he owns personally as well as all his investments in business, other corporations, etc. The children injured on the steps of 4 Main, owned by the corporation, can only sue the corporation for all of *its* assets. They cannot get any of Mr. A's other assets (unless he was personally negligent), neither his personal assets nor his other business assets, *even though he is the sole owner of X Corporation.*

This attribute of limited liability, the risking of only those assets held by the corporation and not the shareholders' other assets, is the most frequently cited reason for using a corporation to hold property. For example, should the income from a parcel of real estate diminish so that its expenses exceed its income, the mortgage holder may not recover from the individual stockholders of the corporation, unless, of course, they have given personal guarantees of payment.

The fact that the stockholders are often called upon to guarantee personally the debts of a corporation should not be overlooked. Many times, for example, a corporation is formed upon advice to "limit liability." Yet, under practical circumstances, the stockholders must personally endorse the notes. As a result, the limitation of liability is not really available, and the formation of the corporation may have deprived the individuals of the tax losses that would have been available to them to offset their personal income, or may result in double taxation.

It should also be remembered that the limitation of liability may be accomplished by means other than incorporating. A person holding property as an individual may arrange for the mortgage debt to apply only to the mortgaged property and not to any of his personal or other business assets. Similarly, he may take out liability insurance to cover possible injuries to people caused by defects in the premises. The cost of such insurance might be prohibitive, especially in a run-down or slum area.

Another aspect of the corporate form is its continuity. The life of a corporation may be set up as perpetual or for a fixed term. Death of one or more shareholders does not require that corporate activity be stilled. Corporate life goes on with the estate of the deceased or his beneficiaries as shareholders.

Another advantage is that management can be vested in representatives of the owners who usually operate without unanimous consent, thus permitting widely split ownership (including minors) without making management decisions cumbersome or impractical.

S corporations Certain corporations may take on special status for tax purposes. Provisions for this special status are found in Subchapter S of the Internal Revenue Code. These corporations have all of the nontax aspects of regular corporations, but if certain requirements are met, their income may escape taxation at the corporate level. Instead, the profits and losses are passed through to the stockholders who then report their proportionate shares of the corporate profits or losses on their individual tax returns. The rules applying to S corporations are explained in Chapter 7.

S corporations versus limited partnerships Inasmuch as profits and losses of S corporations pass through to the shareholders in the same manner as from partnerships, might it not be preferable to use the S corporation rather than the limited partnership for real estate ventures? This might be especially true since passive income from rents no longer disqualifies an S corporation (see Chapter 7).

On the surface there may seem to be an advantage to using the S corporation since it has limited liability. (Of course, if there are more than 35 investors, the S corporation cannot be used because an S corporation may not have more than 35 shareholders.) However, there is one major difference between the S corporation and the limited partnership that makes the limited partnership more attractive for real estate ventures.

Losses that pass through from a real estate limited partnership to the limited partners are deductible by those partners to the extent of their bases for their partnership interests. In the real estate limited partnership (not any other kind), each partner has allocated to his basis for his partnership interest his ratable share of the limited partnership's nonrecourse liabilities (generally the mortgages on the real estate held by the partnership). This allocation increases his basis and allows him to absorb a larger loss than he could absorb were his basis limited to his cash investment. In an S corporation, on the other hand, the corporation's liabilities do *not* increase each shareholder's basis for the S corporation stock he owns. The corporation's loss allocable to him is deductible by him only to the extent of his basis for his stock and for any loans he has made to the corporation. Thus, all other things being equal, the limited partner can deduct a larger loss than his counterpart S corporation shareholder.

Summary of ownership forms

The preceding discussion has considered in some detail the various forms of entities which may be owners of real estate. Figure 14 is a summary of the types of ownership entities and their various legal and tax attributes.

Determining basis of property

Basis is a tax term that describes a taxpayer's investment in property. It is an important term to the real estate investor and broker because, for income tax purposes, it is an essential ingredient in determining gain or loss on the sale or exchange of property and the amount of depreciation deductions allowable.

The concept of basis is required for tax purposes because cost is not an adequate reflection of the owner's investment in the property. Cost is generally the starting point for determining basis, but subsequent events call for adjustments to that cost. The owner may have made improvements to the property, or he may deduct depreciation. Each of these actions adjusts his investment.

Even the concept of cost is not clear-cut. If an individual pays $100,000 cash for a property and the property is not subject to any liens, clearly his cost is $100,000. But suppose he pays only $20,000 and borrows the balance of $80,000 by mortgaging the property. What is his cost? Or suppose he acquires the property other than by purchase—by inheritance, gift, exchange. What is his cost?

The term basis, therefore, is an all-encompassing term. It reflects the various possibilities of acquisition and the changing level of the investment during ownership as a result of improvements, depreciation, partial disposition and any other pertinent events.

How the original basis, referred to as unadjusted basis, is subsequently altered to arrive at adjusted basis is explained below. The adjusted basis is used in determining gain or loss on the sale or exchange of property. How basis affects the calculation of depreciation deductions is described in Chapter 9.

Figure 14 Ownership Forms

Owner	Limited Liability	Authorized To Act	Taxable Status	Ownership Transferability
Corporation	Yes	Officers, employees and agents	Pays tax	Easily assigned, sold or divided
S Corporation	Yes	Officers, employees and agents	Conduit	Easily assigned, sold or divided
Individual	No	Himself, agents and employees	Pays Tax	Easily assigned or sold but less divisible (spouse may have to join)
General Partnership	No	Partners, agents and employees	Conduit	Partners must join or authorize
Limited Partnership	No—for general partners	General partners, agents and employees	Conduit	General partners must join or authorize; no inchoate interest in spouse
	Yes—for limited partners			Limited partnership interest may be assigned or sold; no inchoate interest in spouse
Trusts	Yes	Trustee, agents and employees	May pay tax, be a conduit or be a combination of both	Easy assignment or sale depends on powers granted to trustee
Joint Ownership	No	Joint owners, agents and employees	Conduit (each owner pays tax on his share)	May be assigned or sold; may require spouse to join

Allocation of basis

When property is acquired, it may consist of several elements—for example, land, building (referred to as improvements) and personal property (furniture, fixtures). One overall basis for the entire property may be the starting point when a lump sum is paid for the entire property. This basis

199

must then be allocated among the various items making up the entire property. Allocation is required because land is not depreciable, and the building's basis may be subject to one cost recovery schedule while the personal property may be subject to another schedule. (Cost recovery is a term for depreciation introduced by the 1981 tax law; see Chapter 9.)

It is possible for a purchase contract to specify how much is being paid for the land and how much for each of the improvements and the personal property. These figures are usually accepted for income tax purposes if they were arrived at by unrelated parties in an "arm's length" transaction. If, however, the sale is between related parties, such an allocation in the contract may be given less credence.

In the absence of a bona fide allocation in the contract, an allocation must be made on the basis of relative market values. Land and improvement values may be determined through competent appraisals.

Example

A parcel consisting of land and building is purchased for a total of $100,000. An appraiser estimates the allocation of the purchase price in proportion to the relative market values of the land and building. The appraisal indicates that 80 percent of the value of the parcel is due to the value of the building. Therefore, $80,000 of the total $100,000 purchase price will be allocated to the building and will be subject to depreciation. The remaining $20,000 will be allocated to the land and will not be subject to depreciation.

In the absence of fair market value appraisals, it is possible to allocate between land and improvements based on the relative assessed values of land and building for real estate ad valorem tax purposes. This procedure is one of the methods frequently used, but might not be acceptable to IRS.

Example

An individual buys a parcel consisting of land and building. He pays $100,000 for the parcel; the purchase contract contains no allocation of price between land and building. Assessed values on the real estate tax bills of the land and building are $10,000 and $40,000 respectively. The ratio of the value of the land to the entire value of the parcel is 20 percent—$10,000/$50,000. Therefore, in allocating basis to the building for the purpose of computing depreciation deductions, $80,000 (80 percent of $100,000) will be allocated to the building, and $20,000 of the $100,000 purchase price will be allocated to the land.

Basis of purchased property

It is clear that if property is purchased for $50,000, the basis of that property is $50,000. It makes no difference whether the buyer pays all cash or meets part of the purchase obligation by giving a mortgage or by assuming (or taking subject to) an existing mortgage. The basis is still $50,000.

Examples

1. The purchase price of a parcel is $50,000. There is an existing mortgage on the property of $20,000. The buyer pays $30,000 cash and assumes the existing mortgage. The buyer's basis is $50,000.

2. Assume the same facts as above, but the buyer pays only $20,000 in cash and, in addition to assuming the $20,000 existing mortgage, he also gives the seller a second mortgage of $10,000. His basis is still $50,000.

3. Again, the same facts, but there is no existing mortgage on the property. The buyer secures a $30,000 mortgage from a bank on the property purchased. He uses the $30,000 he received from the bank plus $20,000 of his own funds to make the purchase. Again, his basis is $50,000.

The above examples deal with real estate; the same rules apply whether or not the buyer is "personally" liable on the mortgage obligation. However, if the property is other than real estate and the loan is a "nonrecourse" loan—the lender's only recourse on default is to the property (no recourse to the buyer)—then the buyer's basis does not include the amount of the nonrecourse loan for purposes of claiming losses. The nonrecourse nature of the debt has no effect on the basis of the property for depreciation purposes. Depreciation deductions on the property may be computed in accordance with a basis that includes the nonrecourse loan.

If the buyer pays a fee to secure the mortgage, that fee is not deductible for tax purposes. Nor can the buyer add the fee to the basis of the property he is acquiring, says IRS. However, assuming that the property is either income-producing or business property, he can deduct the fee by amortizing it over the life of the mortgage. For example, if he paid a $300 fee to secure a 15-year mortgage, he can deduct $20 per year.

Property can be purchased with commodities other than cash or mortgage. For example, other assets—a car, boat, diamond ring, stocks or bonds—might be used as part payment. The fair market value of the assets used to make the purchase are part of the purchase price. If, however, the basis of an asset the buyer uses as part of the purchase price is less than that asset's market value, the difference between basis and market value will be treated as a gain realized by the buyer.

Example

Williams buys land for $35,000. He pays for it by transferring to the seller stock in AT&T which has a market value of $35,000. Williams' basis for the land he has acquired is $35,000. However, if Williams' basis for the AT&T stock was $20,000, he will have realized a $15,000 gain on the transaction.

Exchange

In the above example, Williams gave up stock in part payment for the property he acquired. Suppose, however, he exchanged "like-kind" property—for example, land held for investment or an apartment building held for investment. In that case, even though the basis of the land he gave up was less than the market value of the building he received, the gain would not be taxable if he received nothing else but the building.

When property is exchanged for other like-kind property, there may be no immediate tax consequences; that is, the transaction may be tax free. In such cases, the basis of the property received is computed by reference to the basis of the property given up. But because the net debt against the property may change (as in the case in which the mortgage on the property given up is larger or smaller than the mortgage on the property received) and because cash or other unlike-kind property may be given or received to equalize the equities of the properties given up and received in the exchange, the basis of the property acquired may be higher or lower than the basis of the property given up. Further, the allocation of the basis between land and building on the acquired property may be made in proportions other than the proportions applied to the property given up. A discussion of the effect of exchanges on basis is included in Chapter 11.

Basis of inherited property

The basis of the property to the person inheriting is the property's market value at the date of death of the person from whom it was inherited.

An estate required to file a Federal Estate Tax Return (see Appendix E) may, however, choose an alternate valuation date to value the property in the estate. Instead of using the date-of-death values, it may elect to use values six months after the date of death. (If property is *sold* or *distributed* to the beneficiaries *during* the six months after death and the alternate valuation date option is chosen, the alternate valuation date for the property is the date of sale or distribution.) If the alternate valuation date is used, the basis of the property inherited becomes the value on the alternate valuation date, the value at which it was included on the Federal Estate Tax Return.

At one time, it was permissible to use the alternative valuation date value whether that value was greater or smaller than the value at the date of death. Often the greater value was used to step up the basis to increase depreciation and reduce gains on the subsequent disposition of inherited property; the added estate tax stemming from the increased value of the property was far less than the income tax saved via the step-up in basis.

Now, however, for estates of decedents dying after July 18, 1984, the alternate valuation date value may be used *only if* that will *decrease* the value of the decedent's gross estate *and* decrease the amount of estate tax. Thus, the alternate valuation date value may not be used if the property increased in value after the decedent's death.

Basis of jointly-held property

When two or more people hold property jointly, they may be holding the property as tenants in common or as joint tenants.

Tenants in common   If property was held by the parties involved as tenants in common, each has his own interest in the property and his own basis. If one of the tenants in common should die, the basis of his interest to whomever inherits it is determined by the basis rules concerning inherited property (discussed previously).

Joint tenancy When property is held in joint tenancy, upon the death of one of the joint tenants his or her interest in the property automatically passes to the surviving joint tenant or tenants. For example, if property is held by husband and wife as joint tenants (in some states, this type of ownership is referred to as a tenancy by the entirety), when the husband dies his interest automatically passes to his wife.

How does the surviving joint tenant figure his or her basis following the death of the other tenant(s)? The answer depends upon several factors: who paid for the property, how state law allocates income among the joint tenants and whether the joint tenants were husband and wife.

Indeed, most joint tenancies are between husband and wife. Special rules apply in determining the basis of the property in the hands of the surviving spouse when the other spouse dies.

To understand the implications of the special rules for joint tenancies of husband and wife, let us first look at the general rules applying to basis when one joint tenant dies and the surviving tenant was not the spouse of the decedent. These rules are best explained by a series of examples.

Examples

1. A brother and sister purchased a tract of land for $10,000 in 1972, each contributing $5,000. They took ownership as joint tenants. In 1974, they spent $60,000 for an improvement (again, sharing the cost equally). They added another improvement in 1979 at a total cost of $12,000. The brother died on January 1, 1984. Depreciation claimed on the $60,000 improvement totaled $7,500. Depreciation on the $12,000 improvement totaled $1,200. The market value of the property at the brother's death was $180,000.

The federal estate tax rules (with an exception discussed below) require that the full value of jointly-held property be included in the estate of the first joint tenant to die unless it can be shown that the surviving joint tenant contributed his or her own funds toward the acquisition of the property. To the extent that the survivor did contribute to the property's acquisition, the value of the property included in the deceased joint tenant's estate is reduced.

In this example, the sister actually contributed half of the funds used to acquire the property and make the two improvements. So, only half of the property's value—$90,000—is taxed in the brother's estate. The sister's basis for the entire property, after the brother's death, is computed on the premise that she owned half from the beginning and inherited the other half:

Cost of land	$10,000
Cost of 1974 improvement	60,000
Cost of 1979 improvement	12,000
Total cost	$82,000
Depreciation allowed	8,700
Adjusted basis of property at time of brother's death in 1984	$73,300
Sister's basis for half-interest (half of $73,300)	36,650
Value of brother's half-interest included in his estate	90,000
Basis of property to sister after brother's death on entire property	$126,650

2. Assume the same facts of Example 1 with one exception: the brother paid for everything with his own funds although he took title to the property jointly with his sister. Assume further that under state law income from the property would be allocated equally between joint tenants.

In these circumstances, when the brother dies, the *entire* $180,000 value of the property would be included in his estate. Hence, the sister's basis for the property would then become $180,000 less half the depreciation allowed on the property during the brother's lifetime. So, the sister's basis for the property after her brother's death becomes $175,650 ($180,000 minus $4,350, which is half the $8,700 depreciation previously deducted).

The date-of-death value has to be reduced by half the depreciation because the sister was entitled to half the income from the property during the brother's lifetime. Hence, she should be charged with half the depreciation deduction allowable in computing her basis.

3. Assume the same facts as in Example 2 except that under state law, during the brother's life all of the income was allocated to him. In that case, the entire $180,000 value at the date of death becomes the sister's basis for the property.

The general rules outlined in these examples must be modified in the case of a joint tenancy between husband and wife when one of them dies after 1982. In that case, only half the value of the joint property at the time of death (or applicable alternate valuation date) is included in the estate. Hence, the surviving spouse's basis of the property is the amount included in the estate plus half of the basis of the joint property at the time of death.

Example

Assume, in a husband-wife joint tenancy, the same figures as in the brother-sister examples. The husband died in April, 1984. Assume, too, that the husband paid for all the property and the improvements.

Under the rules applying to husband-wife joint tenancies, half the value of the property ($90,000) is included in the husband's estate. Assume that under state law all of the income was allocable to the husband. As a result, the wife's basis for the property after the husband's death is $126,650—$90,000 included in the husband's estate plus $36,650 (half the $73,300 basis of the property at the time of the husband's death).

Compare this result with the $180,000 basis the sister had in Example 3 (when the full $180,000 was included in the brother's estate). While, under the husband-wife rule, the estate tax is cut (since only $90,000 instead of $180,000 is included in the husband's estate), the wife's basis is also severely cut. On subsequent sale of the property, she may incur a substantial taxable gain. Since the estate tax law now allows for an unlimited marital deduction (see Appendix E), estate tax could be avoided even if the entire $180,000 were included in the husband's estate.

Thus, although the special provision for property held jointly by husband and wife was intended to be a relief provision (for estate tax purposes), it may not turn out to be that valuable because it may impose a greater income tax cost to the surviving spouse. It is possible that many tax advisors may now question the advisability of spouses holding property as joint tenants. **205**

Community property Suppose property is held by husband and wife in a community property state and constitutes community property so that each spouse is deemed to own half the property. When the husband dies, half the property will be included in his estate. Nevertheless, the date-of-death value of the entire property will become the wife's basis for the property after her husband's death (assuming, of course, that she inherits the husband's half of the property).

Example

Using the figures in our examples above, upon the husband's death and the wife's inheriting his half of the community property, her basis for the property will be $180,000.

Life estates

Sometimes an individual acquires a life estate in a piece of property.

Example

When Brown died, he left an apartment house he owned to his wife for her life; at her death the property was to go to their son. During her life, Mrs. Brown has a life estate in the property. On her death the property automatically goes to the son.

During her life, Mrs. Brown is entitled to collect the rents from the property. In computing her net taxable income from the property she is, of course, entitled to take a deduction for depreciation. How does she compute her basis for depreciation?

The tax law provides that Mrs. Brown's basis is the basis she would use if she owned the property outright. For example, if the property, when included in Brown's estate, had a value of $100,000, that $100,000 becomes Mrs. Brown's basis. If $80,000 of that $100,000 is allocable to the building, she uses $80,000 as her basis for figuring her depreciation.

On Mrs. Brown's death, her son gets the property outright. What is his basis for the property? The son's basis is the basis remaining to Mrs. Brown after deducting the depreciation she took during her lifetime.

If Mrs. Brown sells her life interest, she has to use a zero basis for determining gain. Hence, everything she receives is gain. If, however, Mrs. Brown's son joins with Mrs. Brown in the sale, so that the purchaser is acquiring the entire property and not only Mrs. Brown's life interest, the remaining basis of the property (i.e. the original basis to Mrs. Brown minus the depreciation deductions she took) is divided between Mrs. Brown and her son according to factors in an IRS table (based on Mrs. Brown's life expectancy). Mrs. Brown and her son figure their respective gain or loss by comparing the basis assigned to each by the table with the share of the total sale price received by each.

What about the purchaser? If he purchases Mrs. Brown's life estate only, he is entitled to keep the property only as long as Mrs. Brown lives. In that case, he can take the entire cost of the life estate and deduct that cost over the life expectancy of Mrs. Brown. In other words, he divides the cost to him of the entire property by the number of years Mrs. Brown is expected to live and deducts that amount each year. (If he paid $100,000 for the property and Mrs. Brown's life expectancy is ten years, he deducts $10,000 a year for ten years. If Mrs. Brown dies before he has fully deducted the $100,000, he deducts the remaining amount of the cost in the year Mrs. Brown dies. If she lives longer than ten years, he gets no further deductions after he has recovered his $100,000 cost.)

Basis of property received as a gift

When property is received as a gift, the general rule is that the donee (the one who receives the gift) takes as his basis the adjusted basis to the donor of the property at the time of the gift. If the donor had to pay a gift tax on the gift, the donee adds to his basis the amount of the gift tax. However, in no case can the donee's basis be increased beyond the market value of the property at the time of the gift.

Example

A father has an adjusted basis of $25,000 for a property. The market value of the property is $30,000. He makes a gift of the property to his son and pays a gift tax of $2,000. His son's basis of the property is $25,000 (father's adjusted basis) plus the $2,000 gift tax for a total of $27,000.

If the gift tax had been $6,000, the son's basis would be $30,000. Although the total of the father's basis plus the gift tax is $31,000, the son's basis cannot be increased above the market value at the time of the gift.

Property sold at a loss Special basis rules apply if the donee sells at a loss property received as a gift.

1. If at the time of the gift the market value of the property is higher than the donor's adjusted basis, the general rule explained above applies.

Example

Green makes a gift of land to his daughter. Green's basis was $10,000. The fair market value of the property at the time of the gift was $12,000. No gift tax was payable. Green's daughter subsequently sells the land for $8,000. Her basis is $10,000 (donor's basis, i.e., the general rule) and her loss is $2,000.

2. If at the time of the gift the market value is less than the donor's basis, the donee's basis for the purpose of computing the loss is the property's market value.

Example

Brown makes a gift of land to his brother. Brown's basis is $20,000. Fair market value at the time of the gift is $18,000. No gift tax is due. Later, the brother sells the land for $15,000. Although the general rule is that the donee takes the donor's basis, the exception applies here. Since the market value was less than the value at the time of the gift and the property was subsequently sold at a loss, the donee takes as his basis the lower value. Hence, his loss on the sale at $15,000 is $3,000.

3. In some cases the special basis rule creates a situation in which neither gain nor loss can be computed on the subsequent sale; therefore, no gain or loss is reported.

Example

Smith makes a gift of land to his mother. The fair market value at the time of the gift is $5,000; Smith's basis is $10,000. No gift tax is due. Smith's mother later sells the land for $7,000. If Smith's mother uses the donor's basis ($10,000) as her basis, there would be a loss of $3,000. But when there is a loss and at the time of the gift the fair market value is less than the donor's basis, the donee is supposed to use the fair market value as her basis. However, if Smith's mother uses the fair market value of $5,000 as her basis, the subsequent sale results in a $2,000 gain. Since basis for gain is always the donor's basis, in a case like this neither gain nor loss can be computed; so, Smith's mother has no gain or loss to report.

Note that the rule dealing with gift property sold at a loss does not apply to gifts between spouses made after July 18, 1984. As to those gifts, the donee takes as basis for the gift property the basis it had in the hands of the donor immediately before the gift, regardless of whether the property is subsequently sold by the donee at a gain or a loss.

Basis of property received for services rendered

If the person who is rendering services is paid with property instead of with cash, the market value of the property received is ordinary income to the recipient since that is compensation for his services. The fair market value of his services becomes the basis for the property he receives.

Example

A real estate broker receives his fee in property rather than cash. He is entitled to a $5,000 commission but instead receives a parcel of land worth $5,000. He has commission income of $5,000 and the basis of the land to him is $5,000.

Suppose, instead of receiving land worth $5,000, he receives improved property worth $25,000 subject to a mortgage of $20,000. He still has $5,000 of income since his compensation is the net value of the property received. But his basis for the property is $25,000. The situation is the same as if the broker purchased the parcel for $25,000, using his $5,000 fee as down payment, and financed the balance with a mortgage.

Basis of property acquired through foreclosure or other repossession

When the seller receives a purchase money mortgage as part of the purchase price, he may subsequently repossess the property on default of the buyer. If that happens, the seller must determine whether he has realized a gain or loss on the repossession by applying special tax rules regarding repossessions. The tax rules differ, depending upon whether the property repossessed is real estate or personal property.

Repossession of real property When the seller repossesses the property in full or partial satisfaction of the purchase money mortgage, the tax rules provide that no loss may be recognized for tax purposes on the transaction and that gain, if any, will be taxed only to a limited extent. (Losses are not recognized in these situations on the theory that the seller really has not lost anything since he has his property back.)

On the other hand, he may have a gain. This would be the case if the seller received some money (and possibly also some other property such as marketable securities) and then regained his property as well. For income tax purposes, the seller has realized a gain equal to the amount of the cash and the other property received less that portion of the gain on the original transaction already reported.

(Note that in the examples that follow distinction is made between situations in which installment sale reporting was used and those in which it was not. Under the installment sale provisions of a tax law enacted in October, 1980, all sales calling for payments in a year subsequent to the year of sale qualify as installment sales, unless the taxpayer elects not to have a sale treated as an installment sale [see Chapter 10]. Hence, there will be very few situations in which installment sale reporting will not have been used when the sale took place in 1980 or thereafter. Nevertheless, some repossessions may involve sales in which the installment method of reporting was not used, either because the taxpayer elected to avoid installment sale reporting or because the original sale occurred prior to the effective date of the 1980 tax law change. The distinctions between cases where installment reporting was used and those where it was not used are set forth in the following examples.)

Example

Barton sold a parcel of real estate, which had a basis of $15,000, for $25,000. He received $5,000 cash and a purchase money mortgage for $20,000, bearing 12-percent interest, payable $4,000 annually commencing the next year. The following year he received the $4,000 payment (plus interest) but the year after that the buyer defaulted and Barton repossessed the property.

Assuming that Barton had treated the sale as an installment sale (discussed in Chapter 10), the tax treatment would be as follows:

Total cash received ($5,000 + $4,000)	$9,000
Reduced by gain previously reported	
Gross profit = $10,000 ($25,000 minus $15,000)	
Gross profit percentage = 40% ($10,000/$25,000)	
40% of $9,000 collected	3,600
Gain on repossession	$5,400

Had the installment method not been used and if the entire $10,000 gain had been reported in the year of sale, there would have been no gain on Barton's repossession.

But this is not the complete story. There is another tax rule, applied in some cases, which limits the gain on repossession. This limitation is the amount of gain on the original sale of the property reduced by the total of the gain already reported plus the cost of repossession.

Example

Using the same facts as above and assuming that costs of repossession amount to $1,200, the limitation on gain would be computed this way:

Original gain		$10,000
($25,000 sale price less $15,000 adjusted basis)		
Reduced by		
Gain previously reported	$3,600	
Repossession costs	1,200	4,800
Limitation		$ 5,200

The limitation would apply to reduce the gain of $5,400 to $5,200.

Tax basis of repossessed real estate The basis of the repossessed property is the basis of the unpaid obligation plus the sum of any gain required to be recognized by the rules above and the costs (if any) of repossession. This rule applies even if there is no gain and even if there is a loss which cannot be deducted for tax purposes. Its effect in situations where there is a nonrecognized loss on repossession is to add that loss to basis.

Example

Continuing the above illustration to compute the basis of the property repossessed, we find the following:

Face value of the unpaid notes ($20,000 - $4,000)	$16,000
Less: Unreported gain (40% of $16,000)	6,400
Basis of unpaid notes	9,600
Plus: Gain on repossession	5,200
Repossession costs	1,200
Basis of repossessed property	$16,000

Had the installment method not been used and had the entire $10,000 gain been reported in the year of sale, the loss on repossession would have been $1,000 ($9,000 total cash received minus $10,000 gain already reported). While this $1,000 loss would not be deductible under the rules relating to repossessions of real estate, it would, in effect, be added to the basis of the property by the application of the previous rule. The computation would be as follows:

Face value of notes (same as basis of unpaid notes)	$16,000
Plus: Repossession costs	1,200
Basis of repossessed property	$17,200

Notice that the new basis of the property can be said to consist of the following items:

Original basis		$15,000
Loss on repossession (not recognized)		
Gain tax on sale	$10,000	
Less: Cash received	9,000	1,000
Repossession costs		1,200
New basis of repossessed property		$17,200

Situations involving principal residence The rules discussed above regarding repossessed real estate may not apply if the realty consists of the seller's principal residence. The law provides that when the principal residence is sold and all or part of the gain is not recognized either under the special rule for persons age 55 or older or the special rule involving reinvestment of the proceeds in a new residence within a prescribed time, then if the seller resells the repossessed residence within one year of repossession, all the rules discussed previously will not apply. In those cases, the resale is treated as part of the original sale, ignoring the repossession. However, if the resale is not made within the year following repossession, all of the rules with respect to gains on repossessions and new basis will apply.

Basis of repossessed personal property The seller of realty will often sell personal property such as furniture within the building. Rules regarding repossessions of such property differ from those involving the real estate.

The market value of the property repossessed becomes the basis of that property after repossession because gain or loss on the repossession is recognized at the time of the repossession.

Gain or loss is the difference between the market value of the property retaken and the seller's basis for the notes canceled or adjusted, when necessary, for other amounts realized or other costs incurred in connection with the repossession. As in the case of real property discussed above, the seller's basis of defaulted notes is their face minus any unreported profit with respect to them.

Examples

1. In connection with the sale of his hotel, Green also sells the furniture for $15,000. His adjusted basis for the furniture at the time of the sale was $10,000. He received $3,000 in the year of the sale and a note for $12,000, payable $1,000 per month, with 10-percent interest, beginning in the year following the sale. Green reports the gain using the installment method. Since his

profit on the sale is $5,000 or one-third of the selling price, he will report one-third of each collection of cash as gain at the time he collects it.

After making three payments, the buyer defaulted and Green repossessed the furniture. Fair market value of the furniture at the time of the repossession was $14,000 and expense of repossession was $1,000. Green computes his gain on the repossession as follows:

Market value of the repossessed furniture		$14,000
Basis of buyer's notes		
Original face amount	$12,000	
Less: Three payments made	3,000	
Face value of unpaid notes	$ 9,000	
Less: Unrealized profit (one-third of $9,000)	3,000	
Basis of unpaid notes		6,000
Gain on repossession		8,000
Less: Repossession costs		1,000
Taxable gain on repossession		$ 7,000

If the installment method of reporting had not been used and the entire gain or loss on the sale was reported in the year of the sale, the basis of the notes or other obligations would be their face amount.

2. Assume that in the previous example the entire gain was reported in the year of sale. That gain was $5,000 and the basis of the unpaid notes was $12,000, their face amount. Subsequently, $3,000 of notes were paid off. So, at the time of repossession, the remaining unpaid notes had a face amount (and a basis) of $9,000. Since the fair market value of the repossessed furniture was $14,000, there was a gain on the repossession of $4,000, computed as follows:

Market value of repossessed furniture		$14,000
Less: Basis of unpaid notes (equal to face)	$9,000	
Repossession costs	1,000	10,000
Gain on repossession		$ 4,000

In either of the two examples, the basis of the repossessed furniture would be $14,000, its market value at time of repossession.

Nature of the gain on repossession If the original sale was reported as an installment sale, any gain or recognized loss on the repossession of either real property or personal property (under the rules spelled out above) is treated the same way as the gain on the installment sale. That means if the sale resulted in capital gain under the installment method, the gain on the repossession is also a capital gain. If part of the gain on a transaction reported as an installment sale constitutes depreciation recapture (explained in Chapter 10), gains realized in the year of sale and subsequent years are first allocated to depreciation recapture. Remaining gain realized is then treated as capital gain. Hence, if prior to the repossession, not all of the depreciation recapture had yet been reported, gain on the repossession would first be applied to the recapture and then any remaining gain would be taxable as capital gain.

Example

Gain on an installment sale was $15,000, of which $5,000 was depreciation recapture and $10,000 was capital gain. After $4,000 of the gain was reported under the installment method, the seller repossessed the property. The gain realized on the repossession was $6,000. Since only $4,000 of the $5,000 depreciation recapture had previously been reported, $1,000 of the $6,000 gain on the repossession is treated as depreciation recapture and the remaining $5,000 gain is treated as capital gain.

If the original sale was not an installment sale, the gain on repossession is treated as a redemption of the notes held by the seller. If the notes were issued to the seller making the repossession before July 2, 1982, there is capital gain on the redemption *only if* the notes are corporate (or government) obligations. If the notes were issued after July 1, 1982, there is capital gain as long as the issuer was not an individual (e.g., a partnership). If the notes were issued by an individual, the gain on repossession is ordinary income. No depreciation recapture problem arises in this case because the entire gain was reported in the year of sale. Hence, the depreciation recapture was reported at that time.

Basis of property foreclosed by third party mortgagees

When money is borrowed from someone other than the seller of property and a mortgage or other pledge is given, the creditor is sometimes called a third party mortgagee. Rules with respect to defaults on such obligations are similar to those applicable to repossessions of personal property.

When mortgaged or pledged property is sold and the net proceeds are less than the amount of the debt, the difference, to the extent it is uncollectible, is deductible as a bad debt loss by the mortgagee. Business bad debts are fully deductible as ordinary losses; however, nonbusiness bad debts are treated as short-term capital losses.

The buyer of such property at a foreclosure sale, if he is not the creditor, has a basis for the property equal to the amount he pays.

Example

Shaw holds a $25,000 mortgage note which is in default. A foreclosure sale is held at which Smith buys the property for $15,000. Expenses of the sale amount to $1,000. The results are as follows: Shaw had a bad debt loss of $11,000 because that is the difference between his basis for the note ($25,000) and the net proceeds ($15,000 less $1,000) he received. Smith has a basis of $15,000 for the property because that is what he paid for it.

When the person buying the property at the foreclosure sale is also the creditor, it is possible for another gain or loss to occur. That is so because the purchase of the property with the defaulted obligation is considered a taxable transaction. Therefore, if the value of the property differs from the creditor's basis for his notes, he will have a gain or a loss. His basis for the property will be its market value at the time he acquired it.

Example

If, in the preceding illustration, Shaw had bid in the foreclosure sale and had purchased the property for $10,000 (assuming that its fair market value was still $15,000) he would have had a loss on the note of $16,000 ($25,000 less net proceeds of $9,000). He also would have had a capital gain of $5,000 on the exchange of note for property (market value of the property less the $10,000 bid price).

Conversely, if he had bid in the property at $20,000, $5,000 in excess of its fair market value, he would have had a loss on the note of $6,000 ($25,000 less net proceeds of $19,000) and a capital loss of the $5,000 excess on the exchange. Whether this is long- or short-term depends on the holding period of the mortgage note.

Finally, if he had bought the property at $15,000, its fair market value, his bad debt loss on the note, as in the case when the property was bought by Smith, would be $11,000 and he would have no gain on the exchange.

His basis for the property would be $15,000, its fair market value, in all three cases.

Note that the bid price is generally deemed to be the fair market value. Treasury regulations make that assumption unless there is clear evidence to the contrary. Further, the Uniform Commercial Code, which applies in most states, requires that bids be made in good faith and presumes that the bid price is the fair market value. Hence, there would be very few situations where there could be a difference between the price at which the property was bid in and its fair market value. Consequently, the first two situations in the example above are not very likely to occur.

Basis of property after involuntary conversions

Sometimes property is converted from one kind to another against the wishes of its owner. Such a conversion occurs when property is condemned by a governmental authority and replaced by cash or state bonds. Similarly, a fire, flood or a natural disaster such as a storm could destroy property which is subsequently replaced with cash by an insurance company. When such an event occurs, a gain may result; that is, the proceeds received exceed the basis of the property destroyed.

When there is a gain as a result of an involuntary conversion, the taxpayer has the option of postponing the taxability of the gain. To achieve such a postponement, the taxpayer must (within a specified time) purchase replacement property which costs as much as or more than the net proceeds received from the conversion. Generally, the replacement has to occur by the end of the second year after the year in which any part of the gain is realized. For example, if any part of the gain is realized any time during 1984, the replacement has to occur by the end of 1986. However, if the real property is used in the taxpayer's trade or business, he has until three years after the close of the taxable year in which the conversion occured to acquire replacement property. If a longer period is needed to make the replacement, IRS, at the request of the taxpayer, has the authority to grant an extension.

If the replacement property costs less than the net proceeds received from the involuntary conversion, the gain is taxed to the extent of the unexpended portion.

Example

Long's factory was condemned by the state and he was awarded $160,000 for the property for which he had a basis of $150,000. Therefore, he realized a $10,000 gain from the condemnation. If he purchases another factory for $160,000 or more within the specified replacement period, he may elect to postpone the tax on his gain. If his new factory cost only $158,000, he would be required to pay tax on $2,000, the part of the gain not reinvested in the new factory.

Note that the *cost* of the new property must equal the proceeds of the involuntary conversion to avoid the tax on the gain. However, cost does not necessarily mean cash. Hence, while a $150,000 cash award on condemnation might have been received, taxable gain is avoided if $150,000 is reinvested in the replacement property within the required time, even if, for example, $20,000 cash is paid and a mortgage of $130,000 is given.

The replacement property has to be property similar or related in service and use to the property which it replaces. That means, says IRS, that it must be functionally the same as the property it replaces; it must serve the same use.

There is an important exception to this rule for real estate, however. This exception applies when real property used in a trade or business or held for production of income or for investment is involuntarily converted as a result of its seizure, requisition or condemnation or is sold because the authorities have indicated their intention to seize the property. (This exception would therefore not apply where the involuntary conversion is a result of a fire loss.)

When the exception applies, the replacement property can be of like kind—that is, any other real property used in the taxpayer's trade or business or held for the production of income or for investment. In other words, it makes no difference that the replacement property is not similar or related in service or use to the property converted. And the property that was given up or the property that was acquired can be either improved or unimproved real property.

Basis of replacement property When replacement property is acquired and an election is made to have the tax postponed on the gain on the involuntary conversion of the old property, the basis of the new (replacement) property must be reduced by the amount of gain which has not been taxed.

Example

In the prior example, assume Long invests $162,000 in a new factory property within the required time. He elects not to report any part of the gain since he has reinvested at least the entire $160,000 proceeds. His basis for the new factory is $152,000, computed as follows:

Amount paid for new factory	$162,000
Less: Gain realized on condemnation but not reported for tax purposes	10,000
Basis of new factory	$152,000

If Long had invested only $156,000 in the new factory, he would have been taxed on $4,000 of the $10,000 gain on the condemnation; $6,000 of the $10,000 gain would be nontaxable. He has to reduce the nontaxable portion of the gain by the $4,000 difference between the $160,000 proceeds from the condemnation and the $156,000 reinvested in the new factory. In that case, the basis of his new factory would be $150,000, computed as follows:

Amount paid for new factory	$156,000
Less: Gain realized on condemnation but not reported for tax purposes	6,000
Basis of new factory	$150,000

Basis of property acquired through exercise of options

Often, prior to the acquisition of real property, the buyer first obtains an option.

Example

Jones pays $1,000 for a three-month option to acquire a property at $15,000. Within the three months, he exercises his option, paying the $15,000 for the property. His basis of the property acquired is $16,000—the $15,000 purchase price plus the $1,000 he paid for the option.

If he lets the three-month period expire without exercising the option, he has a $1,000 loss. The nature of the loss is the same as the kind of loss he would have had if he had sold the property (on which he had the option) at a loss.

Basis of property converted from personal residence to income-producing property

If property has not been used in a trade or business or has not been held for the production of income, such as a former residence which is being converted into rental property, a different rule applies for basis computation. In that case, the basis for computing depreciation is the lower of (1) the property's adjusted basis or (2) the market value of the property. Both of these factors should be determined at the date of the conversion to income-producing status.

Example

Felix bought his personal residence in 1974 for $39,000. In 1984, he moves to an apartment and rents his house to Finch. In 1984, at the time of the rental, the house is worth only $30,000. Felix's basis for it is still the $39,000 he paid; there have been no adjustments (he was not permitted to deduct depreciation on a personal residence).

For the purpose of computing depreciation to reduce Felix's taxable rental income reportable on his 1984 income tax return, the basis to be used for the entire property is $30,000, the lower figure. (An allocation must then be made between land and improvements.)

Adjustments to basis

After the initial, unadjusted basis is determined under the rules we have been discussing, certain adjustments must be made to arrive at *adjusted* basis.

Adjustments can take the form of additions to as well as reductions of the initial, unadjusted basis.

Additions to basis

The cost of improvements to the property increases the basis. As a rule of thumb (and this is IRS' position), improvements which have a useful life of more than one year are added to basis.

Capital improvements must be distinguished from repairs and operating expenses. Repairs and operating costs, as well as improvements with a useful life of one year or less, are current deductions and have no effect on the basis at all. (See Chapter 9 for a discussion of repairs versus capital improvements.)

Capitalized carrying charges, interest and taxes

The lax law gives owners of real estate, in certain instances, the option to deduct or capitalize interest, taxes and carrying charges. If the owner elects to capitalize these items, he adds them to his basis. If he elects to deduct them, then these items have no effect on basis.

In the case of unimproved and unproductive real property, the owner can elect to capitalize annual real estate taxes, interest on a mortgage or other loan and other carrying charges. The election is effective only for the year for which it is made. A new election may be made each year as long as the property remains unimproved and unproductive.

Example

Smith owns land which is both unimproved and unproductive for two years. The third year the land is leased to a department store which uses it as a parking lot. Smith could elect in either or both of the first two years to capitalize taxes, interest and carrying charges. However, in the third year, he could not elect to capitalize those expenses because the property was no longer unproductive in that year.

In the case of real property, whether improved or unimproved, productive or unproductive, the owner may elect to capitalize interest on a loan, taxes measured by the compensation paid for work on construction and development (Social Security taxes, for example), state sales and use taxes paid on materials used in construction or development and other necessary expenditures. These expenses may be capitalized whether the property is improved or unimproved or productive or unproductive but only for such expenses paid or incurred up to the time the development or improvement is completed. Any or all of the taxes or carrying charges for each development or construction project may be capitalized. But once an election is made to capitalize a particular type of tax or carrying charge for a particular project, that type of expenditure must continue to be capitalized until the project is completed.

There is one important exception in this area. Interest and real estate taxes incurred during the time a building or improvement is under construction *must* be capitalized; the owner does not have the option of deducting these expenditures. This rule applies to property other than low-income housing and property that is not to be held in a trade or business or in an activity conducted for profit (e.g., a personal residence). Corporations used to be exempt from this rule as to residential real estate. However, for construction begun after March 15, 1984, in taxable years beginning after 1984, corporations will be subject to capitalization of construction period interest and taxes on residential real estate (other than low income housing). When interest and taxes are required to be capitalized, these items are written off (amortized) over a ten-year period.

On the sale of property, real estate taxes for the current real property tax year are apportioned between seller and buyer. To the extent that the buyer pays taxes allocable to the seller and other prior years' taxes that had been assessed on the property while owned by the seller, they are added to the purchaser's basis of the property.

The costs of purchase commissions, legal fees for perfecting or defending title to the property and title insurance are all items added to the basis of the property.

When property is sold, the cost of selling it (such as brokers' commissions) reduces the gain on the sale or increases the loss. The expenses of sale are not separate deductions against ordinary income (unless the seller is a dealer).

Reductions of basis

Depreciation The major item which reduces basis is the depreciation allowed or allowable during the time the property was held. Thus, if for some reason the property owner deducts less depreciation than the amount he is allowed to deduct under his method of depreciation, his basis must still be reduced by the amount of the depreciation that was *allowable.* Conversely, if the owner deducted more depreciation than he was entitled to deduct under his method or under an improper method, his basis is reduced by the actual depreciation deducted (as long as the depreciation deducted reduced his tax liability in the year it was deducted).

Reduction of basis when there is a partial divestiture of property When property is acquired, it is necessary to make an allocation of basis between land and building. But subsequently, suppose part of the land is sold. Or, perhaps, part is taken by condemnation. How is the basis of the land allocated between the part that is disposed of and the part that is retained? Treasury regulations are not too helpful in this area. They require only that an "equitable" apportionment be made.

If the property was bought on a "square-foot" basis to begin with or for a single purpose and each part of the land has the same value as each other part, a square-foot approach can be used in determining the basis of the portion disposed of and the portion retained.

Example

A 20,000 square-foot parcel of land is bought for $20,000 and a building is erected on half of the land at a cost of $100,000. Immediately the other half of the land is sold. The basis of the sold land would be $10,000 (half the basis of the total land), and the basis of the other half of the property would be $110,000 (the $10,000 basis of the remaining land plus the $100,000 cost of the building).

However, all things are not always equal and a portion of the property (due to favorable frontage, for example, or lack of access to the other portion of the land) may be worth more or less than another portion. In that case, allocation of the basis to the various portions of the land in relation to their relative market values would be in order.

Example

In one tax case, a ten-acre tract of land was acquired for the purpose of developing a shopping center. Later the plans fell through and a portion of the land was sold. IRS argued that the basis should be allocated to the land on a square-foot basis because the entire land was acquired for a single purpose—to erect a shopping center. However, the portion of the land sold, considerably less than 40 percent of the total acreage, was determined by the court to be the most valuable portion of the land because it fronted on two busy streets and was worth about 40 percent of the total value of the land. Hence, 40 percent of the basis was allocated to the portion of the land sold. Subsequently, IRS announced that it would go along with that decision.

Undivided interests If the owner of a tract of land sells an undivided interest in the entire land, rather than a specific portion of it, he allocates to the property sold the same portion of the basis that he has given up in terms of the undivided interest.

Example

If land cost Smith $100,000 and he sells Jones a 25-percent undivided interest in the entire tract, Smith will allocate $25,000 (25 percent of the basis of the entire tract to him) to the interest he sold to Jones. Consequently, if Jones paid $40,000 for his 25-percent undivided interest, Smith would have a $15,000 gain.

Parcels acquired at different times If several parcels of land are acquired at different times at different prices, although they are contiguous and thus form one tract of land, the basis for each parcel is considered separately. Upon subsequent disposition, gain or loss on the parcel disposed of is computed separately by comparing the basis for that parcel with the respective portion of the sale price allocated to that parcel.

Casualty losses If property is partially destroyed by fire, storm or other casualty, the owner may be entitled to a casualty loss deduction. The casualty loss is the difference between the value of the property immediately before and immediately after the casualty (but not more than the adjusted basis at the time of the casualty) reduced by any insurance recovery. (For nonbusiness casualties, the first $100 of each casualty loss is not deductible. Furthermore, the total of all such casualty losses in one year—after reducing each loss by $100—is deductible only to the extent it exceeds 10 percent of adjusted gross income.) The amount of the insurance proceeds received plus any casualty loss deducted reduce the basis of the property.

Example

Stevens owned land and building used in his business for which he had originally paid $40,000, having allocated $35,000 to the building and $5,000 to the land. After it was purchased, Stevens built an addition to the building at a cost of $10,000. On October 1, 1984, the building was completely destroyed by fire. Up to the time of the fire Stevens had been allowed depreciation deductions totaling $23,000. Stevens sold what salvage he could recover for $1,300 and collected $19,700 insurance. He also deducted a $1,000 casualty loss on his 1984 tax return. He spent $19,000 of the insurance proceeds to restore the building. The restoration was completed by the end of 1984. The adjusted basis of his property on January 1, 1985 is computed as follows:

		Land	Building
Original cost of property		$5,000	$35,000
Addition to building			10,000
			45,000
Less: Depreciation			23,000
Basis before casualty		5,000	22,000
Less:			
Casualty loss deduction	$ 1,000		
Insurance proceeds	19,700		
Salvage proceeds	1,300		22,000
Basis after casualty		5,000	none
Add: Cost of restoring building			$19,000
Basis on January 1, 1985		$5,000	$19,000

Easements   If the property owner receives payments for the grant of an easement on the property, the amount received for the easement reduces the basis of the property.

Chapter 9

Operations

The investor's return from a real estate investment consists both of the income produced from operating the property and the profit on its ultimate disposition. In both instances, however, there are income tax consequences with which to reckon. These consequences, of course, affect the net return on the investment.

In this chapter, we will be concerned with the impact of the tax rules on the income from operations of real estate—basically, the investor's return in terms of rental income and the impact of the tax rules on the cash flow from the property.

Nature of income from operations

Typically, the real estate investor receives a current return from his property in the form of rent. This rent is ordinary income. However, since rental income is classified as income from a trade or business, only the net income (after deducting ordinary and necessary business expenses) is subject to taxation. It is possible that after deducting all ordinary and necessary business expenses from the gross rental income, the result will be a taxable loss. As explained earlier, such a loss can be used by the investor to reduce his other taxable income.

Deductible items

The ordinary and necessary business expenses that the real estate owner may deduct in reducing gross rental income to net taxable income (or loss) are utility costs, management and maintenance salaries and wages, real estate taxes, repair and maintenance costs, interest and depreciation.

In some instances, interest, taxes and carrying charges may be capitalized (at the taxpayer's election). Thus, they are not deductible as current expense but, instead, become part of basis.

Cash flow

Any examination of the tax aspects of real estate operations must necessarily include a consideration of the cash flow from the investment.

At the end of this chapter there are several illustrations which show how the application of the tax laws to the income from operations affects the investor's cash flow.

Repairs or Improvements

Sometimes it is difficult to distinguish between a repair and a capital improvement. There are probably more than 1,000 tax cases on the subject. Typically, the courts and IRS say that each case must be decided on the basis of its own particular facts and circumstances, a statement that offers no practical guide to anyone trying to distinguish between a repair and an improvement.

As a general rule an improvement is either *an addition* to the property (with a useful life of more than one year) or something that *prolongs* the useful life of the property. A repair is something more in the way of maintenance, the effect of which merely maintains but does not increase the useful life of the property.

The interest deduction

A major item of deduction for most real estate investors is interest expense. The general rule is that all interest paid on any indebtedness is deductible, whether the interest cost is related to an indebtedness incurred in business, an income-seeking transaction or a personal debt. One major exception is interest paid or incurred to acquire or carry securities yielding interest income, which is tax exempt. For example, if an indebtedness is incurred to buy or carry municipal bonds (the interest income of which is exempt from federal income taxes), the interest paid on such indebtedness is not tax deductible.

Although the general rule is that interest is deductible, there are two problem areas that affect the deductibility of interest. One concerns the prepayment of interest. The other involves the rules governing excess investment interest, under which a portion of the interest expense may not be deductible in the year paid or incurred.

Prepaid Interest

There was a time when as much as five years' interest paid in advance by a cash basis taxpayer was deductible when paid. This is no longer the law. Interest paid or accrued is deductible only insofar as it covers a time period contained within the taxable year in question.

Example

If Green, a cash basis taxpayer, pays $1,500 in interest on January 1, 1984, to cover the period from January 1, 1984, through March 31, 1985, he can deduct only $1,200 in 1984. (The $1,500 paid was for a 15-month period, or $100 a month.) So, Green can deduct the $1,200 covering the 12 months of 1984. The $300 balance would be deductible in 1985.

An exception to the above rule involves mortgage "points" paid in advance. They are deductible when paid, but only if the mortgage is on the taxpayer's principal residence and the amount paid is consistent with the points charged on similar transactions in that market area.

Excess Investment Interest

Part of an individual's interest expense (this rule does not apply to corporations) may be disallowed as a current interest deduction if it constitutes excess investment interest.

Excess investment interest is defined as the amount by which the individual's investment interest expense exceeds the sum of net invesment income plus the excess "net lease" out-of-pocket expenses, plus $10,000.

Example

If investment interest expenses total $45,000 and investment income is $15,000, only $25,000 of the $45,000 would be deductible ($15,000 investment income plus $10,000). The $20,000 difference between the $45,000 investment interest expense and the $25,000 which was deductible is the amount of the excess invesment interest nod deductible in the current year. The full amount of the disallowed investment interest expense may be carried over and deducted in subsequent years (subject to the limitations on investment interest deductions in those years).

Investment interest expense must first be determined. The law says that investment interest expense means "interest paid or accrued on indebtedness incurred or continued to purchase or carry property *held for investment*" (emphasis added). (For short sales of personal property made after July 18, 1984, deductible expenses in connection with the short sale are treated as investment interest paid.) Specifically excluded from investment interest expense is interest on indebtedness incurred or continued in the construction of property to be used in a trade or business.

Net lease   Will interest paid on a mortgage on rental property *not* subject to a net lease fall into the investment interest category? It would seem not because, traditionally, property held for rental income has been considered "trade or business" property by IRS and not investment property. Gains and losses from the sale of this property have been considered Section 1231 gains and losses.

227

Property subject to a net lease   A special provision dealing with property subject to a net lease specifically treats that property as investment property. Interest expense incurred in connection with the purchase or carrying of net lease property *is* subject to the investment interest expense rules.

The law spells out two situations in which it deems a net lease to exist:

1. The lessor is guaranteed a specified return or he is guaranteed, in whole or part, against loss of income.

2. Ordinary and necessary expenses allowed under Section 162 of the Internal Revenue Code in connection with the property are less than 15 percent of the rental income from the property. The expenses included here are reasonable salaries, travel expense while away from home, contributions to the Federal National Mortgage Association in excess of the value of the stock received and certain expenses to lobby against legislation of direct interest to the taxpayer. If any "allowed" expenses are reimbursed to the landlord by the tenant, then the landlord may not include those expenses in determining whether his expenses exceed 15 percent of rental income.

Obviously, very few of these items, other than salaries, would apply to the owner of real estate. Other expenses such as interest, taxes and depreciation are not included in Section 162; they are allowed by other sections of the Code and do not enter into the calculation here. Hence, in most net lease situations, and in some cases in which net leases in the conventional sense are not involved, it would probably be difficult to meet the 15-percent requirement and the interest *would* be investment interest expense.

What happens when there is more than one lease on a single parcel of property? For example, a shopping center may have separate leases with each of its tenants.

For the purposes of determining if there is a net lease, the law allows the taxpayer to elect to combine all the leases and treat them as one. This is a taxpayer election; it does not happen automatically.

Special modifications of the net lease rule   The law provides two special modifications concerning net leases:

1. Expenses in excess of gross rentals   As indicated, expenses such as interest, real estate and personal property taxes, legal and accounting fees in connection with computing taxes or other costs incurred by an investor for the production or collection of income or management, conservation or maintenance of his property are *not* deductible in determining whether the 15-percent rule is met to avoid net lease treatment. However, if the total of these expenses, when added to the expenses allowed in determining whether the 15-percent net lease test is met, exceeds the gross rental from the property, the excess expenses are added to the taxpayer's investment income. Since it is only the interest expenses that *exceed* investment income that are subject to possible disallowances as tax deductions, adding those expenses to the investment income reduces the excess investment interest.

2. *Real property in use for more than five years* If real property has been in use for more than five years, the taxpayer can elect to exempt that property from net lease treatment. In other words, even though there is a net lease on that property, the taxpayer can treat the property as not held for investment; thus the interest paid in connection with that property will not be treated as investment interest. The taxpayer has to elect to have the property treated as noninvestment property; it does not happen automatically.

Net investment income Net investment income is investment income reduced by investment expenses. Investment income is made up of interest, dividends, rents, royalties, net short-term capital gains from investment property and depreciation recapture from property that is not a capital asset or a Section 1231 asset. None of this income can be trade or business income. Thus, rent would be investment income probably only in the "net lease" situations described previously. (Note that if an election is made to treat property subject to a net lease as if it were non-net lease property because it has been in use for more than five years, the rental income from that property would not be investment income. This factor must be taken into consideration before making the election.)

Investment expenses are real and personal property taxes, bad debts, depreciation, amortizable bond premiums, expenses for production of income on investment property and depletion. Of course, these expenses have to be connected directly with the production of investment income. The depreciation allowed in this calculation is straight line depreciation only and the depletion allowed is cost depletion only.

Special deduction rules for vacation homes

It has become fairly common for owners of "second homes" and "vacation homes" to rent these facilities to others for part of the year. The question repeatedly has arisen concerning how much the owner may deduct as expenses because he earns income from the property. After many disputes arose between taxpayers and IRS, Congress enacted a special set of rules which set forth certain limitations on deductions relating to vacation homes.

Under these rules, a vacation home can be a house, apartment, condominium, house trailer or boat. It also can be something like a garage that relates to the use of the dwelling unit. A vacation home is "personally used" if, for any part of the day, it is used by the taxpayer or a relative, an individual who uses it under a reciprocal arrangement or any other individual who is not charged a fair rental.

The rules enacted by Congress provide that:

1. If the house is not rented at all during the year, the owner may deduct the interest on the mortgage, local property taxes and casualty losses (in excess of $100 plus 10 percent of adjusted gross income).

2. If the house is rented for fewer than 15 days, and the owner personally uses the house sometime during the year, no deduction for rental-related expenses (depreciation, maintenance, utilities) is permitted. However, mortgage interest, property taxes and casualty losses (in excess of $100 plus 10 percent of adjusted gross income) are still fully deductible. Any rental income the owner receives is *not* treated as taxable income.

3. If the owner rents his vacation home for fewer than 15 days and does not personally use the home at all, or if he rents it for more than 14 days and uses it personally for fewer than 15 days or 10 percent of the total rental days (whichever is greater), he may or may not be able to deduct all of the rental-related expenses.

   To deduct these expenses in full, the owner must show that by renting his home he is engaged in a profit-making activity. His intent to make a profit is presumed if, during any two years of a period of five consecutive years, the gross rental income exceeds the rental-related deductions. If the owner cannot satisfy this "objective" test, he may still demonstrate his intent to make a profit by other evidence. If the property owner cannot show his rental activity is for profit, the deductions allocable to the rental are deductible. However, they are deductible only to the extent that gross rental income exceeds the total of interest, property taxes and casualty losses (in excess of $100 plus 10 percent of adjusted gross income).

   Actually, there are three levels of deductions. First, mortgage interest, taxes and allowable casualty losses are deducted in full. Then, other rental-related expenses (except depreciation) are allowed to the extent rental income exceeds the first category of expenses. Finally, depreciation is allowed to the extent gross rental income exceeds these two categories of deductions.

4. If the vacation home is rented for more than 14 days and the owner personally uses it for more than 14 days or more than 10 percent of the days it is rented, the following rules apply. Mortgage interest, property taxes and casualty losses (in excess of $100 plus 10 percent of adjusted gross income) are deductible in full. Other expenses attributable to the rental use of the home are deductible only to the extent rental income exceeds the interest, property taxes and allowable casualty losses *allocable* to rental use.

230

To determine the interest, property taxes and casualty losses allocable to rental use of the vacation home, multiply those expenses by a fraction, the numerator of which is the "days of rental use," and the denominator of which is "total days used."

Example

During the year, a taxpayer rents his vacation home for three months and personally uses it for one month. His gross rental income is $2,000. He pays property taxes of $600 and $1,000 of interest on his mortgage. His other expenses allocable to the rental of the house include $200 for utilities, $300 for maintenance and $600 for depreciation.

The deductions he may take on his vacation home are computed as follows:

Rental income	$2,000
Less: Taxes and interest allocable to rental period (3/4 × $1,600)	1,200
Limit on rental expenses other than taxes and interest	800
Less: Utilities and maintenance	500
Limit on depreciation deduction	$ 300

Summary

	Actual Expenses	Deductible Expenses
Taxes and interest	$1,600	
Allocable to rental period		$1,200
Balance deductible in any event		400
Utilities and maintenance allocable to rental period	500	500
Depreciation allocable to rental period	600	300
Totals	$2,700	$2,400

The difference between the actual expenses incurred by the vacation homeowner and the expenses he is allowed to deduct stems from the $300 rental period depreciation which the vacation home rules prohibit the taxpayer from deducting.

Some courts have disagreed with the IRS approach to allocating the fully deductible items (interest, taxes and casualty losses) to the rental period. According to these courts, the allocation should be made in terms of the percentage of the entire year in which the property was rented. Thus, in the example above, only one-fourth of the $1,600 property taxes and mortgage interest expense would be allocated to the rental period because the three-month rental period is equal to one-fourth of the entire year. The $2,000 rental income would be reduced by $400, leaving $1,600 to be offset by the $500 utilities and maintenance expense and the full $600 depreciation. The remaining $1,200 of property taxes and mortgage interest are deductible in any event. Thus, under the courts' approach, the entire $2,700 of expenses would be deductible instead of only $2,400 under the approach required by IRS. (See *Bolton,* 77 TC 104 (1981), *aff'd,* 694 F.2d556 (9th Cir. 1982; *McKinney,* T.C. Memo 1981-377, *aff'd,* 10th Cir., 1983).

Depreciation deductions for real property

From a tax standpoint, depreciation is a cost allocation concept. The cost or, more accurately, the adjusted basis of the property, is allocated over the years of its useful life. The allocation to each year constitutes a tax deduction for that year as a proper charge against the income earned by the property that year.

Put simply, if the basis allocable to a rent-producing property is $75,000 and the property is expected to last 25 years (after which time it is estimated the building will be worthless), it could seem reasonable that 1/25 of the basis, or $3,000, be allocated as an expense to each of the 25 years. As will be pointed out later in this chapter, while a portion of the adjusted basis is apportioned to each year, it does not necessarily have to be done on a straight line basis. Both the Accelerated Cost Recovery System (ACRS) method of the 1981 tax law and the accelerated depreciation methods allowed under prior law permit a greater portion of the basis to be allocated to earlier years of ownership and a lesser amount to later years.

The availability of the depreciation deduction sets real estate apart from many other forms of investment. The deduction does not depend on a cash outlay. Yet it reduces the taxable income arising from the investment and thereby can generate a cash flow by reducing taxes which otherwise would have had to be paid. Examples of this cash flow application are set forth at the end of this chapter.

Depreciation allowed or allowable

During the period property is held for production of income or used in a trade or business, depreciation reduces basis in an amount equal to the greater of the depreciation *allowed* or the depreciation *allowable* according to the depreciation method used by the taxpayer.

Thus, if for some reason the property owner actually deducts less depreciation than the amount he is *allowed* to deduct, his basis must still be reduced by the amount of the depreciation that was *allowable.* Conversely, if a taxpayer has deducted more depreciation than he was entitled to deduct, his basis is reduced by the actual amount of depreciation he has deducted (as long as the depreciation he deducted reduced his tax liability in the year it was deducted).

ACRS—the new depreciation

The Economic Recovery Tax Act of 1981 completely revised the depreciation system. The Accelerated Cost Recovery System (ACRS) was introduced into the law. Instead of depreciation deductions, we have cost recovery deductions (same idea; different name). The computation of cost recovery deductions for real estate is far less complex than for the depreciation calculations under the old law. The ease of calculation under ACRS is mainly attributable to the lack of choices available. The taxpayer will either consult a government table to determine the amount of his cost recovery deduction or use straight line depreciation over 15, 35, or 45 years (as he chooses). For property put into service after March 15, 1984, the straight line choices are 18, 35, or 45 years.

The ACRS rules are effective for all property acquired after 1980. For these acquisitions either the government table or the straight line alternatives must be used. No other depreciation method is available.

Before examining the ACRS rules in detail, and in order to fully comprehend the impact of the changes made by the ACRS provisions, let us briefly review the depreciation rules as they existed prior to the introduction of ACRS. (The old rules continue in effect for properties acquired prior to 1981.)

Pre-ACRS depreciation

In order to determine the depreciation deduction, it was necessary first to determine the useful life of the property. The basis of the property was then written off over its useful life. The shorter the useful life, the larger the depreciation deductions. Useful life was often open to dispute between the taxpayer and IRS, with the taxpayer generally arguing for as short a useful life as possible and IRS seeking to impose a longer useful life.

The amount to be written off over the useful life was the adjusted basis of the property. However, this amount had to be reduced by the salvage value of the property. The salvage value is the amount the taxpayer could reasonably expect to get for the property at the end of its useful life. (Although the property may no longer be useful to the taxpayer, it may still have value to another person.) When declining balance depreciation was used, salvage value did not have to be deducted from adjusted basis, but when the remaining unrecovered basis of the property (after deducting depreciation over a period of time) equaled the salvage value, the taxpayer was not entitled to any additional depreciation deductions. When other methods of depreciation were used, salvage value had to be deducted at the time of acquisition before applying a depreciation method.

A number of depreciation methods were available. The most common was the straight line method under which the amount to be depreciated was divided by the number of years of the useful life. The resulting amount was the depreciation deduction for each year. In other words, it was assumed that the amount to be recovered via depreciation would be recovered ratably over the property's useful life.

Declining balance depreciation allowed for greater deductions in the earlier years of ownership and lesser amounts in the later years. Conceptually, the same total amount would be written off over the useful life of the asset as with straight line. Depending on the nature of the property and whether it was new or used, declining balance deductions could be computed under the 200, 150 or 125-percent methods. The straight line rate was multiplied by one of these three percentages (whichever was appropriate in the situation). The resulting percentage was then applied to the adjusted basis in the first year to determine that year's depreciation deduction. In subsequent years, the same percentage was applied, but in each such succeeding year it was applied to the remaining basis of the property after reducing the starting basis by the prior years' depreciation deductions. Hence, each year the same percentage was applied to a declining balance.

Another accelerated depreciation method permitted in some cases was sum-of-the-years-digits. Assuming, for example, that a property had a 20-year useful life, the sum of the digits of 1 through 20 would be determined (210). To determine the depreciation deduction for the first year, the basis would be multiplied by a fraction the numerator of which was the useful life of the asset for that year (20) and the denominator of which was the sum of the years digits (210). Thus 20/210 of the adjusted basis would be the amount of the first year's depreciation deduction. In the second year, since the remaining useful life was 19, the fraction 19/210 of the original adjusted basis would equal the depreciation deduction. And in each succeeding year the numerator of the fraction would be reduced by 1.

The declining balance and the sum-of-the-years-digits methods—the accelerated methods of depreciation—allowed for a faster recovery of the owner's investment in the property than was available under straight line. On disposition of the property, part or all of the excess of the amount of the accelerated depreciation deducted over the amount of depreciation that would have been allowed had straight line depreciation been used could be "recaptured." That is, the part of the gain on the disposition of the property that was equal to the amount of the depreciation subject to recapture was taxable as ordinary income even though the gain would otherwise qualify as a capital gain.

Depreciation of components rather than of a building as a whole was an approach used to help increase the depreciation deductions in the early years of ownership. Under this approach, the basis of the property was allocated to the various components of the building (e.g., roof, plumbing, wiring). Each component had its own useful life, many of these components' useful lives being much shorter than the useful life of the building as a whole. By constructing a separate depreciation schedule for each component, the total allowable depreciation in one year could be considerably larger than if the depreciation were computed on the building as a single unit. While IRS often resisted this approach, it did concede its availability where the taxpayer had good records and could justify both the useful life of each component and the appropriate amount of basis allocated to each component.

How ACRS applies to real estate

As indicated, the ACRS rules apply to property acquired after 1980 if that property is used in a trade or business or is held for the production of income. Only the ACRS rules, not the previous depreciation rules, apply to such property.

ACRS does away with the need for determining the useful life of any single property. It eliminates salvage value as a factor in determining cost recovery deductions. And it eliminates the need for considering a variety of possible depreciation methods. An annual deduction determined from a government table or straight line depreciation for 15, 35, or 45 years (whichever the property owner chooses) are the only methods allowed. (For property put into service after March 15, 1984, the straight line choices are 18, 35, or 45 years.)

Almost all real property structures fall into a classification called 18-year real property if that property was put into service after March 15, 1984. (Real property put into service before March 16, 1984 is classified as 15-year real property.) Theme parks and manufactured homes fall into a 10-year property classification. Buildings used in particular industries which, according to the asset depreciation range (ADR) classifications IRS issued under the prior law, would have a class life of 12.5 years or less also qualify as 10-year property. (How cost recovery deductions are arrived at for 10-year property is discussed later in this chapter when the ACRS rules for personal property are explained.)

Property placed in service after March 15, 1984 and before 1987 is treated as 15-year real property if the taxpayer or a "qualified person" entered into a binding contract to purchase or construct the property prior to March 16, 1984, or if construction of the property was begun by the taxpayer or a "qualified person" before that date. A "qualified person" is one who transferred to the taxpayer his right in a contract (entered into before March 16, 1984) or property (the construction of which began prior to March 16, 1984), but only if the transfer to the taxpayer was made before the qualified person put that property into service.

The annual cost recovery deductions that are allowed under the ACRS procedure are determined from tables published by the IRS. These assume either a 15-year or an 18-year recovery period. The impact of the Tax Reform Act of 1984 was to lengthen the recovery period for real estate to 18 years.

Figure 15 ARCS Cost Recovery Tables for Real Estate

Table 1	18-Year Real Estate Other Than Low Income Housing Put Into Service After June 22, 1984

If the Recovery Year Is:	And the Month in the First Recovery Year the Property is Placed in Service Is:											
	1	2	3	4	5	6	7	8	9	10	11	12
	The applicable percentage is:											
1	9	9	8	7	6	5	4	4	3	2	1	0.4
2	9	9	9	9	9	9	9	9	9	10	10	10.0
3	8	8	8	8	8	8	8	8	9	9	9	9.0
4	7	7	7	7	7	8	8	8	8	8	8	8.0
5	7	7	7	7	7	7	7	7	7	7	7	7.0
6	6	6	6	6	6	6	6	6	6	6	6	6.0
7	5	5	5	5	6	6	6	6	6	6	6	6.0
8	5	5	5	5	5	5	5	5	5	5	5	5.0
9	5	5	5	5	5	5	5	5	5	5	5	5.0
10	5	5	5	5	5	5	5	5	5	5	5	5.0
11	5	5	5	5	5	5	5	5	5	5	5	5.0
12	5	5	5	5	5	5	5	5	5	5	5	5.0
13	4	4	4	5	4	4	5	4	4	4	5	5.0
14	4	4	4	4	4	4	4	4	4	4	4	4.0
15	4	4	4	4	4	4	4	4	4	4	4	4.0
16	4	4	4	4	4	4	4	4	4	4	4	4.0
17	4	4	4	4	4	4	4	4	4	4	4	4.0
18	4	3	4	4	4	4	4	4	4	4	4	4.0
19		1	1	1	2	2	2	3	3	3	3	3.6

The IRS cost recovery tables (Figure 15, Tables 1 and 2) assume that real property put into service after March 15, 1984 has a useful life of 18 years (the table for property put into service prior to March 16, 1984 assumes a useful life of 15 years and is shown as Figure 15, Table 3). The tables also assume that 175 percent declining balance depreciation is used until the point where straight line depreciation becomes more beneficial. At that point the tables use straight line depreciation.

There is a separate table for low-income housing (Figure 15, Table 4) which applies whether the property was put into service before or after March 15, 1984. This table uses a 15-year useful life and is based on 200 percent declining balance with a switch to straight line.

Note that the different tables in Figure 15 use different conventions. For 15-year property and for 18-year property put into service after March 15 and before June 23, 1984, the property is treated as having been held by the taxpayer for the entire month of acquisition (regardless of when in the month the property was acquired). For 18-year property put into service after June 22, 1984, a mid-month convention is used. That means that the property is deemed to have been held for half a month in the month of acquisition regardless of when during the month the property was acquired.

Figure 15   (continued)

Table 2	18-Year Real Estate Other Than Low Income Housing Put Into Service After March 15, 1984 and Before June 23, 1984									
If the Recovery Year Is:	And the Month in the First Recovery Year the Property is Placed in Service Is:									
	1	2	3	4	5	6	7	8	9	10-11	12
	The applicable percentage is:									
1	10	9	8	7	6	6	5	4	3	2	1
2	9	9	9	9	9	9	9	9	9	10	10
3	8	8	8	8	8	8	8	8	9	9	9
4	7	7	7	7	7	7	8	8	8	8	8
5	6	7	7	7	7	7	7	7	7	7	7
6	6	6	6	6	6	6	6	6	6	6	6
7	5	5	5	5	6	6	6	6	6	6	6
8	5	5	5	5	5	5	5	5	5	5	5
9	5	5	5	5	5	5	5	5	5	5	5
10	5	5	5	5	5	5	5	5	5	5	5
11	5	5	5	5	5	5	5	5	5	5	5
12	5	5	5	5	5	5	5	5	5	5	5
13	4	4	4	5	5	4	4	5	4	4	4
14	4	4	4	4	4	4	4	4	4	4	4
15	4	4	4	4	4	4	4	4	4	4	4
16	4	4	4	4	4	4	4	4	4	4	4
17	4	4	4	4	4	4	4	4	4	4	4
18	4	4	4	4	4	4	4	4	4	4	4
19			1	1	1	2	2	2	3	3	4

The following cost recovery tables are provided in Figure 15:

Table 1. 18-Year Real Estate Other Than Low-Income Housing Put Into Service After June 22, 1984

Table 2. 18-Year Real Estate Other Than Low-Income Housing Put Into Service After March 15, 1984 and Before June 23, 1984

Table 3 15-Year Real Estate Other Than Low-Income Housing Put Into Service Before March 16, 1984

Table 4. Low-Income Housing

Table 1 of Figure 15 will be the most commonly used for 18-year recovery property. It uses the mid-month convention. Table 2 is limited to property put into service after March 15 and before June 23, 1984. This is 18-year recovery property. Property put into service within this limited period is not subject to the mid-month convention. Table 3 applies to property put into service prior to the application of the amendments of the Tax Reform Act of 1984. This property is 15-year recovery property. Table 4 deals with low-income housing, which is 15-year property (before and after the changes of the Tax Reform Act of 1984).

To determine the amount of his cost recovery deduction, the property owner consults the appropriate table in Figure 15. He uses the column

Figure 15 (continued)

Table 3	15-Year Real Estate Other Than Low Income Housing Put Into Service Before March 16, 1984										
If the Recovery Year Is:	The applicable percentage is: (use the column for the month in the first year the property is placed in service)										
	1	2	3	4	5	6	7	8	9	10	11	12
1	12	11	10	9	8	7	6	5	4	3	2	1
2	10	10	11	11	11	11	11	11	11	11	11	12
3	9	9	9	9	10	10	10	10	10	10	10	10
4	8	8	8	8	8	8	9	9	9	9	9	9
5	7	7	7	7	7	7	8	8	8	8	8	8
6	6	6	6	6	7	7	7	7	7	7	7	7
7	6	6	6	6	6	6	6	6	6	6	6	6
8	6	6	6	6	6	6	5	6	6	6	6	6
9	6	6	6	6	5	6	5	5	5	6	6	6
10	5	6	5	6	5	5	5	5	5	5	6	5
11	5	5	5	5	5	5	5	5	5	5	5	5
12	5	5	5	5	5	5	5	5	5	5	5	5
13	5	5	5	5	5	5	5	5	5	5	5	5
14	5	5	5	5	5	5	5	5	5	5	5	5
15	5	5	5	5	5	5	5	5	5	5	5	5
16			1	1	2	2	3	3	4	4	4	5

representing the month in his taxable year in which he acquired the property (more accurately, the month in which he placed the property in service). In that column he will find the percentages that apply to each year of his ownership. Each year, the owner multiplies the appropriate percentage by his original basis for his property to determine the cost recovery deduction for the year.

Example

On May 16, 1985, Arbor acquires an apartment building for $1,125,000. Of this amount $250,000 is allocable to the value of the land. Hence, $1,000,000 is eligible for cost recovery. Assume that Arbor is a calendar-year taxpayer. May is the fifth month of his taxable year. To determine his cost recovery deduction for 1985, Arbor uses Column 5 of Table 1 shown in Figure 15. For year 1, the percentage is six. Therefore, in 1985 Arbor is entitled to deduct 6 percent of $1,000,000, or $60,000. In 1986 he will use the percentage in Column 5, Year 2, which is 9 percent. So, his 1986 deduction is $90,000. In 1987 he will use 8 percent (Column 5, Year 3), and so on.

The use of the cost recovery tables assumes that the property is acquired during a full 12-month taxable year. Suppose, however, that the property is acquired in the first year of the corporation's existence. Assume

Figure 15 (continued)

Table 4 Low Income Housing

If the Recovery Year Is:	The applicable percentage is: (use the column for the month in the first year the property is placed in service)										
	1	2	3	4	5	6	7	8	9	10	11	12
1	13	12	11	10	9	8	7	6	4	3	2	1
2	12	12	12	12	12	12	12	13	13	13	13	13
3	10	10	10	10	11	11	11	11	11	11	11	11
4	9	9	9	9	9	9	9	9	10	10	10	10
5	8	8	8	8	8	8	8	8	8	8	8	9
6	7	7	7	7	7	7	7	7	7	7	7	7
7	6	6	6	6	6	6	6	6	6	6	6	6
5	5	5	5	5	5	5	5	5	5	5	6	6
9	5	5	5	5	5	5	5	5	5	5	5	5
10	5	5	5	5	5	5	5	5	5	5	5	5
11	4	5	5	5	5	5	5	5	5	5	5	5
12	4	4	4	5	4	5	5	5	5	5	5	5
13	4	4	4	4	4	4	5	4	5	5	5	5
14	4	4	4	4	4	4	4	4	4	5	4	4
15	4	4	4	4	4	4	4	4	4	4	4	4
16			1	1	2	2	2	3	3	3	4	4

that in our previous example Arbor organized a corporation on May 2, 1985, and that on May 25, 1985, the corporation acquired the apartment house. Assume, too, that the corporation is going to use the calendar year as its taxable year.

The corporation's first taxable year will run from May 2 through December 31, 1985. In using Table 1 of Figure 15 to determine its cost recovery deduction for 1985, the corporation will use Column 5 and come up with the same deduction as Arbor did. Although the property was acquired in the first month of the corporation's current taxable year, May is the fifth month of the full 12-month taxable year. So the corporation uses Column 5 to calculate the deduction. (Were it allowed to use Column 1, it could have deducted 9 percent instead of 6 percent; but it must use Column 5.)

The straight line depreciation option

If the taxpayer does not want to use the ACRS tables, his only alternative is to use straight line depreciation. He may do so without regard to salvage value. However, he must choose a useful life of either 18, 35, or 45 years for the entire structure; component depreciation is not allowed. (For property put into service before March 16, 1984, 15 rather than 18-year straight line is permitted.)

In figuring straight line for property put into service after March 16, 1984, and before June 23, the taxpayer can take a full month's depreciation for the month the property is put into service at any time during the month. For property put into service after June 22, 1984, the mid-month conven-

239

Figure 16   Straight Line Depreciation Tables

Table 1 18-Year Straight Line Using Mid-Month Convention (For property placed in service after June 22, 1984)					
If the Recovery Year Is:	And the Month in the First Recovery Year the Property Placed in Service Is:				
	1-2	3-4	5-7	8-9	10-11	12
	The applicable percentage is:				
1	5	4	3	2	1	0.2
2	6	6	6	6	6	6.0
3	6	6	6	6	6	6.0
4	6	6	6	6	6	6.0
5	6	6	6	6	6	6.0
6	6	6	6	6	6	6.0
7	6	6	6	6	6	6.0
8	6	6	6	6	6	6.0
9	6	6	6	6	6	6.0
10	6	6	6	6	6	6.0
11	5	5	5	5	5	5.8
12	5	5	5	5	5	5.0
13	5	5	5	5	5	5.0
14	5	5	5	5	5	5.0
15	5	5	5	5	5	5.0
16	5	5	5	5	5	5.0
17	5	5	5	5	5	5.0
18	5	5	5	5	5	5.0
19	1	2	3	4	5	5.0

tion must be used; that is, the taxpayer gets one-half month's depreciation for the month when the property was placed in service regardless of when during the month that took place.

Figure 16 shows IRS tables for use in calculating straight line depreciation. Table 1 is for 18-year straight line using the mid-month convention (i.e., for property put into service after June 22, 1984). Table 2 is for property placed in service after March 15, but before June 23, 1984; it does not use the mid-month convention. Tables 3 and 4 deal with property placed in service after June 22, 1984 (using the mid-month convention) where the taxpayer chooses to use either 35 or 45-year straight line.

Generally, a taxpayer will prefer to use ACRS (accelerated depreciation). Under that method, his deductions in the early years of ownership are greater than they would be under straight line, while in the later years they are less. Overall, his total depreciation deductions should be about the same. Thus, the taxes he saves in the earlier years are available to him for production of income. The use of these tax savings (until he pays them in later years) is the equivalent of an interest-free loan from the government. Nevertheless, as is explained below in the discussion of depreciation recapture, in the case of commercial real estate it may be advantageous to use 18-year straight line depreciation instead of the ACRS table, based on the 18-year recovery period.

Figure 16 (continued)

Table 2	18-Year Straight Line Without Using Mid-Month Convention (For property placed in service after March 15, 1984 and before June 23, 1984)						

If the Recovery Year Is:	And the Month in the First Recovery Year the Property is Placed in Service Is:						
	1	2-3	4-5	6-7	8-9	10-11	12
	The applicable percentage is:						
1	6	5	4	3	2	1	0.5
2	6	6	6	6	6	6	6.0
3	6	6	6	6	6	6	6.0
4	6	6	6	6	6	6	6.0
5	6	6	6	6	6	6	6.0
6	6	6	6	6	6	6	6.0
7	6	6	6	6	6	6	6.0
8	6	6	6	6	6	6	6.0
9	6	6	6	6	6	6	6.0
10	6	6	6	6	6	6	6.0
11	5	5	5	5	5	5	5.5
12	5	5	5	5	5	5	5.0
13	5	5	5	5	5	5	5.0
14	5	5	5	5	5	5	5.0
15	5	5	5	5	5	5	5.0
16	5	5	5	5	5	5	5.0
17	5	5	5	5	5	5	5.0
18	5	5	5	5	5	5	5.0
19		1	2	3	4	5	5.0

Substantial improvements and components

Under the ACRS rules, a substantial improvement is treated as a separate building. A substantial improvement requires at least a 25-percent addition to the building's capital account over a 24-month period. However, an improvement made within three years of the time that the building was placed in service will not qualify as a substantial improvement.

Inasmuch as a substantial improvement is treated as a separate structure, the owner may choose to use the ACRS 18-year table for that improvement even though he chose the straight line method for the basic structure or vice versa.

Components, as distinguished from substantial improvements, are subject to the same recovery method as applies with respect to the building. The recovery period for the component begins on the later of (1) the date the component is put into service, or (2) the date on which the building is put into service. The first component put into service after March 15, 1984, with respect to a building placed in service before March 16, 1984, uses the treatment applicable to property put into service after March 15, 1984 (so it becomes 18-year real property). Subsequent components use the same method.

Figure 16   (continued)

Table 3	35-Year Straight Line Using Mid-Month Convention (For property placed in service after June 22, 1984)				
If the Recovery Year Is:	And the Month in the First Recovery Year the Property is Placed in Service Is:				
	1-2	3-6	7-10	11	12
	The applicable percentage is:				
1	3	2	1	0.4	0.1
2	3	3	3	3.0	3.0
3	3	3	3	3.0	3.0
4	3	3	3	3.0	3.0
5	3	3	3	3.0	3.0
6	3	3	3	3.0	3.0
7	3	3	3	3.0	3.0
8	3	3	3	3.0	3.0
9	3	3	3	3.0	3.0
10	3	3	3	3.0	3.0
11	3	3	3	3.0	3.0
12	3	3	3	3.0	3.0
13	3	3	3	3.0	3.0
14	3	3	3	3.0	3.0
15	3	3	3	3.0	3.0
16	3	3	3	3.0	3.0
17	3	3	3	3.0	3.0
18	3	3	3	3.0	3.0
19	3	3	3	3.0	3.0
20	3	3	3	3.0	3.0
21	3	3	3	3.0	3.0
22	3	3	3	3.0	3.0
23	3	3	3	3.0	3.0
24	3	3	3	3.0	3.0
25	3	3	3	3.0	3.0
26	3	3	3	3.0	3.0
27	3	3	3	3.0	3.0
28	3	3	3	3.0	3.0
29	3	3	3	3.0	3.0
30	3	3	3	3.0	3.0
31	2	2	2	2.6	2.9
32	2	2	2	2.0	2.0
33	2	2	2	2.0	2.0
34	2	2	2	2.0	2.0
35	2	2	2	2.0	2.0
36		1	2	2.0	2.0

Figure 16 (continued)

Table 4 45-Year Straight Line Using Mid-Month Convention
(For property placed in service after June 22, 1984)

If the Recovery Year Is:	And the Month in the First Recovery Year the Property is Placed in Service Is:											
	1	2	3	4	5	6	7	8	9	10	11	12
	The applicable percentage is:											
1	2.1	1.9	1.8	1.6	1.4	1.2	1.0	0.8	0.6	0.5	0.3	0.1
2	2.3	2.3	2.3	2.3	2.3	2.3	2.3	2.3	2.3	2.3	2.3	2.3
3	2.3	2.3	2.3	2.3	2.3	2.3	2.3	2.3	2.3	2.3	2.3	2.3
4	2.3	2.3	2.3	2.3	2.3	2.3	2.3	2.3	2.3	2.3	2.3	2.3
5	2.3	2.3	2.3	2.3	2.3	2.3	2.3	2.3	2.3	2.3	2.3	2.3
6	2.3	2.3	2.3	2.3	2.3	2.3	2.3	2.3	2.3	2.3	2.3	2.3
7	2.3	2.3	2.3	2.3	2.3	2.3	2.3	2.3	2.3	2.3	2.3	2.3
8	2.3	2.3	2.3	2.3	2.3	2.3	2.3	2.3	2.3	2.3	2.3	2.3
9	2.3	2.3	2.3	2.3	2.3	2.3	2.3	2.3	2.3	2.3	2.3	2.3
10	2.3	2.3	2.3	2.3	2.3	2.3	2.3	2.3	2.3	2.3	2.3	2.3
11	2.3	2.3	2.3	2.3	2.3	2.3	2.3	2.3	2.3	2.3	2.3	2.3
12	2.2	2.2	2.2	2.2	2.2	2.2	2.2	2.2	2.2	2.2	2.2	2.2
13	2.2	2.2	2.2	2.2	2.2	2.2	2.2	2.2	2.2	2.2	2.2	2.2
14	2.2	2.2	2.2	2.2	2.2	2.2	2.2	2.2	2.2	2.2	2.2	2.2
15	2.2	2.2	2.2	2.2	2.2	2.2	2.2	2.2	2.2	2.2	2.2	2.2
16	2.2	2.2	2.2	2.2	2.2	2.2	2.2	2.2	2.2	2.2	2.2	2.2
17	2.2	2.2	2.2	2.2	2.2	2.2	2.2	2.2	2.2	2.2	2.2	2.2
18	2.2	2.2	2.2	2.2	2.2	2.2	2.2	2.2	2.2	2.2	2.2	2.2
19	2.2	2.2	2.2	2.2	2.2	2.2	2.2	2.2	2.2	2.2	2.2	2.2
20	2.2	2.2	2.2	2.2	2.2	2.2	2.2	2.2	2.2	2.2	2.2	2.2
21	2.2	2.2	2.2	2.2	2.2	2.2	2.2	2.2	2.2	2.2	2.2	2.2
22	2.2	2.2	2.2	2.2	2.2	2.2	2.2	2.2	2.2	2.2	2.2	2.2
23	2.2	2.2	2.2	2.2	2.2	2.2	2.2	2.2	2.2	2.2	2.2	2.2
24	2.2	2.2	2.2	2.2	2.2	2.2	2.2	2.2	2.2	2.2	2.2	2.2
25	2.2	2.2	2.2	2.2	2.2	2.2	2.2	2.2	2.2	2.2	2.2	2.2
26	2.2	2.2	2.2	2.2	2.2	2.2	2.2	2.2	2.2	2.2	2.2	2.2
27	2.2	2.2	2.2	2.2	2.2	2.2	2.2	2.2	2.2	2.2	2.2	2.2
28	2.2	2.2	2.2	2.2	2.2	2.2	2.2	2.2	2.2	2.2	2.2	2.2
29	2.2	2.2	2.2	2.2	2.2	2.2	2.2	2.2	2.2	2.2	2.2	2.2
30	2.2	2.2	2.2	2.2	2.2	2.2	2.2	2.2	2.2	2.2	2.2	2.2
31	2.2	2.2	2.2	2.2	2.2	2.2	2.2	2.2	2.2	2.2	2.2	2.2
32	2.2	2.2	2.2	2.2	2.2	2.2	2.2	2.2	2.2	2.2	2.2	2.2
33	2.2	2.2	2.2	2.2	2.2	2.2	2.2	2.2	2.2	2.2	2.2	2.2
34	2.2	2.2	2.2	2.2	2.2	2.2	2.2	2.2	2.2	2.2	2.2	2.2
35	2.2	2.2	2.2	2.2	2.2	2.2	2.2	2.2	2.2	2.2	2.2	2.2
36	2.2	2.2	2.2	2.2	2.2	2.2	2.2	2.2	2.2	2.2	2.2	2.2
37	2.2	2.2	2.2	2.2	2.2	2.2	2.2	2.2	2.2	2.2	2.2	2.2
38	2.2	2.2	2.2	2.2	2.2	2.2	2.2	2.2	2.2	2.2	2.2	2.2
39	2.2	2.2	2.2	2.2	2.2	2.2	2.2	2.2	2.2	2.2	2.2	2.2
40	2.2	2.2	2.2	2.2	2.2	2.2	2.2	2.2	2.2	2.2	2.2	2.2
41	2.2	2.2	2.2	2.2	2.2	2.2	2.2	2.2	2.2	2.2	2.2	2.2
42	2.2	2.2	2.2	2.2	2.2	2.2	2.2	2.2	2.2	2.2	2.2	2.2
43	2.2	2.2	2.2	2.2	2.2	2.2	2.2	2.2	2.2	2.2	2.2	2.2
44	2.2	2.2	2.2	2.2	2.2	2.2	2.2	2.2	2.2	2.2	2.2	2.2
45	2.2	2.2	2.2	2.2	2.2	2.2	2.2	2.2	2.2	2.2	2.2	2.2
46	0.1	0.3	0.4	0.6	0.8	1.0	1.2	1.4	1.6	1.7	1.9	2.1

Depreciation recapture on disposition of real estate

Since depreciation (or cost recovery) deductions reduce basis, gain on the subsequent sale of the property may be attributable to a great extent to the depreciation that was previously deducted.

Example

If property is acquired for $100,000, cost recovery deductions of $40,000 are taken, and the property is subsequently sold for $120,000, there will be a gain of $60,000. This is so because the $100,000 basis was reduced to $60,000 by the cost recovery deductions. Hence, the difference between the basis and the sale price is $60,000. Of that gain, $40,000 is attributable to the cost recovery deductions. (If no cost recovery deductions had been taken, the basis would have remained $100,000 and the gain would have been $20,000.)

Cost recovery deductions are ordinary deductions, reducing ordinary income. Gain on the sale is generally a capital gain. Thus, the $40,000 of ordinary deductions is subsequently recovered as capital gain. This, of course, is a good trade-off. Ordinary deductions can reduce income which may be taxable at as much as 50 percent. The maximum tax rate of capital gains is 20 percent.

Consequently, the concept of depreciation recapture was written into the tax law. That part of the gain which is equal to depreciation deductions is treated as ordinary income under that concept. However, under the law prior to ACRS, there was a special rule for real estate. Only as much of the depreciation deducted which exceeded the amount of depreciation that *would have been deducted* had straight line depreciation been used was subject to recapture as ordinary income. (The rule is different for personal property as is explained later in this chapter.) Thus, for real estate, depreciation recapture applied only if accelerated depreciation was used.

The ACRS table is based on an accelerated depreciation method. So, the new tax law also provides for depreciation recapture, although the rules are somewhat different than under the old law, with separate provisions for residential property and commercial property. For residential property, the old recapture rule applies. That is, if the ACRS table is used, the recapturable cost recovery deduction is the excess of the amounts actually deducted (via the use of the ACRS table) over the depreciation that would have been deducted had the 18-year straight line method been used (15-year straight line if the property was placed in service before March 16, 1984).

For commercial property, however, the entire amount of the cost recovery deduction is subject to recapture (a sharp departure from the previous rule). Hence, taxpayers acquiring commercial property may prefer to use 18-year straight line depreciation rather than the deductions available under the ACRS table. When straight line is used, there cannot be any depreciation recapture. While the straight line method may yield smaller deductions in the earlier years of ownership, there will be a complete trade-off of ordinary deductions for capital gain on later sale of the property. On the other hand, while ACRS will give larger deductions (and current use of the tax savings), these deductions will subsequently be recaptured as ordinary income.

Special rule for subsidized low-income housing

As indicated above, depreciation recapture on residential property is limited to the excess of the ACRS deductions over the amount that would have been deducted as straight line depreciation. However, if the property is subsidized low-income housing, this excess is further reduced before it becomes recapturable depreciation. It is reduced by one percentage point per month for every month that this subsidized low-income housing property is held in excess of 100 months.

Example

If excess depreciation on subsidized low-income housing was $50,000 and the property was held for 120 months before it was sold, the $50,000 would be reduced by 20 percent (or $10,000). Thus, only $40,000 would be subject to depreciation recapture.

Five-year write-off for rehabilitation of low-income rental housing

To encourage the rehabilitation of low-income rental housing, the tax law includes a special depreciation provision for rehabilitation expenses. These expenses can be written off over a 60-month period under the straight line method. Salvage value need not be considered, and the investment credit is not available.

To qualify for the rapid write-off, the following requirements concerning the rehabilitation expense must be met:

1. The expenditure has to take place after July 24, 1969, and before January 1, 1987. If the expenditure takes place after this date it qualifies only if it is made under a contract entered into before January 1, 1987.

2. The total amount of rehabilitation expense spent on one dwelling unit (defined below) cannot exceed $20,000. (It can be as high as $40,000 if certain requirements are met; see below.)

3. The special write-off applies only if expenses for the rehabilitation of a dwelling unit in two consecutive years (including the taxable year) exceed $3,000.

What are rehabilitation expenditures? These are amounts spent in connection with the rehabilitation of an existing building for low-income rental housing. They have to be for additions or improvements to the property with a useful life of five years or more. They do not include the cost of the building or an interest (e. g., a lease) in the building.

What is low-income rental housing? This is a building in which the dwelling units are rented to families and individuals with low or moderate incomes. The Commissioner of Internal Revenue will determine which buildings qualify, using as his guide Section 8 of the U. S. Housing Act of 1937.

What is a dwelling unit? A dwelling unit is defined as a house or an apartment used to provide living accommodations in a building or structure. It is not a unit in a hotel, motel, inn or other establishment in which more than half the units are used on a transient basis.

How the $3,000/$20,000 limit works

Example

Assume the following amounts are spent on rehabilitation on one dwelling unit in the years indicated.

1982	$ 1,000
1983	1,500
1984	4,000
1985	6,000
1986	10,000

The 1982 expenditure is not eligible for the 60-month write-off because, when combined with the 1983 expenditure, the more-than-$3,000 requirement is not met. The 1983 expenditure is eligible for the 60-month write-off because, when added to the 1984 expenditure, the more-than-$3,000 requirement is met. The 1984 and 1985 expenditures are eligible for the 60-month write-off because each, on its own, meets the more-than-$3,000 requirement.

Of the $10,000 expended in 1986, only $8,500 is eligible for the 60-month write-off because the previous expenditures eligible for the special write-off (i.e., the $1,500 in 1983, the $4,000 in 1984 and the $6,000 in 1985) already total $11,500. Since not more than $20,000 of expenditures are eligible for the special write-off on one dwelling unit, there is only room for another $8,500 to bring the total up to $20,000. (Note that the $1,000 in 1982 which was not eligible for the special 60-month write-off is not counted in totaling up the $20,000.)

What happens to the $1,000 expended in 1982 and the excess $1,500 expended in 1986? They are not eligible for the 60-month write-off. But these expenses are recoverable via the regular cost recovery method.

Note that amortization in excess of straight line depreciation may be subject to depreciation recapture on disposition of the property.

When the $20,000 limitation can be increased to $40,000

For expenditures made after 1980, the $20,000 limitation on rehabilitation expenses that may be written off over 60 months is increased to $40,000 if the following tests are met:

1. The program under which the rehabilitation takes place and the development costs are certified by the Secretary of Housing and Urban Development or by a state or local government.

2. The tenants occupy the units as their principal residences and the program provides for sale of the units to tenants who demonstrate home ownership responsibility.

3. The amount realized from leasing the units plus the amounts received on the sale of the units cannot exceed the difference between the cost of such units and the tax benefits derived from them. The tax benefits derived equal the 60-month write-offs minus any taxes paid on the income received from leasing the property.

Depreciation of personal property

Many acquisitions of real property include personal property as well. A hotel includes furniture, kitchen equipment and other such property. An apartment building may include window air conditioners, movable refrigerators and furniture. (Generally, personal property is any property which is not real property, i.e., not permanently attached to the building structure.)

Prior to the enactment of ACRS, personal property was depreciable under the various accelerated methods or by straight line depreciation. Useful life for each item had to be determined (although tables published by IRS—so-called ADR tables based on asset depreciation range—could be used to determine useful life). Salvage value had to be taken into account.

For personal property put into service in 1981 or thereafter, ACRS rules apply.

How ACRS applies to personal property

All personal property is divided into four classes: three-year property, five-year property, ten-year property and 15-year public utility property. The 15-year public utility property is only of interest to public utilities and will not be discussed here.

While ten-year property covers mostly public utility property as well, this class includes theme park structures and manufactured homes. Three-year property generally covers automobiles and light trucks. Five-year property covers all personal property not covered by the other three classes. Most of the personal property with which investors in real estate will be concerned is five-year property.

A table has been published which specifies what percentage of the cost of the property is to be written off each year as cost recovery. The table reflects 150 percent declining balance depreciation with a switch to straight line.

The ACRS rules do not require that salvage value be taken into account. Nor is any distinction made between new and used property.

The ACRS tables for personal property are constructed to employ a half-year convention. Under this approach, the assumption is made that all property acquired during a year (regardless of when in the year it was acquired) was in service for one-half year. Thus, regardless of when in the year a piece of personal property was acquired, the cost recovery deduction for that property for that year will be the same. The ACRS table for personal property is shown in Figure 17 and an example follows.

Figure 17   ARCS Cost Recovery Table for Personal Property
[Recovery percentage]

Class of Investment			
	3-year	5-year	10-year	15-year public utility property
If the recovery year is:				
1	25	15	8	5
2	38	22	14	10
3	37	21	12	9
4		21	10	8
5		21	10	7
6			10	7
7			9	6
8			9	6
9			9	6
10			9	6
11				6
12				6
13				6
14				6
15				6
Total	100	100	100	100

Example

In 1984, Brown buys two refrigerators to install in apartments in the building he owns. Each costs $600. One was bought on February 17, 1984, and the other on September 11, 1984. On February 9, 1984, he bought a light truck for $8,000 to use in his real estate business. To calculate his cost recovery deductions, he goes to the table in Figure 17.

The refrigerators are five-year property. In the five-year recovery column, he finds that he is entitled to recover 15 percent of his cost in the first year. Thus, he can deduct 15 percent of $1,200 (or $180) as cost recovery for the refrigerators in 1984. (Note that although one refrigerator was purchased in February and the other in September, the amount of cost recovery for each is the same.) The light truck is three-year property.

In the three-year column of the table he finds that in the first year he is entitled to a cost recovery deduction of 25 percent of the cost of the truck, or $2,000 (25 percent of $8,000). In 1985, he will deduct 22 percent of the $1,200 cost of the refrigerators and 38 percent of the $8,000 cost of the truck. In 1986, he will recover the remaining 37 percent of the cost of the truck, while in 1986, 1987, and 1988, he will recover 21 percent of the cost of the refrigerators in each of these three years.

249

Election to use straight line As in the case of real estate, the taxpayer must either use the ACRS tables for personal property acquired in 1981 or thereafter or elect to use straight line depreciation. If he elects straight line, he must choose the useful life from the following table:

3-year property	3, 5 or 12 years
5-year property	5, 12 or 25 years
10-year property	10, 25 or 35 years

If he uses straight line depreciation, the taxpayer must use the half-year convention to calculate the cost recovery deduction in the year he acquires the property. That is, one-half of a full year's depreciation is allowed in the year of acquisition regardless of when during the year the property was acquired. The straight line life elected must be used for all property in that class acquired that year. This rule differs from the rule applying to real estate, which allows the straight line lives to be elected on a property-by-property basis.

When personal property is disposed of, no cost recovery deductions are allowed in the year of disposition. This, however, makes no difference because, as explained later in this chapter, the application of the depreciation recapture provisions would bring about the same result.

It should be borne in mind that while the above discussion deals with personal property, the same rules apply to ten-year property which is not personal property—for example, theme park structures and manufactured homes after they are installed.

Depreciation recapture The entire amount of cost recovery deductions claimed becomes depreciation recapture on the sale of the property. Thus, that portion of the gain on the disposition of the property which is equal to the total amount of cost recovery deductions taken is treated as ordinary income. Consequently, the fact that cost recovery is not allowed in the year of sale makes no difference. Denying the cost recovery in the year of sale reduces the gain on the sale because the basis of the property sold is that much higher. If the cost recovery deduction were allowed in the year of sale, the gain would be larger, but the amount of the cost recovery deduction would increase that portion of the gain which would be recapturable as ordinary income.

Complete write-off of cost of personal property
Beginning in 1982, taxpayers are permitted to write off the entire cost of some personal property (up to a dollar limitation; see below) in the year it is acquired.

The dollar limitations under the complete write-off rules are as follows:

If the acquisition is made in the taxable year beginning in:	The maximum amount eligible for complete write-off is:
1982-1987	$ 5,000
1988, 1989	7,500
1990 and thereafter	10,000

For a married individual filing a separate return, the above maximum amounts are cut in half.

The property eligible for this treatment is personal property eligible for the investment credit and used in a trade or business (not merely held for the production of income). The rules applying to the investment credit are explained later in this chapter.

To get the complete write-off in the year of acquisition (up to the dollar limitation applicable for that year), the taxpayer must make an election to take the write-off. He signifies this election on his tax return. Once the election is made, it cannot be revoked.

If the election for the complete write-off is made, the investment credit is not available. (Where the regular cost recovery method is used, the investment credit is available as well.)

The property on which the complete write-off is taken must be purchased, but it cannot be acquired from family members and related corporations, partnerships, trusts and estates. Inherited property also does not qualify.

Trusts and estates are not entitled to take this complete write-off. A partnership taking a complete write-off is limited to the dollar limitations listed above. The amount deducted is then allocated among the partners. Each partner adds his portion of the write-off to any other complete write-offs he may have taken on his own or acquired from other partnerships. His total write-off cannot exceed the dollar limits for that year.

The amount deducted as a complete write-off is treated as depreciation recapture should the property be sold. Thus, for example, if the cost of the entire property was written off in the year of acquisition, the property's basis would be zero. Hence, whatever was received on the subsequent sale of that property would all be gain. And to the extent that the gain did not exceed the amount written off in the year of acquisition, the gain would be depreciation recapture, taxable as ordinary income.

Investment credit

Quite apart from deductions for depreciation, a property owner may obtain a credit—a dollar-for-dollar reduction of his tax bill—based on investments in certain cost-recovery (i.e., depreciable) property. The property eligible for investment credit is generally tangible personal property. Buildings and their structural components do not qualify. However, elevators and escalators do qualify.

Personal property used to furnish nontransient lodging (in an apartment house, for example) is not eligible for the investment credit. However, coin-operated vending machines, washers and dryers are eligible. If, however, furnishings are leased directly to tenants of nontransient housing by outside lessors (not the landlord of the building), the lessors may claim the investment credit on their investments in those furnishings. A landlord of transient housing (a hotel or motel, for example) may claim an investment credit on the property he invests in to furnish that building.

The credit is 6 percent for property with a three-year recovery period. For property with a five-year, ten-year or 15-year recovery period, the credit is 10 percent. A maximum of $125,000 of used property acquired in one year is eligible for the credit. Beginning after 1987, the $125,000 limit will be increased to $150,000. (There is no limit on new property.)

There is also a limit as to how much credit may be applied in one year to reduce the tax bill. The credit allowed in one year may not exceed the total of $25,000 plus 85 percent of the taxpayer's tax liability in excess of $25,000.

Example

If the taxpayer's tax before applying the credit is $100,000, the maximum amount of credit which would be allowed is $88,750 ($25,000 plus $67,500—85 percent of $75,000).

The use of the investment credit has an effect on the basis of the property acquired. The basis is reduced by half the investment credit. Thus, where a 10 percent credit is claimed, only 95 percent of the basis of the property is recoverable via cost recovery deductions.

If the investment credit is subsequently recaptured (as explained later in this chapter), half of the recaptured credit is added to the basis of the asset. Since the recapture occurs when the property is disposed of, the addback of the credit to the basis is deemed to occur just before the disposition.

If the basis is reduced by half of the credit, but the credit is not fully utilized (i.e., there is insufficient income in the current year and years of carryover to absorb the full credit), half the unused credit becomes a deduction in the year following the last year to which the credit carryover applied.

The reduction in basis by half the amount of the credit is treated as if it were a deduction for cost recovery when depreciation recapture is calculated. Thus, although the taxpayer did not get a cost recovery deduction for the reduction in basis by half the amount of the credit, that amount is recapturable as ordinary income on the disposition of the property.

The taxpayer can avoid the basis reduction by agreeing to reduce the amount of the investment credit by two percentage points (i.e., take an 8 percent credit instead of a 10 percent credit, or a 4 percent credit instead of a 6 percent credit.

Carryback and carryforward of credit

If the entire credit cannot be used in the taxable year it arises (because of the percentage-of-tax limitation), it may be carried back three years and carried forward 15 years. The credit is carried back to the third year before the taxable year in which it arose to see if it could have been applied in that year. If so, the tax of that prior year is reduced and the taxpayer receives a refund. If the entire credit cannot be used in the third year before the year in which the credit arose, the unused portion is carried to the second year before the year in which it arose. Then, to the extent unused, it is carried to the year before the year in which it arose. Any unused credit still remaining then goes forward, being added to whatever credit arises in the following year and applied to that year, and so on for 15 years if necessary.

At-risk requirement for investment credit

The tax law requires that the taxpayer be at-risk with respect to the property on which he claims an investment credit. This means that in figuring the amount of the credit, he can use only as much of its cost for which he actually paid or is personally liable. To the extent the cost is covered by a nonrecourse debt (a debt on which he is not at-risk) it cannot be included in the cost on which the investment credit is calculated.

This at-risk rule applies to individuals, Subchapter S corporations and closely-held corporations (where more than 50 percent of the stock is owned by five or fewer individuals).

Exceptions to at-risk requirement If the taxpayer is at-risk in an amount equal to at least 20 percent of the property's basis and he did not acquire the property from a "related person," he will be considered to be at-risk on funds borrowed from a "qualified person." A "qualified person" is any person actively and regularly engaged in the business of lending money. This does *not*, however, include (1) someone related to the taxpayer, (2) a person from whom the taxpayer acquired the property (or someone related to that person), and (3) a person who receives a fee with respect to the taxpayer's investment in that property (or someone related to that person). In addition to borrowing from a "qualified person," borrowings are also permitted from federal, state, or local governments as well as loans guaranteed by the federal, state, or local government (but not including convertible debt).

The "related person" may include spouses, children, grandchildren, parents, grandparents; corporations and shareholders (where a shareholder owns more than 10 percent of the stock directly or indirectly); grantors, fiduciaries, and the beneficiaries of certain trusts; two personal holding companies where more than 10 percent of the stock in each is owned by the same individual; and partnerships and their more-than-10-percent partners.

Recapture of investment credit

Because the 6-percent credit assumes that property will be held for three years and the 10-percent credit assumes that property will be held for five years, if the property on which the credit was claimed is held for a shorter period of time, all or part of the credit may have to be returned to the government—that is, recaptured. To the extent that the credit is recaptured, it is added to the taxpayer's tax in the year of recapture (remember, the credit originally *reduced* the taxpayer's tax).

Figure 18 explains how much of the credit is recaptured when the property on which the credit was claimed is not held long enough to warrant the full amount of the credit originally claimed:

Figure 18

If the recovery property is disposed of within	The recapture percentage is:	
	For 15-year, 10 year and 5-year property	For 3-year property
One full year after placed in service	100	100
Two full years after placed in service	80	66
Three full years after placed in service	60	33
Four full years after placed in service	20	0
Five full years after placed in service	20	0

Thus, if three-year property is held for two years and three months (i.e., less than three full years), one-third of the 6-percent investment credit claimed is recaptured. So, the taxpayer ends up enjoying a 4-percent investment credit. If that property had been five, ten or 15-year property, 60 percent of the 10-percent investment credit would have been recaptured. Again, the taxpayer would enjoy only a 4-percent credit.

So, another way of expressing the recapture rule is to say that the taxpayer keeps a 2-percent credit for each full year that he holds the property. (With three-year property, he keeps the entire 6 percent if he holds the property at least three full years. With five, ten or 15-year property, he keeps the entire 10-percent credit if he holds the property at least five full years.)

Investment credit for rehabilitation of real estate

Buildings and structural components (except elevators and escalators) are normally not eligible for the investment credit. However, there is a special investment credit for qualified expenditures incurred in the rehabilitation of older *nonresidential* real estate. For expenditures incurred after 1981, there is a three-tier system of credits (for expenditures before 1981, there is a 10-percent credit), as follows:

1. A 15-percent credit on qualified expenditures incurred in rehabilitating a nonresidential building at least 30 but less than 40 years old.
2. A 20-percent credit if the building is at least 40 years old.
3. A 25-percent credit for rehabilitation of a certified historic structure *(residential or nonresidential;* more on that below).

Qualified rehabilitation expenditure The rehabilitation expenditure on which the investment credit may be claimed must involve a substantial expenditure on property with an 18-year recovery period on which the taxpayer has elected 18-year straight line depreciation (15-year recovery period and 15-year straight line for low-income housing and for other property placed in service before March 16, 1984). The expenditures during the 24-month period ending on the last day of the taxable year must exceed *the greater of* the property's basis on the first day of the 24-month period, or $5,000. If the rehabilitation is done in phases, a 60-month period may be used to apply this test. But if the 60-month period is used, there must be architectural plans and specifications for all phases of the rehabilitation and there must be a reasonable expectation that all phases of the plan will be completed.

The basis of the property has to be reduced by the amount of the investment credit claimed for rehabilitation expenditures (unless the property is a certified historic structure). If any part of the investment credit is recaptured, the increase in tax resulting from the recapture is added to the basis of the building.

Rehabilitation of certified historic structures If the above qualified rehabilitation expenditure rules are met and the rehabilitation is certified by the Secretary of the Interior as a rehabilitation of an historic structure, a 25 percent investment credit applies.

In the case of historic structures the rehabilitation rules differ from those dealinng with nonhistoric structures in two important respects:

1. The rehabilitation can be of either a residential or nonresidential property. (The other rehabilitation credits apply only in respect to nonresidential property.)

2. There is no basis adjustment required for the amount of the investment credit. In the case of other rehabilitation credits, the amount of the credit allowed reduces the basis of the property.

Cash flow

Real estate investors commonly examine their investment results in terms of cash flow; e.g., how much actual cash (often referred to as "spendable dollars") is available to them after taxes from their investment. They are not content merely with the bookkeeping result of net profit or loss from the operation.

The major reason for a difference between net operating income (or loss) and cash flow stems from the interaction of the cost recovery (depreciation) deduction and the principal payments made on any mortgages on the property. Depreciation reduces net taxable income from the property but requires no outlay of cash. On the other hand, principal payments require an outlay of cash but are not deductible for tax purposes. Further, a net taxable loss from operations reduces the property owner's other taxable income and thereby reduces the cash outlay required for income taxes.

To illustrate the interaction of the factors discussed in this chapter and their impacts on cash flow, let us consider the following three examples. (The figures are somewhat arbitrary and are used merely to illustrate the principles involved.)

Examples

1. Assume that Brown, a single individual, has rental property which produces $100,000 in gross rents. He has operating expenses of $60,000, mortgage interest of $9,000, principal payments of $10,000, real estate taxes of $12,000 and a depreciation deduction of $15,000.

His taxable income from the property would be computed as follows:

Rental income		$100,000
Operating expenses	$60,000	
Mortgage interest	9,000	
Real estate taxes	12,000	
Depreciation	15,000	96,000
Taxable income		$ 4,000

His cash flow from the property, however, would be computed as follows:

Rental income		$100,000
Operating expenses	$60,000	
Mortgage interest	9,000	
Real estate taxes	12,000	
Principal payments	10,000	91,000
Cash flow before taxes		9,000
Less: Tax on $4,000 taxable income (assuming a 38% marginal rate)		1,520
Cash flow after taxes		$ 7,480

The $3,480 excess of cash flow over taxable income is accounted for as follows:

Excess of depreciation over principal payments	$5,000
Less: Income tax on taxable income	1,520
Difference between cash flow and taxable income	$3,480

2. Even though the result of operations is a taxable loss, it is still possible to have a positive cash flow from the property. Assume the same facts as in Example 1 except that the depreciation deduction is $22,000 instead of $15,000. Taxable income (loss) would be computed as follows:

Rental income		$100,000
Operating expenses	$60,000	
Mortgage interest	9,000	
Real estate taxes	12,000	
Depreciation	22,000	103,000
Taxable loss		($ 3,000)

257

Cash flow from the property would be computed as follows:

Rental income		$100,000
Operating expenses	$60,000	
Real estate taxes	12,000	
Mortgage interest	9,000	
Principal payments	10,000	91,000
Cash flow before taxes		9,000
Plus: Income taxes saved by applying $3,000 loss to owner's other		
income (assuming 38% marginal rate)		1,140
Cash flow after taxes		$ 10,140

The $13,140 difference between the net taxable loss from operations of the property and the cash flow after taxes is accounted for as follows:

Excess of depreciation over principal payments	$12,000
Income tax savings generated by loss from operations	1,140
	$13,140

3. It is of course possible to have a negative cash flow (the investor has to add cash from his pocket to the operations). This will generally result when the amount of the principal payments during the year exceeds the depreciation deductions. Assume the same facts as in the first example except that the depreciation deduction is $10,000 while the principal payments are $20,000. Taxable income would be calculated as follows:

Rental income		$100,000
Operating expenses	$60,000	
Mortgage interest	9,000	
Real estate taxes	12,000	
Depreciation	10,000	91,000
		$ 9,000

Cash flow from the property would be calculated as follows:

Rental income		$100,000
Operating expenses	$60,000	
Mortgage interest	9,000	
Real estate taxes	12,000	
Principal payments	20,000	101,000
Cash outflow		(1,000)
Tax on taxable income (38% marginal rate)		(3,420)
Negative cash flow after taxes		($ 4,420)

The $13,420 difference between the taxable income of $9,000 and the negative outflow of cash of $4,420 is accounted for as follows:

Excess of principal payments over depreciation deductions	$10,000
Tax on taxable income from operations	3,420
Difference between taxable income and negative cash flow	$13,420

Chapter 10

Dispositions

Whenever property is sold or exchanged for cash, obligations or other property, gain or loss is realized.

Gain or loss is the difference between the basis of the property given up and the amount or value received. The gain is reduced (or the loss increased) by the cost of the transaction (e.g., brokers' commissions).

The gain or loss realized is not always immediately taxable or deductible. Like-kind exchanges, for example, have the effect of deferring the gain or loss. (Tax-deferred exchanges are discussed in the next chapter.) In addition, it is possible, by using the installment method, to spread the taxation of the gain over the period during which the sale price is collected.

Unless the seller is a dealer, gain on the sale of real estate generally results in a capital gain. More accurately, it is usually a Section 1231 gain. (The tax treatment of these gains is explained in detail in Chapter 7.) Furthermore, even though conceptually the gain qualifies for capital gain treatment, part or all of the gain may be treated as ordinary income if the rules for recapture of depreciation apply.

In this chapter the questions of who is a dealer, how to use installment and other deferred sales and when and how depreciation recapture rules apply are explored in detail. In addition, other methods of disposition such as sales and leasebacks, involuntary conversions, demolition, charitable contributions and other gifts, and corporate liquidations and reorganizations are examined for their tax consequences.

Dealer or investor

Whether a seller is a dealer or investor makes no difference in the economic sense. However, in terms of taxation this makes a huge difference. That difference involves the treatment of gain on sale as ordinary income when realized by a dealer or as capital gain (a Section 1231 gain in most cases) when realized by an investor. This difference may often mean the difference of many tax dollars. For individuals and trusts the maximum tax rate for ordinary income can be as much as 50 percent as compared to a maximum of 20 percent for capital gains.

Expressed briefly, gain on the sale of real property will be treated as ordinary income when the property was "held by the taxpayer *primarily* for sale to customers in the ordinary course of his trade or business" (emphasis added). The definition of the word "primarily" is so elusive that it took a decision of the United States Supreme Court to settle the controversy between taxpayers and the government. In that case, the Supreme Court held that the word "primarily" means "of first importance" or "principally." It does not mean merely a "substantial" purpose.

Therefore, a taxpayer must make the determination (and be able to support it if his tax return is examined by IRS) as to whether each parcel of property is being held principally as (1) an investment, (2) property used in trade or business or (3) property held for sale in the ordinary course of trade or business. Generally, the first two categories yield capital gain if sold at a profit; the third yields ordinary income. More precisely, the tax treatment for real estate is as follows:

1. Non-income-producing investment property (such as nonproductive land) when sold at a gain will yield capital gain. When such property is sold at a loss, the result is capital loss, which, as explained in Chapter 7, is of limited value.

2. Property used in the trade or business of a taxpayer and held for more than six months (more than one year if acquired prior to June 23, 1984) is called Section 1231 property. (Included in this category is property held for rental purposes.) All gains (other than those representing recapture of depreciation) and losses from such property for the taxable year are combined. If the net result is profit, it is taxed as a capital gain; if the net result is loss, it is taxed as an ordinary loss.

3. Property held for sale to customers in the ordinary course of trade or business yields ordinary income or ordinary loss. It is this type of property that is designated as dealer property.

Factors indicating dealer status

In some cases, the taxpayer is obviously a dealer—for example, a developer of a tract of residential properties which he sells individually to separate buyers. In other cases, he is clearly an investor; he buys one rental property, holds it for a number of years for the investment return and subsequently sells it, never previously having made a similar sale.

The difficulty arises in the "gray area" as when someone who claims he is an investor is involved in numerous sales transactions.

The issue is considered to be a factual one and each case is considered on its own merits. However, there are certain factors which are usually examined in cases such as these to decide whether property is being held for sale in the ordinary course of business. No one of them is all-important and the relative degree of importance of each factor varies with the individual case. Of course, if a taxpayer declares (by advertising or some such means) that he is in the business of buying and selling real estate, and he sells one of the parcels he holds as part of the inventory of properties he has for sale, he would be hard-pressed later to claim that he was really holding that parcel for investment purposes and not as a dealer in real estate. But that is the extreme case.

Quite often, the taxpayer is not in the real estate business on a full-time basis. He may be a doctor, a lawyer, a police chief, etc. In these cases it is often difficult to determine the principal purpose for holding the real estate.

Following are some of the factors that tend to cause a taxpayer to be classified as a dealer:

- The taxpayer has a real estate license and lists his occupation as "real estate dealer" on his income tax returns.
- He belongs to various real estate dealer organizations.
- He makes frequent, quick turnover transactions.
- His business stationery, advertising and publicity releases all refer to him as a real estate dealer.
- He employs a staff of salespeople to solicit offers from purchasers.
- He develops property by making substantial improvements and subdividing; then he advertises the individual parcels for sale.
- He receives a large part of his total income from the sale of real estate.
- He spends most of his working time on real estate purchase and sale activities.
- His purpose at the time of acquisition and/or sale is quick resale.

All these factors and more must be examined in each case with respect to *each property* sold in order to determine the proper income tax treatment. Thus, if a taxpayer in the business of renting real property decides to liquidate, the sale of the rental property would be considered the sale of property used in trade or business. Hence, any gain would be a Section 1231 gain, taxable as a capital gain. However, if that taxpayer then engaged in a large degree of such activity—subdividing, improving, sales promotion, etc.—his status might be converted to dealer status.

Dealer as an investor

It is possible for a real estate dealer to hold some of his property for use in his trade or business or for investment purposes and not for sale to clients. A real estate dealer or broker who owns the building in which his office is located is holding that building for use in his business and not for sale to customers in the ordinary course of his business. If he were to decide to move his office and sell the building, the gain would be treated as a Section 1231 gain.

Since a dealer may also be an investor, it is important that some designation be made, not only in the taxpayer's mind but also tangibly on paper and by action, to indicate which property he is holding for investment and which for use in his trade or business.

Example

Roberts is a real estate dealer. He buys and sells real estate in the ordinary course of business. When he buys real estate for his own investment and not for sale to customers, he segregates the purchase on his books. His financial records have separate accounts for (1) his inventory property, (2) his investment property and (3) the building in which his office is located—his business property.

Depreciation recapture

When depreciable property is sold at a gain the likelihood is that part of the gain is attributable to depreciation deductions which reduce the basis of the property.

Example

Depreciable property is purchased for $100,000; depreciation deductions totaling $40,000 are taken over a period of years. The adjusted basis of the property becomes $60,000. A subsequent sale of the property at $100,000 (same as the original purchase price) results in a $40,000 gain. In this case, the entire gain arises from the fact that $40,000 of depreciation was deducted. If the property were sold for $110,000, the resulting gain would be $50,000 of which $40,000 would be due to the depreciation deductions taken.

The idea behind depreciation recapture is to prevent converting an ordinary deduction (depreciation deductions reduce ordinary income) into a capital gain when the amount of the previously deducted depreciation is recovered in the sale price.

Consequently, the depreciation recapture rules are designed to treat as ordinary income as much of the gain on the sale as is attributable to the recapture of depreciation deductions by the seller. The rules accomplish this in the case of the sale of depreciable personal property (furniture, machinery, etc.) In the case of depreciable real property, for the most part the recapture is limited to the excess of the amount deducted as depreciation over the amount which would have been deductible as straight line depreciation.

Under the cost recovery approach (the Accelerated Cost Recovery System rules are discussed in detail in Chapter 9), the depreciation recapture rules have been modififed somewhat as is explained both in Chapter 9 and below.

Depreciation recapture on disposition of personal property

The rules governing the recapture of depreciation deducted on personal property are found in Section 1245 of the Internal Revenue Code. Such property is commonly referred to as Section 1245 property.

The depreciation recapture rules apply to depreciation deducted after 1962 on any Section 1245 property. Elevators and escalators acquired after June 30, 1963 and before January 1, 1981 are included in the definition of Section 1245 property.

Section 1245 does not include elevators or escalators which have been acquired after 1980 (they are treated as 18-year real estate if they are put into service after March 15, 1984, and 15-year real estate if put into service before March 16, 1984). Section 1245 property *does* include nonresidential real estate acquired after 1980 if the 15-year (18-year, for property put into service after March 15, 1984) cost recovery table is used. If, however, the nonresidential real estate is being depreciated under a straight line method, then the property is *not* Section 1245 property. The straight line lives that are available are 15 years (18 for property put into service after March 15, 1984), 35 years, or 45 years.

It is to the taxpayer's advantage to have property treated as Section 1250 property (real estate) rather than Section 1245 property. The reason is that *all* depreciation deducted on Section 1245 property is subject to recapture; only depreciation in excess of straight line is subject to recapture under Section 1250.

How section 1245 depreciation recapture works   When the property is disposed of, the gain on the sale is compared with the amount of the depreciation which has been deducted (whether it was depreciation deducted under the pre-1981 depreciation rules or as cost recovery deductions under the post-1980 ACRS rules). *All* depreciation deducted is taken into account except depreciation deducted prior to 1962.

The amount of the gain is compared to the amount of the depreciation deducted:

- If the gain is equal to or less than the amount of the depreciation deducted, the entire gain is ordinary income.
- If the gain is greater than the depreciation deducted, that portion of the gain equal to the depreciation deducted is treated as ordinary income. The balance of the gain is treated as a Section 1231 gain (which usually translates into a capital gain).

• If the property is sold at a loss there is no depreciation recapture.

Example

Smith sells furniture and fixtures used in his hotel. His adjusted basis for the items sold is $15,000. Depreciation claimed on these items during the time he held the property (after 1961) totaled $4,000. Tax treatment of the gain or loss on the transaction, for each of the sale prices indicated, is as follows:

- Sale price is $17,000; gain is $2,000. Since the depreciation total is $4,000, the entire gain of $2,000 is treated as ordinary income.
- Sale price is $19,000; gain is $4,000, exactly equal to the depreciation deducted. Hence, the entire gain of $4,000 is treated as ordinary income.
- Sale price is $21,000; gain is $6,000, which is greater than the total depreciation deducted. In this case, $4,000 of the gain is treated as ordinary income and $2,000 as a Section 1231 gain.
- Sale price is $12,000; since there is a loss of $3,000, depreciation recapture rules do not apply. The loss is a Section 1231 loss.

Depreciation recapture on disposition of real property acquired after 1980

As indicated in Chapter 9, the ACRS rules continue the concept of depreciation recapture. Basically, these rules divide real property *acquired after 1980* into three categories:

1. **Nonresidential real estate** As indicated above, this real estate is treated as Section 1245 property. Hence, *all* cost recovery deductions are treated as recaptured depreciation. However, the taxpayer may elect not to use the cost recovery table (shown in Figure 15) and instead use straight line depreciation based on a useful life of 15 (18 for property put in service after March 15, 1984), 35 or 45 years. If he elects straight line, there is no depreciation recapture at all.

2. **Residential real estate** Here, the excess of the depreciation deducted under the 18-year cost recovery table over the depreciation that would have been deductible under 18-year straight line depreciation is subject to treatment as recaptured depreciation. (For property put in service prior to March 16, 1984, use the 15-year cost recovery table and 15-year straight line.) Therefore, if straight line depreciation was used, there is no depreciation to be recaptured.

3. Subsidized low-income housing The excess depreciation deducted under the cost recovery table over the amount that would have been deductible under 15-year straight line depreciation is first determined. This excess is then reduced by 1 percent for each month in excess of 100 months that the property was held. The excess depreciation remaining after the reduction under the more-than-100-month rule is the amount subject to depreciation recapture. Again, if straight line depreciation was used, there is no recapture.

The above rules apply if the property was held for more than one year prior to disposition. If the property was held for one year or less, the full amount of the cost recovery (depreciation) deducted is subject to recapture even if the straight line method was used.

Depreciation recapture on disposition of real property acquired prior to 1981

The ACRS rules do not apply to property acquired prior to 1981. Taxpayers continue to deduct depreciation under the depreciation schedules established for the property prior to 1981. On disposition after 1981, the depreciation recapture rules applied previously continue to apply. Therefore, it is important to understand the depreciation recapture rules which were in effect prior to the enactment of the 1981 tax law in order to apply them on the disposition of property acquired prior to 1981.

The old rules (applying to depreciation deducted on real estate after 1963) recaptured all or part of what is referred to as "excess depreciation" —the depreciation deduction in excess of the amount that was deductible under the straight line method. The portion of the excess depreciation subject to recapture is called the "applicable amount."

The applicable amount depends on a number of factors:

- The holding period of the property
- The depreciation method used
- How much depreciation was deducted
- When the depreciation was deducted
- Whether the property qualified for special uses

Straight line depreciation used If only straight line depreciation has been used for the property being sold or disposed of, there cannot be any depreciation recapture under Section 1250 as long as the property was held for more than one year.

Property held not more than one year If the property being sold or otherwise disposed of has been held for one year or less, all of the depreciation deducted, regardless of the depreciation method used, becomes subject to recapture. (This is essentially the same procedure used to recapture depreciation on personalty under Section 1245.) Of course, if the gain is less than the depreciation deducted, only the amount of the gain is treated as ordinary.

Property held more than one year When the property has been held for more than one year, the *maximum* amount of depreciation which can be recaptured is the excess depreciation.

Except in the case of new residential rental property and special-purpose properties (discussed later in this chapter) depreciation claimed during two periods of time are considered in calculating depreciation recapture on real estate. It must be determined how much *excess* depreciation was deducted (1) *after* 1963 but *before* 1970, and (2) after 1969. (Depreciation deducted before 1964 is never recaptured.)

In practical terms, however, it is only necessary to determine the excess depreciation deducted after 1969. The reason is that only a portion of excess depreciation deducted after 1963 and before 1970 is recapturable. The longer the property is held, the smaller the portion subject to recapture. Once the property is held more than ten years, no part of the excess depreciation deducted during the years 1964 through 1969 is recapturable. Any sales made currently are more than ten years removed from 1969. Therefore, any depreciation deducted during the years 1964 through 1969 on property sold today would not be subject to recapture.

Consequently, except for the properties subject to the special rules, it is necessary to look only at the excess depreciation deducted after 1969. That portion of the depreciation deducted after 1969 which exceeds the depreciation which *would have been* deductible had straight line depreciation been used is the amount subject to recapture.

As in the case of personal property, the recapturable amount, (i.e., excess depreciation) is compared to the gain. That portion of the gain which is equal to the excess depreciation is "recaptured" as ordinary income. The portion of the gain which exceeds the excess depreciation is treated as a Section 1231 gain. Of course, if there is a loss, there is no depreciation recapture.

Examples

1. An office building acquired in 1968 is sold in 1984 for $1,000,000. The gain is $300,000. The amount of depreciation claimed after 1969 exceeds by $200,000 the amount of straight line depreciation which would be allowed for that period. Of the $300,000 gain, $200,000 is ordinary income; $100,000 is Section 1231 gain. While all depreciation deducted prior to 1970 and after 1969 is used in determining the basis of the property sold, only depreciation deducted after 1969 is used in the calculation of excess depreciation subject to recapture.

2. Assume the gain in Example 1 was $150,000. The entire gain would be subject to depreciation recapture.

3. Assume the sale in Example 1 resulted in a $50,000 loss. There is no depreciation recapture.

Residential rental property   In the case of residential rental property, two periods of time in calculating depreciation recapture must be considered. (We do not consider the depreciation deducted prior to 1970 because sales today would be more than ten years removed from 1969 and the rule discussed applies here as well.) The periods we must consider are (1) the years 1970 through 1975 and (2) after 1975.

Only a *portion* of the *excess* depreciation deducted during 1970–1975 is subject to recapture. For every full month (fractions are disregarded) the property was held (taking into account the entire holding period before 1970 and after 1975) in excess of 100 months, the amount of excess depreciation for the 1970–1975 period is reduced by 1 percent.

Example

If property was held for ten years—120 months—the amount of the excess depreciation would be reduced by 20 percent. Hence, 80 percent of the excess depreciation taken during 1970–1975 would be subject to the depreciation recapture rules.

An easy way to calculate the percentage of the excess depreciation that *is* subject to the depreciation recapture rules is to subtract the number of months in the holding period from 200. In our example above, since 200 minus 120 (the months in the holding period) equals 80, 80 percent of the excess depreciation deducted in 1970–1975 is subject to depreciation recapture.

For depreciation deducted after 1975, the same rules which apply to other properties apply here—that is, the entire amount of the excess depreciation for the period after 1975 is subject to the depreciation recapture rules.

Residential rental property is defined as property from which 80 percent or more of the gross rental income comes from dwelling units. Dwelling units are living accommodations in houses or apartment buildings and do not include hotels, motels, inns or other establishments in which more than half of the units are used on a transient basis.

Example

Assume a residential rental property was acquired on June 1, 1970, and sold on January 15, 1984. The gain on the sale was $60,000. The excess depreciation for the period June 1, 1970, through December 31, 1975, was $40,000. And the excess depreciation for the period January 1, 1976, through January 15, 1984, was $28,000.

The holding period of the property was 13 years, seven months and 14 days. The 14 days are ignored for the purposes of determining the portion of the 1970-1975 excess depreciation subject to recapture. So, we have a holding period of 163 months. Subtracting 163 from 200 gives us 39. Thus, 39 percent of the $40,000 excess depreciation deducted during 1970-1975, or $15,600, is subject to recapture.

The entire $28,000 excess depreciation deducted after 1975 is also subject to recapture. Therefore, the total amount subject to the depreciation recapture rules is $43,600. Of the $60,000 gain, $43,600 is treated as ordinary income and $16,400 as a Section 1231 gain.

Additional depreciation recapture for corporations

A corporation disposing of real estate after 1982 is subject to additional recapture. First it determines what the depreciation recapture would have been had the property been personal (Section 1245) property and then subtracts the recapture calculated under the real property (Section 1250) rules.

If the property was disposed of before 1985, it calculates 15 percent of the excess of the Section 1245 recapture over the Section 1250 recapture. If the disposition occurs after 1984, it calculates 20 percent of that excess. (If straight line depreciation had been used, the amount of Section 1250 depreciation is zero, so 15 or 20 percent, whichever is applicable, of the full amount of the Section 1245 depreciation is used.

The 15 or 20 percent of the excess is added to the depreciation recapture calculated under the real estate (1250) method. This total then becomes the depreciation recapture the corporation must apply.

Tax-free exchanges and depreciation recapture

It is possible to have a so-called tax-free exchange of property of a like-kind without *any* gain being recognized for tax purposes. In other cases, while the *entire* gain may not be recognized for tax purposes, *part* of the gain may be taxable. That occurs when property other than like-kind is received in the exchange. Often that "other property" is cash.

In the case of an exchange of Section 1245 property, the amount of the depreciation deducted is compared to the portion of the gain taxable in the exchange. In other words, the recognized portion of the gain is treated as total gain.

270   The maximum amount of depreciation recapture on real property which can be taxable as ordinary income is the larger of two amounts. These amounts are determined by the following rules:

1. The amount equal to the portion of the gain on the exchange taxable under exchange rules (see Chapter 11).

2. The excess of (a) the potential depreciation recapture on the exchange (computed as though a sale were made for cash) over (b) the fair market value of the depreciable real property received in the exchange. The purpose of this rule is to permit IRS to impose the real estate recapture rules when a good portion of the property being received in exchange is not depreciable real property and hence will not be subject to depreciation recapture in the future.

Similar rules are applied where property is replaced after an involuntary conversion (see Chapter 8).

Installment sales

It is quite common for real estate to be sold using an installment sale in which the buyer pays the purchase price over a number of years. Commonly, the purchaser will be paying part of the purchase price via mortgage principal payments. Of course, if the mortgage is being held by a bank or other lending institution, the seller will receive all that he is going to in the year of the sale. This is *not* an installment sale, and the entire gain on the sale will be reportable by him for tax purposes in the year of sale.

Examples

1. Seller has an adjusted basis for his property of $70,000. He sells it for $100,000, resulting in a $30,000 gain. The buyer pays the $100,000 price by paying $40,000 of his own cash and securing a mortgage on the property for $60,000 from a bank. In this case, the seller gets the full $100,000 at the time of the sale and the buyer ends up owing the bank the $60,000. So, the seller reports the full gain in the year of sale. As far as he is concerned the sale is not an installment sale. The buyer is paying installments by way of mortgage principal payments, but to the bank, not to the seller. In other cases, however, the installment payments are made to the seller.

2. In the preceding case, if instead of borrowing $60,000 from the bank, the buyer pays $40,000 in cash and gives the seller a purchase money mortgage of $60,000, the seller will collect the $60,000 balance of the sale price over the term of the mortgage. Here, the seller considers the transaction an installment sale.

3. Seller sells for $100,000, but there is an existing mortgage of $25,000 on the property. The buyer pays the $100,000 by paying $40,000 cash, taking subject to the $25,000 mortgage and giving the seller a second mortgage of $35,000. Here, too, part of the sale price will be paid to the

seller over a number of years, the term of the second mortgage. Again, an installment sale exists as far as the seller is concerned.

When there is an installment sale, the gain on the transaction is calculated in the usual way. The seller's adjusted basis is subtracted from the sale price to determine the gain. And if the gain qualifies as a capital gain, it is taxed as such. But since the seller will not get all his money in the year of sale, he would like to avoid paying the tax on the full gain in that year. He would like to spread the tax burden over the period during which he will collect that portion of the selling price he has not received in the year of the sale. The tax law permits this spreadout via the installment method of reporting the gain. Losses on installment sales, however, must be reported in full in the year of the sale.

Electing installment sales

Any sale calling for payments in future years is automatically treated as an installment sale. This is so even if there is no payment at all in the year of sale and only one payment is called for (to be made in a future year). The taxpayer is not required to make an election. If he does not want installment sale treatment, he must "elect out" by reporting the full gain on his tax return for the year of sale. If a taxpayer has a large available loss, he may prefer to forgo installment sale treatment and use the loss to offset the entire gain—or most of it—by reporting the gain in full in the year of sale.

Mortgage over basis and wraparound mortgages

If the buyer assumes or takes subject to an existing mortgage on the property and if that mortgage is greater than the seller's basis for the property, the seller is deemed to have received that excess amount in the year of sale. Two troublesome problems arise in this area. One deals with selling expenses; the other, with wraparound mortgages.

Selling expenses Suppose the sale price of a property is $500,000 and brokers' commissions paid by the seller are $30,000. If the seller's basis for the property is $300,000, his gain on the sale is $170,000 (the $500,000 selling price minus the total of the basis plus selling expenses, $330,000). The $170,000 gain can be determined by reducing the selling price by the commissions and then subtracting the basis, or by adding the $30,000 commissions to the $300,000 basis and then subtracting the new basis of $330,000 from the selling price.

If the mortgage on the property which the buyer is assuming or taking subject to is no greater than $300,000, it would make no difference which method was used to arrive at the $170,000 gain. But suppose the mortgage on the property was $350,000.

If the selling expenses merely reduced the selling price by $30,000, the excess of the mortgage over the basis would be $50,000 (and that amount would be treated as received by the seller in the year of sale). However, if the $30,000 were added to the basis to arrive at the $170,000 gain, the new basis would be $330,000 and the excess of the mortgage over the basis would be reduced to $20,000.

IRS' Temporary Regulations establish that the selling expenses should be added to basis. This is, of course, beneficial to sellers in that it permits them to defer a greater portion of the gain when the mortgage exceeds the seller's basis.

When a wraparound mortgage is used, the buyer gives the seller a mortgage for an amount greater than the existing mortgage on the property and purports not to assume or take subject to the existing mortgage.

Example

Wilson has a property with a basis of $200,000. There is an existing mortgage on the property of $300,000. He sells the property for $450,000. The buyer pays $50,000 in cash and gives Wilson a mortgage of $400,000. Under the agreement, the buyer claims he is not taking subject to the $300,000 mortgage on the property. Instead, it is agreed that as he pays off the $400,000, Wilson will use the necessary portion of the payments he receives to make payments on the $300,000 mortgage. This is an example of a wraparound mortgage.

IRS, in its Temporary Regulations, has taken the position that when a wraparound mortgage is used, the buyer is deemed (for tax purposes) to have taken the property subject to the existing mortgage. Furthermore, says IRS, it makes no difference whether the buyer receives title immediately or the title-passing is postponed. In either case, according to IRS, the buyer has taken the property subject to the existing mortgage.

Example

Thus, in the example above, under the IRS view, the seller received $150,000 in the year of sale—$50,000 in cash and the $100,000 excess of the existing mortgage over the seller's basis in the property.

Related person sales

Suppose the seller wants an installment sale, but the buyer wants to pay all cash. One device which had been used was to have the seller sell to a related person on an installment sale basis. The related buyer would then immediately sell to the ultimate buyer for cash. The related buyer would have no gain or loss. Then, he would pay the seller according to the installment sale agreement.

IRS had attacked these sales, and Congress has put some specific rules into the law to eliminate this device in certain instances.

If the seller makes an installment sale to a related person, and if that related person sells the property within two years, the original seller has to pick up the balance of his gain at the time the related person makes the sale. If the property sold is marketable securities, then it makes no difference when the related person makes the sale—even if it is more than two years after the original sale; the original seller still has to pick up the balance of his gain when the related person makes the sale. So, the sale to a related person with an immediate resale defeats the installment sale. However, if the second sale is an "involuntary conversion" (e.g., a condemnation of property), this is not a sale that triggers income to the first seller.

Who is a related person? Related persons are defined as the seller's spouse, children, grandchildren and parents. Also included are trusts of which the seller is a beneficiary (or part of whose property he is deemed to own), estates in which he is a beneficiary, partnerships in which he is a partner and corporations in which he owns at least 50 percent of the stock. (In each of these cases, indirect ownership is also counted.)

The related person rule will not apply, however, if it is established to the satisfaction of IRS that neither the original sale nor the resale "had as one of its principal purposes the avoidance of federal income tax." Of course, it will be difficult to convince IRS that there was no tax avoidance motive present when the second sale takes place almost immediately after the first, or when it is apparent that the original seller could have made an all cash sale to the ultimate buyer in the first place.

Even if the person to whom the seller makes the initial sale (with the idea that the buyer will resell) is not a related person, IRS could still attack the installment sale as a sham. Then the seller could present evidence that there was a real sale. However, if the transaction comes under the related-person rules, the installment sale is more easily knocked out.

Imputed interest

Normally, an installment sale will call for interest on the unpaid installments (the seller expects the buyer to pay him for the use of his money during the deferral period). In the past, transactions were structured calling for no interest or a very low rate of interest. The price was adjusted to reflect some interest (perhaps less than would normally be called for); thus the seller's gain was increased, and he expected to treat this increase as a capital gain. In exchange for losing the interest deduction, the buyer was given some concession on the "interest factor" and the price was raised accordingly.

To prevent this "abuse," Congress created the concept of imputed interest. If a minimum amount of interest was not called for in the sales agreement, the law would impute interest. Thus, each installment, although ostensibly all principal, is segmented into a principal payment and an "imputed interest" payment. Part of the payment becomes interest income to the seller (ordinary income) and an interest deduction to the buyer.

The rules dealing with imputed interest were substantially changed by the Tax Reform Act of 1984 for taxable years ending after July 18, 1984. Before discussing the new rules, however, it is important to see how the old rules applied to transactions governed by the old law to better understand the significance of the changes made by the new law.

Under the old law, the minimum interest rate required to avoid imputed interest was changed from time to time by IRS. If the minimum rate (in terms of simple interest) was not used, IRS imputed a rate one percentage point higher than the minimum rate and applied it on a semiannual compound interest basis. Thus, as each installment was received, a portion of it, based on semiannual compound interest from the date of sale until the date of payment, was considered as interest and the balance was treated as payment of part of the purchase price. This was referred to as discounting back each installment.

Under the new law, there are two sets of rules: one deals with original issue discount, the other revises the old imputed interest rules. The revised imputed interest rules apply to a sale of a principal residence, a farm for $1,000,000 or less, other sales transactions involving total payments of $250,000 or less, and sales of land between related parties (explained below). In all other transactions, the original issue discount rules apply.

Original issue discount is the difference between the issue price of an obligation and its redemption price at maturity. If there is original issue discount, it is accrued on a daily basis and reported as income and deduction. IRS provides a formula for the accrual of the interest which uses a constant rate with periodic compounding. So the interest accruing in the earlier part of the period is relatively small, while the interest accruing in the later part of the period is relatively large.

When the original issue discount rules apply, it is first necessary to determine if the obligation has adequate stated interest. This is done by reference to an applicable rate based on interest paid on federal obligations. The present values of all payments due under the obligation are determined using a discount rate of 110 percent of the applicable federal rate. (IRS regulations will explain the discounting method.) If the total of the present values are equal to or greater than the total amounts of principal to be paid under the obligation, there is adequate stated interest and no interest is imputed.

If, under the 110 percent test, there is inadequate interest, the issue price of the obligation is determined by discounting the payments due under the obligation by 120 percent of the applicable federal rate. This discounted amount is then compared to the principal amounts to be received under the obligation to determine the amount of the original issue discount.

The original issue discount rules do not apply to those sales listed above to which the revised imputed interest rules apply. Under the revised imputed interest rules, the present value of all future payments is first determined and is then subtracted from the sum of the principal payments to be received. The result of this subtraction is then reduced by the interest stated in the agreement (if any). The balance is the unstated, or imputed, interest. To determine the present value of the future payments, they are discounted at 120 percent of the applicable federal rate.

Just as in the old law, there is a minimum amount of interest that acts as a safe harbor. If interest called for in the agreement is at least equal to that minimum, the imputed interest rules do not apply. The minimum is determined by discounting the future principal and interest payments at a rate equal to 110 percent of the applicable federal rate. If the discounted amount is not less than the total of the future principal payments, the safe harbor test is met.

A special rule applies to the sale of a principal residence for up to $250,000 or of a farm. Instead of using the 120/110 percent of the applicable federal rates, the *old* imputed interest rules apply. That is, if the interest called for meets the minimum IRS rate, there is no imputed interest. If not, interest will be imputed at 1 percent higher, compounded semiannually. (Of course, if the sale of the farm is for more than $1,000,000, the original issue discount rules apply).

Another special rule provides a safe harbor for sales of land between family members when the sales price does not exceed $500,000. (This maximum is reduced by the amounts of prior sales between the family members in the same calendar year.) Family members include brothers, sisters, spouse, ancestors, (parents, grandparents, etc.) and lineal descendants (children, grandchildren, etc.). In determining the present value of future payments, a rate of 7 percent, compounded semiannually, is used. This present value is then subtracted from the total of the future payments. If the actual interest called for in the agreement is at least equal to this difference, there is no imputed interest.

Reporting gain under the installment method

We have discussed the qualifications for installment reporting, but once a sale qualifies for installment reporting, how is the gain reported? (Note that installment reporting applies to gains only; losses may not be spread over a number of years via installment reporting.)

Installment reporting of gains requires the following steps:

1. Determine the gain in the usual manner as if the installment method were not being used.

2. Determine the contract price. The contract price is the sale price reduced by mortgages (or other indebtedness) assumed (or taken subject to) by the buyer and *payable to third parties*.

3. Divide the gain (determined in Step 1) by the contract price (determined in Step 2) to determine the percentage of the contract price which the gain equals.

4. In each year in which payment is received from the buyer (the year of sale and subsequent years), multiply the amount received by the percentage determined in Step 3. This procedure determines the amount of the gain to be reported in each year.

The following two examples illustrate installment reporting. The first example details a situation in which there are no existing mortgages on the property; the second deals with a case where there is an existing mortgage.

Examples

1. In March, 1984, Smith sells a parcel of land which cost her $20,000, for $50,000. The land is unencumbered. The buyer pays $10,000 in the year of sale and will pay $5,000 a year for the next eight years (plus sufficient interest on the unpaid balance to avoid imputed interest). Smith pays a broker a commission of $2,500 for bringing about the sale. The sale is reported as an installment sale, according to the following procedure:

Sale price		$50,000
Less: Commission	$ 2,500	
Adjusted basis	20,000	
Total basis		22,500
Gain on sale		$27,500

The contract price is the same as the sale price because there is no indebtedness taken over by the buyer payable to third parties. Hence, the contract price is $50,000. The gain is 55 percent of the contract price ($27,500 divided by $50,000).

In the year of sale, $10,000 was received by the seller. Therefore, 55 percent of the $10,000, or $5,500, is reported as gain in that year.

In each subsequent year, $5,000 will be received by the seller. In each of these years, the seller will report a gain of $2,750 (55 percent of $5,000). And in each of these years, the seller will receive interest payments. The interest will be reported separately as ordinary income.

2. In November, 1984, Brown sells land and building for $100,000. His

adjusted basis for the property at the time of sale is $59,600. He pays a sales commision of $5,000. Terms of the sale are:

Cash paid at time of sale	$ 25,000
Existing mortgage on property assumed by buyer	40,000
Second mortgage given to seller (purchase money mortgage)	35,000
Total	$100,000

The second mortgage is to be paid in seven equal annual installments of principal plus sufficient interest to avoid imputed interest.

Brown reports the transaction as an installment sale. The gain on the sale is $35,400, determined this way:

Sale price		$100,000
Less: Adjusted basis	$59,600	
Sales commissions	5,000	
Total basis		64,600
Gain		$ 35,400

The contract price is $60,000, determined as follows:

Sale price	$100,000
Less: Mortgage assumed by buyer payable to third party	40,000
Contract price	$ 60,000

The gain is 59 percent of the contract price ($35,400 divided by $60,000).

In the year of sale, Brown received payments totaling $25,000. He reports 59 percent of the $25,000, or $14,750, as gain in the year of sale.

In each of the succeeding seven years, Brown will receive $5,000 as principal payment on the $35,000 second mortgage. Each year, Brown will report as gain on the sale $2,950 (59 percent of $5,000). The interest received each year will be reported separately as ordinary income.

Including the year of sale, Brown is to receive total payments of $60,000. (The remaining $40,000 of the sale price will be paid by the buyer to the mortgagee under the mortgage assumed by the buyer.) His total gain is $35,400. Under the installment method of reporting, here is how the gain is reported over the years of collection:

Year	Payment Received	Taxable Gain
1	$25,000	$14,750
2	5,000	2,950
3	5,000	2,950
4	5,000	2,950
5	5,000	2,950
6	5,000	2,950
7	5,000	2,950
8	5,000	2,950
Totals	$60,000	$35,400

Installment sales which include like-kind exchanges

Gain on a like-kind exchange is not taxable. Generally, basis of the old property becomes the basis of the new property. In effect, the tax on the gain is postponed. Suppose, however, that in addition to the like-kind exchange, the seller receives an amount of money which is to be paid over a period of years. It is clear that the gain attributable to the money is taxable as boot (see Chapter 11). It is also clear that if the installment sale rules apply, the gain attributable to the money received will be spread out over the period of payment. There had been some question as to how the gain should be reported. This was cleared up in the revised installment sale law for sales made after October 19, 1980.

Example

A taxpayer exchanges property with a basis of $400,000 for like-kind property worth $200,000 and an $800,000 installment obligation; $100,000 is to be paid in the year of sale and the balance in succeeding years. In effect, the total sale price is $1,000,000 and the gain is $600,000 ($1,000,000 minus the $400,000 basis). Since the seller is to receive $800,000 in cash, the entire $600,000 gain is taxable. But when?

The contract price is $800,000 (the like-kind property is not included in the contract price). Hence, the $600,000 gain is 75 percent of the contract price. *But the $200,000 value of the like-kind property is not included in the amount received in the year of sale.* So, in the year of sale, the seller reports a gain of $75,000 (75 percent of the $100,000 cash received). The balance of the gain is reported as the remainder of the $800,000 is received. Again, only $600,000 is taxable.

How installment sales gains are taxed

We have seen how to determine the gain on an installment sale and how to spread the gain over the years of collection. But does the fact that installment sale reporting is used affect the nature of the gain? That is, if the gain, but for installment sale reporting, would have been a long-term capital gain, are the gains reported in the subsequent years treated as capital gains?

The answer is yes. The nature of the gain is determined at the time of the sale. If, under the rules previously discussed, the gain is a long-term capital gain, in each year that a part of the gain is reported that portion of the gain is treated as a long-term capital gain.

Depreciation recapture in installment sales

If part of the gain on the transaction that is being reported as an installment sale is subject to depreciation recapture, that portion of the gain is treated as ordinary income. The question arises in an installment sale as to *when* that ordinary income is to be reported. The answer depends on whether the disposition took place before June 7, 1984 (old rule) or after June 6, 1984 (new rule). The old rule also applies to dispositions taking place after June 6, 1984 if they were made pursuant to contracts that were binding on March 22, 1984.

Under the old rule, the first amounts received in the installment sale are attributable to depreciation recapture. After the depreciation recapture is accounted for, the balance of the payments is treated as capital gain.

Example

In Example 2, on p. 277-78, Brown had a gain of $35,400. Assume that $15,000 of that gain was depreciation recapture. Since $14,750 is reported in the year of sale which is less than the total $15,000 of depreciation recapture, the entire $14,750 would be reported as ordinary income in the year of sale. In the second year, $2,950 of the gain is reportable. Since $250 of the $15,000 depreciation recapture is still to be reported, $250 of the $2,950 gain will be reported as ordinary income in the second year, and the remaining $2,700 of gain will be reportable as long-term capital gain. In the third through the eighth years, the full $2,950 gain reported each year will be reported as long-term capital gain because the entire depreciation recapture will have been accounted for in previous years.

The new rule takes a much more drastic approach. The amount of the depreciation recapture is reported as ordinary income in the year of sale *regardless of when* the actual installment payments are received. The amount of the depreciation recapture is then added to the basis of the property sold and the installment sale is recalculated.

Example

Going back to Example 2, Brown has a sales price of $100,000, a basis of $64,600, and a gain of $35,400. But since $15,000 was depreciation recapture, that amount has to be reported as ordinary income in the year of sale. The gain on the sale is recomputed by adding $15,000 to the $64,600 basis, producing a new basis of $79,600.

The gain is now $20,400, or 34 percent of the $60,000 contract price. In the year of sale, Brown receives $25,000; he reports a capital gain of 34 percent of $35,000, or $8,500. In each of the subsequent seven years, he will receive a payment of $5,000, of which 34 percent, or $1,700, will be reported as capital gain. Thus, Brown will report $15,000 of ordinary income (in the year of sale) and $20,400 of capital gain which is made up of $8,500 in the year of sale and $11,900 in the subsequent seven years ($1,700 multiplied by seven).

Overall, this is the same result as under the old rule. But under the new rule, the $15,000 depreciation recapture has to be reported in the year of sale even if *no* payments were received in that year; and the gain attributable to the amount that *was* received in the year of sale is reported *in addition to* the depreciation recapture reported that year.

Advantages of installment reporting

Under the installment method, the tax cost of the gain is matched to the collections. In other words, the taxpayer does not have to pay out cash in the form of taxes before actually receiving the payments in which his gain is included.

To the extent that the taxpayer can defer the payment of the tax, he has the use of the tax money at no interest cost for the period of deferral.

To the extent that the gain is spread over a number of years, it may be subject to lower marginal tax rates than if the entire gain were reported in one year. This is obviously true to the extent the gain is reportable as ordinary income (i.e. depreciation recapture). It may also be true as to the capital gains.

Only 40 percent of the capital gain is included in ordinary income. By spreading the gain over a number of years, the amount of the gain included each year may be subject to lower marginal rates than the marginal rates which would apply if the entire gain were included in one year.

Contingent sale price

If the sale price was not readily determinable (for example, part of the sale price depended on future events, such as the amount of income produced by the property sold), IRS took the position that the installment sale rules did not apply.

In other cases, taxpayers argued that the value of the obligations had no ascertainable value—as where the buyer's obligation was in the form of a "bare" contractual promise rather than in the form of negotiable notes. (Some courts sustained the taxpayers in this view.) Then, the seller could apply the first proceeds he received to recover his basis. When the payments he received had accounted for his basis, future payments were treated as gain.

Congress has finally set forth rules dealing with a contingent sales price. The law now treats as installment sales those sales which have contingent sale prices and those in which the price is not readily ascertainable. This new provision affects sales made after October 19, 1980. IRS regulations detail how the installment sale reporting should be made in these cases.

Since almost all contingent sale-price sales are to be treated as installment sales, it will be almost impossible to argue that the installment obligations do not have ascertainable values. That being the case, the seller will not have any basis for asserting that he could apply the first proceeds received to recover his basis and then report gain only after he recovered his basis. (As indicated above, this argument was accepted by some courts before Congress amended the law.)

Sale and leaseback

A sale and leaseback is a transaction in which the owner of the property sells the property and immediately leases it back from the new owner. Consequently, during the term of the lease, the seller-lessee's physical relationship to the property remains unchanged.

A sale-leaseback transaction is often looked upon as a financing transaction. In other words, it is often a substitute for refinancing by the owner via a new mortgage. There is one major difference between a sale-leaseback and a mortgage: at the end of the lease term the former owner (now lessee) loses possession of the property; in the case of a mortgage, he retains the property. Consequently, the residual value of the property (the value at the end of the lease term) is an important factor in comparing the economic results of sale-leasebacks and mortgages.

In this section we are concerned primarily with the tax consequences to the seller-lessee. The tax consequences, of course, weigh heavily in calculating the net financial results of the transaction.

Tax consequences

Two distinct transactions are involved in a sale-leaseback.

Upon the sale, the seller realizes gain or loss in the same manner as upon any other sale. The tax consequences are the same as for any other sale: possible Section 1231 gain or loss, possible depreciation recapture.

Upon becoming a lessee, the former owner pays rent for the occupancy rights to the property. Normally, rent is a fully deductible expense for tax purposes, assuming that the property is used in the lessee's trade or business (including the business of holding the property for rent to others). If the rent agreement constitutes a Section 467 Rental Agreement, special rules apply as to when rent is deductible (and reportible as income). See the discussion in Chapter 7.

These are the general tax rules that apply to a sale-leaseback. There are, however, a number of problems that can arise which may modify these rules.

Lease term for 30 years or more   If the lease term is for 30 years or more, IRS says the lease itself is property of a like-kind to other real estate. Hence, the sale-leaseback is to be treated as a tax-deferred exchange. Since in a sale-leaseback the seller usually receives cash (if the result of the sale-leaseback is a gain), even if it is deemed to be a like-kind exchange, the gain would be taxable to the extent of the cash received.

The difficulty arises if the sale portion of the sale-leaseback results in a loss. In that case, if the IRS view prevails and a 30-year lease is treated as like-kind property, the loss would not be recognized for tax purposes.

The courts have sustained the IRS view in some cases, and the safer approach (when there is a loss) is to use a lease term of less than 30 years. In this respect, it should also be noted that a shorter lease term with an unrealistic renewal term (either unusual length of time or greatly reduced rent) may cause IRS to attempt to combine the lease terms for the purposes of its 30-year rule.

Repurchase option   As has been pointed out, one of the unfavorable aspects of the sale-leaseback (from the seller's viewpoint) is that, as lessee, he loses the property at the end of the lease term.

To overcome this objection to the sale-leaseback, the seller may be given an option to reacquire the property at the termination of the lease. The difficulty with this arrangement, from a tax viewpoint, is that it may upset the treatment of the lease as a lease. If, for example, the seller-lessee may reacquire the property at the end of the lease term for a nominal payment, IRS will likely contend that the arrangement was not a lease from the outset but rather that it was merely a financing arrangement similar to a mortgage. In that case, the rental deductions the lessee expected each year would be disallowed. Instead, the lessee would be allowed that portion of his "rent" payments which represent a reasonable interest rate on borrowed money as a deduction. He would also be entitled to depreciation deductions (since he would be considered the owner of the property).

To avoid having the lease treated as a loan, any repurchase option contained in the arrangement must call for a purchase price which can be sustained as representing the fair market value of the property at the time the lease expires. A repurchase price to be determined by professional appraisers at the time of the repurchase is probably one satisfactory approach. Other reasonable approaches resulting in the equivalent of an arm's-length purchase price at the end of the lease term may be used.

The tax law has special provisons dealing with finance leases. These provisions apply only to personal property eligible for the investment credit.

"Tax arithmetic" of leasebacks

Owners of property are entitled to depreciation deductions and deductions for interest paid. Lessees are entitled to tax deductions for rent paid.

The owner of property will at one point find that his depreciation deductions are declining under ACRS. He recognizes that the portion of his basis allocable to the underlying land is nondepreciable for tax purposes; yet the value of his property has increased. So he looks to convert that appreciation into cash for use in his business or for further investment. If he sells the property, he realizes the appreciation but loses the use of the property (which he may need in his business—a factory or warehouse, for example).

If he refinances, he may not be able to borrow as much as he can realize on the sale. A sale-leaseback may give him the best of both possible worlds (however, the loss of the property at the end of the lease term should not be overlooked).

Sale-leaseback Assuming that the sale is made at a gain, the seller will have a cash amoung equal to the sale price minus selling costs and the tax on the gain. The "cost" of this after-tax cash is the net cash outlay of the rental payments over the term of the lease. Since the rent payments constitute tax deductions, the net cash outlay is the difference between the rent called for in the lease and the tax saved by the deductibility of the rent (the amount of the rent multiplied by the taxpayer's marginal rate).

The total after-tax outlay for rent over the lease term will likely exceed the net after-tax cash realized on the sale. In that sense, then, the sale-leaseback is financing. An additional cost of after-tax cash on the sale is the loss of the property at the end of the lease term.

Without the sale-leaseback, the owner's depreciation deductions are limited in total to his basis in the improvements (land is nondepreciable). After the sale and leaseback, he has realized the proceeds from the sale of both the land and improvements and is paying rent on both. To that extent, he has converted the nondepreciable land into an investment amortizable over the life of the lease.

Mortgage financing If, instead of selling and leasing back, the owner seeks to refinance, he must obtain a loan equal to the after-tax sale proceeds (in the sale-leaseback) to have the same cash availability at that point.

Assuming that the mortgage term is as long as the lease term, the after-tax cash outlay in repaying the loan may be compared with the after-tax cash outlay for the rents. In determining the after-tax cash outlay, principal payments on the loan are not considered tax deductible. However, the interest payments are deductible for income tax purposes, thereby reducing the effective cash outlay for the interest. Furthermore, when the mortgage financing route is used, the borrower continues to own the property and is therefore entitled to depreciation deductions. These deductions do not require a cash outlay but reduce taxable income and the cash required for tax payments. Hence, in determining the total cash outlay over the mortgage term (in order to compare it with the total net cash outlay over the lease term were a sale-leaseback employed), it is proper to subtract from the total of the principal and interest payments to be made over that period the tax savings arising from the deductibility of both the interest payments and the depreciation on the property.

Other dispositions of property

In addition to the more conventional dispositions of property, there are a number of less common types of disposition which have special tax consequences.

Involuntary conversions

A disposition of property can arise involuntarily, as when property is condemned or when property is destroyed by fire or other casualty. Gain or loss may then arise. The condemnation award or insurance proceeds are compared to the basis of the converted property to determine the gain or loss. Typically, the gain or loss is treated the same way it would be treated on a sale. Tax on the gain may be deferred, however, if reinvestment in similar property is made to a sufficient extent and within a prescribed time. Rules for tax deferral when there is no involuntary conversion are detailed in Chapter 8.

Demolition

Existing structures may be demolished to make room for other structures. For taxable years beginning before 1984, the tax treatment of the loss resulting from demolition depended on the owner's intentions at the time the property was acquired. If there was no intent to demolish at the time of acquisition, subsequent demolition resulted in an ordinary loss for tax purposes. If there was an intent to demolish at the time of acquisition, all "losses" resulting from demolition became part of the basis of the land.

For taxable years beginning after 1983, all demolition "losses" must be capitalized (regardless of intent at time of acquisition) and become part of the basis of the land.

Gifts and charitable contributions

One method of disposing of property is to give it away. A gift may be made to a family member as part of an estate plan, or a gift may be contributed to a charitable organization. Many tax factors are involved in either type of disposition; estate and income taxes may be saved and capital gains may be avoided. Planning methods and tax consequences of these types of dispositions are examined in Appendices E and F.

Corporate liquidations and reorganizations

Because a corporation is an entity separate from its shareholders (the owners), a disposition of corporate property may create a double tax in the process of getting the sale proceeds in the hands of the shareholders. This may be avoided in some instances by using one of several methods of liquidation. In some cases, it may be possible to avoid all taxes and convert the shareholders' equity in the corporation into equity in a larger corporation with more diversified holdings (somewhat equivalent to a tax-deferred exchange) by going through a corporate reorganization.

The liquidation and reorganization route require compliance with a number of technical tax rules (as well as compliance with the requisite state corporation laws). The tax advantages and pitfalls of liquidations and reorganizations are set forth in Appendix D.

Chapter 11

Exchanges

11

Motivations for exchange

Exchanging real estate,[1] rather than selling it outright and reinvesting the proceeds, generally stems from one of two motivations. First, exchanging properties is a method of marketing real estate when a sale does not appear to be possible for one of a number of reasons, including the following:

- Buyers with cash are not available.
- A sale on "terms" does not give the seller sufficient funds with which to acquire another property.
- The seller will not price his property realistically so that it will attract a purchaser.

The second, and probably the most important, motivating force for exchanging property is the available income tax deferral. The capital gains tax that would normally be paid on the gain from the sale may be postponed or even avoided in full or in part with use of an exchange. The following example dramatically illustrates why tax deferral is such an important motivation for an exchange.

Example

Wilson, a married man filing a joint return, has property with a market value of $100,000. His adjusted basis for the property is $10,000. In 1984, were he to sell the property for $100,000 in cash, he would have a capital gain of $90,000. Assuming the maximum tax on capital gains applies, he would have a tax of $18,000 (20 percent of $90,000). Hence, he would have $82,000 to reinvest ($100,000 sale price minus $18,000 tax).

Were he to engage in an exchange, Wilson would receive property worth $100,000. He could, in essence, reinvest the full $100,000 value of his present property. Thus, a tax-free exchange could preserve $18,000 of his capital (the amount he would owe in taxes on a sale). Assuming a 10-percent capitalization rate on Wilson's investment, the $18,000 would produce $1,800 per year of ordinary income. Consequently, a tax deferral for ten years, for example, would build up capital for this investor of $36,000 —the $18,000 of capital preserved via the tax-free exchange plus the $18,000 return on that investment at 10 percent per year. (Actually, the amount would be reduced by the taxes paid on the annual interest income and would be increased by the compounding effect of reinvesting the after-tax income.)

Exchange or sell?

Before discussing the rules of tax deferral in detail, it is important to keep in mind that a sale at a taxable gain, coupled with reinvestment in another property, has the effect of stepping up basis. In an exchange, however, (subject to adjustments discussed later) the basis of the property given up becomes the basis of the property acquired. Consequently, a question presents itself: is the property owner better off selling, paying a capital gains tax and reinvesting to get a higher basis and larger depreciation deductions in the future or will he fare better by avoiding current taxation via a tax-deferred exchange and forgo larger depreciation deductions in the future?

The tax dollars saved currently by going through a tax-deferred exchange rather than realizing a capital gain can easily be calculated. This amount can then be compared to the total of the discounted values of the future tax savings that would arise from additional depreciation deductions which would be available had there been a sale and reinvestment in property with a higher adjusted basis.

There cannot be one answer to the question of choosing between exchanging or selling and reinvesting. With the same properties taxpayers with different marginal tax rates can get different tax results. Hence, individual calculations should be made.

Since the current values of future tax savings are, at best, a good guess (future tax rates can change or the taxpayer's other income streams may be altered, thus increasing or decreasing his marginal rate), many investors prefer the "bird in the hand" of a current tax saving via a tax-deferred exchange. Be that as it may, the value of future tax savings via larger depreciation deductions (when basis is stepped up through a sale and reinvestment) is mentioned here so that it may be considered among all of the other factors in determining whether to exchange or to sell outright.

In connection with the future tax savings via depreciation deductions, keep in mind that for real property put into service after March 15, 1984, the ACRS recovery rate is based on an 18- rather than a 15-year life. This change diminishes the early-year depreciation deductions. (For a full discussion of the ACRS rules as they apply to real estate, see Chapter 9.)

Whenever a decision to exchange is made, it is important to carefully follow the tax rules set forth in this chapter.

Tax law requirements for tax-deferred exchanges

Section 1031 of the Internal Revenue Code provides that when certain property is exchanged for other property, some or all of the gain which is *realized* economically may not have to be *recognized* for tax purposes.

Example

Davidson has property which is worth $100,000. His adjusted basis for that property is only $40,000. If he sells that property for its value, he will *realize* a gain of $60,000. If he sells for cash, that gain will also be *recognized* for tax purposes; he would have to pay tax on a gain of $60,000. If, instead, he exchanges it for another property worth $100,000, he would still realize a gain of $60,000. However, that gain would not be recognized for tax purposes; he would pay no tax because of that transaction.

This example illustrates the difference between gain which is *realized* and that which is *recognized*. "Realized" is an economic concept—how much gain actually results from the transaction. "Recognized" is a tax concept—how much gain (if any) is taxable.

Section 1031 provides that no gain or loss is to be recognized (taxed) if certain business or investment property is exchanged solely for property of a like-kind which is also to be held for use in business or as an investment. To the extent that the exchange is not *solely* for like-kind property, some of the gain might be recognized; the balance of the gain may still be deferred.

The provisions of Section 1031 are not discretionary with the taxpayer or with the government. *If a transaction fits within the statutory requirements, no gain or loss is recognized.*

It should be made clear that when a transaction is described as tax-free in this discussion, it does not necessarily mean that the gain escapes taxation completely. What is meant is that the tax on the gain is deferred or postponed. Since the appreciation on the original property is not recognized for tax purposes, it does not increase the basis of the new property.

Example

A owns a parcel of land with a market value of $50,000 and a basis of $10,000. He exchanges it for another piece of land which is also worth $50,000. A's basis for the new land acquired is $10,000, the same as his basis for the land he gave up. There is no tax on this exchange. But if some years later A should sell the second parcel of land for $50,000, he would have a $40,000 recognized gain *at that time*. Consequently, the effect of Section 1031 on that exchange was to defer the $40,000 taxable gain until the subsequent disposition; it did not eliminate the gain forever.

Of course, a tax deferral is very valuable. As was illustrated in a prior example (where the tax of $18,000 was deferred), the deferral permitted the accumulation of an additional $18,000 of income over a ten-year period. Looking at it another way, whenever a tax can be deferred, in effect, money is borrowed from the U.S. Treasury without interest. (And, should an individual die without having disposed of the property in a taxable transaction, that deferred income tax will never have to be paid. When property is inherited, the basis to the heirs is the market value of that property on the date of the owner's death.)

Elements required for section 1031 exchange

In order to qualify for no recognition of gain or loss on an exchange under Section 1031, certain elements must be present.

1. Both the property received and the property given up must be held either for productive use in a trade or business or for investment. Specifically excluded from the benefits of this section are stock in trade or other property primarily held for sale (inventory), stocks, bonds, notes, choses in action, certificates of trust or beneficial interest, any other securities or evidences of indebtedness or interests, and interests in a partnership transferred after March 31, 1984.

2. To qualify, both properties must be of a *like-kind* to each other; that is, the nature or character of both properties must be alike.

3. Finally, the properties must be *exchanged* for each other.

Property used in a trade or business

This may include any kind of property which is used in the taxpayer's trade or business, such as machinery, office equipment, automobiles, factory buildings and land on which a building is situated. Property held for rental purposes, such as an apartment house or office building, is property used in a trade or business.

Held for Investment

This is property held for appreciation in value (and for the income therefrom) and not held for resale or in business. Since rental property (which is held for income) is defined as trade or business property, in terms of real estate, property held for investment is generally limited to vacant land. However, since property used in a trade or business also qualifies for a Section 1031 exchange, the distinction between trade or business property and investment property has no particular significance in terms of tax-free exchanges of real estate.

Like-kind

This concept relates to the nature of the property rather than its grade or quality. Improved real estate is considered to be of the same nature as unimproved real estate. They are both of a like-kind. The fact of improvement or unimprovement relates only to the grade or quality of the property and not to its kind or class. For this purpose, real estate is considered to be the same kind of property as a leasehold for real estate if the leasehold has 30 years or more to run.

Property used in a trade or business may be exchanged for other property used in a trade or business or may be exchanged for investment property. Similarly, property held for investment may be exchanged for other investment property or may be exchanged for property used in a trade or business.

The following exchanges are illustrations of like-kind properties permitted to be exchanged: city real estate for a ranch or farm; truck for a truck; vacant lot for land and building; or a leasehold of real estate with 30 or more years to run for a parcel of real estate owned outright.

There had been considerable controversy over whether interests in partnerships qualify as like-kind property. If both partnerships have the same type of underlying property, the courts have ruled that exchange of some partnership interests can qualify for like-kind, tax-free exchange treatment. However, the Tax Reform Act of 1984 provides that partnership interests exchanged after March 31, 1984 do *not* qualify as like-kind property.

Requirement of exchange

To enable the gain to be deferred under Section 1031, property must actually be exchanged. Care must be taken to avoid a sale and a purchase when an exchange is intended.

A typical situation in which the exchange requirement must be carefully observed arises when the seller wants an exchange for like-kind property and the buyer does not own suitable property to exchange. In such a situation, the seller and buyer can agree that the buyer will first acquire suitable property and then exchange it for the seller's property.

In this case the seller has a tax-free exchange, but the buyer does not. The property he acquires and exchanges was not held by him for investment or for productive use in a trade or business. However, since he has just bought the property, chances are that his basis will be close to the fair market value and thus he will have little or no taxable gain on the transaction.

In a transaction of this sort, the seller can even direct the buyer to make specific improvements to the property the seller is to acquire, prior to the exchange. For example, he can direct that a plant be built on the property to his specifications.

Sometimes a middle man is used in these transactions. If, for example, the buyer does not wish to acquire the property that he is then to exchange with the seller, the middle man buys the property and exchanges that property for the seller's property. The buyer then buys from the middle man the property formerly owned by the seller.

Four-way exchange

With three judges dissenting, the Tax Court, in *Coupe*, 52 TC 394 (1969), held a four-way exchange to be tax-free under the circumstances described in the example below.

Example

Taxpayer owned farmland which Southern Pacific contracted to buy for $2,500 an acre, for a total of $330,000. The taxpayer's basis in the property was only $17,000. His attorney suggested that the capital gains tax could be deferred if he were willing to take other farmlands rather than cash. The taxpayer agreed, and the attorney obtained acceptable farmlands. Southern Pacific was not willing to take title to the other farmlands but was willing to cooperate in other ways—that is, to deposit the purchase price in escrow, payable to the titleholder of the property it had contracted to buy.

The transaction was arranged by way of simultaneous closings: (1) taxpayer's property was deeded to the attorney; (2) the attorney then immediately deeded that property to Southern Pacific; (3) the attorney used the escrow deposit to acquire the deeds to the other farmlands; (4) the attorney deeded the other farmlands to the taxpayer.

Future exchange

What can be done when the buyer has no suitable property to exchange? That problem was solved in the *Starker* case, where the court found a tax-free exchange when property was exchanged for a *promise* by the buyer to acquire suitable properties and exchange them. The court held that the promise was a "fee equivalent."

However, for transfers made after March 31, 1984, the Tax Reform Act of 1984 has effectively outlawed certain future exchanges. If a taxpayer transfers his property for property to be received later, the exchange will *not* qualify as like-kind, unless:

1. The property to be received in the future is identified no later than 44 days after the taxpayer transferred his property, *and*
2. The property to be received is received no later than 180 days after the taxpayer transferred his property. If the taxpayer's tax return for the taxable year in which he transferred the property is due before the end of the 180-day period, then the taxpayer must have received the property no later than the due date of that tax return which includes any extension of time allowed.

Disqualification from section 1031

Let us examine more closely those attributes of a transaction which will disqualify it from nonrecognition treatment of Section 1031.

The first attribute concerns the nature of the property *received:* If the property received is not the same kind as that given up, the transaction will not qualify under Section 1031. If the property received is totally cash, notes, stocks, bonds, inventory or any of the other kinds of property referred to on page 289, which are specifically excluded from the beneficial treatment accorded by the section, the transaction will not qualify.

The exclusion of inventory-type property prevents a real estate dealer from exchanging any of his *real estate inventory* under the umbrella of Section 1031. (For a detailed discussion of when one is deemed to be a real estate dealer and when a dealer may be holding property for investment rather than as inventory see Chapter 10.)

Both the property received as well as that given up must have been held either (1) for productive use in a trade or business or (2) for investment. Thus, property which is held for personal use, such as an automobile or a yacht, does not qualify. Similarly, if the property received is immediately resold or exchanged, the inference is that the property received is not acquired for investment or for use in business but rather for the purpose of resale. This could destroy the tax-free nature of the transaction.

Also, when the property received is not the same kind as that given up, the exchange will not qualify. Thus if investment real estate is exchanged for factory machinery, the exchange would not qualify because real estate is not the same kind of property as factory machinery, which is personal property.

Computation of indicated gain

The presence of unlike property in the exchange may cause some gain to be taxed. Before the amount of taxable gain can be determined, however, it is necessary to compute the amount of gain *realized* on the exchange. Another term for "realized" is "indicated" gain. Both mean the amount of gain the property owner would have had if the property was sold rather than exchanged.

Example

Simon has a parcel with an adjusted basis to him of $6,000 and a fair market value of $10,000. On a cash sale, his realized gain would be $4,000.

Market value (cash received)	$10,000
Adjusted basis	6,000
Realized (indicated) gain	$ 4,000

If Simon had exchanged his parcel for one which also had a fair market value of $10,000, the computation and the result would be the same, so the gain is the difference between the adjusted basis of the property transferred and its fair market value. The total of what is received in exchange (net equity in real estate, cash, other property, etc.) normally will have a market value equal to the total given up.

Effect of receipt of unlike property

It is a rare situation when two or more properties being exchanged will have identical equities. Before the exchange is made the equities must be balanced. The equity in a property is its market value less any encumbrances on it.

Example

1. Property A has a market value of $50,000 and a first mortgage of $10,000. The equity in that property is $40,000. If Property B has a market value of $150,000 with a mortgage of $110,000, it too has an equity of $40,000. Thus, on the basis of equal equities, these two properties can be exchanged evenly.

2. Suppose we have this set of facts, however: Stone owns property with a market value of $100,000, subject to a mortgage of $40,000. His equity is therefore $60,000. Brown's property has a market value of $80,000, subject to a mortgage of $40,000, giving him an equity of $40,000. Obviously, Stone and Brown cannot make an even exchange.

Brown might pay Stone $20,000 in cash *in addition* to exchanging the buildings to balance the equities. Or he might give Stone other property—a boat, a car or other property—having a total value of $20,000.

Brown might give Stone promissory notes totalling $20,000, perhaps as a mortgage on the property Brown is acquiring in the exchange.

Stone might put an additional encumbrance on his property before the exchange, borrowing another $20,000 on a second mortgage on his property, and then transferring the property to Brown subject to mortgages totaling $60,000. He thereby reduces the equity in his property to $40,000 before the exchange.

In these situations, the process of balancing the equities brings about a situation in which either something in addition to the exchange property passes from one party to the other or one party is relieved of a greater amount of loan on the property he is giving up than he will bear on the property he is acquiring. It is the presence of cash, other property or net loan relief that can produce a partial (or total) taxable gain in an exchange which is subject to Section 1031.

If, under the circumstances mentioned, some of the property received qualifies for the nonrecognition treatment and some does not, realized gain will be recognized and taxed only to the extent of the value of the unlike property. There are, generally speaking, three kinds of unlike property: cash, other unlike property (called "boot") and net mortgage (loan) relief.

The mortgage debt attached to the property given up, which the former owner will now not have to pay, is considered to be unlike property. However, a special rule applies when the former owner takes his new property also subject to a mortgage. In that case, the unlike property received is deemed to be only the *net* loan relief; the two mortgages are netted and unlike property is considered to have been received only to the extent the mortgage on the property given up exceeds the mortgage on the property received. These rules apply regardless of whether the mortgage is assumed or the property received is merely taken subject to the mortgage with no personal liability assumed; it makes no difference.

Example

Arthur and Baker wish to exchange their properties. Prior to the exchange, the pertinent facts concerning each property are as follows:

Arthur's Property		Baker's Property
$50,000	Market value	$70,000
30,000	Mortgages on property	40,000
20,000	Equity	30,000

Since Baker's equity is greater than Arthur's by $10,000, Arthur will also pay Baker $10,000 cash. Each will acquire the other's property subject to mortgages on the properties. On the exchange, Baker will be relieved of a $40,000 mortgage and acquire a property subject to a $30,000 mortgage. He will therefore have net loan relief of $10,000. In addition, he will receive $10,000 cash. Hence, he will have received $20,000 of unlike property. Arthur will have an *increased* loan and will *pay* $10,000 cash. He will not have received any unlike property.

There can be situations in which one party to the exchange has net loan relief but also pays cash. In that case, he may reduce the net loan relief by the cash paid in determining the net unlike property received. On the other hand, if he *receives* cash and also assumes a greater loan than he gives up, he is not permitted to reduce the amount of cash received by the increase in his loan burden. Therefore, the full amount of the cash received will be treated as unlike property in determining the amount of the recognized gain.

Effect of transaction costs   Transaction costs (brokerage commissions paid on the transfers, excise taxes on deeds, etc.) are considered reductions of the proceeds of the sale and thereby reduce the indicated gain. They then become part of the basis of the property acquired in the exchange.

IRS has ruled that cash paid for transaction costs is to be treated as cash paid in the exchange transaction. Therefore, the IRS ruling provides that the transaction cost paid in cash reduces any cash received in the exchange in calculating the amount of unlike property received. Presumably, the same logic allows for the reduction of net loan relief by the amount of the transaction costs paid in cash in determining the amount of unlike property received in the exchange.

Application of exchange rules

The following example illustrates the tax effects of exchanges, including the calculation of the recognized gain and the treatment of the giving and receiving of unlike property.

Example

Dr. Brown owns an apartment house which has an adjusted basis of $100,000 and a market value of $220,000 but is subject to a mortgage of $80,000. Prof. Smith also owns an apartment house. His apartment house has an adjusted basis of $175,000 and a market value of $250,000 and is subject to a mortgage of $150,000. Dr. Brown exchanges his apartment house for Prof. Smith's apartment house and $40,000 cash. Each apartment house was exchanged subject to the mortgage on it. Dr. Brown's realized or indicated gain would be computed as follows:

Received

Value of Prof. Smith's apartment house	$250,000
Cash	40,000
Mortgage on property given up	80,000
Total received	$370,000

Given up

Adjusted basis of old building	$100,000	
Transaction costs	16,500	
Mortgage on property received	150,000	
Total given up		266,500
Gain realized (indicated gain)		$103,500

A quick way to calculate the indicated gain is as follows:

Market value of Brown's property		$220,000
Less: Adjusted basis of his property	$100,000	
Transaction costs	16,500	116,500
Indicated gain		$103,500

A similar computation would apply to Prof. Smith:

Received

Value of Dr. Brown's property	$220,000
Mortgage on property given up	150,000
Total received	$370,000

Given up

Adjusted basis of old building	$175,000	
Transaction costs	19,000	
Cash paid to Dr. Brown	40,000	
Mortgage on property received	80,000	
Total given up		314,000
Gain realized (indicated gain)		$ 56,000

Here, too, the indicated gain for Prof. Smith can be calculated as follows:

Market value of Prof. Smith's property		$250,000
Less: Adjusted basis of his property	$175,000	
Transaction costs	19,000	194,000
Indicated gain		$ 56,000

Dr. Brown received $40,000 in cash. He surrendered a property with an $80,000 mortgage but acquired a property subject to a mortgage of $150,000. Hence, he had no net loan relief. The only unlike property he received was the $40,000 cash. He paid $16,500 in transaction costs, which reduces the cash received by that amount. His net unlike property received was $23,500. Since the $23,500 is less than his indicated gain of $103,500 he has a recognized (taxable) gain of $23,500.

Prof. Smith gave up property subject to a mortgage of $150,000. He acquired property subject to an $80,000 mortgage. He had a loan relief of $70,000. However, he paid out in cash $40,000 to Dr. Brown and $19,000 in transaction costs. This total of $59,000, when subtracted from the $70,000 net loan relief, gives him net unlike property received of $11,000. Thus, of his indicated gain of $56,000, $11,000 is recognized gain.

Losses in a section 1031 exchange

If a transaction qualifies fully under Section 1031—that is, if there is a like-kind exchange of qualifying property with no unlike property—then neither gain nor loss is recognized. Presence of unlike property *received* may cause some gain to be recognized but will never cause the recognition of loss.

Example

Green exchanges his apartment house which has a basis of $16,000 and a market value of $12,000 for an apartment house having a $10,000 market value plus $2,000 cash. Although Green has an indicated loss of $4,000, no part of that loss is deductible.

If, however, unlike property is *transferred,* it is possible for the transferor to realize and to deduct his loss on the unlike property that he is transferring.

Example

Phillips exchanges investment real estate plus stock for another piece of real estate to be held for investment. The real estate given up has an adjusted basis of $10,000 and a market value of $11,000. The stock given up has a basis of $4,000 and a market value of $2,000. The real estate received has a fair market value of $13,000.

Phillips is deemed to have received a $2,000 portion of the new real estate in exchange for the stock he gave up because that is its fair market value at the time of the exchange. A loss of $2,000 is recognized on the transfer of the stock by Phillips. No gain or loss is recognized on the transfer of the real estate because that was an exchange completely within the provisions of Section 1031—no unlike property was *received* by Phillips.

Multiple exchange

It is often difficult to find two people who are willing to exchange parcels of real estate with each other. Very often one of them will be willing to take the parcel owned by the second, but the second has no desire to receive the parcel owned by the first. In such cases, sometimes a third parcel can be found which the second individual may be willing to take. Then a three-way exchange may be executed.

For federal income tax purposes, such an exchange will still satisfy the requirements of Section 1031. Each owner will compute his realized and recognized gain in the same manner as described previously. The mechanics of the exchange may be performed as follows.

Example

A, B and C each hold parcels of real estate for investment purposes. They agree to exchange lots, with any difference in acreage to be made up the rate of $100 per acre.

In the exchange, C acquires the lot owned by B; B acquires the lot owned by A and A acquires the lot owned by C. The position of the Treasury Department, expressed in *Rev. Rul. 57-244,* is that the transaction constitutes exchanges within the scope of Section 1031 and gain, if any, is recognized only to the extent of the cash received.

The importance of this ruling is that for Section 1031 to apply, it is *not* necessary to receive the property in an exchange from the person to whom the property is being transferred. As is demonstrated in the example, although A transferred his lot to B, he acquired the lot owned by C. In other words, only three deeds were needed to carry out the transaction: A gave the deed to his land to B, B gave the deed to his land to C and C gave the deed to his land to A.

There may be a practical difficulty with the three-way exchange as described here: the difficulty of documentation. Not all exchanges are "text book" exchanges with all of the parties to the entire multiple exchange sitting around one table. The multiplicity of the exchange is usually developed by the broker who, after analyzing a number of different situations, is able to put together a multiple exchange for the benefit of all of the parties concerned. Consequently, a round-robin deeding of property, as described in the preceding paragraph, may not always be practical. (And where it is practical, it may be a good idea to have all the parties sign a document indicating that an exchange took place as described so that on a future tax examination, any one of the three parties can document the entire transaction.)

An alternative to the use of only three deeds, where for practical reasons not all the parties are available to do the direct deeding as would be required, is to follow a procedure such as this: (1) A deeds his property to B and B deeds his property to A; (2) B then deeds the property he acquired from A to C and C deeds his property to B.

This arrangement clearly indicates that exchanges were made. The difficulty with this type of arrangement is that B will not have a tax-free exchange on his acquisition of A's property because he has not acquired it for use in his trade or business or for investment (he has acquired it for the purpose of exchanging it). Of course, if B wants to "cash out"—really sell his property—it makes no difference to him because he expected to have a taxable transaction. However, if he too wants a tax-free exchange, in order to follow the deeding procedure described above, a fourth party (probably the broker) would have to get involved. He would act as a conduit; the various parties would transfer properties to him and he would exchange with the other parties. Thus, A, B and C would deed their properties to D (the broker); D would then deed the A property to C, the B property to A and the C property to B.

Items which affect basis in an exchange

The reason there is really only a tax deferral as the result of an exchange is that, generally, basis of the old property carries over to the new. Adjustments have to be made, however, for the unlike property that passed in the exchange, the payment of transaction costs and the recognition of some gain in many cases. Just how is the adjusted basis of the property acquired in an exchange computed?

If the gain on a transaction escapes recognition for tax purposes, the tax result is often that the new piece of property, the property received, will be penalized by having a basis that is less than its fair market value by the amount of nonrecognized or nontaxed gain. Conversely, to maintain the symmetry of the tax concepts, any loss which is not recognized will have the effect of increasing the basis of the property received.

Before the basis of the property received can be calculated, certain items of information must be known. We will now consider these items and their effects on the basis of the property acquired.

To arrive at the adjusted basis of the property acquired in the exchange, we start with the basis of the property given up. To this basis, we add the gain recognized plus the net amount, in addition to the property, the taxpayer parted with—that is, cash paid to balance the equities, payments of transaction costs and net increase in the mortgage indebtedness (the excess of the mortgage on the property received over the mortgage on the property given up).

From the above total is subtracted the amount of cash or other unlike property received, including net mortgage relief (the excess of the mortgage on the property given up over the mortgage on the property received).

Example

Refer back to the exchange between Dr. Brown and Prof. Smith (see page 295). Here is how each would calculate the basis of the property acquired in the exchange.

Dr. Brown

Basis of the property given up	$100,000
Add:	
Gain recognized	23,500
Transaction costs	16,500
Excess of mortgage on property received	
over mortgage on property given up	70,000
Total	210,000
Subtract:	
Cash received	40,000
Basis of property acquired	$170,000

Prof. Smith

Basis of property given up	$175,000
Add:	
Gain recognized	11,000
Transaction costs	19,000
Cash paid	40,000
Total	245,000
Subtract:	
Net mortgage relief (excess of mortgage	
given up over mortgage acquired)	70,000
Basis of property acquired	$175,000

If we now examine the situation after the new basis computations have been made, we can see the net effect of what has happened. Dr. Brown acquired an apartment house with a value of $250,000. In the process he benefited from a nonrecognized gain of $80,000. Remember that only a $23,500 gain was recognized out of his total realized (indicated) gain of $103,500. Therefore, the basis for his new property is $170,000, which is the same as the value of the property acquired ($250,000) minus the portion of the gain that was not recognized ($80,000).

Similarly, Prof. Smith acquired an apartment house with a market value of $220,000. His nonrecognized gain was $45,000 ($56,000 indicated gain minus $11,000 recognized gain). His basis for the property acquired ($175,000) is equal to the value of the property acquired ($220,000) less the nonrecognized gain ($45,000).

From this it should become apparent that the penalty for the benefit of being able to defer gain is a decrease in basis below the market value of the parcel received by the amount of the gain which is deferred.

Increases in basis for depreciation

It may be noticed from the example that it is possible for basis to be built up—actually increased—as a result of an exchange. Dr. Brown started with a parcel having an adjusted basis of $100,000. When he was finished he had a parcel of greater value, with a basis of $170,000. That increase of $70,000 was due largely to the increase in mortgage liability attributable to his new parcel.

Thus, it is possible to increase the basis of a property which is subject to depreciation and thereby gain the advantage of additional depreciation deductions reducing taxable income without the expenditure of cash. What can be accomplished by this method is an increase in the leverage factor and the value of the investment.

Example

Green owns a property with a market value of $100,000, a mortgage of $20,000 and an adjusted basis of $45,000. He holds that parcel for the production of rental income; therefore it is property used in a trade or business. He exchanges it for another rental building which is worth $150,000 and has a mortgage of $70,000. The equity in each building is therefore $80,000.

Green has a tax-free exchange under Section 1031. No gain is recognized because he has received no cash, no other property and no net mortgage relief. But what about his basis for the property received? It is as follows:

Basis of property given up	$ 45,000
Add: Amount of loan on property received	70,000
Total	$115,000
Subtract: Loan on property given up	20,000
Basis of property received	$ 95,000
(Transaction costs have been omitted to simplify the example.)	

As indicated, Green has increased the value of the property he holds from a $100,000 parcel to a $150,000 parcel. He has also increased his basis for depreciation from $45,000 to $95,000. And he has not paid out any cash. **301**

Although the basis for depreciation may be increased via an exchange, not all of the basis acquired will necessarily qualify for Accelerated Cost Recovery (ACRS) under the 1981 tax law. (How ACRS works is described in Chapter 9.) ACRS applies only to property acquired after 1980. In the case of a tax-free exchange which takes place after 1980, the property surrendered by the taxpayer may very well have been held by him during 1980. In that case, the basis of the property acquired is compared to the basis of the property given up. Only to the extent that the basis of the property acquired exceeds the basis of the property given up do the ACRS rules apply. That portion of the basis of the property acquired which is equal to the basis of the property given up is subject to depreciation under the rules which applied prior to the enactment of ACRS.

Allocation of basis between land and buildings   Another possibility for increasing the basis of property subject to the allowance for depreciation arises from the requirement that basis be allocated between land (which is not depreciable) and building (which is depreciable).

This principle can be applied to a common situation where the adjusted basis of a building has been reduced because of depreciation deductions to such a point that it is far below the basis for the land, and the relative market values are such that the building is worth considerably more than the land. When two such situations exist, an exchange of the properties can result in a dramatic increase in the basis for depreciation of both buildings.

Example

Assume that Smith and Green each owns land and buildings having a value in excess of basis, as follows:

	Adjusted Basis	Market Value	
Smith			
Land	$40,000	$ 40,000	33⅓%
Building	10,000	80,000	66⅔
	$50,000	$120,000	100%
Green			
Land	$30,000	$ 30,000	25%
Building	30,000	90,000	75
	$60,000	$120,000	100%

If Green and Smith should exchange properties, here are the tax results (ignoring transaction costs).

Smith's basis for the total property acquired from Green would be $50,000. But he can allocate that basis between the acquired land and building according to their relative market values. Since 75 percent of the fair market value of the property acquired from Green is attributable to the building, Smith can allocate $37,500 of his $50,000 basis to the building and the remaining $12,500 to the land. Hence, as a result of the exchange, Smith has boosted his basis for depreciable property from $10,000 to $37,500 and stepped down his basis for land from $40,000 to $12,500.

On acquiring Smith's property, Green would use $60,000 as his basis for that property, the same basis he had for the property he exchanged. But he, too, would allocate that basis between land and building according to relative fair market values. Hence, he would allocate two-thirds of his $60,000 basis, or $40,000, to the building and the remaining one-third, or $20,000, to the land. So he too will have increased his basis for depreciable property, from $30,000 to $40,000.

Hence Green and Smith *both* get stepped up bases for their buildings and increased depreciation deductions as a result of the exchange.

Depreciation recapture and the section 1031 exchange

As has been explained in Chapter 10, part or all of the gain on the sale or exchange of depreciable property may be treated as the recapture of previously deducted depreciation and taxed as ordinary income. How does this depreciation recapture rule affect exchanges made under Section 1031 when part or all of the gain is not recognized for tax purposes?

If the property is personal property (e.g. furniture, equipment, etc. not part of the real estate), Section 1245 provides that the amount of the depreciation deducted after 1961 (or after June, 1963, for elevators and escalators) is compared to the portion of the gain that is taxable in the exchange. In other words, for purposes of depreciation recapture, the *recognized* portion of the gain is treated as the total gain. That amount is the maximum amount subject to depreciation recapture.

In the case of real property, Section 1250 applies. It provides that although depreciation recapture can convert capital gain into ordinary income on the sale of real estate, ordinary income from depreciation recapture can be avoided in a Section 1031 exchange. Ordinary income is recognized on the exchange due to depreciation recapture *only if:*

1. There is some recognized gain on the exchange due to the receipt of unlike property; or
2. The amount of Section 1250 gain that would have been recognized had this been an outright sale rather than exchange exceeds the market value of Section 1250 property (depreciable real estate) received in the exchange.

If neither (1) nor (2) is true, there is no ordinary income due to depreciation recapture on the exchange. If either (1) or (2) is true, the maximum amount of ordinary income due to depreciation recapture on the exchange is the amount computed in (1) or (2). If both (1) *and* (2) are true, the larger amount is taxable.

Allocation of basis   After the exchange, if any ordinary income due to depreciation recapture has been avoided under the above rules, basis of all the property acquired in the exchange is first computed in the usual way. Then, an allocation of the basis must be made.

First, basis is allocated between Section 1250 property and other property received in the exchange. For example, if land and building were acquired, the land is not Section 1250 property while the building is. The total basis is allocated in proportion to the properties' fair market values. But the fair market value of the Section 1250 property is reduced by the amount of ordinary income avoided on the exchange because the Section 1250 rules did not apply under the provisions explained.

Examples

1. Brown exchanges his land and building for Spencer's land and building. This is a tax-free exchange in which no gain or loss is recognized. Had this been a taxable transaction, Brown would have realized $10,000 of ordinary income under the Section 1250 depreciation recapture rules. Since no unlike property was received in the exchange, Item 1 does not apply. Since the market value of the building received is greater than the $10,000 of ordinary income from depreciation recapture which would have resulted in a taxable transaction, Item 2 does not apply. Hence, there is no ordinary income from depreciation recapture recognized on this transaction.

Assume that Brown's basis for the total property he acquired, under the usual rules for computing basis in a tax-free exchange, is $42,000. Assume, too, that the market value of the building is $70,000 and the market value of the land is $30,000.

The $42,000 basis must be allocated to building and land. To do this, the market value of the building (the Section 1250 property) is reduced by the $10,000 that would have constituted ordinary income from depreciation recapture if the transaction had been fully taxable. Thus, the market value of the building becomes $60,000 and the market value of the land remains $30,000. Since $60,000 is two-thirds of the total market value of $90,000, two-thirds of the $42,000 basis, or $28,000, is allocated to the building and one-third, or $14,000, to the land.

2. Suppose instead of getting one building in the exchange, there were two whose total value was $70,000, with the remaining $30,000 market value attributable to the land on which they stand. The $28,000 basis for buildings (calculated previously) must be allocated between the two buildings in relation to their market values. But here the market values of the buildings are not reduced by the ordinary income from depreciation recapture which was avoided on the exchange. Thus, assume the $70,000 market value is allocable $40,000 to Building 1 and $30,000 to Building 2. In that case four-sevenths of the $28,000 basis allocable to the Section 1250 properties, or $16,000, is allocable to Building 1 and three-sevenths, or $12,000, is allocable to Building 2.

What happens to the ordinary income from depreciation recapture that was avoided on the tax-free exchange? It carries over to the new properties as excess depreciation. If only one building was acquired, the full $10,000 is allocated to the building. If two buildings were acquired, the allocation is made in proportion to the bases of the two buildings, i.e. four-sevenths of $10,000, or $5,715, to Building 1; and three-sevenths of $10,000, or $4,285, to Building 2.

3. Suppose $5,000 of the $10,000 ordinary income due to excess depreciation arose before 1970. (Under the rules applying to the depreciation recapture for that period, the total excess depreciation is reduced by 1 percent for each month in excess of 20 that the property was held.) Assume the property is held two more years and sold at a gain of $50,000. During the two years the property was held, there was excess depreciation of $735.

Since the property sold was acquired in a tax-free exchange, for *depreciation recapture purposes only* it is necessary to use a holding period commencing with the acquisition of the property. Here, we use two years. Consequently, the depreciation recapture (ordinary income) portion of the $50,000 gain is calculated as follows:

Excess depreciation since the acquisition of the exchanged property	$ 735
$5,000 of depreciation recapture after 1969 (carried over from prior property)	5,000
$5,000 of depreciation recapture prior to 1970 (carried over from prior property) reduced by 4 percent because property was held 24 months (using new holding period)	4,800
Portion of $50,000 gain subject to ordinary income treatment due to depreciation recapture	$10,535

Notes

1. For a complete volume on exchanges, see Mark Lee Levine, *Real Estate Exchanges* (Chicago: REALTORS NATIONAL MARKETING INSTITUTE®, 1981).

Section III

Case Studies in Real Estate Brokerage

The real estate investment broker's role is to combine into a meaningful investment proposal his knowledge of properties, clients, investment analysis and income tax regulations.

The previous sections of this book have been devoted to the presentation of a framework of real estate investment analysis. Much attention has been given to the methods of calculating rate of return for use in comparing all forms of investments. Income tax impact on real estate investments has been given consideration in order that the cash flow analysis can be calculated in an after-tax situation.

The purposes of this section are to discuss and demonstrate the practical aspects of cash flow analysis, to provide illustrative case studies of a limited number of important brokerage operations and to introduce and demonstrate the use of several standard forms developed by the Commercial-Investment Council of the REALTORS NATIONAL MARKETING INSTITUTE® of the NATIONAL ASSOCIATION OF REALTORS®. The purpose of using these forms is to ease and simplify the accumulation and evaluation of data necessary to understand a particular investment property.

The forms address themselves to the major problem of real estate investment analysis—defining or estimating the future income stream and measuring this stream by discounting it to a present value or measuring its rate in terms of an investment amount.

Some of the most widely used forms presented in this section are the Annual Property Operating Data form, the Cash Flow Analysis form and the Exchange Worksheet.

Practical aspects of cash flow analysis

No facet of the real estate brokerage business is as controversial as that concerned with cash flow forecasting and analysis of investment real estate. Extreme views are expressed on both sides of the issue.

Rabid opponents to this kind of forecasting argue:

"Future cash flows cannot be accurately predicted."

"Future resale prices are impossible to forecast."

"The process is too technical—buyers and sellers do not understand it."

"Figures can lie and liars can figure—the numbers can be made to show any desired result."

Enthusiastic advocates counter with:

"The only things an investor is interested in are

1. How much money do I put in?
2. When do I put it in?
3. How much do I get out?
4. When do I get it?

That's the essence of cash flow analysis."

"If real estate is acquired for its future benefit, one must estimate the annual and disposition income in order to make a decision to acquire, hold or dispose of property."

"The computer capability of cash flow analysis brings a greater professionalism to the industry."

These extremes of viewpoints create two extremes of salesperson. One is a "people person" who is never involved with numbers. This salesperson has the ability to locate properties for sale and clients who want properties. Valuation and/or analysis is left to the buyer or his advisors. The salesperson's role in the negotiation is to let the principals negotiate; sales are made (or lost) by the principals. The salesperson has little or no influence on the market or the transaction other than keeping clients happy and driving people around.

At the other end of the spectrum is the "numbers person" who is not too adept at personal relationships. This salesperson loves numbers, the computer and analyzing the properties under all possible variables. Filling out forms, passing out computer runs and stressing the percentages and ratios is how this salesperson thinks and operates. Finding clients, negotiating and compromising do not come easily. (Of these two types of salespeople, the former probably makes more money and is usually in more trouble.)

There is a great need, however, for a middle position—for the professional investment brokerage salesperson—one who recognizes that the popular rules of thumb are poor yardsticks for measuring future benefits of real estate and who understands the strengths and limitations of the internal rate of return calculations. This salesperson knows cash flow analysis thoroughly, yet understands the human aspects of brokerage. Investment clients, whether sellers or buyers, are entitled to more than a personable salesperson. They are entitled to assistance from a real estate professional as well as from the fields of law and accounting.

Forecasting as art and science

Cash flow forecasting may be viewed as more an art than a science because of the variety of types of real estate income. The income from a long-term net lease is simplest to define because the lease itself usually states the rental stream. This estimation could become more complicated if a percentage rent is also required. At the other extreme, income from a vacant portion of land can account for a negative income stream created by real estate taxes and loan payments, until the land is sold.

Between these extremes is the apartment, the store building or other improved real estate with short-term leases where the owner pays all or most of the expenses. Other examples include vacant buildings as well as properties to be developed where all income and expense items must be estimated and projected.

The estimation of future cash flows for income-producing real estate requires a variety of judgments and assumptions concerning the future. Among these are judgments concerning the property itself, the future of the neighborhood in which it is located, the general market conditions that are expected to prevail and their impact on the specific property, future developments in the federal income tax laws that may influence the after-tax cash flows of the property and myriad other factors which may affect the cash flows of the specific property over time. The task of income estimation requires both experience in and knowledge of the operation of the real estate market. It is not simply an extrapolation of the known market behavior of preceding years, nor can the estimation problem be refined completely to objective statistical probabilities. In its final form, the estimate of future benefits from an investment in real estate must relate to the *amount, timing, duration* (or term) and *stability* of after-tax cash flows to be received by the investor.

The mathematical logic employed in discounting future cash flows is fundamentally essential in analyzing real estate investments. Of equal importance, however, is the process by which the future cash flows of a specific property (or group of properties) are estimated. Generally speaking, this process stands in marked contrast to the inexorable precision of the discounting process. Because estimates of cash flows which are generated by real estate necessarily involve estimates of the future, they are more often than not significantly less precise than the mathematical technique used to discount them to the present.

Cash flow analysis assumptions

1. The real estate investment broker uses cash flow analysis in order to determine whether or not the future benefits to be derived from the property, based on the asking price and terms, will provide a yield competitive with other real estate and non-real estate investment alternatives available in the market. If such a study indicates the property is not competitive or cannot be made competitive, the broker is foolish to waste his time, money and energy trying to market the property.

2. Cash flow projections and internal rate of return calculations may or may not be used in marketing the property. How all or parts of the study are utilized with the seller, buyer and/or their advisors depends upon human factors and the education, training and experience of the parties involved. The investment broker uses what he needs for each party to the transaction and in such form as can be understood by the parties involved.

3. Although it is impossible to predict future cash flows, it is easy to calculate yields on any series of *projected* cash flows. Therefore, it is essential that the investment broker do his homework in order to make the most logical and honest projections of future cash flows. This may not necessarily be one projection. Most logically it might be three. One might be the broker's "best guesstimate" projection, the next a more optimistic one, the third a more pessimistic one. Yields can then be calculated from the three projections. Potential buyers can be shown the range of possible yields and the rationale for each projection. They can assess the future of the property based on their own viewpoints of the future and the yields available from alternative investments.

4. Cash flow analysis has no purpose other than to compare the potential yields of two or more investment opportunities. Therefore, it is essential not only that the cash flow analysis process is understood but also that clients understand under which circumstances comparisons may or may not be valid.

The case studies in this section are grouped under three chapters:

Cash Flow Forecasting

Differential Cash Flow Analysis

Special Investment Problems

The case studies presented are by no means an exhaustive presentation, but rather are intended to serve as a foundation for the broker who will use the fundamentals presented in solving his specific brokerage or counseling problems. The potential for other applications is unlimited.

Most of the case studies presented are from actual experiences of the authors—in some instances simplified to eliminate extraneous data and calculations.

Although the case studies reflect the most recent 1984 tax changes, some studies will have interest rates and/or mortgage terms that may not be compatible with lending policies at the date of publication and/or the exact date of reading of this material. These inconsistencies, however, should not distract the reader from the principles involved in "making the transaction" nor diminish the value of the analysis process.

Chapter 12

Cash Flow Forecasting

12

Case Study 1
After-tax analysis of income-producing property

The purpose of this case study is to demonstrate how the effective investment broker makes cash flow forecasts or projections and calculates yield (Internal Rate of Return) from the projection. Two standard forms, the Annual Property Operating Data form and the Cash Flow Analysis form, are used extensively in this case study.

Situation

At a recent civic club meeting Bill Broker met John Seller. During the course of the meeting, Seller indicated to Broker that he had an apartment building he wanted to sell. Broker made an appointment to see the property for the following week. After the inspection, Seller indicated he wanted $540,000 for the property. He also gave the following information to Broker:

Rents collected in previous year		$78,000
Expenses:	Taxes	$6,200
	Insurance	1,800
	Utilities	2,400
	Supplies	250
	Maintenance	1,000

Seller also said there was an existing mortgage on the property of approximately $210,000 payable at $2,300 per month including 8-percent interest. Broker told Seller he wanted to analyze the property and would get back to him.

Owner's statement

The first step in the process of property analysis is to obtain all possible financial and physical data about the property from the owner and his records. The Annual Property Operating Data (APOD) form acts as a checklist in the gathering of the financial data. It must be emphasized, however, that at this stage the broker is collecting and recording data, not evaluating, interpreting or analyzing it.

Upon his return to his office Bill Broker begins his analysis by preparing the Owner's Statement on an APOD. He systematically enters information supplied by the owner without verifying or evaluating it. Figure 19 shows the completed Owner's Statement. Note the indicated cash flow before income taxes of $38,750. It is apparent from just looking over the Owner's Statement that some income and expense boxes are unfilled. Broker must decide whether or not these items need further investigation.

Broker gets an overall look at the property income stream from a quantity standpoint. The owner's reported income of $78,000 and expenses of $11,650 indicate that the property produces $66,350 before debt service. Reported expenses are 15 percent of reported income. If this is a low expense ratio for the type of property, perhaps further investigation of the statement is needed. Is the income too high or are the expenses too low? The cash flow of 11.7 percent on equity is good—but is it too good? It is apparent that Broker should delve deeper to better understand the property. His next step is the preparation of a Broker's Forecast.

Broker's forecast (pro forma)

Up to this point Broker has merely organized Seller's figures in an orderly manner; however, there is no assurance that the numbers on the Owner's Statement are realistic or reflect the future potential of the property. Last year's results may or may not be an indication of future income.

To test the validity of the information submitted by Seller and to analyze the potential income of the property in terms of quantity, quality and durability, Broker must develop a new operating statement based upon the Owner's Statement and other market data.

This Broker's Forecast is prepared by Broker on another blank APOD form. This statement reflects how the property is *expected* to perform financially for the next full calendar year. A projected operating statement for a shorter period is more valid than for a longer period—that is, the possibility of projecting a valid income and expense statement for next year is greater than a projection of income and expenses 15 years from now.

When the Broker's Forecast is completed, it is possible that not one single item of income or expense on it is the same as for any previous year, yet it should more accurately reflect the income that the property will produce for the next full calendar year than will the Owner's Statement.

Figure 19 Owner's Statement

Annual Property Operating Data

Date _____

Price $ __540,000_____

Purpose _Owner's Statement_
Loans $ __210,000_____
Name _John Seiler_
Equity $ __330,000_____
Location _16752 SW Cedar Way_
Type of Property _32 Unit Apt._

FINANCING

	Existing	Balance	Payment	# Pymt/Yr.	Interest	Term
1st	$210,000	2300	12	8 %		

Assessed/Appraised Values

Land	$_____ _____ %	2nd	$_____ _____ _____ _____ % _____
Improvement	$_____ _____ %	3rd	$_____ _____ _____ _____ % _____
Personal Property	$_____ _____ %	Potential	
Total	$_____ 100 %	1st	_____ _____ _____ _____ % _____
Adjusted Basis as of _____	$_____	2nd	$_____ _____ _____ _____ % _____

		%	2	3	Comments
1	SCHEDULED RENTAL INCOME				
2	Less: Vacancy and Credit Losses				
3	EFFECTIVE RENTAL INCOME				
4	Plus: Other Income				
5	GROSS OPERATING INCOME			78 000	
6	Less: Operating Expenses				
7	Accounting and Legal				
8	Advertising, Licenses and Permits		1 800		
9	Property Insurance				
10	Property Management				
11	Payroll–Resident Management				
12	Other				
13	Taxes–Worker's Compensation				
14	Personal Property Taxes		6 200		
15	Real Estate Taxes				
16	Repairs and Maintenance		1 000		
17	Services–Elevator				
18	Janitorial				
19	Lawn				
20	Pool				
21	Rubbish				
22	Other				
23	Supplies		250		
24	Utilities–Electricity		2 400		
25	Gas and Oil				
26	Sewer and Water				
27	Telephone				
28	Other				
29	Miscellaneous				
30					
31	TOTAL OPERATING EXPENSES	15		11 650	
32	NET OPERATING INCOME			66 350	
33	Less: Annual Debt Service			27 600	
34	CASH FLOW BEFORE TAXES	11.7		38 750	

Broker
Prepared by _(Owner's Data)_

315

The Broker's Forecast was prepared in the following series of steps. From the local assessor's office, Broker obtained the assessed value of land and improvements and entered them on the APOD form. (The percentage of the improvement to value enables the broker to estimate the improvement value and to calculate annual depreciation from that amount.) Broker also obtained a verbal opinion from a lender as to the amount and terms of a maximum new loan that might be available for a qualified purchaser of the property. These figures are entered under the potential financing section of the Annual Property Operating Data form (Figure 20). From the seller's accountant, it was determined that the owner's adjusted basis (depreciated value or book value) was $290,000, which is entered beside the adjusted basis (see Figure 20).

The first item entered on the Broker's Forecast for actual operating figures (see Figure 21) is scheduled rental income. This is the income that the property will produce during the coming year if rented at market or economic rents 100 percent of the time.

To estimate scheduled rental income, it is necessary to know what typical rentals are in the neighborhood for a comparable apartment building. Studies must therefore be made to estimate economic rents for Seller's property. This is done by analyzing competitive rents to determine unit comparability on a square-foot, cubic-foot, per-room or per-apartment basis. The unit basis is then applied to the property being studied. In this case Broker went to similar apartment units and inquired into rental rates. In addition, he reviewed his own (or other friendly brokers') rental rates. He found market rents as follows:

One-bedroom rents	Two-bedroom rents
$175.00	$230.00
195.00	270.00
187.50	285.00
200.00	265.00
195.00	310.00

Adjustments upward or downward of these figures were then made by Broker, judging how the comparable units varied from those owned by John Seller and how much more or less they would rent for per month as compared to the subject units. Did they have fireplaces, swimming pools, furniture, central heat, or were they in better or worse condition? Then Broker compared the adjusted rents to the square footage area to indicate unit rents. The results are as follows:

Figure 20 Financing Information

Annual Property Operating Data

Date _____

Price $ _____

Loans $ _____

Equity $ _____

Purpose **Broker's Forecast**

Name **John Seller**

Location **16752 SW Cedar Way**

Type of Property **32 Unit Apt.**

Assessed/Appraised Values

Land	$42,000	19.6 %
Improvement	$168,000	78.5 %
Personal Property	$ 4,000	1.9 %
Total	$214,000	100 %

Adjusted Basis as of **Dec. 31** $290,000

FINANCING

Existing	Balance	Payment	# Pymt/Yr.	Interest	Term
1st	$210,000	2,300	12	8 %	
2nd	$			%	
3rd	$			%	
Potential					
1st	400,000	3,634.80	12	10 %	25
2nd	$			%	

		%	2	3	Comments
1	SCHEDULED RENTAL INCOME				
2	Less: Vacancy and Credit Losses				
3	EFFECTIVE RENTAL INCOME				
4	Plus: Other Income				
5	GROSS OPERATING INCOME				
6	Less: Operating Expenses				
7	Accounting and Legal				
8	Advertising, Licenses and Permits				
9	Property Insurance				
10	Property Management				
11	Payroll–Resident Management				
12	Other				
13	Taxes–Worker's Compensation				
14	Personal Property Taxes				
15	Real Estate Taxes				
16	Repairs and Maintenance				
17	Services–Elevator				
18	Janitorial				
19	Lawn				
20	Pool				
21	Rubbish				
22	Other				
23	Supplies				
24	Utilities–Electricity				
25	Gas and Oil				
26	Sewer and Water				
27	Telephone				
28	Other				
29	Miscellaneous				
30					
31	TOTAL OPERATING EXPENSES				
32	NET OPERATING INCOME				
33	Less: Annual Debt Service				
34	CASH FLOW BEFORE TAXES				

Prepared by _____

317

Estimated rent roll:

No. Units	Unit Rent	Monthly Rent	Annual
16	$200	$3200	$38,400
16	250	4000	48,000
		Total	86,400

Vacancies and credit losses were determined by comparing rent rolls of several other apartment complexes to actual rents collected.

	100% Rent Roll	Collected Rents	Indicated Vacancy Rate
Cavalier Apts.	$ 98,000	$93,765	4.3%
Thunderbird	102,000	98,445	3.5%
No Name	76,000	72,865	4.1%
Wellman Apts.	82,000	78,490	4.3%

(Vacancy of the subject property is estimated at 4 percent.)

Broker's study also estimates vacancies and credit losses at 4 percent of scheduled gross rents, or $3,500. These are deducted from the total income, resulting in a gross operating income of $84,100. After investigation, Broker estimated $100 per month income from the use of leased washers and dryers.

Operating expenses   Next, an analysis of operating expenses is made. Broker developed estimates of these expenses based on his experience with this kind of property and by asking questions of people who had better information than he. His investigation produced the following estimates which are shown recorded on the Broker's Forecast in Figure 21.

1. Accounting and Legal (Line 7 on the form). $300 based on experience with managing similar-size properties.

2. Advertising, Licenses and Permits (Line 8). $135 based on experience of this property, for the latter two items only.

3. Property Insurance (Line 9). $2,200; obtained from Broker's insurance agent who recommended typical coverage.

4. Property Management (Line 10). $4,200; typical professional property management for this type of building is 5 percent with managing office paying all advertising costs.

5. Resident Manager (Line 11). $5,100; investigation indicates a resident manager could be obtained for $175 a month plus the use of a two-bedroom apartment ($250 monthly). Owner's taxes for the manager are estimated at 10 percent, or $510 annually. (Although Seller now acts as resident manager and property manager, these costs must be reflected as expenses of the property. A new owner may not wish to be so actively involved.)

6. Personal Property Taxes (Line 14) are estimated at $400.

7. Real Estate Taxes (Line 15). Although Seller reported $6,200 for the previous year, Broker determined that a new school bond levy will go in effect next year and raise the taxes to approximately $8,800.

8. Repairs and Maintenance (Line 16). $3,840; the property is in good repair; Broker's contact with property managers indicates $10 per month per apartment per year should provide adequate coverage (about 4.5 percent of the gross operating income).

9. Lawn (Line 19). Broker estimates $120 a month will handle this.

10. Rubbish (Line 21) is estimated at $360.

11. Supplies (Line 23). $575 was based on an estimate of $1.50 per month per unit.

12. Utilities (Line 24). $2,880; tenants pay for electricity, heating, cooling and hot water. Past experience and records of the utility company indicate that $7.50 per month per unit will cover the cost of house electricity, washer, dryer, etc.

13. Sewer-Water (Line 26). Investigation indicates $40 per month average; $480 per year.

14. Telephone (Line 27). $15 per month; $180 annually.

15. Miscellaneous Expenses (Line 29). Estimated at $600 per year.

Total operating expenses came to $32,000 which is 38 percent of gross operating income. Broker knows that 37 to 40 percent is a typical expense ratio for properties of this type which helps him confirm that his Broker's Forecast has greater validity than the Owner's Statement.

After deducting Seller's annual debt service, there is a cash flow from the property to the owners of $24,500, or 7.4 percent on the $330,000 equity. The Owner's Statement indicates a cash flow of $38,750. This discrepancy was probably caused by not accounting for all costs and not differentiating between property income and management income the owner paid himself.

The completed Broker's Forecast (shown in Figure 21) enables Bill Broker to better understand the owner's realistic position in the property. If the property as an investment will produce approximately $52,100 for a new owner, it cannot be expected to produce any more than that for the present owner. Perhaps the present owner could obtain more cash by doing his own management or maintenance, but this is income from sources other than the investment. It is readily apparent that the owner's real cash flow before taxes for next year (assuming a valid projection) would be $24,500 under present financing if he continues to hold the property.

Using the broker's forecast for the potential client   Another important use of the Broker's Forecast is for a potential client (see Figure 22, Potential Client Statement). This statement indicates the cash flow before taxes available to a potential buyer who acquires the property at the owner's asking price, while obtaining the maximum financing available. Other Potential Client Statements can be prepared using different financing assumptions as well (such as acquiring the property with secondary financing or "buying down" to existing financing). In any event, the Potential Client Statement forms the basis for the Cash Flow Analysis.

Cash flow analysis

Before demonstrating the steps of this analysis, it is necessary to point out the purpose, the limitations and the assumptions of a cash flow analysis, as well as some suggestions for projecting future years' cash flows.

Purpose   The cash flow analysis is a projection of an investor's cash flows from the real estate under study after income tax. The cash flows derive from annual operations and resale proceeds. The projection is usually made for a typical real estate investment holding period of 10 to 15 years. Although some believe this period is too long, studies indicate that yield increases with the holding period up to about 12 to 14 years. Our case study's holding period will be 15 years. In real life, investors evaluate holdings periodically. They will switch investments (sell one to acquire another) only if a new one appears to have greater potential yield.

Limitations and assumptions   No one can accurately predict exact future annual operating statements, exact holding periods or exact resale prices, but projections can be made based on certain assumptions. Therefore, the mathematics of the projections are valid if we recognize the limitations of our ability to project.

We have said that the Broker's Forecast is the best estimate for the next full calendar year's operation. Projections based on these numbers must be done cautiously, however. If it is felt that over the study period the Net Operating Income will increase or decrease, the "next year's operating

Figure 21

Annual Property Operating Data

Date _____
Price $ 540,000
Loans $ 210,000
Equity $ 330,000

Purpose **Broker's Forecast**
Name **John Seller**
Location **16752 SW Cedar**
Type of Property **32 Unit Apt.**

Assessed/Appraised Values
Land $ 42,000 19.6 %
Improvement $ 168,000 78.5 %
Personal Property $ 4,000 1.9 %
Total $ 214,000 100 %
Adjusted Basis as of **Dec. 31** $ 290,000

FINANCING

	Balance	Payment	# Pymt/Yr.	Interest	Term
Existing					
1st	$210,000	2,300	12	8 %	
2nd	$			%	
3rd	$			%	
Potential					
1st	400,000	3,634.80	12	10 %	25
2nd	$			%	

		%	2	3	Comments
1	SCHEDULED RENTAL INCOME			86,400	16 @ $200/mo.+16 @ $250/mo.
2	Less: Vacancy and Credit Losses	4		3,500	
3	EFFECTIVE RENTAL INCOME			82,900	
4	Plus: Other Income			1,200	$100/mo.
5	GROSS OPERATING INCOME			84,100	
6	Less: Operating Expenses				
7	Accounting and Legal		300		
8	Advertising, Licenses and Permits		135		
9	Property Insurance		2,200		
10	Property Management	5	4,200		
11	Payroll-Resident Management		5,100		2 BR UNIT+$175/mo.
12	Other				
13	Taxes-Worker's Compensation		510		
14	Personal Property Taxes		400		
15	Real Estate Taxes		8,800		
16	Repairs and Maintenance	4.5	3,840		$10/mo/UNIT
17	Services-Elevator				
18	Janitorial				
19	Lawn		1,440		$120/mo.
20	Pool				
21	Rubbish		360		$30/mo.
22	Other				
23	Supplies		575		$1.50/mo./UNIT
24	Utilities-Electricity		2,880		$7.50/mo./UNIT
25	Gas and Oil				
26	Sewer and Water		480		$40/mo.
27	Telephone		180		$15/mo.
28	Other				
29	Miscellaneous		600		$50/mo.
30					
31	TOTAL OPERATING EXPENSES	38		32,000	
32	NET OPERATING INCOME			52,100	
33	Less: Annual Debt Service			27,600	
34	CASH FLOW BEFORE TAXES	7.4		24,500	

Prepared by **Broker**

Figure 22

Annual Property Operating Data

Date _____

Price $ __540,000__

Purpose **Broker's Forecast**   Loans $ __400,000__

Name **Potential Client**   Equity $ __140,000__

Location _____

Type of Property **32 Unit Apt.**

FINANCING

Assessed/Appraised Values			Existing	Balance	Payment	# Pymt/Yr.	Interest	Term
Land	$_____	___%	1st	$	___	___	___%	___
Improvement	$_____	___%	2nd	$	___	___	___%	___
Personal Property	$_____	___%	3rd	$	___	___	___%	___
Total	$_____	100 %	Potential					
			1st	400,000	3,634.80	12	10 %	25
Adjusted Basis as of _____	$_____		2nd	$	___	___	___%	___

		%	2	3	Comments
1	SCHEDULED RENTAL INCOME			86 400	
2	Less: Vacancy and Credit Losses			3 500	
3	EFFECTIVE RENTAL INCOME			82 900	
4	Plus: Other Income			1 200	
5	GROSS OPERATING INCOME			84 100	
6	Less: Operating Expenses				
7	Accounting and Legal				
8	Advertising, Licenses and Permits				
9	Property Insurance				
10	Property Management				
11	Payroll–Resident Management				
12	Other				
13	Taxes–Worker's Compensation				
14	Personal Property Taxes				
15	Real Estate Taxes				
16	Repairs and Maintenance				
17	Services–Elevator				
18	Janitorial				
19	Lawn				
20	Pool				
21	Rubbish				
22	Other				
23	Supplies				
24	Utilities–Electricity				
25	Gas and Oil				
26	Sewer and Water				
27	Telephone				
28	Other				
29	Miscellaneous				
30					
31	TOTAL OPERATING EXPENSES			32 000	
32	NET OPERATING INCOME			52 100	
33	Less: Annual Debt Service			43 618	
34	CASH FLOW BEFORE TAXES			8 482	

NATIONAL ASSOCIATION OF REALTORS®
developed in cooperation with its affiliate, the
© REALTORS NATIONAL MARKETING INSTITUTE®
1976. 3-76-F051

The statements and figures presented
herein, while not guaranteed, are secured
from sources we believe authoritative.

Prepared by **Broker**

statement'' can be adjusted accordingly. Projections can also show outlays for further capital costs (carpets, major repairs, etc.) at some particular time during this study period. Reserves could be set aside each year for these purposes, thereby reducing annual cash flows. As an alternative, no funds need be set aside, but capital expenditures can be made from cash flows of the year of the improvement (and even by additional capital at that time), thereby possibly creating a negative cash flow in the year that the improvement is added.

Since the projection may be made on any basis, it is imperative that each cash flow analysis be evaluated not only in terms of the final resulting numbers but also *by the assumptions under which the study was made*. This also pertains to the resale price. The resale price can be indicated the same as the purchase price, or higher or lower. When the projected investment is evaluated, the broker must question how reasonable the assumptions are.

Suggestions for projections

Projecting annual cash flows from the cash flow of the Broker's Forecast is more than a mathematical exercise. Here the investment broker's experience and knowledge of the market become important.

The major projection problems arise in determining the resale price and the pattern of the Net Operating Income streams. If there is no long-term lease which controls the rent, there are several approaches the investment broker may take in determining these factors.

First, he can assume that income and expenses will increase by the same amounts, thereby projecting Net Operating Income each year to be the same. Secondly, he can assume that income will increase by a greater amount than expenses. Experience may show that expenses increase annually, but rental increases may take place every two to three years. For projection purposes it is more convenient to estimate the rent increase over five-year periods and prorate this annually. For example, if the Net Operating Income is projected to increase 10, 15 or 20 percent over five-year periods, an annual growth rate of 2, 3 or 4 percent can be projected. It is also possible that the Net Operating Income would be projected to decrease because of the age of the improvements or a declining or transitional neighborhood.

The resale price could be projected to be the same as the acquisition price. This would assume actual depreciation and/or declining net income were offset equally by inflation. The resale price could also be projected higher than the acquisition price which assumes an increase of Net Operating Income and a relatively stable capitalization rate, or a stable Net Operating Income and a decreasing capitalization rate.

A resale price less than acquisition price could be attributed to a declining income and/or increased capitalization rate. In the case of a special-purpose building, it is logical to assume the improvement at the end of a lease to be valueless and the land to have equal or greater value than it had when the building was built.

323

As stated previously, the assumptions of the projections are as important as the projection analysis itself. It is essential that the broker understand the ramifications of his assumptions.

Recognizing the possibilities for great differences due to the assumptions, the following are suggested guidelines to projecting cash flows.

Conservative projection Project Net Operating Income as stable over the life of the projection and project resale prices as equal to acquisition, 25 percent over acquisition and 15 percent less than acquisition. The spread of resulting yields will give a fairly conservative projection and give the broker and client an opportunity to study a range of probabilities.

Aggressive projection Increase Net Operating Income from 2 to 5 percent annually with resale price calculated by capitalizing last year's income by the acquisition capitalization rate. Or, increase Net Operating Income as above but increase the sale price by 10 to 20 percent over acquisition price.

Pessimistic projection Decrease Net Operating Income from 1 to 3 percent annually and have resale price equal to acquisition price.

It must be understood that projections may be in the range of pessimistic-conservative to overly optimistic. However, if the reader of the projection understands the assumptions made, he can make an investment decision based on what he feels the probability is of the projection becoming reality.

For example, if a study shows an investor can expect a 15-percent yield if the property doubles in value, an 11-percent yield if the property value remains the same and an 8-percent return if the property declines 25 percent, the investor can make his judgment to buy or not, based on some correlation of all the alternatives, not just on the optimistic one, and then by comparing other investments available.

Cash flow analysis procedure

In our case study Broker made these initial assumptions:

1. A projection period of 15 years.

2. Net Operating Income will remain level.

3. Marginal tax bracket of the investor is 40 percent. (To make an after-tax analysis, the tax bracket of the investor must be taken into account. Even if the investor and his tax bracket are known, the tax position can change during the projection period. The broker can make the assumption of a constant tax bracket or a changing one. It is less important what the broker uses than it is how the projections are interpreted.)

4. Capital gain taxes will be at 50 percent of 40 percent of the gain (20 percent of the total capital gain). Capital gain taxes are determined by taking 40 percent of the gain, adding it to other taxable income and multiplying the total amount by the applicable rate, not to exceed 50 percent. Under the 1984 tax act,

the minimum holding period for long-term capital gain treatment of qualifying property is more than six months.

5. Depreciation on the improvement will be straight line for an 18-year economic life; for the personal property it will be straight line for a five-year life.

6. Resale price will be same as the acquisition price.

7. Purchase price, $540,000; cash down payment of $140,000 and a new mortgage of $400,000.

8. Resale costs, 6 percent.

To assist the reader, the step-by-step analysis procedures are outlined on the respective portions of the Cash Flow Analysis form, as shown in Figures 23 through 30. A completed composite form is shown in Figure 31.

Step 1 Step 1 (Figure 23) includes basic data from the Broker's Forecast (Figure 21) for a potential client using the assumptions previously discussed.

1. Line 1 indicates the $400,000 potential loan, its term, payments per year, interest rate and monthly and annual debt service.

2. On Lines 6 through 8 are the Gross Operating Income ($84,100), the Operating Expenses ($32,000) and the Net Operating Income ($52,100). These are also taken from the Broker's Forecast.

3. Line 10 indicates the annual mortgage interest rate of 10 percent.

4. Line 13 indicates the assumption of straight line depreciation.

5. Line 21 indicates the potential client's marginal tax bracket of 40 percent.

6. Lines 15 and 16 indicate the Net Operating Income ($52,100) minus Annual Debt Service of $43,618 to obtain on Line 19 the Cash Flow Before Taxes of $8,482.

Step 2 Figure 24 indicates the interest payable each year under the mortgage. This was calculated on a hand-held calculator (as detailed in Appendix B) and is entered on Line 10 for each of the 15 years of the projection.

Step 3 Figure 25 calculates depreciation for the 15-year projection period. When the Broker's Forecast (Figure 21) was made, the following assessed values and percentages were entered:

Figure 23

For Potential Client
Purpose 15 yr. Projection
Date _____

Cash Flow Analysis

Purchase Price 540,000
Encumbrances 400,000
Investment 140,000

Mortgage Data

	Encumbrances	Beginning Balance	Remaining Term	Number of Payments Per Year	Interest Rate	Payment	Annual Debt Service	Remarks
1	1st Mortgage	400,000	25yr.	12	10%	3,634.80	43,618	
2	2nd Mortgage							
3	3rd Mortgage							

		Year: 1	Year: 2	Year: 3	Year: 4	Year: 5	EOY	Mortgage Balance
	Ownership Analysis of Property Income:		Taxable Income					1st Mortgage
4	Gross Scheduled Income	87,600						
5	Less: Vcy. & Credit Losses	3,500						
6	Gross Operating Income	84,100						
7	– Operating Expenses	32,000						
8	Net Operating Income	52,100						
9	– Non-Operating Expense							
10	– Interest – 1st Mortgage							2nd Mortgage
11	– Interest – 2nd Mortgage							
12	– Interest – 3rd Mortgage							
13	– Cost Recovery							
14	Real Est. Taxable Income							
			Cash Flows					
15	Net Operating Income	52,100						3rd Mortgage
16	– Annual Debt Service	43,618						
17	– Funded Reserves							
18	– Capital Additions							
19	Cash Flow before Taxes	8,482						
20	– Minimum Tax							
21	– Tax Liability on Real Est.							
22	Cash Flow after Taxes							

Analysis of Sale Proceeds — Year:

	Adjusted Basis		Excess Cost Recovery (CR)		Tax Liability on Sale	
23	Original Basis		Total CR		Excess Recapture Tax	
24	+ Capital Improvements		S/L CR		Capital Gain Tax	
25	– Cost Recovery		Excess CR*		Tax Liability on Sale	
26	– Partial Sales		Exc. CR Carryover			
27	AB		Gain		Sale Proceeds	
28			Sale Price		Sale Price	
			– Cost of Sale		– Costs of Sale	
			– AB		– Mortgage	
			Gain		Proceeds before Taxes	
			– Excess CR		– Tax Liability on Sale	
			Capital Gain		Proceeds after Taxes	

*NOTE: On non-residential property, if accelerated CR system is elected, all CR claimed is recaptured as ordinary income in the year of sale.

The statements and figures presented herein, while not guaranteed are secured from sources we believe authoritative

Prepared by _____

Land	$ 42,000	19.6%
Improvements	168,000	78.5
Personal Property	4,000	1.9
Total	$214,000	100 %

The investment broker can use these allocations to determine depreciation amounts for projection studies (providing the numbers are logical). This
would mean that on a $540,000 acquisition price the allocation would be as
follows:

Land	$105,840	19.6%
Improvements	423,900	78.5
Personal Property	10,260	1.9
Total	$540,000	100 %

Using 18-year straight line depreciation for the improvements (because
of the negligible impact upon the IRR, the mid-month convention has been
ignored during the year of disposition) and 5-year straight line depreciation
for the personal property, the amounts of depreciation are:

YEAR	1	2-5	6	7-10	11-15
Improvements	$21,195	$25,434	$25,434	$25,434	$21,195
Personal Property	1,026	2,052	1,026	-0-	-0-

The total of these amounts is entered on Line 13 of Figure 25. Then both
the depreciation amount (Line 13) and the amount of interest (Line 10)
are deducted from Net Operating Income (Line 8) to obtain Real Estate
Taxable Income (Line 14).

Step 4   Step 4 (Figure 26) is the calculation of Cash Flow After Taxes.
Line 14 of Figure 26 has the annual entry for Taxable Income. Taxable
Income multiplied by the tax bracket of the potential client (40 percent) will
result in the annual income tax attributable to the real estate income. This is
entered on Line 21 (Tax Liability on Real Estate); then it is deducted from
Cash Flow Before Taxes (Line 19) to obtain Cash Flow After Taxes
(Line 22).

When the taxable income is negative (such as in Year 1—($9,950))
that amount can be deducted from other taxable income. If taxable income
is taxed at 40 percent, that means the individual's taxes will be reduced by
$3,980. Because it was the real estate that brought this about, the saving is
attributed to the real estate income and shows up as an income item on Line
21 when the minus tax is subtracted (thereby added) to the Cash Flow Before Taxes. This creates a Cash Flow After Taxes greater than Before Taxes.

Figure 24

For _Potential Client_

Purpose _15 yr. Projection_

Date _____

Cash Flow Analysis

Purchase Price _540,000_

Encumbrances _400,000_

Investment _140,000_

Mortgage Data

	Encumbrances	Beginning Balance	Remaining Term	Number of Payments Per Year	Interest Rate	Payment	Annual Debt Service	Remarks
1	1st Mortgage	400,000	25yr.	12	10%	3,634.80	43,618	
2	2nd Mortgage							
3	3rd Mortgage							

		Year: 1	Year: 2	Year: 3	Year: 4	Year: 5	EOY	Mortgage Balance
	Ownership Analysis of Property Income:		**Taxable Income**					
4	Gross Scheduled Income	87,600						1st Mortgage
5	Less: Vcy. & Credit Losses	3,500						
6	Gross Operating Income	84,100						
7	– Operating Expenses	32,000						
8	Net Operating Income	52,100	52,100	52,100	52,100	52,100		
9	– Non-Operating Expense							
10	– Interest – 1st Mortgage	39,829	39,433	38,995	38,511	37,976		2nd Mortgage
11	– Interest – 2nd Mortgage							
12	– Interest – 3rd Mortgage							
13	– Cost Recovery							
14	Real Est. Taxable Income							
		Cash Flows						
15	Net Operating Income	52,100						3rd Mortgage
16	– Annual Debt Service	43,618						
17	– Funded Reserves							
18	– Capital Additions							
19	Cash Flow before Taxes	8,482	8,482	8,482	8,482	8,482		
20	– Minimum Tax							
21	– Tax Liability on Real Est.							
22	Cash Flow after Taxes							

Analysis of Sale Proceeds   Year:

	Adjusted Basis			Excess Cost Recovery (CR)			Tax Liability on Sale		
23	Original Basis			Total CR			Excess Recapture Tax		
24	+ Capital Improvements			S/L CR			Capital Gain Tax		
25	– Cost Recovery			Excess CR*			Tax Liability on Sale		
26	– Partial Sales			Exc. CR Carryover					
27	AB				Gain			Sale Proceeds	
28				Sale Price			Sale Price		
				– Cost of Sale			– Costs of Sale		
				– AB			– Mortgage		
				Gain			Proceeds before Taxes		
				– Excess CR			– Tax Liability on Sale		
				Capital Gain			Proceeds after Taxes		

*NOTE: On non-residential property, if accelerated CR system is elected, all CR claimed is recaptured as ordinary income in the year of sale.

The statements and figures presented herein, while not guaranteed, are secured from sources we believe authoritative

Prepared by _____

Figure 24 (continued)

For Potential Client

Purpose 15 yr. Projection

Date _____

Cash Flow Analysis

Purchase Price **540,000**

Encumbrances **400,000**

Investment **140,000**

Mortgage Data

Encumbrances	Beginning Balance	Remaining Term	Number of Payments Per Year	Interest Rate	Payment	Annual Debt Service	Remarks
1 1st Mortgage	400,000	25 yr.	12	10%	3,634.80	43,618	
2 2nd Mortgage							
3 3rd Mortgage							

	Year: 6	Year: 7	Year: 8	Year: 9	Year: 10	EOY	Mortgage Balance
Ownership Analysis of Property Income:		**Taxable Income**					1st Mortgage
4 Gross Scheduled Income							
5 Less: Vcy. & Credit Losses							
6 Gross Operating Income							
7 − Operating Expenses							
8 Net Operating Income	52,100	52,100	52,100	52,100	52,100		
9 − Non-Operating Expense							
10 − Interest − 1st Mortgage	37,385	36,732	36,011	35,215	34,335		2nd Mortgage
11 − Interest − 2nd Mortgage							
12 − Interest − 3rd Mortgage							
13 − Cost Recovery							
14 Real Est. Taxable Income							
		Cash Flows					
15 Net Operating Income							3rd Mortgage
16 − Annual Debt Service							
17 − Funded Reserves							
18 − Capital Additions							
19 Cash Flow before Taxes	8,482	8,482	8,482	8,482	8,482		
20 − Minimum Tax							
21 − Tax Liability on Real Est.							
22 Cash Flow after Taxes							

Analysis of Sale Proceeds   Year: ____

Adjusted Basis		Excess Cost Recovery (CR)		Tax Liability on Sale	
23 Original Basis		Total CR		Excess Recapture Tax	
24 + Capital Improvements		S/L CR		Capital Gain Tax	
25 − Cost Recovery		Excess CR*		Tax Liability on Sale	
26 − Partial Sales		Exc. CR Carryover			
27 AB		**Gain**		**Sale Proceeds**	
28		Sale Price		Sale Price	
		− Cost of Sale		− Costs of Sale	
		− AB		− Mortgage	
		Gain		Proceeds before Taxes	
		− Excess CR		− Tax Liability on Sale	
		Capital Gain		Proceeds after Taxes	

*NOTE: On non-residential property, if accelerated CR system is elected, all CR claimed is recaptured as ordinary income in the year of sale.

The statements and figures presented herein, while not guaranteed are secured from sources we believe authoritative

Prepared by_____

Figure 24 (continued)

For **Potential Client**	**Cash Flow Analysis**	
Purpose **15 yr. Projection**	Purchase Price **540,000**	
Date _____	Encumbrances **400,000**	
	Investment **140,000**	

Mortgage Data

	Encumbrances	Beginning Balance	Remaining Term	Number of Payments Per Year	Interest Rate	Payment	Annual Debt Service	Remarks
1	1st Mortgage	400,000	25yr.	12	10%	3,634.80	43,618	
2	2nd Mortgage							
3	3rd Mortgage							

		Year: 11	Year: 12	Year: 13	Year: 14	Year: 15	EOY	Mortgage Balance
	Ownership Analysis of Property Income:		**Taxable Income**					
4	Gross Scheduled Income							1st Mortgage
5	Less: Vcy. & Credit Losses							
6	Gross Operating Income							
7	– Operating Expenses							
8	Net Operating Income	52 100	52 100	52 100	52 100	52 100		
9	– Non-Operating Expense							
10	– Interest – 1st Mortgage	33 363	32 289	31 103	29 793	28 348		2nd Mortgage
11	– Interest – 2nd Mortgage							
12	– Interest – 3rd Mortgage							
13	– Cost Recovery							
14	Real Est Taxable Income							
			Cash Flows					
15	Net Operating Income							3rd Mortgage
16	– Annual Debt Service							
17	– Funded Reserves							
18	– Capital Additions							
19	Cash Flow before Taxes	8 482	8 482	8 482	8 482	8 482		
20	– Minimum Tax							
21	– Tax Liability on Real Est.							
22	Cash Flow after Taxes							

Analysis of Sale Proceeds

Year:

	Adjusted Basis			Excess Cost Recovery (CR)				Tax Liability on Sale			
23	Original Basis			Total CR				Excess Recapture Tax			
24	+ Capital Improvements			S/L CR				Capital Gain Tax			
25	– Cost Recovery			Excess CR*				Tax Liability on Sale			
26	– Partial Sales			Exc. CR Carryover							
27	AB				Gain				Sale Proceeds		
28				Sale Price				Sale Price			
				– Cost of Sale				– Costs of Sale			
	*NOTE: On non-residential property, if			– AB				– Mortgage			
	accelerated CR system is elected, all CR			Gain				Proceeds before Taxes			
	claimed is recaptured as ordinary income in the year of sale.			– Excess CR				– Tax Liability on Sale			
				Capital Gain				Proceeds after Taxes			

The statements and figures presented herein, while not guaranteed are secured from sources we believe authoritative

Prepared by _____

Figure 25

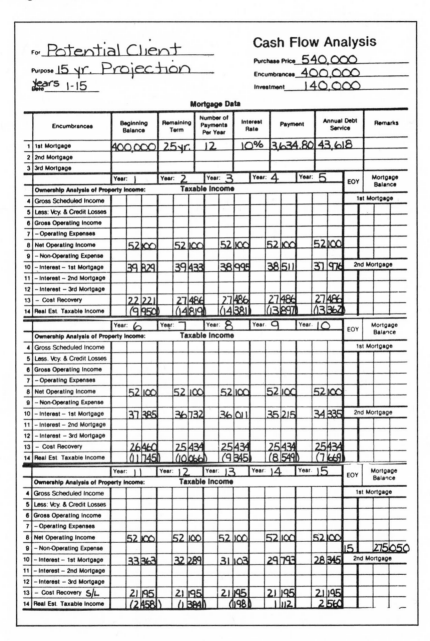

For **Potential Client**

Purpose **15 yr. Projection**

Years **1-15**

Cash Flow Analysis

Purchase Price **540,000**

Encumbrances **400,000**

Investment **140,000**

Mortgage Data

Encumbrances	Beginning Balance	Remaining Term	Number of Payments Per Year	Interest Rate	Payment	Annual Debt Service	Remarks
1 1st Mortgage	400,000	25 yr.	12	10%	3,634.80	43,618	
2 2nd Mortgage							
3 3rd Mortgage							

Ownership Analysis of Property Income:	Year: 1	Year: 2	Year: 3	Year: 4	Year: 5	EOY	Mortgage Balance
	Taxable Income						1st Mortgage
4 Gross Scheduled Income							
5 Less: Vcy. & Credit Losses							
6 Gross Operating Income							
7 – Operating Expenses							
8 Net Operating Income	52,100	52,100	52,100	52,100	52,100		
9 – Non-Operating Expense							2nd Mortgage
10 – Interest – 1st Mortgage	39,829	39,433	38,995	38,511	37,976		
11 – Interest – 2nd Mortgage							
12 – Interest – 3rd Mortgage							
13 – Cost Recovery	22,221	27,486	27,486	27,486	27,486		
14 Real Est. Taxable Income	(9,950)	(14,819)	(14,381)	(13,897)	(13,362)		

Ownership Analysis of Property Income:	Year: 6	Year: 7	Year: 8	Year: 9	Year: 10	EOY	Mortgage Balance
	Taxable Income						1st Mortgage
4 Gross Scheduled Income							
5 Less: Vcy. & Credit Losses							
6 Gross Operating Income							
7 – Operating Expenses							
8 Net Operating Income	52,100	52,100	52,100	52,100	52,100		
9 – Non-Operating Expense							2nd Mortgage
10 – Interest – 1st Mortgage	37,385	36,732	36,011	35,215	34,335		
11 – Interest – 2nd Mortgage							
12 – Interest – 3rd Mortgage							
13 – Cost Recovery	26,460	25,434	25,434	25,434	25,434		
14 Real Est. Taxable Income	(11,745)	(10,066)	(9,345)	(8,549)	(7,669)		

Ownership Analysis of Property Income:	Year: 11	Year: 12	Year: 13	Year: 14	Year: 15	EOY	Mortgage Balance
	Taxable Income						1st Mortgage
4 Gross Scheduled Income							
5 Less: Vcy. & Credit Losses							
6 Gross Operating Income							
7 – Operating Expenses							
8 Net Operating Income	52,100	52,100	52,100	52,100	52,100		
9 – Non-Operating Expense						15	275,050
10 – Interest – 1st Mortgage	33,363	32,289	31,103	29,793	28,345		2nd Mortgage
11 – Interest – 2nd Mortgage							
12 – Interest – 3rd Mortgage							
13 – Cost Recovery S/L	21,195	21,195	21,195	21,195	21,195		
14 Real Est. Taxable Income	(2,458)	(1,384)	(198)	1,112	2,560		

Figure 26

Cash Flow Analysis

For _Potential Client_

Purpose _15 yr. Projection_

Years _1-15 (cont.)_

Purchase Price _540,000_

Encumbrances _400,000_

Investment _140,000_

Mortgage Data

Encumbrances	Beginning Balance	Remaining Term	Number of Payments Per Year	Interest Rate	Payment	Annual Debt Service	Remarks
1 1st Mortgage	400,000	25yr.	12	10%	3,634.80	43,618	
2 2nd Mortgage							
3 3rd Mortgage							

	Year: 1	Year: 2	Year: 3	Year: 4	Year: 5	EOY	Mortgage Balance
Ownership Analysis of Property Income:			**Taxable Income**				
4 Gross Scheduled Income							1st Mortgage
5 Less. Vcy. & Credit Losses							
6 Gross Operating Income							
7 – Operating Expenses							
8 Net Operating Income							
9 – Non-Operating Expense							
10 – Interest – 1st Mortgage							2nd Mortgage
11 – Interest – 2nd Mortgage							
12 – Interest – 3rd Mortgage							
13 – Cost Recovery							
14 Real Est Taxable Income	(9,950)	(14,819)	(14,381)	(13,897)	(13,362)		
			Cash Flows				
15 Net Operating Income	52,100	52,100	52,100	52,100	52,100		3rd Mortgage
16 – Annual Debt Service	43,618	43,618	43,618	43,618	43,618		
17 – Funded Reserves							
18 – Capital Additions							
19 Cash Flow before Taxes	8,482	8,482	8,482	8,482	8,482		
20 – Minimum Tax							
21 – Tax Liability on Real Est.	(3,980)	(5,928)	(5,752)	(5,559)	(5,345)		
22 Cash Flow after Taxes	12,462	14,410	14,234	14,041	13,827		

	Year: 6	Year: 7	Year: 8	Year: 9	Year: 10		
14 Real Est Taxable Income	(11,745)	(10,066)	(9,345)	(8,549)	(7,669)		
			Cash Flows				
15 Net Operating Income	52,100	52,100	52,100	52,100	52,100		3rd Mortgage
16 – Annual Debt Service	43,618	43,618	43,618	43,618	43,618		
17 – Funded Reserves							
18 – Capital Additions							
19 Cash Flow before Taxes	8,482	8,482	8,482	8,482	8,482		
20 – Minimum Tax							
21 – Tax Liability on Real Est.	(4,698)	(4,026)	(3,738)	(3,420)	(3,068)		
22 Cash Flow after Taxes	13,180	12,508	12,220	11,902	11,550		

	Year: 11	Year: 12	Year: 13	Year: 14	Year: 15		
14 Real Est Taxable Income	(2,458)	(1,384)	(198)	1,112	2,560		
			Cash Flows				
15 Net Operating Income	52,100	52,100	52,100	52,100	52,100		3rd Mortgage
16 – Annual Debt Service	43,618	43,618	43,618	43,618	43,618		
17 – Funded Reserves							
18 – Capital Additions							
19 Cash Flow before Taxes	8,482	8,482	8,482	8,482	8,482		
20 – Minimum Tax							
21 – Tax Liability on Real Est.	(983)	(554)	(79)	445	1,024		
22 Cash Flow after Taxes	9,465	9,036	8,561	8,037	7,458		

Step 5 Step 5 is the calculation of resale proceeds (see Figures 27, 28, 29 and 30). Assume the following:

1. Resale with a purchase price of $540,000 (see Figure 27)

2. Resale cost, 6 percent

3. Capital gain taxes at 50 percent of 40 percent of capital gain

4. Mortgage balance at end of the fifteenth year is $275,050.

Resale proceeds are also calculated as though the property would resell for $490,000 (negative growth, .65 percent per annum—see Figure 28), at $625,000 (positive growth at 1 percent per annum—see Figure 29) and $725,000 (positive growth at 2 percent per annum—see Figure 30).

Figure 31 shows the entire projection completed, calculated on the $540,000 resale price.

Internal rate of return calculation

The broker now has completed the one-year after-tax analysis (Broker's Forecast—Figure 21) and the 15-year after-tax cash flow analysis (Figure 31). The results of these studies are indicated below. (Annual cash flows are based on the projection assumptions and at four resale prices.)

Period	$540,000 Resale Cash Flows After Taxes	$490,000 Resale Cash Flows After Taxes	$625,000 Resale Cash Flows After Taxes	$725,000 Resale Cash Flows After Taxes
0	($140,000)	($140,000)	($140,000)	($140,000)
1	12,462	12,462	12,462	12,462
2	14,410	14,410	14,410	14,410
3	14,234	14,234	14,234	14,234
4	14,041	14,041	14,041	14,041
5	13,827	13,827	13,827	13,827
6	13,180	13,180	13,180	13,180
7	12,508	12,508	12,508	12,508
8	12,220	12,220	12,220	12,220
9	11,902	11,902	11,902	11,902
10	11,550	11,550	11,550	11,550
11	9,465	9,465	9,465	9,465
12	9,036	9,036	9,036	9,036
13	8,561	8,561	8,561	8,561
14	8,037	8,037	8,037	8,037
15	7,458	7,458	7,458	7,458
Resale Proceeds After Taxes	$165,063	$128,163	$229,683	$304,883

Figure 27 $540,000 Resale Price

Analysis of Sale Proceeds Year: 15

Adjusted Basis		Excess Cost Recovery (CR)		Tax Liability on Sale	
23 Original Basis	540000	Total CR	366336	Excess Recapture Tax	-0-
24 + Capital Improvements		S/L CR	366336	Capital Gain Tax 20%	66787
25 – Cost Recovery	366336	Excess CR*	-0-	Tax Liability on Sale	66787
26 – Partial Sales		Exc. CR Carryover			
27 AB	173664	**Gain**		**Sale Proceeds**	
28		Sale Price	540000	Sale Price	540000
		– Cost of Sale	32400	– Costs of Sale	32400
*NOTE: On non-residential property, if accelerated CR system is elected, all CR claimed is recaptured as ordinary income in the year of sale.		– AB	173664	– Mortgage	275050
		Gain	333936	Proceeds before Taxes	232550
		– Excess CR	-0-	– Tax Liability on Sale	66787
		Capital Gain	333936	Proceeds after Taxes	165763

REALTORS NATIONAL MARKETING INSTITUTE® of the NATIONAL ASSOCIATION OF REALTORS®, 1982 All rights reserved 2-81-F812   The statements and figures presented herein, while not guaranteed are secured from sources we believe authoritative   Prepared by_____

Figure 28 $490,000 Resale Price

Analysis of Sale Proceeds Year: 15

Adjusted Basis		Excess Cost Recovery (CR)		Tax Liability on Sale	
23 Original Basis	540000	Total CR	366336	Excess Recapture Tax	-0-
24 + Capital Improvements		S/L CR	366336	Capital Gain Tax 20%	57387
25 – Cost Recovery	366336	Excess CR*	-0-	Tax Liability on Sale	57387
26 – Partial Sales		Exc. CR Carryover			
27 AB	173664	**Gain**		**Sale Proceeds**	
28		Sale Price	490000	Sale Price	490000
		– Cost of Sale	29400	– Costs of Sale	29400
*NOTE: On non-residential property, if accelerated CR system is elected, all CR claimed is recaptured as ordinary income in the year of sale.		– AB	173664	– Mortgage	275050
		Gain	286936	Proceeds before Taxes	185550
		– Excess CR	-0-	– Tax Liability on Sale	57387
		Capital Gain	286936	Proceeds after Taxes	128163

REALTORS NATIONAL MARKETING INSTITUTE® of the NATIONAL ASSOCIATION OF REALTORS®, 1982 All rights reserved 2-81-F812   The statements and figures presented herein, while not guaranteed are secured from sources we believe authoritative   Prepared by_____

The final calculation is now made to determine the investor's yield *under the projected assumptions*. Everything done thus far has been estimated, projected or assumed. The final step will give a definitive number. The validity of the number, however, is only as good as the earlier input estimates.

By definition, the Internal Rate of Return (IRR) is that rate which discounts an income stream so that the total equals the initial investment. The purpose of our calculation is to find an interest rate which will discount the total income stream so that the total present values will equal the initial investment (investment amount).

Figure 29 $625,000 Resale Price

			Analysis of Sale Proceeds				Year: 15		
	Adjusted Basis		**Excess Cost Recovery (CR)**			**Tax Liability on Sale**			
23	Original Basis	540000	Total CR	366336		Excess Recapture Tax		-0-	
24	+ Capital Improvements		S/L CR	366336		Capital Gain Tax 20%		82767	
25	– Cost Recovery	366336	Excess CR*	-0-		Tax Liability on Sale		82767	
26	– Partial Sales		Exc. CR Carryover						
27	AB	173664		Gain			Sale Proceeds		
28			Sale Price	625000		Sale Price		625000	
	*NOTE: On non-residential property, if accelerated CR system is elected, all CR claimed is recaptured as ordinary income in the year of sale.		– Cost of Sale	37500		– Costs of Sale		37500	
			– AB	173664		– Mortgage		275050	
			Gain	413836		Proceeds before Taxes		312450	
			– Excess CR	-0-		– Tax Liability on Sale		82767	
			Capital Gain	413836		Proceeds after Taxes		229683	

REALTORS NATIONAL MARKETING INSTITUTE® of the NATIONAL ASSOCIATION OF REALTORS®, 1982 All rights reserved 2-81-F612

The statements and figures presented herein, while not guaranteed are secured from sources we believe authoritative   Prepared by_____

Figure 30 $725,000 Resale Price

			Analysis of Sale Proceeds				Year: 15		
	Adjusted Basis		**Excess Cost Recovery (CR)**			**Tax Liability on Sale**			
23	Original Basis	540000	Total CR	366336		Excess Recapture Tax		-0-	
24	+ Capital Improvements		S/L CR	366336		Capital Gain Tax 20%		101567	
25	– Cost Recovery	366336	Excess CR*	-0-		Tax Liability on Sale		101567	
26	– Partial Sales		Exc. CR Carryover						
27	AB	173664		Gain			Sale Proceeds		
28			Sale Price	725000		Sale Price		725000	
	*NOTE: On non-residential property, if accelerated CR system is elected, all CR claimed is recaptured as ordinary income in the year of sale.		– Cost of Sale	43500		– Costs of Sale		43500	
			– AB	173664		– Mortgage		275050	
			Gain	507836		Proceeds before Taxes		406450	
			– Excess CR	-0-		– Tax Liability on Sale		101567	
			Capital Gain	507836		Proceeds after Taxes		304883	

REALTORS NATIONAL MARKETING INSTITUTE® of the NATIONAL ASSOCIATION OF REALTORS®, 1982 All rights reserved 2-81-F612

The statements and figures presented herein, while not guaranteed are secured from sources we believe authoritative   Prepared by_____

The calculation of IRR recently has been simplified by the advent of hand-held financial calculators. Here we have calculated the IRR using a Hewlett Packard HP-12C calculator. (Appendix B shows a manual method, using any four-function calculator or the compound interest tables.)

The calculation indicates the following Internal Rates of Return for all the assumed resale prices, as follows.

Resale Value	IRR (After Income Tax)
$540,000	9.38
490,000	8.43
625,000	10.74
725,000	12.04

In looking at the IRR above it is well to review some of the key results.

1. The Net Operating Income (NOI) remained level.

2. The acquisition price was $540,000 with a Net Operating Income of $52,100, resulting in a capitalization rate of 9.6 percent.

3. The mortgage interest rate was 10 percent, indicating negative before-tax leverage.

4. Projected resale capitalization rates at EOY 15 with the same Net Operating Income would be:

Resale Price	NOI	Capitalization Rate
$540,000	$52,100	9.6%
490,000	52,100	10.6%
625,000	52,100	8.3%
725,000	52,100	7.2%

Therefore, the study is based on a constant NOI, but with a fluctuating overall capitalization rate increasing to 10.6 percent and reducing as low as 7.2 percent.

Alternative projection

It is not at all illogical to assume that a prudent or knowledgeable investor who acquires a property with negative before-tax leverage might do so because he believes rents will increase (because of inflation) faster than expenses. If this happens and the overall capitalization rate remains the same, the resale price would increase; the larger NOI divided by the same capitalization rate produces a higher price.

Another cash flow study of the property will be made, with the following changes in the assumptions:

1. Net Operating Income will increase 3 percent per year.

2. Two resale prices will be used. The first ($490,000) will be based on a 16-percent capitalization rate.

3. The second ($788,000) reflects an increased Net Operating Income, indicating a capitalization rate of 10 percent.

These cash flow projections are shown in Figure 32.

Figure 31

Cash Flow Analysis

For Potential Client
Purpose 15 yr. Projection
Date _____

Purchase Price 540,000
Encumbrances 400,000
Investment 140,000

Mortgage Data

Encumbrances	Beginning Balance	Remaining Term	Number of Payments Per Year	Interest Rate	Payment	Annual Debt Service	Remarks
1 1st Mortgage	400,000	25 yr	12	10%	3,634.80	43,618	
2 2nd Mortgage							
3 3rd Mortgage							

	Year: 1	Year: 2	Year: 3	Year: 4	Year: 5	EOY	Mortgage Balance
Ownership Analysis of Property Income:		Taxable Income					1st Mortgage
4 Gross Scheduled Income	87,600						
5 Less: Vcy. & Credit Losses	3,500						
6 Gross Operating Income	84,100						
7 – Operating Expenses	32,000						
8 Net Operating Income	52,100	52,100	52,100	52,100	52,100		
9 – Non-Operating Expense							
10 – Interest – 1st Mortgage	39,829	39,433	38,995	38,511	37,976		2nd Mortgage
11 – Interest – 2nd Mortgage							
12 – Interest – 3rd Mortgage							
13 – Cost Recovery	22,221	27,486	27,486	27,486	27,486		
14 Real Est. Taxable Income	(9,950)	(14,819)	(14,381)	(13,897)	(13,362)		
		Cash Flows					3rd Mortgage
15 Net Operating Income	52,100						
16 – Annual Debt Service	43,618						
17 – Funded Reserves							
18 – Capital Additions							
19 Cash Flow before Taxes	8,482	8,482	8,482	8,482	8,482		
20 – Minimum Tax							
21 – Tax Liability on Real Est.	(3,980)	(5,928)	(5,752)	(5,559)	(5,345)		
22 Cash Flow after Taxes	12,462	14,410	14,234	14,041	13,827		

Analysis of Sale Proceeds
Year: ____

Adjusted Basis				Excess Cost Recovery (CR)				Tax Liability on Sale			
23 Original Basis				Total CR				Excess Recapture Tax			
24 + Capital Improvements				S/L CR				Capital Gain Tax			
25 – Cost Recovery				Excess CR*				Tax Liability on Sale			
26 – Partial Sales				Exc. CR Carryover							
27 AB					Gain				Sale Proceeds		
28				Sale Price				Sale Price			
				– Cost of Sale				– Costs of Sale			
				– AB				– Mortgage			
				Gain				Proceeds before Taxes			
				– Excess CR				– Tax Liability on Sale			
				Capital Gain				Proceeds after Taxes			

*NOTE: On non-residential property, if accelerated CR system is elected, all CR claimed is recaptured as ordinary income in the year of sale.

The statements and figures presented herein, while not guaranteed, are secured from sources we believe authoritative.

Prepared by _____

Figure 31 (continued)

For _Potential Client_

Purpose _15 yr. Projection_

Date _____

Cash Flow Analysis

Purchase Price __540,000__

Encumbrances __400,000__

Investment __140,000__

Mortgage Data

	Encumbrances	Beginning Balance	Remaining Term	Number of Payments Per Year	Interest Rate	Payment	Annual Debt Service	Remarks
1	1st Mortgage	400,000	25 yr.	12	10%	3,634.80	43,618	
2	2nd Mortgage							
3	3rd Mortgage							

		Year: 6	Year: 7	Year: 8	Year: 9	Year: 10	EOY	Mortgage Balance
	Ownership Analysis of Property Income:		**Taxable Income**					
4	Gross Scheduled Income							1st Mortgage
5	Less: Vcy. & Credit Losses							
6	Gross Operating Income							
7	– Operating Expenses							
8	Net Operating Income	52,100	52,100	52,100	52,100	52,100		
9	– Non-Operating Expense							
10	– Interest – 1st Mortgage	37,385	36,732	36,011	35,215	34,335		2nd Mortgage
11	– Interest – 2nd Mortgage							
12	– Interest – 3rd Mortgage							
13	– Cost Recovery	26,460	25,434	25,434	25,434	25,434		
14	Real Est. Taxable Income	(11,745)	(10,066)	(9,345)	(8,549)	(7,669)		
			Cash Flows					
15	Net Operating Income	52,100						3rd Mortgage
16	– Annual Debt Service	43,618						
17	– Funded Reserves							
18	– Capital Additions							
19	Cash Flow before Taxes	8,482	8,482	8,482	8,482	8,482		
20	– Minimum Tax							
21	– Tax Liability on Real Est.	(4,698)	(4,026)	(3,738)	(3,420)	(3,068)		
22	Cash Flow after Taxes	13,180	12,508	12,220	11,902	11,550		

Analysis of Sale Proceeds   Year: _____

	Adjusted Basis			Excess Cost Recovery (CR)				Tax Liability on Sale		
23	Original Basis			Total CR				Excess Recapture Tax		
24	+ Capital Improvements			S/L CR				Capital Gain Tax		
25	– Cost Recovery			Excess CR*				Tax Liability on Sale		
26	– Partial Sales			Exc. CR Carryover						
27	AB				Gain			Sale Proceeds		
28				Sale Price				Sale Price		
				– Cost of Sale				– Costs of Sale		
				– AB				– Mortgage		
				Gain				Proceeds before Taxes		
				– Excess CR				– Tax Liability on Sale		
				Capital Gain				Proceeds after Taxes		

*NOTE: On non-residential property, if accelerated CR system is elected, all CR claimed is recaptured as ordinary income in the year of sale.

The statements and figures presented herein, while not guaranteed are secured from sources we believe authoritative.

Prepared by_____

Figure 31 (continued)

Cash Flow Analysis

For **Potenial Client**

Purpose **15 yr. Projection**

Date _____

Purchase Price **540,000**

Encumbrances **400,000**

Investment **140,000**

Mortgage Data

	Encumbrances	Beginning Balance	Remaining Term	Number of Payments Per Year	Interest Rate	Payment	Annual Debt Service	Remarks
1	1st Mortgage	400,000	25 yr.	12	10%	3,634.80	43,618	
2	2nd Mortgage							
3	3rd Mortgage							

	Ownership Analysis of Property Income:	Year: 11	Year: 12	Year: 13	Year: 14	Year: 15	EOY	Mortgage Balance
		Taxable Income						1st Mortgage
4	Gross Scheduled Income							
5	Less: Vcy. & Credit Losses							
6	Gross Operating Income							
7	– Operating Expenses							
8	Net Operating Income	52 100	52 100	52 100	52 100	52 100		
9	– Non-Operating Expense						15	275 050
10	– Interest – 1st Mortgage	33 363	32 289	31 103	29 793	28 345	2nd Mortgage	
11	– Interest – 2nd Mortgage							
12	– Interest – 3rd Mortgage							
13	– Cost Recovery	21 195	21 195	21 195	21 195	21 195		
14	Real Est. Taxable Income	(2 458)	(1 384)	(198)	1 112	2 560		
		Cash Flows						
15	Net Operating Income	52 100						3rd Mortgage
16	– Annual Debt Service	43 618						
17	– Funded Reserves							
18	– Capital Additions							
19	Cash Flow before Taxes	8 482	8 482	8 482	8 482	8 482		
20	– Minimum Tax							
21	– Tax Liability on Real Est.	(983)	(554)	(79)	445	1 024		
22	Cash Flow after Taxes	9 465	9 036	8 561	8 037	7 458		

Analysis of Sale Proceeds

Year: 15

	Adjusted Basis		Excess Cost Recovery (CR)		Tax Liability on Sale	
23	Original Basis	540 000	Total CR	366 336	Excess Recapture Tax	– 0 –
24	+ Capital Improvements		S/L CR	366 336	Capital Gain Tax 20%	66 787
25	– Cost Recovery	366 336	Excess CR*	– 0 –	Tax Liability on Sale	66 787
26	– Partial Sales		Exc. CR Carryover			
27	AB	173 664	**Gain**		**Sale Proceeds**	
28			Sale Price	540 000	Sale Price	540 000
			– Cost of Sale	32 400	– Costs of Sale	32 400
	*NOTE: On non-residential property, if accelerated CR system is elected, all CR claimed is recaptured as ordinary income in the year of sale.		– AB	173 664	– Mortgage	275 050
			Gain	333 936	Proceeds before Taxes	232 550
			– Excess CR	0 –	– Tax Liability on Sale	66 787
			Capital Gain	333 936	Proceeds after Taxes	165 763

REALTORS NATIONAL MARKETING INSTITUTE®
of the NATIONAL ASSOCIATION OF REALTORS®, 1982
All rights reserved 2-81-F612

The statements and figures presented herein, while not guaranteed are secured from sources we believe authoritative

Prepared by _____

Figure 32

For **Potential Client**

Purpose **15 yr. Alternative Projection**

Date _____

Cash Flow Analysis

Purchase Price **540,000**

Encumbrances **400,000**

Investment **140,000**

Mortgage Data

	Encumbrances	Beginning Balance	Remaining Term	Number of Payments Per Year	Interest Rate	Payment	Annual Debt Service	Remarks
1	1st Mortgage	400,000	25 yr	12	10%	3,634.80	43,618	
2	2nd Mortgage							
3	3rd Mortgage							

		Year: 1	Year: 2	Year: 3	Year: 4	Year: 5	EOY	Mortgage Balance
	Ownership Analysis of Property Income:		**Taxable Income**					
4	Gross Scheduled Income	87,600						1st Mortgage
5	Less: Vcy. & Credit Losses	3,500						
6	Gross Operating Income	84,100						
7	– Operating Expenses	32,000						
8	Net Operating Income	52,100	53,663	55,273	56,931	58,639		
9	– Non-Operating Expense							
10	– Interest – 1st Mortgage	39,829	39,433	38,995	38,511	37,976		2nd Mortgage
11	– Interest – 2nd Mortgage							
12	– Interest – 3rd Mortgage							
13	– Cost Recovery S/L	22,221	27,486	27,486	27,486	27,486		
14	Real Est. Taxable Income	(9,950)	(13,256)	(11,208)	(9,066)	(6,823)		
		Cash Flows						
15	Net Operating Income	52,100	53,663	55,273	56,931	58,639		3rd Mortgage
16	– Annual Debt Service	43,618	43,618	43,618	43,618	43,618		
17	– Funded Reserves							
18	– Capital Additions							
19	Cash Flow before Taxes	8,482	10,045	11,655	13,313	15,021		
20	– Minimum Tax							
21	– Tax Liability on Real Est.	(3,980)	(5,302)	(4,483)	(3,626)	(2,729)		
22	Cash Flow after Taxes	12,462	15,347	16,138	16,939	17,750		

Analysis of Sale Proceeds
Year: ___

	Adjusted Basis				Excess Cost Recovery (CR)				Tax Liability on Sale			
23	Original Basis				Total CR				Excess Recapture Tax			
24	+ Capital Improvements				S/L CR				Capital Gain Tax			
25	– Cost Recovery				Excess CR*				Tax Liability on Sale			
26	– Partial Sales				Exc. CR Carryover							
27	AB				**Gain**				**Sale Proceeds**			
28	**3% Annual Growth in NOI**				Sale Price				Sale Price			
					– Cost of Sale				– Costs of Sale			
	*NOTE: On non-residential property, if accelerated CR system is elected, all CR claimed is recaptured as ordinary income in the year of sale.				– AB				– Mortgage			
					Gain				Proceeds before Taxes			
					– Excess CR				– Tax Liability on Sale			
					Capital Gain				Proceeds after Taxes			

The statements and figures presented herein, while not guaranteed, are secured from sources we believe authoritative

Prepared by _____

Figure 32 (continued)

<table>
<tr><td colspan="2">For Potential Client</td><td colspan="4">Cash Flow Analysis</td></tr>
<tr><td colspan="2">Purpose 15 yr. Alternative Projection</td><td colspan="2">Purchase Price 540,000</td></tr>
<tr><td colspan="2"></td><td colspan="2">Encumbrances 400,000</td></tr>
<tr><td colspan="2">Date</td><td colspan="2">Investment 140,000</td></tr>
</table>

Mortgage Data

	Encumbrances	Beginning Balance	Remaining Term	Number of Payments Per Year	Interest Rate	Payment	Annual Debt Service	Remarks
1	1st Mortgage	400,000	25 yrs	12	10%	3,634.80	43,618	
2	2nd Mortgage							
3	3rd Mortgage							

	Ownership Analysis of Property Income:	Year: 6	Year: 7	Year: 8	Year: 9	Year: 10	EOY	Mortgage Balance
				Taxable Income				
4	Gross Scheduled Income							1st Mortgage
5	Less: Vcy. & Credit Losses							
6	Gross Operating Income							
7	− Operating Expenses							
8	Net Operating Income	60398	62210	64076	65999	67979		
9	− Non-Operating Expense							
10	− Interest − 1st Mortgage	37385	36737	36011	35215	34335		2nd Mortgage
11	− Interest − 2nd Mortgage							
12	− Interest − 3rd Mortgage							
13	− Cost Recovery S/L	26460	25434	25434	25434	25434		
14	Real Est. Taxable Income	(3447)	44	2631	5350	8210		
				Cash Flows				
15	Net Operating Income	60398	62210	64076	65999	67979		3rd Mortgage
16	− Annual Debt Service	43618	43618	43618	43618	43618		
17	− Funded Reserves							
18	− Capital Additions							
19	Cash Flow before Taxes	16780	18592	20458	22381	24361		
20	− Minimum Tax							
21	− Tax Liability on Real Est.	(1379)	18	1052	2140	3284		
22	Cash Flow after Taxes	18159	18574	19406	20241	21077		

Analysis of Sale Proceeds   Year:

	Adjusted Basis				Excess Cost Recovery (CR)				Tax Liability on Sale			
23	Original Basis				Total CR				Excess Recapture Tax			
24	+ Capital Improvements				S/L CR				Capital Gain Tax			
25	− Cost Recovery				Excess CR*				Tax Liability on Sale			
26	− Partial Sales				Exc. CR Carryover							
27	AB						Gain				Sale Proceeds	
28	**3% Annual Growth in NOI**				Sale Price				Sale Price			
					− Cost of Sale				− Costs of Sale			
	*NOTE: On non-residential property, if accelerated CR system is elected, all CR claimed is recaptured as ordinary income in the year of sale.				− AB				− Mortgage			
					Gain				Proceeds before Taxes			
					− Excess CR				− Tax Liability on Sale			
					Capital Gain				Proceeds after Taxes			

The statements and figures presented herein, while not guaranteed are secured from sources we believe authoritative

Prepared by_____

Figure 32 (continued)

Cash Flow Analysis

For **Potential Client**

Purpose **15 yr. Alternative Projection**

Date _____

Purchase Price **540,000**
Encumbrances **400,000**
Investment **140,000**

Mortgage Data

Encumbrances	Beginning Balance	Remaining Term	Number of Payments Per Year	Interest Rate	Payment	Annual Debt Service	Remarks
1 1st Mortgage	400,000	25 yrs	12	10%	3,634.80	43,618	
2 2nd Mortgage							
3 3rd Mortgage							

	Year: 11	Year: 12	Year: 13	Year: 14	Year: 15	EOY	Mortgage Balance
Ownership Analysis of Property Income:		Taxable Income					1st Mortgage
4 Gross Scheduled Income							
5 Less: Vcy. & Credit Losses							
6 Gross Operating Income							
7 – Operating Expenses							
8 Net Operating Income	70,018	72,119	74,282	76,511	78,806		
9 – Non-Operating Expense						15	275,050
10 – Interest – 1st Mortgage	33,363	32,289	31,103	29,793	28,345	2nd Mortgage	
11 – Interest – 2nd Mortgage							
12 – Interest – 3rd Mortgage							
13 – Cost Recovery S/L	21,195	21,195	21,195	21,195	21,195		
14 Real Est Taxable Income	15,460	18,635	21,984	25,523	29,266		
Cash Flows							
15 Net Operating Income	70,018	72,119	74,282	76,511	78,806	3rd Mortgage	
16 – Annual Debt Service	43,618	43,618	43,618	43,618	43,618		
17 – Funded Reserves							
18 – Capital Additions							
19 Cash Flow before Taxes	26,400	28,501	30,664	32,893	35,188		
20 – Minimum Tax							
21 – Tax Liability on Real Est.	6,184	7,454	8,794	10,209	11,706		
22 Cash Flow after Taxes	20,216	21,047	21,870	22,684	23,482		

Analysis of Sale Proceeds
Year: 15

Adjusted Basis		Excess Cost Recovery (CR)		Tax Liability on Sale	
23 Original Basis	540,000	Total CR	366,336	Excess Recapture Tax	-0-
24 + Capital Improvements		S/L CR	366,336	Capital Gain Tax 20%	57,387
25 – Cost Recovery	366,336	Excess CR*	-0-	Tax Liability on Sale	57,387
26 – Partial Sales		Exc. CR Carryover			
27 AB	173,664	Gain		Sale Proceeds	
28 3% ANNUAL GROWTH in NOI		Sale Price	490,000	Sale Price	490,000
		– Cost of Sale	29,400	– Costs of Sale	29,400
*NOTE: On non-residential property, if accelerated CR system is elected, all CR claimed is recaptured as ordinary income in the year of sale.		– AB	173,664	– Mortgage	275,050
		Gain	286,936	Proceeds before Taxes	185,550
		– Excess CR	-0-	– Tax Liability on Sale	57,387
		Capital Gain	286,936	Proceeds after Taxes	128,163

The statements and figures presented herein, while not guaranteed are secured from sources we believe authoritative

Prepared by _____

Figure 32 (continued)

Cash Flow Analysis

For _____ Purchase Price_____

Purpose _____ Encumbrances_____

Date _____   Investment_____

Mortgage Data

	Encumbrances	Beginning Balance	Remaining Term	Number of Payments Per Year	Interest Rate	Payment	Annual Debt Service	Remarks
1	1st Mortgage							
2	2nd Mortgage							
3	3rd Mortgage							

	Ownership Analysis of Property Income:	Year:	Year:	Year:	Year:	Year:	EOY	Mortgage Balance
	Taxable Income							1st Mortgage
4	Gross Scheduled Income							
5	Less: Vcy. & Credit Losses							
6	Gross Operating Income							
7	– Operating Expenses							
8	Net Operating Income							
9	– Non-Operating Expense							
10	– Interest – 1st Mortgage							2nd Mortgage
11	– Interest – 2nd Mortgage							
12	– Interest – 3rd Mortgage							
13	– Cost Recovery							
14	Real Est. Taxable Income							
	Cash Flows							
15	Net Operating Income							3rd Mortgage
16	– Annual Debt Service							
17	– Funded Reserves							
18	– Capital Additions							
19	Cash Flow before Taxes							
20	– Minimum Tax							
21	– Tax Liability on Real Est.							
22	Cash Flow after Taxes							

Analysis of Sale Proceeds   Year: 15

	Adjusted Basis		Excess Cost Recovery (CR)		Tax Liability on Sale	
23	Original Basis	540000	Total CR	366336	Excess Recapture Tax	–0–
24	+ Capital Improvements		S/L CR	366336	Capital Gain Tax 20%	113411
25	– Cost Recovery	366336	Excess CR*	–0–	Tax Liability on Sale	113411
26	– Partial Sales		Exc. CR Carryover			
27	AB	173664		Gain		Sale Proceeds
28	3% ANNUAL GROWTH in NOI		Sale Price	788000	Sale Price	788000
			– Cost of Sale	47280	– Costs of Sale	47280
	*NOTE: On non-residential property, if accelerated CR system is elected, all CR claimed is recaptured as ordinary income in the year of sale.		– AB	173664	– Mortgage	275050
			Gain	567056	– Proceeds before Taxes	465670
			– Excess CR	–0–	– Tax Liability on Sale	113411
			Capital Gain	567056	Proceeds after Taxes	352259

The statements and figures presented herein, while not guaranteed are secured from sources we believe authoritative

Prepared by_____

The resulting cash flows or yields (from Figure 32) are:

EOY	$	EOY	$
0	($140,000)	0	($140,000)
1	12,462	1	12,462
2	15,347	2	15,347
3	16,138	3	16,138
4	16,939	4	16,939
5	17,750	5	17,750
6	18,159	6	18,159
7	18,574	7	18,574
8	19,406	8	19,406
9	20,241	9	20,241
10	21,077	10	21,077
11	20,216	11	20,216
12	21,047	12	21,047
13	21,870	13	21,870
14	22,684	14	22,684
15	23,482 + 352,259	15	23,482 + 128,163
Resale: $788,000		Resale: $490,000	
IRR: 15.45%		IRR: 12.38%	

After-tax investment analysis

This step-by-step analysis creates no miraculous real estate investments. In fact, some brokers dislike the method because they say it does not show real estate yields as "high" as do other types of investment analysis. The purpose of the procedure, however, is not to show real estate investments as high or low; it is used merely to show what happens under *projected* circumstances. IRR uses a yield measurement that is similar to the measurement used and understood by the public on alternative investments such as stocks and bonds.

As we have shown in our case study, the foundation of cash flow analysis is the Broker's Forecast, an estimate of the operations for the next year. If the broker finds reliability in this statement, his next step is to prepare the cash flow analysis. In making this analysis, he gives consideration to many factors—the type of tenant or improvement, the location and demographics of the area, increases or decreases of the quantity of income projected over succeeding years and how these items will affect the durability of the income.

While these items are impossible to predict accurately, both the broker and the client have some ability to project future trends. They are able to understand the present condition of the property and can make some estimate as to whether it can be maintained at the cost indicated in the projection for the period indicated. They have some idea as to whether the rents will increase or decrease due to the improvements, neighborhood trends and so forth. And they can form an opinion as to whether the projected resale price, if it is the same as the acquisition price, is a reasonable, a conservative or an optimistic estimate. If the property is to sell at more or less than at acquisition, is that because of increased or decreased income or decreasing or increasing yield demands? These are all logical points of discussion between the broker and the seller or the broker and the buyer.

If a projection process is followed, such discussions can concern themselves with the assumptions; but if such a process is ignored, the negotiation process reduces itself to who is the best salesperson.

The seller? "I won't take a cent less." "They don't build them like they used to." "This is the finest piece of real estate in the country."

The buyer? "I'm looking for a deal." "Don't talk to me about taxes; my brother-in-law is the best accountant there is." "I'll only offer $_____." "The price is too high."

The salesperson to the seller? "You know the market is quiet." "You probably have overpriced." "You've got to be reasonable."

The salesperson to the buyer? "Real estate is the best investment." "This property really will increase in value and you'll come out well on your investment." "But you're getting shelter."

If a property is analyzed properly, projected logically and compared fairly with alternative investments, such cliches will be shown to be unnecessary, superfluous and unproductive.

Buyers must understand that they are buying the future benefits of the property, and that although these cannot be predicted, yields can be calculated on projections. They must understand the ingredients of the projections and must compare the projected yields with available alternative investments. With proper guidance, investors can understand that even if some properties sell for less than the purchase price, the yield can still be better than on alternative investment opportunities.

On the other hand, when a seller can be shown what yield a prospective purchaser would have obtained by acquiring an overpriced property, he will understand why it did not sell and hopefully will reduce his price. But before this can happen, the broker must understand how to project yields at various prices, terms and conditions. The process is less for clients than it is for brokers. Only when the broker understands the process and the reasons for it can he assist clients by talking in a language they already understand.

If investment value is a reflection of an investment's future benefits, then an analysis of its potential cash flows from operations and resale is a must for anyone to understand the investment. If real estate brokers are unable or unwilling to do the analysis, clients have only two ways to turn— to soothsayers who promise the impossible or to other professionals who have the capability.

Case Study 2
Discounted cash flow analysis—a listing tool

One of the most common (and often the most difficult) problems that brokers face in listing income-producing property is offering it at a price that will accomplish the transaction within a reasonable period of time.

Over the years, brokers have relied on gross multipliers, overall capitalization rates and other rules of thumb to convince sellers of marketplace realities. All too often, however, a difference of only 1 percent in overall capitalization rate can stand between the seller and his agent in reaching an agreement on listing price.

This case study illustrates a situation where discounting cash flows is used as a means of bringing the sellers to list at a reasonable price.

Situation

The subject property is a small office building which the owners wish to sell for $290,000. A property analysis indicated a Net Operating Income (NOI) of $24,725 and thus an overall capitalization rate of 8.5 percent at the asking price. The broker recommended a sale price of $260,000, indicating a capitalization rate of 9.5 percent. The owners disagreed and the salesperson was unable to list the property at $260,000.

A new listing approach has been conceived based on the methodology and philosophy of discounted cash flows discussed in this book. In essence, the approach is based on the idea of placing the seller in the position of a prospective buyer. What would his income stream be if he acquired the property? This can be projected with data and assumptions on mortgage, amortization, depreciation, interest rates, tax brackets, term of holding and resale price. These assumptions form the basis of projections which are presented to the current owner.

Mortgage amount

Many people believe that the mortgage is always estimated as a percentage of the sale price; this is not necessarily true. Although loans may be as high as 75 percent, it is generally accepted that a $50,000 property sold at $100,000 will not necessarily command a $75,000 mortgage.

So, instead of estimating a mortgage based on a sale price for the subject property, the broker in this case used a debt coverage ratio (DCR) of 1.25 at the current interest rate (10 percent) for a loan period typical of this kind of property (25 years). Therefore:

$$\frac{NOI}{DCR} = \frac{\$24,725}{1.25} = \$19,780 \text{ available for annual debt service}$$
$$(\$1,648.33 \text{ per month})$$

Payments of $1,648.33 monthly at 10 percent for 25 years will repay a loan of $181,394.15. Specifically, the broker estimated a loan of $180,000, payable at $1,635.66 per month for 25 years including 10-percent interest (which comes to $19,627.92 annual debt service).

Depreciation (cost recovery)

Brokers tend to think of land/building allocations in terms of ratios or percentages. Such thinking conditions them to believe that as price rises so does the amount of depreciation. It is possible, however, to change thinking habits to establish a logical amount of depreciation with a change in the price being dependent on a change in land value. Under such a premise, depreciation becomes a constant amount at various projected sale prices.

In this case study, improvements were estimated at $200,000 and an 18-year straight line depreciation method was selected. Land was estimated at $60,000.

Projection period

Experience shows that the internal rate of return (IRR) in Year One is usually negative; it generally increases until some time between 12 and 16 years when it levels off and then declines. For this case study, 15 years was selected as the projection period.

Tax bracket of the investor

It is unusual to find low tax-bracket investors buying million-dollar buildings; conversely, not too many duplexes are acquired by investors in high tax brackets.

In this particular case, it was assumed that a property priced in the $200,000 to $300,000 range would be sold to someone with a 40-percent marginal tax rate.

Reversion (resale proceeds)

Estimating the future value of a property 15 years hence is actually not as difficult as estimating current value, at least from the standpoint of present value of money. An error in judgment as to future value is minimized in terms of present value by the discounting process.

In this case the future value at the time of sale was estimated at $300,000. Marketing costs were estimated at 7 percent and capital gains taxes were calculated at 50 percent of 40 percent of the gain (or 20 percent of the gain) because the larger gain would probably raise the investor's marginal tax bracket to the maximum marginal bracket of 50 percent.

Projected income stream

A complete cash flow analysis was done on the subject property (see Figure 33), with the resulting projected income stream:

EOY	$
1	$6,376
2	7,105
3	7,026
4	6,939
5	6,843
6	6,736
7	6,619
8	6,489
9	6,346
10	6,187
11	5,212
12	5,019
13	4,805
14	4,570
15	4,309 + 117,828 (net proceeds after taxes)

This income stream becomes the total future benefits to a prospective purchaser. It therefore follows that the prospective purchaser's yield will depend upon the price he pays for the income stream.

The income stream was then discounted at seven different rates to determine equity values *over* the proposed mortgage. The results were as follows:

Yield	Equity Value	Mortgage	Investment Value
6%	$109,758	$180,000	$289,758
8%	91,037	180,000	271,037
10%	76,498	180,000	256,498
12%	65,096	180,000	245,096
14%	56,065	180,000	236,065
16%	48,841	180,000	228,841
18%	43,007	180,000	223,007

Bringing buyer and seller together

It was pointed out to the sellers that a buyer of the property at $290,000 could only expect an approximate 6-percent yield. It was agreed that no one (including the sellers) buys real estate for that yield. The sellers agreed that 10 to 12 percent was a reasonable minimum expected return in light of competitive investments which a prospective purchaser could make.

The property was listed at $250,000 after these points were made, in spite of the fact that the sellers previously had refused to list at $260,000.

Within six days a client who had been searching for an investment for many months was shown the analysis. He wanted to offer $225,00, but it was brought to his attention that such an offer would, if accepted, return a yield of more than 17 percent which was much higher than he could expect from competitive investments. It was also pointed out that his current equity

Figure 33

Cash Flow Analysis

For **Mr. Seller**

Purpose **15 yr. Projection**

Date _____

Purchase Price **?**

Encumbrances **180,000**

Investment **?**

Mortgage Data

Encumbrances	Beginning Balance	Remaining Term	Number of Payments Per Year	Interest Rate	Payment	Annual Debt Service	Remarks
1 1st Mortgage	180,000	25 yrs	12	10%	1,635.66	19,628	
2 2nd Mortgage							
3 3rd Mortgage							

	Year: 1	Year: 2	Year: 3	Year: 4	Year: 5	EOY	Mortgage Balance
Ownership Analysis of Property Income:	Taxable Income						1st Mortgage
4 Gross Scheduled Income							
5 Less: Vcy. & Credit Losses							
6 Gross Operating Income							
7 – Operating Expenses							
8 Net Operating Income	24,725	24,725	24,725	24,725	24,725		
9 – Non-Operating Expense							
10 – Interest – 1st Mortgage	17,923	17,745	17,548	17,330	17,089		2nd Mortgage
11 – Interest – 2nd Mortgage							
12 – Interest – 3rd Mortgage							
13 – Cost Recovery S/L	10,000	12,000	12,000	12,000	12,000		
14 Real Est. Taxable Income	(3,198)	(5,020)	(4,823)	(4,605)	(4,364)		
	Cash Flows						
15 Net Operating Income	24,725						3rd Mortgage
16 – Annual Debt Service	19,628						
17 – Funded Reserves							
18 – Capital Additions							
19 Cash Flow before Taxes	5,097	5,097	5,097	5,097	5,097		
20 – Minimum Tax							
21 – Tax Liability on Real Est.	(1,279)	(2,008)	(1,929)	(1,842)	(1,746)		
22 Cash Flow after Taxes	6,376	7,105	7,026	6,939	6,843		

Analysis of Sale Proceeds   Year: ____

Adjusted Basis			Excess Cost Recovery (CR)			Tax Liability on Sale		
23 Original Basis			Total CR			Excess Recapture Tax		
24 + Capital Improvements			S/L CR			Capital Gain Tax		
25 – Cost Recovery			Excess CR*			Tax Liability on Sale		
26 – Partial Sales			Exc. CR Carryover					
27 AB			Gain			Sale Proceeds		
28			Sale Price			Sale Price		
			– Cost of Sale			– Costs of Sale		
			– AB			– Mortgage		
			Gain			Proceeds before Taxes		
			– Excess CR			– Tax Liability on Sale		
			Capital Gain			Proceeds after Taxes		

*NOTE: On non-residential property, if accelerated CR system is elected, all CR claimed is recaptured as ordinary income in the year of sale.

REALTORS NATIONAL MARKETING INSTITUTE of the NATIONAL ASSOCIATION OF REALTORS. 1982 All rights reserved 2-81-F812

The statements and figures presented herein, while not guaranteed are secured from sources we believe authoritative.

Prepared by _____

Figure 33 (continued)

Cash Flow Analysis

For **Mr. Seller**

Purpose **15 yr. Projection**

Date _____

Purchase Price **?**

Encumbrances **180,000**

Investment **?**

Mortgage Data

	Encumbrances	Beginning Balance	Remaining Term	Number of Payments Per Year	Interest Rate	Payment	Annual Debt Service	Remarks
1	1st Mortgage	180,000	25 yrs	12	10%	1,635.66	19,628	
2	2nd Mortgage							
3	3rd Mortgage							

	Ownership Analysis of Property Income:	Year: 6		Year: 7		Year: 8		Year: 9		Year: 10		EOY	Mortgage Balance
		Taxable Income											
4	Gross Scheduled Income												1st Mortgage
5	Less: Vcy. & Credit Losses												
6	Gross Operating Income												
7	– Operating Expenses												
8	Net Operating Income	24,725		24,725		24,725		24,725		24,725			
9	– Non-Operating Expense												
10	– Interest – 1st Mortgage	16,823		16,530		16,205		15,847		15,451			2nd Mortgage
11	– Interest – 2nd Mortgage												
12	– Interest – 3rd Mortgage												
13	– Cost Recovery	12,000		12,000		12,000		12,000		12,000			
14	Real Est. Taxable Income	(4,098)		(3,805)		(3,480)		(3,122)		(2,726)			
		Cash Flows											
15	Net Operating Income												3rd Mortgage
16	– Annual Debt Service												
17	– Funded Reserves												
18	– Capital Additions												
19	Cash Flow before Taxes	5,097		5,097		5,097		5,097		5,097			
20	– Minimum Tax												
21	– Tax Liability on Real Est.	(1,639)		(1,522)		(1,392)		(1,249)		(1,090)			
22	Cash Flow after Taxes	6,736		6,619		6,489		6,346		6,187			

Analysis of Sale Proceeds Year: _____

	Adjusted Basis			Excess Cost Recovery (CR)			Tax Liability on Sale		
23	Original Basis			Total CR			Excess Recapture Tax		
24	+ Capital Improvements			S/L CR			Capital Gain Tax		
25	– Cost Recovery			Excess CR*			Tax Liability on Sale		
26	– Partial Sales			Exc. CR Carryover					
27	AB			**Gain**			**Sale Proceeds**		
28				Sale Price			Sale Price		
				– Cost of Sale			– Costs of Sale		
				– AB			– Mortgage		
				Gain			Proceeds before Taxes		
				– Excess CR			– Tax Liability on Sale		
				Capital Gain			Proceeds after Taxes		

*NOTE: On non-residential property, if accelerated CR system is elected, all CR claimed is recaptured as ordinary income in the year of sale.

The statements and figures presented herein, while not guaranteed are secured from sources we believe authoritative

Prepared by _____

Figure 33 (continued)

Cash Flow Analysis

For **Mr. Seller**

Purpose **15 yr. Projection**

Date _____

Purchase Price ___?___

Encumbrances **180,000**

Investment ___?___

Mortgage Data

	Encumbrances	Beginning Balance	Remaining Term	Number of Payments Per Year	Interest Rate	Payment	Annual Debt Service	Remarks
1	1st Mortgage	180,000	25 yrs	12	10%	1,635.66	19,628	
2	2nd Mortgage							
3	3rd Mortgage							

	Ownership Analysis of Property Income:	Year: 11	Year: 12	Year: 13	Year: 14	Year: 15	EOY	Mortgage Balance
				Taxable Income				1st Mortgage
4	Gross Scheduled Income							
5	Less: Vcy. & Credit Losses							
6	Gross Operating Income							
7	– Operating Expenses							
8	Net Operating Income	24,725	24,725	24,725	24,725	24,725		
9	– Non-Operating Expense						15	123,772
10	– Interest – 1st Mortgage	15,013	14,530	13,996	13,407	12,755		2nd Mortgage
11	– Interest – 2nd Mortgage							
12	– Interest – 3rd Mortgage							
13	– Cost Recovery	10,000	10,000	10,000	10,000	10,000		
14	Real Est. Taxable Income	(288)	195	729	1,318	1,970		

Cash Flows

								3rd Mortgage
15	Net Operating Income							
16	– Annual Debt Service							
17	– Funded Reserves							
18	– Capital Additions							
19	Cash Flow before Taxes	5,097	5,097	5,097	5,097	5,097		
20	– Minimum Tax							
21	– Tax Liability on Real Est.	(115)	78	292	527	788		
22	Cash Flow after Taxes	5,212	5,019	4,805	4,570	4,309		

Analysis of Sale Proceeds   Year: 15

	Adjusted Basis		Excess Cost Recovery (CR)		Tax Liability on Sale	
23	Original Basis	260,000	Total CR	168,000	Excess Recapture Tax	– 0 –
24	+ Capital Improvements		S/L CR	168,000	Capital Gain Tax 20%	37,400
25	– Cost Recovery	168,000	Excess CR*	– 0 –	Tax Liability on Sale	37,400
26	– Partial Sales		Exc. CR Carryover			
27	AB	92,000	Gain		Sale Proceeds	
26			Sale Price	300,000	Sale Price	300,000
			– Cost of Sale	21,000	– Costs of Sale	21,000
			– AB	92,000	– Mortgage	123,772
			Gain	187,000	Proceeds before Taxes	155,228
			– Excess CR	– 0 –	– Tax Liability on Sale	37,400
			Capital Gain	187,000	Proceeds after Taxes	117,828

*NOTE: On non-residential property, if accelerated CR system is elected, all CR claimed is recaptured as ordinary income in the year of sale.

funds were earning only 6 percent (before taxes) and that his yield could be dramatically increased by acquiring the subject property. His ultimate purchase of the property at $250,000 confirmed the broker's analysis.

It is obvious that this type of analysis by the broker lays the foundation for a more intelligent and profitable business.

Within a period of 90 days the broker did similar analyses on two apartment complexes, each having a different owner. In both instances, the yield projected, at the owner's price and terms, was less than 5 percent. Neither investment was competitive in the market; however, the broker's knowledge and experience in the market added another dimension which ultimately resulted in listing one property and rejecting the other.

The apartment building that eventually was listed consisted of two and three-bedroom units in a stable neighborhood which made the building a natural for conversion to condominiums.

The other building consisted of one-bedroom apartments in a highly transient area of the city. Condominium buyers would not be attracted to the area. The broker knew that the owner will have to revise his price and terms to dispose of the property. When the time comes for the owner to accept this fact, a transaction will probably be made.

Case Study 3
The sandwich lease

The "sandwich" lease is a further example of how value is estimated by the discounted cash flow process and, in fact, demonstrates that none of the other historically used methods of valuation are feasible when applied to this type of property.

Once a lease is executed by a tenant on a property, an income stream is defined. The stream may be above, below or equal to the rent on comparable properties at the time of execution or at later times. Therefore, care must be taken to account for the differences between contract rent and market rent when analyzing the property as a potential investment.

When the contract rent is less than market rent, an interest is established for the lessee called a leasehold interest. Such interest may be valued by the discounted cash flow techniques discussed throughout this book (applying the appropriate discount factor to the future income stream). The discount rate used will reflect the quantity, quality and durability of the income of the leasehold.

The income stream is represented by the difference between the annual contract rent and the market rent over the remaining period of the lease. If the lessee subleases the property, the income stream is defined as the difference between the rent he pays and the rent he receives.

Situation

Twelve years have elapsed since Able leased his 50,000 square-foot warehouse to Bon Bon Corporation of America for $2,500 per month net rent for a period of 30 years. Two years ago the space became inadequate for Bon Bon; the broker subleased the building to two local tenants as follows:

> Cable TV: 30,000 sq. ft.; term: 20 years, $2,400 per month net net
> Dental Supply: 20,000 sq. ft.; term: 20 years, $1,600 per month

Recently Dental Supply moved and the broker subleased its space for the balance of the term for $2,000 per month net to Farmer's Tractors.

Income stream and present value

We will try to accomplish two aims in this case study:

1. Describe each lessor's and sublessor's projected income stream, assuming Able's resale price at the end of the lease is $400,000.

2. Estimate the present value of each leasehold interest.

The following will be our assumptions:

Able's income stream is discounted at 10 percent.

Bon Bon's stream is discounted at 15 percent because of greater risk.

Dental Supply leasehold is discounted at 25 percent to reflect the fact that Farmer's Tractors is a new local business with untested staying power and credit.

Able has 18 years left to collect on the original 30-year lease. Thus, he will receive 216 monthly rentals of $2,500 at the beginning of the month (BOM). In addition, it is assumed that he will obtain $400,000 from resale proceeds at the end of the leases.

Able's cash flows to be discounted at 10 percent can be described as:

BOM		
	1	$2,500
	2	2,500
	3	2,500
	4	2,500
	–	–
	–	–
	–	–
	214	2,500
	215	2,500
	216	2,500 + $400,000 (EOM)

353

By calculator:

Present Value $\boxed{\text{PV}}$ of $2,500 BOM for 216 months $252,123
discounted at 10 percent on monthly basis

$\boxed{\text{PV}}$ of $400,000 end of 216 months discounted at   66,615
10 percent on monthly basis

Total $\boxed{\text{PV}}$ Able position $318,738

Bon Bon position (discounted at 15 percent):

Receives from Cable T.V.		Receives from Dental Supply		Pays to Able		Bon Bon's Net Cash Flows	
BOM 1	$2,400	BOM 1	$1,600	BOM 1	$2,500	BOM 1	$1,500
2	2,400	2	1,600	2	2,500	2	1,500
3	2,400	3	1,600	3	2,500	3	1,500
–	–	–	–	–	–	–	–
–	–	–	–	–	–	–	–
–	–	–	–	–	–	–	–
214	2,400	214	1,600	214	2,500	214	1,500
215	2,400	215	1,600	215	2,500	215	1,500
216	2,400	216	1,600	216	2,500	216	1,500

By calculator:

$\boxed{\text{PV}}$ of $1,500 per month BOM for 216 months
discounted at 15 percent on monthly basis $113,197

Dental Supply Co. position (discounted at 25 percent):

Payable to Bon Bon		Receivable from Farmer's Tractor		Dental Supply's Net Cash Flow	
BOM 1	$1,600	BOM 1	$2,000	BOM 1	$400
2	1,600	2	2,000	2	400
3	1,600	3	2,000	3	400
–	–	–	–	–	–
–	–	–	–	–	–
–	–	–	–	–	–
214	1,600	214	2,000	214	400
215	1,600	215	2,000	215	400
216	1,600	216	2,000	216	400

By calculator:

$\boxed{\text{PV}}$ of $400 monthly BOM for 216 months
discounted at 25 percent on monthly basis $19,372

This example illustrates how a broker can create a valuable asset for a lessee who no longer needs a property by finding a sublessee who will pay a greater rent than the lessee pays the lessor. The broker should be aware of this possibility of creating a leasehold interest for the lessee when market rents exceed contract rents negotiated years before. He also should learn the technique of assigning value to the income stream produced.

Case Study 4
After-tax yields from wraparound loans

A technique of financing that has been popular, particularly in situations with owner carry-back financing, is the wraparound mortgage. As explained in Chapter 6 the wraparound mortgage is a junior loan subordinate to the underlying mortgages. The wraparound offers a potentially higher yield than the typical second or junior mortgage.

The usual problems associated with wraparound mortgages are the calculation of the true yield on the investment and the tax impact of the wraparound. This case study illustrates the calculations of the yield before and after taxes.

Situation

Johnson is selling a property for $150,000; it has an existing loan of $81,770.50, an interest rate of 8.5 percent and monthly payments of $805.23 for the remaining 15-year term. The terms of the sale are $25,000 down with Johnson taking back a $125,000 wraparound loan at 10-percent interest with monthly payments of $1,074.59 which represents a 35-year amortization. The wraparound loan has a term of ten years. Therefore, the entire balance remaining is due and payable at the end of Year Ten. Johnson's marginal income tax rate is 50 percent.

Before-tax analysis

The before-tax analysis and calculation of rate of return for the wraparound lender is illustrated in the table on page 356.

The before-tax yield to the wraparound lender is 11.84 percent. The borrower pays 10-percent interest on the total loan amount of $125,000. The wraparound lender (Johnson) loans $125,000 at 10 percent, but $81,770.50 of the $125,000 is borrowed at 8.5 percent. Therefore, the wraparound lender benefits from positive leverage, thus increasing his yield to 11.84 percent for the ten-year loan term.

355

End of Month	Wraparound Loan	−	Existing Loan	=	Wraparound Lender's Cash Flows Before Tax
0	(125,000.00)	−	(81,770.50)	=	(43,229.50)
1	1,074.59	−	805.23	=	269.36
↓	↓		↓		↓
120	1,074.59	−	805.23	=	269.36
Balloon 120	118,255.82	−	39,247.02	=	79,008.80
IRR (Monthly)	.833333		.708333		.986356
X12 =	× 12		× 12		× 12
Annualized	10.00%		8.50%		11.84%

The impact of taxes can alter both the yield and the cash flows substantially. To fully appreciate this effect, the cash flows after tax must be derived and measured. The interest collected by the wraparound lender is ordinary income and the interest he pays out on the underlying ("existing") loan is an ordinary deduction. Tax is calculated on the net difference. As always, cash flow after tax equals cash flow before tax less the resulting tax.

After-tax cash flows

Following is an analysis of the after-tax cash flows. The analysis has been annualized to simplify the process, and thus the resulting solution will not be quite as accurate as it would be if it were calculated on a monthly basis, but it is extremely close. The calculation of net interest income and tax to the wraparound lender is summarized on page 357.

Note that the *net* interest income increases each year in this case study. The interest portion of the wraparound loan payment is greater than the interest portion of each corresponding underlying loan payment. This relationship is explained by the greater interest rate, longer amortization term and larger principal balance of the wraparound loan compared to the underlying loan.

Cash flows before taxes were identified in the before-tax analysis of this loan. The wraparound lender's initial investment is $43,229 ($125,000–$81,771). Total annual debt service received by the wraparound lender pays annual debt services of $9,663 ($805.23 × 12). The net annual cash flows before taxes to the wraparound lender from annual debt service is $3,232 ($12,895–$9,663). The net loan balance received by the wraparound lender at the end of Year Ten is $79,009 ($118,256–$39,247). Cash flows after taxes are summarized on page 357.

The IRR of annualized cash flows after tax is 6.03 percent—approximately 50 percent less than the before-tax IRR. Certainly, the amount of tax

	Summary of Net Interest to the Wraparound Lender and Resulting Tax			
	INTEREST			
EOY	Interest Received	Interest Paid on Underlying Loan	Net Interest Income	Tax (50%)
1	$12,481	$6,842	$5,639	$2,820
2	12,438	6,593	5,845	2,923
3	12,390	6,322	6,068	3,034
4	12,337	6,026	6,311	3,156
5	12,279	5,705	6,574	3,287
6	12,214	5,355	6,859	3,430
7	12,143	4,974	7,169	3,585
8	12,064	4,560	7,504	3,752
9	11,977	4,109	7,868	3,934
10	11,881	3,618	8,263	4,132

	Summary of Cash Flows Before Tax and Cash Flows After Tax to the Wraparound Lender		
EOY	Cash Flows Before Tax	Tax	Cash Flows After Tax
0	($43,229)		($43,229)
1	3,232	$2,820	412
2	3,232	2,923	309
3	3,232	3,034	198
4	3,232	3,156	76
5	3,232	3,287	(55)
6	3,232	3,430	(198)
7	3,232	3,585	(353)
8	3,232	3,752	(520)
9	3,232	3,934	(702)
10	3,232 + 79,009	4,132	(900) + 79,009

paid on net interest to the wraparound lender will affect the cash flows after tax and the after-tax yield. As the amount of tax increases, the cash flows after tax decreases. In this example, cash flows after taxes are negative after Year Four.

Principal amortization

Notice that the wraparound lender's initial cash investment was $43,229 and the net loan balance EOY 10 was $79,009. The wraparound lender's net balance is increased with this wraparound loan because the principal portion of each payment on the underlying loan exceeds the principal portion of each corresponding payment on the wraparound loan. The differential principal payments depend on the loan amounts, interest rates, and remaining terms of both the underlying and wraparound loans. In this case, the wraparound loan payments are based on a 35-year amortization schedule at a 10-percent interest rate. The principal portion of each wraparound loan payment is less than the principal portion of each underlying loan payment at 8.5-percent interest with a 15-year remaining term. The annual principal amortization for the wraparound and underlying loans is summarized in the following table:

EOY	Principal Amortization		Difference*
	Wraparound Loan*	Underlying Loan*	
1	$ 414	$2,821	($2,407)
2	457	3,070	(2,613)
3	505	3,341	(2,836)
4	558	3,636	(3,079)
5	616	3,958	(3,342)
6	681	4,308	(3,627)
7	752	4,688	(3,936)
8	831	5,103	(4,272)
9	918	5,554	(4,636)
10	1,014	6,045	(5,031)
Total			($35,779)
*Adjusted for rounding error			

With this loan, the wraparound lender receives less principal each year than the underlying lender. The difference is an additional capital investment in the loan by the wraparound lender. The sum of the increased principal during the ten-year loan term, $35,779, plus the wraparound lender's original investment of $43,229 is equal to the net loan balance EOY 10 of $79,009 (adjusted for rounding error). The annual increase of principal by the wraparound lender is taxed as ordinary income each tax period. For example, the wraparound lender's taxable income for the first year may be allocated between two elements as follows:

Net cash flow before tax EOY 1	$3,232
Net principal increase EOY 1	+2,407
Wraparound lender's taxable income EOY 1	$5,639

The wraparound lender's taxable income, as calculated above, is equal to the net interest income calculated on page 357. Taxable income exceeds cash flows before taxes for this loan. Tax is paid on the net principal increase each tax period even though the net principal increase is not received until the end of the loan term.

It is important to analyze wraparound loans on an after-tax basis. In this case study the wraparound lender is a seller. Indeed, the terms of this wraparound loan may be necessary to consummate the transaction. However, the forecast negative cash flows after tax may be unacceptable to the wraparound lender. Negative cash flows after tax could be eliminated by changing one or more of the loan terms. For example, the loan could be due at the end of Year Five, the amortization term of the wraparound loan could be decreased or the wraparound loan interest rate could be increased. Each of these variables will affect the wraparound lender's cash flows and yield.

Conclusion

We have examined the seller's position when a portion of equity is "loaned" to the buyer in a wraparound loan. The same concepts apply when deriving before- and after-tax cash flows and before- and after-tax yields when negotiating a wraparound mortgage for a traditional lender who is actually putting dollars in the mortgage investment.

Notes

1. Although the 1984 Tax Act requires that a mi-month convention be used for 18-year real property, the following case studies ignore this minor adjustment in the cost recovery amount for the years of purchase and disposition.

Chapter 13

Differential Cash Flow Analysis

13

One of the difficulties in real estate investing is choosing among the many variables that are available with just one property or between two or more properties. Once a property has been purchased, this dilemma is not over. There are many options available almost on a daily basis during the life of the investment.

A useful process in choosing between various alternatives is differential cash flow analysis. This analysis is done by reducing each alternative to its cash flows for the entire anticipated holding period. Once the investments are reduced to cash flows, the difference between two alternatives can be derived and compared. The framework of the process will be outlined in this chapter and then various examples of application will be given.

Before the process can be outlined, an understanding of investment base, or End of Year 0 cash flow, is necessary. A detailed explanation of investment base is in Chapter 4. Simply stated, investment base is the dollar amount at risk in an investment on any given day as determined by loss of opportunity in alternative investments. For a new investment, it is the total acquisition cost or money paid for an investment by the buyer. In a currently owned investment, the investment base is equal to the proceeds of sale after tax if that investment were sold during the initial time period of the analysis. This amount is not available for alternative investments if the present investment is held. Investment base changes during the holding period when the value of the investment, loan amounts, or owner's tax posture changes. Therefore, the investment base is probably not equal to the original cash investment amount throughout the holding period. The investment base amount is the initial investment End of Year 0 of the cash flow forecast and is usually a negative value.

The steps in the process are as follows:

Step 1 Reduce all alternatives to cash flows from EOY 0 to end of forecast period. Be consistent by using only before-tax *or* after-tax cash flows. It may be helpful to use a Cash Flow Analysis form.

360 Step 2 Isolate the differential cash flows between alternatives.

Step 3 Calculate IRR of differential cash flows.

Step 4 Compare calculated IRR to other comparable investment
opportunities in the marketplace.

At this point a reminder is necessary: the basic objective of any pure investment strategy is to accumulate wealth. The investor does not necessarily seek the investment which will produce the highest "return," but the investment which will produce the most dollars at some time in the future. The following case studies illustrate this procedure in a variety of commercial/investment brokerage applications.

Case Study 5
Comparison of two installment sale offers

Very often the terms of a real estate transaction are as important as the sale price itself to the outcome of the sale. In the process of negotiating the terms of the contract, the seller may have to accept a smaller down payment in return for a higher sale price. Terms of purchase money financing will also affect the sale price. Differential cash flow analysis can be used to determine which alternative purchase offer will produce the greater future wealth for the seller.

Differential cash flow analysis of two possible installment sale offers, or any financial alternative, is accomplished by comparing the cash flows created by each alternative. A forecast of cash flows after taxes produced by each sale offer is made based on the proposed terms of the offer. The differential cash flow stream is the difference between one offer and another. Of course, the seller would choose an offer where all cash flows exceed the cash flows from all other offers, given equal risk characteristics. Usually, one offer will produce a greater initial cash flow at the time of sale and smaller future cash flows than the other offers. The IRR of the differential cash flows will indicate the minimum yield required on intermediate cash flows to produce greater future wealth by accepting the offer with a larger initial cash flow and smaller future cash flows.

Situation

In this situation, the seller is taxed at a marginal tax rate of 50 percent. The adjusted basis of the property is $500,000. There is no depreciation recapture since the straight line method was used. Brokerage fees and other costs of sale are estimated to be 6 percent of the sale price. Each potential buyer will assume the existing mortgage balance of $600,000. Both buyers will close at the end of the seller's tax year so that only the taxable amount received at the time of closing is taxed during the year of sale. The terms of the two offers are summarized below:

	Offer A	Offer B
Sale Price	$1,100,000	$1,075,000
Cash Down Payment	$ 200,000	$ 250,000
Purchase Money Mortgage		
Amount	$ 300,000	$ 225,000
Interest Rate	12%	15%
Amortization	15 years	30 years
Monthly Payment	$ 3,600.50	$ 2,845.00

The seller requires that either purchase money mortgage balance is paid at the end of Year Five (i.e., balloon payment, EOY 5). Offer A has a greater sale price, but a smaller cash down payment. The seller will take back a smaller purchase money mortgage at a higher interest rate and longer amortization term if Offer B is accepted.

Analysis of Offer A	
Sale Price	$1,100,000
Mortgage Balance	−600,000
Cash Down Payment	−200,000
Purchase Money Mortgage	$ 300,000

Annual debt service on the $300,000 purchase money mortgage is $43,206 ($3,600.50/mo. × 12), based on an interest rate of 12% and a 15-year amortization term.

Sale Price		$1,100,000
Sale Costs (6%)	$ 66,000	
Adjusted Basis	+500,000	
Adjusted Basis at Sale		−566,000
Capital Gain		$ 534,000
Down Payment		$ 200,000
Mortgage Balance	$600,000	
Adjusted Basis at Sale	−566,000	
Excess Mortgage Over Basis		+34,000
Total Taxable Portion of Down Payment		$ 234,000
Sale Price		$1,100,000
Excess Mortgage Over Basis (from above)		+34,000
Mortgage Balance		−600,000
Contract Price		$ 534,000
Capital Gain		$ 534,000
Contract Price		÷534,000
Portion of Gain Reportable		100%

After-Tax Cash Flows for Offer A			
Year	0	1	2
Taxable Income			
Excess Mortgage Over Basis	$ 34,000		
Principal	200,000	$ 7,614	$ 8,582
Taxable Portion of Principal*	93,600	3,046	3,433
Interest	0	35,590	34,624
Total	$ 93,600	$38,626	$38,057
Marginal Tax Rate	×50%	×50%	×50%
Tax from Sale	$ 46,800	$19,318	$19,028
Cash Flows After Tax			
Down Payment	$200,000		
less: Sale Costs	66,000		
Proceeds Before Taxes	$134,000		
Annual Debt Service		$43,206	$43,206
less: Tax from Sale	46,800	19,318	19,028
Cash Flows After Taxes	$ 87,200	$23,888	$24,178
Year	3	4	5
Taxable Income			
Principal	$ 9,670	$10,897	$ 12,278 +250,957
Taxable Portion of Principal*	3,868	4,359	105,294
Interest	33,536	32,309	30,928
Total	$37,404	$36,668	$136,222
Marginal Tax Rate	×50%	×50%	×50%
Tax from Sale	$18,702	$18,334	$ 68,111
Annual Debt Service	$43,206	$43,206	$ 43,206 +250,957
less: Tax from Sale	18,702	18,334	68,111
Cash Flows After Taxes	$24,504	$24,872	$226,052

*Principal plus excess mortgage over basis times portion of gain reportable of 100% times taxable portion of long-term capital gain of 40%. Under the 1984 tax act, *all* excess recapture must be recognized in the year of sale, regardless of the amount of principal received that year.

Comparing offer

The tables on pages 362–65 reduce both offers to a stream of cash flows after taxes for comparison.

Analysis of Offer B		
Sale Price	$1,075,000	
Mortgage Balance	−600,000	
Cash Down Payment	−250,000	
Purchase Money Mortgage	$ 225,000	

Annual debt service on the $225,000 purchase money mortgage is $34,140 ($2,845.00/mo. × 12), based on an interest rate of 15% and a 30-year amortization term.

Sale Price		$1,075,000
Sale Costs (6%)	$ 64,500	
Adjusted Basis	+500,000	
Adjusted Basis at Sale		−564,500
Capital Gain		$ 510,500
Down Payment		$ 250,000
Mortgage Balance	$600,000	
Adjusted Basis at Sale	−564,500	
Excess Mortgage Over Basis		+35,500
Total Taxable Portion of Down Paymen.		$ 285,500
Sale Price		$1,075,000
Excess Mortgage Over Basis (from above)		+35,500
Mortgage Balance		−600,000
Contract Price		$ 510,500

Each year 100 percent of principal payments will be reportable because the capital gain is equal to the contract price. This will always be the case when there is excess mortgage over basis at the time of sale.

After-Tax Cash Flows for Offer B			
Year	0	1	2
Taxable Income			
Excess Mortgage Over Basis	$ 35,500		
Principal	250,000	$ 418	$ 485
Taxable Portion of Principal*	114,200	167	194
Interest	0	33,722	33,655
Total	$114,200	$33,889	$33,849
Marginal Tax Rate	×50%	×50%	×50%
Tax from Sale	$ 57,100	$16,945	$16,924
Cash Flows After Tax			
Down Payment	$250,000		
less: Sale Costs	64,500		
Proceeds Before Taxes	$185,500		
Annual Debt Service		$34,140	$34,140
less: Tax from Sale	57,100	16,945	16,924
Cash Flows After Tax	$128,400	$17,195	$17,216
Year	3	4	5
Taxable Income			
Principal	$ 563	$ 654	$ 759 +222,121
Taxable Portion of Principal*	225	261	89,152
Interest	33,557	33,486	33,381
Total	$33,802	$33,748	$122,533
Marginal Tax Rate	×50%	×50%	×50%
Tax from Sale	$16,901	$16,874	$ 61,267
Annual Debt Service	$34,140	$34,140	$ 34,140 +222,121
less: Tax from Sale	16,901	16,874	61,267
Cash Flows After Tax	$17,239	$17,266	$194,995

*Principal plus excess mortgage over basis times portion of gain reportable of 100% times taxable portion of long term capital gain of 40%.

The cash flows after taxes from each offer and the differential cash flows are summarized in the following table:

EOY	Offer A	Offer B	A−B
0	$ 87,200	$128,400	$(41,200)
1	23,888	17,195	6,693
2	24,178	17,216	6,962
3	24,504	17,239	7,265
4	24,872	17,266	7,606
5	226,052	194,995	31,057

Conclusion

Offer A has a higher sale price, a smaller cash down payment, a larger purchase money loan amount at a lower interest rate and is amortized over a shorter term than Offer B. As a result, Offer A produces a smaller initial cash flow after tax and then greater cash flows after tax for the next five years. The IRR on the differential cash flows (summarized in the table above) is 10.42 percent. By forgoing the difference of $41,200 if accepting Offer A, the seller will receive 10.42 percent after tax on the future differential cash flows. Therefore, if all else is equal, Offer A will produce greater future wealth if cash flows after taxes can be invested at an after-tax rate of return less than 10.42 percent. Offer B will produce greater future wealth if cash flows after taxes can be invested at an after-tax rate of return greater than 10.42 percent.

To demonstrate this conclusion, suppose that the seller will invest cash flows at a 12-percent rate of return after tax. Since 12 percent is greater than 10.42 percent, Offer B should produce the greater future wealth. The future values of the cash flows after taxes (CFAT) at the end of Year Five, invested at 12 percent after taxes, are summarized in the following table:

	Offer A		Offer B	
EOY	CFAT	FV @ 12%, EOY 5	CFAT	FV @ 12%, EOY 5
0	$ 87,200	$153,676	$128,400	$226,285
1	23,888	37,588	17,195	27,057
2	24,178	33,968	17,216	24,187
3	24,504	30,738	17,239	21,625
4	24,872	27,857	17,266	19,338
5	226,052	226,052	194,995	194,995
Total		$509,879		$513,487

Note that Offer B does indeed produce greater future wealth than does Offer A when the cash flows are invested at a rate greater than the IRR on the differential cash flows. The sale price and terms of the sale are required to estimate the cash flows after taxes from the proposed transactions. Once the offers have been reduced to cash flows, the seller may base a decision on the results of a differential cash flow analysis. It should be noted that an offer for an outright cash sale could also be considered within the framework of this analysis.

Case Study 6
Measuring the impact of refinancing

A common rule of thumb used by investors in years past has been to refinance whenever possible and thus to use maximum leverage. If analyzed as an alternative investment decision, however, it might become obvious that refinancing may not always maximize the investor's future wealth.

Situation

Consider a property that has a value of $100,000 now, net operating income of $11,000 and an existing loan of $50,000 at 8-percent interest with monthly payments of $465. The owner's basis is $40,000. The straight line cost recovery amount is $2,000 per year. At the end of five years, the cost of sale will be 7 percent of the sale price. The owner's marginal tax bracket is 40 percent. Assume there is no increase in net operating income and a 5-percent annual increase in value. The anticipated holding period is five years.

A new loan is available for 75 percent of the property value with 12-percent interest, a 25-year term and monthly payments. The origination fee of this loan is three points (3 percent of the loan amount).

Reducing alternatives to cash flows

The analytical process is the same as in Case Study Five. The first step is to reduce the alternatives to their cash flows after tax. The next step is to isolate the differential cash flows and then calculate the IRR on the differential cash flows.

The investment base, or End of Year 0 cash flow, without refinancing is as follows:

Sale Price	$100,000
less: Mortgage	50,000
less: Cost of sale	7,000
less: Tax on sale	8,480
Proceeds of sale after tax EOY 0	$ 34,520

(continued on next page.)

Calculation of Tax on Sale

Gross sale price		$100,000
Adjusted basis	$40,000	
Plus: Cost of sale	7,000	
Adjusted basis at sale		−47,000
Long-term capital gain		$ 53,000
		×40%
Taxable portion of long-term capital gain		$ 21,200
Marginal tax rate		×40%
Tax on sale		$ 8,480

The cash flows after tax without refinancing the property are as follows:

| End of Year | Without Refinance | | | | |
	1	2	3	4	5
Net Operating Income	$11,000	$11,000	$11,000	$11,000	$11,000
Interest	3,941	3,805	3,657	3,498	3,325
Cost Recovery	2,000	2,000	2,000	2,000	2,000
Taxable Income	$ 5,059	$ 5,195	$ 5,343	$ 5,502	$ 5,675
Net Operating Income	$11,000	$11,000	$11,000	$11,000	$11,000
Annual Debt Service	5,580	5,580	5,580	5,580	5,580
Cash Flow Before Tax	$ 5,420	$ 5,420	$ 5,420	$ 5,420	$ 5,420
Tax 40%	2,024	2,078	2,137	2,201	2,270
Cash Flow After Tax	$ 3,396	$ 3,342	$ 3,283	$ 3,219	$ 3,150

Proceeds of Sale After Tax EOY 5:

Sale price		$127,628
less: Mortgage balance EOY 5		−40,326
less: Cost of sale		−8,934
less: Tax from sale		−14,191
Proceeds of sale after tax EOY 5		$ 64,177

Calculation of Tax on Sale:

Gross sale price		$127,628
Adjusted basis BOY 0	$40,000	
less: Cost recovery		
(5 × $2,000)	−10,000	
plus: Cost of sale	+8,934	
Adjusted basis at sale		−38,934
Long-term capital gain		$ 88,694
		×40%
Taxable portion of long-term capital gain		$ 35,478
Marginal tax rate		×40%
Tax on sale		$ 14,191

The new loan amount is greater than the existing loan balance. Proceeds of the new loan will first be used to repay the underlying loan. The difference between the new loan amount and the existing loan balance is a tax-free cash flow received by the owner immediately—that is, at End of Year 0. Since the owner receives a portion of equity in the form of proceeds of refinancing, the investment base is reduced. The revised investment base is calculated below:

New loan amount	$75,000
Orgination fee (3% × $75,000)	−2,250
Net loan proceeds	$72,750
Existing loan balance EOY 0	−50,000
Net proceeds of refinancing	$22,750
Investment base before refinancing	$34,520
Net proceeds of refinancing	−22,750
Investment base after refinancing	$11,770

	With Refinance				
End of Year	1	2	3	4	5
Net Operating Income	$11,000	$11,000	$11,000	$11,000	$11,000
Interest	8,973	8,909	8,836	8,755	8,663
Cost Recovery	2,000	2,000	2,000	2,000	2,000
Taxable Income	$ 27	$ 91	$ 164	$ 245	$ 337
Net Operating Income	$11,000	$11,000	$11,000	$11,000	$11,000
Annual Debt Service	9,479	9,479	9,479	9,479	9,479
Cash Flow Before Tax	$ 1,521	$ 1,521	$ 1,521	$ 1,521	$ 1,521
Tax 40%	11	36	66	98	135
Cash Flow After Tax	$ 1,510	$ 1,485	$ 1,455	$ 1,423	$ 1,386

Proceeds of Sale After Tax End of Year 5:

Sale price	$127,628
less: Mortgage balance EOY 5	71,740
Cost of sale	8,934
Tax from sale	14,191
Proceeds of sale after tax	$ 32,763

Tax is the same as without refinancing because financing does not affect the amount of capital gain.

The following table is a summary of cash flows after taxes from both alternatives and the differential cash flows:

EOY	Without Refinance A	With Refinance B	Differential A–B
0	($34,520)	($11,770)	(22,750)
1	3,396	1,510	1,886
2	3,342	1,485	1,857
3	3,283	1,455	1,828
4	3,219	1,423	1,796
5	3,150 + 64,177	1,386 + 32,763	33,178
IRR	20.90%	31.60%	13.84%

Conclusion

Refinancing will reduce the investment base and increase the loan-to-value ratio. Since the investor benefits from positive leverage, additional leverage will increase the IRR. The investor is faced with the decision to do nothing and receive an after-tax yield of 20.90 percent on $34,520 or refinance the property and receive an after-tax yield of 31.60 percent on $11,770. Based on IRR alone, refinancing would appear to be the better alternative. However, the $22,750 net proceeds of refinancing should be considered.

Refinancing reduces the investment base. There is a size disparity between the two initial investment amounts. Subsequent cash flows after taxes with refinancing are less because the annual debt service is increased and the loan balance at the end of Year Five is greater with the new loan. The dollar cost to the investor of taking the $22,750 is the differential cash flows. The IRR of the differential cash flows is 13.84 percent. To maximize future wealth, the property should be refinanced at this time if the net proceeds of refinancing can be reinvested at an after-tax yield in excess of 13.84 percent. Stated another way, the opportunity cost of withdrawing capital ($22,750, in this case) is 13.84 percent. It is as if the investor borrowed $22,750 at an after-tax interest rate of 13.84 percent. To get positive leverage, these funds must be invested at a greater rate of return.

To illustrate this conclusion, assume that the most suitable investment alternative for the net proceeds of refinancing will produce an after-tax rate of return of 12 percent. In addition, all cash flows after taxes will also be reinvested at an after-tax rate of 12 percent. It should be noted that these rates may be different and changed each year according to assumptions consistent with the investor's financial planning. The future wealth from all cash flows after taxes are summarized in the following table:

EOY	Without Refinance CFAT	FV EOY 5 @ 12%	With Refinance CFAT	FV EOY 5 @ 12%	Net Proceeds of Refinance
0	($34,520)		($11,770)		($22,750)
1	3,396	$ 5,344	1,510	$ 2,376	
2	3,342	4,695	1,485	2,086	
3	3,283	4,118	1,455	1,825	
4	3,219	3,605	1,423	1,594	
5	3,150	67,327	1,386	34,149	40,093
	+64,177		+32,763		
Total		$85,089		$42,030 +40,093 =$82,123	

As expected, with an after-tax reinvestment rate less than the IRR on the differential cash flows, it is better not to refinance the property. In both cases, the total initial investments are the same. With refinancing, the total initial investments are the investment base in the property plus the net proceeds of refinancing. The future wealth End of Year Five is the sum of the future values of all cash flows invested at 12-percent after tax. Future wealth End of Year Five for the refinancing alternative includes the future value of net proceeds of refinancing invested at 12-percent after tax.

The future wealth position of the two alternatives can be graphed using alternative after-tax opportunity rates of return (see Figure 34). Calculation of several data points on this graph are summarized below. Note that the sum of cash flows after tax is equal to the total future value if the reinvestment rate is 0 percent.

		Without Refinance			
		FV at End of Year 5			
EOY	CFAT	5%	10%	15%	20%
1	$ 3,396	$ 4,128	$ 4,972	$ 5,940	$ 7,042
2	3,342	3,869	4,448	5,083	5,775
3	3,283	3,620	3,972	4,342	4,728
4	3,219	3,380	3,541	3,702	3,863
5	3,150	3,150	3,150	3,150	3,150
Sale 5	64,177	64,177	64,177	64,177	64,177
Total	$80,567	$82,234	$84,260	$86,394	$88,735

(continued on next page)

With Refinance					
		FV at End of Year 5			
EOY	CFAT	5%	10%	15%	20%
1	$ 1,510	$ 1,835	$ 2,211	$ 2,641	$ 3.131
2	1,485	1,719	1,977	2,259	2,566
3	1,455	1,604	1,761	1,924	2,095
4	1,423	1,494	1,565	1,636	1,708
5	1,386	1,386	1,386	1,386	1,386
Sale 5	32,763	32,763	32,763	32,763	32,763
FV of Net Proceeds of Refinancing EOY 5	22,750	29,035	36,639	45,758	56,609
TOTAL	$62,772	$69,836	$78,302	$88,367	$100,258

The wealth positions at End of Year Five for various rates are plotted on the Figure 34 graph. The curves in Figure 34 intercept where the after-tax rate of return on reinvested cash flows equal 13.84 percent, the IRR on the differential cash flows. Figure 34 illustrates the original conclusions: to maximize future wealth, under the assumptions of this case study, the investor would refinance the property if the opportunity cost of capital exceeds 13.84 percent.

This analysis may also be useful in choosing among alternative loans available for refinancing. The interest rate, loan-to-value ratio, holding period and other variables are required to reduce the problem to cash flows after tax. Differential cash flow analysis is then applied to the alternative cash flows as we have done here.

Case Study 7
Own/lease decisions

Another useful application of differential cash flow analysis is in making the decision to own or to lease. The occupancy and/or use of any asset can be accomplished by either buying/owning the asset or by leasing it. Many individual investors or firms make the own-versus-lease decision by looking at lease payments as an operating cost. A more meaningful analysis is to view the outlays of capital for owning or leasing, either on the first or subsequent time periods, as investments. This allows the decision maker to approach

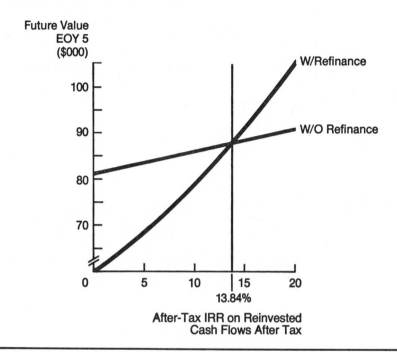

Figure 34 Future Wealth Position

the problem as one of selecting among investment alternatives. As a first step, each alternative must be reduced to after-tax cash flows. Then these flows must be compared as to their size and timing.

There are other considerations involved when deciding between owning or leasing which are not investment-related. Leasing or lease financing, as it is sometimes called, permits the user to acquire an asset and finance it in the same process. Leasing is similar to 100-percent financing and has the characteristics of an interest-only loan. Leasing may not change the capital structure of a firm's balance sheet, but most accounting procedures do include provisions for capitalizing long-term leases so that they appear as long-term obligations. A lease obligation has a lower priority in bankruptcy than debt financing. Leasing may also involve fewer debt restrictions than a mortgage loan or a deed of trust.

Generally, in leasing the total amount of the payment is deductible in computing taxes, whereas only the interest portion of a loan payment is deductible. In real estate ownership, no cost recovery deduction is allowed on the land portion of the property. In leasing, the total cost of use and/or occupancy—rent—is deducted as an ordinary business expense. Finally, although leasing generally requires a lower initial outlay than debt financing, the lessee usually gives up any reversion at the end of the lease term.

373

There are certain tax caveats that must be considered when choosing the lease alternative. These have to do with term, reasonable rate of return and option of purchase. The IRS may determine that the "lease" is actually a "financing" agreement. This would limit certain tax deductions asssociated with the lease. Also, under certain conditions the lessor may pass investment tax credits through to the lessee. This aspect may be a critical factor in the buy/lease decision. It is always best to obtain competent tax advice with any transaction, but special care must be taken when arranging a lease.

Situation

This case study will deal primarily with the investment decision-making process. The following assumptions are used throughout this analysis:

Cost of asset	$100,000
Property income	None, property is occupied by user
Available financing	75% loan @ 12%, 25-year amortization, monthly payments
Lease term	10 years
Rental payments	$1,000 per month net to owner for 5 years with 15% increase 2nd 5 years
Value EOY 10	$150,000
Investor's marginal tax bracket	48%
After-tax opportunity cost of money	12%
Cost recovery	18-year real property, straight line method
Building/land allocation	80%/20%
Holding period	10 Years
Cost of sale EOY 10	7% of sale price

Present value technique

There are two approaches to making the lease/own decision: the present value (or cost) approach and the differential cash flow approach. The present value approach involves three basic steps:

1. Estimate cash outflows associated with both the lease and purchase alternatives.

2. Discount these cash flows at an appropriate rate. The discount rate may be the firm's cost of capital or opportunity cost of capital. Use of the latter is more common since capital available for investment must be used for acquisition of the asset. A hybrid weighted cost of capital, including return to equity reflecting the appropriate debt leverage, may be used.

3. Decision rule: the alternative with the least present value is most desirable since the cash flows are the respective after-tax costs of each alternative.

Figure 35

Cash Flow Analysis

For __Own vs. Lease__

Purpose __Ownership Alternative__

Date _____

Purchase Price __100,000__

Encumbrances __75,000__

Investment __25,000__

Mortgage Data

Encumbrances	Beginning Balance	Remaining Term	Number of Payments Per Year	Interest Rate	Payment	Annual Debt Service	Remarks
1	1st Mortgage	75,000	25 yrs	12	12%	789.92	9,479	
2	2nd Mortgage							
3	3rd Mortgage							

	Year: 1	Year: 2	Year: 3	Year: 4	Year: 5	EOY	Mortgage Balance
Ownership Analysis of Property Income:	**Taxable Income**						1st Mortgage
4 Gross Scheduled Income							
5 Less: Vcy. & Credit Losses							
6 Gross Operating Income							
7 − Operating Expenses							
8 Net Operating Income	-0-	-0-	-0-	-0-	-0-		
9 − Non-Operating Expense							
10 − Interest − 1st Mortgage	8,973	8,909	8,836	8,755	8,663		2nd Mortgage
11 − Interest − 2nd Mortgage							
12 − Interest − 3rd Mortgage							
13 − Cost Recovery	4,000	4,800	4,800	4,800	4,800		
14 Real Est. Taxable Income	(12,973)	(13,709)	(13,636)	(13,555)	(13,463)		
	Cash Flows						
15 Net Operating Income	-0-	-0-	-0-	-0-	-0-		3rd Mortgage
16 − Annual Debt Service	9,479	9,479	9,479	9,479	9,479		
17 − Funded Reserves							
18 − Capital Additions							
19 Cash Flow before Taxes	(9,479)	(9,479)	(9,479)	(9,479)	(9,479)		
20 − Minimum Tax							
21 − Tax Liability on Real Est.	(6,227)	(6,580)	(6,545)	(6,506)	(6,462)		
22 Cash Flow after Taxes	(3,252)	(2,899)	(2,934)	(2,973)	(3,017)		

Analysis of Sale Proceeds   Year:

Adjusted Basis			Excess Cost Recovery (CR)			Tax Liability on Sale		
23 Original Basis			Total CR			Excess Recapture Tax		
24 + Capital Improvements			S/L CR			Capital Gain Tax		
25 − Cost Recovery			Excess CR*			Tax Liability on Sale		
26 − Partial Sales			Exc. CR Carryover					
27 AB			Gain			Sale Proceeds		
28			Sale Price			Sale Price		
			− Cost of Sale			− Costs of Sale		
			− AB			− Mortgage		
			Gain			Proceeds before Taxes		
			− Excess CR			− Tax Liability on Sale		
			Capital Gain			Proceeds after Taxes		

*NOTE: On non-residential property, if accelerated CR system is elected, all CR claimed is recaptured as ordinary income in the year of sale.

REALTORS NATIONAL MARKETING INSTITUTE* of the NATIONAL ASSOCIATION OF REALTORS*, 1982 All rights reserved 2-81-F812

The statements and figures presented herein, while not guaranteed are secured from sources we believe authoritative

Prepared by_____

Figure 35 (continued)

Cash Flow Analysis

For __Own vs. Lease__
Purpose __Ownership Alternative__
Date _____

Purchase Price __100,000__
Encumbrances __75,000__
Investment __25,000__

Mortgage Data

Encumbrances	Beginning Balance	Remaining Term	Number of Payments Per Year	Interest Rate	Payment	Annual Debt Service	Remarks
1 1st Mortgage	75,000	25yrs	12	12%	789.92	9,479	
2 2nd Mortgage							
3 3rd Mortgage							

	Year: 6	Year: 7	Year: 8	Year: 9	Year: 10	EOY	Mortgage Balance
Ownership Analysis of Property Income:		**Taxable Income**					1st Mortgage
4 Gross Scheduled Income							
5 Less: Vcy. & Credit Losses							
6 Gross Operating Income							
7 – Operating Expenses							
8 Net Operating Income	-0-	-0-	-0-	-0-	-0-		
9 – Non-Operating Expense						10	65,817
10 – Interest – 1st Mortgage	8,559	8,443	8,311	8,163	7,996	2nd Mortgage	
11 – Interest – 2nd Mortgage							
12 – Interest – 3rd Mortgage							
13 – Cost Recovery	4,800	4,800	4,800	4,800	4,800		
14 Real Est. Taxable Income	(13,359)	(13,243)	(13,111)	(12,963)	(12,796)		
		Cash Flows					
15 Net Operating Income	-0-	-0-	-0-	-0-	-0-	3rd Mortgage	
16 – Annual Debt Service	9,479	9,479	9,479	9,479	9,479		
17 – Funded Reserves							
18 – Capital Additions							
19 Cash Flow before Taxes	(9,479)	(9,479)	(9,479)	(9,479)	(9,479)		
20 – Minimum Tax							
21 – Tax Liability on Real Est.	(6,412)	(6,357)	(6,293)	(6,222)	(6,142)		
22 Cash Flow after Taxes	(3,067)	(3,122)	(3,186)	(3,257)	(3,337)		

Analysis of Sale Proceeds　　Year:

Adjusted Basis		Excess Cost Recovery (CR)		Tax Liability on Sale	
23 Original Basis	100,000	Total CR	47,200	Excess Recapture Tax	-0-
24 + Capital Improvements		S/L CR	47,200	Capital Gain Tax .192	16,646
25 – Cost Recovery	47,200	Excess CR*	-0-	Tax Liability on Sale	16,646
26 – Partial Sales		Exc. CR Carryover			
27 AB	52,800	Gain		Sale Proceeds	
28		Sale Price	150,000	Sale Price	150,000
		– Cost of Sale	10,500	– Costs of Sale	10,500
		– AB	52,800	– Mortgage	65,817
		Gain	86,700	Proceeds before Taxes	73,683
		– Excess CR	-0-	– Tax Liability on Sale	16,646
		Capital Gain	86,700	Proceeds after Taxes	57,037

*NOTE: On non-residential property, if accelerated CR system is elected, all CR claimed is recaptured as ordinary income in the year of sale.

The statements and figures presented herein, while not guaranteed, are secured from sources we believe authoritative

Prepared by _____

The ownership cash flows after tax are derived from a Cash Flow Analysis form (see Figure 35). Once the cash flows are derived for End of Year 0 to End of Year 10, including the tenth year proceeds of sale, the present value is established by discounting these cash flows at the after-tax opportunity cost of capital. In our example, this rate is 12 percent.

The ownership after-tax cash flows, as calculated on the Cash Flow Analysis form, are as follows:

EOY	$
0	($25,000)
1	(3,252)
2	(2,899)
3	(2,934)
4	(2,973)
5	(3,017)
6	(3,067)
7	(3,122)
8	(3,186)
9	(3,257)
10	(3,337) + $57,037

$\boxed{\text{PV}}$ = ($24,042)

The present value of all cash flows after tax, discounted at 12 percent, is ($24,042). Therefore, for an investor with opportunity to invest funds at a 12-percent after-tax rate, the after-tax cost of occupancy for ten years through the ownership alternative is $24,042 in today's dollars.

The after-tax cash flows from the leasing alternative, with the rent being paid in arrears, are calculated on another Cash Flow Analysis form (see Figure 36).

The leasing cash flows are as follows:

EOY	$
0	—0—
1	($6,240)
2	(6,240)
3	(6,240)
4	(6,240)
5	(6,240)
6	(7,176)
7	(7,176)
8	(7,176)
9	(7,176)
10	(7,176)

$\boxed{\text{PV}}$ = ($37,172)

Figure 36

Cash Flow Analysis

For _OWN vs. LEASE_

Purpose _LEASING ALTERNATIVE_

Date _____

Sales Price _____

Encumbrances _____

Investment _____

Mortgage Data

	Encumbrances	Beginning Balance	Remaining Term	Number of Payments Per Year	Interest Rate	Payment	Annual Debt Service	Remarks
1	1st Mortgage							
2	2nd Mortgage							
3	3rd Mortgage							

		Year: 1	Year: 2	Year: 3	Year: 4	Year: 5	EOY	Mortgage Balance
	Ownership Analysis of Property Income:		**Taxable Income**					
4	Gross Scheduled Income							1st Mortgage
5	Less: Vcy. & Credit Losses							
6	Gross Operating Income							
7	– Operating Expenses							
8	Net Operating Income	(12 000)	(12 000)	(12 000)	(12 000)	(12 000)		
9	– Non-Operating Expense							
10	– Interest – 1st Mortgage							2nd Mortgage
11	– Interest – 2nd Mortgage							
12	– Interest – 3rd Mortgage							
13	– Cost Recovery							
14	Real Est. Taxable Income	(12 000)	(12 000)	(12 000)	(12 000)	(12 000)		
			Cash Flows					
15	Net Operating Income	(12 000)	(12 000)	(12 000)	(12 000)	(12 000)		3rd Mortgage
16	– Annual Debt Service							
17	– Funded Reserves							
18	– Capital Additions							
19	Cash Flow before Taxes	(12 000)	(12 000)	(12 000)	(12 000)	(12 000)		
20	– Minimum Tax							
21	– Tax Liability on Real Est.	5 760	5 760	5 760	5 760	5 760		
22	Cash Flow after Taxes	6 240	6 240	6 240	6 240	6 240		

Analysis of Sale Proceeds   Year: _____

	Adjusted Basis		Excess Cost Recovery (CR)		Tax Liability on Sale	
23	Original Basis		Total CR		Excess Recapture Tax	
24	+ Capital Improvements		S/L CR		Capital Gain Tax	
25	– Cost Recovery		Excess CR		Tax Liability on Sale	
26	– Partial Sales		Exc. CR Carryover			
27	AB		Gain		Sale Proceeds	
28			Sale Price		Sale Price	
29			– Cost of Sale		– Costs of Sale	
30			– AB		– Mortgage	
31			Gain		Proceeds before Taxes	
32			– Excess		– Tax Liability on Sale	
33			Capital Gain		Proceeds after Taxes	

The statements and figures presented herein, while not guaranteed, are secured from sources we believe authoritative.

Prepared by _____

Figure 36 (continued)

Cash Flow Analysis

For_____

Purpose_____

Date_____

Sales Price_____

Encumbrances_____

Investment_____

Mortgage Data

	Encumbrances	Beginning Balance	Remaining Term	Number of Payments Per Year	Interest Rate	Payment	Annual Debt Service	Remarks
1	1st Mortgage							
2	2nd Mortgage							
3	3rd Mortgage							

	Ownership Analysis of Property Income:	Year: 6	Year: 7	Year: 8	Year: 9	Year: 10	EOY	Mortgage Balance
	Taxable Income							
4	Gross Scheduled Income							1st Mortgage
5	Less: Vcy. & Credit Losses							
6	Gross Operating Income							
7	− Operating Expenses							
8	Net Operating Income	13 800	13 800	13 800	13 800	13 800		
9	− Non-Operating Expense							
10	− Interest − 1st Mortgage							2nd Mortgage
11	− Interest − 2nd Mortgage							
12	− Interest − 3rd Mortgage							
13	− Cost Recovery							
14	Real Est. Taxable Income	13 800	13 800	13 800	13 800	13 800		
	Cash Flows							
15	Net Operating Income	13 800	13 800	13 800	13 800	13 800		3rd Mortgage
16	− Annual Debt Service							
17	− Funded Reserves							
18	− Capital Additions							
19	Cash Flow before Taxes	13 800	13 800	13 800	13 800	13 800		
20	− Minimum Tax							
21	− Tax Liability on Real Est.	6 624	6 624	6 624	6 624	6 624		
22	Cash Flow after Taxes	7 176	7 176	7 176	7 176	7 176		

Analysis of Sale Proceeds   Year:

	Adjusted Basis			Excess Cost Recovery (CR)			Tax Liability on Sale		
23	Original Basis			Total CR			Excess Recapture Tax		
24	+ Capital Improvements			S/L CR			Capital Gain Tax		
25	− Cost Recovery			Excess CR			Tax Liability on Sale		
26	− Partial Sales			Exc. CR Carryover					
27	AB			**Gain**			**Sale Proceeds**		
28				Sale Price			Sale Price		
29				− Cost of Sale			− Costs of Sale		
30				− AB			− Mortgage		
31				Gain			Proceeds before Taxes		
32				− Excess			− Tax Liability on Sale		
33				Capital Gain			Proceeds after Taxes		

● REALTORS NATIONAL MARKETING INSTITUTE® of the NATIONAL ASSOCIATION OF REALTORS® , 1981

The statements and figures presented herein, while not guaranteed, are secured from sources we believe authoritative.

Prepared by_____

The present value for all cash flows after tax discounted at 12 percent is ($37,172). Therefore, an investor who has opportunities to invest funds at a 12-percent after-tax rate has an after-tax cost of occupancy for ten years through the leasing alternative of $37,172.

The comparison can now be made between the present values of owning and leasing. The present values of both alternatives are negative, or costs. Therefore, the least cost is the best alternative. In this case, the ownership cost of $24,042 is less than the leasing cost of $37,172. Therefore, with a 12-percent after-tax opportunity cost of capital, owning is a better alternative than leasing.

Differential cash flow technique

The other approach to making the decision of own versus lease is the differential cash flow technique. The procedure is to determine the difference between the ownership cash flows and the leasing cash flows and then to calculate a rate of return on the differential cash flows. This rate of return is the after-tax opportunity cost of capital which would make the investor indifferent to either alternative. The procedure is illustrated as follows:

Summary of Cash Flows After Tax and Differential Cash Flows			
EOY	Ownership	Lease	Differential
0	($25,000)	—0—	($25,000)
1	(3,252)	($6,240)	2,988
2	(2,899)	(6,240)	3,341
3	(2,934)	(6,240)	3,306
4	(2,973)	(6,240)	3,267
5	(3,017)	(6,240)	3,223
6	(3,067)	(7,176)	4,109
7	(3,122)	(7,176)	4,054
8	(3,186)	(7,176)	3,990
9	(3,257)	(7,176)	3,919
10	(3,337) + 57,037	(7,176)	$60,876
			IRR = 19.87%

By owning the real estate in this example, the out-of-pocket net investment is the down payment of $25,000. The difference between the after-tax cash flows of ownership and the after-tax cash flows of leasing are the cash flow benefits of the net investment of $25,000 in the real estate. In other words, the investor would have an annual cash flow savings if the property were purchased instead of leased because the after-tax cost to own is less than the after-tax cost to lease. The savings is the result of an additional initial investment of $25,000 to buy the property. The cash flow savings produce an after-tax rate of return of 18.97 percent on the initial investment. Therefore, the investor should purchase the property if the after-tax opportunity cost of capital is less than 18.97 percent.

Differential cash flow analysis is useful when choosing between alternatives which produce cost savings. For example, the technique could be applied to alternative heating, ventilating and air conditioning systems where a more expensive system would produce a cost savings in energy consumption in the future. In this type of case study, future wealth is maximized by choosing the alternative which will cost less *after the time value of money has been considered.*

Case Study 8
Differential cash flow analysis of cost recovery

The method of cost recovery used on income-producing real estate improvements may have a substantial influence on the after-tax yield and future wealth of the investor. Comparison of internal rate of return of cash flows after taxes for alternative cost recovery schedules may not lead the analyst to the appropriate conclusion because such a comparison implicitly assumes all cash flows are reinvested at the internal rate. Differential cash flow analysis can overcome this problem and also isolate the critical variables.

Situation
Consider this new residential income property:

Cost	$160,000
NOI	$15,750 EOY 1, NOI will increase 5% per year
Land	$32,500
Improvements	$127,500
Holding period	5 years
Sale price EOY 5	$204,205 (5% appreciation per year)
Cost of sale EOY 5	$12,252 (6% of sale price EOY 5)
Financing	$120,000, 12% fixed rate, 25-year amortization with monthly payments of $1,263.87
Equity investment:	$40,000 ($160,000 − $120,000)

The investor in this instance has a high ordinary income which is taxed at the marginal rate of 40 percent. The gain on sale will push the owner into the maximum tax bracket; thus recapture will also be taxed at a marginal rate of 50 percent.

Cash flow analysis
The two cash flow analyses shown in Figures 37 and 38 have been prepared under the preceding assumptions. Only the method of cost recovery

is different. Cash Flow Analysis A (Figure 37) uses the straight line method and Cash Flow Analysis B (Figure 38) uses the accelerated method.

The cash flows and differential cash flows are summarized below:

	Analysis A	Analysis B	A—B
EOY	S/L	Accelerated	Differential
0	($40,000)	($40,000)	—0—
1	2,576	4,616	($2,040)
2	3,518	5,048	(1,530)
3	3,968	4,988	(1,020)
4	4,437	4,947	(510)
5	4,925 + 63,383	5,435 + 56,370	6,503
IRR	17.51%	18.10%	8.32%

The after-tax yields are within one percentage point for either alternative. IRR alone, therefore, may not indicate the most appropriate strategy. Notice in Figures 37 and 38 that the cash flows before taxes are the same for each cash flow analysis, including the proceeds of sale before taxes. The only source of the differential cash flows are the after-tax savings caused by the cost recovery deductions. Cash flows after taxes from operations of the property are greater with the accelerated cost recovery method during the holding period. However, the sale proceeds after taxes are less if the accelerated method is used. This occurs because the tax savings from the accelerated cost recovery is 40 percent for years with negative taxable income, but cost recovery recapture is taxed at the maximum rate of 50-percent upon the sale of the property.

The IRR of the differential cash flows is 8.32 percent. This is the return on forgoing larger cash flows each year which would result from using the accelerated cost recovery method in order to receive greater proceeds after taxes in the year of sale by using the straight line method. The investor must reinvest the cash flows after taxes at an after-tax rate in excess of 8.32 percent in order for the accelerated method to maximize future wealth. Conversely, if cash flows are invested at a rate less than 8.32 percent, the straight line method will produce greater future wealth.

To illustrate, assume cash flows are reinvested at an after-tax rate of 10-percent. The future wealth amounts for each alternative are summarized in the table on page 385.

Figure 37

Cash Flow Analysis

For **Cash Flow Analysis A**

Purpose **Straight Line Method**

Date _____

Purchase Price **160,000**

Encumbrances **120,000**

Investment **40,000**

Mortgage Data

	Encumbrances	Beginning Balance	Remaining Term	Number of Payments Per Year	Interest Rate	Payment	Annual Debt Service	Remarks
1	1st Mortgage	120,000	25 yrs	12	12%	1,263.87	15,166	Fixed Rate
2	2nd Mortgage							
3	3rd Mortgage							

	Ownership Analysis of Property Income:	Year: 1	Year: 2	Year: 3	Year: 4	Year: 5	EOY	Mortgage Balance
		Taxable Income						
4	Gross Scheduled Income							1st Mortgage
5	Less: Vcy. & Credit Losses							
6	Gross Operating Income							
7	– Operating Expenses							
8	Net Operating Income	15,750	16,538	17,364	18,233	19,144		
9	– Non-Operating Expense						5	114,784
10	– Interest – 1st Mortgage	14,356	14,254	14,138	14,008	13,861	2nd Mortgage	
11	– Interest – 2nd Mortgage							
12	– Interest – 3rd Mortgage							
13	– Cost Recovery	6,375	7,650	7,650	7,650	7,650		
14	Real Est Taxable Income	(4,981)	(5,366)	(4,424)	(3,425)	(2,367)		
		Cash Flows						
15	Net Operating Income	15,750	16,538	17,364	18,233	19,144	3rd Mortgage	
16	– Annual Debt Service	15,166	15,166	15,166	15,166	15,166		
17	– Funded Reserves							
18	– Capital Additions							
19	Cash Flow before Taxes	584	1,372	2,198	3,067	3,978		
20	– Minimum Tax							
21	– Tax Liability on Real Est.	(1,992)	(2,146)	(1,770)	(1,370)	(947)		
22	Cash Flow after Taxes	2,576	3,518	3,868	4,437	4,925		

Analysis of Sale Proceeds

Year: _____

	Adjusted Basis		Excess Cost Recovery (CR)		Tax Liability on Sale	
23	Original Basis	160,000	Total CR	36,975	Excess Recapture Tax	-0-
24	+ Capital Improvements		S/L CR	36,975	Capital Gain Tax 20%	13,786
25	– Cost Recovery	36,975	Excess CR*	-0-	Tax Liability on Sale	13,786
26	– Partial Sales		Exc. CR Carryover			
27	AB	123,025		Gain		Sale Proceeds
28			Sale Price	204,205	Sale Price	204,205
			– Cost of Sale	12,252	– Costs of Sale	12,252
	*NOTE: On non-residential property, if accelerated CR system is elected, all CR claimed is recaptured as ordinary income in the year of sale.		– AB	123,025	– Mortgage	114,784
			Gain	68,928	Proceeds before Taxes	77,169
			– Excess CR	-0-	– Tax Liability on Sale	13,786
			Capital Gain	68,928	Proceeds after Taxes	63,383

The statements and figures presented herein, while not guaranteed, are secured from sources we believe authoritative

Prepared by_____

Figure 38

Cash Flow Analysis

For **Cash Flow Analysis B**
Purpose **Accelerated Method**
Date _____

Purchase Price **160,000**
Encumbrances **120,000**
Investment **40,000**

Mortgage Data

Encumbrances	Beginning Balance	Remaining Term	Number of Payments Per Year	Interest Rate	Payment	Annual Debt Service	Remarks
1 1st Mortgage	120,000	25yrs	12	12%	1,263.87	15,166	Fixed Rate
2 2nd Mortgage							
3 3rd Mortgage							

	Year: 1	Year: 2	Year: 3	Year: 4	Year: 5	EOY	Mortgage Balance
Ownership Analysis of Property Income:		**Taxable Income**					1st Mortgage
4 Gross Scheduled Income							
5 Less: Vcy. & Credit Losses							
6 Gross Operating Income							
7 – Operating Expenses							
8 Net Operating Income	15750	16538	17364	18233	19144		
9 – Non-Operating Expense						5	114784
10 – Interest – 1st Mortgage	14356	14254	14138	14008	13861	2nd Mortgage	
11 – Interest – 2nd Mortgage							
12 – Interest – 3rd Mortgage							
13 – Cost Recovery	11475	11475	10200	8925	8925		
14 Real Est Taxable Income	(10081)	(9191)	(6974)	(4700)	(3642)		
		Cash Flows					
15 Net Operating Income	15750	16538	17364	18233	19144	3rd Mortgage	
16 – Annual Debt Service	15166	15166	15166	15166	15166		
17 – Funded Reserves							
18 – Capital Additions							
19 Cash Flow before Taxes	584	1372	2198	3067	3978		
20 – Minimum Tax							
21 – Tax Liability on Real Est.	(4032)	(3676)	(2790)	(1880)	(1457)		
22 Cash Flow after Taxes	4616	5048	4988	4947	5435		

Analysis of Sale Proceeds   Year:

Adjusted Basis		Excess Cost Recovery (CR)		Tax Liability on Sale	
23 Original Basis	160000	Total CR	51000	Excess Recapture Tax 50%	7013
24 + Capital Improvements		S/L CR	36975	Capital Gain Tax 20%	13786
25 – Cost Recovery	51000	Excess CR*	14025	Tax Liability on Sale	20799
26 – Partial Sales		Exc. CR Carryover			
27 AB	109000	Gain		Sale Proceeds	
28		Sale Price	204205	Sale Price	204205
		– Cost of Sale	12252	– Costs of Sale	12252
*NOTE: On non-residential property, if accelerated CR system is elected, all CR claimed is recaptured as ordinary income in the year of sale.		– AB	109000	– Mortgage	114784
		Gain	82953	Proceeds before Taxes	77169
		– Excess CR	14025	– Tax Liability on Sale	20799
		Capital Gain	68928	Proceeds after Taxes	56370

The statements and figures presented herein, while not guaranteed are secured from sources we believe authoritative

Prepared by _____

	Analysis A (S/L)			Analysis B (Accelerated)	
EOY	Cash Flows After Taxes	Future Value EOY 5		Cash Flows After Taxes	Future Worth EOY 5
1	$2,576	$ 3,772		$4,616	$ 6,758
2	3,518	4,682		5,048	6,719
3	3,968	4,801		4,988	6,035
4	4,437	4,881		4,947	5,442
5	4,925 + 63,383	68,308		5,435 + 56,370	61,805
Total		$86,444			$86,759
IRR	17.51%			18.10%	

As expected with an after-tax reinvestment rate greater than 8.2 percent, the accelerated method produces the greater future wealth. IRR is the rate of return on each dollar that remains at risk in an investment. *Forgoing the greater annual cash flow from the accelerated method by using the straight line method is like investing the differential cash flows in the same property at the 17.51 percent rate.*

Cost recovery

The differential cash flows from operations in this example are the after-tax result of one variable—cost recovery. This analysis can be abbreviated by isolating cost recovery and deriving the same differential cash flows. The amount of cost recovery, the tax savings and differential tax savings are shown for each year in the table below:

	Analysis A (S/L)		Analysis B (Accelerated)		B — A
EOY	Cost Recovery	Tax Savings (40%)	Cost Recovery	Tax Savings (40%)	Differential Tax Savings
1	$ 6,375	$ 2,550	$11,475	$ 4,590	($2,040)
2	7,650	3,060	11,475	4,590	(1,530)
3	7,650	3,060	10,200	4,080	(1,020)
4	7,650	3,060	8,925	3,570	(510)
5	7,650	3,060	8,925	3,570	(510)
Total	$36,975	$14,790	$51,000	$20,400	($5,610)

The sale proceeds before taxes are the same for both analyses. The difference in the tax liability on sale results from the 50-percent tax on the cost recovery recapture. (Refer to the lower right hand corner of the Cash Flow Analysis forms in Figures 37 and 38.)

The difference in the sale proceeds after taxes is:

A (S/L)	$63,383
B (accelerated)	− 56,370
A less B	$ 7,013

As expected, the difference is equal to the 50-percent tax on the cost recovery recapture:

Total cost recovery	$51,000
Less: Straight-line cost recovery	−36,975
Cost recovery recapture	$14,025
Tax rate	x50%
Tax on cost recovery recapture	$ 7,013

The total tax savings is $5,610 as shown in the table above. Each dollar of cost recovery in excess of straight line cost recovery which was deducted each year produced a tax savings of 40 cents because the marginal tax rate for each year of operations was 40 percent. The accumulated accelerated cost recovery in excess of straight line cost recovery is recaptured upon the disposition and taxed at 50 percent. The difference creates a differential cash flow to the investor. The investor may choose the annual differential tax savings at a marginal rate of 40 percent at the cost of the increased marginal tax rate of 50 percent on the total difference at the time of sale.

The differential tax savings are summarized below:

EOY	Differential Tax Savings
0	—0—
1	($2,040)
2	(1,530)
3	(1,020)
4	(510)
5	(510) + $7,013 = $6,503
IRR	8.32%

The differential cash flows after taxes from cost recovery are exactly the same as the differential cash flows after taxes on the entire property. Thus, the selection of appropriate cost recovery method can be made by isolating only the cost recovery cash flows.

386   Note that the yield on the differential cash flows after taxes from cost recovery is the result of the higher tax rate on the cost recovery recapture during the year of sale. The IRR on these differential cash flows will be 0 percent if the same tax rate is used on the cost recovery recapture. The cost recovery recapture is the total cost recovery in excess of straight line taken during the investment holding period for a residential property. If the annual tax savings is at the 40-percent rate and is then recaptured at the same rate, the total tax savings must equal the tax on the recapture. To demonstrate, the tax on the cost recovery recapture at a 40-percent marginal rate would be:

Cost recovery	$14,025
Tax rate	x40%
Tax on recapture	$ 5,610

The tax on recapture at 40 percent, $5,610, is equal to the total differential tax savings shown in the table on page 385.

The differential cash flows after tax from cost recovery under this new assumption are summarized below:

EOY	Differential Tax Savings
0	—0—
1	($2,040)
2	(1,530)
3	(1,020)
4	(510)
5	(510) + $5,610
IRR	0%

In this case, the accelerated method will produce the greater future wealth if the after-tax reinvestment rate exceeds 0 percent.

All cost recovery is recaptured upon the sale of nonresidential property if the accelerated cost recovery method is used. This will affect the amount of tax liability on the sale of the property. Cash flows from operations will not be affected. This will influence the choice of cost recovery method. To illustrate, assume that the property in this case study is *not* a residential property. All cash flows after taxes would be the same except the proceeds of sale after taxes if the accelerated method were used. The tax on sale, if the accelerated method were used, would be:

Total gain	$82,953
Total accelerated cost recovery	– 51,000
Long-term capital gain	$31,953
	×40%
Taxable portion of long-term capital gain	$12,781
Marginal tax rate	×50%
Tax on long-term capital gain (continued)	$ 6,391

Accelerated cost recovery recapture	$51,000	
Marginal tax rate	×50%	
Tax on cost recovery recapture		+25,500
Total tax on sale		$31,891
Proceeds after taxes would be:		
Proceeds before tax	$77,169	
Total tax on sale	− 31,891	
Proceeds after taxes	$45,278	

The cash flows after taxes and differential cash flows are summarized below:

EOY	S/L	Accelerated	Differential
0	($40,000)	($40,000)	—0—
1	2,860	4,616	($1,756)
2	3,292	5,048	(1,756)
3	3,741	4,988	(1,247)
4	4,210	4,947	(737)
5	4,698 + 63,695	4,924 + 45,915	17,554
IRR	17.41%	14.44%	47.00%

The increase in tax on sale as a result of cost recovery recapture on the nonresidential property has reduced the after-tax IRR from 17.99 percent to 14.44 percent. The IRR on the differential cash flows has increased from 8.42 percent to 47.00 percent. In this case, cash flows after taxes would have to be reinvested at an after-tax rate greater than 47.00 percent in order for the accelerated method to be the alternative which will maximize future wealth.

Conclusion

The use of the accelerated method of cost recovery will usually increase annual cash flows after taxes. The "cost" of the greater annual cash flows is the tax on cost recovery recapture at the time of sale. The investor may maximize future wealth by using straight line cost recovery if the cost recovery recapture is taxed at a higher rate than the tax rate on annual taxable income from operations. Straight line cost recovery will maximize future wealth if cash flows after taxes are reinvested at an after-tax rate *less* than the IRR on the differential cash flows after taxes of the straight line method less cash flows after taxes of the accelerated method. Use of IRR of cash flows after taxes for both alternatives may not indicate the appropriate cost recovery method.

Accelerated cost recovery may become more advantageous to the investor in several circumstances. Note from this example that the differential cash flows decline each year as the amount of the accelerated cost recovery deduction declines each tax year. The additional tax on the cost recovery is repaid at the end of the holding period or, perhaps, deferred in the case of an exchange. Therefore, an accelerated method may become more advantageous as the holding period is extended.

The marginal tax rate will affect the decision regarding the method of cost recovery. The appeal of the accelerated method will increase as the difference in the marginal tax rate on cost recovery recapture at the time of disposition and during each year of operation decreases. Since Congress can influence tax rates with tax legislation, the analyst may input some assumptions regarding the investor's anticipated taxable income. If taxable income is expected to decline over the years ahead, the marginal tax rates may go down and the accelerated method may be appealing. Conversely, if taxable income is expected to increase, the straight line method may be appropriate.

Cost recovery recapture also depends on the property type. All cost recovery is recaptured if the accelerated method is used on nonresidential properties. The accelerated cost recovery in excess of straight line is recaptured only on residential properties. The amount of cost recovery recapture which is subject to ordinary income tax rates will affect the decision to use straight line or accelerated cost recovery.

The method of cost recovery which will maximize future wealth depends on several factors. Anticipated future taxable income will indicate appropriate marginal tax rates. The "best" method of cost recovery which maximizes future wealth may be between the maximum amount permitted and the minimum amount allowable. Recall the straight line cost recovery for real property may be based upon an 18, 35, or 45-year cost recovery period. The longer terms will decrease the cost recovery deduction. Holding period will also influence the decision. Finally, the after-tax rate at which cash flows are reinvested affects the choice among alternative methods of cost recovery.

Chapter 14

Special Investment Problems

This chapter presents case studies designed to illustrate "special" problems or issues in real estate investments. Case Study 9 illustrates the process used to test the feasibility of exchanging properties. The Exchange Worksheet Form is used to organize information and to "balance" the equities among parties to a proposed exchange.

Case Study 10 is the analysis of a real estate exchange, comparing the financial implications of exchanging versus sale/reinvestment.

Case Study 11 is actually a collection of illustrations which sequentially analyze several key implications of investing in raw land.

Case Study 12 demonstrates the impact which holding period has on the selection of financing alternatives.

The final case study illustrates the use of Financial Management Rate of Return analysis.

Case Study 9
Determining exchange feasibility

The exchange worksheet

The investment broker involved in the exchange of real estate, whether tax deferred under Revenue Code Section 1031 or simply the barter-type exchange, must have the ability to "balance" equities. It is vital to understand the difference in value of respective properties and who owes whom how much.

In its simplest form, an exchange between two parties can be balanced as follows:

	Owner A (Vacant Land)	Owner B (Commercial Store)
Market Value	$100,000	$200,000
Encumbrance	55,000	100,000
Equity	45,000	100,000

A's equity is smaller than B's by $55,000. In fact, A must pay this amount to B to effect the exchange—that is, to "balance equities."

However, there are other complications. What about the sale costs? How are they paid? What if A does not have $55,000? How is the loan handled? What if A wants B's property, but B doesn't want A's and would rather have C's? What if there are four or five parties to the exchange—will it work? Is there enough money in the transaction to pay title costs, loan costs, commissions and deficiencies in equities?

The broker's best tool for threading through this complicated maze of exchanging is the Exchange Worksheet. This is a simple and valuable tool for those who take the time to understand its use. In this case study, we will proceed step-by-step through the analysis of a typical two-way exchange, using the Exchange Worksheet as illustrated in Figures 39, 40 and 41.

Situation

Refer back to A and B above, the owners respectively of the vacant land and the commercial store. Let's get all the facts.

A's land is valued at $100,000. It is encumbered with a $55,000 loan. A can only put in an additional $5,000 to make the transaction. Commission to sell the property is 10 percent and other transaction costs are estimated at $800.

B's store is valued at $200,000, on which B owes $100,000. There is a potential loan available on the property for $150,000. B is willing to take the land but is not willing to add cash. He will pay a 6-percent commission "if you can get it out of the transaction," he tells the broker. Other costs are estimated at $1,500.

Is this exchange possible and, if it is made, is there sufficient money to pay the costs and the commissions? The Exchange Worksheet will be used to find these answers.

Step 1   Inventory the assets of each party

In the first column of the worksheet (see Figure 39 and note the spacing between each party to allow for other entries) we indicate that A has land. Its market value (Column 2) is $100,000. Existing loans (Column 3) are $55,000. Column 4 shows the equity of A (Column 2 less Column 3).

A is willing to put in $5,000 which is indicated in Column 5. The 10-percent commission to make the transaction is indicated in Column 9, and transaction costs of $800 are listed in Column 10. Column 11 (Net Equity) is A's gross equity (Column 4) increased $5,000 by the cash he is willing to add and diminished by the commission and transaction costs to be paid if the exchange is made. In a slightly different format, the calculation is as follows:

Figure 39   Exchange Worksheet

Date _____

Property 1	Market Value 2	Existing Loans 3	Equity 4	Cash Gives (In) 5	Cash Gets (Out) 6	Paper Gives 7	Paper Gets 8	Comm. 9	Trans. Costs 10	Net Equity 11	New Loan 12	Old Loan 13	Net Loan Proceeds 14
1. A HAS LAND	100,000	55,000	45,000	5,000				10,000	800	39,200			
2.													
3.													
4. B HAS STOCKS	200,000	100,000	100,000					12,000	1,500	86,500	150,000	100,000	50,000
5.													
6.													
7.													
8.													
9.													
10.													

Prepared by _____

Market value	$100,000
less: Encumbrances	−55,000
Equity	45,000
plus: Cash to be added	+5,000
less: Commission	−10,000
less: Transaction costs	−800
Net equity	$ 39,200 (Column 11, Figure 39)

B is similarly "inventoried" on Line 4 of the Exchange Worksheet (Figure 39).

Step 2   Provide for maximum financing of hard money

At this stage it is unknown how much financing is needed to make the transaction possible. It isn't even known whether or not the financing should be utilized before or after the exchange or by which party. Maximum financing may not be needed or desired, but at this stage financing is maximized (at least on paper). If, under maximum financing, the transaction is not workable, so be it. If less financing is needed, the completed worksheet will tell us that and the exchange can be restructured with less financing.

A owns land; in his case there are not readily available refinancing possibilities. B's property can be refinanced up to $150,000, however. This is indicated by inserting that amount under New Loan (Column 12) on Line 4 of Figure 39. Under Old Loan (Column 13) the present loan on B's property ($100,000) is indicated and in Column 14, Net Loan Proceeds, the difference between the two previous columns—$50,000—is shown.

For simplification in this example, loan costs will be disregarded. In practice, they could be added to Transaction Costs (Column 10) or reduced in Net Loan Proceeds (Column 4).

Step 3   Balance equities under maximum financing available

In this step, new figures are added to the Exchange Worksheet (see Figure 40). Under "A has land," "A gets store" is inserted (see Line 2, Column 1). Since A is to get the store, its market value of $200,000 is inserted on Line 2 of Column 2.

At this stage it is assumed that A will take the store with maximum financing of $150,000; that amount is inserted on Line 2, Column 3, making the equity (Column 4) that A is to get $50,000.

Recall that the net equity A "put in" (Column 11) is $39,200. If A put in that amount and is ready to take out $50,000 (Line 2), we can see A is taking out $10,800 ($50,000 − $39,200) too much. A *must* add this amount to the exchange to keep it "in balance." From the information supplied, we know A has no further money to put in. Therefore, he will put in (give) "paper" for that amount. ("Paper" can be a note, unsecured or secured with a mortgage, a deed of trust, a wraparound mortgage or contract or a

393

Figure 40   Exchange Worksheet

Date _____

Property 1	Market Value 2	Existing Loans 3	Equity 4	Cash Gives (in) 5	Cash Gets (Out) 6	Paper Gives 7	Paper Gets 8	Comm. 9	Trans. Costs 10	Net Equity 11	New Loan 12	Old Loan 13	Net Loan Proceeds 14
1. A Has Land	100,000	55,000	45,000	5,000				10,000	800	39,200			
2. A Gets Stores	200,000	150,000	50,000			10,800				39,200			
3.													
4. B Has Stores	200,000	100,000	100,000					12,000	1,500	86,500	150,000	100,000	50,000
5. B Gets Land	100,000	55,000	45,000				41,500			86,500			
6.													
7.													
8.													
9.													
10.													

Prepared by _____

myriad of other security instruments.) So, on Line 2, Column 7, we insert $10,800. (At this stage we are not concerned with who gets the paper; we are merely indicating its need.)

As indicated in Line 2, Column 11, the net equity A is to receive is:

Store valued at	$200,000
less: Mortgage	150,000
less: "Paper"	10,800
Net equity	$ 39,200

It is now apparent that the net equity A put in of $39,200 will be equalized by the equity A will get of $39,200; therefore, A is in balance. This is indicated by the curved line connecting the two $39,200s in Column 11.

Balancing B poses another problem. On Line 5, Column 1, "B gets land" is inserted. In Column 2 the value of the land ($100,000) is inserted and in Column 3 the existing loan on the land ($55,000) is indicated, making Column 4 $45,000, which is the amount of equity B is getting at this point.

Looking at Column 11, Line 4, it can be seen that B has a net equity of $86,500 but so far is only getting $45,000. He is $41,500 short of his net equity. We do not know if there is sufficient cash in the transaction to pay B this amount. Therefore, at this point we indicate that B is going to "get paper" of that amount. We are not concerned whether or not B wants "paper"; we just insert on the worksheet on Line 5, Column 8 $41,500. Line 5 is completed by inserting in Column 11 (Net Equity) the total of what B gets;

$45,000	equity in the land
41,500	in paper
$86,500	Net Equity

which is equal to the net equity, $86,500, B had. We indicate that the amounts balance with a bracket (see Column 11).

Step 4   Balance paper

In Figure 40, Column 7 (Gives Paper) is $10,800 while Column 8 (Gets Paper) is $41,500. If the only "paper" coming into the transaction is $10,800, it will be impossible to take out $41,500. Therefore, $41,500 is changed to $10,800, and in order to keep Column 8 in balance, we put the difference ($41,500 − $10,800 = $30,700) on Line 5 of Column 6, "Gets Cash" (see Figure 41).

Now, we will check to see if B is still in balance:

B put in $86,500

B will take out:	Equity	$45,000
	Cash	30,700
	Paper	10,800
	Total	$86,500

Therefore, B is in balance.

Step 5   Total the active columns

Again, in Figure 41 (Line 7), the "active" columns are each totaled:

Column 5	Gives Cash	$ 5,000
Column 6	Gets Cash	30,700
Column 7	Gives Paper	10,800
Column 8	Gets Paper	10,800
Column 9	Commission	22,000
Column 10	Transaction Cost	2,300
Column 14	Net Loan Proceeds	50,000

Step 6   Close all accounts except paper account to cash

Think of the cash columns (5 and 6) in Figure 41 as the "broker's trust account." To this point the only "cash in" is the $5,000 of A. However, Column 14 shows $50,000 to come from loan proceeds.

The $50,000 loan proceeds are taken out of Column 14 and put in Column 5 (Cash In). The commissions are to be paid from escrow, so they are subtracted from Column 9 and added to Column 6 (Cash Out). Transaction costs are also to be paid from escrow. There are subtracted from Column 10 and added to Column 6 (Cash Out).

Step 7   Check that cash and paper accounts are in balance.

Columns 5 and 6 of Figure 41 add up to $55,000, showing that Cash is in balance. A glance at the "Gives Paper" and "Gets Paper" columns shows that they are also in balance. So the exchange works—on paper at least.

Step 8   Evaluation

Now is the time to review the feasibility of the exchange.

The completed worksheet in Figure 41 graphically illustrates how the exchange can be implemented.

1. A will convey his equity to B plus $5,000, and in exchange A will receive B's property with a new $150,000 mortgage and will owe an additional $10,800.

2. B will exchange his property for A's subject to the existing $55,000 loan. In addition, B will receive $30,700 in cash and a note (or other security instrument) for $10,800.

Figure 41 Exchange Worksheet

Date _____

Property	Market Value 2	Existing Loans 3	Equity 4	Cash Gives (In) 5	Cash Gets (Out) 6	Paper Gives 7	Paper Gets 8	Comm. 9	Trans. Costs 10	Net Equity 11	New Loan 12	Old Loan 13	Net Loan Proceeds 14
1. A HAS LAND	100,000	55,000	45,000	5,000				10,000	800	39,200)			
2. A GETS STORES	200,000	150,000	50,000			10,800				39,200)			
3.													
4. B HAS STORES	200,000	100,000	100,000		30,700		10,800	12,000	4,500	86,500)	150,000	100,000	50,000
5. B GETS LAND	100,000	55,000	45,000							86,500)			
6.													
7.				5,000	30,700	10,800	10,800	22,000	2,300				50,000
8.			+50,000	+50,000	+22,000			-22,000	-2,300				-50,000
9.				+2,300		0	0	0	0				0
10.				55,000	55,000								
					0								

Prepared by _____

It is also evident that there will be sufficient funds for transaction costs and commissions.

What if B won't take the $10,800 in paper?—That really is not too big a problem. There is $22,000 in commissions. Perhaps the broker will take the note, or buy it at a discount, with part of the commissions he has earned.

The Exchange Worksheet can be used in the same manner for multiple exchanges or for a two-way exchange with a cash-out. In Case Study 10, a slightly different approach is used. In that example, A's property is exchanged to B (who doesn't want it) and then B sells A's property to C, the ultimate owner. Such a procedure makes certain that A will not receive any cash, boot or net loan relief, thereby ensuring a tax deferred exchange under Section 1031.

Case Study 10
The tax deferred exchange and cash flow analysis

The most typical tax deferred exchange under Section 1031 of the Internal Revenue Code occurs because of these circumstances:

1. A owns a property

2. He has held it for some time

3. The equity is large

4. The adjusted basis is low because of low cost and/or depreciation taken

5. The market price is substantially over basis and the sale will cause a large capital gain tax

6. The property no longer fits A's investment needs

7. A wants to stay in real estate and is willing to step up to a larger property

8. A has found a property he wants or is willing to look for another property

9. B is the owner of the property A wants, but
     B doesn't want A's property
     B usually wants to sell for cash or terms

10. C is a person who wants to buy A's property.

11. D is an advisor to A, probably a real estate broker, accountant or

lawyer familiar with the processing of 1031 exchanges discussed in Chapter 11.

In order to better illustrate the actions of all parties and their resulting positions, consider the following data.

Situation

A's property can be described:

20-Unit Apartment Building

Value	$425,000	
Net Operating Income	39,500	
Existing mortgage	165,000	(8.5%; $2,013 monthly)
Adjusted basis	190,000	(no excess depreciation)
Transaction costs	6%	
Potential loan	320,000	(25 years, 10%; $2,908 monthly)

A wishes to acquire an office building without further cash outlay except the loan costs, if any. His marginal tax bracket is 50 percent.

B's property can be described:

Office Building

Value	$850,000	
Net Operating Income	81,000	
Existing mortgage	265,000	
Potential mortgage	600,000	(25 yrs; 10%; $5,452.20 monthly; $65,426 annually)
Transaction costs	6%	
Land/building allocation	25/75	
Depreciation schedule	18 years, straight line	

C has $150,000 cash available to acquire A's property.

In order to show the advantages of a 1031 exchange, most practitioners show A his position in the B property if he acquires it by selling his own property and purchasing B's, or if he exchanges into B.

Buying and selling alternative

If A sells his property his net sales proceeds would be:

Sale price		$425,000
less: Existing loan	$165,000	
Transaction costs	25,500	190,500
Gross proceeds		$234,500
Sale price		$425,000
Adjusted basis before sale	$190,000	
Transaction costs	25,500	

(continued)

Total basis at sale	215,500	
Gain	209,500	
Taxable gain (40%)	83,800	
Capital gain tax on sale (50%)	41,900	
Gross proceeds		234,500
Tax on sale		41,900
Net proceeds (if sold)		192,600

Therefore, if A sells to C, A will have net sale proceeds of $192,600. The office building could then be acquired by A as follows:

Purchase price	$850,000	
Down payment	$192,600	(net proceeds on sale of apartment building)
First mortgage	600,000	
Second mortgage	57,400	
	$850,000	

Exchange alternative

On the other hand, if A exchanges into the B property and B sells the A property to C, the results would be as shown on the Exchange Worksheet in Figure 42. The results can then be summarized.

A acquires the office building for his net equity ($234,500) and owes a first mortgage of $600,000 and a second mortgage of $15,500. For the purpose of this problem assume the $15,500 is payable monthly, amortized over 25 years at 11 percent and payable in full at the end of the fifteenth year.

B gets his net equity of $534,500—$518,500 in cash and the $15,500 second mortgage. C acquires A's property for $425,000 with $105,000 down and a $320,000 first mortgage loan. If C wishes to utilize the balance of his funds ($45,000) he can reduce the loan to (or obtain a lower loan of) $275,000.

A has exchanged his property (the apartment building) to B and acquired B's property (the office building). B then sells the apartment building to C. If A had sold directly to C, he would have created a taxable event that would cost him $41,900 in capital gains taxes.

By exchanging with B, A owes loans of $600,000 and $15,500, a total of $615,500. If he had sold instead of exchanged, paid capital gains taxes and bought the office building, his debt would have been $657,400. The difference is the tax saved on the exchange.

It is apparent that by the exchange taxes were avoided and the equity of A is $41,900 larger—not bad considering the only difference was how the steps of conveyance of property were taken and how all the parties were educated to the transaction. Finally, if the equities were capable of earning 10 percent, the $41,900 larger equity would earn nearly $4,200 more per year—in ten years nearly $42,000.

Figure 42 Exchange Worksheet

Property 1	Market Value 2	Existing Loans 3	Equity 4	Cash Gives (In) 5	Cash Gets (Out) 6	Paper Gives 7	Paper Gets 8	Comm. 9	Trans. Costs 10	Net Equity 11	New Loan 12	Old Loan 13	Net Loan Proceeds 14
1. A Has	425,000	165,000	260,000						25,500	234,500			
2. A Gets	850,000	600,000	250,000			15,500				234,500			
3.													
4. B Has	850,000	265,000	585,000						51,000	534,000	600,000	265,000	335,000
5. B Gets	425,000	165,000	260,000		244,000					534,000			
6.													
7. B Has	425,000	165,000	260,000		244,500					260,000	320,000	165,000	155,000
8. B Gets							15,500			260,000			
9.													
10. C Has				105,000						105,000			
11. C Gets	425,000	320,000	105,000	105,000	518,500	15,500	15,500		76,500	105,000			490,000
				490,000	76,500		0		76,500				492,000
				595,000	515,000				74,500				0
					0				0				

401

Comparing Cash Flows

Let us, however, check these benefits by another method. Wouldn't it be interesting to compare the after-tax cash flows of the sale and the after-tax cash flows of the exchange and to calculate the yields therefrom to confirm the advantages of the exchange?

Figures 43 and 44 show the annual cash flows of both the sale/purchase and the exchange outlined above. The differences between these two transaction methods are due to mortgage and depreciation differences.

In the sale/purchase, the adjusted basis of the office building is $850,000 allocated $212,500 (25 percent) to land and $637,500 (75 percent) to improvements. This is depreciated on a straight line basis over 18 years.

In the exchange (see Figure 44), the adjusted basis of the office building is $850,000 less the unrecognized gain of $209,500, or $640,500. Of this, 75 percent ($480,375) is allocated to the improvements and depreciated over 18 years on a straight line basis. (This example assumes that anti-churning rules do not apply and that the office building could be depreciated under the 1981 tax act.)

Other assumptions of the cash flow studies are as follows:

1. The Net Operating Income is projected to increase at 2 percent per year.

2. The resale price at end of Year 15 will be $1,000,000 and sale costs will be 6 percent.

3. Resale capital gains tax will be 20 percent (50 percent of 40 percent of the gain).

4. The second mortgage loan will be amortized on a 25-year, 11-percent monthly schedule, payable in full at the end of the fifteenth year.

The T-charts on page 403 are composed of the Annual Cash Flows After Taxes (Line 22 of Figures 43 and 44) and the Sale Proceeds After Taxes (Line 33).

The equal initial investment for each projection is based on the premise from Chapter 4 that the investment base for an alternative investment analysis is the net sale proceeds after taxes plus any cash added or less any cash received. In both the exchange and the sale/purchase the transaction was made from the net after-tax equity of $192,600.

The comparative cash flows show practically the same yield (the sale/purchase being only slightly higher). It is apparent that the cash flows of the sale/purchase are greater and sooner, however. This indicates that the 1031 exchange is not as beneficial as it may appear on the surface.

Conclusion

402   Much of the literature (and salesmanship) of 1031 exchanging only

Sale/Purchase		Exchange	
Year	$	Year	$
0	($192,600)	0	($192,600)
1	$ 17,278	1	$ 15,982
2	20,952	2	18,889
3	21,420	3	19,379
4	21,867	4	19,850
5	22,288	5	20,298
6	22,681	6	20,721
7	23,039	7	21,113
8	23,360	8	21,471
9	23,635	9	21,788
10	23,860	10	22,060
11	20,841	11	19,878
12	20,943	12	20,038
13	20,972	13	20,132
14	20,917	14	20,150
15	20,769	15	20,082
	+361,481		+375,793
	$382,250		$395,875
IRR: 13.22%		IRR: 12.64%	

takes the tax consequences of the sale into consideration and completely omits the after-tax cash flows of the property's operation over the holding period. Investment brokers would be wise, however, to test the future after-tax benefits of the exchange with those of the sale/purchase so that they completely understand the differences.

Some investors and/or their advisors may not be interested in your studies, however, and will insist on going through the complications of an exchange. The promise of deferral or avoidance of taxes is sometimes easier to believe than maximizing wealth. The machinations of exchange are difficult and in most cases not worth the effort, especially for high tax bracket investors who are oversold on the benefits.

We are not saying "never utilize 1031." Under some circumstances it may be beneficial, but generally not under the normal circumstances of high leverage, high improvement ratio and high marginal tax bracket.

Some major points to be learned from this case:

1. All 1031 exchanges are not as beneficial to the taxpayer as sometimes purported by well-meaning advisors.

2. The investment broker should be able to make the cash flow analyses of both the potential sale/purchase and the potential exchange.

3. Investors should demand (and pay for) such studies before they attempt the complicated negotiations and paperwork of a technically competent exchange.

Figure 43

For Mr A

Purpose Sale / Purchase Analysis

Date _____

Cash Flow Analysis

Purchase Price 850,000

Encumbrances 657,400

Investment 192,600

Mortgage Data

	Encumbrances	Beginning Balance	Remaining Term	Number of Payments Per Year	Interest Rate	Payment	Annual Debt Service	Remarks
1	1st Mortgage	600,000	25 yrs	12	10%	5452.20	65,426	
2	2nd Mortgage	57,400	25 yrs.	12	11%	562.58	6,751	Payable
3	3rd Mortgage							EOY 15

		Year: 1	Year: 2	Year: 3	Year: 4	Year: 5	EOY	Mortgage Balance
	Ownership Analysis of Property Income:			**Taxable Income**				1st Mortgage
4	Gross Scheduled Income							
5	Less: Vcy. & Credit Losses							
6	Gross Operating Income							
7	– Operating Expenses							
8	Net Operating Income	81,000	82,620	84,272	85,958	87,677		
9	– Non-Operating Expense							
10	– Interest – 1st Mortgage	59,744	59,149	58,492	57,766	56,964		2nd Mortgage
11	– Interest – 2nd Mortgage	6,291	6,238	6,179	6,113	6,039		
12	– Interest – 3rd Mortgage							
13	– Cost Recovery S/L	31,875	38,250	38,250	38,250	38,250		
14	Real Est. Taxable Income	(16,910)	(21,017)	(18,649)	(16,171)	(13,576)		
				Cash Flows				
15	Net Operating Income	81,000	82,620	84,272	85,958	87,677		3rd Mortgage
16	– Annual Debt Service	72,177	72,177	72,177	72,177	72,177		
17	– Funded Reserves							
18	– Capital Additions							
19	Cash Flow before Taxes	8,823	10,443	12,095	13,781	15,500		
20	– Minimum Tax							
21	– Tax Liability on Real Est.	(8,455)	(10,509)	(9,325)	(8,086)	(6,788)		
22	Cash Flow after Taxes	17,278	20,952	21,420	21,867	22,288		

Analysis of Sale Proceeds

Year: _____

	Adjusted Basis				Excess Cost Recovery (CR)				Tax Liability on Sale		
23	Original Basis				Total CR				Excess Recapture Tax		
24	+ Capital Improvements				S/L CR				Capital Gain Tax		
25	– Cost Recovery				Excess CR*				Tax Liability on Sale		
26	– Partial Sales				Exc. CR Carryover						
27	AB					Gain			Sale Proceeds		
28					Sale Price				Sale Price		
					– Cost of Sale				– Costs of Sale		
	*NOTE: On non-residential property, if accelerated CR system is elected, all CR claimed is recaptured as ordinary income in the year of sale.				– AB				– Mortgage		
					Gain				Proceeds before Taxes		
					– Excess CR				– Tax Liability on Sale		
					Capital Gain				Proceeds after Taxes		

The statements and figures presented herein, while not guaranteed are secured from sources we believe authoritative

Prepared by _____

Figure 43 (continued)

Cash Flow Analysis

For **Mr. A**

Purpose **Sale/Purchase Analysis**

Date _____

Purchase Price **850,000**

Encumbrances **657,400**

Investment **192,600**

Mortgage Data

	Encumbrances	Beginning Balance	Remaining Term	Number of Payments Per Year	Interest Rate	Payment	Annual Debt Service	Remarks
1	1st Mortgage	600,000	25yrs	12	10%	5,452.20	65,426	
2	2nd Mortgage	57,400	25yrs	12	11%	562.58	6,751	Payable EOY 15
3	3rd Mortgage							

	Ownership Analysis of Property Income:	Year: 6	Year: 7	Year: 8	Year: 9	Year: 10	EOY	Mortgage Balance
		Taxable Income						
4	Gross Scheduled Income							1st Mortgage
5	Less: Vcy. & Credit Losses							
6	Gross Operating Income							
7	– Operating Expenses							
8	Net Operating Income	89,431	91,219	93,044	94,904	96,802		
9	– Non-Operating Expense							
10	– Interest – 1st Mortgage	56,078	55,099	54,017	52,822	51,503		2nd Mortgage
11	– Interest – 2nd Mortgage	5,956	5,864	5,762	5,647	5,519		
12	– Interest – 3rd Mortgage							
13	– Cost Recovery	38,250	38,250	38,250	38,250	38,250		
14	Real Est. Taxable Income	(10,853)	(7,994)	(4,985)	(1,815)	1,530		
		Cash Flows						
15	Net Operating Income	89,431	91,219	93,044	94,904	96,802		3rd Mortgage
16	– Annual Debt Service	72,177	72,177	72,177	72,177	72,177		
17	– Funded Reserves							
18	– Capital Additions							
19	Cash Flow before Taxes	17,254	19,042	20,867	22,727	24,625		
20	– Minimum Tax							
21	– Tax Liability on Real Est.	(5,427)	(3,997)	(2,493)	(908)	765		
22	Cash Flow after Taxes	22,681	23,039	23,360	23,635	23,860		

	Analysis of Sale Proceeds Year:					
	Adjusted Basis		Excess Cost Recovery (CR)		Tax Liability on Sale	
23	Original Basis		Total CR		Excess Recapture Tax	
24	+ Capital Improvements		S/L CR		Capital Gain Tax	
25	– Cost Recovery		Excess CR*		Tax Liability on Sale	
26	– Partial Sales		Exc. CR Carryover			
27	AB		Gain		Sale Proceeds	
28			Sale Price		Sale Price	
			– Cost of Sale		– Costs of Sale	
	*NOTE: On non-residential property, if accelerated CR system is elected, all CR claimed is recaptured as ordinary income in the year of sale.		– AB		– Mortgage	
			Gain		Proceeds before Taxes	
			– Excess CR		– Tax Liability on Sale	
			Capital Gain		Proceeds after Taxes	

The statements and figures presented herein, while not guaranteed are secured from sources we believe authoritative

Prepared by _____

Figure 43 (continued)

Cash Flow Analysis

For **Mr. A**

Purpose **Sale/Purchase Analysis**

Date _____

Purchase Price **850,000**

Encumbrances **657,400**

Investment **192,600**

Mortgage Data

	Encumbrances	Beginning Balance	Remaining Term	Number of Payments Per Year	Interest Rate	Payment	Annual Debt Service	Remarks
1	1st Mortgage	600,000	25yrs	12	10%	5452.20	65,426	
2	2nd Mortgage	57,400	25yrs	12	11%	562.58	6,751	Payable EOY 15
3	3rd Mortgage							

		Year: 11	Year: 12	Year: 13	Year: 14	Year: 15	EOY	Mortgage Balance
	Ownership Analysis of Property Income:			**Taxable Income**				**1st Mortgage**
4	Gross Scheduled Income							
5	Less: Vcy. & Credit Losses							
6	Gross Operating Income							
7	– Operating Expenses							
8	Net Operating Income	98,739	100,713	102,728	104,782	106,878		
9	– Non-Operating Expense						15	412,576
10	– Interest – 1st Mortgage	50,045	48,434	46,655	44,689	42,517		**2nd Mortgage**
11	– Interest – 2nd Mortgage	5,377	5,218	5,041	4,843	4,622		
12	– Interest – 3rd Mortgage							
13	– Cost Recovery	31,875	31,875	31,875	31,875	31,875		
14	Real Est Taxable Income	11,442	15,186	19,157	23,375	27,864		
				Cash Flows				15 40,843
15	Net Operating Income	98,739	100,713	102,728	104,782	106,878		**3rd Mortgage**
16	– Annual Debt Service	72,177	72,177	72,177	72,177	72,177		
17	– Funded Reserves							
18	– Capital Additions							
19	Cash Flow before Taxes	26,562	28,536	30,551	32,605	34,701		
20	– Minimum Tax							
21	– Tax Liability on Real Est.	5,721	7,593	9,579	11,688	13,932		
22	Cash Flow after Taxes	20,841	20,943	20,972	20,917	20,769		

Analysis of Sale Proceeds

Adjusted Basis		Excess Cost Recovery (CR)		Tax Liability on Sale Year:	
23 Original Basis	850,000	Total CR	535,500	Excess Recapture Tax	– 0 –
24 + Capital Improvements		S/L CR	535,500	Capital Gain Tax 20%	125,100
25 – Cost Recovery	535,500	Excess CR*	– 0 –	Tax Liability on Sale	125,100
26 – Partial Sales		Exc. CR Carryover			
27 AB	314,500	**Gain**		**Sale Proceeds**	
28		Sale Price	1,000,000	Sale Price	1,000,000
		– Cost of Sale	60,000	– Costs of Sale	60,000
*NOTE: On non-residential property, if accelerated CR system is elected, all CR claimed is recaptured as ordinary income in the year of sale.		– AB	314,500	– Mortgage	453,419
		Gain	625,500	Proceeds before Taxes	486,581
		– Excess CR	– 0 –	– Tax Liability on Sale	125,100
		Capital Gain	625,500	Proceeds after Taxes	361,481

The statements and figures presented herein, while not guaranteed are secured from sources we believe authoritative

Prepared by _____

Figure 44

For Mr. A

Purpose Exchange Analysis

Date _____

Cash Flow Analysis

Purchase Price 850,000

Encumbrances 615,500

Equity Investment 234,500

Investment Base 192,600

Mortgage Data

	Encumbrances	Beginning Balance	Remaining Term	Number of Payments Per Year	Interest Rate	Payment	Annual Debt Service	Remarks
1	1st Mortgage	600,000	25 yrs	12	10%	5,452.20	65,426	
2	2nd Mortgage	15,500	25 yrs	12	11%	151.92	1,823	
3	3rd Mortgage							

Taxable Income

	Ownership Analysis of Property Income:	Year: 1	Year: 2	Year: 3	Year: 4	Year: 5	EOY	Mortgage Balance
4	Gross Scheduled Income							1st Mortgage
5	Less: Vcy. & Credit Losses							
6	Gross Operating Income							
7	– Operating Expenses							
8	Net Operating Income	81,000	82,620	84,272	85,958	87,677		
9	– Non-Operating Expense							
10	– Interest – 1st Mortgage	59,744	59,149	58,492	57,766	56,964		2nd Mortgage
11	– Interest – 2nd Mortgage	1,699	1,684	1,668	1,651	1,631		
12	– Interest – 3rd Mortgage							
13	– Cost Recovery	24,019	28,823	28,823	28,823	28,823		
14	Real Est Taxable Income	(4,462)	(7,036)	(4,711)	(2,282)	259		

Cash Flows

		Year: 1	Year: 2	Year: 3	Year: 4	Year: 5		
15	Net Operating Income	81,000	82,620	84,272	85,958	87,677		3rd Mortgage
16	– Annual Debt Service	67,249	67,249	67,249	67,249	67,249		
17	– Funded Reserves							
18	– Capital Additions							
19	Cash Flow before Taxes	13,751	15,371	17,023	18,709	20,428		
20	– Minimum Tax							
21	– Tax Liability on Real Est.	(2,231)	(3,518)	(2,356)	(1,141)	130		
22	Cash Flow after Taxes	15,982	18,889	19,379	19,850	20,298		

Analysis of Sale Proceeds   Year:

	Adjusted Basis			Excess Cost Recovery (CR)			Tax Liability on Sale		
23	Original Basis			Total CR			Excess Recapture Tax		
24	+ Capital Improvements			S/L CR			Capital Gain Tax		
25	– Cost Recovery			Excess CR*			Tax Liability on Sale		
26	– Partial Sales			Exc. CR Carryover					
27	AB			Gain			Sale Proceeds		
28				Sale Price			Sale Price		
				– Cost of Sale			– Costs of Sale		
				– AB			– Mortgage		
				Gain			Proceeds before Taxes		
				– Excess CR			– Tax Liability on Sale		
				Capital Gain			Proceeds after Taxes		

*NOTE: On non-residential property, if accelerated CR system is elected, all CR claimed is recaptured as ordinary income in the year of sale.

The statements and figures presented herein, while not guaranteed are secured from sources we believe authoritative

Prepared by _____

Figure 44 (continued)

Cash Flow Analysis

For **Mr. A**

Purpose **Exchange Analysis**

Date _____

Purchase Price **850,000**

Encumbrances **615,500**

Equity ~~Investment~~ **234,500**

Investment Base **192,600**

Mortgage Data

	Encumbrances	Beginning Balance	Remaining Term	Number of Payments Per Year	Interest Rate	Payment	Annual Debt Service	Remarks
1	1st Mortgage	600,000	25 yrs	12	10%	5,452.20	65,426	
2	2nd Mortgage	15,500	25 yrs	12	11%	151.92	1,823	
3	3rd Mortgage							

Taxable Income

	Ownership Analysis of Property Income:	Year: 6	Year: 7	Year: 8	Year: 9	Year: 10	EOY	Mortgage Balance
4	Gross Scheduled Income							1st Mortgage
5	Less: Vcy. & Credit Losses							
6	Gross Operating Income							
7	− Operating Expenses							
8	Net Operating Income	89,431	91,219	93,044	94,904	96,802		
9	− Non-Operating Expense							
10	− Interest − 1st Mortgage	56,078	55,099	54,017	52,822	51,503		2nd Mortgage
11	− Interest − 2nd Mortgage	1,608	1,584	1,556	1,525	1,490		
12	− Interest − 3rd Mortgage							
13	− Cost Recovery	28,823	28,823	28,823	28,823	28,823		
14	Real Est. Taxable Income	2,922	5,713	8,648	11,734	14,986		

Cash Flows

15	Net Operating Income	89,431	91,219	93,044	94,904	96,802		3rd Mortgage
16	− Annual Debt Service	67,249	67,249	67,249	67,249	67,249		
17	− Funded Reserves							
18	− Capital Additions							
19	Cash Flow before Taxes	22,182	23,970	25,795	27,655	29,553		
20	− Minimum Tax							
21	− Tax Liability on Real Est.	1,461	2,857	4,324	5,867	7,493		
22	Cash Flow after Taxes	20,721	21,113	21,471	21,788	22,060		

Analysis of Sale Proceeds   Year:

	Adjusted Basis			Excess Cost Recovery (CR)			Tax Liability on Sale		
23	Original Basis			Total CR			Excess Recapture Tax		
24	+ Capital Improvements			S/L CR			Capital Gain Tax		
25	− Cost Recovery			Excess CR*			Tax Liability on Sale		
26	− Partial Sales			Exc. CR Carryover					
27	AB				Gain			Sale Proceeds	
28				Sale Price			Sale Price		
				− Cost of Sale			− Costs of Sale		
	*NOTE: On non-residential property, if accelerated CR system is elected, all CR claimed is recaptured as ordinary income in the year of sale.			− AB			− Mortgage		
				Gain			Proceeds before Taxes		
				− Excess CR			− Tax Liability on Sale		
				Capital Gain			Proceeds after Taxes		

The statements and figures presented herein, while not guaranteed are secured from sources we believe authoritative

Prepared by _____

Figure 44 (continued)

Cash Flow Analysis

For __Mr. A__

Purpose __Exchange Analysis__

Date _____

Purchase Price __850,000__
Encumbrances __615,500__
Equity Investment __234,500__
Investment Base __192,600__

Mortgage Data

	Encumbrances	Beginning Balance	Remaining Term	Number of Payments Per Year	Interest Rate	Payment	Annual Debt Service	Remarks
1	1st Mortgage	600,000	25 yrs	12	10%	5,452.20	65,426	
2	2nd Mortgage	15,500	25 yrs	12	11%	151.92	1,823	
3	3rd Mortgage							

		Year: 11	Year: 12	Year: 13	Year: 14	Year: 15	EOY	Mortgage Balance
	Ownership Analysis of Property Income:		**Taxable Income**					
4	Gross Scheduled Income							1st Mortgage
5	Less: Vcy. & Credit Losses							
6	Gross Operating Income							
7	– Operating Expenses							
8	Net Operating Income	98,739	100,713	102,728	104,782	106,878		
9	– Non-Operating Expense						15	412,576
10	– Interest – 1st Mortgage	50,045	48,434	46,655	44,689	42,517	2nd Mortgage	
11	– Interest – 2nd Mortgage	1,452	1,409	1,361	1,308	1,248		
12	– Interest – 3rd Mortgage							
13	– Cost Recovery	24,019	24,019	24,019	24,019	24,019		
14	Real Est Taxable Income	23,223	26,851	30,693	34,766	39,094		
			Cash Flows				15	11,027
15	Net Operating Income	98,739	100,713	102,728	104,782	106,878	3rd Mortgage	
16	– Annual Debt Service	67,249	67,249	67,249	67,249	67,249		
17	– Funded Reserves							
18	– Capital Additions							
19	Cash Flow before Taxes	31,490	33,464	35,479	37,533	39,629		
20	– Minimum Tax							
21	– Tax Liability on Real Est.	11,612	13,426	15,347	17,383	19,547		
22	Cash Flow after Taxes	19,878	20,038	20,132	20,150	20,082		

Analysis of Sale Proceeds   Year:

	Adjusted Basis		Excess Cost Recovery (CR)		Tax Liability on Sale	
23	Original Basis	640,500	Total CR	403,521	Excess Recapture Tax	– 0 –
24	+ Capital Improvements		S/L CR	403,521	Capital Gain Tax 20%	140,604
25	– Cost Recovery	403,521	Excess CR*	– 0 –	Tax Liability on Sale	140,604
26	– Partial Sales		Exc. CR Carryover			
27	AB	236,979		**Gain**		**Sale Proceeds**
28			Sale Price	1,000,000	Sale Price	1,000,000
			– Cost of Sale	60,000	– Costs of Sale	60,000
			– AB	236,979	– Mortgage	423,603
			Gain	703,021	Proceeds before Taxes	516,397
			– Excess CR	– 0 –	– Tax Liability on Sale	140,604
			Capital Gain	703,021	Proceeds after Taxes	375,793

*NOTE: On non-residential property, if accelerated CR system is elected, all CR claimed is recaptured as ordinary income in the year of sale.

REALTORS NATIONAL MARKETING INSTITUTE® of the NATIONAL ASSOCIATION OF REALTORS®, 1982
All rights reserved 2-81-F612

The statements and figures presented herein, while not guaranteed are secured from sources we believe authoritative.

Prepared by _____

Case Study 11
Land and land analysis

Land is the most misunderstood and the most mysterious of investments. There is very little literature on the subject and what is available quotes platitudes of wealthy historical figures:

John Jacob Astor   "Buy land near a growing city."

Andrew Carnegie   "The wise young man or wage earner of today invests his money in real estate, suburban real estate."

Grover Cleveland   "No investment on earth is so safe, so sure, so certain to enrich its owner as undeveloped realty. I always advise my friends to place their savings in realty near some growing city. There is no such savings bank anywhere."

Most investors' opinions about land as an investment result in other platitudes. For example:

"Land is a good investment because it always increases in value. In fact, if I'm not satisfied with an offer on my land because it's too low, all I have to do is wait and prices will catch up to mine."

"Land is a bad investment—it's not liquid, it's an alligator, it keeps eating and I, as owner, have to support it."

"Land is a good investment. As an owner I can write off the interest and taxes I pay. As a result Uncle Sam is paying my costs. It's a good tax shelter."

"Land is a bad investment—it lacks cash flow—and any investment without cash flow is foolhardy."

"Land is a good investment. God stopped making land, but He didn't stop making people; therefore land prices must go up. In fact, I have a friend who doubled his money in land in only ten years. Not only that, but land can be bought on leverage."

Such thinking results in some people buying, some people not buying, and some people buying, accomplishing their goals, but losing money. In fact, ask a room full of people. Is investment land a good long-term investment or a good short-term investment? You'll find the answer mixed. Let us then start at the beginning and try to resolve the conflicting opinions.

First, let us define investment land (or speculative land). Investment lands are vacant properties acquired with no specific plan in mind except to hold for appreciation. Contrast this with a tract acquired to subdivide or to build a specific building thereon within a relatively short period of time.

Investment in land is unique to any other investment in several ways. First, all the expenses of land ownership, interest on debt, real estate taxes and any liability insurance—that is, all of the carrying costs—may be expensed and therefore deducted from income at ordinary tax rates, whereas all the income in excess of basis (if held for more than one year by someone other than a dealer) is taxed at capital gain rates.

Secondly, at the time land is acquired, all cash flows are negative—the down payment, the debt service and the carrying charges. The only positive cash flow (excluding the possibility of rental income) comes from the eventual disposition of the property.

A t-Chart of a land acquisition would appear as:

0	(Initial Investment)
1	Annual Debt Service (ADS) + Carrying Costs (CC)
2	[ADS + CC]
3	
–	
–	
–	
Year of Sale	[ADS + CC] + Resale Proceeds

Most investors are aware that investment land has greater risk than most other investments, as well as less liquidity and negative cash flows; because of these factors, land should yield greater returns than savings (5 to 7 percent) or mortgages (10 to 15 percent). Investors are often unable to translate this awareness into the price necessary to obtain the yield they desire for the period they expect to hold the property. Furthermore, they are unable to evaluate this type of investment on a before- or after-tax basis and to make comparisons with alternative investments available. Therefore, most tend to rely on the platitudes heretofore expressed in justifying their "Go" or "No Go" decisions on a land investment opportunity.

Situation

The purpose of this section, then, is to provide some guidelines and processes for understanding land investments. This will be done through a series of illustrations based upon the following "facts" about a hypothetical piece of property:

> Property: 24 acres, at $5,000 per acre
> Price: $120,000
> Annual real estate taxes: $2,200
> Other annual carrying costs: $200
> Resale costs: 10%

Illustration 1   Holding period

Resale prices necessary for a five, ten or fifteen-year holding period to obtain yields of 15, 20 and 25-percent are shown below. These figures assume the property is acquired free and clear (no mortgage) and they do not take holding costs into consideration.

Resale Prices Necessary To Achieve Desired Yield			
Before-Tax	Holding Period		
Yield	5 Years	10 Years	15 Years
25%	$406,901	$1,241,763	$3,789,561
20%	331,776	825,565	2,054,270
15%	268,181	539,408	1,084,942

The resale prices above were calculated with a hand-held calculator determining future value for each period at each growth rate. The future values found were divided by .90 to reflect the resale price necessary to include sale costs of 10 percent yet yield the given rate. For example, $120,000 compounded at 20 percent annually for ten years is $743,008. Dividing by .90 the result is $825,565, which is the gross sale price needed to obtain 20 percent per annum yield (disregarding carrying costs and income taxes).

A quick glance at the resulting graph (Figure 45) tells the story of how rapid the growth must be as the holding period lengthens.

At 15 years the $120,000 must increase as follows to attain the indicated yields:

15%	9 times
20%	17 times
25%	31.6 times

Most investors are unaware of the impact of long holding periods. Instead, they buoy their spirits by recalling what a low price they paid for the property instead of recognizing their present investment base (see Chapter 4).

Illustration 2   Impact of carrying costs

If the subject property is acquired free and clear and the carrying costs are $2,400, the income stream and the IRR, using the resale proceeds after 10-percent selling costs, can be calculated as shown in the table below. Assume a 15-percent per year increase in value.

Sale proceeds are calculated by taking 90 percent of resale price to indicate after-sale proceeds. For example:

10 yr. sale price: $539,408 × .90 = $485,467.

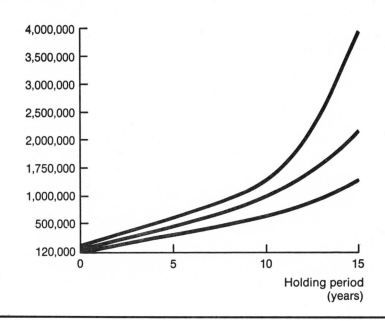

Figure 45 Holding Periods

5 Years		10 Years		15 Years	
EOY	Cash Flow	EOY	Cash Flow	EOY	Cash Flow
0	($120,000)	0	($120,000)	0	($120,000)
1	(2,400)	1	(2,400)	1	(2,400)
–	–	–	–	–	–
–	–	–	–	–	–
–	–	–	–	–	–
5	(2,400)+	5	(2,400)+	5	(2,400)+
Sale proceeds after 10% selling costs:	$241,363		$485,467		$976,448
Yield:	13.66%		13.86%		14.12%

Projected yields before income taxes, giving consideration to holding costs and resale costs are:

413

at 20%

5 Years		10 Years		15 Years	
EOY	Cash Flow	EOY	Cash Flow	EOY	Cash Flow
0	($120,000)	0	($120,000)	0	($120,000)
1	(2,400)	1	(2,400)	1	(2,400)
–	–	–	–	–	–
–	–	–	–	–	–
–	–	–	–	–	–
5	(2,400)+	10	(2,400)+	15	(2,400)+
Sale proceeds after 10% selling costs:	$298,598		$743,008		$1,843,843
Yield	18.57%		19.01%		19.27%

at 25%

5 Years		10 Years		15 Years	
EOY	Cash Flow	EOY	Cash Flow	EOY	Cash Flow
0	($120,000)	0	($120,000)	0	($120,000)
1	(2,400)	1	(2,400)	1	(2,400)
–	–	–	–	–	–
–	–	–	–	–	–
–	–	–	–	–	–
5	(2,400)+	10	(2,400)+	15	(2,400)+
Sale proceeds after 10% selling costs:	$366,211		$1,117,587		$3,410,605
Yield	23.66%		24.12%		24.37%

From this projection and calculation, it is evident that the carrying costs have reduced the before-tax yield. Expressed another way, an even higher resale price is necessary to attain the desired before-tax yield because of the impact of negative cash flows of the carrying costs.

Illustration 3   Impact on the yield of tax savings of carrying costs and capital gains at resale

We will now look at the ten-year holding period for the three before-tax yields and at the tax impact on 30-percent and 50-percent marginal taxpayers. Capital gain taxes are considered to be at 20 percent of the total gain (which is the same as 40 percent of the total gain at a maximum rate of 50 percent) for both hypothetical taxpayers under the assumption that the larger gain will move the 30-percent taxpayer up into the 50-percent marginal bracket. The differences in the income streams are shown below and in Figures 46, 47 and 48.

	Before Tax		After Tax 30% Marginal Rate		After Tax 50% Marginal Rate

			10 Years/15% Growth			
EOY	Cash Flow	EOY	Cash Flow	EOY	Cash Flow
0	($120,000)	0	($120,000)	0	($120,000)
1	(2,400)	1	(1,680)	1	(1,200)
–	–	–	–	–	–
–	–	–	–	–	–
–	–	–	–	–	–
–	–	–	–	–	–
10	(2,400)	10	(1,680)+	10	(1,200)+

Sale proceeds after 10% selling costs:

	$485,467		$412,374		$412,374
Yield	13.86%		12.39%		12.5%
					(see Figure 46)

			10 Years/20% Growth			
EOY	Cash Flow	EOY	Cash Flow	EOY	Cash Flow
0	($120,000)	0	($120,000)	0	($120,000)
1	(2,400)	1	(1,680)	1	(1,200)
–	–	–	–	–	–
–	–	–	–	–	–
–	–	–	–	–	–
–	–	–	–	–	–
10	(2,400)+	10	(1,680)+	10	(1,200)+

Sale proceeds after 10% selling costs:

	$743,008		$618,406		$618,406
Yield	19.01%		17.1%		17.3%
					(see Figure 47)

			10 Years/25% Growth			
EOY	Cash Flow	EOY	Cash Flow	EOY	Cash Flow
0	($120,000)	0	($120,000)	0	($120,000)
1	(2,400)	1	(1,680)	1	(1,200)
–	–	–	–	–	–
–	–	–	–	–	–
–	–	–	–	–	–
–	–	–	–	–	–
10	(2,400)+	10	(1,680)+	10	(1,200)+

Sale proceeds after 10% selling costs:

	$1,117,587		$918,070		$918,070
Yield	24.12%		21.9%		21.1%
					(see Figure 48)

Figure 46 Sale Proceeds After Taxes (10 yrs., 15% growth, 50% tax bracket)

	Analysis of Sale Proceeds			Year:	
Adjusted Basis		**Excess Cost Recovery (CR)**		**Tax Liability on Sale**	
23 Original Basis	/20 000	Total CR		Excess Recapture Tax	
24 + Capital Improvements		S/L CR		Capital Gain Tax 20%	73 093
25 − Cost Recovery	−0−	Excess CR		Tax Liability on Sale	
26 − Partial Sales		Exc. CR Carryover			
27 AB	/20 000	Gain		Sale Proceeds	
28		Sale Price	485 467	Sale Price	485 467
29		− Cost of Sale	−0−	− Costs of Sale	−0−
30		− AB	/20 000	− Mortgage	−0−
31		Gain	365 467	Proceeds before Taxes	485 467
32		− Excess	−0−	− Tax Liability on Sale	73 093
33		Capital Gain	365 467	Proceeds after Taxes	412 374

● REALTORS NATIONAL MARKETING INSTITUTE®
of the NATIONAL ASSOCIATION OF REALTORS® , 1981
The statements and figures presented herein, while not guaranteed, are secured from sources we believe authoritative.   Prepared by_____

Figure 47 Sale Proceeds After Taxes (10 yrs., 20% growth, 50% tax bracket)

	Analysis of Sale Proceeds			Year:	
Adjusted Basis		**Excess Cost Recovery (CR)**		**Tax Liability on Sale**	
23 Original Basis	/20 000	Total CR		Excess Recapture Tax	
24 + Capital Improvements		S/L CR		Capital Gain Tax 20%	124 602
25 − Cost Recovery	−0−	Excess CR		Tax Liability on Sale	
26 − Partial Sales		Exc. CR Carryover			
27 AB	/20 000	Gain		Sale Proceeds	
28		Sale Price	743 008	Sale Price	743 008
29		− Cost of Sale	−0−	− Costs of Sale	−0−
30		− AB	/20 000	− Mortgage	−0−
31		Gain	623 008	Proceeds before Taxes	743 008
32		− Excess	−0−	− Tax Liability on Sale	124 602
33		Capital Gain	623 008	Proceeds after Taxes	618 406

● REALTORS NATIONAL MARKETING INSTITUTE®
of the NATIONAL ASSOCIATION OF REALTORS® , 1981
The statements and figures presented herein, while not guaranteed, are secured from sources we believe authoritative.   Prepared by_____

Calculation of after-tax cash flows The annual $2,400 expenditure for carrying costs is deducted from ordinary income. For the 30-percent marginal rate taxpayer, this yields a savings of $720 which, in effect, reduces the negative $2,400 cash flow to negative $1,680.

For the 50-percent marginal rate taxpayer, the $2,400 deduction results in a tax savings of $1,200, making the after-tax negative cash flow ($1,200).

In the ten-year, 15-percent growth rate, the resale proceeds after sales costs are $485,467. Capital gains and capital gains tax and after-tax proceeds are calculated as follows:

Figure 48 Sale Proceeds After Taxes (10 yrs, 25% growth, 50% tax bracket)

Adjusted Basis			Excess Cost Recovery (CR)			Tax Liability on Sale		
Analysis of Sale Proceeds						**Year:**		
23 Original Basis	120 000		Total CR			Excess Recapture Tax			
24 + Capital Improvements			S/L CR			Capital Gain Tax 20%		199 517
25 − Cost Recovery	−0−		Excess CR			Tax Liability on Sale		
26 − Partial Sales			Exc. CR Carryover					
27 AB	120 000		**Gain**			**Sale Proceeds**		
28			Sale Price	1 117 587	Sale Price	1 117 587	
29			− Cost of Sale	−0−	− Costs of Sale	−0−	
30			− AB	120 000	− Mortgage	−0−	
31			Gain		Proceeds before Taxes	1 117 587	
32			− Excess		− Tax Liability on Sale	199 517	
33			Capital Gain	997 587	Proceeds after Taxes	918 070	

● REALTORS NATIONAL MARKETING INSTITUTE®
of the NATIONAL ASSOCIATION OF REALTORS®, 1981

The statements and figures presented herein, while not guaranteed, are secured from sources we believe authoritative.

Prepared by _____

Proceeds after sales costs		$485,467
Original basis	$120,000	
Capital gain (long-term)	365,467	
Tax rate (40% × 50% = 20%)	.20	
Tax		73,093
After-tax proceeds		$412,374

A study of the preceding cash flows points to two important conclusions. First, it is evident that the higher margial-rate taxpayer has a greater tax savings, thereby creating a smaller negative after-tax annual cash flow. This, coupled with the same sales proceeds after taxes, gives the 50-percent taxpayer a slightly higher yield at the same resale price. (This slight advantage could be negated if the long-term capital gain is not so large as to put the 30-percent taxpayer into the 50-percent bracket.)

The most significant result, however, has to do with the "shelter" obtained from the write-off of the annual carrying costs at ordinary rates and the capital gains treatment of the gain.

Normally it might be expected that a 13.86-percent yield will be reduced to 9.7 percent for a 30-percent taxpayer or 6.9 percent for a 50-percent taxpayer. Instead, the after-tax yields are 12.39 percent and 12.5 percent respectively (in the ten-year, 15-percent example).

Obviously there are tax benefits from the ordinary rate "write-offs" and from the capital gain rates on resale. However, the benefits are never great enough to give an after-tax yield equal to or greater than the before-tax yield.

Illustration 4 Impact of adding expenses to basis instead of taking annual deductions

If no annual deduction of expenses were taken, the before- and after-tax annual cash flows would be the same—a negative $2,400. The carrying costs, however, would be added to basis, changing after-tax resale proceeds. For the ten-year, 15-percent growth rate, the after-tax resale proceeds would be calculated as follows:

Proceeds after sales costs		$485,467
Original basis	$120,000	
Expenses added to basis	24,000	
Basis at time of sale	144,000	
Capital gains	341,467	
Tax rate (20%)	.20	
Tax		68,293
After-tax proceeds		$417,174

The cash flow diagram for both the 30-percent and 50-percent marginal tax rate would be the same (assuming the capital gains tax rate was at the maximum rate):

EOY	Cash Flow
0	($120,000)
1	(2,400)
–	–
–	–
–	–
10	(2,400)+
After-tax proceeds	$417,174

This gives a yield of 12.1 percent which is less than the yield obtained by taking the deduction of expenses annually.

Illustration 5 Impact of financing on land

Assume the subject property is acquired with a 25-percent down payment and an interest-only loan for the remaining $90,000 at 10 percent, with the principal payable upon resale at the end of the ten-year holding period. The property will be analyzed at the 15, 20 and 25-percent growth rates on an after-tax basis for both a 30-percent and 50-percent marginal rate taxpayer. Capital gains will be 20 percent.

Comparisons will be made on a before- and after-tax basis. Annual cash outlay will be $2,400 for carrying costs and $9,000 for interest (10 percent of $90,000), or a total of $11,400. Deducting $11,400 from the taxpayer's other income results in a reduced income tax on other income. For a 30-percent taxpayer, the tax reduction is $3,420, thereby reducing the $11,400 before-tax outgo to $7,980 outgo. For a 50-percent taxpayer, the tax reduction would be $5,700, thereby reducing the $11,400 before-tax outgo to $5,700 outgo.

Resale proceeds after sales costs, but before taxes, are reduced by the $90,000 outstanding loan balance. After-tax proceeds are calculated by reducing resale proceeds before tax by 20 percent of the gain.

Creating leverage by financing confirms the conclusions of Illustration 3, but it adds another dimension. As we saw in Illustration 3, there are tax benefits resulting from write-offs at ordinary rates and from long-term capital gain rates. Also, it is apparent that the higher-bracket taxpayer obtains higher yields at the same growth rate or can have a lower growth rate than the lower-rate taxpayer to obtain an equal yield.

	Before Tax		After Tax 30% Marginal Rate		After Tax 50% Marginal Rate	
	10 Years/15% Growth					
	EOY	Cash Flow	EOY	Cash Flow	EOY	Cash Flow
	0	($30,000)	0	($30,000)	0	($30,000)
	1	(11,400)	1	(7,980)	1	(5,700)
	–	–	–	–	–	–
	–	–	–	–	–	–
	–	–	–	–	–	–
	10	(11,400)	10	(7,980)	10	(5,700)
Resale Proceeds		$ 485,467		$ 485,467		$ 485,467
Mortgage Balance		$ 90,000		$ 90,000		$ 90,000
Income Tax		0		$ 73,093		$ 73,093
Yield		16.84%		16.97%		19.49%
	10 Years/20% Growth					
	EOY	Cash Flow	EOY	Cash Flow	EOY	Cash Flow
	0	($30,000)	0	($30,000)	0	($30,000)
	1	(11,400)	1	(7,980)	–	(5,700)
	–	–	–	–	–	–
	–	–	–	–	–	–
	–	–	–	–	–	–
	10	(11,400)	10	(7,980)	10	(5,700)
Resale Proceeds		$ 743,008		$ 743,008		$ 743,008
Mortgage Balance		$ 90,000		$ 90,000		$ 90,000
Income Tax		0		$ 124,602		$ 124,602
Yield		24.87%		24.5%		26.8%

419

(continued)

		10 Years/25% Growth			
EOY	Cash Flow	EOY	Cash Flow	EOY	Cash Flow
0	($30,000)	0	($30,000)	0	($30,000)
1	(11,400)	1	(7,980)	1	(5,700)
–	–	–	–	–	–
–	–	–	–	–	–
10	(11,400)	10	(7,980)	10	(5,700)
Resale Proceeds	$1,117,587		$1,117,587		$1,117,587
Mortgage Balance	$ 90,000		$ 90,000		$ 90,000
Income Tax	0		$ 199,517		$ 199,517
Yield	32.15%		31.46%		33.49%

The point illustrated here is that the leverage has boosted yield substantially on both before- and after-tax projections. The comparisons are:

	Before Tax		After Tax (30% Rate)	
	No Mortgage	25% Equity	No Mortgage	25% Equity
15%/10 Yr.	13.86%	16.84%	12.3%	16.97%
20%/10 Yr.	19.01%	24.87%	17.1%	24.5%
25%/10 Yr.	24.12%	32.15%	21.9%	31.46%

Many investors erroneously attribute yields which are higher than the growth rate to tax savings involved in the write-off of expenses at ordinary rates while gains are taken at lower capital gain rates. In reality it is leverage that effects the higher yields.

Illustration 6 Another land analysis technique

In Chapter 4 it was pointed out that negative cash flows, especially coupled with high Internal Rates of Return (IRR), could be responsible for misleading results. Discounting future negative cash flows at high rates suggests that an investor could have invested the funds at the IRR rate until needed. This is practically impossible at 15- to 20-percent rates, however. As Chapter 4 pointed out, it is probably more realistic to discount future negative cash flow needs at a lower, safe rate.

It is also realistic to assume that not all land purchases are made for cash, or on interest-only-until-sold loans. More probable is some kind of level payment loan where the payment includes principal and interest for a specified period of time. Finally, the investor should have some way to calculate what a property should sell for sometime in the future in order to obtain a specified yield either before or after taxes.

This illustration is concerned with a process to accomplish these ends. **420** The subject property is the same as before, but with a few different assumptions:

Price	$120,000
Down payment	30,000
Loan	90,000
Interest rate	10%
Loan period	10 years
Annual payment	$ 14,647
Marginal tax bracket	50%
Capital gains	20%
Resale costs	10%
Safe rate (after tax)	5%
Operating costs	$ 2,400

The problem will be to determine what the property must resell for at any year from EOY 1 through EOY 10 in order to yield the investor 15 percent before income taxes and/or after income taxes.

The first step is to determine the investor's cash flows both before and after taxes if the property is held for ten years. See Figure 49 for this cash flow analysis.

The cash flows from Figure 49 can be diagramed as:

Before Tax		After Tax	
EOY	Cash Flow	EOY	Cash Flow
0	($30,000)	0	($30,000)
1	(17,047)	1	(11,347)
2	(17,047)	2	(11,629)
3	(17,047)	3	(11,940)
4	(17,047)	4	(12,266)
5	(17,047)	5	(12,657)
6	(17,047)	6	(13,071)
7	(17,047)	7	(13,525)
8	(17,047)	8	(14,025)
9	(17,047)	9	(14,576)
10	(17,047)	10	(15,181)

In a typical IRR study the information available is the initial investment, the annual cash flows and the resale proceeds. From this an IRR, or yield, is calculated. In a net present value study, the annual cash flows, resale proceeds and yield are known and the calculation is to determine the appropriate initial investment. In this illustration the knowns are the initial investment and the annual cash flows (which are negative).

If it is assumed that a potential investor desired a minimum yield of 15 percent, then the unknown would be the resale price needed to attain that yield for the time the property was held. Because the holding period is also unknown, the resale price needed both before and after taxes will be calculated for each of the ten years. This will give the investor insight into how

421

Figure 49

Cash Flow Analysis

For _Mr. Investor_

Purpose _10 yr. Cash Flow Analysis_

Date_____

Sales Price _120,000_

Encumbrances _90,000_

Investment _30,000_

Mortgage Data

	Encumbrances	Beginning Balance	Remaining Term	Number of Payments Per Year	Interest Rate	Payment	Annual Debt Service	Remarks
1	1st Mortgage	90,000	10 yrs.	1	10%	14,647	14,647	
2	2nd Mortgage							
3	3rd Mortgage							

		Year: 1	Year: 2	Year: 3	Year: 4	Year: 5	EOY	Mortgage Balance
	Ownership Analysis of Property Income:			**Taxable Income**				1st Mortgage
4	Gross Scheduled Income	0						
5	Less: Vcy. & Credit Losses							
6	Gross Operating Income	0						
7	– Operating Expenses	2 400						
8	Net Operating Income	(2 400)	(2 400)	(2 400)	(2 400)	(2 400)		
9	– Non-Operating Expense							
10	– Interest – 1st Mortgage	9 000	8 435	7 814	7 131	6 379		2nd Mortgage
11	– Interest – 2nd Mortgage							
12	– Interest – 3rd Mortgage							
13	– Cost Recovery							
14	Real Est. Taxable Income	(11 400)	(10 835)	(10 214)	(9 531)	(8 779)		
				Cash Flows				
15	Net Operating Income	(2 400)	(2 400)	(2 400)	(2 400)	(2 400)		3rd Mortgage
16	– Annual Debt Service	14 647	14 647	14 647	14 647	14 647		
17	– Funded Reserves							
18	– Capital Additions							
19	Cash Flow before Taxes	(17 047)	(17 047)	(17 047)	(17 047)	(17 047)		
20	– Minimum Tax							
21	– Tax Liability on Real Est.	(5 700)	(5 418)	(5 107)	(4 781)	(4 390)		
22	Cash Flow after Taxes	(11 347)	(11 629)	(11 940)	(12 266)	(12 657)		

Analysis of Sale Proceeds   Year:

	Adjusted Basis			Excess Cost Recovery (CR)			Tax Liability on Sale		
23	Original Basis			Total CR			Excess Recapture Tax		
24	+ Capital Improvements			S/L CR			Capital Gain Tax		
25	– Cost Recovery			Excess CR			Tax Liability on Sale		
26	– Partial Sales			Exc. CR Carryover					
27	AB				Gain		Sale Proceeds		
28				Sale Price			Sale Price		
29				– Cost of Sale			– Costs of Sale		
30				– AB			– Mortgage		
31				Gain			Proceeds before Taxes		
32				– Excess			– Tax Liability on Sale		
33				Capital Gain			Proceeds after Taxes		

Figure 49 (continued)

Cash Flow Analysis

For _____

Purpose _____

Date _____

Sales Price _____

Encumbrances _____

Investment _____

Mortgage Data

Encumbrances	Beginning Balance	Remaining Term	Number of Payments Per Year	Interest Rate	Payment	Annual Debt Service	Remarks
1 1st Mortgage							
2 2nd Mortgage							
3 3rd Mortgage							

Ownership Analysis of Property Income:	Year: 6	Year: 7	Year: 8	Year: 9	Year: 10	EOY	Mortgage Balance
	Taxable Income						
4 Gross Scheduled Income						1st Mortgage	
5 Less: Vcy. & Credit Losses						10	0 —
6 Gross Operating Income							
7 – Operating Expenses							
8 Net Operating Income	(2 400)	(2 400)	(2 400)	(2 400)	(2 400)		
9 – Non-Operating Expense							
10 – Interest – 1st Mortgage	5 532	4 643	3 643	2 542	1 331	2nd Mortgage	
11 – Interest – 2nd Mortgage							
12 – Interest – 3rd Mortgage							
13 – Cost Recovery							
14 Real Est. Taxable Income	(7 952)	(7 043)	(6 043)	(4 942)	(3 731)		
	Cash Flows						
15 Net Operating Income	(2 400)	(2 400)	(2 400)	(2 400)	(2 400)	3rd Mortgage	
16 – Annual Debt Service	14 647	14 647	14 647	14 647	14 647		
17 – Funded Reserves							
18 – Capital Additions							
19 Cash Flow before Taxes	(17 047)	(17 047)	(17 047)	(17 047)	(17 047)		
20 – Minimum Tax							
21 – Tax Liability on Real Est.	3 976	3 522	(3 022)	(2 471)	1 866		
22 Cash Flow after Taxes	13 071	13 525	(14 025)	(14 576)	(15 181)		

Analysis of Sale Proceeds   Year:

Adjusted Basis		Excess Cost Recovery (CR)		Tax Liability on Sale	
23 Original Basis		Total CR		Excess Recapture Tax	
24 + Capital Improvements		S/L CR		Capital Gain Tax	
25 – Cost Recovery		Excess CR		Tax Liability on Sale	
26 – Partial Sales		Exc. CR Carryover			
27 AB		Gain		Sale Proceeds	
28		Sale Price		Sale Price	
29		– Cost of Sale		– Costs of Sale	
30		– AB		– Mortgage	
31		Gain		Proceeds before Taxes	
32		– Excess		– Tax Liability on Sale	
33		Capital Gain		Proceeds after Taxes	

Prepared by _____

the sale price must increase for him to attain his investment goals.

Figure 50 shows the format used to obtain the resale price needed for each year.

Financial management rate of return

Column 1 of Figure 50 shows the $17,047 negative cash flow which was taken from Figure 49, Line 19, Cash Flow Before Taxes. Column 2, Line 1 is the amount that must be deposited at the safe rate (5 percent) at the time of acquisition (EOY 0) in order to have $17,047 available for payment EOY 1. This is the Financial Management Rate of Return (FMRR) process of assuring the funding of future negative cash flows from an increased initial investment when no sufficient positive cash flows precede a negative cash flow. (See Chapter 4 for a complete discussion of FMRR.) Line 2 and subsequent lines in Column 2 of Figure 50 discount the subsequent negative cash flows at a safe rate back to EOY 0.

For Column 3 (Year 1) the $16,235 in Column 2 is added to the initial investment of $30,000, thereby creating an adjusted initial investment of $46,235. Line 2 of Column 3 is the adjusted initial investment from Line 1 increased by the present value of the Year 2 negative cash flow discounted to EOY 1.

To continue the example the process for EOY 4 (Line 4) can be diagramed as:

```
EOY   0   ($30,000) + (16,235) + (15,462) + (14,726) + (14,025)
      1   ( 17,047) ————↑          ↑          ↑           ↑
      2   ( 17,047) ————————————————┘          │           │
      3   ( 17,047) ———————————————————————————┘           │
      4   ( 17,047) ———————————————————————————————————————┘
```

making the adjusted cash flows:

EOY	
0	($90,448)
1	0
2	0
3	0
4	0

The adjusted initial investment of $90,448 (Column 3, Line 4) is the original $30,000 initial investment plus the total of the first four years' cash flows discounted at the safe rate for the appropriate number of years until needed.

Column 4 is the amount of net proceeds the investor must take out of the investment (upon resale) to obtain 15 percent on his adjusted initial investment, compounded for the number of years until the property is disposed of.

Figure 50 Calculation Format

EOY	1 Cash Flows	2 Present Value	3 Adjusted Initial Investment	4 Proceeds for 15%	5 Mortgage Balance	6 Total (4 + 5)	7 After Tax Gain 6-Basis	8 Taxable Gain 7 ÷ .80	9 Sale Price 8 + Basis	10 Sale Price ÷ .90	11 Rounded	12 Price Per Sq Ft	13 Annual Growth Rate	14 % Over Cost
						Before Taxes								
1	(17,047)	(16,235)	46,235	53,170	84,353	137,523				152,803	153,000	14.6	27.5	27.5
2	(17,047)	(15,462)	61,697	81,594	78,141	159,735				177,483	178,000	17.0	21.8	48.3
3	(17,047)	(14,726)	76,423	116,230	71,308	187,538				208,375	208,000	19.9	20.1	73.3
4	(17,047)	(14,025)	90,448	158,194	63,792	221,986				246,651	247,000	23.6	19.8	105.8
5	(17,047)	(13,357)	103,805	208,789	55,524	264,313				293,681	294,000	28.1	19.6	145.0
6	(17,047)	(12,721)	116,526	269,532	46,429	315,961				351,068	351,000	33.6	19.6	192.5
7	(17,047)	(12,115)	128,641	342,188	36,425	378,613				420,681	420,000	40.2	19.6	250.0
8	(17,047)	(11,538)	140,179	428,811	25,421	454,232				504,702	505,000	48.3	19.7	320.8
9	(17,047)	(10,989)	151,168	531,790	13,316	545,106				605,673	606,000	58.0	19.7	405.0
10	(17,047)	(10,465)	161,633	653,896	0	653,896				726,551	727,000	69.5	19.7	505.8
						After Taxes								
1	(11,347)	(10,807)	40,807	46,928	84,353	131,281	11,281	14,101	134,101	149,001	149,000	14.3	24.2	24.2
2	(11,629)	(10,548)	51,355	67,917	78,141	146,058	26,058	32,573	152,573	169,525	170,000	16.3	19.0	41.7
3	(11,940)	(10,314)	61,669	93,791	71,308	165,099	45,099	56,374	176,374	195,971	196,000	18.7	17.8	63.3
4	(12,266)	(10,091)	71,760	125,509	63,792	189,301	69,301	86,625	206,626	229,585	230,000	22.0	17.7	91.7
5	(16,657)	(9,917)	81,677	164,282	55,524	219,806	99,806	124,758	244,756	271,953	272,000	26.0	17.8	126.7
6	(13,071)	(9,754)	91,431	211,485	46,429	257,914	137,914	172,393	292,393	324,881	325,000	31.1	18.1	170.8
7	(13,525)	(9,612)	101,043	268,776	36,429	305,205	185,205	231,506	351,506	390,562	391,000	37.4	18.4	225.8
8	(14,025)	(9,493)	110,536	338,132	25,421	363,553	243,553	304,441	424,441	471,601	472,000	45.1	18.7	293.3
9	(14,576)	(9,396)	119,932	421,906	13,316	435,222	315,222	394,028	514,028	571,142	571,000	54.6	18.9	375.8
10	(15,181)	(9,320)	129,252	522,896	0	522,896	402,896	503,620	623,620	692,911	693,000	66.3	19.2	477.5

For example:

Line 1 $53,170 is $46,235 at 15 percent for one year.
Line 3 $116,230 is $76,423 at 15 percent for three years.
Line 8 shows that $140,179 (Column 3) invested for eight years at 15
     percent compounded must grow to $428,811 (Column 4).

The cash flow t-charts for the above three examples:

	EOY 1		EOY 3		EOY 8
0	($46,235)	0	($76,423)	0	($140,179)
1	0 + 53,170	1	0	1	0
	FMRR 15%	2	0	2	0
		3	0 + 116,230	3	0
			FMRR 15%	4	0
				5	0
				6	0
				7	0
				8	0 + 428,811
					FMRR 15%

Column 5 indicates the unpaid balance of the $90,000 loan at the end of each year. This is obtained from Lines 5 in Figure 50.

Column 6 (total of Columns 4 plus 5) is the amount the investor must receive at the end of the indicated year to obtain sufficient funds to yield 15 percent on his adjusted initial investment for the number of years the investment was held, plus the amount needed to pay off the existing mortgage balance.

The total described in Column 6 is an after-sales cost amount. If sale costs are 10 percent, Column 6 represents 90 percent of the sale price. Therefore, dividing the Column 6 amount by .90 indicates the gross sales price needed to:

1. Pay sales costs
2. Pay the existing debt
3. Give the investor 15-percent on the initial investment compounded for the holding period.

This figure is shown in Column 10 for the various years. Column 11 is the sale price from Column 10 rounded to a typical market price.

The acquisition price of $120,000 for 24 acres was 11.47 cents per square foot. Column 12 indicates the resale price per square foot.

Column 13 (annual growth rate) is calculated by entering the acquisition price of $120,000 as the present value, the resale price (say for Year 8— $505,000) as the future value and using a hand-held calculator to solve for i (interest rate) for eight years—19.7 percent for Year 8.

Column 14 (percentage over cost) is obtained by dividing the increased value by the purchase price and multiplying by 100 to get a percentage figure:

$$\frac{\$505,000 - \$120,000}{\$120,000} \times 100 = 320.8\%$$

A review of this column shows that, in this example, the property must double (105.8 percent) in four years to obtain 15 percent and must grow two and one-half times in seven years and five times in ten years for the investor to reach his desired goal of 15 percent. The growth necessary to obtain a 20- or 25-percent yield, of course, has to be even more rapid.

After-tax cash flows

The first six after-tax columns in Figure 50 use the same techniques as described above, except that the cash flows (Column 1) are the after-tax cash flows from Figure 49, Line 22.

The after-tax gain (Column 7) is calculated by reducing the amount in Column 6 by the basis of the property, $120,000.

Using EOY 5 as an example, Column 6 indicates the investor must have $219,806 to obtain sufficient funds to yield 15 percent compounded for five years on the adjusted initial investment and pay off the mortgage of $55,524. If the $219,806 is to be an after-tax amount, that means that the investor must receive $99,806 after taxes in addition to his basis of $120,000.

If at EOY 5, the after-tax gain must be $99,806 and the capital gains tax rate is 20 percent, then the $99,806 represents the 80 percent after taxes. Therefore, dividing $99,806 by .80 gives the before-tax gain of $124,758 (Column 8).

If the before-tax gain is $124,758, this must be increased by the basis of $120,000 to obtain the sale price after sale costs (Column 9).

Columns 10 to 14 are calculated as described previously for before taxes, but of course represent after-tax amounts.

Conclusion

It is interesting to compare the before- and after-tax sale prices necessary to produce the projected yield (see Figure 50, Column 11). The differences are slight. And it is well to note that in this example the resale prices on an after-tax basis are lower than the before-tax prices. This indicates that the conversion of annual expenses at regular rates to capitalization rates at resale was advantageous. Prior to the reduced capital gain rates in the 1981 law, this was not necessarily the case. See Figure 51 for a graph of resale prices needed for each year of holding to obtain the 15-percent projected yields after taxes under the assumptions of the study.

Figure 51   Resale Prices/Holding Period

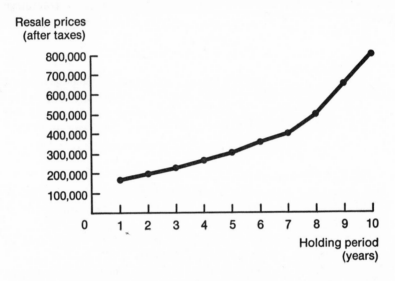

Several important conclusions become evident.

The longer an investor holds a parcel of investment land, the faster it must appreciate for a desired yield to be obtained.

Many land investors have conflicting investment strategies which usually result in working against their best interests. Most wish a high yield, say 20 to 40 percent because of the speculative nature and lack of liquidity of investment land, and they couple these dreams with the concept that the investment is the small price they originally paid for the property instead of its worth today. In addition, they are reluctant to sell the property because of the capital gains that would create, so they hold onto it for long periods of 15 to 30 years. This ensures the impossibility of attaining the yields they originally hoped for.

This study did not take into consideration the IRS's limitation on investment interest discussed in Chapter 9. The interest limitation in effect delays the tax savings caused by the deduction, which must be deferred, thereby increasing early negative cash flows and thus requiring higher resale prices.

The study also disregards syndicators' portions of profits and perhaps even management fees. Real estate taxes in the example are considered level, but they could increase as the property value increases. These additional costs would require an even further boost in sale price to obtain the desired yield.

Our example was of 24 acres to be acquired at $5,000 per acre. A potential investor who wants a 15-percent yield and realizes that the selling price in five years must be approximately $12,000 per acre and in ten years approximately $30,000 per acre must project what trends, zoning, utilities capability and development potential must occur to make the needed sale price a probability.

We might want to relate these findings with the land investment platitudes discussed earlier:

"Land is a good investment because it always goes up in value."

"Land is a bad investment—it's not liquid . . . ."

There is nothing wrong with a nonliquid investment—if it has a good yield—and in land that means a good and rapid growth.

"Land is a good investment. I can write off carrying costs—it's a good shelter."

The costs written off are not shelter. They are actual out-of-pocket expenses. Yes, they can be deducted from ordinary income and this results in tax savings which can be described as the government paying a portion of the costs. But the deduction is not like depreciation, which is a noncash expense against ordinary income. When reduced from basis the deduction is repaid at capital gains rates. Land is sold at an amount over the original basis, and if qualified, the gain is taxed at long-term capital gain rates. This, however, is not tax shelter.

"Land is a good investment—its amount is finite and it must go up in value."

As before, the timing of the growth is the overriding factor. There are some who believe that getting an appraisal is the answer, but that only indicates what others have been doing in the past. It does not indicate what will happen.

If there are any conclusions about land investments they must be these:

1. Because investment land has all negative cash flows until it is sold, because it is difficult to project when it can be sold and to whom and because such land is difficult to borrow against, it has greater risk than many other traditional investments and should therefore have a potential for greater yield than these other investments.

2. The longer land is held the longer is the period for compounding all the negative cash flows that increase in total each year. This means that the sale price needed increases more rapidly with each additional year of holding—especially after the first four or five years. Therefore, investment land tends to be a better short-term investment than a long-term one.

3. Although an investor in land may not be able to project when it will resell nor at what price, prior to acquisition he should have some idea what it must sell for at some future time in order to earn a yield commensurate with the risks.

4. Nothing here should be construed to imply that land is not or cannot be an attractive investment. However, in order for land to be an intelligent investment decision it should be acquired with a basic understanding of what it must sell for.

5. The greatest error committed by many investors who hold speculative land is their tendency to regard what they paid for it many years ago as their investment in the property. In reality, their investment today is the amount they would *net* from a sale after expenses, including taxes.

6. The decision to keep or sell should not be based on potential income taxes, but rather on whether the proceeds *after* taxes would earn more by investing in the land for a further period (holding on to it) or by investing in some other holding that will yield a larger return.

Case Study 12
Impact of holding period on equity yield

Before-tax equity yield will virtually always change throughout the holding period of an investment. Yield is affected by changes in income and expenses during the holding period, the sale price at the end of the holding period, and the financing. Interest rates, amortization terms and loan-to-value ratio will each affect the equity return on investment. For any investment financed with an amortizing loan, the loan-to-value ratio changes after each payment which includes principal; thus, leverage will change each period. The related equity yield, if calculated for each individual period, will be different for each period if only because of the constantly changing financial structure. Therefore, holding period can be an important variable when choosing among alternative financing with different amortization terms.

Situation

To illustrate the impact of holding period on equity yield, consider a property with constant NOI of $12,000 and a constant value of $100,000. Constant value and income are assumed in order to isolate the impact of financing. Notice that this property would produce a 12-percent equity yield for any holding period if it were acquired without any debt financing. The investors' cash flows before taxes are summarized below.

EOY	$
0	($100,000)
1	12,000
↓	↓
$\boxed{n}$	12,000 + 100,000

The income will be the same for any number of periods, and the sale price will be $100,000 no matter when it is sold. Equity yield, in this case, is calculated as if the cash flows were a perpetuity or interest-only loan:

$$y = \frac{\text{NOI}}{\text{value}} = \frac{\$12,000}{\$100,000} = 12\%$$

The IRR of these cash flows will be 12 percent for any number of years exceeding zero.

Financing alternatives

Consider three alternative loans to finance this property.

Loan A   An $85,000 loan at 10.75-percent interest per year with a balloon payment of $80,000 due EOY 15 and monthly payments of $772.71. The annual debt constant is:

0.1091   [($772.71 × 12) ÷ $85,000]

Loan B   An $85,000 loan at 10-percent interest per year with monthly payments of $913.41 which will fully amortize the loan in 15 years. The annual debt constant is:

0.1290   [($913.41 × 12) ÷ $85,000].

Loan C   An $85,000 loan at 9.5-percent interest per year plus 2.5 points at origination and 20-year amortization with monthly payments of $792.31. Loan proceeds are $82,875 (85,000 less 2.5 percent). The annual debt constant is:

0.1147   [($792.31 × 12) ÷ $82,875].

If equity yield before tax is used as the decision criterion, the highest yielding choice will depend on the *investment holding period*. Monthly cash flows before taxes (CFBT) for each financing alternative are constant for each month the property is owned. (CFBT is the monthly NOI of $1,000 less the monthly loan payment.) Proceeds before taxes (PBT) are equal to the constant sale price of $100,000 less the outstanding loan balance at the end of the month. The initial investment end of month (EOM) 0 is equal to the $100,000 purchase price less the loan proceeds. In the case of Loan C, the 2.5 points have been added to the initial investment. The cash flows

before taxes and proceeds before taxes for all three financing alternatives
have been summarized below for three-, eight- and fifteen-year holding periods.

EOM	Loan A	
	CFBT	PBT
0	($15,000.00)	
1	$227.29	
↓		
3×12=36	$227.29	$15,475.69
↓		
8×12=96	$227.29	$16,701.40
↓		
15×12=180	$227.29	$20,000.00

EOM	Loan B	
	CFBT	PBT
0	($15,000.00)	
1	$86.59	
↓		
3×12=36	$86.59	$23,568.66
↓		
8×12=96	$86.59	$44,978.96
↓		
15×12=180	$86.59	$100,000.00

EOM	Loan C	
	CFBT	PBT
0	($17,125.00)	
1	$207.69	
↓		
3×12=36	$207.69	$19,950.80
↓		
8×12=96	$207.69	$32,070.50
↓		
15×12=180	$207.69	$62,274.22

Equity yields before taxes are summarized in the following table, using
the monthly cash flows above. The resulting monthly IRRs have been annualized.

Summary of Equity Yield Before Taxes			
Holding Period (Years)	Financing Alternative		
	A	B	C
3	19.0%	20.8%*	18.7%
8	18.8%	18.2%	19.2%*
15	18.6%*	16.0%	18.0%

The asterisk indicates the financing alternative that will produce the highest equity yield before taxes for each holding period. The "best" of these financing alternatives actually depends on holding period. The original loan-to-value ratio is the same for each alternative, but the interest rate and terms vary for each.

Effects of holding period

The effects, over time, of the different financing alternatives can be seen in Figure 52. The equity yields before taxes for each financing alternative for holding periods up to 15 years have been summarized in this graph. Each point on each curve indicates the equity yield for that corresponding holding period. This graph also illustrates the highest-yielding financing alternative for every holding period during the 15-year projection.

Figure 52 shows that Loan B would be higher for holding periods less than five years. If the property is held for approximately five to eleven years, Loan C has the highest yield; for holding periods beyond eleven years, Loan A would provide the highest yield.

Note that each loan shown on Figure 52 would maximize equity yield before tax for some holding periods, but not for all holding periods. Some generalizations can be made for each of these loans which may clarify the equity yield trends.

Loan A has the highest interest rate but the lowest monthly payment. Among the three financing alternatives monthly CFBT is greater for this loan. Proceeds before taxes, for any holding period, is less for Loan A, compared to B and C. The $80,000 balloon payment EOY 15 reduces the amount of amortization required as part of the debt service. Alternatively stated, it would take more than 39 years to amortize $85,000 at 10.75-percent interest with monthly payments of $772.71. Thus, the loan-to-value ratio does not decline a great deal during the 15-year projection due to the small amount of principal amortization. Since the loan-to-value ratio is fairly constant, the resulting equity yield is likewise relatively stable during the 15-year projection. (Recall from Chapter 6 that the equity yield would be constant over time with an interest-only loan.)

Loan B illustrates the impact of a short amortization term. The 10-percent interest rate is less than for Loan A. Equity yields for holding periods less than about five years are greatest with Loan B because of the low effective interest rate. Monthly cash flows before taxes are less for Loan B than the other loans because B requires the greater debt service. The high debt service is required to fully amortize the loan balance in 15 years, the shortest term among the three loans.

For any holding period, the equity proceeds before taxes are greater for Loan B. The benefit of positive leverage decreases as equity increases. The rate of equity increase per period, from loan amortization, is greatest for Loan B. Therefore, the equity yield will decrease more rapidly for longer holding periods. The equity yields for holding periods up to 15 years decline over 600 basis points (a basis point is 1/100th of a percentage point) for Loan B compared to about 45 basis points for Loan A.

The steady decline in equity yields for longer holding periods for Loans A and B can be explained by changes in the loan-to-value ratios over time. The effective interest rates for these alternatives are constant over any holding period. This is not the case, however, for Loan C.

Loan C produces a humped equity yield curve (see Figure 52) which indicates that it is the highest-yielding financing alternative for holding periods over five years and less than eleven years. Loan C's cash flows before taxes and sales proceeds before taxes, for any holding period, are always between those resulting from the other two financing alternatives. The shape of the equity yield curve for Loan C is caused by two variables which change for different holding periods—the loan-to-value ratio and the effective interest rate.

Loan B has the lowest nominal interest rate among the three choices, but it is the only loan with discount points payable at origination. Recall that the effective interest rate of a loan with discount points decreases as the term of the loan is increased. If Loan C is paid in full after a short holding period, the effective interest rate will be very high; therefore, the equity yield will be low. The effective interest rate of Loan C is more than 10 percent, the interest rate of Loan B, for holding periods of less than eight years.

The equity yields produced with this financing alternative increase for holding periods of less than approximately five years because the effective interest rate decreases significantly for each additional period up to that time. The decreasing loan-to-value ratio becomes the dominant influence on equity yield for longer holding periods. The benefit of positive leverage declines for long holding periods as it does for the other alternative loans; therefore, the equity yield will be less for longer holding periods.

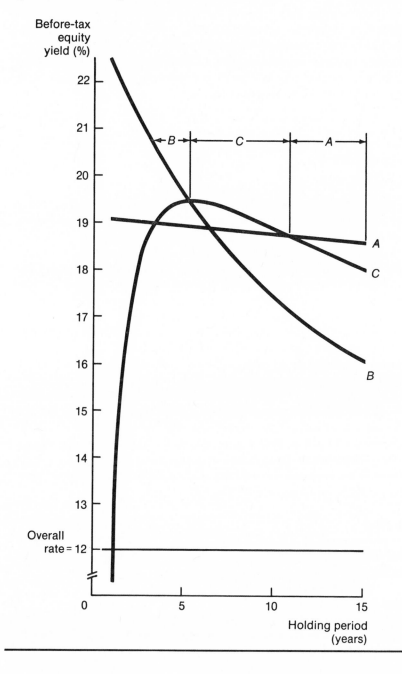

Figure 52 Financing Alternatives

Before-tax
equity
yield (%)

Holding period
(years)

Conclusion

It is obvious that the anticipated holding period of an investment can be an important consideration in the selection among financing alternatives. The effective interest rate and amortization terms affect the volatility of equity yield over time. An understanding of the influence of interest rates and repayment terms over time will assist in negotiating financing terms which are most consistent with investment objectives.

Case Study 13
FMRR analysis

The Financial Management Rate of Return (FMRR) model was designed to provide a flexible analytical framework which can reflect present and anticipated market realities in the form of cash flow projections.

Recall from Chapter 4 that all cash flows processed within the context of the FMRR model are after tax and after all available financing. Cash flows may be modified with after-tax discount and compounding rates commensurate with the investment amount, level of risk and duration of the investment. The "safe rates" used to discount projected after-tax cash outflows are chosen to reflect anticipated after-tax market yields for investments which provide *both* liquidity and preservation of capital.

After-tax yields on reinvested after-tax cash inflows are based on the investor's risk and liquidity preferences. Yields on "safe" or "speculative" investments change with market conditions. An analyst may choose a reinvestment rate based on treasury bill or municipal bond yields as of the date of the analysis or he may use the average yield on AA utility bonds in the past ten years. FMRR analysis can incorporate an investor's total investment portfolio management strategy, including risk preference, with the current and anticipated economic environment in choosing among investment alternatives based upon estimated future wealth.

Situation

Consider a client with a total of $100,000 available to invest who is trying to choose between two investment alternatives. The cash flows after taxes for each are summarized on page 437.

FMRR analysis

Investment A has a greater IRR with half the initial investment of Investment B. If A is acquired, some provisions must be made to meet the $30,000 cash outflow EOY 2. Investment B has a duration of only four years, compared to six years for Investment A. The after-tax cash flows must be modified for the time and size disparities in order to compare the

EOY	Investment A	Investment B
0	($50,000)	($100,000)
1	5,000	–0–
2	(30,000)	–0–
3	10,000	–0–
4	30,000	200,000
5	35,000	–0–
6	115,000	–0–
IRR	22.3%	18.9%

investment alternatives on a par basis, assuming that each has similar risk characteristics.

Three after-tax investment rates will be used to adjust the cash flows. Cash required to meet future obligations will be invested in treasury bonds at an after-tax yield of 7 percent. After-tax income from investments will be reinvested at an after-tax rate of 12 percent. At any time in the future the investor can buy limited partnership shares in block amounts at $60,000 which will produce an after-tax yield of 18 percent.

The after-tax cash flows for Investment A are modified in a three-step procedure.

Step 1 Modify cash outflows The $5,000.00 received EOY 1 will be invested at the safe rate of 7 percent and will grow to $5,350 by EOY 2. The $30,000 cash outflow at EOY 2 will be reduced by that amount, leaving a balance of ($24,650). This amount must be available EOY 2 from a safe investment of $21,530.26 (the present value of $24,650 discounted at 7 percent for two years) made EOY 0 to anticipate the payment. The actual initial investment is $71,530.26: $50,000 plus the reserve account balance EOY 0 of $21,530.26.

EOY	Cash Flows	Adjustments	Modified Cash Flows
0	($50,000)	+ ($21,530.26)	($71,530.26)
1	5,000	7% ↑ 7%	–0–
2	(30,000)	+$5,350 =($24,650)	–0–
3	10,000		10,000
4	30,000		30,000
5	35,000		35,000
6	115,000		115,000

Step 2 Adjust for investment size disparity Investment B required an initial investment of $100,000 compared to $71,530.26 for Investment

A. If Investment A is acquired, the investor will have $28,469.74 ($100,000 − $71,530.26) to invest at 12 percent.

Step 3 Adjust for reinvestment income The remaining $28,469.74 of the $100,000 investment base grows at 12 percent to $39,997.93 by EOY 3. The $10,000 after-tax investment income plus $39,997.93 grows at 12 percent to $55,997.68 by EOY 4. The $55,997.68 plus investment income of $30,000 totals $85,997.68 by EOY 4. At EOY 4 the investor will purchase one limited partnership share for $60,000 which grows at 18 percent to $83,544 by EOY 6. The remaining $25,997.68 grows at 12 percent to $29,117.40 by EOY 5. The $35,000 investment income EOY 5 plus $29,117.40 is $64,117.40, enough money to buy another limited partnership share for $60,000. The balance of $4,117.40 ($64,117.40-$60,000) is invested at 12 percent and grows to $4,611.49 by EOY 6. Total wealth by EOY 6 from Investment Alternative A is estimated to be $273,955.49. This is the sum of the $115,000 investment income, plus $4,611.49, plus $70,800 (from the second limited partnership share), plus $83,544 (from the first limited partnership share).

Investment A				
EOY	Cash Flows		Adjustments	Modified Cash Flows
0	($71,530.26) +	($28,469.74)	=	($100,000)
1	−0−			−0−
2	−0−		↓ 12%	−0−
3	10,000 +	39,997.93=49,997.93		−0−
		12% ↙		
4	30,000 +	55,997.68=85,997.68		
		=25,997.68+60,000		−0−
		↓ 12%		
5	35,000 +	29,117.40=64,117.40		
		=4,117.40+60,000	18%	−0−
		↓12% ↓18%		
6	115,000 +	4,611.49+70,800+ 83,544 =		**$273,955.49**

Step 4 Adjust cash flows of Investment B for the time disparity The $200,000 received at EOY 4 will be used to buy three limited partnership shares at $60,000 each. Thus, $180,000 (three shares times $60,000) is compounded forward at 18 percent for two years to $250,632. The remaining $20,000 ($200,000 − $180,000) is compounded at 12 percent to $25,088. Total wealth at EOY 6 from Investment Alternative B is estimated to be $275,720: the $250,632 from limited partnership shares plus $25,088.

Investment B			
EOY	Cash Flows	Adjustments	Modified Cash Flows
0	($100,000)		($100,000)
1	-0-		-0-
2	-0-		-0-
3	-0-		-0-
4	$200,000	= $180,000 + $20,000	-0-
5	-0-	↓ 18% ↓ 12%	-0-
6	-0-	$250,632 + $25,088 =	$275,720

Comparing the investment alternatives

Investment alternatives A and B can now be compared. The total available initial investment base of $100,000 was assumed to have been fully invested in both investment analyses. Only after-tax cash flows and after-tax rates of return were used. Some cash was invested in a safe and liquid investment to meet the $30,000 future obligation for Alternative A. After-tax income was reinvested to earn yields consistent with the economic environment and the investor's financial objectives and risk preferences. Cash flows from Investment B were adjusted for the time disparity between the alternatives. Results of the comparison are summarized below:

	Investment A		Investment B	
EOY	Cash Flows	Modified Cash Flows	Cash Flows	Modified Cash Flows
0	($50,000)	(100,000)	($100,000)	($100,000)
1	$5,000	-0-	-0-	-0-
2	($30,000)	-0-	-0-	-0-
3	$10,000	-0-	-0-	-0-
4	$30,000	-0-	$200,000	-0-
5	$35,000	-0-	-0-	-0-
6	$115,000	$273,955.49	-0-	$275,720
IRR	22.3%		18.9%	
FMRR	18.3%		18.4%	

Future wealth will be maximized with Investment B based upon the assumptions employed in this analysis. The IRR of Investment A is greater **439** than the IRR of Investment B. However, the IRR is the *internal* rate earned on capital which remains at risk in the investment. The geometric mean compound rate of growth of wealth, measured by FMRR, will be lower if investment income is reinvested at a rate lower than the IRR. Different financial management assumptions with regard to the after-tax yields on safe or more speculative investments may indicate a different conclusion.

To summarize the factors which may be imputed in the estimate of future wealth using the FMRR model:

- Alternative reinvestment and safe rates may be used to reflect the economic environment.

- Several criteria should be considered when selecting after-tax reinvestment rates for cash flows.

- Before-tax market yields should be adjusted for the investor's particular tax posture.

- Investment duration may affect the yield as well as the amount of capital available for investment.

- Risk and liquidity have a fundamental impact on the reinvestment rates used in the analysis.

Appendix A

Compound Interest Tables

The tables are reprinted from *Ellwood Tables for Real Appraising and Financing*, 4th edition, by L. W. Ellwood, with the permission of the American Institute of Real Estate Appraisers.

5%   **MONTHLY COMPOUND INTEREST TABLE**   **5%**

EFFECTIVE RATE = 5/12%   **BASE = 1.00416666+**

	1 AMOUNT OF 1 AT COMPOUND INTEREST $S^n=(1+i)^n$	2 ACCUMULATION OF 1 PER PERIOD $S_{\overline{n}\|}=\frac{S^n-1}{i}$	3 SINKING FUND FACTOR $1\,S_{\overline{n}\|}=\frac{i}{S^n\,1}$	4 PRES. VALUE REVERSION OF 1 $v^n=\frac{1}{S^n}$	5 PRESENT VALUE ORD. ANNUITY 1 PER PERIOD $a_{\overline{n}\|}=\frac{1-v^n}{i}$	6 INSTALMENT TO AMORTIZE 1 $1\,a_{\overline{n}\|}=\frac{i}{1-v^n}$	n MONTHS
MONTHS							
1	1.004167	1.000000	1.000000	.995851	.995851	1.004167	1
2	1.008351	2.004167	.498960	.991718	1.987569	.503127	2
3	1.012552	3.012517	.331948	.987603	2.975173	.336115	3
4	1.016771	4.025070	.248443	.983506	3.958678	.252610	4
5	1.021008	5.041841	.198340	.979425	4.938103	.202507	5
6	1.025262	6.062848	.164939	.975361	5.913463	.169106	6
7	1.029534	7.088110	.141081	.971313	6.884777	.145248	7
8	1.033824	8.117644	.123188	.967283	7.852060	.127355	8
9	1.038131	9.151467	.109272	.963269	8.815329	.113439	9
10	1.042457	10.189599	.098139	.959272	9.774602	.102306	10
11	1.046800	11.232055	.089031	.955292	10.729894	.093198	11
YEARS							
1	1.051162	12.278855	.081441	.951328	11.681222	.085608	12
2	1.104941	25.185921	.039705	.905025	22.793898	.043872	24
3	1.161472	38.753336	.025804	.860976	33.365701	.029971	36
4	1.220895	53.014885	.018863	.819071	43.422956	.023030	48
5	1.283359	68.006083	.014705	.779205	52.990706	.018872	60
6	1.349018	83.764259	.011938	.741280	62.092777	.016105	72
7	1.418036	100.328653	.009967	.705201	70.751835	.014134	84
8	1.490585	117.740513	.008493	.670877	78.989441	.012660	96
9	1.566847	136.043196	.007351	.638225	86.826108	.011518	108
10	1.647010	155.282280	.006440	.607161	94.281350	.010607	120
11	1.731274	175.505671	.005698	.577609	101.373733	.009865	132
12	1.819849	196.763730	.005082	.549496	108.120917	.009249	144
13	1.912956	219.109392	.004564	.522751	114.539704	.008731	156
14	2.010826	242.598300	.004122	.497308	120.646077	.008289	168
15	2.113704	267.288945	.003741	.473103	126.455243	.007908	180
16	2.221845	293.242810	.003410	.450076	131.981666	.007577	192
17	2.335519	320.524524	.003120	.428170	137.239108	.007287	204
18	2.455008	349.202023	.002864	.407331	142.240661	.007031	216
19	2.580611	379.346717	.002636	.387505	146.998780	.006803	228
20	2.712640	411.033670	.002433	.368645	151.525313	.006600	240
21	2.851424	444.341789	.002251	.350702	155.831531	.006418	252
22	2.997308	479.354014	.002086	.333633	159.928159	.006253	264
23	3.150656	516.157530	.001937	.317394	163.825396	.006104	276
24	3.311850	554.843985	.001802	.301946	167.532948	.005969	288
25	3.481290	595.509712	.001679	.287250	171.060047	.005846	300
26	3.659400	638.255975	.001567	.273269	174.415476	.005734	312
27	3.846622	683.189218	.001464	.259968	177.607590	.005631	324
28	4.043422	730.421330	.001369	.247315	180.644338	.005536	336
29	4.250291	780.069928	.001282	.235278	183.533282	.005449	348
30	4.467744	832.258641	.001202	.223827	186.281617	.005369	360
31	4.696323	887.117429	.001127	.212933	188.896185	.005294	372
32	4.936593	944.782896	.001058	.202569	191.383497	.005225	384
33	5.189161	1005.398638	.000995	.192709	193.749748	.005162	396
34	5.454648	1069.115596	.000935	.183330	196.000829	.005102	408
35	5.733719	1136.092435	.000880	.174407	198.142346	.005047	420
36	6.027066	1206.495936	.000829	.165918	200.179632	.004996	432
37	6.335423	1280.501414	.000781	.157843	202.117759	.004948	444
38	6.659555	1358.293153	.000736	.150160	203.961554	.004903	456
39	7.000270	1440.064865	.000694	.142852	205.715609	.004861	468
40	7.358417	1526.020172	.000655	.135899	207.384290	.004822	480
41	7.734888	1616.373117	.000619	.129284	208.971754	.004786	492
42	8.130620	1711.348689	.000584	.122992	210.481953	.004751	504
43	8.546598	1811.183392	.000552	.117006	211.918649	.004719	516
44	8.983858	1916.125828	.000522	.111311	213.285417	.004689	528
45	9.443489	2026.437318	.000493	.105893	214.585663	.004660	540
46	9.926636	2142.392554	.000467	.100739	215.822623	.004634	552
47	10.434501	2264.280279	.000442	.095836	216.999379	.004609	564
48	10.968350	2392.404012	.000418	.091171	218.118860	.004585	576
49	11.529512	2527.082798	.000396	.086734	219.183853	.004563	588
50	12.119383	2668.652007	.000375	.082512	220.197012	.004542	600

EFFECTIVE RATE = 1¼%   BASE = 1.0125

	1 AMOUNT OF 1 AT COMPOUND INTEREST $S^n = (1+i)^n$	2 ACCUMULATION OF 1 PER PERIOD $S_{\overline{n}|} = \frac{S^n-1}{i}$	3 SINKING FUND FACTOR $1\,S_{\overline{n}|} = \frac{i}{S^n\,1}$	4 PRES. VALUE REVERSION OF 1 $v^n = \frac{1}{S^n}$	5 PRESENT VALUE ORD. ANNUITY 1 PER PERIOD $a_{\overline{n}|} = \frac{1-v^n}{i}$	6 INSTALMENT TO AMORTIZE 1 $1\,a_{\overline{n}|} = \frac{i}{1-v^n}$	n QUARTERS
QUARTERS							
1	1.012500	1.000000	1.000000	.987654	.987654	1.012500	1
2	1.025156	2.012500	.496894	.975461	1.963115	.509394	2
3	1.037971	3.037656	.329201	.963418	2.926534	.341701	3
YEARS							
1	1.050945	4.075627	.245361	.951524	3.878058	.257861	4
2	1.104486	8.358888	.119633	.905398	7.568124	.132133	8
3	1.160755	12.860361	.077758	.861509	11.079312	.090258	12
4	1.219890	17.591164	.056847	.819746	14.420292	.069347	16
5	1.282037	22.562979	.044320	.780009	17.599316	.056820	20
6	1.347351	27.788084	.035987	.742197	20.624235	.048487	24
7	1.415992	33.279384	.030049	.706219	23.502518	.042549	28
8	1.488131	39.050441	.025608	.671984	26.241274	.038108	32
9	1.563944	45.115506	.022165	.639409	28.847267	.034665	36
10	1.643619	51.489557	.019421	.608413	31.326933	.031921	40
11	1.727354	58.188337	.017186	.578920	33.686395	.029686	44
12	1.815355	65.228388	.015331	.550856	35.931481	.027831	48
13	1.907839	72.627097	.013769	.524153	38.067734	.026269	52
14	2.005034	80.402736	.012437	.498745	40.100431	.024937	56
15	2.107181	88.574508	.011290	.474568	42.034592	.023790	60
16	2.214532	97.162593	.010292	.451563	43.874992	.022792	64
17	2.327353	106.188201	.009417	.429673	45.626178	.021917	68
18	2.445920	115.673621	.008645	.408844	47.292474	.021145	72
19	2.570529	125.642280	.007959	.389025	48.877995	.020459	76
20	2.701485	136.118795	.007347	.370167	50.386657	.019847	80
21	2.839113	147.129040	.006797	.352223	51.822185	.019297	84
22	2.983753	158.700206	.006301	.335148	53.188125	.018801	88
23	3.135761	170.860868	.005853	.318902	54.487850	.018353	92
24	3.295513	183.641059	.005445	.303443	55.724570	.017945	96
25	3.463404	197.072342	.005074	.288733	56.901339	.017574	100
26	3.639849	211.187886	.004735	.274737	58.021064	.017235	104
27	3.825282	226.022551	.004424	.261419	59.086509	.016924	108
28	4.020162	241.612973	.004139	.248746	60.100305	.016639	112
29	4.224971	257.997654	.003876	.236688	61.064957	.016376	116
30	4.440213	275.217058	.003633	.225214	61.982847	.016133	120
31	4.666421	293.313711	.003409	.214297	62.856242	.015909	124
32	4.904154	312.332304	.003202	.203909	63.687298	.015702	128
33	5.153998	332.319805	.003009	.194024	64.478068	.015509	132
34	5.416570	353.325577	.002830	.184619	65.230505	.015330	136
35	5.692519	375.401494	.002664	.175669	65.946467	.015164	140
36	5.982526	398.602077	.002509	.167153	66.627722	.015009	144
37	6.287308	422.984621	.002364	.159051	67.275953	.014864	148
38	6.607617	448.609342	.002229	.151340	67.892760	.014729	152
39	6.944244	475.539523	.002103	.144004	68.479668	.014603	156
40	7.298021	503.841671	.001985	.137023	69.038124	.014485	160
41	7.669821	533.585681	.001874	.130381	69.569509	.014374	164
42	8.060563	564.845011	.001770	.124061	70.075135	.014270	168
43	8.471211	597.696857	.001673	.118047	70.556250	.014173	172
44	8.902779	632.222352	.001582	.112324	71.014042	.014082	176
45	9.356334	668.506759	.001496	.106879	71.449643	.013996	180
46	9.832996	706.639689	.001415	.101698	71.864128	.013915	184
47	10.333941	746.715313	.001339	.096768	72.258520	.013839	188
48	10.860408	788.832603	.001268	.092078	72.633794	.013768	192
49	11.413695	833.095572	.001200	.087614	72.990876	.013700	196
50	11.995169	879.613534	.001137	.083367	73.330649	.013637	200
51	12.606267	928.501369	.001077	.079326	73.653950	.013577	204
52	13.248498	979.879811	.001021	.075480	73.961580	.013521	208
53	13.923447	1033.875745	.000967	.071821	74.254296	.013467	212
54	14.632781	1090.622520	.000917	.068340	74.532824	.013417	216
55	15.378253	1150.260278	.000869	.065027	74.797849	.013369	220
56	16.161704	1212.936303	.000824	.061875	75.050027	.013324	224
57	16.985067	1278.805378	.000782	.058875	75.289980	.013282	228
58	17.850377	1348.030176	.000742	.056021	75.518302	.013242	232
59	18.759771	1420.781655	.000704	.053306	75.735556	.013204	236
60	19.715494	1497.239482	.000668	.050722	75.942278	.013168	240

5%   SEMI-ANNUAL COMPOUND INTEREST TABLE   5%
EFFECTIVE RATE = 2½%   BASE = 1.025

	1 AMOUNT OF 1 AT COMPOUND INTEREST $S^n = (1+i)^n$	2 ACCUMULATION OF 1 PER PERIOD $S_{\overline{n}|} = \dfrac{S^n-1}{i}$	3 SINKING FUND FACTOR $1\,S_{\overline{n}|} = \dfrac{i}{S^n-1}$	4 PRES. VALUE REVERSION OF 1 $v^n = \dfrac{1}{S^n}$	5 PRESENT VALUE ORD. ANNUITY 1 PER PERIOD $a_{\overline{n}|} = \dfrac{1-v^n}{i}$	6 INSTALMENT TO AMORTIZE 1 $1'a_{\overline{n}|} = \dfrac{i}{1-v^n}$	n HALF YEARS
HALF YEARS 1	1.025000	1.000000	1.000000	.975610	.975610	1.025000	1
YEARS							
1	1.050625	2.025000	.493827	.951814	1.927424	.518827	2
2	1.103813	4.152516	.240818	.905951	3.761974	.265818	4
3	1.159693	6.387737	.156550	.862297	5.508125	.181550	6
4	1.218403	8.736116	.114467	.820747	7.170137	.139467	8
5	1.280085	11.203382	.089259	.781198	8.752064	.114259	10
6	1.344889	13.795553	.072487	.743556	10.257765	.097487	12
7	1.412974	16.518953	.060537	.707727	11.690912	.085537	14
8	1.484506	19.380225	.051599	.673625	13.055003	.076599	16
9	1.559659	22.386349	.044670	.641166	14.353364	.069670	18
10	1.638616	25.544658	.039147	.610271	15.589162	.064147	20
11	1.721571	28.862856	.034647	.580865	16.765413	.059647	22
12	1.808726	32.349038	.030913	.552875	17.884986	.055913	24
13	1.900293	36.011708	.027769	.526235	18.950611	.052769	26
14	1.996495	39.859801	.025088	.500878	19.964889	.050088	28
15	2.097568	43.902703	.022778	.476743	20.930293	.047778	30
16	2.203757	48.150278	.020768	.453771	21.849178	.045768	32
17	2.315322	52.612885	.019007	.431905	22.723786	.044007	34
18	2.432535	57.301413	.017452	.411044	23.556251	.042452	36
19	2.555682	62.227297	.016070	.391285	24.348603	.041070	38
20	2.685064	67.402554	.014836	.372431	25.102775	.039836	40
21	2.820995	72.839808	.013729	.354485	25.820607	.038729	42
22	2.963808	78.552323	.012730	.337404	26.503849	.037730	44
23	3.113851	84.554034	.011827	.321146	27.154170	.036827	46
24	3.271490	90.859582	.011006	.305671	27.773154	.036006	48
25	3.437109	97.484349	.010258	.290942	28.362312	.035258	50
26	3.611112	104.444494	.009574	.276923	28.923081	.034574	52
27	3.793925	111.756996	.008948	.263579	29.456829	.033948	54
28	3.985992	119.439694	.008372	.250879	29.964858	.033372	56
29	4.187783	127.511329	.007842	.238790	30.448407	.032842	58
30	4.399790	135.991590	.007353	.227284	30.908656	.032353	60
31	4.622529	144.901164	.006901	.216332	31.346728	.031901	62
32	4.856545	154.261786	.006482	.205908	31.763691	.031482	64
33	5.102407	164.096289	.006094	.195986	32.160563	.031094	66
34	5.360717	174.428663	.005733	.186542	32.538311	.030733	68
35	5.632103	185.284114	.005397	.177554	32.897857	.030397	70
36	5.917228	196.689122	.005084	.168998	33.240078	.030084	72
37	6.216788	208.671509	.004792	.160855	33.565809	.029792	74
38	6.531513	221.260504	.004520	.153104	33.875844	.029520	76
39	6.862170	234.486817	.004265	.145726	34.170940	.029265	78
40	7.209568	248.382713	.004026	.138705	34.451817	.029026	80
41	7.574552	262.982087	.003803	.132021	34.719160	.028803	82
42	7.958014	278.320556	.003593	.125659	34.973620	.028593	84
43	8.360888	294.435534	.003396	.119605	35.215819	.028396	86
44	8.784158	311.366333	.003212	.113841	35.446348	.028212	88
45	9.228856	329.154253	.003038	.108356	35.665768	.028038	90
46	9.696067	347.842687	.002875	.103135	35.874616	.027875	92
47	10.186931	367.477223	.002721	.098165	36.073400	.027721	94
48	10.702644	388.105758	.002577	.093435	36.262606	.027577	96
49	11.244465	409.778612	.002440	.088933	36.442694	.027440	98
50	11.813716	432.548654	.002312	.084647	36.614105	.027312	100
51	12.411786	456.471430	.002191	.080569	36.777257	.027191	102
52	13.040132	481.605296	.002076	.076686	36.932546	.027076	104
53	13.700289	508.011564	.001968	.072991	37.080354	.026968	106
54	14.393866	535.754649	.001867	.069474	37.221039	.026867	108
55	15.122556	564.902228	.001770	.066126	37.354944	.026770	110
56	15.888135	595.525404	.001679	.062940	37.482398	.026679	112
57	16.692472	627.698877	.001593	.059907	37.603710	.026593	114
58	17.537528	661.501133	.001512	.057021	37.719177	.026512	116
59	18.425366	697.014628	.001435	.054273	37.829080	.026435	118
60	19.358150	734.325993	.001362	.051658	37.933687	.026362	120

5% ANNUAL COMPOUND INTEREST TABLE 5%
EFFECTIVE RATE = 5%   BASE = 1.05

	1 AMOUNT OF 1 AT COMPOUND INTEREST $S^n = (1+i)^n$	2 ACCUMULATION OF 1 PER PERIOD $S_{\overline{n}|} = \dfrac{S^n - 1}{i}$	3 SINKING FUND FACTOR $1\,S_{\overline{n}|} = \dfrac{i}{S^n - 1}$	4 PRES. VALUE REVERSION OF 1 $V^n = \dfrac{1}{S^n}$	5 PRESENT VALUE ORD. ANNUITY 1 PER PERIOD $a_{\overline{n}|} = \dfrac{1 - V^n}{i}$	6 INSTALMENT TO AMORTIZE 1 $1/a_{\overline{n}|} = \dfrac{i}{1 - V^n}$	
YEARS							n YEARS
1	1.050000	1.000000	1.000000	.952381	.952381	1.050000	1
2	1.102500	2.050000	.487805	.907029	1.859410	.537805	2
3	1.157625	3.152500	.317209	.863838	2.723248	.367209	3
4	1.215506	4.310125	.232012	.822702	3.545951	.282012	4
5	1.276282	5.525631	.180975	.783526	4.329477	.230975	5
6	1.340096	6.801913	.147017	.746215	5.075692	.197017	6
7	1.407100	8.142008	.122820	.710681	5.786373	.172820	7
8	1.477455	9.549109	.104722	.676839	6.463213	.154722	8
9	1.551328	11.026564	.090690	.644609	7.107822	.140690	9
10	1.628895	12.577893	.079505	.613913	7.721735	.129505	10
11	1.710339	14.206787	.070389	.584679	8.306414	.120389	11
12	1.795856	15.917127	.062825	.556837	8.863252	.112825	12
13	1.885649	17.712983	.056456	.530321	9.393573	.106456	13
14	1.979932	19.598632	.051024	.505068	9.898641	.101024	14
15	2.078928	21.578564	.046342	.481017	10.379658	.096342	15
16	2.182875	23.657492	.042270	.458112	10.837770	.092270	16
17	2.292018	25.840366	.038699	.436297	11.274066	.088699	17
18	2.406619	28.132385	.035546	.415521	11.689587	.085546	18
19	2.526950	30.539004	.032745	.395734	12.085321	.082745	19
20	2.653298	33.065954	.030243	.376889	12.462210	.080243	20
21	2.785963	35.719252	.027996	.358942	12.821153	.077996	21
22	2.925261	38.505214	.025971	.341850	13.163003	.075971	22
23	3.071524	41.430475	.024137	.325571	13.488574	.074137	23
24	3.225100	44.501999	.022471	.310068	13.798642	.072471	24
25	3.386355	47.727099	.020952	.295303	14.093945	.070952	25
26	3.555673	51.113454	.019564	.281241	14.375185	.069564	26
27	3.733456	54.669126	.018292	.267848	14.643034	.068292	27
28	3.920129	58.402583	.017123	.255004	14.898127	.067123	28
29	4.116136	62.322712	.016046	.242946	15.141074	.066046	29
30	4.321942	66.438848	.015051	.231377	15.372451	.065051	30
31	4.538039	70.760790	.014132	.220359	15.592811	.064132	31
32	4.764941	75.298829	.013280	.209866	15.802677	.063280	32
33	5.003189	80.063771	.012490	.199873	16.002549	.062490	33
34	5.253348	85.066959	.011755	.190355	16.192904	.061755	34
35	5.516015	90.320307	.011072	.181290	16.374194	.061072	35
36	5.791816	95.836323	.010434	.172657	16.546852	.060434	36
37	6.081407	101.628139	.009840	.164436	16.711287	.059840	37
38	6.385477	107.709546	.009284	.156605	16.867893	.059284	38
39	6.704751	114.095023	.008765	.149148	17.017041	.058765	39
40	7.039989	120.799774	.008278	.142046	17.159086	.058278	40
41	7.391988	127.839763	.007822	.135282	17.294368	.057822	41
42	7.761588	135.231751	.007395	.128840	17.423208	.057395	42
43	8.149667	142.993339	.006993	.122704	17.545912	.056993	43
44	8.557150	151.143006	.006616	.116861	17.662773	.056616	44
45	8.985008	159.700156	.006262	.111297	17.774070	.056262	45
46	9.434258	168.685164	.005928	.105997	17.880067	.055928	46
47	9.905971	178.119422	.005614	.100949	17.981016	.055614	47
48	10.401270	188.025393	.005318	.096142	18.077158	.055318	48
49	10.921333	198.426663	.005040	.091564	18.168722	.055040	49
50	11.467400	209.347996	.004777	.087204	18.255925	.054777	50
51	12.040770	220.815395	.004529	.083051	18.338977	.054529	51
52	12.642808	232.856165	.004294	.079096	18.418073	.054294	52
53	13.274949	245.498974	.004073	.075330	18.493403	.054073	53
54	13.938696	258.773922	.003864	.071743	18.565146	.053864	54
55	14.635631	272.712618	.003667	.068326	18.633472	.053667	55
56	15.367412	287.348249	.003480	.065073	18.698545	.053480	56
57	16.135783	302.715662	.003303	.061974	18.760519	.053303	57
58	16.942572	318.851445	.003136	.059023	18.819542	.053136	58
59	17.789701	335.794017	.002978	.056212	18.875754	.052978	59
60	18.679186	353.583718	.002828	.053536	18.929290	.052828	60

10% MONTHLY COMPOUND INTEREST TABLE 10%

EFFECTIVE RATE = 5/6%   BASE = 1.00833333

MONTHS	1 AMOUNT OF I AT COMPOUND INTEREST $S^n = (1+i)^n$	2 ACCUMULATION OF I PER PERIOD $S_{\overline{n}} = \frac{S^n-1}{i}$	3 SINKING FUND FACTOR $1/S_{\overline{n}} = \frac{i}{S^n-1}$	4 PRES. VALUE REVERSION OF I $V^n = \frac{1}{S^n}$	5 PRESENT VALUE ORD.ANNUITY 1 PER PERIOD $a_{\overline{n}} = \frac{1-V^n}{i}$	6 INSTALMENT TO AMORTIZE I $1/a_{\overline{n}} = \frac{i}{1-V^n}$	n MONTHS
1	1.008333	1.000000	1.000000	.991735	.991735	1.008333	1
2	1.016736	2.008333	.497925	.983539	1.975274	.506258	2
3	1.025208	3.025069	.330570	.975410	2.950685	.338904	3
4	1.033752	4.050278	.246896	.967349	3.918035	.255229	4
5	1.042366	5.084030	.196694	.959355	4.877390	.205027	5
6	1.051053	6.126397	.163228	.951426	5.828817	.171561	6
7	1.059812	7.177450	.139325	.943563	6.772380	.147658	7
8	1.068643	8.237262	.121399	.935765	7.708146	.129732	8
9	1.077549	9.305906	.107458	.928031	8.636177	.115791	9
10	1.086528	10.383456	.096307	.920362	9.556540	.104640	10
11	1.095583	11.469984	.087184	.912755	10.469295	.095517	11
YEARS							
1	1.104713	12.565568	.079582	.905212	11.374508	.087915	12
2	1.220390	26.446915	.037811	.819409	21.670854	.046144	24
3	1.348181	41.781821	.023933	.741739	30.991235	.032267	36
4	1.489354	58.722491	.017029	.671432	39.428160	.025362	48
5	1.645308	77.437072	.012913	.607788	47.065369	.021247	60
6	1.817594	98.111313	.010192	.550177	53.978665	.018525	72
7	2.007920	120.950418	.008267	.498027	60.236667	.016601	84
8	2.218175	146.181075	.006840	.450820	65.901488	.015174	96
9	2.450447	174.053712	.005745	.408088	71.029355	.014078	108
10	2.707041	204.844978	.004881	.369406	75.671163	.013215	120
11	2.990504	238.860492	.004186	.334391	79.872985	.012519	132
12	3.303648	276.437875	.003617	.302695	83.676528	.011950	144
13	3.649584	317.950100	.003145	.274003	87.119542	.011478	156
14	4.031743	363.809198	.002748	.248031	90.236200	.011082	168
15	4.453919	414.470344	.002412	.224521	93.057438	.010746	180
16	4.920303	470.436373	.002125	.203239	95.611258	.010459	192
17	5.435523	532.262776	.001878	.183974	97.923008	.010212	204
18	6.004693	600.563212	.001665	.166536	100.015632	.009998	216
19	6.633463	676.015596	.001479	.150750	101.909902	.009812	228
20	7.328073	759.368830	.001316	.136461	103.624619	.009650	240
21	8.095418	851.450237	.001174	.123526	105.176801	.009507	252
22	8.943114	953.173772	.001049	.111817	106.581857	.009382	264
23	9.879575	1065.549089	.000938	.101218	107.853729	.009271	276
24	10.914096	1189.691570	.000840	.091624	109.005045	.009173	288
25	12.056944	1326.833392	.000753	.082939	110.047230	.009087	300
26	13.319464	1478.335753	.000676	.075078	110.990629	.009009	312
27	14.714186	1645.702391	.000607	.067961	111.844605	.008940	324
28	16.254544	1830.594505	.000546	.061519	112.617636	.008879	336
29	17.957060	2034.847238	.000491	.055688	113.317391	.008824	348
30	19.837399	2260.487900	.000442	.050409	113.950820	.008775	360
31	21.914633	2509.756088	.000398	.045631	114.524207	.008731	372
32	24.209382	2785.125915	.000359	.041306	115.043244	.008692	384
33	26.744421	3089.330559	.000323	.037390	115.513083	.008657	396
34	29.544691	3425.389403	.000292	.033846	115.938387	.008625	408
35	32.638649	3796.638004	.000263	.030638	116.323378	.008596	420
36	36.056343	4206.761180	.000237	.027734	116.671875	.008571	432
37	39.831913	4659.829611	.000214	.025105	116.987341	.008547	444
38	44.002835	5160.340233	.000193	.022725	117.272903	.008527	456
39	48.610506	5713.260852	.000175	.020571	117.531398	.008508	468
40	53.700662	6324.079483	.000158	.018621	117.765390	.008491	480
41	59.323823	6998.858807	.000142	.016856	117.977204	.008476	492
42	65.535802	7744.296352	.000129	.015258	118.168940	.008462	504
43	72.398257	8567.790939	.000116	.013812	118.342502	.008450	516
44	79.979301	9477.516170	.000105	.012503	118.499611	.008438	528
45	88.354179	10482.501530	.000095	.011318	118.641830	.008428	540
46	97.606016	11592.721980	.000086	.010245	118.770568	.008419	552
47	107.826641	12819.197020	.000078	.009274	118.887103	.008411	564
48	119.117491	14174.100030	.000070	.008395	118.992592	.008403	576
49	131.590658	15670.879080	.000063	.007599	119.088082	.008397	588
50	145.369919	17324.390450	.000057	.006879	119.174520	.008391	600

10 × QUARTERLY COMPOUND INTEREST TABLE 10 ×

EFFECTIVE RATE = 2½%   BASE = 1.025

	1 AMOUNT OF 1 AT COMPOUND INTEREST $S^n = (1 + i)^n$	2 ACCUMULATION OF 1 PER PERIOD $S_{\overline{n}|} = \frac{S^n - 1}{i}$	3 SINKING FUND FACTOR $1/S_{\overline{n}|} = \frac{i}{S^n - 1}$	4 PRES. VALUE REVERSION OF 1 $V^n = \frac{1}{S^n}$	5 PRESENT VALUE ORD. ANNUITY 1 PER PERIOD $a_{\overline{n}|} = \frac{1 - V^n}{i}$	6 INSTALMENT TO AMORTIZE 1 $1/a_{\overline{n}|} = \frac{i}{1 - V^n}$	n
QUARTERS							QUARTERS
1	1.025000	1.000000	1.000000	.975610	.975610	1.025000	1
2	1.050625	2.025000	.493827	.951814	1.927424	.518827	2
3	1.076891	3.075625	.325137	.928599	2.856024	.350137	3
YEARS							
1	1.103813	4.152516	.240818	.905951	3.761974	.265818	4
2	1.218403	8.736116	.114467	.820747	7.170137	.139467	8
3	1.344889	13.795553	.072487	.743556	10.257765	.097487	12
4	1.484506	19.380225	.051599	.673625	13.055003	.076599	16
5	1.638616	25.544658	.039147	.610271	15.589162	.064147	20
6	1.808726	32.349038	.030913	.552875	17.884986	.055913	24
7	1.996495	39.859801	.025088	.500878	19.964889	.050088	28
8	2.203757	48.150278	.020768	.453771	21.849178	.045768	32
9	2.432535	57.301413	.017452	.411094	23.556251	.042452	36
10	2.685064	67.402554	.014836	.372431	25.102775	.039836	40
11	2.963808	78.552323	.012730	.337404	26.503849	.037730	44
12	3.271490	90.859583	.011006	.305671	27.773154	.036006	48
13	3.611112	104.444494	.009574	.276923	28.923081	.034574	52
14	3.985992	119.439695	.008372	.250879	29.964858	.033372	56
15	4.399790	135.991590	.007353	.227284	30.908657	.032353	60
16	4.856545	154.261786	.006482	.205908	31.763692	.031482	64
17	5.360717	174.428664	.005733	.186542	32.538311	.030733	68
18	5.917228	196.689123	.005084	.168998	33.240078	.030084	72
19	6.531513	221.260505	.004520	.153104	33.875844	.029520	76
20	7.209568	248.382713	.004026	.138705	34.451817	.029026	80
21	7.958014	278.320556	.003593	.125659	34.973620	.028593	84
22	8.784158	311.366333	.003212	.113841	35.446348	.028212	88
23	9.696067	347.842688	.002875	.103135	35.874616	.027875	92
24	10.702644	388.105759	.002577	.093435	36.262606	.027577	96
25	11.813716	432.548655	.002312	.084647	36.614105	.027312	100
26	13.040132	481.605297	.002076	.076686	36.932546	.027076	104
27	14.393866	535.754651	.001867	.069474	37.221039	.026867	108
28	15.888135	595.525406	.001679	.062940	37.482398	.026679	112
29	17.537528	661.501135	.001512	.057021	37.719177	.026512	116
30	19.358150	734.325996	.001362	.051658	37.933687	.026362	120
31	21.367775	814.711016	.001227	.046799	38.128022	.026227	124
32	23.586026	903.441037	.001107	.042398	38.304081	.026107	128
33	26.034559	1001.382378	.000999	.038410	38.463581	.025999	132
34	28.737282	1109.491294	.000901	.034798	38.608080	.025901	136
35	31.720583	1228.823308	.000814	.031525	38.738989	.025814	140
36	35.013588	1360.543523	.000735	.028560	38.857586	.025735	144
37	38.648450	1505.937994	.000664	.025874	38.965030	.025664	148
38	42.660657	1666.426286	.000600	.023441	39.062368	.025600	152
39	47.089383	1843.575332	.000542	.021236	39.150552	.025542	156
40	51.977868	2039.114732	.000490	.019239	39.230442	.025490	160
41	57.373841	2254.953642	.000443	.017430	39.302818	.025443	164
42	63.329985	2493.199414	.000401	.015790	39.368388	.025401	168
43	69.904454	2756.178168	.000363	.014305	39.427790	.025363	172
44	77.161438	3046.457506	.000328	.012960	39.481606	.025328	176
45	85.171790	3366.871582	.000297	.011741	39.530361	.025297	180
46	94.013719	3720.548769	.000269	.010637	39.574530	.025269	184
47	103.773555	4110.942208	.000243	.009636	39.614545	.025243	188
48	114.546588	4541.863516	.000220	.008730	39.650797	.025220	192
49	126.438000	5017.520012	.000199	.007909	39.683639	.025199	196
50	139.563895	5542.555784	.000180	.007165	39.713393	.025180	200
51	154.052426	6122.097036	.000163	.006491	39.740348	.025163	204
52	170.045054	6761.802144	.000148	.005881	39.764768	.025148	208
53	187.697922	7467.916888	.000134	.005328	39.786892	.025134	212
54	207.183386	8247.335444	.000121	.004827	39.806934	.025121	216
55	228.691692	9107.667692	.000110	.004373	39.825092	.025110	220
56	252.432838	10057.313520	.000099	.003961	39.841542	.025099	224
57	278.638621	11105.544820	.000090	.003589	39.856445	.025090	228
58	307.564901	12262.596050	.000082	.003251	39.869946	.025082	232
59	339.494103	13539.764110	.000074	.002946	39.882178	.025074	236
60	374.737967	14949.518680	.000067	.002669	39.893259	.025067	240

447

10 × SEMI-ANNUAL COMPOUND INTEREST TABLE 10 ×

EFFECTIVE RATE = 5%   BASE = 1.05

	1 AMOUNT OF I AT COMPOUND INTEREST $S^n = (1+i)^n$	2 ACCUMULATION OF I PER PERIOD $S_{\overline{n}|} = \frac{S^n - 1}{i}$	3 SINKING FUND FACTOR $1/S_{\overline{n}|} = \frac{i}{S^n - 1}$	4 PRES. VALUE REVERSION OF I $V^n = \frac{1}{S^n}$	5 PRESENT VALUE ORD.ANNUITY I PER PERIOD $a_{\overline{n}|} = \frac{1 - V^n}{i}$	6 INSTALMENT TO AMORTIZE I $1/a_{\overline{n}|} = \frac{i}{1 - V^n}$	n
HALF YEARS							HALF YEARS
1	1.050000	1.000000	1.000000	.952381	.952381	1.050000	1
YEARS							
1	1.102500	2.050000	.487805	.907029	1.859410	.537805	2
2	1.215506	4.310125	.232012	.822702	3.545951	.282012	4
3	1.340096	6.801913	.147017	.746215	5.075692	.197017	6
4	1.477455	9.549109	.104722	.676839	6.463213	.154722	8
5	1.628895	12.577893	.079505	.613913	7.721735	.129505	10
6	1.795856	15.917127	.062825	.556837	8.863252	.112825	12
7	1.979932	19.598632	.051024	.505068	9.898641	.101024	14
8	2.182875	23.657492	.042270	.458112	10.837770	.092270	16
9	2.406619	28.132385	.035546	.415521	11.689587	.085546	18
10	2.653298	33.065954	.030243	.376889	12.462210	.080243	20
11	2.925261	38.505214	.025971	.341850	13.163003	.075971	22
12	3.225100	44.501999	.022471	.310068	13.798642	.072471	24
13	3.555673	51.113454	.019564	.281241	14.375185	.069564	26
14	3.920129	58.402583	.017123	.255094	14.898127	.067123	28
15	4.321942	66.438847	.015051	.231377	15.372451	.065051	30
16	4.764941	75.298829	.013280	.209866	15.802677	.063280	32
17	5.253348	85.066959	.011755	.190355	16.192904	.061755	34
18	5.791816	95.836323	.010434	.172657	16.546852	.060434	36
19	6.385417	107.709546	.009284	.156605	16.867893	.059284	38
20	7.039989	120.799774	.008278	.142046	17.159086	.058278	40
21	7.761588	135.231751	.007395	.128840	17.423208	.057395	42
22	8.557150	151.143005	.006616	.116861	17.662773	.056616	44
23	9.434258	168.685164	.005928	.105997	17.880066	.055928	46
24	10.401270	188.025393	.005318	.096142	18.077158	.055318	48
25	11.467400	209.347996	.004777	.087204	18.255925	.054777	50
26	12.642808	232.856165	.004294	.079096	18.418073	.054294	52
27	13.938696	258.773922	.003864	.071743	18.565146	.053864	54
28	15.367412	287.348249	.003480	.065073	18.698545	.053480	56
29	16.942572	318.851445	.003136	.059023	18.819542	.053136	58
30	18.679186	353.583718	.002828	.053536	18.929290	.052828	60
31	20.593802	391.876049	.002552	.048558	19.028834	.052552	62
32	22.704667	434.093344	.002304	.044044	19.119124	.052304	64
33	25.031896	480.637912	.002081	.039949	19.201019	.052081	66
34	27.597665	531.953298	.001880	.036235	19.275301	.051880	68
35	30.426426	588.528511	.001699	.032866	19.342677	.051699	70
36	33.545134	650.902683	.001536	.029811	19.403788	.051536	72
37	36.983510	719.670208	.001390	.027039	19.459218	.051390	74
38	40.774320	795.486404	.001257	.024525	19.509495	.051257	76
39	44.953688	879.073761	.001138	.022245	19.555098	.051138	78
40	49.561441	971.228821	.001030	.020177	19.596460	.051030	80
41	54.641489	1072.829775	.000932	.018301	19.633978	.050932	82
42	60.242241	1184.844827	.000844	.016600	19.668007	.050844	84
43	66.417071	1308.341422	.000764	.015056	19.698873	.050764	86
44	73.224821	1444.496418	.000692	.013657	19.726869	.050692	88
45	80.730365	1594.607301	.000627	.012387	19.752262	.050627	90
46	89.005227	1760.104549	.000568	.011235	19.775294	.050568	92
47	98.128263	1942.565265	.000515	.010191	19.796185	.050515	94
48	108.186410	2143.728204	.000466	.009243	19.815134	.050466	96
49	119.275517	2365.510344	.000423	.008384	19.832321	.050423	98
50	131.501258	2610.025154	.000383	.007604	19.847910	.050383	100
51	144.980137	2879.602732	.000347	.006897	19.862050	.050347	102
52	159.840601	3176.812012	.000315	.006256	19.874875	.050315	104
53	176.224262	3504.485244	.000285	.005675	19.886508	.050285	106
54	194.287249	3865.744982	.000259	.005147	19.897060	.050259	108
55	214.201692	4264.033842	.000235	.004668	19.906630	.050235	110
56	236.157366	4703.147310	.000213	.004234	19.915311	.050213	112
57	260.363496	5187.269910	.000193	.003841	19.923184	.050193	114
58	287.050754	5721.015076	.000175	.003484	19.930326	.050175	116
59	316.473456	6309.469122	.000158	.003160	19.936804	.050158	118
60	348.911985	6958.239706	.000144	.002866	19.942679	.050144	120

YEARS	1 AMOUNT OF I AT COMPOUND INTEREST $S^n = (1+i)^n$	2 ACCUMULATION OF I PER PERIOD $S_{\overline{n}} = \frac{S^n - 1}{i}$	3 SINKING FUND FACTOR $1/S_{\overline{n}} = \frac{i}{S^n - 1}$	4 PRES. VALUE REVERSION OF I $v^n = \frac{1}{S^n}$	5 PRESENT VALUE ORD. ANNUITY I PER PERIOD $a_{\overline{n}} = \frac{1 - v^n}{i}$	6 INSTALMENT TO AMORTIZE I $1/a_{\overline{n}} = \frac{i}{1 - v^n}$	n YEARS
1	1.100000	1.000000	1.000000	.909091	.909091	1.100000	1
2	1.210000	2.100000	.476190	.826446	1.735537	.576190	2
3	1.331000	3.310000	.302115	.751315	2.486852	.402115	3
4	1.464100	4.641000	.215471	.683013	3.169865	.315471	4
5	1.610510	6.105100	.163797	.620921	3.790787	.263797	5
6	1.771561	7.715610	.129607	.564474	4.355261	.229607	6
7	1.948717	9.487171	.105405	.513158	4.868419	.205405	7
8	2.143589	11.435888	.087444	.466507	5.334926	.187444	8
9	2.357948	13.579477	.073641	.424098	5.759024	.173641	9
10	2.593742	15.937425	.062745	.385543	6.144567	.162745	10
11	2.853117	18.531167	.053963	.350494	6.495061	.153963	11
12	3.138428	21.384284	.046763	.318631	6.813692	.146763	12
13	3.452271	24.522712	.040779	.289664	7.103356	.140779	13
14	3.797498	27.974983	.035746	.263331	7.366687	.135746	14
15	4.177248	31.772482	.031474	.239392	7.606080	.131474	15
16	4.594973	35.949730	.027817	.217629	7.823709	.127817	16
17	5.054470	40.544703	.024664	.197845	8.021553	.124664	17
18	5.559917	45.599173	.021930	.179859	8.201412	.121930	18
19	6.115909	51.159090	.019547	.163508	8.364920	.119547	19
20	6.727500	57.274999	.017460	.148644	8.513564	.117460	20
21	7.400250	64.002499	.015624	.135131	8.648694	.115624	21
22	8.140275	71.402749	.014005	.122846	8.771540	.114005	22
23	8.954302	79.543024	.012572	.111678	8.883218	.112572	23
24	9.849733	88.497327	.011300	.101526	8.984744	.111300	24
25	10.834706	98.347059	.010168	.092296	9.077040	.110168	25
26	11.918177	109.181765	.009159	.083905	9.160945	.109159	26
27	13.109994	121.099942	.008258	.076278	9.237223	.108258	27
28	14.420994	134.209936	.007451	.069343	9.306567	.107451	28
29	15.863093	148.630930	.006728	.063039	9.369606	.106728	29
30	17.449402	164.494023	.006079	.057309	9.426914	.106079	30
31	19.194342	181.943425	.005496	.052099	9.479013	.105496	31
32	21.113777	201.137767	.004972	.047362	9.526376	.104972	32
33	23.225154	222.251544	.004499	.043057	9.569432	.104499	33
34	25.547670	245.476699	.004074	.039143	9.608575	.104074	34
35	28.102437	271.024368	.003690	.035584	9.644159	.103690	35
36	30.912681	299.126805	.003343	.032349	9.676508	.103343	36
37	34.003949	330.039486	.003030	.029408	9.705917	.103030	37
38	37.404343	364.043434	.002747	.026735	9.732651	.102747	38
39	41.144778	401.447778	.002491	.024304	9.756956	.102491	39
40	45.259256	442.592556	.002259	.022095	9.779051	.102259	40
41	49.785181	487.851811	.002050	.020086	9.799137	.102050	41
42	54.763699	537.636992	.001860	.018260	9.817397	.101860	42
43	60.240069	592.400692	.001688	.016600	9.833998	.101688	43
44	66.264076	652.640761	.001532	.015091	9.849089	.101532	44
45	72.890484	718.904837	.001391	.013719	9.862808	.101391	45
46	80.179532	791.795321	.001263	.012472	9.875280	.101263	46
47	88.197485	871.974853	.001147	.011338	9.886618	.101147	47
48	97.017234	960.172338	.001041	.010307	9.896926	.101041	48
49	106.718957	1057.189572	.000946	.009370	9.906296	.100946	49
50	117.390853	1163.908529	.000859	.008519	9.914814	.100859	50
51	129.129938	1281.299382	.000780	.007744	9.922559	.100780	51
52	142.042932	1410.429320	.000709	.007040	9.929599	.100709	52
53	156.247225	1552.472252	.000644	.006400	9.935999	.100644	53
54	171.871948	1708.719477	.000585	.005818	9.941817	.100585	54
55	189.059142	1880.591425	.000532	.005289	9.947106	.100532	55
56	207.965057	2069.650567	.000483	.004809	9.951915	.100483	56
57	228.761562	2277.615624	.000439	.004371	9.956286	.100439	57
58	251.637719	2506.377186	.000399	.003974	9.960260	.100399	58
59	276.801490	2758.014905	.000363	.003613	9.963873	.100363	59
60	304.481640	3034.816395	.000330	.003284	9.967157	.100330	60

449

15%   ANNUAL COMPOUND INTEREST TABLE   15%

EFFECTIVE RATE = 15%   BASE = 1.15

YEARS	1 AMOUNT OF 1 AT COMPOUND INTEREST $s^n = (1+i)^n$	2 ACCUMULATION OF 1 PER PERIOD $s_{\overline{n}|} = \frac{s^n - 1}{i}$	3 SINKING FUND FACTOR $1\,s_{\overline{n}|} = \frac{i}{s^n - 1}$	4 PRES. VALUE REVERSION OF 1 $v^n = \frac{1}{s^n}$	5 PRESENT VALUE ORD. ANNUITY 1 PER PERIOD $a_{\overline{n}|} = \frac{1 - v^n}{i}$	6 INSTALMENT TO AMORTIZE 1 $1'a_{\overline{n}|} = \frac{i}{1 - v^n}$	n YEARS
1	1.150000	1.0000	1.000000	.869565	.869565	1.150000	1
2	1.322500	2.1500	.465116	.756144	1.625709	.615116	2
3	1.520875	3.4725	.287976	.657516	2.283225	.437976	3
4	1.749006	4.9934	.200265	.571753	2.854978	.350265	4
5	2.011357	6.7424	.148315	.497177	3.352155	.298315	5
6	2.313061	8.7537	.114236	.432328	3.784483	.264236	6
7	2.660020	11.0668	.090360	.375937	4.160420	.240360	7
8	3.059023	13.7268	.072850	.326902	4.487322	.222850	8
9	3.517876	16.7858	.059574	.284262	4.771584	.209574	9
10	4.045558	20.3037	.049252	.247185	5.018769	.199252	10
11	4.652391	24.3493	.041068	.214943	5.233712	.191068	11
12	5.350250	29.0017	.034480	.186907	5.420619	.184480	12
13	6.152788	34.3519	.029110	.162528	5.583147	.179110	13
14	7.075706	40.5047	.024688	.141329	5.724476	.174688	14
15	8.137062	47.5804	.021017	.122894	5.847370	.171017	15
16	9.357621	55.7175	.017947	.106865	5.954235	.167947	16
17	10.761264	65.0751	.015366	.092926	6.047161	.165366	17
18	12.375454	75.8364	.013186	.080805	6.127966	.163186	18
19	14.231772	88.2118	.011336	.070265	6.198231	.161336	19
20	16.366537	102.4436	.009761	.061100	6.259331	.159761	20
21	18.821518	118.8101	.008416	.053131	6.312462	.158416	21
22	21.644746	137.6316	.007265	.046201	6.358663	.157265	22
23	24.891458	159.2764	.006278	.040174	6.398837	.156278	23
24	28.625176	184.1678	.005429	.034934	6.433771	.155429	24
25	32.918953	212.7930	.004699	.030378	6.464149	.154699	25
26	37.856796	245.7120	.004069	.026415	6.490564	.154069	26
27	43.535315	283.5688	.003526	.022970	6.513534	.153526	27
28	50.065612	327.1041	.003010	.019974	6.535508	153010	28
29	57.575454	377.1697	.002651	.017369	6.550877	.152651	29
30	66.211772	434.7451	.002300	.015103	6.565980	.152300	30

EFFECTIVE RATE = 20%   **BASE = 1.20**

	1 AMOUNT OF 1 AT COMPOUND INTEREST $S^n = (1+i)^n$	2 ACCUMULATION OF 1 PER PERIOD $S_{\overline{n}|} = \frac{S^n-1}{i}$	3 SINKING FUND FACTOR $1/S_{\overline{n}|} = \frac{i}{S^n-1}$	4 PRES. VALUE REVERSION OF 1 $V^n = \frac{1}{S^n}$	5 PRESENT VALUE ORD. ANNUITY 1 PER PERIOD $a_{\overline{n}|} = \frac{1-V^n}{i}$	6 INSTALMENT TO AMORTIZE 1 $1/a_{\overline{n}|} = \frac{i}{1-V^n}$	n
YEARS							**YEARS**
1	1.200000	1.000000	1.000000	.833333	.833333	1.200000	1
2	1.440000	2.200000	.454545	.694444	1.527777	.654545	2
3	1.728000	3.640000	.274725	.578704	2.106481	.474725	3
4	2.073600	5.368000	.186289	.482253	2.588734	.386289	4
5	2.488320	7.441600	.134380	.401878	2.990612	.334380	5
6	2.985984	9.929920	.100706	.334898	3.325510	.300706	6
7	3.583181	12.915904	.077424	.279082	3.604592	.277424	7
8	4.299817	16.499085	.060609	.232568	3.837160	.260609	8
9	5.159780	20.798902	.048079	.193807	4.030967	.248079	9
10	6.191736	25.958682	.038523	.161506	4.192473	.238523	10
11	7.430083	32.150418	.031104	.134588	4.327061	.231104	11
12	8.916100	39.580501	.025265	.112157	4.439218	.225265	12
13	10.699320	48.496601	.020620	.093464	4.532682	.220620	13
14	12.839184	59.195921	.016893	.077887	4.610569	.216893	14
15	15.407021	72.035105	.013882	.064905	4.675474	.213882	15
16	18.488514	87.442126	.011436	.054088	4.729562	.211436	16
17	22.186217	105.930640	.009440	.045073	4.774635	.209440	17
18	26.623460	128.116857	.007805	.037561	4.812196	.207805	18
19	31.948153	154.740317	.006462	.031301	4.843497	.206462	19
20	38.337783	186.688470	.005357	.026085	4.869582	.205357	20
21	46.005340	225.026253	.004444	.021737	4.891319	.204444	21
22	55.206408	271.031593	.003690	.018114	4.909433	.203690	22
23	66.247690	326.238001	.003065	.015095	4.924528	.203065	23
24	79.497228	392.485691	.002548	.012579	4.937107	.202548	24
25	95.396675	471.982919	.002119	.010483	4.947590	.202119	25
26	114.476010	567.379594	.001762	.008735	4.956325	.201762	26
27	137.371212	681.855604	.001467	.007280	4.963605	.201467	27
28	164.845454	819.226816	.001221	.006066	4.969671	.201221	28
29	197.814545	984.072270	.001016	.005055	4.974726	.201016	29
30	237.377454	1181.886815	.000846	.004213	4.978939	.200846	30

EFFECTIVE RATE = 25%   **BASE = 1.25**

	1 AMOUNT OF 1 AT COMPOUND INTEREST $S^n = (1+i)^n$	2 ACCUMULATION OF 1 PER PERIOD $S_{\overline{n}|} = \frac{S^n-1}{i}$	3 SINKING FUND FACTOR $1/S_{\overline{n}|} = \frac{i}{S^n-1}$	4 PRES. VALUE REVERSION OF 1 $V^n = \frac{1}{S^n}$	5 PRESENT VALUE ORD. ANNUITY 1 PER PERIOD $a_{\overline{n}|} = \frac{1-V^n}{i}$	6 INSTALMENT TO AMORTIZE 1 $1/a_{\overline{n}|} = \frac{i}{1-V^n}$	n
YEARS							**YEARS**
1	1.250000	1.000000	1.000000	.800000	.800000	1.250000	1
2	1.562500	2.250000	.444444	.640000	1.440000	.694444	2
3	1.953125	3.812500	.262295	.512000	1.952000	.512295	3
4	2.441406	5.765625	.173442	.409600	2.361600	.423442	4
5	3.051758	8.207031	.121847	.327680	2.689280	.371847	5
6	3.814697	11.258789	.088819	.262144	2.951424	.338819	6
7	4.768372	15.073486	.066342	.209715	3.161139	.316342	7
8	5.960465	19.841858	.050399	.167772	3.328911	.300399	8
9	7.450581	25.802323	.038756	.134218	3.463129	.288756	9
10	9.313226	33.252904	.030073	.107374	3.570503	.280073	10
11	11.641532	42.566130	.023493	.085899	3.656402	.273493	11
12	14.551915	54.207662	.018448	.068719	3.725121	.268448	12
13	18.189893	68.759577	.014544	.054976	3.780097	.264544	13
14	22.737366	86.949470	.011501	.043980	3.824077	.261501	14
15	28.421708	109.686836	.009117	.035184	3.859261	.259117	15
16	35.527134	138.108544	.007241	.028147	3.887408	.257241	16
17	44.408918	173.635678	.005759	.022518	3.909926	.255759	17
18	55.511147	218.044596	.004586	.018014	3.927940	.254586	18
19	69.388934	273.555743	.003656	.014412	3.942352	.253656	19
20	86.736167	342.944677	.002916	.011529	3.953881	.252916	20
21	108.420208	429.680844	.002327	.009223	3.963104	.252327	21
22	135.525260	538.101052	.001858	.007379	3.970483	.251858	22
23	169.406575	673.626312	.001485	.005903	3.976386	.251485	23
24	211.758219	843.032887	.001186	.004722	3.981108	.251186	24
25	264.697727	1054.791106	.000948	.003778	3.984886	.250948	25

451

Appendix B

Conversion and Expansion of Tables and Use of Financial Calculators

The compound interest tables, as published in *Ellwood Tables* (see Appendix A), may be modified or expanded quite simply for use in solving an even greater variety of compound interest and discount problems.

Converting table factors from EOP to BOP

In many instances, compound interest problems involve the receipt or investment of funds at the "beginning of the period" (BOP) rather than at the end of the period (EOP). Of course, Column 1 Factors of the tables are already based upon the assumption that the investment takes place at the beginning of the period or at the present. Thus, there is generally no need to convert such factors to BOP, although it is possible to do so.

Of much greater relevance is the conversion of those columns which are based upon either receipt or payment (investment) at EOP, Columns 2 through 6. Conversion of all columns may be accomplished using the base of the factor as follows.

Columns					
1	2	3	4	5	6
$F_1 \div$ Base	$F_2 \times$ Base	$F_3 \div$ Base	$F_4 \times$ Base	$F_5 \times$ Base	$F_6 \div$ Base

---

Example

Suppose an investor wishes to invest $10,000 today and each year thereafter for three years at 10-percent compounded annually. How much is accumulated by the end of the third year? It is not appropriate to use the Column 2 Factor at 10 percent interest compounded annually for three years because this factor of 3.310000 is based on the assumption that the first investment takes place at the end of the first period, not the beginning.

EOP	Amount Invested	Interest Earned From Prior Period	EOP Balance
1	$10,000	-0-	$10,000
2	$10,000	$1,000	$21,000
3	$10,000	$2,100	$33,100

The case described, however, indicates that the first $10,000 investment is made at the beginning of the first period, or at the period zero (0), as follows:

BOP	Amount Invested	Interest Earned During Period	EOP Balance
1	$10,000	$1,000	$11,000
2	$10,000	$2,100	$23,100
3	$10,000	$3,310	$36,410

It may be seen that when the series of three investments of $10,000 each is made at the beginning of each period rather than at the end, the amount accumulated by the end of three years with 10 percent annual compounding is $36,410. This same result is achieved using the following procedure:

$$\underset{3.310000}{\frac{\text{EOP Factor}}{10\%, n = 3}} \times \underset{(1.10)}{\frac{\text{Base}}{\text{(Annual, 10\%)}}} = \underset{3.641000}{\frac{\text{BOP Factor}}{10\%, n = 3}}$$

$$\text{and}$$

$$3.641000 \times \$10,000 = \$36,410$$

The conversion of all factors at 10 percent, annual compounding, $n=3$, is shown this way:

Column	EOP Factors	Function	Base	BOP Factors
1	1.331000	÷	1.1	1.210000
2	3.310000	×	1.1	3.641000
3	.302115	÷	1.1	.274650
4	.751315	×	1.1	.826447
5	2.486852	×	1.1	2.735537
6	.402115	÷	1.1	.365559

Converting EOP to BOP factors for compounding periods of less than a year is accomplished in exactly the same manner as for annual compounding. It is also possible to convert the present value of a variable income stream from EOP to BOP receipts by multiplying the proper base value times the present value (originally calculated using EOP factors).

Expansion of compound interest factors

It is often necessary to obtain factors which extend into periods beyond the published tables. This situation can occur if a factor is needed for a greater number of periods than provided for in the table. A similar situation occurs when a factor is needed for a fractional compounding period beyond one year (such as nine years, seven months) since only annual factors are provided beyond the first year. In either situation, the expansion procedure is exactly the same.

Columns 1 and 4

These columns may be expanded *directly* by multiplication of those factors where the sum of the number of periods is equal to the desired number of periods. For example, suppose that a Column 1 Factor at 10 percent annual compounding is needed for a period of 65 years. This may be calculated as follows:

Column 1 Factor ($10\%, n = 60$)	Column 1 Factor ($10\%, n = 5$)	Column 1 Factor ($10\%, n = 65$)
304.481640	$\times$ 1.610510	490.37072

or

Column 1 Factor ($10\%, n = 35$)	Column 1 Factor ($10\%, n = 30$)	Column 1 Factor ($10\%, n = 65$)
28.102437	$\times$ 17.449402	= 490.37072

or

any combination of two or more factors whose periods' sum is equal to $n = 65$ multiplied times each other:

$$F_1^n \times F_1^m = F_1^{n+m}$$
and
$$F_4^n \times F_4^m = F_4^{n+m}$$

If a Column 1 Factor for three years, seven months, (43 months) at 5 percent compounded monthly, is needed, it would be calculated in the following manner:

Column 1 Factor ($5\%, n = 36$)	Column 1 Factor ($5\%, n = 7$)	Column 1 Factor ($5\%, n = 43$)
1.161472	$\times$ 1.029534	= 1.195775

Columns 2 and 3

The procedure for expanding Columns 2 and 3 may be generalized as follows.

$$F_2^n + (F_1^n \times F_2^m) = F_2^{n+m}$$
$$\text{and}$$
$$\frac{1}{F_2^{n+m}} = F_3^{n+m}$$

Thus, the Column 2 Factor for three years, seven months, (43 months) at 5 percent, compounded monthly, is calculated this way:

Column 2 Factor (5%, n = 36)	Column 1 Factor (5%, n = 36)	Column 2 Factor (5%, n = 7)	Column 2 Factor (5%, n = 43)
38.753336 +	(1.161472 ×	7.088110) =	46.985977

To calculate the comparable Column 3 Factor, simply find the reciprocal.

$$\frac{1}{46.985977} = .021283 = F_3^{43}$$

Columns 5 and 6

Expanding Columns 5 and 6 may be generalized:

$$F_5^n + (F_4^n \times F_5^{n+m})$$
$$\text{and}$$
$$\frac{1}{F_5^{n+m}} = F_6^{n+m}$$

Thus, the Column 5 Factor for three years, seven months, (43 months) at 5 percent compounded monthly, would be calculated this way:

Column 5 Factor (5%, n = 36)	Column 4 Factor (5%, n = 36)	Column 5 Factor (5%, n = 7)	Column 5 Factor (5%, n = 43)
33.365701 +	(.860976 ×	6.884777) =	39.293328

To calculate the comparable Column 6 Factor, simply find the reciprocal:

$$\frac{1}{39.293328} = .0254496 = F_6^{43}$$

Interpolation

It is often necessary to "interpolate" between compound interest rates as a means of estimating an intermediate value not found in the tables or as a short-cut means of finding an approximate rate of return. The concept of interpolation is simple; it involves applying proportionate distances between known quantities so that the corresponding values found between such quantities can be estimated.

Conversion and Expansion of Tables/Calculators   Appendix B

Example

Suppose that the following relationships are given:

	Production Time	Output of Product
	10.0 hours	90 units
	4.0 hours	30 units
Distance (value dffi.)	6.0 hours	60 units

How much time would be required to produce 45 units?

The distance between the lower production level and 45 units is 15 units or a distance of 25 percent (15 ÷ 60) of the total distance. The same percentage of distance on the time scale would be 25 percent of the total distance—1.5 (6 × .25). When this amount is added to the minimum time of four hours, the suggested solution is that it would take 5.5 hours to produce 45 units.

The same technique may be used to *estimate* compound interest factors, but again it must be recognized that the method of estimation assumes a proportionate (linear) relationship between factors and values which does not actually exist. Thus, while the technique is reasonably useful, it loses accuracy as the distance between rates increases.

Example

The following rates and factors are given:

n	Rate	Factor (Column 1)
10	15	4.045558
	10	
10	5	1.628895
Diff.	10	2.416663

Suppose now that the interpolation method is used to calculate the factor for 10 percent. The estimated factor would be as follows:

$$5 \div 10 \times 2.416663 = 1.208332$$
$$+ 1.628895$$
$$2.837227$$

However, the actual factor is 2.593742. If the same estimate of the ten-year, 10-percent factor is made with an interpolation between 20 and 5 percent, the resulting solution is 3.149842, producing an even greater error than the earlier estimate.

Perhaps the most useful and frequent application of the interpolation technique is the calculation of Internal Rate of Return (IRR).

Example

Assume an investment of $10,000 in return for the following after-tax cash flows:

n	After-Tax Cash Flows
1	$2,000
2	1,500
3	1,200
4	1,000
5	800
6	600
7	300 + $10,700 sales proceeds

Present Values of After-Tax Cash Flows					
		Discounted at 10%		Discounted at 15%	
End of Year	After-Tax Cash Flow	PV of 1	Amount	PV of 1	Amount
1	$ 2,000	.909091	$1,818	.869565	$1,739
2	1,500	.826446	1,240	.756144	1,134
3	1,200	.751315	902	.657516	789
4	1,000	.683013	683	.571753	572
5	800	.620921	497	.497177	398
6	600	.564474	339	.432328	259
7	11,000	.513158	5,645	.375937	4,135
Total			$11,124		$9,026

Interpolation		
% Rate	Present Value Amount	
Smaller .10	$11,124 ⟶	$11,124
Larger .15	$ 9,026 Initial investment	$10,000

Absolute difference [.05 ÷ $2,098] × $1,124 + smaller rate .10 = .126787

or

12.68% IRR (correct answer is 12.48%)

Short-cut method for calculating the present value of a variable cash flow

The typical method of calculating the present value of a variable stream of cash flows is to find the sum of the present values of each cash flow using the appropriate Column 4 Factors.

Example

The following procedure would be used to calculate the present value of the indicated cash flows with a discount rate of 8.5 percent.

EOP (Year)	Cash Flows	×	Discount Factor Column 4, 8.5%	=	Present Value
1	$ 2,000		.921659		$1,843.32
2	–0–		—		–0–
3	(3,000)		.782908		(2,348.72)
4	11,000		.721574		7,937.31
					$7,431.91

The "short-cut" procedure is designed for speed of calculation but also eliminates the need for any compound interest tables, thus reducing the risk of errors from copying factors. The procedure is based upon the table on p. 459.

Thus, by utilizing the following procedure, each cash flow is divided by $(1 + i)$ n times according to when it is received. The steps are as follows:

Step 1   Enter the *last* period cash flow and divide by the appropriate base. (Enter the base in the calculator as a constant if possible.)

458

$11,000 ÷ 1.085 = $10,138.25

EOP (Years)	Cash Flows	×	Discount Factors	=	Present Value
1	$ 2,000	×	$1/(1 + i)$	=	PV
2	–0–	×	$1/(1 + i) \times 1/(1 + i)$	=	PV
3	(3,000)	×	$1/(1 + i) \times 1/(1 + i)$ $\times 1/(1 + i)$	=	PV
4	11,000	×	$1/(1 + i) \times 1/(1 + i)$ $\times 1/(1 + i) \times 1/(1 + i)$	=	PV

Step 2   Add *next* cash flow to the previously calculated product and divide the sum by the constant base.

$$(\$3,000) + \$10,138.25 = \$7,138.25$$
$$\$7,138.25 \div 1.085 = \$6,579.03$$

Step 3   Repeat Step 2 for each remaining cash flow.

$$0 + \$6,579.03 = \$6,579.03$$
$$\$6,579.03 \div 1.085 = \$6,063.62$$
$$\text{and}$$
$$\$2,000 + \$6,063.62 = \$8,063.62$$
$$\$8,063.62 \div 1.085 = \$7,431.91$$

This procedure illustrates the treatment of positive, zero and negative cash flows and can save a considerable amount of time in most present value calculations.

Example

The cash flows in the previous problem under "Interpolation" were the following:

n	$
1	$ 2,000
2	1,500
3	1,200
4	1,000
5	800
6	600
7	11,000

The present value of this cash flow stream discounted at 10 percent may be calculated, with modest practice, in less than 40 seconds using the short-cut procedure. Compare this time with the conventional method using Column 4 Factors.

Financial calculators

Financial calculators can solve a multitude of quantitative financial problems. To maximize the utility of any calculator, it is certainly very helpful to read the instruction manual of the particular calculator model. Many manuals have detailed explanations of procedures to solve common financial problems.

The following discussion will present an analytical format for financial problem-solving with financial calculators. The first step in any analytical process is to determine what data are known. For simple financial problems, there are three categories of data: the number of time *periods* during the holding period, the effective compound interest or discount *rate per period* and the cash flows. The appropriate data can usually be matched easily to the financial input of the financial calculator.

Number of time periods

The number of time periods $\boxed{n}$ for an investment is the only measure of time. Each period is assumed to be of equal duration and consistent with the periodic interest rate. When the number of periods is not given directly, it is usually easy to determine. The number of time periods is equal to the number of compounding periods per year times the number of years. For example, $\boxed{n}$ is 360 months for an amortizing loan for 30 years with 12 monthly payments per year. If the number of periods is the unknown value, an interest rate and a minimum of two cash flow values (explained below) are required.

Periodic interest rate

The periodic interest rate $\boxed{i}$ is usually stated as an annualized value. It must be consistent with the duration of the compounding period used (e.g., monthly, semiannual). Some financial calculators require input of $\boxed{i}$ as a decimal value (0.0075 for $3/4$ percent). Check the operating manual for the input format for a specific calculator. If the interest rate is stated as an annualized value, compute $\boxed{i}$ by dividing the annualized rate by the number of compounding periods per year. For example, the periodic interest rate for a problem with 12-percent interest per year and quarterly compounding would be:

$$12\% \div 4 = 3\% \text{ per period}$$

If $\boxed{i}$ is the unknown value, the number of compounding periods and, at least, two cash flows are required. The result of the calculation will be the effective *periodic* interest rate. The annualized effective interest rate is the periodic rate times the number of compounding periods per year. For example, the annualized effective interest rate (or yield) for a problem with a monthly rate of 1.25 percent is:

$$12 \times 1.25\% = 15\%$$

Check the manual to determine if the calculated rate is displayed as a percentage or a decimal value. Some calculators will display the calculated rate as a percentage when it is calculated, but display the rate as a decimal if it is recalled from memory.

Cash flows

Financial calculators will require and calculate the three types of cash flows described below:

Present Value $\boxed{\text{PV}}$ is always one lump sum cash flow that occurs at the *beginning* of the *first* compounding period (sometimes labeled EOP O).

Future Value $\boxed{\text{FV}}$ is always one lump sum cash flow that occurs at the *end* of the *last* compounding period.

Periodic Payment $\boxed{\text{PMT}}$ is always assumed to be the amount of equal periodic cash flows made at the end of each and every compounding period during the investment time horizon. Some calculators have a built-in function to accommodate payments made at the beginning of each period. If not, see the discussion on cash flows received at the beginning of each period on page 452.

Required data input

The following combinations of data input are required to solve for the listed unknown financial quantity. Most financial calculators can solve for one unknown financial value from any three known values.

To solve for $\boxed{\text{n}}$: known values for $\boxed{\text{i}}$ and two cash flows are required.

To solve for $\boxed{\text{i}}$: known values for $\boxed{\text{n}}$ and two cash flows are required.

To solve for $\boxed{\text{PV}}$: known values for $\boxed{\text{n}}$, $\boxed{\text{i}}$ and either $\boxed{\text{PMT}}$ *or* $\boxed{\text{FV}}$ are required

To solve for $\boxed{\text{PMT}}$: known values for $\boxed{\text{n}}$, $\boxed{\text{i}}$ and either $\boxed{\text{PV}}$ *or* $\boxed{\text{FV}}$ are required

To solve for $\boxed{\text{FV}}$: known values for $\boxed{\text{n}}$, $\boxed{\text{i}}$ and either $\boxed{\text{PV}}$ *or* $\boxed{\text{PMT}}$ are required

Notice that $\boxed{\text{n}}$ and $\boxed{\text{i}}$ are *always* required to solve for an unknown cash flow value.

The data input combinations above are true for all financial calculators. However, some financial calculators, such as the Hewlett-Packard HP-38E, can solve for one unknown financial value from three *or* four known financial values. The above generalizations are also true for such calculators.

461

One other type of known cash flow *may* be input for any of the five types of calculations generalized above. Consult the owner's manual of your calculator regarding algebraic sign convention. In some cases, the calculator will distinguish cash flow receipts as positive values and cash flow payments as negative values.

Rounding

Financial calculators vary in the number of digits in the display, the number of internal significant digits and the method of automatic rounding of the last significant digit in the display. Consequently, results may vary slightly between calculators. The result of a particular problem may also be slightly different if rounded results are input into the same calculator to verify a calculation. The rounding error will be a small part of 1 percent of the answer. It should not negate the validity of the analysis. Of course, a large error may *not* be a rounding error.

Example

A loan will be paid in full at the end of six years and 11 months. The balance today is $6,210.37 and monthly payments are $100. What is the annual interest rate?

The unknown value is $\boxed{i}$, the periodic interest rate. The known values are:

$$\boxed{n} = 83 \text{ months, } ((6 \times 12) + 11 \text{ months})$$
$$\boxed{PV} = \$6,210.37, \text{ loan balance today}$$
$$\boxed{PMT} = \$100 \text{ per month}$$

Input the known values above and solve for $\boxed{i}$. The result is 0.729165 percent, the *monthly* periodic interest rate. The annual interest rate is:

$$
\begin{array}{ll}
0.729165\% & \\
\times \quad 12 & \text{months per year} \\
\hline
8.749980\% & \text{rounded to } 8.75\% \text{ per year}
\end{array}
$$

Summary

Using a financial calculator to solve simple financial problems is a matter of determining the known values and the unknown value. The known values must be input in the correct format. The periodic interest rate, $\boxed{i}$, must be consistent with the number of compounding periods per year. The total number of compounding periods, $\boxed{n}$, must likewise be consistent with the periodic interest rate. It is always advisable to consult the owner's manual of a particular calculator to identify specific operating characteristics.

Financial calculations with handheld electronic calculators

Many of the financial calculations discussed in this book may be performed easily with any one of the many handheld electronic financial calculators currently available. Financial calculators have at least five "financial keys":

$\boxed{\text{n}}$ or $\boxed{\text{N}}$ = number of compounding periods

$\boxed{\text{i}}$ or $\boxed{\text{\%i}}$ = interest rate *per period* (this will be stated as a percent, not a decimal)

$\boxed{\text{PMT}}$ = equal payment made at the end of each period

$\boxed{\text{PV}}$ = present value of an amount invested at the beginning of the first investment period

$\boxed{\text{FV}}$ = future value of a cash flow invested or received at the end of the last compounding period

Financial calculators vary in operating logic and data input format. Some calculators use an algebraic sign convention to indicate cash inflows (positive cash flows) and cash outlays or payments (negative cash flows). We will use this sign convention. Computation of the unknown value may be automatic (as with Hewlett-Packard calculators) or may require some kind of "compute" instruction (as do certain Texas Instrument calculators) to initiate the computation. The "compute" instruction will be used here.

Most financial calculators will take only three known financial values to solve for the fourth unknown value; they are called "four value" calculators. For example, with the givens, (1) number of payments $\boxed{\text{n}}$; (2) periodic interest rate $\boxed{\text{i}}$; (3) present value of a loan $\boxed{\text{PV}}$, these calculators can compute the payment to amortize the loan $\boxed{\text{PMT}}$, the unknown fourth value. In contrast, some calculators will accept any four known values, although only three are required, and solve for the fifth value; these are called "five value" calculators.

Some of the following procedures may not function with some calculators. Again, the reader is advised to consult the operating manual of a particular calculator to identify subtle data input requirements and other operating characteristics. In many cases, financial calculators will have additional preprogrammed financial functions that will save steps in some financial calculations. For example, many financial calculators have preprogrammed Internal Rate of Return, Net Present Value, loan balance and amortization functions. Most financial problems may be solved with any one of many keystroke procedures; however, only one procedure will be given here.

In most cases, the format of this section will list the type of financial problem and the known values, with the instruction to solve for the unknown values. All of these problems usually may be solved by merely identifying the known values and the unknown value.

Unless otherwise indicated, it is assumed that the calculator is reset and/or all financial registers are cleared at the beginning of each problem.

Compound interest and discount factors

All compound interest and discount factors are calculated with three known values; therefore, only one set of keystrokes will be summarized here. In each case $\boxed{n}$ and $\boxed{i}$ are known. Recall that the interest per period, $\boxed{i}$, must be consistent with the period (e.g., monthly interest for monthly compounding of payments). Here are the factors:

Elwood Column Number	Factor	Input these Known Values	Input 1 Into this Register	Solve for this Value
1	Amount of 1 at compound interest	$\boxed{n}$, $\boxed{i}$	$\boxed{PV}$	$\boxed{FV}$
2	Accumulation of 1 per period	$\boxed{n}$, $\boxed{i}$	$\boxed{PMT}$*	$\boxed{FV}$
3	Sinking fund factor	$\boxed{n}$, $\boxed{i}$	$\boxed{FV}$	$\boxed{PMT}$*
4	Present value reversion of 1	$\boxed{n}$, $\boxed{i}$	$\boxed{FV}$	$\boxed{PV}$
5	Present value of an ordinary annuity of 1 per period	$\boxed{n}$, $\boxed{i}$	$\boxed{PMT}$*	$\boxed{PV}$
6	Installment to amortize 1	$\boxed{n}$, $\boxed{i}$	$\boxed{PV}$	$\boxed{PMT}$*

*All calculations involving $\boxed{PMT}$ assume that payments are received or paid at the *end* of each period.

Converting factors for payments to be received or paid at the beginning of each period

In many instances, compound interest problems involve the receipt or investment of funds at the beginning of the period (BOP) rather than at the end of the period (EOP). Many financial calculators have a preprogrammed instruction or function to make these adjustments. For example, Hewlett-Packard financial calculators have a "Begin/End" switch, and Texas Instruments financial calculators have an annuity "DUE" instruction to use prior to the calculation. Of course, the amount of 1 at compound interest and the present value reversion of 1 factors are based on the assumptions that the investment takes place at the beginning of the first period and reversion, $\boxed{FV}$, is received at the end of the last period. Thus, there is generally no need to convert these factors to BOP, although it is possible to do so.

Loan analysis

To calculate the payment for a fully amortized loan input the known values:

$\boxed{n}$ = number of payments during loan term

$\boxed{i}$ = interest rate per period

$\boxed{PV}$ = loan amount

Solve for $\boxed{PMT}$ = periodic loan payment

To calculate the payment for a partially amortized loan with known balloon payments, do the following: For a five-value calculator, input the known values:

$\boxed{n}$ = number of payments during loan term (including last payment)

$\boxed{i}$ = interest rate per period

$\boxed{PV}$ = loan amount

$\boxed{FV}$ = dollar amount of balloon payment

Solve for $\boxed{PMT}$ = periodic loan payment

Examples

1. Calculate the quarterly payment for a $100,000 loan at 12 percent per annum with a balloon payment of $95,000 due EOY 15.

$\boxed{n}$ = 60 (15 years × 4 quarterly payments per year)

$\boxed{i}$ = 3 percent (12 percent ÷ 4)

$\boxed{PV}$ = $100,000

$\boxed{FV}$ = ($95,000) (negative because it will be *paid* EOY 15)

Solve for $\boxed{PMT}$ = ($3,030.66)

For a four-value calculator, first compute the payment on total amount, then compute the sinking fund payment of the balloon payment. The payment is the difference of the payment on the total amount less the sinking fund payment on the balloon. The process is as follows:

Step 1   Compute the payment on total amount from known values:

$\boxed{n}$ = number of payments

$\boxed{i}$ = periodic interest rate

$\boxed{PV}$ = loan amount

Solve for $\boxed{PMT}$ = payment for fully amortized loan

465

Step 2   Compute sinking fund factor of the balloon payment:

$$\boxed{n} = \text{number of payments (same as Step 1)}$$
$$\boxed{i} = \text{periodic interest rate (same as Step 1)}$$
$$\boxed{FV} = \text{amount of balloon payment}$$
$$\text{Solve for } \boxed{PMT} = \text{sinking fund factor for balloon}$$

Step 3   Compute the payment by simple substraction:

Payment for fully amortized loan
less: Sinking fund payment for balloon
_____
Equals: Loan payment

2. Use the facts in the preceding example.

Step 1   Compute the payment on total amount from known values:

$$\boxed{n} = 60$$
$$\boxed{i} = 3\%$$
$$\boxed{PV} = \$100,000$$
$$\text{Solve for } \boxed{PMT} = \$3,613.30$$

Step 2   Compute the sinking fund payment on the balloon payment from known values:

$$\boxed{n} = 60$$
$$\boxed{i} = 3\%$$
$$\boxed{FV} = \$95,000$$
$$\text{Solve for } \boxed{PMT} = \$582.63$$

Step 3   Compute the loan payment:

Payment to fully amortize the loan	\$3,613.30
less: Sinking fund payment for balloon	582.63
Loan payment	\$3,030.67

Remaining term of a fully amortized loan

The remaining term of a straight amortizing loan is calculated using the same procedure for both four-value and five-value calculators from the following known data:

$$\boxed{i} = \text{periodic interest rate}$$
$$\boxed{PMT} = \text{periodic payment}$$
$$\boxed{PV} = \text{current loan balance}$$

The remaining term is the unknown value $\boxed{n}$.

Example

Calculate the remaining term of a loan at 12-percent interest, with monthly payments of $100 and a remaining balance of $7,000.

The known values are:

$$\boxed{i} = 1\% \ (12\% \div 12)$$
$$\boxed{PMT} = \$100$$
$$\boxed{PV} = \$7,000$$

Solving for the unknown value, $\boxed{n} = 121$ months.
The remaining term is 121 months or 10 years, 1 month.

Loan balance

The procedure for figuring loan balances is the same for both four-value and five-value calculators. The loan balance is equal to the present value of the *remaining* payments, discounted at the nominal rate of the loan. Therefore, the known values are:

$$\boxed{n} = \text{remaining number of payments}$$
$$\boxed{i} = \text{periodic nominal interest rate}$$
$$\boxed{PMT} = \text{periodic loan payment}$$
$$\text{Solve for } \boxed{PV} = \text{loan balance}$$

Example

Calculate the loan balance of a loan with a remaining term of nine years, 11 months; monthly payments are $1,780.91 at 11 $\frac{7}{8}$ percent (11.875 percent). The known values are:

$$\boxed{n} = 119 \text{ months, } [\ (9 \times 12) + 11]$$
$$\boxed{i} = 0.99\% \ (11.875 \div 12)$$
$$\boxed{PMT} = \$1,780.91$$

Solving for the unknown value, $\boxed{PV} = \$124,211.58$.

Number of payments to reduce the loan balance to a specified balance

For a four-value calculator, first calculate the number of payments from the *end* of the loan term to a specified balance. The number of payments to reduce a loan balance to a specific sum is the total remaining payments less the number of payments from the end of the loan term to the specified balance.

Calculate the number of payments from the end of the loan term to the specified balance from the known values:

$$\boxed{\text{i}} = \text{periodic interest rate}$$
$$\boxed{\text{PMT}} = \text{periodic loan payment}$$
$$\boxed{\text{PV}} = \text{specified loan balance}$$

Solve for number of payments $\boxed{\text{n}}$ until the *end* of the loan term from the specified loan balance. The number of payments to reduce the loan balance to a specified balance is the total remaining term less the number of payments until the end of the loan term from the specified loan balance.

Example

How many monthly payments of $1,028.61 are required to reduce a $100,000 loan at 12 percent to a balance of $50,000? This loan would be fully amortized in 30 years (360 months).

Calculate the number of payments from the end of the loan term from the known values:

$$\boxed{\text{i}} = 1\% \ (12\% \div 12)$$
$$\boxed{\text{PMT}} = 1,028.61$$
$$\boxed{\text{PV}} = 50,000$$
$$\text{Solve for } \boxed{\text{n}} = 66.90.$$

The loan balance will be $50,000 when there are 66.90 remaining payments. The number of payments required to reduce the loan balance to $50,000 is:

Total remaining payments	360.00
Payments to the end of the loan term from the specified balance	66.90
Number of payments to reduce loan balance to $50,000	293.10

The fractional portion of the result indicates that the balance is slightly more than $50,000 after the 293rd payment.

For a five-value calculator, solve for $\boxed{n}$ from the known values:

$$\boxed{i} = 1\% \ (12\% \div 12)$$
$$\boxed{PMT} = (\$1,028.61)$$
$$\boxed{PV} = \$100,000$$
$$\boxed{FV} = (\$50,000)$$
$$\text{Solve for } \boxed{n} = 293.11 \text{ (difference due to rounding)}$$

Amortization schedules*

Amortization may be computed for any number of periods. The basic principal reduction formula is:

> Loan balance at the beginning of amortization period
> Less: loan balance at the end of amortization period
> _____
> Equals: principal reduction during amortization period

Accumulated interest is:

> Total of loan payments during amortization period
> Less: principal reduction during amortization period
> _____
> Equals: accumulated interest during amortization period

Calculation of the loan balances is the only financial calculation required.

Example

An investor assumes a loan balance of $75,000 at 12.6-percent interest with monthly payments of $824.97 for the remaining term of 24 years, eight months (296 months). Calculate the principal reduction and accumulated interest for the last four months of the current tax year and for the next tax year.

Amortization for the remaining four months of the current tax year is calculated first. Loan balance at the beginning of the amortization period is $75,000. The loan balance after four payments is calculated from the following known data:

$$\boxed{n} = 292 \ (296 - 4 \text{ remaining payments})$$
$$\boxed{i} = 1.05\% \ (12.60\% \div 12)$$
$$\boxed{PMT} = \$824.97$$

*Some hand-held financial calculators, such as the HP-12c, have a built-in amortization function which can calculate the interest and principal accumulated over any period directly and much more quickly than this section illustrates.

To find the balance after the first four payments, solve for $\boxed{\text{PV}}$ = $74,847.71. Principal reduction for the first four months is:

Beginning balance	$75,000.00
Ending balance	−74,847.71
Principal reduction	$152.29

Accumulated interest is:

Total loan payments (4 × $824.97)	$ 3,299.88
Principal reduction	− 152.29
Accumulated interest	$ 3,147.59

Amortization in the following tax year (12 months) is calculated as follows. Beginning balance is $74,847.71 from above. Ending balance, after 12 payments, is calculated from the following known data:

$\boxed{\text{n}}$ = 280 (292 − 12 remaining payments at the end of the next tax year)

$\boxed{\text{i}}$ = 1.05% (12.60% ÷ 12)

$\boxed{\text{PMT}}$ = $824.97

Calculate the ending balance by solving for $\boxed{\text{PV}}$ = $74,350.83
Principal reduction during the next tax year is:

Beginning balance	$ 74,847.71
Ending balance	−74,350.83
Principal reduction	$ 496.88

Accumulated interest is:

Total loan payments (12 × $824.97)	$ 9,899.64
Principal reduction	− 496.88
Accumulated interest	$ 9,402.76

Calculation of IRR

Many financial calculators can solve for the periodic interest rate, $\boxed{\text{i}}$. The IRR for three types of cash flows can be calculated directly on such four-value financial calculators: (1) a present lump sum and a future sum, (2) a present lump sum and an ordinary annuity and (3) a future lump sum and an ordinary annuity. In each case, the number of periods, $\boxed{\text{n}}$, must be known. Simply input the three known values and solve for $\boxed{\text{i}}$.

Examples

470   1. An investor bought a vacant site five years ago for $100,000 and recently sold it for $250,000. Holding costs were paid by a nominal rent for a billboard on the property. What is the investor's before-tax yield? The known values are:

$$\boxed{n} = 5 \text{ (number of periods)}$$
$$\boxed{PV} = \$100,000 \text{ (initial investment)}$$
$$\boxed{FV} = \$250,000 \text{ (future value of reversion)}$$

Solving for the yield, $\boxed{i}$ = 20.11 percent.

2. An investor pays $10,000 for quarterly payments of $875 for four years. Calculate the yield. The known values are:

$$\boxed{n} = 16 \text{ (4} \times \text{4 payments)}$$
$$\boxed{PV} = \$10,000$$
$$\boxed{PMT} = \$875$$

The quarterly yield is calculated by solving for $\boxed{i}$ = 4.264 percent. The annual yield is 17.06 percent (4 × 4.264 percent).

3. A condominium association will make monthly deposits of $100 for ten years for the roof replacement reserve account. The new roof is expected to cost $20,000. What minimum rate of return will produce the required funds EOY 10? The known values are:

$$\boxed{n} = 120 \text{ (10} \times \text{12 periods)}$$
$$\boxed{PMT} = \$100 \text{ per month}$$
$$\boxed{FV} = \$20,000$$

Solving for the unknown yield, $\boxed{i}$ = 0.7984 percent per month. The annual minimum required yield is 9.58 percent (12 × 0.7984 percent).

Compound rate of growth

The compound rate of growth of populations, company earnings, securities values, land or other values over time may be figured with a financial calculator. The known values are:

$$\boxed{n} = \text{number of periods during growth}$$
$$\boxed{PV} = \text{value at beginning of projection}$$
$$\boxed{FV} = \text{value at end of projection}$$

Solve for $\boxed{i}$ to get the geometric mean compound rate of growth during the projection period.

Example

During the past five years, the population of a certain market area has **471** grown from 121,000 to 162,000 people. Calculate the geometric mean compound rate of growth of the population for the five-year period. The known values are:

$$\boxed{n} = 5 \text{ years}$$
$$\boxed{PV} = 121,000 \text{ (population at beginning of projection)}$$
$$\boxed{FV} = 162,000 \text{ (population at the end of projection)}$$

The compound rate of growth is $\boxed{i}$ = 6.01 percent per year.

IRR of cash flows with level annuities, present value sum and a sum in the future for four-value calculators

We will present two procedures for estimating IRR. The first will work for a cash flow with an annuity, present sum and future sum, which can be described as follows:

EOY	$
0	$\boxed{PV}$
1	$\boxed{PMT}$
↓	↓
$\boxed{n}$	$\boxed{PMT}$ + $\boxed{FV}$

Note that the last payment is *not* included in the future reversion.

Step 1   Calculate the "cash-on-cash" (c/c) per period (not annualized) as a percent:

$$\frac{\boxed{PMT}}{\boxed{PV}} \times 100 = \text{c/c (save this value in the calculator's memory)}$$

Step 2   Calculate the change in value (Δ V—positive or negative) from the $\boxed{PV}$ to $\boxed{FV}$ as a percent:

$$\frac{\boxed{FV} - \boxed{PV}}{\boxed{PV}} \times 100 = \Delta \text{ V}$$

This value is $\boxed{FV}$ for this calculation.

Step 3   Input the following values:

$$\boxed{n} = \text{number of periods}$$
$$\boxed{i} = \text{c/c from Step 1 and save this value}$$
$$\boxed{FV} = \Delta \text{ V from Step 2}$$

Step 4 Solve for $\boxed{\text{PMT}}$, then add result to c/c. This will produce an approximation of the yield.

Step 5 Replace the value of $\boxed{\text{i}}$ with the result of Step 4.

Step 6 Repeat Steps 4 and 5 until the same value is repeated after Step 4.

Example

A bank loans $100,000 at 12 percent per annum with monthly payments of $1,028.61. The lender charges four points to make the loan. The borrower repays the loan balance of $97,663.43 at EOY 5. Calculate the lender's IRR on this loan. The lender's cash flows are summarized in the following T-chart:

EOM	$
0	(96,000) = ($100,000 less 4 pts)
1	$1,028.61
↓	↓
12 × 5 = 60	$1,028.61 + $97,663.43

Step 1 Calculate the "cash-on-cash" as a percent:

$$\text{c/c} = \frac{\$1,028.61}{\$96,000} \times 100 = 1.0715\% \quad \text{(use internal answer from calculator, (not rounded value)}$$

Save in memory if possible.

Step 2 Calculate the change in value as a percent:

$$\Delta V = \left[\frac{\$97,663.43 - \$96,000}{\$96,000}\right] \times 100 = 1.7327\%$$

Step 3 Input the following data (to improve estimate of IRR, do not use rounded values):

$$\boxed{\text{n}} = 60 \ (12 \times 5 \text{ periods})$$
$$\boxed{\text{i}} = 1.0715\% \ (\text{c/c})$$
$$\boxed{\text{FV}} = 1.7327\% \ (\Delta V)$$

Step 4
$$\begin{array}{rr}
\text{Solve for PMT} = & 0.0207 \\
\text{Add c/c} & +1.7327 \\
\hline
\text{First approximation of IRR} & 1.0922
\end{array}$$

Step 5 Replace $\boxed{\text{i}}$ with approximation of IRR from above.

Step 6   Repeat Steps 4 and 5 until the same result from Step 4 is repeated (to more decimal places for more accuracy). The steps may be repeated several times, depending on the particular calculation.

First approximation   1.0922
Second approximation   1.0921
Third approximation   1.0921

The monthly IRR is approximately 1.0921 percent. The lender's annual yield is 13.10 percent.

Estimation of IRR of variable cash flows by interpolation

The following procedure is based on the definition of IRR—that rate at which all future cash flows are discounted to equal the initial investment.

Step 1   Discount cash flows at a trial rate. Save results. Use a periodic discount rate consistent with the cash flows.

Step 2   Discount cash flows at a second trial rate, preferably closer to the IRR based on the first estimate. If the $\boxed{\text{PV}}$ of the cash flows discounted at the first trial rate is greater than the initial investment, try a greater discount rate, and vice-versa. The estimate of IRR will be better for smaller intervals between the trial rates.

Step 3   Compute:

First trial discount rate
less: Second trial rate
─────────────────────────
Difference in discount rates

Step 4   Compute:

$\boxed{\text{PV}}$ of cash flows at first trial discount rate

less: $\boxed{\text{PV}}$ of cash flows at second trial discount rate
──

Difference in trial $\boxed{\text{PV}}$ s

Step 5*   Compute:

Initial investment
less: $\boxed{\text{PV}}$ of cash flows at first trial discount rate
──

Difference of first trial $\boxed{\text{PV}}$ to initial investment

Step 6* the estimated IRR is:

$$\text{First trial rate} + \left[\frac{\text{Difference in discount rates} \times \text{difference of trial } \boxed{\text{PV}} \text{ to initial investment}}{\text{Difference in trial } \boxed{\text{PV}}} \right]$$

Examples

1. Estimate the IRR of the following cash flows:

EOY	$	
0	$10,000	(treat initial investment as
1	1,000	a positive number)
2	(2,000)	
3	3,000	
4	4,000	
5	11,000	

Step 1 Discount cash flows at first trial rate, say 10 percent:

EOY	$	$\boxed{\text{PV}}$ @ 10%
1	$1,000	$ 909.09
2	(2,000)	(1,652.89)
3	3,000	2,253.94
4	4,000	2,732.05
5	11,000	6,830.13
Total $\boxed{\text{PV}}$ @ 10%		$11,072.32

Notice that the negative cash flow EOY 2 maintains the negative algebraic sign.

Step 2 Discount the cash flows at a second trial rate. The first trial rate, 10 percent, is too low because the $\boxed{\text{PV}}$ of $11,072.32 is greater than the initial investment of $10,000. Therefore, a greater trial rate will be used, say 15 percent.

---

*These values must correlate to first and second trial discount rates although they may be reversed if done consistently.

EOY	$	PV @ 15%
1	$1,000	$ 869.57
2	(2,000)	(1,512.29)
3	3,000	1,972.55
4	4,000	2,287.01
5	11,000	5,468.94

Total PV @ 15% | $ 9,085.78

The IRR is between 10 percent and 15 percent since the total PV of the cash flows is greater and less than, respectively, the initial investment.

Step 3   Difference in discount rates:

First trial discount rate	10%	
Second trial discount rate	15%	
Difference in discount rates	−5%	(keep appropriate algebraic signs)

Step 4   Difference in trial PV s:

First trial PV @ 10%	$11,072.32
Second trial PV @ 15%	9,085.78
Difference in trial PV s	$1,986.54

Step 5   Difference of first trial PV to initial investment:

Initial investment	$10,000.00
First trial PV @ 10%	11,072.32
	(−$1,072.32)

Step 6   The estimated IRR is:

$$10 + \left[\frac{(-.05) \times (-1,072.32)}{1,986.54} \right] = .10 + .0272 = .1270 = 12.7\%$$

The actual IRR is 12.54 percent.

2. This procedure could be used to estimate the IRR of the lender from the previous example on page 473. Recall that the *monthly* cash flows were:

EOM	$	
0	$96,000.00	(treat initial investment
1	1,028.61	as a positive number)
60	1,028.61 + 97,663.43	

Step 1 $\boxed{\text{PV}}$ at first trial rate of say 12 percent per annum, or 1 percent per month:

$\boxed{\text{PV}}$ @ 1% of annuity of $1,028.61 for 60 months is $46,241.20

$\boxed{\text{PV}}$ @ 1% of loan balance EOM 60 of $97,663.43 is   53,758.80

˙Total $100,000.00

This result could have been predicted because the payments and balance were based on a $100,000 loan at 12 percent per year with monthly payments.

Step 2 The IRR is greater than 12 percent per year since the $\boxed{\text{PV}}$ at 12 percent, $100,000, is greater than the initial investment of $96,000. Try 1.1 percent per month.

$\boxed{\text{PV}}$ @ 1.1% per month of annuity of $1,028.61 per month is $45,004.75

$\boxed{\text{PV}}$ @ 1.1% of loan balance EOM 60 of $97,663.43 is   50,659.70

Total $95,664.45

Step 3 Difference in discount rates:

First trial discount rate	1.0%
Second trial discount rate	1.1%
Difference in discount rates	−0.1%

Step 4 Difference in trial $\boxed{\text{PV}}$s:

First trial $\boxed{\text{PV}}$ @ 1.0%	$100,000.00
Second trial $\boxed{\text{PV}}$ @ 1.1%	95,664.45
Difference in trial $\boxed{\text{PV}}$s	$4,335.55

Step 5 Difference in first trial $\boxed{\text{PV}}$ to initial investment:

Initial investment	$96,000
First trial $\boxed{\text{PV}}$ @ 1.0%	100,000
	$4,000

Step 6 The estimated monthly IRR is:

$$.010000 + \left[\frac{(-.001000 \times (-4,000))}{4,335.55} \right] = .010000 + .000923 + .010923$$

$$= 1.0923\%$$

The estimated *annual* IRR is:

$$1.0923\%$$
$$\times \quad 12$$
$$13.1076\%$$

This is close to the estimate of 13.1 percent found on page 474. The calculations were carried to several decimal places because of the small difference in the trial discount rates. This procedure is valid for discount rates for any consistent time period (quarter, semi-annual, etc.)

The estimate of IRR is improved by using trial discount rates which produce a small difference in discount rates (Step 3). The estimated IRR for cash flows using trial discount rates with a one-percentage-point difference is better than using discount rates with a five-percentage-point difference.

Appendix C

Limited Partnership

The use of the partnership form of ownership and the significance of limited partnership were discussed in Chapter 8. However, because the limited partnership is of special significance to real estate ventures, especially where a substantial investor participation is involved, such as the real estate syndicate or the so-called "tax shelter," the tax aspects of this form of ownership will be examined in some detail here.

Major reasons for using the limited partnership

Before going into a detailed explanation of the limited partnership, it is appropriate to review the principal reasons for using this form of ownership in syndications:

1. The liability of the limited partners (the investors) is limited to the amount of the investment they agree to make. This is similar to the treatment of stockholders in a corporation.

2. There is no double taxation on operating income or gains from sales; the partnership is a mere conduit and is not a tax-paying entity. Profits and capital gains pass directly through to the partners without first being taxed.

3. Losses, as well as profits, pass through to the partners. These losses include tax losses generated by noncash outlays such as depreciations. Thus, while the partnership may have an actual cash surplus over cash outlay for the year (and the cash may be distributed to the partners), a tax loss is available to the partners to offset their other personal income.

In this respect, the availability of increased basis to each partner for his share of the partnership's liabilities becomes important because a partner may not deduct that part of the partnership losses which exceed his basis. While a limited partner may not increase his basis for a share of liabilities that are specifically those of the partnership, he *may* increase his basis by a **479** share of the liabilities that are of a nonrecourse nature (those liabilities se-cured by liens on the partnership property where the only recourse of the creditor in case of default is to foreclose on the property and where the creditor has no recourse to the other partnership assets or to the assets of any of the partners) but *only if the partnership is involved in investment in real estate*. In all other cases, neither the limited partners nor the general partners may increase their bases by the amounts of the nonrecourse liabili-ties when measuring the amount of losses they may deduct. The availability of nonrecourse loans to increase limited partners' bases is the heart of the so-called real estate tax shelter. It is also the reason why real estate invest-ment has become the major form of tax shelter.

Comparison with corporation

A corporation offers the shareholders limited liability but it presents the problem of double taxation. The corporation is a tax-paying entity so that income and gains realized by the corporation are subject to corporate income tax and there may be another tax on distribution to the shareholders. Further, because the corporation is a separate entity, losses and deductions of the corporation do not pass through to the shareholders.

The S Corporation

Some of the tax objections to a corporation can be avoided if the cor-poration elects Subchapter S status. In that case, the shareholders retain the benefits of limited liability, avoid the corporate income tax and obtain the benefit of a pass-through of losses and deductions. However, in an S corporation the liabilities of the corporation or the liens on the corpora-tion's property do not enter into the calculation of the basis of the shareholder's stock as in the case of a limited partnership. Yet, as in the case of a partnership, an S corporation shareholder may not deduct losses in excess of his basis. For additional analysis of the pros and cons of limited partnerships versus S corporations, see Chapter 8.

Assuring partnership status

If the limited partnership is chosen as the vehicle for a real estate invest-ment, it is essential that the partnership be classified by the tax law as a partnership rather than what the law calls an association which is taxed as a corporation. (As will be explained, even though a business form is a partnership under state law, it may still be treated as a corporation under the tax law if it has enough "corporate attributes.")

Avoiding corporate status

Treasury Regulations (Reg. Section 301.7701-2(a)(b)) provide four criteria for determining whether an association is a corporation or a partnership. These four criteria are (1) continuity of life, (2) centralized management, (3) transferability of interest and (4) limited ability. The regulations further say that the unincorporated organization will not be considered a corporation unless it has more corporate characteristics than partnership characteristics. Thus, if an organization resembles a corporation as to two of the tests and resembles a partnership as to the other two, the regulations say that the organization is to be classified as a partnership. Let's consider the four criteria in greater detail.

Continuity of life   This means, say the regulations, that the death, resignation, etc. of a member does not cause the dissolution of the organization. In a partnership agreement, provision can be made for the continuation of the venture despite the death, resignation, etc. of a general partner. But the regulations say that the partnership agreement does not determine whether continuity exists. If under state law, death or resignation, etc. causes a technical dissolution of the partnership, that is it; the partnership does not meet the "continuity of life" test. Under just about every state law, death, resignation, etc. of a general partner *does* create a technical dissolution.

Centralized management   The regulations take the position that centralized management exists only if management is substantially divorced from ownership. So, in a limited partnership there is centralized management only if the general partner has a 20 percent or less investment interest. The 20 percent, of course, is only a rule of thumb. In any event, most limited partnerships meet the centralized management standard. Usually the limited partners supply the bulk of the investment and the general partners operate the partnership without any voice in management by the limited partners.

Transferability   The regulations seem to indicate that if there is any substantial restriction on transfer of interest (i.e. if the approval of the general partner is needed before a limited partner may transfer his interest or the general partner has a right of first refusal) the transferability-of-interest test may not be met. The regulations are not specific here; they simply indicate that a substantial restriction on transferability of the interest may prevent the organization from being considered a corporation.   **481**

Limited liability   The last test is limited liability, a corporate characteristic. An organization has the characteristic of limited liability if there is *no* member who is personally liable for the debts of the organization. In a limited partnership, limited liability would exist if the general partner is a person without substantial assets other than his interest in the partnership and if he is a mere dummy, an agent for the limited partners.

Example

In a major case (*Phillip G. Larson*, 66 TC 159 [1976]) over the status of a limited partnership, the Tax Court determined that a limited partnership qualified as a partnership because it did not have continuity of life nor did it have limited liability. Of major significance was the IRS announcement that it would follow this case (*Acq., 1979–12 IRB 6*).

There was some question about whether under the California law which applies in this case the partnership would be dissolved in the case of the general partner's bankruptcy. The court found that it would. California law, however, is somewhat different than the Uniform Limited Partnership Act, which most states have adopted. Under the Uniform Limited Partnership Act, death, resignation, bankruptcy, etc. of a general partner *does* dissolve the partnership.

More important, however, was the fact that the general partner in this case did not have substantial assets. As indicated above, the regulations require the general partner to have substantial assets *and* not be a mere dummy. The court pointed specifically to the word "and" in the regulations. While he did not have substantial assets, the general partner was *not* a "mere dummy." The limited partners did not use him as a screen to conceal their own involvement in the limited partnership. Since *both* requirements of the regulations' definition were not met, the general partner was considered to have unlimited liability. Therefore, the partnership was considered to have unlimited liability.

Since the partnership did not have continuity of interest and did not have limited liability, it lacked two of the four corporate characteristics. Consequently, its status as a partnership was recognized. As indicated above, IRS agreed to follow this court opinion.

IRS attitude on partnership status

Although, under the regulations discussed previously, it would seem relatively simple to assure partnership status of a limited partnership real estate syndicate, imaginative maneuvering on the part of syndicate promoters in setting up many of these arrangements has caused IRS to take a careful look at this area. It has imposed restrictions, indirectly, through its power to issue advance rulings.

While IRS will issue advance rulings on proposed transactions, it can also refuse to rule. This is a powerful tool in the hands of IRS. In a specific case, the government may feel it does not have sufficient basis to rule adversely. However, if the facts do not meet IRS guidelines for a favorable ruling, it can refuse any ruling at all. Thus, while ostensibly the guidelines for issuing favorable rulings deal only with whether IRS will or will not issue a ruling, its power to withhold a ruling can have the practical effect of an adverse ruling.

Furthermore, although the guidelines for issuing a ruling technically do not affect the substance of a transaction, tax practitioners often feel that these will still influence revenue agents examining returns. For example, a taxpayer need not get an advance ruling to proceed with a transaction. He may feel he is on safe ground or he may be advised by counsel that his syndicate will meet the requirements of partnership status. Subsequently, when the tax return is examined, although the IRS guidelines for rulings were not issued as substantive rules, many tax advisers fear that the revenue agent examining the return will apply those guidelines in determining the status of the already existing syndicate.

Two sets of IRS guidelines for favorable rulings regarding limited partnership status take on substantial significance. One of these sets of guidelines (*Rev. Proc. 74-17*) deals in general with when IRS will rule with regard to limited partnership status. The other (*Rev. Proc. 72-13*) sets forth requirements for the recognition of a corporation as a general partner in a limited partnership.

General requirements of a limited partnership

Rev. Proc. 74-17, issued May 3, 1974, provides that IRS will refuse to rule that a limited partnership will be taxed as a partnership and not as a corporation unless the following requirements are met:

1. The interests of all the general partners, taken together, in each material item of partnership income, gain, loss, deduction or credit is equal to at least 1 percent of each such item at all times during the existence of the partnership. In determining the general partners' interests in such items, limited partnership interests owned by the general partners will not be taken into account.

2. The aggregate deductions to be claimed by the partners as their distributive shares of partnership losses for the first two years of

483

operation of the limited partnership will not exceed the amount of equity capital invested in the limited partnership.

3. A creditor who makes a nonrecourse loan to the limited partnership must not have or acquire, at any time as a result of making the loan, any direct or indirect interest in the profits, capital or property of the limited partnership other than as a secured creditor.

The first of these requirements is apparently aimed at the arrangements under which all of the partnership losses are attempted to be allocated to the limited partners or other special allocations of the various items made to make the investment in the syndicate more attractive. The requirement that the general partners must have at least a 1-percent interest in each item can be significant where the total amounts are substantial.

The second requirement seems to be an attempt to curb the practice of promising investors loss deductions far in excess of their cash investments (via large depreciation and other deductions) made possible by substantial increases of limited partners' bases due to nonrecourse loans.

The third requirement, which is consistent with other IRS rulings, is aimed at preventing the boosting of partners' bases via nonrecourse loans when these loans come from investors in the project. IRS apparently does not want to recognize the validity of a nonrecourse loan unless it is from a true outsider.

As mentioned previously, and as must be emphasized, these requirements are ostensibly *not* substantive requirements. They are merely the guidelines IRS has set up for issuing favorable advance rulings. Taxpayers are free to set up limited partnerships that do not meet these requirements and may very well prevail on the ground that they meet the tests of the regulations (i.e. that the organization does not have more corporate attributes than partnership attributes).

Corporation as a general partner

Rev. Proc. 72-13 deals with the current tendency to use a corporation as the general partner in a limited partnership. As was pointed out, an organization is treated as having limited liability (a corporate characteristic) if no member of the organization is personally liable for the debts of the organization.

Since most states now permit corporations to be partners in partnerships, the idea arose to have a corporation be the general partner. In a limited partnership of this type, the other partner with personal liability is the corporate general partner. The limited partners do not have personal liability and the shareholders of the general-partner corporation (as in the case of the shareholders of *any* corporation) do not have personal liability.

484   If the corporation is the only entity personally liable for the debts of the limited partnership, will the organization be classified as a partnership or taxed as a coporation? IRS, in *Rev. Proc. 72-13*, provides the guidelines as to when IRS will issue a ruling that a limited partnership with a corporation as general partner is taxable as a partnership and not as a corporation:

1. The limited partners may not own more than 20 percent of the stock of the general-partner corporation or its affiliates. Attribution rules apply in determining stock ownership (i.e. one is deemed to own stock owned by his spouse, children, etc.).

2. The corporate general partner must have a net worth *at all times* of at least 15 percent of the total contributions to the limited partnership or $250,000, whichever is less, if the total contributions to the partnership are less than $2,500,000. If total contributions to the partnership are $2,500,000 or more, the corporation's net worth must at all times be at least 10 percent of the total contributions.

3. The net worth computation is based on current market values but *excludes* the corporation's interest in the partnership as well as receivables from and payables to the partnership.

4. If the corporation has interests in more than one limited partnership, the minimum net worth must equal the aggregate of the amounts required for each individual partnership.

5. The purchase of an interest in a limited partnership may not carry with it the right or obligation to purchase a security of the general-partner corporation or its affiliates.

In addition, the guidelines issued by the IRS require that the specific minimum capital requirements of the corporate partner be met "at all times." This requirement undoubtedly gives tax advisers a difficult time. What kind of assurances and guarantees should they insist that their investor clients get to ensure that the corporate general partner retain the capital levels "at all times" in the future?

Even if the syndicate promoters give contractual assurances to the investors, the failure to maintain the minimum capital levels in the corporate general partner might destroy the tax shelter to the investor (if the IRS guideline is subsequently upheld as a proper substantive criterion as well as a guideline for advance ruling). The investor (limited partner) may bring a lawsuit against the syndicator but that may be small solace (or of limited economic value, depending on the syndicator's liquidity) to the investor.

Basis of limited partner's interest

As previously explained, the real estate limited partnership has great appeal as a vehicle for tax-sheltered investments because of the potential for increasing the limited partner's basis far beyond his investment. A partner, including a limited partner, can deduct partnership losses only to the extent

485

of his basis. However, the tax rules are that a limited partner's basis includes his share of those liabilities of the partnership for which *no* partner is personally liable—so-called "subject to" or nonrecourse liabilities—provided that the partnership is involved in investment in real estate.

Partnership liabilities are normally allocated for basis purposes according to the ratio for sharing losses. If the agreement provides one ratio for losses and another for profits, the loss ratio may be used. When the partnership has no recourse liabilities, regulations require that the profit ratio be used.

If any of the partners are personally liable for a partnership liability, that liability cannot increase the limited partner's basis beyond his subscription liability. If no one is personally liable, then the limited partner can increase his basis by his share of that liability.

In 1983, the Claims Court (in the *Raphan* case) ruled that a nonrecourse note guaranteed by a general partner was not his personal liability, and hence the liability could be shared by the partners (including the limited partners) in determining their bases. IRS took a contrary position in *Rev. Rul. 83-151*. The 1984 tax act sides with the IRS, providing that the *Raphan* case should not be followed for transactions after March 1, 1984.

Furthermore, Congress directed the IRS to revise and update its regulations regarding conditions under which recourse and nonrecourse liabilities are to be reflected in the basis of partnership interests. In its report accompanying the Tax Reform Act of 1984, the Conference Committee said, in regard to the regulations IRS is directed to issue:

> The conferees intend that the revision to the Section 752 regulations will be based largely on the manner in which the partners, and persons related to the partners, share the economic risk or loss with respect to partnership debt (other than bona fide nonrecourse debt, as defined by such regulations). With respect to bona fide nonrecourse debt, the conferees do not expect that such regulations will make major changes to the manner in which the partners' shares are determined, but may attempt to provide more certainty than presently exists.

Consequences of including liabilities in the basis of a partner's interest

We have seen that a partner's allocable share of the liabilities of the partnership enter into the computation of the basis of his partnership interest. To the extent that a partner shares partnership liabilities, it is the same as if he made a money contribution to the partnership which is exactly what Section 752 of the Internal Revenue Code says. Correspondingly, any decrease in a partner's share of partnership liabilities is considered the same as a distribution of money to the partner by the partnership.

Partnership agreements in many real estate tax-sheltered transactions provide that limited partners will have allocated to them a high proportion of the profits during the early years of the venture. During its early years, the venture is going to operate at a substantial loss because of the use of accelerated depreciation and other initial deductible expenses. By allocating a high proportion of the profits to the limited partners, they are able to use almost all the losses. As was pointed out previously, a limited partner adds to his basis a proportion of the partnership's nonrecourse liabilities *in accordance with the profit ratio*. So if 90 percent of the profits are allocated to the limited partners, the limited partners can include in their basis 90 percent of the nonrecourse liabilities of the partnership. However, while the general partner may not object to giving the limited partners the profits for the years when there will be losses, he likely wants a larger share of the profits in the years when there will be profits. So these arrangements often provide that down the line the profit ratio will change. The limited partner's share of the profits will change, for example, from 90 percent to 50 percent.

This change may be a trap for the limited partners. Suppose a limited partner has invested $10,000 and the real estate partnership nonrecourse liabilities amount to $100,000. Because of the 90-percent profit ratio, $90,000 of the liabilities are allocated to the limited partner and the basis of his interest is $100,000. Losses pass through to him and, over the years, he takes deductions of $50,000.

Let us assume that at that time partnership nonrecourse liabilities stand at $70,000. The basis of the limited partner's interest, the 90-percent profit ratio still being in effect, is $23,000 (investment, $10,000, plus share of liabilities, $63,000, minus losses deducted, $50,000). Now there is a profit switch to 50 percent. The limited partner is considered to have received a distribution from the partnership of $28,000 since his allocable share of partnership liabilities has been reduced from $63,000 to $35,000. To the extent that this constructive distribution exceeds his basis before the distribution, he realizes a gain which is considered a gain from the sale of his partnership interest. Thus, all of a sudden, because of a profit-ratio switch and without receiving any real money, the limited partner will incur a tax.

Disposition of property or partnership interest

It is clear that if the property of the partnership were sold for a price that exceeded the amount of the mortgage or other nonrecourse liability to which it was subject, the partnership would realize a gain allocable among the partners, general and limited, according to the partnership agreement.

Suppose, however, that the property has declined in value, that debt service payments cannot be met and the mortgage is foreclosed. Assume that the market value of the property is less than the mortgage liability outstanding at that time. Nevertheless, on a disposition of the property or a foreclosure, the partnership would be regarded as receiving income to the extent of the liability of which it was relieved.

Example

Suppose there is a nonrecourse mortgage of $500,000 on the partnership real estate and the limited partner had an original basis of $90,000. Over the years he deducted losses of $70,000 and reduced his basis to $20,000. On foreclosure of the mortgage, the partner is relieved of his $50,000 share of the liability; that is treated as a sale for $50,000. Since the limited partner's basis has been reduced to $20,000, he has a taxable gain of $30,000.

In 1981, the Court of Appeals for the Fifth Circuit rejected the idea that the amount of the nonrecourse mortgage on the disposition of the partnership property was *automatically* to be treated as proceeds received on the sale of property. That court held that only so much of the nonrecourse mortgage which did not exceed the value of the property was to be treated as sales proceeds. So, if the property declined in value—so that it was worth less than the unpaid mortgage—only the amount of the value of the property was to be treated as sales proceeds. *(See Tufts, 651F.2d1058.)*

However, in 1983, the United States Supreme Court reversed the Fifth Circuit's decision in *Tufts*. The Supreme Court held that the *entire* amount of the nonrecourse mortgage was treated as sales proceeds regardless of the value of the property.

The IRS position is further illustrated in examples set forth in a Revenue Ruling *(Rev. Rul. 74-40)* in which IRS deals with nonrecourse debt when a limited partner disposes of his partnership interest (rather than the partnership disposing of the property).

Examples

1. A limited partner invests $10,000 cash. His share of the partnership's nonrecourse liabilities is $15,000. He later sells his interest for $10,000 cash. At the time of the sale, his basis for his interest is $20,000. (Presumably, he reduced his original $25,000 basis by deducting a $5,000 loss.) Although he receives the same amount of cash as he invested ($10,000), he is treated as having realized a taxable gain of $5,000. The sale price of his partnership interest is calculated to be $25,000 ($10,000 cash plus $15,000 of partnership liabilities of which he is now relieved). Subtracting his $20,000 basis, he has a $5,000 gain.

2. The same as above, except that instead of selling his partnership interest, the partner receives $10,000 from the partnership in liquidation of his interest. The tax result is the same as in the first situation.

3. The taxpayer above has claimed sufficient losses to bring his basis down to zero. At that point, he simply withdraws from the partnership and *re-*

ceives nothing for his interest. He is treated as having realized a taxable gain of $15,000. The $15,000 of liabilities of which he is relieved is considered an amount received by him. He has no basis to subtract from that, so the whole $15,000 is taxable gain.

The gains in each of the three instances can be capital gains if the partnership had no unrealized receivables and no substantially appreciated inventory and there was no depreciation recapture at the time of disposition.

Allocation of income and deductions

It is common for a real estate syndication intended to offer the limited partners a tax shelter to provide for a plan for sharing of profits and losses. This plan has the effect of providing losses to the limited partner in the beginning years with the probability of future income realization, preferably capital gain.

However, the plan of allocation must have "substantial economic effect." Thus, allocations which may be deemed to be "shams" or having no business purpose can be set aside by IRS even though such allocations are pursuant to partnership agreements.

Retroactive allocations

Suppose a limited partner were to enter a partnership after the partnership has started and after some of the initial deductible expenses, such as interest and taxes during construction, have been paid. Can the new partner get the benefit of these deductions, assuming, of course, that he comes in before the end of the partnership year?

In 1976, Congress amended the law to prevent retroactive allocations of profits and losses. In 1984, Congress decided the law needed to be amended again to close up loopholes that developed in its prior law. Under the 1976 law, two acceptable methods were allowed to allocate the profits or losses when there is a change in partnership interests during the year.

Proration method   The net profit or loss is prorated over the year on a daily basis and allocated among those partners who were partners on each day.

Example

Mr. A, a 50-percent partner, sells half of his partnership interest to Mr. B on July 1. After the sale, Mr. A and Mr. B are 25-percent partners. Assume the partnership (on a calendar year) has a net loss of $10,000 for the year. Mr. A is entitled to half the loss prorated to the first half of the year (one-half of $5,000, or $2,500). He is entitled to 25 percent of the loss prorated to the second half of the year (one-quarter of $5,000, or $1,250). So, his share of the loss is $3,750. Mr. B is entitled to 25 percent of the loss prorated to the second half of the year, or $1,250.

Hypothetical closing-of-the-books method In the above example, the partnership would determine its profits or losses for the period ended June 30. Mr. A would be entitled to half of the profits or losses. The difference between the partnership's year-end results and the results as of June 30 would be allocated to the second half of the year, and Mr A and B would each be entitled to 25 percent of the second-half's profits or losses.

Some taxpayers took advantage of the closing-of-the-books method to load deductions into the end of the year, thus benefiting the income partner. Cash basis partnerships delayed paying expenses until near the end of the year. A partner coming into the partnership near the end of the year benefited from the high deductions achieved near year-end because the closing-of-the-books method was used to allocate losses.

Another approach involved the use of tiered partnerships. Partnership A became a partner of Partnership B. Both used the same taxable years (e.g., calendar years) and both were cash basis. If Partnership B had losses that passed through to Partnership A, it was the position of both that those losses passed through to Partnership A on the last day of its taxable year. So if Partnership A used the closing-of-the-books method after admitting partners near year-end, the new partners would get the full benefit of Partnership B's losses that passed through, even though the B losses arose during the entire calendar year.

Because of these techniques employed by taxpayers to circumvent the prohibition against retroactive allocations, the Tax Reform Act of 1984 instituted some new rules regarding allocations. They apply to amounts attributable to periods after March 31, 1984.

These new rules require IRS to issue regulations for allocations of profits and losses after there is a change in partnership interests. Taxpayers will be permitted to use any method allowed by these regulations.

The new rules set up a special treatment of "allocable cash basis items." These items must be allocated on a daily basis to each day of the period to which they are attributable. Each partner picks up his proportionate share of the total for each day on which he was a partner. "Allocable cash basis items" are the following (if the partnership uses the cash basis of accounting): interest, taxes, payments for services or the use of property, and any other items specified in regulations IRS is to issue.

Principles similar to the ones dealing with "allocable cash basis items" are to be applied when Partnership A is a partner in Partnership B. The items are allocated on a daily basis in B, with A picking up its share based on the days during the year on which it was a partner in B. These items are then further allocated among the partners of Partnership A based on their proportionate interests in A on each of the days for which Partnership B items were allocated to A.

All of these allocation rules are subject to modification by regulations.

Appendix D

Corporate Liquidations/ Reorganizations

In the discussion of the forms of ownership of real estate, it was pointed out that real estate is often acquired in corporate form in order to avoid personal liability but that in some situations corporate ownership may create tax disadvantages which would outweigh whatever advantages may flow from limited liability (see Chapter 8). In other situations, corporate ownership may present an opportunity for tax free diversification of the investment.

One of the major problems of corporate ownership arises when the time comes to dispose of the property owned by the corporation. The problem is especially acute when the corporation is owned by just one or a few shareholders—the so-called closely-held corporation. Since the corporation is a separate entity, any gain realized on the disposition will be taxable to the corporate entity. However, if corporate reinvestment is not intended at that point and if each of the shareholders would like to reinvest his share in different investments and not in conjunction with the other shareholders, the problem arises of how to get the after-tax proceeds into the hands of the shareholders. As was pointed out in Chapter 7, distributions to the shareholders by the corporation of after-tax corporate profits are again taxed to the shareholders as dividends.

This problem of double taxation may be solved by astute use of the rules applying to corporate liquidations.

In some cases, an investor may be seeking to diversify his investments. However, he may be deterred by the tax cost involved in disposing of his current holdings to acquire the funds with which to reinvest. Sometimes, if he holds the property in unincorporated form this problem may be solved via so-called "like-kind" exchanges (described in detail in Chapter 11.) In other situations, the fact that the property is held in corporate form may present an opportunity to diversify without incurring a tax. This result may be achieved via a corporate reorganization.

Corporate liquidations

The general tax rule pertaining to complete liquidations of corporations must first be understood in order to apply the special rules that are available to avoid double taxation.

If a corporation is completely liquidated, the shareholders receive all of the corporate assets in exchange for their shares in the corporation. The transaction is treated as a sale or an exchange. Assuming the shareholder's holding period for his stock is sufficiently long (see Chapter 7), he will realize a long-term capital gain or loss on the transaction (it is treated as if he sold his stock to the corporation for the assets he received). The gain or loss will be equal to the difference between the market value of everything he receives from the corporation and the basis for the stock he surrenders. Had there not been a complete liquidation and if the corporation distributed accumulated earnings to the stockholder as a dividend, he would have ordinary income. If, however, these earnings are paid to the shareholder as part of the total liquidation of the corporation, they are part of the total proceeds used to measure his long-term capital gain on liquidation.

The corporation is normally not taxable on the transaction. However, if the corporation distributes depreciable property as part of the liquidation, whatever depreciation recapture would have arisen had the corporation sold the property to a third party at its market value at that time arises upon the liquidation distribution. (The rules pertaining to depreciation recapture are explained in Chapter 10.) Although the corporation is completely liquidated, it may still be liable for some taxes attributable to the distribution of property on which depreciation recapture is realized. (If the corporation has not retained assets with which to pay the taxes, IRS may pursue each of the shareholders who received a distribution in liquidation for his pro rata share of the taxes payable by the corporation.)

The twelve-month (section 337) liquidation

The problem with using the corporate liquidation rules as a vehicle for the sale of property held in a corporation can be seen from the following simplified example.

Example

Assume a corporation with two equal stockholders holds a piece of property worth $1,000,000. Its basis for the property is $200,000. If in 1984 the corporation sells the property it will realize a gain of $800,000. (For illustrative purposes, assume that there is no depreciation recapture and that the entire gain qualifies as a Section 1231 gain.)

The corporation has a long-term capital gain of $800,000 and pays a 28-percent tax, or $224,000. The corporation now has $776,000 in cash, and the two equal shareholders would like to get that money. The corporation can now go through a complete liquidation, distributing $388,000 to each shareholder. If each shareholder has a basis for his stock of $88,000, each will have a long-term capital gain of $300,000. Taking into account each shareholder's other income, assume each pays an effective overall rate on his capital gain of 20 percent (the maximum rate), of $60,000. (The rules for calculating the tax on long-term capital gain are set forth in Chapter 7.) Thus, the $800,000 gain on the sale of the property by the corporation is subject to a total tax of $344,000 ($224,000 on the corporate level and $120,000 on the shareholder level).

With this problem of double taxation before them, the taxpayers in this example attempt to circumvent the double tax by going through the liquidation prior to the sale. Had the corporation in the example distributed the property to the shareholders in total liquidation, they would have had a capital gain on the distribution of $824,000 (the $1,000,000 market value of the property received minus the combined basis of the stock in the hands of both shareholders of $176,000). Again, assuming a 20-percent tax on the capital gains, the tax would come to $164,800. If the shareholders then sold the property for $1,000,000 they would have no gain or loss on the transaction since their basis for the property would be $1,000,000, the value they picked up computing their taxable capital gain on the liquidation.

If the corporation liquidated the property and the stockholders then sell it, they would have cash remaining after taxes of $835,200 ($1,000,000 sales proceeds minus the $164,800 capital gain tax paid on the liquidation), or $417,600 each.

On the other hand, if the corporation sold the property first, each stockholder would receive a distribution of $388,000, pay a capital gain tax of $60,000 and have $328,000 left after taxes.

Obviously, the preferred tax route is to liquidate first and then sell. However, a famous U. S. Supreme Court decision, the *Court Holding Company* case, presents a major problem. In that case, the court agreed with IRS that although the liquidation took place before the sale, the negotiations prior to the transaction made it clear that the sale was really being made on behalf of the corporation. So the court said the case should be decided on what it considered to be the *substance* of the transaction, not its formal form, and it treated the transaction as if the sale was made by the corporation and then the liquidation took place; hence the double tax. In a later case, the *Cumberland Public Service Company* case, the Supreme Court held that the facts concerning sales negotiations indicated that the liquidation took place first and the sale was truly made by the shareholders after liquidation; a double tax was avoided.

The result of these cases was to create great uncertainty: fine distinctions between fact patterns made all the difference, and no one could be sure exactly how the facts in his case would ultimately be interpreted. Finally, Congress came to the rescue and enacted Section 337 of the Internal Revenue Code.

Section 337 is intended to take the uncertainty out of the result and remove the problems that would arise if it were ultimately determined that the fact pattern resembled *Court Holding Company* rather than *Cumberland Public Service*.

If the rules of Section 337 are met, the corporation makes the sale. However, the gain to the corporation is not taxed to the corporation. On the liquidation that follows, the shareholders utilize the regular rules applying to corporate liquidations and report a capital gain for the difference between the proceeds they receive and the basis for their stock.

Example

If Section 337 were applied to the example above, the corporation would sell the property for $1,000,000. It would not recognize any gain on the transaction and thus pay no tax. It could then distribute the $1,000,000 to the two shareholders who would have a combined capital gain of $824,000, a combined capital gain tax of $164,800 and proceeds remaining of $835,200, or $417,600 each. These are the same results that would arise if they liquidated first and then sold and were not subsequently upset by the *Court Holding Company* ruling.

Section 337 rules   For Section 337 to apply, certain rules must be followed. First, a plan of complete liquidation must be adopted. This can be a simple matter of having a resolution passed by the corporation's board of directors. While the Treasury regulations will recognize some informal arrangements as having the effect of the adoption of a plan of liquidation (especially where the existence of such a plan will produce adverse tax effects), if a Section 337 liquidation is desired, it is the safe and prudent practice to have the formal adoption of a plan in writing.

The next requirement is to liquidate the entire corporation (all of its assets distributed to the shareholders) within one year of the adoption of the plan of liquidation. The corporation may retain such assets as are required to meet those liabilities which are not distributed.

Within the one-year period, gains and losses on the sale of property by the corporation are not recognized for tax purposes; they are tax-free. The term property here means all property other than inventory. (Thus, if the corporation were a dealer in real estate, sale of individual pieces of real estate would be taxable to the corporation as sale of inventory.) If, however, the entire inventory is sold to one customer in one transaction, gain or loss on that sale, too, is not recognized for tax purposes.

Note that the nonrecognition applies to both gains and losses. If some of the property sold by the corporation during the one year after the adoption of the plan of liquidation were sold at a loss, that loss would not be deductible by the corporation to offset other income. To avoid this result it is advisable to sell the loss property prior to the adoption of the plan of liquidation. After the sale at a loss, the plan can be adopted and subsequent sales by the corporation at gains within the one-year period would not be taxable at the corporate level. (It is important here to avoid any informal understanding that resembles a plan of liquidation before the loss property is sold. It is in these situations that IRS may seek to establish that *in fact* a plan of liquidation was adopted prior to the sale of the loss property and thus deny the corporation a deduction for those losses.)

Installment sales Prior to April 1, 1980, a major problem arose if the sale by the corporation during the one-year period was an installment sale. While the corporation would not be taxed on the sale, when it distributed the installment notes to the shareholders in the liquidation process, the value of these notes was included in the total received by the shareholders. Hence, although the sale qualified for installment sale reporting in the first instance (at the corporate level) it did not continue as an installment sale at the stockholder level. The shareholders had to report the entire gain even though they would not receive payment on the installment notes until sometime in the future. This was considered a major defect in the Section 337 solution to the *Court Holding Company* problem.

Congress finally came to the rescue. In revising the entire installment-sale process in the tax law, Congress decreed that where there is a liquidation under the rules of Section 337, if the corporation made a sale during the one-year period which qualified as an installment sale, the equivalent to an installment-sale status carries over to the shareholders in the liquidation process.

The way IRS interprets this provision is to treat the liquidation as an installment sale (unless the shareholder elects not to have it treated this way). The installment sales rules are explained in Chapter 10.

The total value of what the shareholder receives as a distribution in liquidation is treated as the sales price of his stock in an installment sale. His basis for his stock is subtracted from the sales price to determine the gross profit on the sale. This gross profit is then translated into a percentage.

The percentage is applied to the amount of cash and other property received in the year of liquidation to determine the portion of those proceeds that is treated as capital gain in the year of liquidation. In subsequent years, when he collects on the installment obligation distributed to him by the corporation, the shareholder applies the same gross profit percentage to each payment to determine the portion of each payment that is treated as capital gain.

Example

Mr. Brown is the sole shareholder of Alpha Corporation. Alpha adopts a plan of complete liquidation. Within the 12-month period after the adoption of the plan, it sells an apartment house it owns for $1,000,000. The terms are $300,000 cash in the year of sale and installment notes of $70,000 payable over 10 years. Any gain on the sale is not recognized to Alpha because it will be completedly liquidated within 12 months after adopting the plan of liquidation. In addition to the building it sold, Alpha also has other assets and cash totalling $200,000. Brown's basis for his stock in Alpha is $480,000.

Within 12 months of adopting the plan of liquidation, Alpha distributes all of its assets to Brown in complete liquidation of the corporation. This distribution consists of the $700,000 of installment notes it received on the sale of the building, the $300,000 in cash it received on the sale, and the other $200,000 in assets. Brown thus receives a total of $1,200,000. Since his basis for his stock is $480,000, his gain is $720,000.

Because this transaction is treated as an installment sale of Brown's stock to his corporation, he compares his $720,000 gain to the sales price of $1,200,000 and arrives at a gross profit percentage of 60 percent.

In the year of liquidation, he receives $500,000—the $300,000 cash the corporation received on the sale plus the $200,000 of other assets the corporation had. So in that year he reports a capital gain of $300,000 (60 percent of $500,000). In each of the succeeding 10 years he will receive $70,000 on the $700,000 installment obligation. So in each of those years he will report a gain of $42,000 (60 percent of $70,000). Thus, over the 10-year priod, he will report a capital gain of $420,000. This, plus the gain of $300,000 he reported in the year of liquidation, gives a total of $720,000, the total gain he realized on the liquidation.

The one-month (section 333) liquidation

This special form of liquidation (in which the distribution in liquidation must all take place within one calendar month) is designed to permit the property to be distributed to the shareholders in a transaction in which the shareholders do not recognize any gain. However, they retain as the basis for the property they have received the basis of the stock they have surrendered. On subsequent sale, the gain is taxable to the shareholders (since they have then sold their own property).

The foregoing is a simplified explanation of the one-month liquidation rules. As may be expected, there are a number of complexities involved. Certain rules must be followed and, notwithstanding the broad description of the purpose of Section 333, there are situations where part or all of the gain to the shareholders on liquidation may be taxed, even as ordinary income.

Before getting into the specific rules of Section 333, it should be noted that this section is most beneficial when the corporation holds property which has appreciated considerably in value and has little or no earnings and profits (accumulated or current) and little or no cash or securities acquired after 1953.

To qualify as a liquidation under Section 333, a plan of liquidation has to be adopted. Thereafter, at least 80 percent of the shareholders must consent to the liquidation. If enough shareholders consent, those who do not consent treat their distributions in liquidation under the general rules pertaining to liquidations (they realize capital gain or loss for the difference between the market value of what they received in the liquidation and the bases for their shares in the corporation.)

Once the plan is adopted and the necessary consents obtained, the complete liquidation of the corporation must take place within one calendar month. Note that the entire distribution must take place within that one month (a calendar month and *not* a 30-day period spanning two calendar months).

If the Section 333 rules are met, the shareholder computes his gain in the usual manner (i.e. the difference between the market value of what he receives and the basis for the stock he surrenders). However, all or part of that gain may not be recognized.

1. If, at the time of the liquidation, the corporation had earnings and profits accumulated from prior years or current year's earnings or both, the shareholder is deemed to have received his pro rata share of those earnings and profits. The portion of his gain equal to his pro rata share of earnings and profits is taxable to him as a dividend (ordinary income).

2. If the distribution to the shareholder includes cash, stock or securities acquired by the corporation after 1953, that portion of his gain remaining (after applying the rules on earning and profits) which is equal to the value of such cash and stock or securities is taxable to him as a capital gain.

3. Any remaining gain, after applying the rules above, is not recognized. The bases for these items are allocable portions of the remaining basis of his stock.

Obviously, if there are little or no earnings and profits and no cash or securities, then most or all of the gain on liquidation is not recognized. Thereafter, the shareholder can sell the property to a third party, recognize the gain and pay the tax.

Earnings and profits When a one-month liquidation is employed and if the corporation distributes depreciable property, depreciation recapture on the corporate level can occur. The corporation is deemed to have the same amount of depreciation recapture as it would have had had it sold the property at the time of liquidation at a price equal to the market value at the time of liquidation. If depreciation recapture occurs, the corporation has income and a tax to pay. In addition, the income remaining after the tax adds to the corporation's earnings and profits and thereby creates (or adds to) a dividend to the shareholders at the time of liquidation.

Basis It was explained earlier that in a Section 333 liquidation the shareholders allocate their bases for their stock to the properties received in the liquidation (where gain is not recognized). It should be noted that where the property is subject to a mortgage or other lien, the liability that comes with the property is added to the basis of the property received, thus increasing the shareholder's basis.

Corporate reorganizations

For the real estate investor, the corporate reorganization can provide a means of diversification of investment without reducing the amount available for reinvestment.

For example, if an investor should sell his current investment, he is left with *after-tax* proceeds for reinvestment. On the other hand if he is able to combine his corporation with another and thus become an investor in the combined enterprise (thereby diversifying or expanding his investment) without paying a tax, he has the full value of the original investment working for him. This latter result can be accomplished via a corporate reorganization.

From a potential seller's viewpoint, the corporate reorganization is most attractive when the seller's corporation (usually closely-held) is acquired by a much larger corporation whose stock is publicly traded. After the acquisition, the former shareholder of the closely-held company is now a stockholder in a corporation whose stock is traded publicly. He is now in a position to dispose of part of his investment as the situation dictates, picking up capital gains along the way. He is also in a position to make gifts and otherwise plan his estate using determined values (stock quotations).

Statutory pattern of reorganization

The tax law in this area is very complex. What follows, therefore, is an outline of the structures of the various forms of corporate reorganization and the basic rules without an examination of all of the fine points and complexities.

There are seven forms of reorganizations. Only three will be considered here, the "A," "B" and "C" types. The other four do not apply to acquisition transactions.

Basically, in a corporate reorganization, the shareholders and bondholders of the corporation that is being acquired end up as shareholders or bondholders of the corporation doing the acquiring. Part or all of the gain on the transaction may be nonrecognized (i.e. not currently taxed) depending on how the transaction is structured.

Typically, if a shareholder gets stock only in return for his stock, the gain on the transaction is not taxed. If he gets securities (bonds, notes, etc.), they are considered "boot" to the extent that the face amount of the securities received exceeds the face amount of the securities surrendered (obviously, if no securities are surrendered, the face amount of any securities received constitutes "boot"). Cash and property other than stock or securities also constitute "boot." Basically, "boot" is taxable to the extent it does not exceed the total gain. ("Boot" is further explained under each type of reorganization below.)

"A" type of reorganization

The "A" type is defined as a "statutory merger or consolidation." Evidently all that is required to consummate an "A" type reorganization is to effect, under the corporation laws of any state, a merger of two or more corporations whereby one retains its corporate existence and absorbs the others.

Unlike the "B" and "C" types, in an "A" reorganization no restrictions are imposed by the tax law as to the amount of money or other property that may be used nor the type of stock or securities that may be issued. True, any money or other property will constitute "boot" and result in some tax incidence but the issuance of "boot" in and of itself will not disqualify the transaction as an "A" organization.

Thus, considerable flexibility is available in an "A" organization. Should some shareholders want cash and others stock it can be worked out within the framework of an "A" type. However, there is some peril inherent in this very flexibility. Excessive use by the acquiring or resulting corporation of bonds, cash and other property may violate the requirement of "continuity of interest." This concept requires that there be a continuity of interest through stock ownership in the acquiring corporation on the part of the former stockholders of the acquired corporation. How much "boot," therefore, may be given and yet preserve the reorganization?

IRS takes the position that the "continuity of interest" is satisfied if at least 50 percent in value of the former stock interest is continued in the acquiring corporation. IRS would thus permit not more than 50 percent of the value of the stock to be exchanged for "boot."

Note also that after receiving the required stock interest in the acquiring corporation, it is necessary to retain it for a relatively reasonable period of time. Otherwise IRS will probably argue that there was a pre-existing plan to sell off the stock, thereby destroying the "continuity of interest" at the time of the reorganiztion.

Treatment of "boot" in "A" reorganizations If "boot" is given in an otherwise qualifying reorganization, gain is recognized to the recipient of the "boot" but in an amount not in excess of the "boot." A loss sustained on the reorganization is not deductible whether or not "boot" is received. If gain is recognized, it may be treated as a dividend to the extent of the recipient's share of the corporation's accumulated earnings and profits.

"B" type of reorganization

In this type of reorganization, the acquiring corporation acquires the stock of the acquired corporation directly from that corporation's stockholders. The acquiring corporation must have at least 80-percent control of the acquired corporation after the exchange. In effect, the acquiring corporation ends up with a subsidiary corporation which it controls.

What do the shareholders of the acquired corporation get? They must get voting stock *only* in the acquiring corporation or its parent *and nothing else*.

Should the acquiring corporation issue any cash or "boot" to finance the redemption or purchase of the stock of any dissenting shareholders, this will destroy the "B" type reorganization status and a fully taxable trans-action will result.

Minimal cash may be given in lieu of fractional shares. If any other amount of "boot" is given, the *entire* transaction is fully taxable and the gain is to be reported as capital gain to the extent the value of the stock and other property received by the shareholder exceeds his basis in the stock exchanged. IRS has ruled that the issuance of contingent rights to receive additional shares will not violate the "solely for voting stock" requirement provided the right is not represented by a negotiable certificate. The acquiring corporation may acquire debentures of the acquired corporation for cash or by issuance of its own bonds without invalidating the reorganization.

"C" type of reorganization

A "C" type of reorganization resembles an "A" type in that it generally achieves a merger of the assets of the acquired corporation with that of the acquiring corporation although it need not go that far.

In a "C" type there must be an acquisition of substantially all of the properties of the acquired corporation in exchange solely for voting stock of either the acquiring corporation or its parent corporation. The assets received may also be transferred directly to a subsidiary of the acquiring corporation.

Initially, the exchange is between the two corporations; one corporation transfers its assets in exchange for the other corporation's stock. After the exchange, the corporation whose assets were acquired is required to distribute the stock received (plus any other assets it has) to its shareholders in liquidation of the corporation. This second exchange is tax-free to the shareholders (subject to the "boot" provisions). After the liquidation of the corporation whose assets were acquired, there is, in effect, the same result as in a merger. In fact, the "C" reorganization followed by the liquidation is often referred to as a "practical merger."

Unlike an "A" reorganization, the "C" type lacks flexibility in that *solely voting stock* must be used. Peculiarly, here the statute expands the phrase "solely for voting stock" to permit a limited amount of "boot" to be given by the acquiring corporation.

As mentioned, in an "A" reorganization the "continuity of interest" requirement acts as the only limitation on the issuance of "boot." In a "C" type, the acquired corporation or its shareholders may receive cash or other property in addition to voting stock but only up to a value equal to 20 percent of the total value of the corporation's property. On the face of it, this would seem to allow for a sizable amount of "boot." However, there is this additional provision: in applying this 20-percent "boot" test, liabilities taken over are treated as if they constituted cash paid to the transferor corporation. Yet, where no "boot" whatsoever is given in addition to the voting stock, the liabilities taken over will *not* be treated as cash. In other words, if the acquiring corporation gives no "boot," only voting stock, then it can take over the liabilities regardless of the amount involved. But should any amount of "boot" be given, say $100 in cash, then *all* liabilities taken over suddenly become the equivalent of cash for the purposes of the 20-percent test.

As can be assumed, most corporations will have liabilities equal to at least 20 percent of the value of the assets. Hence, a "C" reorganization in practical effect precludes the issuance of any "boot."

Another problem may arise in a "C" reorganization with reference to the requirement for a transfer of "substantially all" of the acquired company's properties. Obviously, where all assets are taken over without exception, no question arises. But should the acquiring corporation reject some of the assets, the "substantially all" requirement may prevent consummation of a "C" reorganization. Although courts have found that 86 percent of the acquired corporation's net worth is "substantially all," while 68 percent is not, IRS maintains no percentage is controlling and that the facts in each individual case will be studied.

words, if the acquiring corporation gives no "boot," only voting stock, then it can take over the liabilities regardless of the amount involved. But should any amount of "boot" be given, say $100 in cash, then *all* liabilities taken over suddenly become the equivalent of cash for the purposes of the 20-percent test.

As can be assumed, most corporations will have liabilities equal to at least 20 percent of the value of the assets. Hence, a "C" reorganization in practical effect precludes the issuance of any "boot."

Another problem may arise in a "C" reorganization with reference to the requirement for a transfer of "substantially all" of the acquired company's properties. Obviously, where all assets are taken over without exception, no question arises. But should the acquiring corporation reject some of the assets, the "substantially all" requirement may prevent consummation of a "C" reorganization. Although courts have found that 86 percent of the acquired corporation's net worth is "substantially all," while 68 percent is not, IRS maintains no percentage is controlling and that the facts in each individual case will be studied.

Appendix E

Gift and Estate Planning

Throughout this book we have been concerned with the income stream and cash flow from a property (including the income and cash flow arising from the disposition of the property). In doing so, we have necessarily taken into account the impact of the federal income tax on these cash flows.

The types of dispositions of property with which we have been concerned thus far are sales and exchanges. However, there are other dispositions that should be considered: lifetime gifts and dispositions arising because of death. Each of these dispositions may have federal (and, in most cases, state) tax consequences. The taxes involved are the gift and estate taxes.

The real estate broker should have some familiarity with these taxes because just about every investor with a substantial amount of property will be concerned about passing his estate on to his family. In the vast majority of cases he will want to pass on the maximum amount possible. Consequently, he will be concerned with planning devices which will reduce the estate and gift taxes as much as possible. (It should be emphasized that the property owner's personal desires should take precedence over tax savings. There are numerous situations where personal and family considerations, emotional or otherwise, may call for plans which save less taxes than other available alternatives.) Knowing the gift and estate tax rules will help the real estate broker understand the needs of the investor and thereby enable the broker to present purchase or sale situations intelligently and usefully

The unified tax

Prior to 1977, the federal government imposed separate taxes on lifetime gifts and on estates of decedents. Beginning with 1977, a unified tax for this purpose was instituted. Although there is a separate tax imposed on litetime gifts, these gifts are then included in the estate to determine the overall tax. Then, the calculated tax is reduced by any gift taxes paid by the decedent after 1977. Thus, in the end, there is a unified tax on all the transfers.

The gift tax and the estate tax, just like the income tax, is a progressive tax. The taxable amount is segregated into layers (tax brackets) with each additional bracket subject to a higher rate.

Thus, if taxable gifts are made for the first time, the tax is computed (according to the rate table) on the amount of those taxable gifts for the period covered by the gift tax return. If additional taxable gifts are made in subsequent periods, the total of all taxable gifts is first determined (the current period's taxable gifts plus all prior taxable gifts). The tax is computed on that total (the total may have pushed some of the gifts into a higher tax bracket). After the tax is computed, there is subtracted from that tax all prior gift taxes paid, and the taxpayer then pays the difference.

The same procedure is followed when the donor dies and his estate tax is computed. All his lifetime taxable gifts are added to his taxable estate to determine the total tax due (using the same tax table used to compute the gift taxes). Again, the amount of this combined total will cause part of this total to end up in higher tax brackets. After the tax is computed, any gift taxes paid by the decedent during his life are subtracted. As a result, the total tax paid is based on the total of the taxable gifts and the taxable estate.

The unified tax removes some of the tax advantage of lifetime gifts. Prior to the 1977 tax changes, there were two separate tax tables—one for lifetime gifts and another for estates. The gift tax table rates were 75 percent of the estate tax table rates. Thus, it was less costly (in terms of taxes) to make gifts than to pass property by inheritance. Furthermore, property given away was removed from the estate, leaving a smaller amount to be subject to the higher estate tax rates. Under the new unified tax structure these two advantages of lifetime gifts have been removed.

There are still some advantages to lifetime gifts. If, for example, the property given away subsequently increased in value to a great extent, the gift tax (based on the value at the time of the gift) could be considerably less than the tax would have been at the time of death (which would have been based on the higher value at the time of death). Of course, the reverse is true if the property declines in value after the gift is made.

Only taxable gifts are included in the estate when the final calculation is made. Since some parts of gifts are subject to annual exclusions (more on that later), the total of these exclusions are not subject to any tax (gift or estate). Had the gifts not been made (and thus the exclusions not been taken) the total of those exclusions would have been included in the estate. Since the exclusions are based on the number of donees involved in the gifts, the total of the exclusions can be considerable when gifts are given regularly over a period of time to many donees.

How the gift tax works

The unified tax applies to lifetime gifts, but not all gifts are fully taxable. **504** Annual exclusions, split gifts, the marital deduction and the unified credit reduce (or eliminate) the gift tax.

Annual exclusion Beginning in 1982, each person is entitled to an annual gift tax exclusion of $10,000 per donee per year. Thus, if an individual makes ten $10,000 gifts to ten different donees (e.g. children, grandchildren) in one year (a total of $100,000), no part of those gifts would be subject to the gift tax. And he could repeat the process every year.

Split gifts If a married person makes a gift (and his spouse consents by signing the consent clause on the gift tax return), the annual exclusion on that gift is increased to $20,000. This is so even if only one spouse owns the property being given away and the other merely "consents." Thus, in the preceding example if the donor's wife consented, he could give away a total of $200,000 per year without any gift tax liability.

Gift tax marital deduction Beginning in 1982, there is an unlimited gift tax marital deduction. That means all outright gifts to spouses—regardless of the amount of value involved—are not subject to gift tax. (Previously, only a portion of the gift was subject to the marital deduction.) The unlimited marital deduction for gift tax is consistent with the change made (effective in 1982) concerning the marital deduction for estate tax. For that tax, too, an unlimited marital deduction is allowed (see below).

The unified credit After the tax on a gift is calculated it is reduced by the unified credit. If the calculated tax is less than the credit, there is no tax to pay, and the credit is reduced by the amount of the tax. The remaining credit is available to offset future gift taxes. Thus, no gift tax is actually paid until the full credit is exhausted.

On death, all of the taxable gifts are added to the taxable estate to determine the full tax liability on the combination of the taxable gifts and the estate. Then, the combined tax is reduced by any gift tax paid by the decedent during his life, and the full unified credit is applied against the remaining tax liability.

The amount of the unified credit for gifts made in 1987 and thereafter or for estates of decedents dying in 1987 and thereafter is $192,800. Based on the unified gift and estate tax rates, this means that there is an equivalent tax exemption of $600,000—no tax until the taxable gifts or taxable estate exceeds $600,000. (In other words, the tax on the first $600,000 is $192,800 and that is wiped out by the credit.) For the years prior to 1987, the unified credit and the equivalent exemption from tax are shown on the table at the top of p. 506.

How the estate tax works

The estate tax is imposed on the value of the property owned by the decedent on his death as well as certain other property which he is deemed to have owned because of the control he was able to exercise over it.

Decedent dying in, or gift made in—	Unified Credit	Equivalent Exemption
1981	$ 47,000	$175,625
1982	62,800	225,000
1983	79,300	275,000
1984	96,300	325,000
1985	121,800	400,000
1986	155,800	500,000
1987 and thereafter	192,800	600,000

The starting point is the gross estate which includes all property just described. From the gross estate are subtracted debts of the decedent and the cost of administering the estate. The resulting amount is the adjusted gross estate. From this is subtracted the estate tax marital deduction (described below). What remains may be further reduced by charitable bequests. The amount of the taxable gifts made during the decedent's lifetime are then added. The estate tax is then calculated on this total.

The tax thus computed is then reduced by (1) gift taxes paid during the decedent's life, (2) the unified credit and (3) credit for state death taxes paid. (The federal tax law sets a maximum amount permitted to be deducted as a credit for state death taxes paid. If the actual tax imposed by the state is less than the maximum amount set forth in the federal law, then that lesser amount is the amount which is deductible on the federal estate tax return.)

Alternate valuation date

It was previously stated that the gross estate consists of the market value of all the property owned by the decedent at the time of his death. However, the estate has a choice of two dates it can use to determine the value of the property: date of death or six months after date of death (referred to as the alternate valuation date).

If the alternate valuation date is selected, *all* property in the estate must be valued as of the alternate valuation date. It is not permissible to value some of the property as of the date of death and other property as of the alternate valuation date. Furthermore, if the alternate valuation date is chosen and if some of the estate's property is sold or distributed between the date of death and the alternate valuation date, the value of such property for estate tax purposes is its sale price or the value on the date of distribution.

Why choose the alternate valuation date? Obviously, the value of the property in the estate (or some significant portion of it) may have gone up or down six months after the date of death. If the value has gone down, the alternate valuation date may be used to reduce the value of the estate and thereby reduce the amount of the estate tax due.

However, it was sometimes deemed advisable to choose the alternate valuation date when the value of the property increased between the date of death and six months thereafter. As pointed out in Chapter 8, when property is inherited, it takes as its basis the market value at the date of death or the alternate valuation date (whichever date is used for estate tax purposes). The higher the basis assigned to the property, the lower the potential capital gain on disposition by the heir to the property. Hence, if the income tax bracket of the person inheriting the property is such that the tax on a capital gain by him would exceed the estate's tax on the difference between the date-of-death value and the higher alternate-valuation-date value, the use of the alternate valuation was favored by that beneficiary.

The Tax Reform Act of 1984 eliminated the option to choose the alternate valuation date when the property's value increased after the date of death. For estates of those dying after July 18, 1984, the alternate valuation date may be used only if, by choosing the alternate valuation date, the value of the gross estate will be *decreased* and the estate tax will also be decreased. Thus, if the value of some of the assets in the estate increased and some decreased, the alternate date may be used for all of the assets, if the result is a *net decrease.*.

The alternate valuation date is elected by the executor on the estate tax return. Once the alternate date is elected, the election is irrevocable.

Estate tax marital deduction

Obviously, the amount of property which passes to the decedent's beneficiaries is the net amount after the estate taxes are paid. Consequently, the usual strategy for people with large estates is to embark on programs which will reduce the tax impact on the property being transferred. One major device for achieving this result is the marital deduction.

Beginning with estates of decedents dying in 1982, the tax law provides for an unlimited marital deduction. Whatever property the decedent leaves to his or her spouse can qualify for the marital deduction and thus be deducted from the adjusted gross estate in arriving at the taxable estate. For example, if, after allowing for the administration expenses of the estate, possible state death taxes and other bequests equal to the equivalent exemption, the decedent left the balance of the estate to his spouse, there would be no federal estate tax to pay regardless of the size of the estate.

Whether or not the maximum marital deduction should be utilized is a matter of arithmetic in many cases. (In other cases, the decedent for other than tax reasons may decide not to utilize the maximum marital deduction.) The arithmetic involves two elements: (1) the estate tax that will have to be paid when the surviving spouse dies and (2) the value of the tax saved by using the maximum marital deduction in the first estate.

When the surviving spouse dies, the amount that was subject to the marital deduction when the first spouse died will be included in the estate of the second spouse. (We are assuming that the surviving spouse did not remarry and thus his or her estate will not have any marital deduction available.) Of course, the surviving spouse may diminish his or her estate by making lifetime gifts and otherwise disposing of property. But for the sake of planning calculations, it is assumed that the amount of the marital deduction allowed in the first estate is included in the second estate.

Since the estate tax is a graduated tax, adding the amount of the marital deduction of the first estate to the property already owned by the surviving spouse may cause the ultimate estate tax on the amount equal to that marital deduction to be greater in the second estate than it would have been in the first estate. This is one of the calculations to be made in planning with the marital deduction.

The other calculation involves the value of the estate tax saved in the first estate by using the full marital deduction. Here we must estimate the remaining life expectancy of the surviving spouse and, using an appropriate interest rate, calculate how much those estate tax savings can earn (after taxes) during the life expectancy of the surviving spouse.

A comparison of the extra estate tax which would be payable in the second estate (by adding the marital deduction of the first estate to that of the second estate) with the after-tax earnings generated by the estate tax saved in the first estate can give some indication of the value of the marital deduction and to what extent it should be utilized.

Of course, since we are dealing with the uncertainties of the time of death, all calculations are based on assumptions.

If an individual determines that it would not be wise to utilize the maximum marital deduction, he may still arrange to have the surviving spouse receive the income from a greater amount of property than the property eligible for the marital deduction. To the extent that he wants to use the marital deduction, a person can leave that property outright to his spouse or in a trust which pays the income to the spouse during that surviving spouse's life (with the trust property passing to some other person on the surviving spouse's death). If the trust is used, special arrangements have to be made to qualify it for the marital deduction.

To the extent that he does not want the property to qualify for the marital deduction, a person can leave it in trust, with the income going to the surviving spouse for the spouse's lifetime and then passing to someone else. If the special arrangements to qualify this trust for the marital deduction are not made, it will not qualify for the marital deduction and will not be included in the estate of the surviving spouse when that spouse dies.

Appendix F

Charitable Contributions

Both the federal income tax and estate tax provisions allow substantial deductions for charitable contributions. As explained in Chapter 7, charitable contributions reduce adjusted gross income in arriving at taxable income. Also, charitable bequests reduce the estate subject to estate taxes.

While there is no limit on charitable bequests as reductions of the estate, the income tax law does provides a series of limitations regarding the charitable contribution deduction for income tax purposes.

Income tax limitations on charitable deductions

The deductible amount of the charitable contributions made to public charities (those which receive their financial support from the public, e.g., the Red Cross, Boy Scouts of America, local churches and synagogues) is limited to 50 percent of adjusted gross income (adjusted gross income is defined in Chapter 7). Contributions to private foundations (entities qualifying as charitable organizations but which do not look to the public for support—generally, foundations set up by individuals for specific charitable purposes whose financial support comes from the founder and a few others) are deductible to the extent of 30 percent of adjusted gross income for gifts made after July 18, 1984 (the limit was 20 percent for gifts made prior to July 19, 1984). If more than the limit is contributed in one year, the excess may be carried forward and be treated as charitable deductions (within the allowable limits) for the following five years. (The carryover is not available for gifts to private foundations made prior to July 19, 1984.)

Contributions of property other than cash

Charitable contributions need not be made in cash in order to be deductible. Thus, contributions of real estate, for example, may be made. In some cases, making such a contribution may be considered an attractive alternative to selling since the donor can thereby satisfy his charitable inclinations while at the same time enjoying tax benefits. He thus reduces the economic impact of parting with the property. In some cases, not only does he get a deduction for the value of property he gives away but he also avoids the capital gain tax on the appreciation (a tax he would have had to pay had he sold the property). The tax savings can be substantial.

As might by expected, there are a number of technical rules which have the effect of limiting the tax benefits available from contributions of appreciated property. These limitations are:

1. Gift to a public charity of appreciated property which, had it been sold, would have produced a long-term capital gain The taxpayer gets a deduction for the fair market value of the property and pays no tax on the appreciation. However, in this case the ceiling on deductible contributions is 30 percent of adjusted gross income instead of 50 percent. Any unused deduction may be carried forward for five years. (The taxpayer may use the 50-percent limitation if he is willing to treat the amount of the gift as the market value of the property minus one-half the appreciation.) The rules of this category of gifts apply not only to real estate but also to stocks and securities as well. They do not apply to tangible personal property (see Number 4 below).

Note that if any part of the gain (had the property been sold) would have been treated as ordinary income due to depreciation recapture, the market value of the property must be reduced by the depreciation recapture in determining the amount of the contribution.

2. Same as item 1 except gift is to a private foundation The amount of the charitable contribution is equal to the fair market value of the property minus 40 percent of the appreciation. Again, the taxpayer is not taxed on the appreciation. If part of the gain, had the property been sold, would have been ordinary income because of depreciation recapture, the amount of the contribution must be reduced by the depreciation recapture.

3. Gift of appreciated property which if sold would have resulted in ordinary income or short-term capital gain The amount of the contribution is equal to the donor's basis. While the appreciation is not taxed neither is it included in the amount of the contribution.

4. Gift of tangible personal property which is sold would have produced a long-term capital gain. The amount of the contribution is the market value of the property minus 40 percent of the capital gain which would have been realized had it been sold. However, if the property contributed is related to the function of the charity receiving it (e.g., a painting to an art museum), the full market value of the property is the amount of the contribution. In neither situation is the appreciation taxable to the donor.

Gift of real estate subject to liens

If property contributed to a charity is subject to liens (a mortgage, liens for taxes, etc.), the value of the gift is the difference between its market value and the amount of the liens. Then, the preceding rules are applied to determine the amount of the deduction available.

Bargain sale to charity

Suppose, instead of making an outright gift of the property, the donor sells appreciated property to the charity for his basis. In this way, he recovers his cost and, in effect, is making a gift of the appreciation. At least that was the way the tax law used to be applied.

Under current law, however, such a sale is treated as two transactions: a sale and a gift, with the donor's basis allocated between the two transactions. Thus, he gets a charitable contribution deduction but he also ends up with a taxable capital gain.

Example

Stimson owns property the sale of which would yield a long-term capital gain. The basis of the property is $40,000 and it has a market value of $100,000. He sells it to a charity for $40,000. As a result, he has the following:

1. A sale at $40,000 of a portion of the property having a basis of $16,000. Since the $40,000 sale price is 40 percent of the total value of the property, 40 percent of the $40,000 basis, or $16,000, is allocable to the portions of the property sold. Hence, he has a taxable long-term capital gain of $24,000.

2. A charitable contribution of $60,000 for the balance of the property subject to the limitations described above relating to the contribution of appreciated property.

Mortgage in excess of basis   If the property contributed to a charity is subject to a mortgage in excess of basis, it is likely to be treated as a bargain sale of the property. The amount of the mortgage will probably be treated as proceeds received on the transfer and will result in a capital gain for the difference between the mortgage and that portion of the basis allocable to the same percentage of the property as the mortgage is a percentage of the total value of the property transferred.

Example

Green has property with a basis of $20,000 and a value of $100,000. He obtains an $80,000 mortgage on the property and transfers the property to a charity subject to the mortgage.

The transaction will probably be considered a sale for $80,000. Hence, he would have a capital gain of $64,000 ($80,000 minus $16,000—80 percent of the $20,000 basis). He would also have a charitable contribution deduction (subject to the limitations previously described) of $20,000.

Bibliography

This Bibliography has been compiled especially for the second edition of *Marketing Investment Real Estate* by the Library of the NATIONAL ASSOCIATION OF REALTORS® Additional valuable reference materials can be found in the Notes to each chapter.

Allen, Roger H. *Real Estate Investment and Taxation.* Cincinnati, O., South-Western Publishing Co., 1984.

American Institute of Real Estate Appraisers *American Institute of Real Estate Appraisers financial tables,* ed. and comp. by James J. Mason Chicago, Ill., 1981. 473p.

American Institute of Real Estate Appraisers *Readings in real estate investment analysis.* Chicago, Ill., 1977. 252p.

Andersen (Arthur) & Co. *Federal taxes affecting real estate.* 5th ed. New York, Matthew Bender, 1981. looseleaf.

Aronsohn, Alan J. B. *Real estate investment and the Economic Recovery Tax Act of 1981.* JOURNAL OF REAL ESTATE TAXATION, Spring 1981, p. 291–300.

Bagby, Joseph R. *Real estate financing desk book.* 3d ed. Englewood Cliffs, N. J., Institute for Business Planning, 1981. 454p.

Boykin, James H. *Financing real estate.* Lexington, Mass., D. C. Heath & Co., 1979. 635p.

Britten, James A. and Kerwood, Lewis O., ed. *Financing income-producing real estate: a theory and casebook.* New York, McGraw-Hill, 1977. 707p.

Brueggeman, William B. and Stone, Leo D. *Real estate finance.* 7th ed. Homewood, Ill., Irwin, 1981. 712p.

Bruss, Robert J. *Effective Real Estate Investing.* Orem, Utah, Investment and Taxation Publications, Inc., 1984.

Commerce Clearing House *U.S. master tax guide.* Chicago, Ill. Annual.

Corgel, John B. and Goebel, Paul R. *Useful life, component depreciation, and the economic characteristics of real estate.* JOURNAL OF REAL ESTATE TAXATION, Winter 1981, p. 125–141.

Crean, Michael J. *Are capitalization rates obsolete?* APPRAISAL JOURNAL, Apr. 1981, p. 248–257.

Dasso, Jerome and Kuhn, Gerald. *Real Estate Finance.* Englewood Cliffs, N.J.,: Prentice-Hall, Inc., 1983.

DCF analysis: the other side of the coin. MORTGAGE AND REAL ESTATE EXECUTIVES REPORT, Jan. 15, 1981, p. 6–7.

Dilmore, Gene *Quantitative techniques in real estate counseling.* Lexington, Mass., Heath, 1981. 256p.

Edwards, Charles E. and Gaines, James P. *Alternative accelerated depreciation methods and rates of return on real estate investments.* REAL ESTATE APPRAISER AND ANALYST, Fall 1981, p. 13–22.

Emory, Meade and Hjorth, Roland L. *An Analysis of the changes made by the Installment Sales Revision Act of 1980.* JOURNAL OF TAXATION, Feb. 1981, p. 66–71; Mar. 1981, p. 130–137

Epley, Donald R. and Miller, James A. *Basic Real Estate Finance and Investment.* Somerset, N.J.,: John Wiley and Sons, 1984.

Feder, Jack M. *Starker: the deferred tax-free exchange resurrected.* JOURNAL OF REAL ESTATE TAXATION, Spring 1980, p. 218–240.

Ferguson, Jerry T. *Fundamentals of Real Estate Investing.* Glenview, Ill., Scott, Foresman and Company, 1984.

Fisher, Jeffrey D. and Lusht, Kenneth M. *Mortgage equity analysis with a debt coverage constraint.* REAL ESTATE APPRAISER AND ANALYST, Fall 1981, p. 5–12.

Fisher, Jeffrey D. and Sanders, Anthony B. *Capitalization rates and market information.* APPRAISAL JOURNAL, Apr. 1981, p. 186–198.

Gibbons, James E. *Equity yield.* APPRAISAL JOURNAL, Jan 1980. p. 31–55.

Goodman, Richard A. *The New Starker case: how it will revolutionize tax-deferred exchanges.* REAL ESTATE SECURITIES JOURNAL, Spring 1980, p. 33–43.

Greer, Gaylon E. and Farrell, Michael D. *Investment Analysis for Real Estate Decisions.* Hinsdale, Ill., Dryden Press, 1984.

Harris, Bridget McInerney *The Effect of the Installment Sales Revision Act of 1980 on like-kind exchanges: nonsimultaneous exchanges.* TAXES, July 1981, p. 448–456.

Howell, A. Harold and Smith, David A. *Independent component analysis; a new way to analyze real estate shelter opportunities.* REAL ESTATE REVIEW, Spring 1981, p. 53–64.

Investment analysis: what's the return? REAL ESTATE INVESTMENT IDEAS, May 1981, 1st issue, p. 1–3.

Jaffe, Austin J. *A Note on the use of capitalization, discount, and forward rates.* APPRAISAL JOURNAL, *Jan. 1980, p. 24–30.*

Johnson, Ross H. and Henderson, Thomas P. *Real Estate Finance.* Columbus, O., Charles E. Merrill Publishing Co., 1985.

Koelsch, James P. *Discounting projected cash flows.* APPRAISAL JOURNAL, Oct. 1981, p. 522–533.

Kurn, Neal and Nutter, Jack O., II *The Installment Sales Revision Act of 1980: in the name of simplification has a measure of complexity been added?* JOURNAL OF REAL ESTATE TAXATION, Spring 1981, p. 195–212.

Levine, Howard J *Tax-free real estate transactions.* JOURNAL OF REAL ESTATE TAXATION, Spring 1981, p. 354–358.

Levine, Mark Lee *Multiple party exchanges: recent decisions support flexibility under Section 1031.* TAXES, Mar. 1981, p. 194–200.

Levine, Mark Lee *Real estate exchanges.* Chicago, Ill., REALTORS NATIONAL MARKETING INSTITUTE®, 1981. 600p.

Lipscomb, Joseph B. *Discount rates for cash equivalent analysis.* APPRAISAL JOURNAL, Jan. 1981, p. 23–33.

A Look at the accelerated cost recovery system. REAL ESTATE INVESTMENT IDEAS, Oct. 1981, 2d issue, p. 1–3.

Luscombe, George A., II and Chevis, Cheryl A. *Faster, simpler depreciation rules available for all property under the new tax legislation.* JOURNAL OF TAXATION, Oct. 1981, p. 194–201.

Lusht, Kenneth M. *Measuring rate of return: two rules of thumb v. the internal rate.* APPRAISAL JOURNAL, April 1978, p. 245–256.

Martin, William B., Jr. *A Risk analysis rate-of-return model for evaluating income-producing real estate investments.* APPRAISAL JOURNAL, July 1978, p. 424–442.

McBirney, James J. *Real estate financing in an inflationary economy*. APPRAISAL JOURNAL, Oct. 1981, p. 494–521.

McGuire, John A. *Tax aspects of income reservations in real estate transactions*. JOURNAL OF REAL ESTATE TAXATION, Spring 1981, p. 213–232.

McMullen, Charles W. *Tax deferred exchanges of real estate investments*. New York, Wiley, 1981. 86p.

Montgomery, J. Thomas and Raper, Charles F. *Equity yields and the reinvestment issue*. APPRAISAL JOURNAL, Oct. 1981, p. 509–521.

Nutter, Jack O., II *Regulations under the Installment Sales Revision Act*. JOURNAL OF REAL ESTATE TAXATION, Fall 1981, p. 46–56.

Peterson, Charles H. *Are capitalization rates obsolete?* APPRAISAL JOURNAL, Apr. 1981, p. 179–185.

Pyhrr, Stephen A. and Cooper, James R. *Real Estate Investment: Strategy, Analysis, Decisions*. Boston, Mass., Warren, Gorham and Lamont, Inc., 1982.

Rohan, Patrick J. *Real estate financing; text; forms; tax analysis*. New York, Matthew Bender. Multi-volume, looseleaf.

Sear, Michael *Choosing a recovery method for non-residential property: an internal rate of return approach*. REAL ESTATE SECURITIES JOURNAL, Fall 1981, p. 38–49.

Seldin, Maury *Real estate investment for profit through appreciation*. Reston, Va., Reston, 1980. 211p.

Shlaes, Jared and Young, Michael S. *Evaluating major investment properties*. APPRAISAL JOURNAL, Jan. 1978, p. 101–111.

Sirota, David. *Essentials of Real Estate Investment*. Chicago, Ill., Longman Group U.S.A., Inc., 1984.

Smith, Halbert C. and others *Real estate and urban development*. 3d ed. Homewood, Ill., Irwin, 1981. 638p.

Special issue: new tax law benefits real estate. REAL ESTATE TAX IDEAS, Oct. 1981 (entire issue).

Special report: depreciation and recapture under new tax law. MORTGAGE AND REAL ESTATE EXECUTIVES REPORT, Oct. 1, 1981, p. 3–8.

Special report: new tax law is good news for investors. MORTGAGE AND REAL ESTATE EXECUTIVES REPORT, Sept. 1, 1981, p. 1–7.

Bibliography

Texas A&M University. College of Agriculture. Texas Real Estate Research Center. *Tax-free exchanges under Section 1031,* by Jack Harris and Jack P. Friedman. College Station, Tex., 1981. 26p.

Tornga, David L. *Tax consequences on the disposition of real property or interests therein by limited partnerships and partners.* JOURNAL OF REAL ESTATE TAXATION, Winter 1981, p. 166–182.

Valachi, Donald J. *On interpreting the internal rate of return on a real estate investment.* REAL ESTATE APPRAISER AND ANALYST, First Quarter 1981, p. 35–42.

Viscione, Jerry A. and Porter, Ronald *IRR analyses may not yield the best results.* REAL ESTATE REVIEW, Summer 1980, p. 97–101.

Walters, David W. *Real estate exchanges.* New York, Wiley, 1982. 205p.

Webb, James R. *Negative cash flows: a current appraisal problem.* APPRAISAL JOURNAL, Jan 1981, p. 95–101.

Weinstein, Marvin W. *Real estate—the "unquestionable" tax shelter.* REAL ESTATE LAW JOURNAL, Summer 1981, p. 67–71.

Which depreciation method should you use? REAL ESTATE INVESTMENT IDEAS, Dec. 1981, 1st issue, p. 5–6.

Whitmire, Robert L. and Reynolds, Kerry M. *Selecting the optimum depreciation method for real estate under the new ACR system.* JOURNAL OF TAXATION, Dec. 1981, p. 360–363.

Young, Michael S. *FMRR: a clever hoax?* APPRAISAL JOURNAL, July 1979, p. 359–369.

Zerbst, Robert H. *Evaluating risks by partitioning the internal rate of return.* REAL ESTATE REVIEW, Winter 1980, p. 80–84.

Index

Index

Index

523

Index

Index

531

539

545